D1556606

THE ONE SHOW

ADVERTISING'S BEST PRINT, DESIGN, RADIO & TV

VOLUME 24

PRESIDENT
John Butler

EXECUTIVE DIRECTOR/EXECUTIVE EDITOR
Mary Warlick

EDITOR
Tiffany Meyers

PRODUCTION EDITORS
Sharon Lange
Steve Marchese
Chris Rosino

BOOK DESIGN

DESIGNER
Lise Mardon Smith

COVER & DIVIDER PAGE DESIGN
Jeffrey Hale, Duffy New York

INITIAL LAYOUTS
Edwin Laguerre

DVD

SPONSOR
Discreet, San Francisco

DVD AUTHORING
Scream DVD, New York

DVD PRODUCER
Mark Ashkinos

PRODUCTION
Todd Gaffney
Kevin Swanepoel
The One Club

PUBLISHED BY

ONE CLUB PUBLISHING
21 East 26th Street
New York, NY 10010
TEL: 212-979-1900
FAX: 212-979-5006
EMAIL: info@oneclub.com
WEBSITE: www.oneclub.com

FIRST PRINTING
ISBN 0-929837-18-5

PRODUCTION AND SEPARATION
AVA Book Production Pte. Ltd.
EMAIL: production@avabooks.com.sg

A note on the alphanumeric identification system in this volume: The digits that appear in the credits for each entry comprise a unique pencil and merit award number. An "A" at the end of unique numbers represents One Show winners. A "D" represents One Show Design winners.

DISTRIBUTED BY

STERLING PUBLISHING CO., INC.
IN USA
387 Park Avenue South
New York, NY 10016-8810
TEL: +1 212 532 7160
FAX: +1 212 213 2495
WEBSITE: www.sterlingpub.com

IN CANADA
STERLING PUBLISHING
C/O CANADIAN MANDA GROUP
One Atlantic Avenue
Suite 105, Toronto
Ontario M6K 3E7

DISTRIBUTED EX-NORTH AMERICA BY
AVA DISTRIBUTION
TEL: +41 78 600 5109
EMAIL: sales@avabooks.ch
WEBSITE: www.avabooks.ch

TABLE OF CONTENTS

BOARD OF DIRECTORS

JOHN BUTLER
PRESIDENT/THE ONE CLUB

This has been a tough year.

Our industry's woes pale in comparison to what's going on in the world right now, and it's probably good to keep that in perspective.

As for my first year on the job as President of The One Club, let's just say it's been quite an education.

This year, we've seen a number of decent agencies disappear, a greater number of talented people lose their jobs, leaving many to reconsider their chosen careers and wonder when it will all just go back to normal.

And then, right in the middle of it all came the One Show Call for Entries. We braced ourselves. And guess what? The entries poured in...and in...and in.

In the face of having to make some extremely difficult business decisions this year, each and every one of you exhibited passion and conviction for creative excellence in our industry. Not surprising. Advertising people are incredibly resilient. I guess we have to be to last more than a few years in this business, watching most of those little gems we create unceremoniously killed off.

The tome you hold in your hands is representative of the stuff that lived. The work that defied a recession and actually got made. That, in and of itself, is probably worthy of an award.

In fact, the work collected in this volume is some of the freshest and most interesting that I've seen in an award show in quite some time. We owe it to this year's jury, which really pushed itself to redefine the definition of "good," and not to reward work that was derivative and familiar. That's a lot harder than it sounds.

Case in point, this year's Best of Show, the BMW "The Hire" campaign. We were proud to be the first show to acknowledge this groundbreaking work, while other shows deemed it ineligible because it "ran" primarily online. Our judges unequivocally agreed it was the freshest thinking this year, decided that it was indeed advertising, and unanimously championed it.

It'll be a tough act to follow if you ask me.

So welcome to the 2002 One Show Annual. As always, we thank you for being here, and appreciate your continued support of the club.

And hang in there. It'll get better.

THE 2002 ONE SHOW JUDGES

SCOTT AAL
Grant Scott & Hurley, San Francisco

ARTHUR BIJUR
Cliff Freeman and Partners
New York

GREG BOKOR
Mullen, Wenham

ROSSANA BARDALES
Cliff Freeman and Partners
New York

ROGER CAMP
Wieden + Kennedy, Portland

EUGENE CHEONG
Ogilvy, Singapore

MARIE CATHERINE DUPUY
TBWA, Paris

RYAN EBNER
Butler Shine & Stern, Sausalito

MICHAEL HART
Fallon, Minneapolis

PAUL HIRSCH
Goodby Silverstein & Partners
San Francisco

LANCE JENSEN
Moderista!, Boston

MIKE MAZZA
Publicis & Hal Riney, San Francisco

RAYMOND MCKINNEY
The Martin Agency, Richmond

AMY NICHOLSON
Freelance, New York

LIZ PARADISE
McKinney & Silver, Raleigh

MICHAEL PATTI
BBDO, New York

HANK PERLMAN
Hungry Man, New York

JEREMY POSTAER
GSD&M, Austin

JEAN ROBAIRE
a.k.a.Robaire, Los Angeles

KIRK SOUDER
Freelance, Marina Del Rey

THE 2002 ONE SHOW DESIGN JUDGES

JOE DUFFY, CHAIR
Duffy Design, Minneapolis

DANA ARNETT
VSA Partners, Chicago

SHEPARD FAIREY
Black Market Design, Los Angeles

RICO LINS
Rico Lins + Studio, São Paulo

THOM MIDDLEBROOK
McKinney & Silver Design, Raleigh

STEVE SANDSTROM
Sandstrom Design, Portland

THE 2002 RADIO JUDGES

ADAM CHASNOW, CHAIR
Cliff Freeman and Partners
New York

WAYNE BEST
Freelance, New York

STEPHANIE CRIPPEN
Leo Burnett, Chicago

AL KELLY
Goodby Silverstein & Partners
San Francisco

CARL LOEB
Bartle Bogle Hegarty, New York

CHUCK MEEHAN
Davidandgoliath, Los Angeles

ARI MERKIN
Crispin Porter & Bogusky, Miami

ZAK MROUEH
Taxi, Toronto

MARK NARDI
Hill Holliday, Boston

EDDIE VAN BLOEM
Lowe, New York

BOB WINTER
DDB, Chicago

MEMBERS

A

Michael Abadi
Jeffrey Abbott
Rick Abbott
Michael Abel
Geoffrey W. Abraham
Ekta Aggarwal
Diane Albergo
B.A. Albert
Christine Aliferis
Kelly Allen
Blythe Alpern
Elyse Altabet
Olivia Altschuler
Gideon Amichay
Stephanie Anderson
Johnas Andre
Frank Anselmo
Marcelo Aragao
Larry Asher
Nader Ashway
Jayson Atienza

B

Kristina Backlund
Ron Bacsa
Chris Baier
Larry Baisden
David Baldwin
Mark Bangerter
Robert Barnwell
Lauren Barrocas
Tim Bayless
Troy Benson
Ron Berger
David Bernstein
Eric Bertuccio
Rahul Bhatia
Christopher Biddle
Arthur Bijur
Bruce Bildsten
Michael Blumberg
John Boone
George Boutilier
Clarence Bradley
Scott Brewer
Bill Brokaw
Michael Brothers
Jane Bryson
Pat Buckley
John Butler
Amy Butterworth

C

Larry Cadman
Ralph Calderon
Michael Campbell
John Carter
Tom Carter
Marie Cavosora
Marco Ceo
Frank Chang
Chung-Mau Cheng
Chris Churchill
Amanda Citrin
Bart Cleveland
Gary Cohen
Christopher Cole
Curt Collinsworth
Regan Colombo
Tom Cordner
Candice Corlett
Andrea Cormier
August Cosentino
Leonardo Costa
Nicole Cota
Katie Coulombe
Jac Coverdale
Steve Crane
George Curi
Hal Curtis

D

Billy D'Ambrosio
Trish Daley
Kevin Daly
Michele Daly
John Danza
Matthew Davis
Jaye Davis
Timothy Delaney
Georgia Demmitt
Sal DeVito
Steve Diamond
Justin Dodd
Christine Doll
Steve Doppelt
Rob Dow
Joe Duffy
Lisa Duke
Andrew Dunn
Patrick Durkin
David Dyer

E

Matt Eastwood
Keri Eisenberg
Grant Elliot
Belinda Ellis
Jackie End
Gary Ennis
Karim Ezzat

F

Niki Faldemolaei
Doran Farnum
John Fawcett
Carlos Fernandez
Miguel Fernandez
Chris Finlay
Tim Fisher
Mike Flegle
Ian Forbes
Melanie Foster
Brian Foughy
Cliff Freeman
Kevin Freidberg
Robert Fremgen
Len Friedland
Glen Fruchter
James Furguson

G

Naoki Ga
Tom Gabriel
Marc Gallucci
Mark Ganton
Trina Gardner
Joe Gatti
Dean Gemmell
Evan Georges
Richard Gerdes
Jennifer Getz
Shelly Gilad
Frank Ginsberg
Samantha Glatzer
Kenneth Gleason
Keith Glen
Prachi Gokhale
Daniel Goldstein
Larry Goldstein
Mort Goldstrom
Melissa Golicewski
Mitch Gordon
Vance Gorham
Allison Graffeo
Mario Granatur
Norm Grey
Philip Growick
Rob Guenette
Ted Guidotti
Juan Carlos Gutierrez

H

Lori Habas
Ad Hackimer
Matthew Hallock
Trace Hallowell
Kevin Hand
Tucker Hasler
Jackie Hathiramani
Naoise Hefferon
Roy Herbert
Armando Hernandez
Lee Hester
Antonio Hidalgo
Woody Hinkle
Charles Hively
Kari Hoerchler
John Hofmeister
Henrik Holen
Dave Holloway
S. Hale Holman
Reid Holmes
Jim Hord
Laurence Horvitz
Hugh Hough
Eric Hughes
Mike Hughes
John Hynes

I

Brenda Innocenti
Lauren Inquye

J

Amanda Jacobellis
Per Robert Jacobson
Rinku Jariwala
Bob Jeffrey
Kathy Jennings
Anthony A. Johnson
Burr Johnson
Stephen Jones

K

Dominique Bigar Kahn
Tom Kaminsky
Tom Kane
Simon Kao
Linus Karlsson
Richard Kaufman
Leslie Kay
Scott Keglovic
Tom Kelly
Jeff Kidwell
Joanne Kim
Jeremy Kinder
Peter Klueger
Joe Knezic
Jeanette Kong
Debbie Koppman
Dennis Koye
Judy Kozuck
Neal Krouse
Paul Kruger

L

Conley La Barr
Jonathan Lafeliece
Ming Lai
Sharon Lange
Andy Langerx
Anthony LaPetri
David Laskarzewski
Leah Lax
Kevin Lecinger
Eun-Jung Lee
Seung Lee
Aimee Lehto
Ann Lemon
Mike Lescarbeau
Kate Levin
Larissa Liberato
Adrian Lim
Ron Lim
Lisa Lipkin-Balser
Mindy Liu
Teddy Lo
Damon Lockett
Carolyn London
Frank Lopresti
James Loughran
Antonia Ludes
John Lutter

M

Sam Maclay
Sharoz Makarechi
Madhu Malhan
Karen Mallia
Bradley Manier
Sarah Marden
Michael Mark
Howard Marks
Joel Maron
Jason Marrotte
Julie Marsh
Rhoda Marshall
Chuck Matzker
Richard May
Scott McAfee
Cal McAllister
Chris McCarthy
Joseph McCarthy
John McClure
Cameron McNaughton
John Melillo
Linda Menck
Mark Mendelis
Frank Meo
Ari Merkin

M
Lyudmila Mikhelzon
Brian Millar
Mark Millar
Chris Miller
Don Miller
Renee Miller
Russell Miyaki
Sakol Mongkolkasetarin
Sara Moore
Adam Morgan
Jacob Morris
Scott Mortimore
Jim Mountjoy
Zak Mroueh
Mark Musto

N
Caroline Naggiar
Bob Needleman
Samuel Nelson
Don Nelson
Arun K. Nemali
Joseph Ney
Jenny Norberg

O
David Oakley
Rip Odell
Ron Ordansa

P
Babita Patel
Paul Patterson
Michael Paxton
Michael Payer
Brantley Payne
Stephen Pederson
Anita Ruth Perez
Dimitrios Petsas
Elizabeth Phillips
Loren Phillips
Ayana Picariello
Gianni Pinello
Jill Pool
Kim Porter
Matthew Proctor
Tony Pucca
Michael Pudin
Dave Pullar

Q
Aldo Quevedo

R
Corey Rawowsky
Rob Reilly
Kerry Reynolds
Anders Rich
Hank Richardson
Robert Gregg Rosenthal
Anne Rudig

S
Neeraj Sabharwal
Diana Samper
Victoria Santiso
Emmanuel Santos
Sal Sardo
Ann Saulnier
Samantha Sayet
Sandra Scher
Dennis Scheyer
Chris Schlegel
Terry Schneider
Jonathan Schoenberg
Trevor Schoenfeld
Michael Schwabenland
Jaime Schwarz
Heinz Schwegler
Joe Sciarrotta
Tod Seisser
Tonice Sgrignoli
Donald Shelford
Steve Simpson
Richard Singer
Lauren Slaff
Robert Slosberg
Claudine Smith
David Smith, Jr.
Laura Soles
Richard Solomon
Mark Spillane
Catherine St. Jean
John Staffin
Todd Stanton
Dean Stefanides
Amy Stewart
Larry Stone
Marcia Stone
Scott Storrs
Will Strain
Jack Supple
Michael Suskind
Steve Swartz
Leslie Sweet

T
Matthew Tarulli
Dow Tate
Chris Tatman
Nick Terzis
Greg Thomas
Laura Toch
Kyle Toyama
Mark Tutssel
Amy Tyler

V
German Silva Vasquez
Paul Vaynerman
Paul Venables
Amy Vensel
Christopher Vercelloni
Andres Vergara
Carol Vick
Ed Vick
Chris Vickers
Danielle Vieth
John Viglione
Meagan Vilsack
Larry Vine
Michael Vitiello
John Vitro
Theodore Voss

W
Elaine Wagner
William Ernest Waites
David Waitz
Judy Wald
Michael Ward
Bob Warren
David Wassell
Steve Waterloo
David Wecal
Iwan Weidmann
Lawrence G. Werner
Robert Shaw West
Nat Whitten
Steve Williams
Stewart Winter
Stefen Wojnarowski

Y
Betsy Yamazaki
Marvin Young

Z
Jsson Ziehm
Mat Zucker

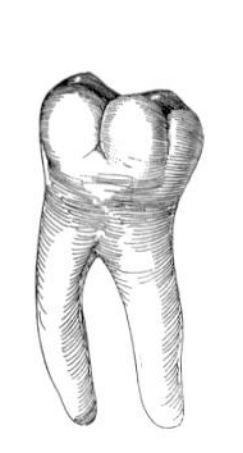

Gold, *Au*
Silver, *Ag*
Bronze, *2/3 Cu + 1/3 Sn*

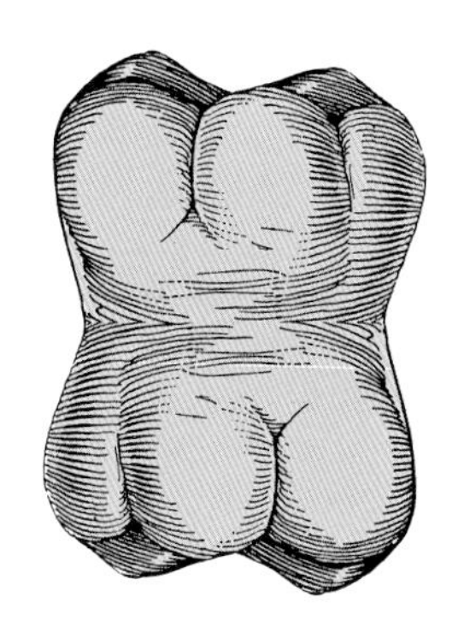

GOLD

Silver

BRONZE

GOLD AWARD
NEWSPAPER OVER 600 LINES
SINGLE

ART DIRECTORS
Mark Mason
Slade Gill

WRITERS
Slade Gill
Mark Mason

PHOTOGRAPHER
Ian Anderson

TYPOGRAPHER
Mark Mason

CREATIVE DIRECTOR
Vanessa Pearson

CLIENT
Procter & Gamble-Oil of Olay

AGENCY
Saatchi & Saatchi/Cape Town

02001A

Also won:
MERIT AWARD
MAGAZINE COLOR
FULL PAGE OR SPREAD: SINGLE

Tock. Tick.

SILVER AWARD
NEWSPAPER OVER 600 LINES
SINGLE

ART DIRECTOR
Gareth Lessing

WRITER
Benjamin Abramowitz

ILLUSTRATOR
Gareth Lessing

PHOTOGRAPHER
Clive Stewart

CREATIVE DIRECTORS
Frances Luckin
Sandra de Witt

CLIENT
Playstation

AGENCY
TBWA Hunt Lascaris/
Johannesburg

02002A

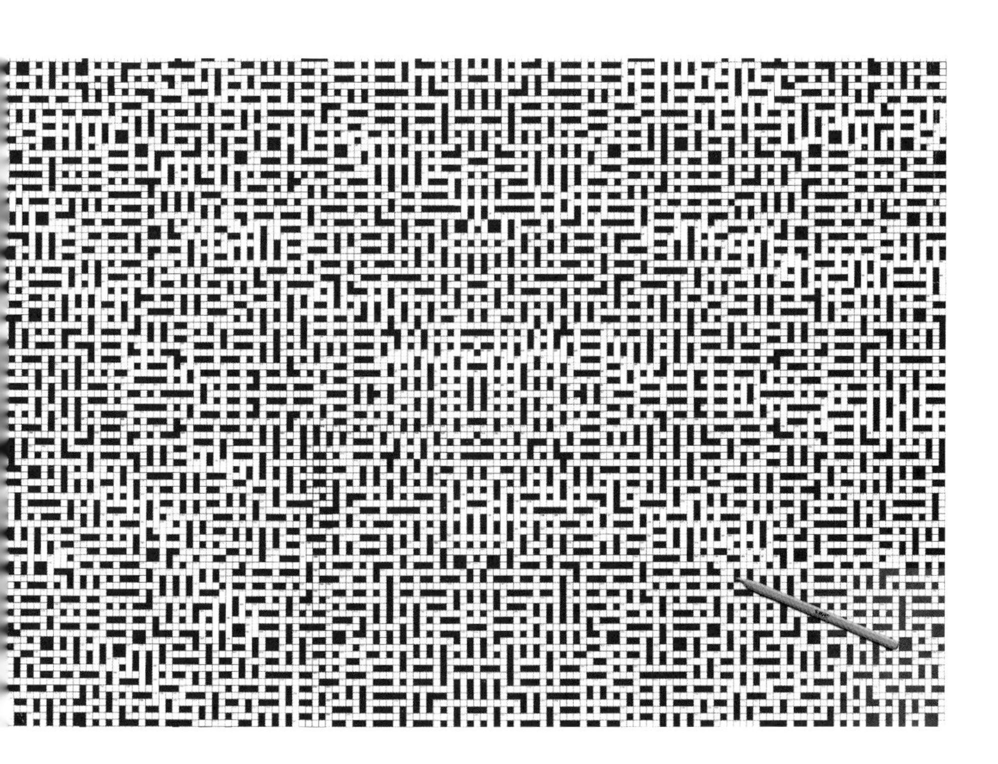

BRONZE AWARD
NEWSPAPER OVER 600 LINES
SINGLE

ART DIRECTORS
Tony Purnell
Nicholas Pereira

WRITER
Xander Smith

ILLUSTRATOR
Nicholas Pereira

CREATIVE DIRECTORS
Chris Garbutt
Sandra de Witt

CLIENT
Bic

AGENCY
TBWA Hunt Lascaris/
Johannesburg

02003A

Also won:
MERIT AWARD
COLLATERAL: POSTERS
SINGLE

GOLD AWARD
NEWSPAPER OVER 600 LINES
CAMPAIGN

ART DIRECTORS
Rob Story
Lou Flores
David Crawford

WRITERS
Michael Buss
Cameron Day
Jeremy Postaer

PHOTOGRPAPHER
Stock

ILLUSTRATORS
Slade Seaholm
Kevin Peake

CREATIVE DIRECTORS
Jeremy Postaer
David Crawford

CLIENT
Land Rover North America

AGENCY
GSD&M/Austin

02004A

Also won:
MERIT AWARDS
NEWSPAPER OVER 600 LINES
SINGLE

MERIT

MERIT

MERIT

SILVER AWARD
NEWSPAPER OVER 600 LINES
CAMPAIGN

ART DIRECTOR
Justin Tindall

WRITER
Adam Tucker

PHOTOGRAPHER
Ben Stockley

CREATIVE DIRECTOR
Mark Reddy

CLIENT
Harvey Nichols

AGENCY
BMP DDB/London

02005A

BRONZE AWARD
NEWSPAPER OVER 600 LINES
CAMPAIGN

ART DIRECTORS
André Nassar
Bruno Prosperi

WRITER
Renato Simões

PHOTOGRAPHER
Márcia Ramalho

CREATIVE DIRECTORS
José Henrique Borghi
Bruno Prosperi

CLIENT
Kelloggs

AGENCY
Leo Burnett/São Paulo

02006A

KEEP THIS AD TO READ IN THE BATHROOM.

All right: we agree that the text of this ad is too long. We know that just looking at so many lines makes us kind of lazy. And we're also aware that most people have less and less time and patience to read (if you're a good observer, you might have noticed that ads and even articles have shorter and shorter texts). But, anyway, what made us write a text as long as this one? We could have been much briefer, much more economical in words and information. But we preferred to make this immense text for a very simple reason. It's because although we know you're a very busy person and have millions of things to do (all of them much more important than reading an ad), we're also sure that there is a time of your day when you have nothing to do. And that's exactly when a big text like this can be a great way to pass the time.

Yes, you know what we're talking about. We're referring to that time when you go to the toilet and stay there for a long time, reading whatever falls into your hands. It can be a book, preferably one with hundreds of pages (Greek philosophers are a fine suggestion). It can be a newspaper, a magazine, a dictionary, medicine directions, a phone book or any other thing. In this case, the size is much more important than the contents of the text. The more words it has, the better it is. After all, in the bathroom you have time to read. Plenty of time, by the way.

If you pay attention you'll notice that a lot of people go to the toilet as if they were going camping. Besides a lot of reading material, some people take video games, walkman and cell phones on this expedition. And lately, more and more people have taken their laptops to the bathroom to update their work. (Before you ask: no, this text was not written inside a bathroom.)

The truth is that people are spending more and more time in the bathroom. Let's count: a guy who stays, in average, 40 minutes a day in the bathroom, by the end of his life will have spent two and a half years in there. That's right. Two and a half years looking at some tiled walls. A little too much, don't you think?

Anyway, is it normal to spend so much time inside a bathroom? (This question does not apply to teenagers, who spend too long in the bathroom, but for completely different reasons.)

The answer is: no, it's not normal at all. A person who spends so much time in the bathroom surely has some sort of intestinal trouble (constipation, lazy bowel, lack of regularity in intestinal functions, etc, etc, etc).

We know that poor functioning intestines is not one of the most pleasant subjects in the world. But consider this point: as long as you're there, at the toilet, completely alone, it's the best time to talk about such a delicate and embarrassing subject.

Let's face the facts: good functioning intestines is 100% related to nutritional habits. People who have fiber-rich nutrition, for example, have intestines that work better. These people don't tend to have gastrointestinal illnesses often. Studies show that Africans, the people that consume the most fiber in the world, seldom have intestinal problems.

So, what makes fiber so important to our body?

In case you don't know, dietary fiber are vegetable substances that are not absorbed by the human digestive system. This means that the fiber we ingest is completely eliminated from our body, or rather, the only function of fiber is to ease and accelerate the working of our intestines, helping them to eliminate all the impurities from our body A fiber-rich diet ends constipation and keeps intestines always at work.

But fiber does much more than improve your intestines' activity and save time in the bathroom. People who eat fiber regularly are preventing themselves from serious diseases, such as diverticulitis, high cholesterol, arteriosclerosis and colon cancer. Recent studies show that fiber also helps controlling diabetes and reduces the risk of breast cancer.

And that's not all: fiber also helps you lose weight ("grow thin while eating" diets are always based on fiber). And that's because, in addition to having very low calories, they are also a natural appetite regulator. When fiber gets in contact with water, it inflates, giving the feeling of full stomach and reducing the desire to eat. And for all that, fibers is more and more recommended by doctors, especially nutritionists and endocrinologists.

Now that you know a little more about the importance of fiber, you may want to know how much fiber you should consume daily. Specialists state that, with 35 daily grams of fiber, your intestines start to work like a clock. You probably consume much less fiber than what is recommended. (Of course, if you ate 35 daily grams of fiber, you'd have already gotten out of the bathroom a long time ago).

So, if you've come to the conclusion that you need to start consuming more fiber, the first thing you must do is rethink your nutritional habits. Take advantage of sitting in the bathroom, with time to spare, and answer some questions about the way you eat.

What do you usually eat every day? What do you usually have for breakfast (I mean, if you do have breakfast)? What are your favorite dishes? What kind of food you don't like?

Probably, you're the kind of person who doesn't like vegetables, fruit and cereal (believe me, you're far from being an exception). Yet, these are the exactly the kinds of foods - which most people hate - that have the greatest amount of fiber. Does this mean that to have healthy, fiber-rich nutrition, you have to become the most orthodox of the vegetarians, right? Wrong.

Fortunately, there are prepared foods with really high concentrations of fiber. All-Bran, Kellogg's whole cereal, is the best example. A small serving of All-Bran with milk has approximately 12 grams of fiber. This represents 1/3 of all the fiber you need per day. If you add some fruit to your All-Bran (which, by the way, is delicious) you're consuming even more fiber in only one meal.

Compare All-Bran with any other kind of fiber-rich food. A small bowl of All-Bran has the same amount of fiber as 10 unpeeled apples. Or 12 bananas. Or, even, 48 plums. Or, if you prefer 57 stems of broccoli. Let's assume you're someone who wants healthy and balanced nutrition, though are not crazy enough to eat 57 stems of broccoli a day. So, you should consider eating All-Bran every morning. Besides its really high fiber concentration, All-Bran is enriched with calcium and eleven vitamins, which makes it a complete, nutritious kind of food, and, even better, low on calories.

And you can prepare All-Bran in many ways. It's perfect for making muffins, pancakes, bread, cheesecakes, pies, cakes and a lot of different delicious recipes. Thanks to All-Bran, having a healthy meal can be a delicious experience.

If you have All-Bran every day, you'll have more balanced nutrition and your intestines will start to work better, faster and much more regularly. This means that you'll spend so little time in the bathroom that you'll never be able to read texts as long as this one.

All-Bran. Fiber to make your intestines work much better.

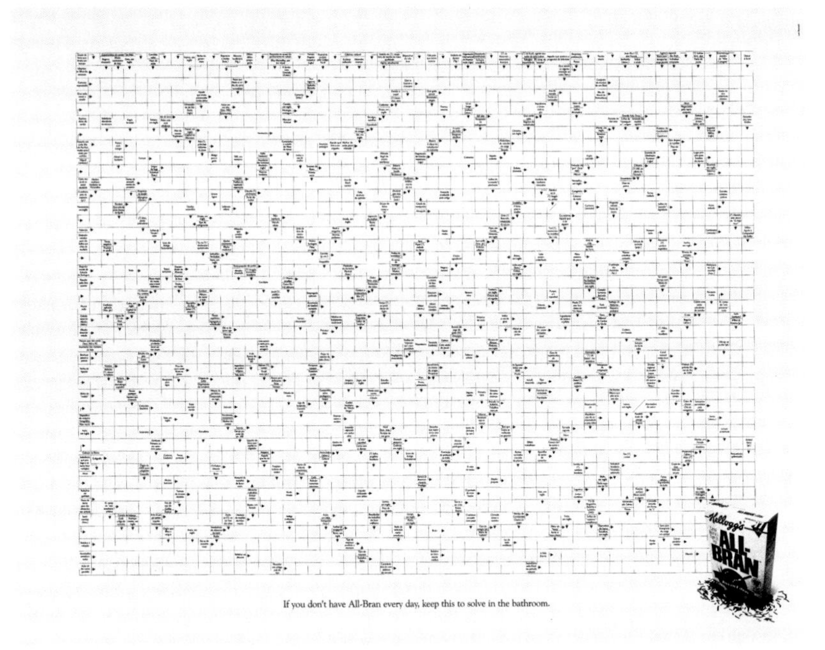

If you don't have All-Bran every day, keep this to solve in the bathroom.

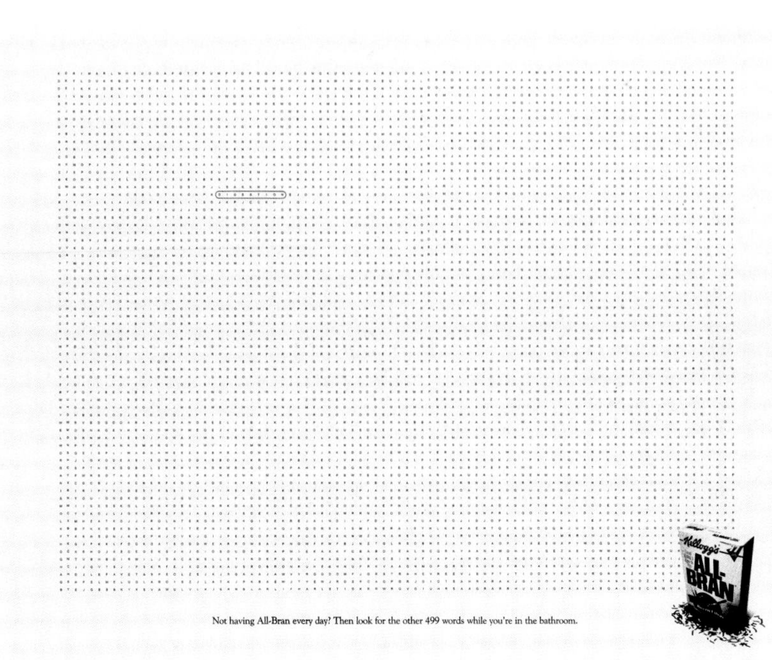

Not having All-Bran every day? Then look for the other 499 words while you're in the bathroom.

SILVER AWARD
NEWSPAPER 600 LINES OR LESS
SINGLE

ART DIRECTOR
Marcus Rebeschini

WRITER
Robert Kleman

PHOTOGRAPHER
Bruce Allan

CREATIVE DIRECTOR
Mark Bamfield

CLIENT
Thule Asia

AGENCY
TBWA/Singapore

02007A

Also won:
MERIT AWARDS
MAGAZINE COLOR
FULL PAGE OR SPREAD: SINGLE

COLLATERAL: POINT OF PURCHASE AND IN-STORE

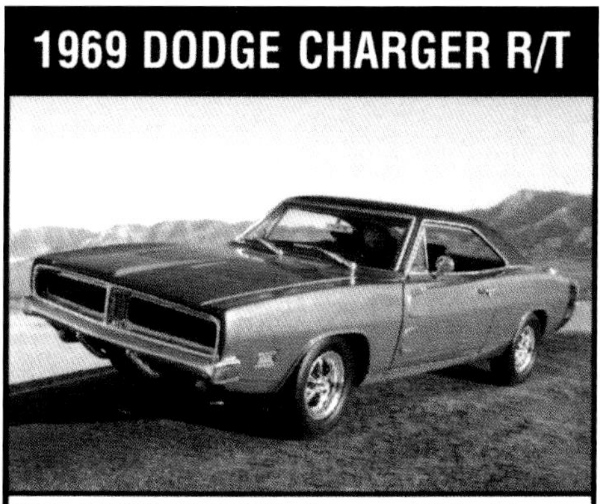

1969 DODGE CHARGER R/T
1969 DODGE CHARGER, Bronze ext/blk. int, mag wheels, hideaway hdlghts, very clean, classic, $25. Serious inquiries only. 1/18 scale. Hotwheels.com

2001 DODGE VIPER GTS-R
2001 DODGE VIPER GTS-R, 8.0-liter V-10 red/wht. trim, fog lamps, rear spoliler, mint, $25. Won't last! 1/18 scale. Hotwheels.com

2001 BMW Z8
2001 BMW Z8, conv, silver, low mi, alloy whls, xclent cond. $25, 1/18 scale. Must see! Hotwheels.com

SILVER AWARD
NEWSPAPER 600 LINES OR LESS
CAMPAIGN

ART DIRECTORS
John Davis
Dana Markee

WRITER
Ben Purcell

CREATIVE DIRECTOR
David Angelo

CLIENT
Mattel

AGENCY
Davidandgoliath/Los Angeles

02008A

GOLD AWARD
MAGAZINE COLOR
FULL PAGE OR SPREAD: SINGLE

ART DIRECTORS
Jayanta Jenkins
Bill Karow

WRITERS
Mark Fitzloff
Simon Mainwaring

PHOTOGRAPHER
Michael Jones

CREATIVE DIRECTORS
Dan Wieden
Hal Curtis
Jim Riswold

CLIENT
Nike

AGENCY
Wieden + Kennedy/Portland

02009A

GOLD AWARD
MAGAZINE COLOR
FULL PAGE OR SPREAD: SINGLE

ART DIRECTORS
Jayanta Jenkins
Bill Karow

WRITERS
Mark Fitzloff
Simon Mainwaring

PHOTOGRAPHERS
Michael Jones
Bruce Forster

CREATIVE DIRECTORS
Dan Wieden
Hal Curtis
Jim Riswold

CLIENT
Nike

AGENCY
Wieden + Kennedy/Portland

02010A

SILVER AWARD
MAGAZINE COLOR
FULL PAGE OR SPREAD: SINGLE

ART DIRECTOR
Antony Nelson

WRITER
Mike Sutherland

PHOTOGRAPHER
Trevor Ray Hart

TYPOGRAPHER
Scott Silvey

CREATIVE DIRECTOR
David Droga

CLIENT
Club 18-30

AGENCY
Saatchi & Saatchi/London

02011A

Also won:
MERIT AWARDS
OUTDOOR: SINGLE

POSTERS: SINGLE

BRONZE AWARD
MAGAZINE COLOR
FULL PAGE OR SPREAD: SINGLE

ART DIRECTORS
Bradley Wood
Christopher Toland

WRITER
Steve Morris

PHOTOGRAPHER
Ken Anderson

ILLUSTRATOR
Christopher Toland

CREATIVE DIRECTORS
Harry Cocciolo
Sean Ehringer

CLIENT
Adidas

AGENCY
Leagas Delaney/San Francisco

02012A

GOLD AWARD
MAGAZINE COLOR
FULL PAGE OR SPREAD:
CAMPAIGN

ART DIRECTOR
Andrew Whitehouse

WRITER
Justin Gomes

PHOTOGRAPHER
Clive Stewart

CREATIVE DIRECTOR
Rob McLennan

CLIENT
Dulux

AGENCY
Lowe Bull Calvert Pace/
Johannesburg

02014A

Also won:
MERIT AWARDS
NEWSPAPER OVER 600 LINES
CAMPAIGN

COLLATERAL: POSTERS
CAMPAIGN

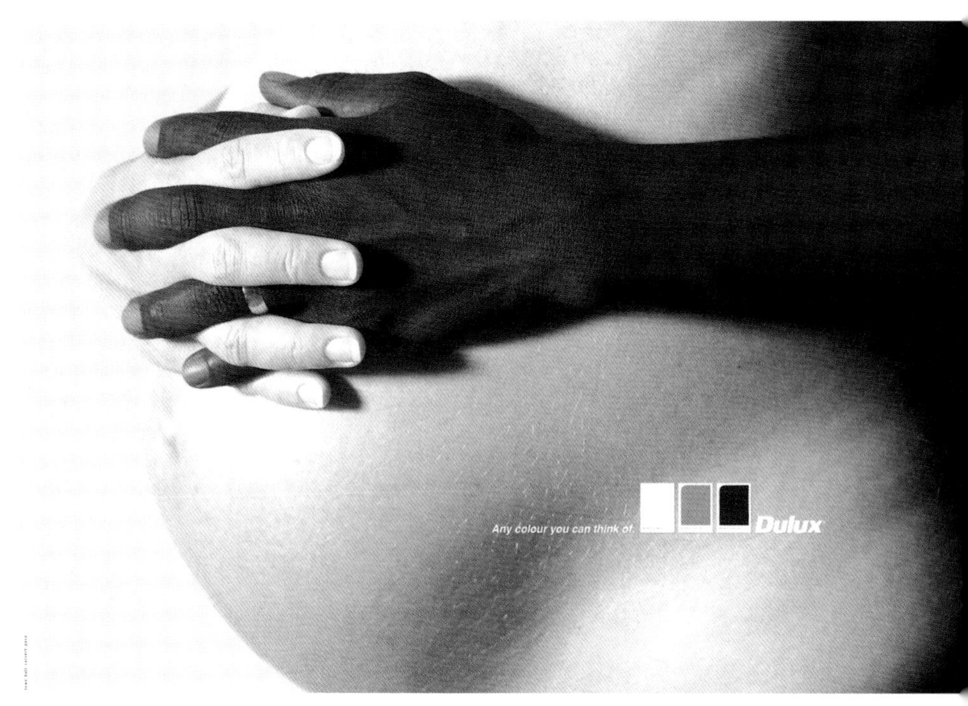

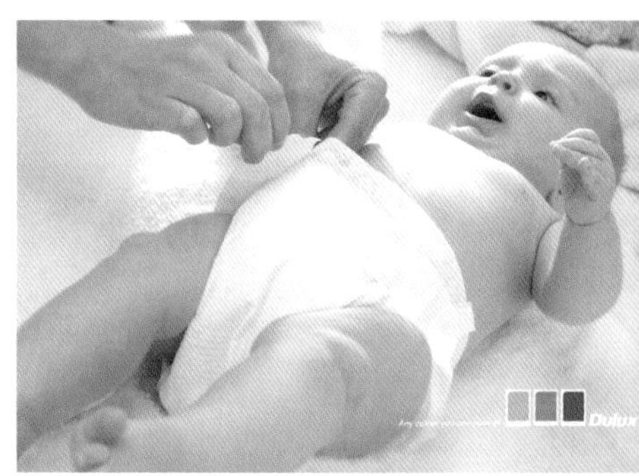

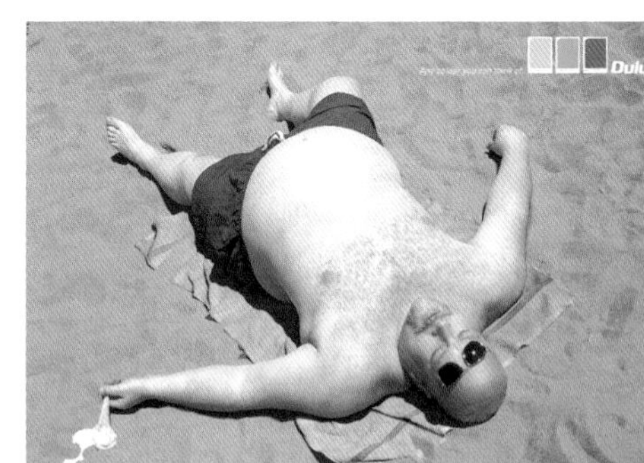

GOLD AWARD
MAGAZINE COLOR
FULL PAGE OR SPREAD:
CAMPAIGN

ART DIRECTOR
Antony Nelson

WRITER
Mike Sutherland

PHOTOGRAPHER
Trevor Ray Hart

TYPOGRAPHER
Scott Silvey

CREATIVE DIRECTOR
David Droga

CLIENT
Club 18-30

AGENCY
Saatchi & Saatchi/London

02013A

Also won:
MERIT AWARDS
OUTDOOR: CAMPAIGN

POSTERS: CAMPAIGN

SILVER AWARD
MAGAZINE COLOR
FULL PAGE OR SPREAD:
CAMPAIGN

ART DIRECTORS
Jayanta Jenkins
Bill Karow

WRITERS
Mark Fitzloff
Simon Mainwaring

PHOTOGRAPHER
Michael Jones

CREATIVE DIRECTORS
Dan Wieden
Hal Curtis
Jim Riswold

CLIENT
Nike

AGENCY
Wieden + Kennedy/Portland

02015A

BRONZE AWARD MAGAZINE COLOR FULL PAGE OR SPREAD: CAMPAIGN

ART DIRECTOR
Paco Marco

WRITER
Javier Valero

PHOTOGRAPHER
Josep M. Roca

CREATIVE DIRECTOR
David Guimaraes

CLIENT
Miguel Torres

AGENCY
Tandem Company Gausch
DDB/Barcelona

02016A

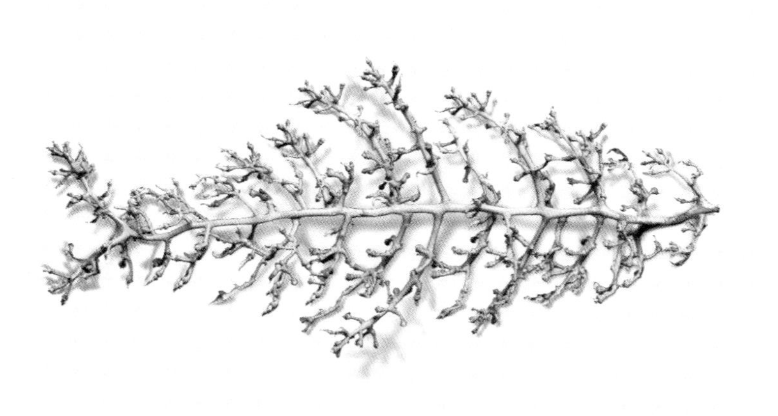

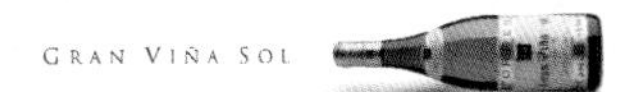

GOLD AWARD
OUTDOOR: SINGLE

ART DIRECTOR
Joseph Mazzaferro

WRITERS
Joseph Mazzaferro
Pete Lewtas

CREATIVE DIRECTOR
David Page

CLIENT
Absolut Vodka

AGENCY
TBWA/Chiat/Day/New York

02017A

SILVER AWARD
OUTDOOR: SINGLE

ART DIRECTOR
Martin Casson

WRITER
Matthew Abbott

CREATIVE DIRECTOR
Peter Souter

CLIENT
The Economist

AGENCY
Abbott Mead Vickers.BBDO/
London

02018A

SILVER AWARD
OUTDOOR: CAMPAIGN

ART DIRECTORS
Staffan Håkanson
Staffan Forsman

WRITERS
Martin Ringqvist
Björn Engström
Emma Zetterholm
Johanna Svernvall

PHOTOGRAPHER
Lennart Sjöberg

CLIENT
Göteborgs Posten

AGENCY
Forsman & Bodenfors/
Göthenburg

02019A

SILVER AWARD
GUERILLA ADVERTISING

ART DIRECTOR
Toh Han Ming

WRITER
Toh Han Ming

CREATIVE DIRECTORS
Patrick Low
Mark Fong

CLIENT
Singapore Cancer Society

AGENCY
Dentsu Young & Rubicam/
Singapore

02020A

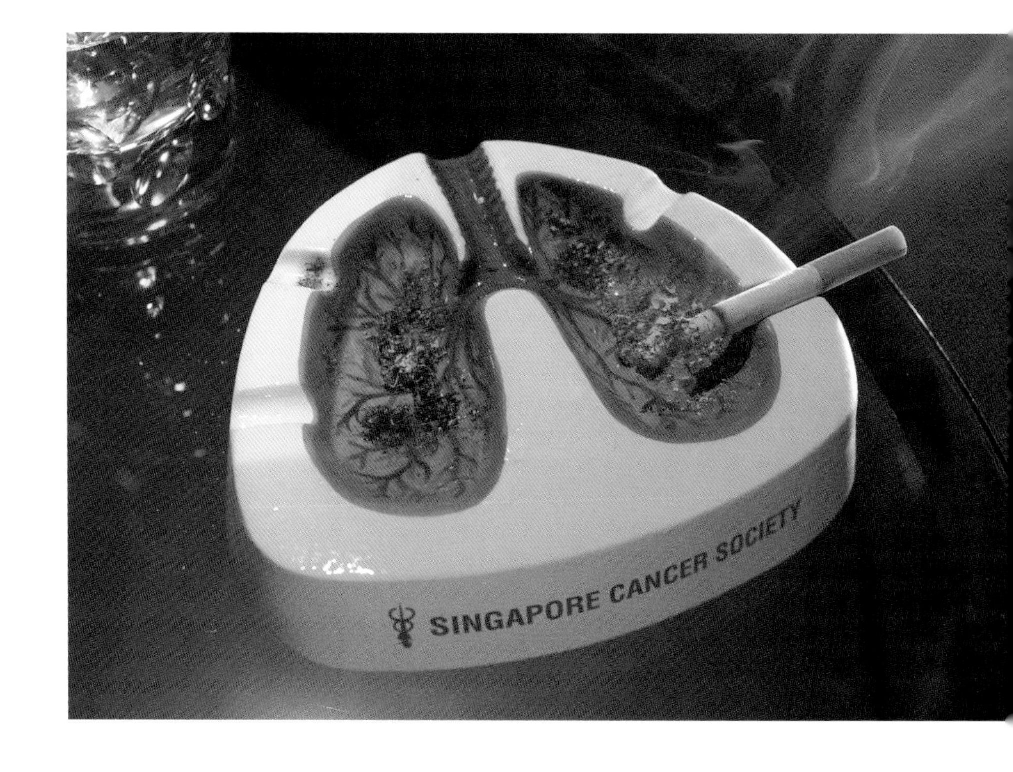

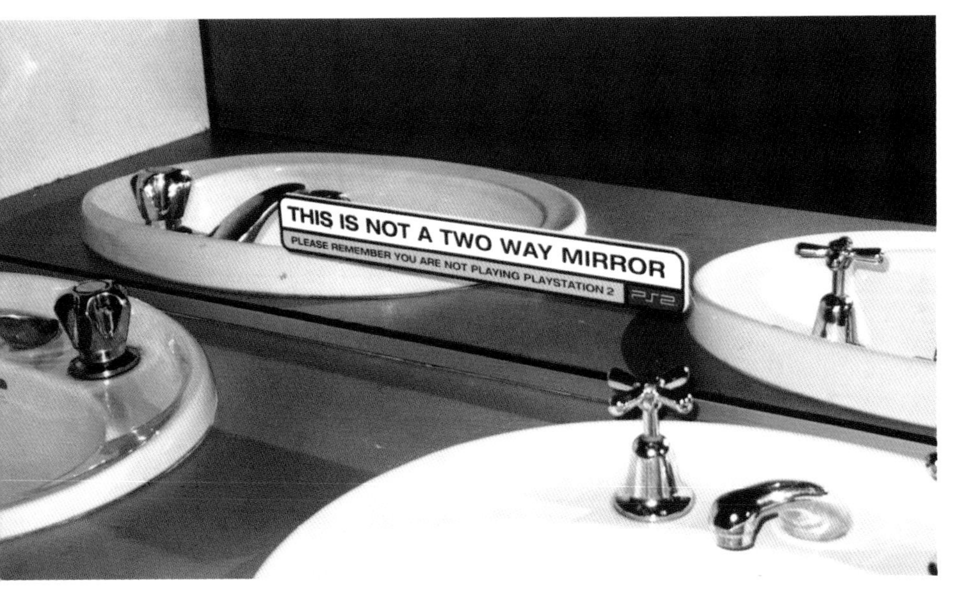

SILVER AWARD
GUERILLA ADVERTISING

ART DIRECTORS
Matty Burton
Christian Finucane

WRITERS
David Bowman
Jon Skinner

CREATIVE DIRECTOR
Ian Sizer

CLIENT
Sony Computer
Entertainment

AGENCY
Whybin Lawrence TBWA/
Sydney

02021A

BRONZE AWARD
GUERILLA ADVERTISING

ART DIRECTOR
Gavin Siakimotu

WRITER
Hywel James

PHOTOGRAPHER
Francois Maritz

CREATIVE DIRECTOR
Jeneal Rohrback

CLIENT
SKY Television

AGENCY
DDB NZ Limited/Auckland

02022A

Fly United and see the world.

For an international business traveler, there's no more welcome destination than the conference room you reach on time. So it may be worth remembering that United's network serves more of the business capitals of Europe, Asia, the South Pacific, and the Americas than any other airline. After all, when your travel arrangements go smoothly, there's much more time to see the world, instead of just working there. For reservations, please see your travel professional, or visit www.cn.ual.com.

SILVER AWARD
TRADE COLOR
FULL PAGE OR SPREAD: SINGLE

ART DIRECTOR
Andy Anema

WRITER
Rob McPherson

PHOTOGRAPHER
Jim Gallop

CREATIVE DIRECTORS
David Lubars
Tom Lichtenheld

CLIENT
United Airlines

AGENCY
Fallon/Minneapolis

02023A

BRONZE AWARD
TRADE COLOR
FULL PAGE OR SPREAD: SINGLE

ART DIRECTOR
James Clunie

WRITER
Michael Atkinson

PHOTOGRAPHER
Ron Crofoot

CREATIVE DIRECTOR
Brian Kroening

CLIENT
American Standard

AGENCY
Carmichael Lynch/
Minneapolis

02024A

GOLD AWARD
TRADE ANY SIZE
B/W OR COLOR: CAMPAIGN

ART DIRECTOR
Maurice Wee

WRITER
Renee Lim

PHOTOGRAPHER
Stanley Wong

ILLUSTRATOR
Edward Loh

CREATIVE DIRECTOR
Craig Davis

CLIENT
Campaign Brief Asia

AGENCY
Saatchi & Saatchi/Hong Kong

02025A

Also won:
MERIT AWARD
COLLATERAL: POSTERS
CAMPAIGN

MERIT AWARDS
TRADE COLOR
FULL PAGE OR SPREAD: SINGLE

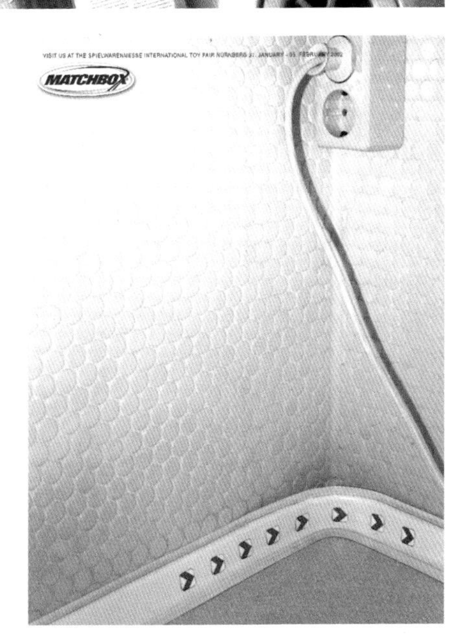

SILVER AWARD
TRADE ANY SIZE
B/W OR COLOR: CAMPAIGN

ART DIRECTORS
Juergen Schanz
Simon Oppmann

WRITER
Olga Potempa

PHOTOGRAPHERS
Joachim Bacherl
Olga Potempa

CREATIVE DIRECTORS
Simon Oppmann
Peter Römmelt

CLIENT
Mattel

AGENCY
Ogilvy & Mather/Frankfurt

02026A

Also won:
MERIT AWARD
COLLATERAL: POSTERS
CAMPAIGN

BRONZE AWARD
TRADE ANY SIZE
B/W OR COLOR: CAMPAIGN

ART DIRECTOR
Joel Rodriguez

WRITERS
Bob Kerstetter
Paul Charney

PHOTOGRAPHER
Joel Rodriguez

CREATIVE DIRECTORS
Bob Kerstetter
Steve Stone

CLIENT
MTV International

AGENCY
Black Rocket/San Francisco

02027A

My life is in the crapper.

I'm 52. I feel 72. I work with young people. I hear them laugh. Their laughs echo in my head. All day long. A year ago, I was looking at boats. Today I'm eating a bag lunch. And my mortgage hangs over me like a cement truck. But there's still hope for you. Let me show you how to dynamically reach a vibrant, optimistic, worldwide youth market. We are the only network that can do this. Are you with me? Please hurry. I'm not getting any younger.

Talk to me. Bring me back.

Please advertise with MTV International.

My pain is real.

I am the new guy. Was it a mistake to come here? Perhaps. My peers ignore me. I don't get their jokes or references. I keep to myself. Try not to make eye contact. Strangely, I have found comfort in data. I am a fountain. I know everything about teenagers in every part of the world. MTV International does not pay me enough for what I can do for you.

Call me. Pray for me.

Please advertise with MTV International.

I am a ticking time bomb.

Call me. I am nice on the phone.

My world has no joy.

Let's meet. My calendar is wide open.

GOLD AWARD
COLLATERAL: POINT OF PURCHASE AND IN-STORE

ART DIRECTORS
Frank Anselmo
Jayson Atienza

WRITERS
Jayson Atienza
Frank Anselmo

CREATIVE DIRECTORS
Ted Sann
Gerry Graf

CLIENT
Guinness

AGENCY
BBDO/New York

02028A

Round for a reason. The New Beetle received the Insurance Institute for Highway Safety's highest rating. Drivers wanted.

SILVER AWARD
COLLATERAL: POINT OF PURCHASE AND IN-STORE

ART DIRECTOR
Don Shelford

WRITER
Susan Ebling Corbo

PHOTOGRAPHER
Jeff Mermelstein

CREATIVE DIRECTORS
Ron Lawner
Alan Pafenbach

CLIENT
Volkswagen of America

AGENCY
Arnold Worldwide/Boston

02029A

BRONZE AWARD
COLLATERAL: POINT OF PURCHASE AND IN-STORE

ART DIRECTOR
Gareth Lessing

PHOTOGRAPHER
Janyon Boschoff

ILLUSTRATOR
Gareth Lessing

CREATIVE DIRECTOR
Chris Garbutt

CLIENT
Colman's Spray and Cook

AGENCY
TBWA Hunt Lascaris/
Johannesburg

02030A

GOLD, SILVER, BRONZE

GOLD AWARD
COLLATERAL: SELF-PROMOTION

ART DIRECTORS
Thomas Hilland
Luke Williamson

WRITER
Ben Mooge

CREATIVE DIRECTORS
Robert Saville
Mark Waites

CLIENT
Mother

AGENCY
Mother/London

02031A

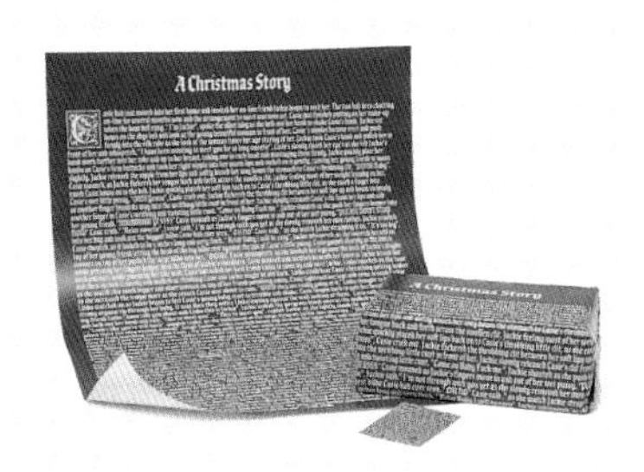

SILVER AWARD
COLLATERAL: SELF-PROMOTION

ART DIRECTOR
Bebemona Yim

WRITER
Marc Lucas

CREATIVE DIRECTORS
Jimmy Lam
Larry Ong
Marc Lucas

CLIENT
D'Arcy HK

AGENCY
D'Arcy/Hong Kong

02032A

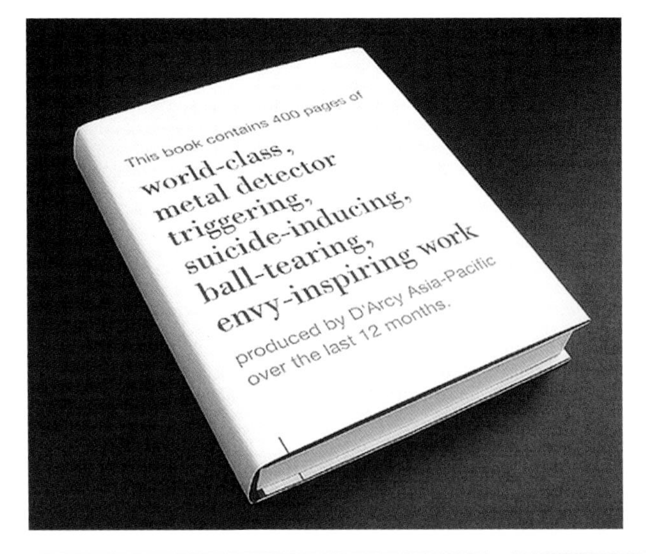

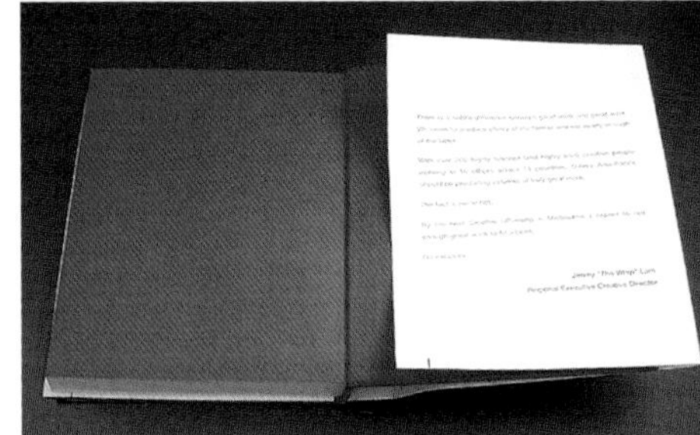

GOLD AWARD
COLLATERAL: POSTERS
SINGLE

ART DIRECTOR
Antony Nelson

WRITER
Mike Sutherland

PHOTOGRAPHER
Trevor Ray Hart

TYPOGRAPHER
Scott Silvey

CREATIVE DIRECTOR
David Droga

CLIENT
Club 18-30

AGENCY
Saatchi & Saatchi/London

02033A

Also won:
MERIT AWARD
MAGAZINE COLOR
FULL PAGE OR SPREAD: SINGLE

SILVER AWARD
COLLATERAL: POSTERS
SINGLE

ART DIRECTORS
Gavin Simpson
Sonal Dabral

WRITERS
Paul Lim
Sonal Dabral

PHOTOGRAPHER
Fai/IFL Studio

CREATIVE DIRECTOR
Sonal Dabral

CLIENT
Mattel Southeast Asia

AGENCY
Ogilvy & Mather/
Kuala Lumpur

02034A

BRONZE AWARD
COLLATERAL: POSTERS
SINGLE

ART DIRECTOR
Thirasak Thanapatanakul

WRITERS
Kitti Chaiyaporn
David Guerrero

PHOTOGRAPHER
Anuchai Sricharunputong

ILLUSTRATOR
Anuchai Sricharunputong

CREATIVE DIRECTOR
Suthisak Sucharittanonta

CLIENT
Federal Express

AGENCY
BBDO/Bangkok

02035A

GOLD AWARD
COLLATERAL: POSTERS
CAMPAIGN

ART DIRECTORS
Brian Capel
Gavin Simpson
Ngow Fei Fei
James Wong
Lydia Lim
Sonal Dabral
Tham Khai Meng
Neil French

WRITERS
Case Deenadayalan
Paul Lim
Ngow Fei Fei
Eddie Azadi
Sonal Dabral

PHOTOGRAPHER
Fai/IFL Studio

CREATIVE DIRECTOR
Sonal Dabral

CLIENT
Mattel Southeast Asia

AGENCY
Ogilvy & Mather/
Kuala Lumpur

02036A

Also won:
MERIT AWARD
COLLATERAL: POSTERS
SINGLE

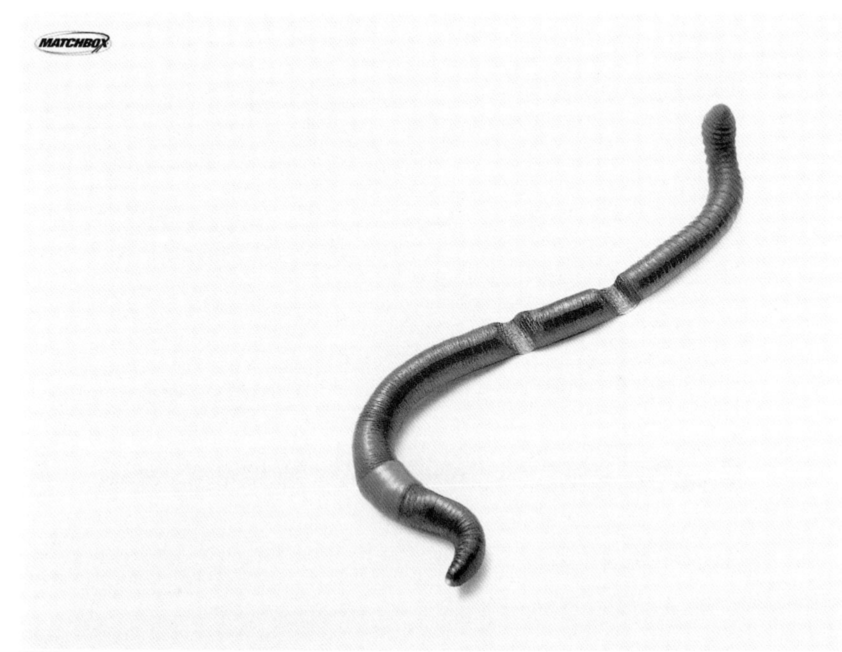

MERIT

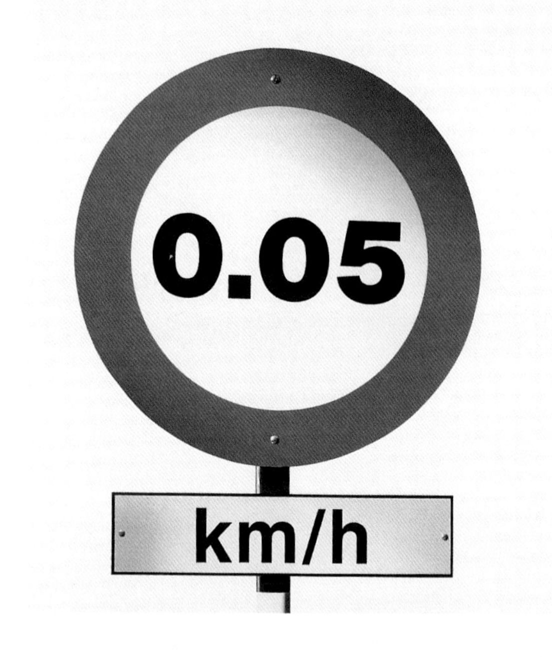

SILVER AWARD
COLLATERAL: POSTERS
CAMPAIGN

ART DIRECTOR
Andrés Grego

WRITERS
Enric Fortea
Àlex Martínez

PHOTOGRAPHER
Miquel Àngel Nalda

CREATIVE DIRECTORS
Àlex Martínez
Enric Fortea

CLIENT
Coty Astor S.A.

AGENCY
J. Walter Thompson/
Barcelona

02037A

BRONZE AWARD
COLLATERAL: POSTERS
CAMPAIGN

ART DIRECTOR
Steve Driggs

WRITER
Greg Hahn

PHOTOGRAPHERS
Mike Powell
Robert Beck
Thomas Kienzle

CREATIVE DIRECTOR
David Lubars

CLIENT
Sports Illustrated

AGENCY
Fallon/Minneapolis

02038A

Also won:
MERIT AWARD
COLLATERAL: POSTERS
SINGLE

GOLD, SILVER, BRONZE

☐ Newspaper

☐ Blanket

Please call 0800 248 964 to make a donation because some people don't have the choice.

AUCKLAND CITY MISSION
WINTER APPEAL

GOLD AWARD
PUBLIC SERVICE/POLITICAL NEWSPAPER OR MAGAZINE SINGLE

ART DIRECTOR
Guy Denniston

WRITER
Karl Fleet

CREATIVE DIRECTOR
Lachlan McPherson

CLIENT
Auckland City Mission

AGENCY
Publicis Mojo/Auckland

02039A

SILVER AWARD
PUBLIC SERVICE/POLITICAL NEWSPAPER OR MAGAZINE SINGLE

ART DIRECTOR
Roberto Fernandez

WRITER
Marcelo Reis

PHOTOGRAPHER
Rafael Costa

CREATIVE DIRECTORS
Erh Ray
Jader Rossetto
Pedro Cappeletti

CLIENT
MASP São Paulo Museum of Art

AGENCY
DM9 DDB Publicidade/São Paulo

02040A

BRONZE AWARD
PUBLIC SERVICE/POLITICAL
NEWSPAPER OR MAGAZINE
SINGLE

ART DIRECTOR
Ajab Singh

WRITER
Ajab Singh

PHOTOGRAPHER
Mejor Samrai

TYPOGRAPHER
Roger Kennedy

CREATIVE DIRECTOR
David Droga

CLIENT
Emma

AGENCY
Saatchi & Saatchi/London

02041A

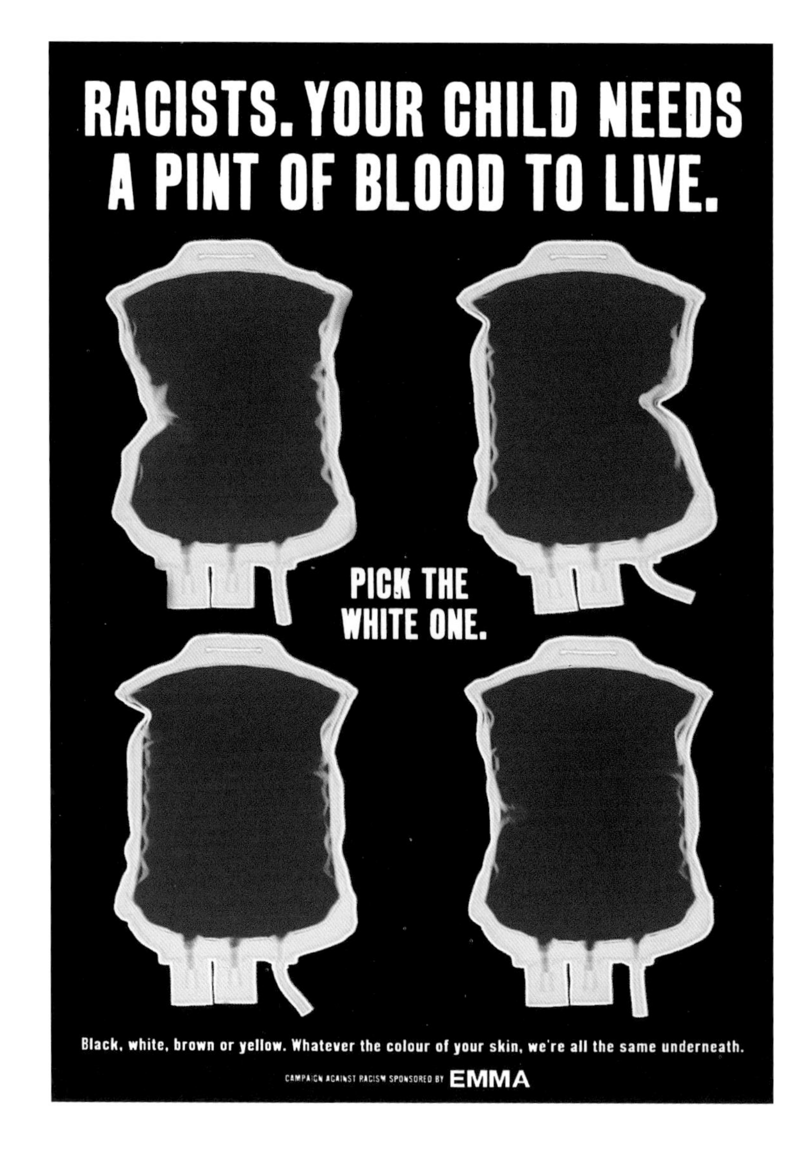

GOLD AWARD
PUBLIC SERVICE/POLITICAL NEWSPAPER OR MAGAZINE CAMPAIGN

ART DIRECTOR
Jon Wyville

WRITER
Ken Erke

CREATIVE DIRECTOR
Mark Figliulo

CLIENT
Misericordia

AGENCY
Young & Rubicam/Chicago

02042A

CIGARS WEREN'T HANDED OUT THE DAY PETER WAS BORN

Peter's dad was so overwhelmed with confusion he didn't know what to do. He and his wife had just been informed that their son was severely mentally disabled and they needed help. Fortunately there was Misericordia, a home dedicated to giving each of its 550 residents the best quality of life possible. With Misericordia at their side, they felt understood and supported and were now able to celebrate the great gift of their child's life.

MISERICORDIA Heart of Mercy FOR MORE INFORMATION OR IF YOU WOULD LIKE TO OFFER YOUR SUPPORT, PLEASE CALL 773.273.4166

JANUARY 22, 1977. 150 BIRTH ANNOUNCEMENTS SIT ON A DESK, UNSENT

22 HOURS OF LABOR, AND THEN THE STRUGGLE BEGAN

SILVER AWARD
PUBLIC SERVICE/POLITICAL
NEWSPAPER OR MAGAZINE
CAMPAIGN

ART DIRECTORS
Alex Burnard
Mike del Marmol

WRITER
Brian Tierney

PHOTOGRAPHERS
Angela Cappetta
Alex Burnard
Mike del Marmol

CREATIVE DIRECTOR
Alex Bogusky

CLIENT
Best Buddies

AGENCY
Crispin Porter & Bogusky/
Miami

02043A

Also won:
MERIT AWARDS
PUBLIC SERVICE/POLITICAL
NEWSPAPER OR MAGAZINE
SINGLE

2:00p.m. – Learned Sherry's IQ was only 54.
2:23 p.m. – Realized the insignificance of IQ tests.

OK, so you go into this Best Buddies thing thinking "Yeah, I'd like to help somebody with developmental disabilities... take them out... give them a chance to socialize... teach them a few things." Then, minutes after meeting your new friend, you realize that you're the one being taught. You're learning about their world. You're looking at your life differently – reassessing your priorities. You're gaining so much, you almost feel guilty. But then, you see the look on their face, and you say to yourself, "Hey, this 'giving' thing isn't so bad.

careful, calling 1-800-89-BUDDY just might change your life.
www.bestbuddies.org

MERIT

6:15 p.m. – PHILLIP IS A DEVELOPMENTALLY DISABLED PERSON.
6:27 p.m. – PHILLIP IS A PERSON.

It's true. Phillip Chai is not like the rest of us. He doesn't sweat the little things in life like the rest of us. He laughs more than the rest of us. He appreciates a simple walk in the park more than the rest of us. When you became his Best Buddy, it didn't take long to see how much he had to offer. You quickly realized that spending time with him wasn't going to be charity work. It wasn't going to be work at all. Just a friendship. A valuable, rewarding friendship. And hey, let's face it, who couldn't use another one of those?

CAREFUL, CALLING 1-800-89-BUDDY JUST MIGHT CHANGE YOUR LIFE.
www.bestbuddies.org

1:03 p.m. – Willie is "Special."
1:14 p.m. – Willie is Special.

So which is it? Are you giving? Are you gaining? Who's helping who here? You joined Best Buddies thinking it would be a nice way to do a little "public service." You'd sacrifice a couple afternoons a month and be a friend to someone with developmental disabilities. Maybe take them to a movie, go out for coffee, brighten their day, you know? Then you met him. He told a joke and it made you laugh. You discovered you both like the same movies. Suddenly, you realized this wasn't going to be charity work. It wasn't going to be work at all. Who knew?

CAREFUL, CALLING 1-800-89-BUDDY JUST MIGHT CHANGE YOUR LIFE. www.bestbuddies.org

MERIT

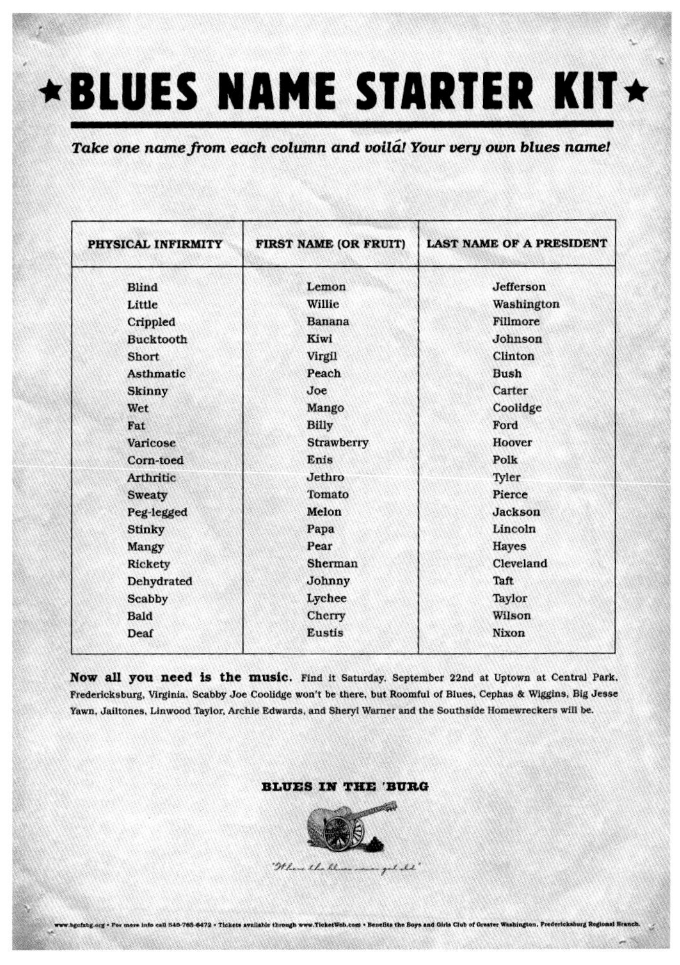

PHYSICAL INFIRMITY	FIRST NAME (OR FRUIT)	LAST NAME OF A PRESIDENT
Blind	Lemon	Jefferson
Little	Willie	Washington
Crippled	Banana	Fillmore
Bucktooth	Kiwi	Johnson
Short	Virgil	Clinton
Asthmatic	Peach	Bush
Skinny	Joe	Carter
Wet	Mango	Coolidge
Fat	Billy	Ford
Varicose	Strawberry	Hoover
Corn-toed	Enis	Polk
Arthritic	Jethro	Tyler
Sweaty	Tomato	Pierce
Peg-legged	Melon	Jackson
Stinky	Papa	Lincoln
Mangy	Pear	Hayes
Rickety	Sherman	Cleveland
Dehydrated	Johnny	Taft
Scabby	Lychee	Taylor
Bald	Cherry	Wilson
Deaf	Eustis	Nixon

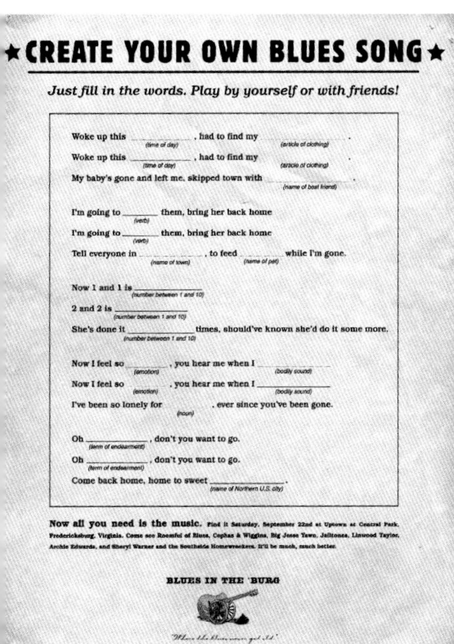

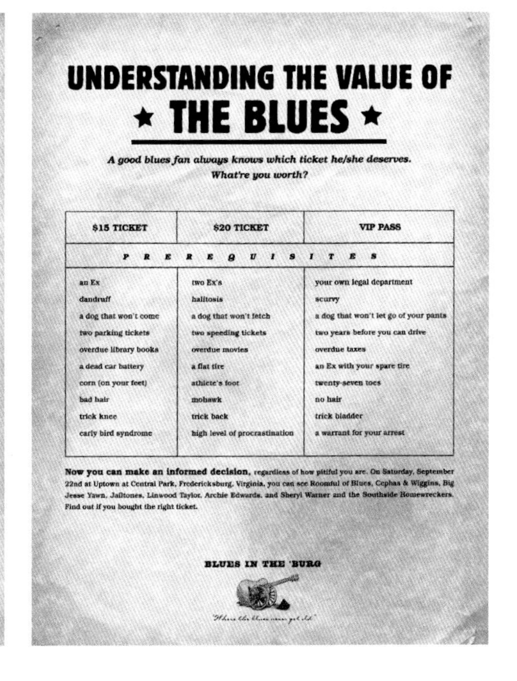

$15 TICKET	$20 TICKET	VIP PASS
P R E R E Q U I S I T E S		
an Ex	two Ex's	your own legal department
dandruff	halitosis	scurvy
a dog that won't come	a dog that won't fetch	a dog that won't let go of your pants
two parking tickets	two speeding tickets	two years before you can drive
overdue library books	overdue movies	overdue taxes
a dead car battery	a flat tire	an Ex with your spare tire
corn (on your feet)	athlete's foot	twenty-seven toes
bad hair	mohawk	no hair
trick knee	trick back	trick bladder
early bird syndrome	high level of procrastination	a warrant for your arrest

BRONZE AWARD
PUBLIC SERVICE/POLITICAL
NEWSPAPER OR MAGAZINE
CAMPAIGN

ART DIRECTORS
Bill Lee
Michael Ashley

WRITERS
Matt Fischvogt
Dinesh Kapoor
Michael Ashley

CREATIVE DIRECTOR
Michael Ashley

CLIENT
Boys & Girls Club of America

AGENCY
Arnika/Richmond

02044A

SILVER AWARD
PUBLIC SERVICE/POLITICAL
OUTDOOR AND POSTERS

ART DIRECTOR
Rajiv Rao

WRITER
Piyush Pandey

PHOTOGRAPHERS
Suresh Natarajan
Dinodia Picture Agency

CREATIVE DIRECTOR
Piyush Pandey

CLIENT
Cancer Patients
Aid Association

AGENCY
Ogilvy & Mather/Mumbai

02046A

Also won:
MERIT AWARD
PUBLIC SERVICE/POLITICAL
NEWSPAPER OR MAGAZINE
SINGLE

SILVER AWARD
PUBLIC SERVICE/POLITICAL
OUTDOOR AND POSTERS

ART DIRECTOR
Mike Sundell

WRITER
Suzanne Pope

PHOTOGRAPHER
Richard Heyfron

CREATIVE DIRECTORS
Zak Mroueh
Paul Lavoie

CLIENT
ABC Canada
Literacy Foundation

AGENCY
Taxi/Toronto

02045A

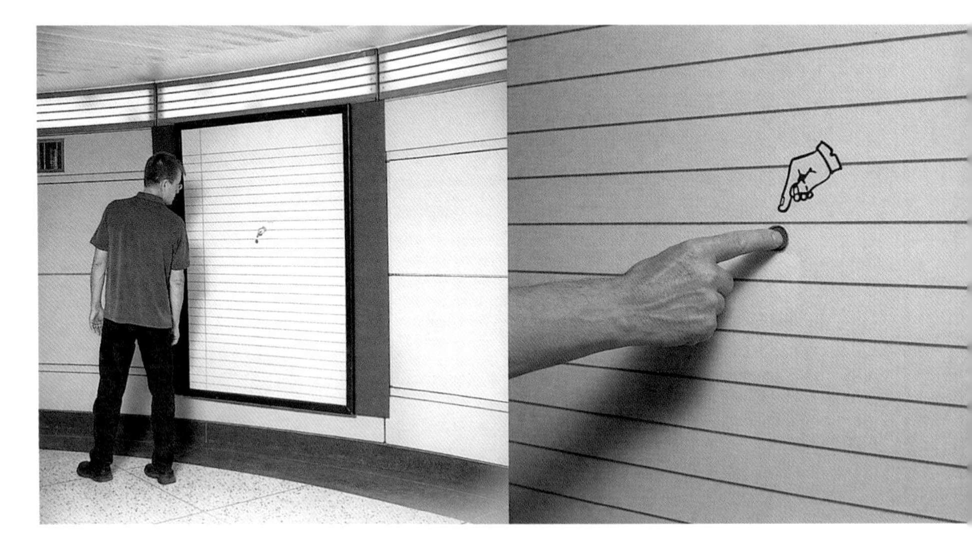

When someone presses the button, they hear a recorded message:

> "You'll notice this poster has no printed words. That's because 5 million adult Canadians would have a hard time reading them. But help is available. If you know someone who needs help with reading, writing, or math, just look under Learn in the Yellow Pages. This message brought to you by ABC Canada Literacy Foundation."

IF ROBERT BACON WERE WHITE, HE WOULD BE IN PRISON FOR LIFE.

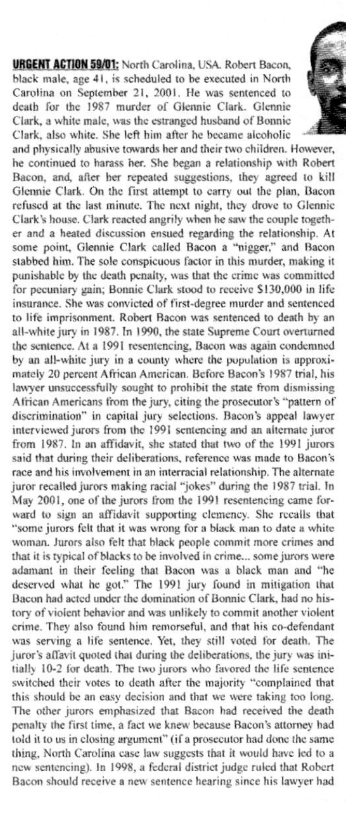

URGENT ACTION 59/01: North Carolina, USA. Robert Bacon, black male, age 41, is scheduled to be executed in North Carolina on September 21, 2001. He was sentenced to death for the 1987 murder of Glennie Clark. Glennie Clark, a white male, was the estranged husband of Bonnie Clark, also white. She left him after he became alcoholic and physically abusive towards her and their two children. However, he continued to harass her. She began a relationship with Robert Bacon, and, after her repeated suggestions, they agreed to kill Glennie Clark. On the first attempt to carry out the plan, Bacon refused at the last minute. The next night, they drove to Glennie Clark's house. Clark reacted angrily when he saw the couple together and a heated discussion ensued regarding the relationship. At some point, Glennie Clark called Bacon a "nigger," and Bacon stabbed him. The sole conspicuous factor in this murder, making it punishable by the death penalty, was that the crime was committed for pecuniary gain; Bonnie Clark stood to receive $130,000 in life insurance. She was convicted of first-degree murder and sentenced to life imprisonment. Robert Bacon was sentenced to death by an all-white jury in 1987. In 1990, the state Supreme Court overturned the sentence. At a 1991 resentencing, Bacon was again condemned by an all-white jury in a county where the population is approximately 20 percent African American. Before Bacon's 1987 trial, his lawyer unsuccessfully sought to prohibit the state from dismissing African Americans from the jury, citing the prosecutor's "pattern of discrimination" in capital jury selections. Bacon's appeal lawyer interviewed jurors from the 1991 sentencing and an alternate juror from 1987. In an affidavit, she stated that two of the 1991 jurors said that during their deliberations, reference was made to Bacon's race and his involvement in an interracial relationship. The alternate juror recalled jurors making racial "jokes" during the 1987 trial. In May 2001, one of the jurors from the 1991 resentencing came forward to sign an affidavit supporting clemency. She recalls that "some jurors felt that it was wrong for a black man to date a white woman. Jurors also felt that black people commit more crimes and that it is typical of blacks to be involved in crime... some jurors were adamant in their feeling that Bacon was a black man and "he deserved what he got." The 1991 jury found in mitigation that Bacon had acted under the domination of Bonnie Clark, had no history of violent behavior and was unlikely to commit another violent crime. They also found him remorseful, and that his co-defendant was serving a life sentence. Yet, they still voted for death. The juror's affavit quoted that during the deliberations, the jury was initially 10-2 for death. The two jurors who favored the life sentence switched their votes to death after the majority "complained that this should be an easy decision and that we were taking too long. The other jurors emphasized that Bacon had received the death penalty the first time, a fact we knew because Bacon's attorney had told it to us in closing argument" (if a prosecutor had done the same thing, North Carolina case law suggests that it would have led to a new sentencing). In 1998, a federal district judge ruled that Robert Bacon should receive a new sentence hearing since his lawyer had failed to present important mitigating evidence. This important evidence was that Bacon had an alcoholic father who engaged in numerous adulterous affairs. When he was very young, Bacon's mother sought his advice and assistance on this adultery, including having the boy eavesdrop on his father's phone calls. He also witnessed various incidents in which his father physically abused his mother. The Fourth Circuit Court reinstated the death sentence, saying that this evidence would not have altered the outcome. One of the three judges dissented, saying that the evidence, "would support the proposition that Bacon's family history uniquely mirrors the circumstances surrounding the crime for which Bacon now faces the death penalty; in both instances (in his family and in his relationship with Clark), a woman was apparently subjected to abuse by her husband; Bacon served as a confidant to the woman, and Bacon was manipulated to take steps he otherwise would not have taken." Two state Supreme Court judges have also dissented in the case, saying that in comparison with other cases and Bonnie Clark's life sentence, Bacon's death sentence was disproportionate.

RECOMMENDED ACTION: Please send faxes/express/airmail letters, in your own words; explaining that you do not condone the manner of Glennie Clark's death and expressing sympathy for his relatives; expressing deep concern about the allegations of racial discrimination that have marked this case; noting that two state Supreme Court judges have stated that Bacon's death sentence is disproportionate when compared to others and his co-defendant's sentence, and that two federal judges have ruled that evidence of Bacon's background not heard by the jury should require a new sentencing hearing; pointing out that the power of executive clemency exists to compensate for the rigidity of the courts, to remedy unfairness and error; noting that the Inter-American Commission on Human Rights has called for a stay of execution in order that it can consider Bacon's petition; calling on the governor to commute Robert Bacon's death sentence in the name of fairness and the reputation of his state and country.

PLEASE SEND APPEALS IMMEDIATELY: Governor Michael F. Easley, Office of the Governor, 20301 Mail Service Center, Raleigh, NC 27699-030, fax 1-919-715-3175 or 1-919-733-2120. Salutation: Dear Governor. You may also write, in not more than 250 words, to "Letters to the Editor": Raleigh News and Observer, PO Box 191, Raleigh, NC 27602, USA, fax 1-919-829-4872, e-mail forum @nando .com. Charlotte Observer, PO Box 20848, Charlotte, NC 28230, USA, fax 1-704-377-6214, e-mail opinion@charlotteobserver.com. Jacksonville News, PO Box 196, Jacksonville, NC 28541, USA, fax 1-910-353-7316, e-mail letters@jdnews.com. Winston-Salem Journal, PO Box 3159, Winston-Salem, NC 27102, USA, fax 1-336-727-7402, e-mail letters@wsjournal.com.

AMNESTY INTERNATIONAL

BRONZE AWARD
PUBLIC SERVICE/POLITICAL
OUTDOOR AND POSTERS

ART DIRECTOR
Philip Bonnery

WRITER
Anselmo Ramos

PHOTOGRAPHER
Public Domain

CREATIVE DIRECTOR
Armando Hernandez

CLIENT
Amnesty International

AGENCY
Young & Rubicam/Miami

02047A

SILVER AWARD
PUBLIC SERVICE/POLITICAL
COLLATERAL: BROCHURES AND DIRECT MAIL

ART DIRECTOR
Ute Sonntag

WRITER
Albrecht Tiefenbacher

PHOTOGRAPHER
Joachim Bacherl

CREATIVE DIRECTOR
Pith Kho

CLIENT
Verein Fur Arbeits und Erziehungshilfe

AGENCY
Ogilvy & Mather/Frankfurt

02048A

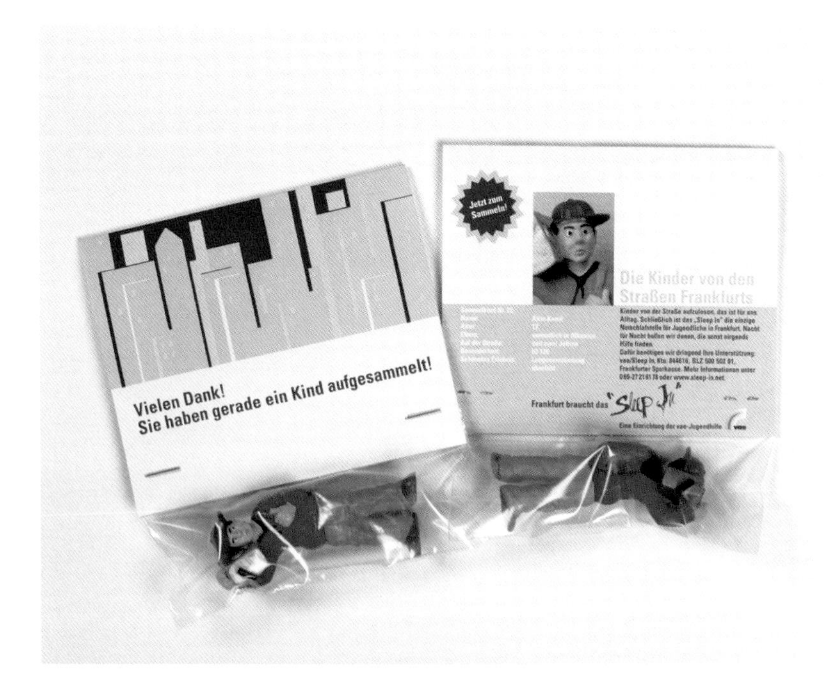

SFX: Baby crying inconsolably for 60 seconds.

ANNOUNCER: No matter how much she cries. No matter how tired you are. No matter how frustrated you get. Never, ever, shake a baby. This message brought to you by The Shaken Baby Association and Milwaukee area radio stations.

BRONZE AWARD
PUBLIC SERVICE/POLITICAL
RADIO: SINGLE

WRITERS
Gary Mueller
Pam Mufson

CREATIVE DIRECTOR
Gary Mueller

CLIENT
Shaken Baby Association

AGENCY
BVK/Milwaukee

02051A

ADAMS: This would have been in '66 or '68, I'm not sure.

ANNOUNCER: Eddie Adams, Associated Press photographer.

ADAMS: And Marines are taking about 50% casualties and guys are getting blown up. And I was scared to death, and facing me was a Marine about four feet away from me. This kid was about 18 years old, he was a poster, a US Marine poster. He was handsome. His face was all sunburned. And he had fear on his face like I'd never seen in my life. And, Jesus, you know. Now this would have been one of the greatest pictures of the war, because his face told it all. And I didn't take the picture because people would read it wrong and they'd call him a coward. He wasn't a coward. And I didn't do it. I knew that was going to screw up his life. I think there are times where you just don't take pictures.

ANNOUNCER: War is hell on journalists, too. Hear the stories behind the headlines, and see war through journalists' eyes at War Stories, now on exhibit at the Newseum. The story behind the news.

SILVER AWARD
PUBLIC SERVICE/POLITICAL
RADIO: CAMPAIGN

WRITER
Lisa Biskin

AGENCY PRODUCERS
Corinne Paulsen
Sandy Mislang

PRODUCTION COMPANY
AudioMaster

CREATIVE DIRECTOR
Mark Greenspun

CLIENT
Newseum

AGENCY
Adworks/Washington, DC

02053A

GOLD AWARD
PUBLIC SERVICE/POLITICAL
TELEVISION: SINGLE

ART DIRECTOR
Paul Brazier

WRITER
Nick Worthington

AGENCY PRODUCER
Francine Linsey

PRODUCTION COMPANY
Four Hundred Films

DIRECTOR
Stuart Douglas

CREATIVE DIRECTOR
Peter Souter

CLIENT
DETR

AGENCY
Abbott Mead Vickers.BBDO/
London

02054A

VOICEOVER: At just 5 mph over the 30 mph limit, how much further does it take to stop? One foot, two feet, three feet, four feet, five feet.

(In slow motion, the car hits a young boy crossing the road. The count continues until the car stops 21 feet later.)

VOICEOVER: Think. Slow down.

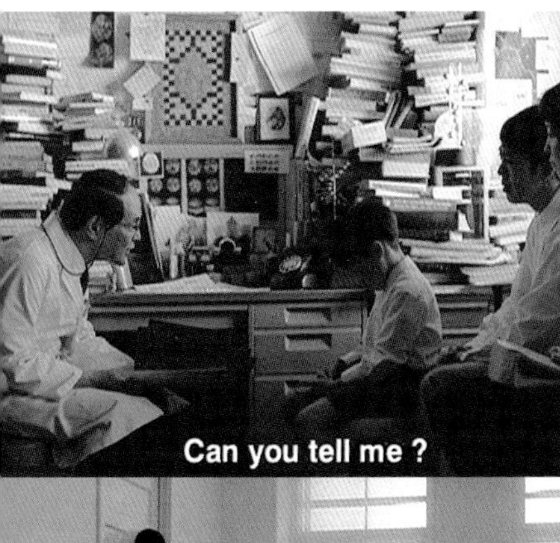

(A young boy's response to his teacher's request to "draw anything that comes up in your mind" is to obsessively color page after page of paper entirely black. He takes it to such extremes that he is sent to an institution for observation where he continues his drawing. Eventually his teacher discovers a puzzle piece in his desk whereupon she realizes the boy had been creating a life-size collage of a whale.)

SUPER: How can you encourage a child? Use your imagination. Support The Children Foundation. Japan Ad Council.

VOICE OF 14-YEAR-OLD: My hobbies are football, cyclin'...I like playin' in the street, an' I like, I like going down to the park an' stuff. Or I like collecting medals, like football medals. I like the way they're presented and stuff 'cuz they, some are shiny and some are like, blue, silver, green, stuff like that, but they're always, the ones I pick are always like blue but with shiny bits on. I always make sure that if I have a football player, it ain't just one with a leg out, it's one with an actual football on it.

(The screen reveals the speaker. It is not a 14-year-old boy but a middle aged man.)

SUPER: People online may not be who they say they are. Paedophiles use the internet. Don't give out your email, mobile or other personal details.

SILVER AWARD
PUBLIC SERVICE/POLITICAL
TELEVISION: SINGLE

ART DIRECTOR
Akira Kagami

WRITER
Takuma Takasaki

AGENCY PRODUCER
Hidehiko Kawasaki

PRODUCTION COMPANY
Dentsu Tec Inc.

DIRECTOR
Masahiro Takata

CLIENT
Japan Ad Council

AGENCY
Dentsu/Tokyo

02055A

BRONZE AWARD
PUBLIC SERVICE/POLITICAL
TELEVISION: SINGLE

ART DIRECTOR
Paul Belford

WRITER
Nigel Roberts

AGENCY PRODUCER
Kim Knowlton

DIRECTOR
Gillian Wearing

CREATIVE DIRECTORS
Nigel Roberts
Paul Belford

CLIENT
COI/Child Protection

AGENCY
Ogilvy/London

02056A

GOLD AWARD
PUBLIC SERVICE/POLITICAL
TELEVISION: CAMPAIGN

ART DIRECTORS
José Heitor
José Carlos Bontempo

WRITERS
Diogo Anahory
Pedro Bidarra

AGENCY PRODUCERS
Manuel Teixeira
Pedro Gaspar

PRODUCTION COMPANY
Ministério dos Filmes

DIRECTOR
Marco Martins

CREATIVE DIRECTOR
Pedro Bidarra

CLIENT
Portuguese Road Safety

AGENCY
BBDO Portugal/Lisbon

02057A

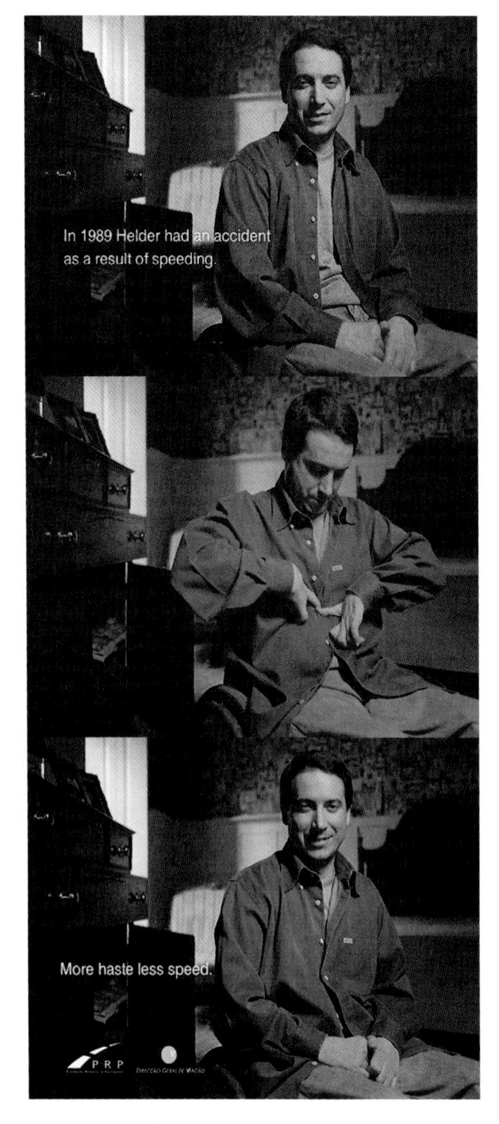

SUPER: In 1989 Helder had an accident as a result of speeding.

(Helder, who is paralyzed from the chest down, takes the entire length of the commercial to button his shirt.)

SUPER: More haste, less speed.

SUPER: In 1989 Henrique was thrown off his motorbike as he tried a dangerous maneuver.

(Henrique, who is paralyzed from the chest down, takes the entire length of the commercial to take off his shoes.)

SUPER: More haste, less speed.

SUPER: At St. Anthony's Feast in 1992 the car in which Teresa was traveling swerved off the road.

(Teresa, who is paralyzed from the chest down, takes the entire length of the commercial to open a letter.)

SUPER: More haste, less speed.

GOLD AWARD
CONSUMER RADIO: SINGLE

WRITERS
Ian Reichenthal
Adam Chasnow

AGENCY PRODUCER
Katherine Cheng

PRODUCTION COMPANY
Kamen Entertainment Group

CREATIVE DIRECTOR
Arthur Bijur

CLIENT
Hollywood Video

AGENCY
Cliff Freeman and Partners/
New York

02058A

HANNIBAL: Hollywood Video presents "60 Second Theater," where we try (unsuccessfully) to pack a two-hour Hollywood production into 60 seconds. Today's presentation...*Hannibal*.

CLARICE: FBI, Agent Starling.

HANNIBAL: Hello, Clarice.

CLARICE: Doctor Lecter! Where are you?

HANNIBAL: I can't say, but I'm about to have...an old friend for dinner.

CLARICE: Uchh! Still doing the cannibalism puns. Listen, I've got to go.

SFX: Phone rings again.

CLARICE: Starling here.

HANNIBAL: Buon giorno, Clarice.

CLARICE: Dr. Lecter, you're in Italy.

HANNIBAL: Well, you know I love...

CLARICE: ...eating Italian?

HANNIBAL: Why, yes.

CLARICE: Don't tell me. You've been picking the locals' brains...

HANNIBAL: Indeed.

CLARICE: Call me back when you get some new material.

SFX: Phone rings again. Someone picks up.

CLARICE: What?

HANNIBAL: Guess what I'm having for lunch...Clarice?...an Ed salad sandwich.

CLARICE: Did you say Ed salad?

HANNIBAL: Yes, as in Ed Perkins, your boss. You said he's a tough boss, and I agree.

CLARICE: Tough boss, Ed salad...that's all you got?

HANNIBAL: Well, I have this bit about your mom's home cooking....Ready?
Your mom's...home...cooking...She's in the pot...She's...Hello?
Clarice, Clarice...

ANNOUNCER: If this doesn't satisfy your urge to see Hannibal (and we can't say we blame you), then rent it today at Hollywood Video. Where every rental is yours for five days, and guaranteed to be in stock or next time it's free. Hollywood Video. Celebrity voices impersonated.

ANNOUNCER: Bud Light presents...Real. American. Heroes.

SINGER: Real American Heroes.

ANNOUNCER: Today we salute you, Mr. Company Computer Guy.

SINGER: Mr. Company Computer Guy.

ANNOUNCER: Though we "worker bees" scarcely know our modems from our scrotums, you are there to guide us.

SINGER: Modums and scrotums.

ANNOUNCER: When we screw up the "boot up," you are there. Without you, computers would mega-bite.

SINGER: Megabyte!

ANNOUNCER: The countless hours we spend surfing the internet and accidentally stumbling upon porn sites would instead be spent...working.

SINGER: Working for the man.

ANNOUNCER: So crack open an ice cold Bud Light, Mr. Company Computer Guy. For it's you who keeps our "log ons"...loggin'...and our hard drives hard.

SINGER: You've got to see this porn site.

ANNOUNCER: Bud Light Beer. Anheuser-Busch. St. Louis, Missouri.

SILVER AWARD
CONSUMER RADIO: SINGLE

WRITER
Bob Winter

AGENCY PRODUCER
Sam Pillsbury

PRODUCTION COMPANY
Chicago Recording Company

CREATIVE DIRECTORS
Bill Cimino
Mark Gross
John Immesoete
Bob Winter

CLIENT
Anheuser-Busch

AGENCY
DDB/Chicago

02059A

ANNOUNCER: Bud Light presents...Real. American. Heroes.

SINGER: Real American Heroes.

ANNOUNCER: Today we salute you, Mr. Camouflage Suit Maker.

SINGER: Mr. Camouflage Suit Maker.

ANNOUNCER: Your amazing skills of deception can trick a deer into thinking we're just a tree out for a walk, or a shrub having a cup of coffee.

SINGER: Shrub having coffee!

ANNOUNCER: Tirelessly you perfect your artistry. The squiggly black line. The blob. The slightly larger blob. All in spectacular shades of green.

SINGER: Green, green, green!

ANNOUNCER: Thanks to you we look fabulous in or out of the forest with a suit that can be easily accessorized with face paint and a few twigs.

SINGER: Dressed to kill.

ANNOUNCER: So crack open an ice cold Bud Light, Mr. Camouflage Suit Maker. Because when it comes to blending in, you really stand out.

SINGER: Mr. Camouflage Suit Makerrrrr.

ANNOUNCER: Bud Light Beer. Anheuser-Busch. St. Louis, Missouri.

BRONZE AWARD
CONSUMER RADIO: SINGLE

WRITER
John Immesoete

AGENCY PRODUCER
Sam Pillsbury

PRODUCTION COMPANY
Chicago Recording Company

CREATIVE DIRECTORS
Bill Cimino
Mark Gross
John Immesoete

CLIENT
Anheuser-Busch

AGENCY
DDB/Chicago

02060A

GOLD AWARD
CONSUMER RADIO: CAMPAIGN

WRITERS
Ian Reichenthal
Adam Chasnow
Greg Gerstner

PRODUCTION COMPANY
Kamen Entertainment Group

CREATIVE DIRECTOR
Arthur Bijur

CLIENT
Hollywood Video

AGENCY
Cliff Freeman and Partners/
New York

02061A

Also won:
MERIT AWARD
CONSUMER RADIO: SINGLE

SEE ALSO 02058A

ANNOUNCER: Hollywood Video presents "60 Second Theater," where we try (unsuccessfully) to pack a two-hour Hollywood production into 60 seconds. Today's presentation, *The Family Man.*

ANGEL: Excuse me, Jack Campbell?

JACK: *(Nicolas Cage soundalike.)* Who are you?

ANGEL: An angel. I've come to make your life better.

JACK: My life couldn't be better.

ANGEL: Do you have a penthouse apartment?

JACK: Yes.

ANGEL: Do you have a Ferrari?

JACK: Yes.

ANGEL: Do you sleep with supermodels?

JACK: Two at a time.

ANGEL: Really? Well, even your life is missing one thing. Love.

JACK: I have plenty of love. I love my penthouse, I love my Ferrari and I love sleeping with supermodels.

ANGEL: No, no, no, Jack, I'll take you to a magical place where you'll be surrounded by true love.

JACK: You mean Thailand?

ANGEL: No, New Jersey.

WOMAN: Hi, honey!

KIDS: Hi, daddy!

JACK: Who are you people?

ALL: We are your loving family!

JACK: Angel, you've taught me something. You can take away a man's Ferrari and all his wealth and power, but as long as he has a loving wife and family...and supermodels willing to entertain his every desire and fantasy...he'll be just fine.

ANGEL: Uh, Jack? The supermodels are gone, too.

ANNOUNCER: If this doesn't satisfy your urge to see *The Family Man* (and we can't say we blame you), then rent it today at Hollywood Video. Where every rental is yours for five days, and where *The Family Man* is guaranteed to be in stock or next time it's free. Hollywood Video. Celebrity voices impersonated.

MERIT

ANNOUNCER: Hollywood Video presents "60 Second Theatre," where we try (unsuccessfully) to pack a two-hour Hollywood production into 60 seconds. Today's presentation, *The Grinch.*

GRINCH: I must stop Christmas. To do so, I'll dress like Santa and go down their chimneys.

CHILD 1: Oh my god, what are you doing in our fireplace, Santa?

GRINCH: I'm going to ruin Christmas for you and your family.

CHILD 1: See any Christmas lights around here? Hello. This is a Jewish neighborhood.

GRINCH: Sorry.

CHILD 2: Whassup, Santa?

GRINCH: Where's your Christmas tree and all your presents?

CHILD 2: Yo, we celebrate Kwanza. The festival of our cultural heritage. Try the white folks next store.

WIFE: Nice touch coming down the chimney. The kids are going to love this, Harold!

GRINCH: I'm not Harold.

WIFE: Right, Santa.

GRINCH: I hate Christmas. Ooh, egg nog. *(Glug, glug.)* I love Christmas.

WIFE: You look green! How much egg nog have you had?

GRINCH: *(Snoring. Wakes up.)* It's Christmas! I blew it! Why am I laying in Grinch vomit?

ANNOUNCER: If this doesn't satisfy your urge to see *The Grinch* (and we can't say we blame you), then rent it today at Hollywood Video. Where *The Grinch* is guaranteed to be in stock or next time it's free. Hollywood Video. Celebrity voices impersonated.

ANNOUNCER:	And with that, the ruminant mammals stepped from the curb just as the Volkswagen appeared. Team 4Motion springs into action.
CHORUS:	Go Team 4Motion!
BACK RIGHTY:	Hey, uh, Right Fronty, is that a deer up ahead?
RIGHT FRONTY:	Yeah, I think it is.
LEFT BACKY:	Hey, fellas, what say we move some of the weight over to the left side, everybody cool with that?
THREE OTHER WHEELS:	Yeah, that's a good idea, sure.
SFX:	Swirling sound indicates Team 4Motion in action.
ANNOUNCER:	Quickly, our four wheels transfer power between them, stabilizing the Passat as it avoids the four-footed felons!
SFX:	Car veering.
DEER 2:	That was close.
DEER 1:	What?
CHORUS:	Team 4Motion!
ANNOUNCER:	Once again, Passat "Team 4Motion" illustrates 4Motion All-wheel Drive makes it better. Available only at your local Volkswagen dealer.

SILVER AWARD
CONSUMER RADIO: CAMPAIGN

WRITER
Joe Fallon

AGENCY PRODUCER
Elisha Goldstein

PRODUCTION COMPANY
Bart Radio

CREATIVE DIRECTORS
Ron Lawner
Alan Pafenbach

CLIENT
Volkswagen of America

AGENCY
Arnold Worldwide/Boston

02062A

ANNOUNCER: And we're down to the final seconds of this one. "Shaving Cream Endorsement" flips the puck through the air, knocked down by "Free Agent Next Year," "Free Agent" slides it over to "5 Million A Year." On the left side, "5 Million's" hit hard by "Spokesman for Athletic Equipment He Doesn't Even Use." And there's a penalty on the play....Wanna see great hockey players before they hit the NHL? Then check out the St. Mike's Majors this Thursday when they take on the Oshawa Generals. St. Mike's Majors, Hard Core Hockey.

SILVER AWARD
CONSUMER RADIO: CAMPAIGN

WRITERS
Kevin Rathgeber
Brent Wheeler

AGENCY PRODUCER
Janice Crondahl

PRODUCTION COMPANY
Griffiths, Gibson & Ramsay Productions

CREATIVE DIRECTOR
Dan Pawych

CLIENT
St. Michael's Majors

AGENCY
Downtown Partners/Toronto

02063A

GOLD AWARD
CONSUMER TELEVISION
OVER :30 SINGLE

ART DIRECTORS
Marcelo Vergara
Rafael Dalvia
Juan Cabral

WRITERS
Sebastian Blezowski
Sebastian Stagno
Sebastian Wilhelm
Alberto Ponte

PHOTOGRAPHER
Víctor Gonzalez

AGENCY PRODUCER
Hernan Carnavale

PRODUCTION COMPANY
La 4 Films

DIRECTOR
El Chirlo

CREATIVE DIRECTORS
Alberto Ponte
Sebastián Wilhelm

CLIENT
HSBC La Buenos Aires Insurance

AGENCY
Agulla & Baccetti/ Buenos Aires

02064A

(In the style of a cops and robbers '70s TV show, two thieves in a getaway car are chased by the police at a ridiculously slow speed. Eventually, the thieves are surrounded at the edge of a cliff. They lock hands, and decide to jump over the cliff. Both thieves explode.)

SUPER: La Buenos Aires logo. Member of the HSBC Group. HSBC logo and phone number.

ANNOUNCER: If you drive carefully, you pay less for your insurance. La Buenos Aires Autoscoring.

GOLD AWARD
CONSUMER TELEVISION
OVER :30 SINGLE

ART DIRECTOR
Gavin Lester

WRITER
Antony Goldstein

AGENCY PRODUCER
Andy Gulliman

PRODUCTION COMPANY
Academy Productions

DIRECTOR
Jonathan Glazer

CREATIVE DIRECTOR
Stephen Butler

CLIENT
Levi Strauss

AGENCY
Bartle Bogle Hegarty/London

02065A

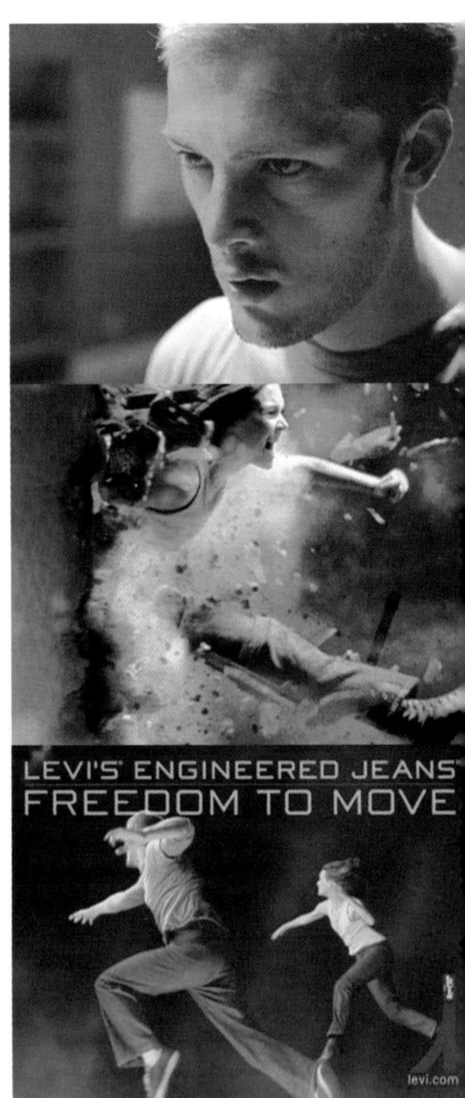

(A young man and woman in Levi's Engineered Jeans run at full pelt through a series of walls. They emerge out of the side of a building and run up a tree. As they approach the top of the tree they jump off, upwards into the night sky.)

SUPER: Levi's Engineered Jeans. Freedom to Move.

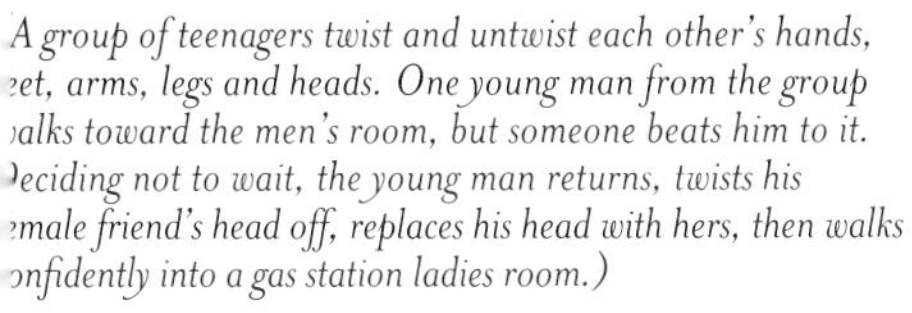

A group of teenagers twist and untwist each other's hands, eet, arms, legs and heads. One young man from the group alks toward the men's room, but someone beats him to it. eciding not to wait, the young man returns, twists his emale friend's head off, replaces his head with hers, then walks onfidently into a gas station ladies room.)

UPER: Levi's Engineered Jeans. Twisted to fit.

(A runner is shown crossing the street, catching up to passing trucks or moving cranes, speeding up or slowing down when necessary—all for the purpose of staying in the shade.)

SUPER: Shade running.

(As the runner leans against a wall, her shoe is in the sun. She moves her shoe so that it is completely shaded.)

SUPER: Swoosh/Play. nike.com/play.

SILVER AWARD
CONSUMER TELEVISION
OVER :30 SINGLE

ART DIRECTOR
Tony McTear

WRITER
Mark Hunter

AGENCY PRODUCER
Andy Gulliman

PRODUCTION COMPANY
Gorgeous Enterprises

DIRECTOR
Frank Budgen

CREATIVE DIRECTOR
Russell Ramsey

CLIENT
Levi Strauss

AGENCY
Bartle Bogle Hegarty/London

02067A

SILVER AWARD
CONSUMER TELEVISION
OVER :30 SINGLE

ART DIRECTORS
Monica Taylor
Andy Fackrell

WRITERS
Mike Byrne
Kash Sree

AGENCY PRODUCER
Andrew Loevenguth

PRODUCTION COMPANY
Gorgeous Enterprises

DIRECTOR
Frank Budgen

CREATIVE DIRECTORS
Dan Wieden
Hal Curtis
Jim Riswold

CLIENT
Nike

AGENCY
Wieden + Kennedy/Portland

02066A

BRONZE AWARD
CONSUMER TELEVISION
OVER :30 SINGLE

ART DIRECTORS
Juan Cabral
Santiago Chaumont
Maximiliano Anselmo

WRITERS
Christian Camean
Javier Mentasti
Sebastián Wilhelm

AGENCY PRODUCER
Hernan Carnavale

PRODUCTION COMPANY
Argentina Cine

DIRECTOR
Fabián Bielinski

CREATIVE DIRECTORS
Maximiliano Anselmo
Sebastián Wilhelm

CLIENT
Telecom

AGENCY
Agulla & Baccetti/
Buenos Aires

02068A

(A girl leaving a dance club yawns. The bouncer sees her and starts yawning. The yawn travels from a garbage collector who sees the bouncer, to passing policemen, even a dog. Eventually, the contagious yawn reaches a building super exactly when the same girl who started the chain gets home. She waves at the super and starts yawning again.)

SUPER: Communicate. It's simple. Telecom.

boy follows a man down the street, dribbling a basketball. e boy's moves get more complex as he navigates around stacles. The man, clearly annoyed, turns to walk down an ey, then throws aside his briefcase, hitches up his trousers d plays one-on-one against the boy.)

PER: Tailgating.

aron Davis walks by with a girl, another boy dribbling behind em.)

PER: nike.com/play. Play logo.

(Someone tags an unsuspecting young man, then runs away. As he tries to tag someone back, everyone manages to get away. In the subway, the people on a train see another person on the platform. They motion for him to get away. The young man chases him across the platform.)

SUPER: Tag. Swoosh/Play. nike.com/play

GOLD AWARD
CONSUMER TELEVISION
OVER :30 CAMPAIGN

ART DIRECTORS
Monica Taylor
Andy Fackrell

WRITERS
Mike Byrne
Kash Sree

AGENCY PRODUCER
Andrew Loevenguth

PRODUCTION COMPANY
Gorgeous Enterprises

DIRECTORS
Frank Budgen
Tom Carty

CREATIVE DIRECTORS
Dan Wieden
Hal Curtis
Jim Riswold

CLIENT
Nike

AGENCY
Wieden + Kennedy/Portland

02069A

SEE ALSO 02066A

**SILVER AWARD
CONSUMER TELEVISION
OVER :30 CAMPAIGN**

ART DIRECTOR
Damon Collins

WRITER
Tony Barry

AGENCY PRODUCER
Charles Crisp

PRODUCTION COMPANY
Gorgeous Enterprises

DIRECTOR
Chris Palmer

CREATIVE DIRECTOR
Paul Weinberger

CLIENT
Interbrew UK

AGENCY
Lowe/London

02070A

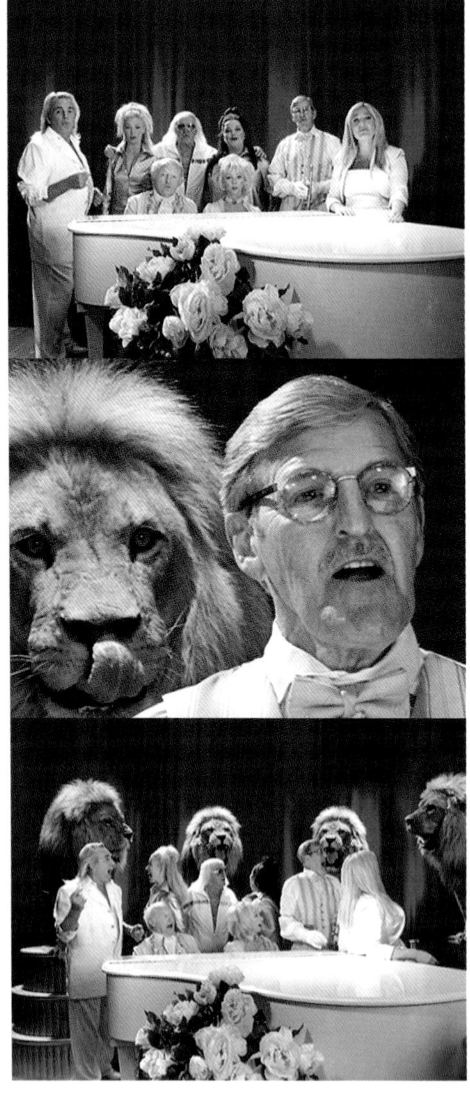

(In this campaign, has-been celebrities croon the Carpenters' classic "Close to You" in an attempt to blackmail consumers to buy their product.)

SUPER: Good news. Heineken sales have risen to a more than acceptable level. So we've got a treat for you. *(A pack of lions is released on the celebrities.)* How refreshing, how Heineken.

**BRONZE AWARD
CONSUMER TELEVISION
OVER :30 CAMPAIGN**

WRITERS
Ryo Honda
Nobuhiro Nakaji
Rika Yukimasa

AGENCY PRODUCERS
Naohiko Iwai
Hiroshi Oba

PRODUCTION COMPANY
Dentsu Tec Inc.

DIRECTOR
Shinji Yokota

CREATIVE DIRECTORS
Ryo Honda
Nobuhiro Nakaji

CLIENT
Otsuka Pharmaceutical

AGENCY
Dentsu/Tokyo

02071A

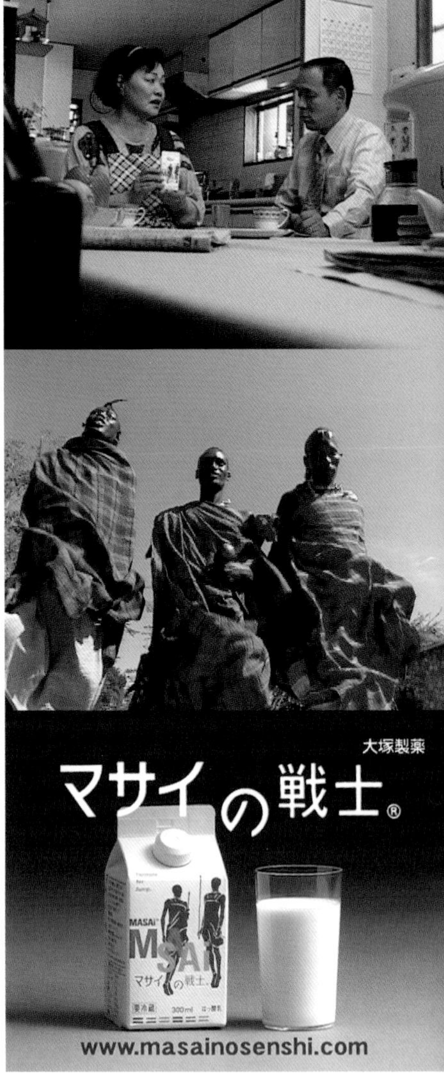

WIFE: Honey, did you know that staple foo for the Masai is this fermented milk? You know the Masai in Africa.

HUSBAND: The who?

WIFE: The Masai! The WHO did this research and they are the healthiest people.

HUSBAND: Ooooh.

WIFE: They're jumping fresh and peppy. Oh, look at you.

HUSBAND: C'mon, these people, they have no stress.

WIFE: They do, too. They've got lions ou there that could bite you any time. Have you been bit by your boss? No, right?

HUSBAND: Right.

WIFE: You complain about getting pushe around in crowded subways. What they were all hippos? That's stress!

HUSBAND: Absolutely.

WIFE: But we are up to our necks in debt What's worse? That or being choke by a monkey?

VOICEOVER: New fermented milk, The Masai. It's a healthy alternative.

SUPER: Otsuka Pharmaceutical.

stream of school children run to their parents' cars. A girl eaks away and runs toward a parked Corolla. She waves thusiastically and jumps in. The woman in the driver's seat ks at the little girl, slightly baffled.)

MAN: Who are you?

RL: Just shut up and drive!

PER: The new Corolla. A car to be proud of.

Beware of things made in October.

(A guy pulls the trigger of a new nail gun. Nothing happens. He heads to the phone to call customer support. Suddenly the nail gun shoots nails into the wall next to his head. The guy scrambles for cover, military style. His wife enters.)

MAN: Get down! Get down!

SUPER: Beware of things made in october.

(A distracted worker on the assembly line in the nail gun factory is glued to the TV. He misses a nail gun as it passes by, leaving the motor badly attached.)

SUPER: MLB Playoffs are coming. Fox logo.

GOLD AWARD
CONSUMER TELEVISION
:30/:25 SINGLE

ART DIRECTORS
Brett Salmons
Jo Stafford

WRITERS
Jo Stafford
Brett Salmons

AGENCY PRODUCER
Chris Moore

PRODUCTION COMPANY
Outsider

DIRECTORS
Dom & Nic

CREATIVE DIRECTOR
David Droga

CLIENT
Toyota GB

AGENCY
Saatchi & Saatchi/London

02072A

SILVER AWARD
CONSUMER TELEVISION
:30/:25 SINGLE

ART DIRECTORS
Jeff Labbe
Eric King

WRITERS
Jeff Labbe
Eric King
Scott Wild

AGENCY PRODUCER
Betsy Beale

PRODUCTION COMPANY
Harvest Productions

DIRECTOR
Baker Smith

CREATIVE DIRECTOR
Chuck McBride

CLIENT
Fox Sports

AGENCY
TBWA/Chiat/Day/
San Francisco

02073A

Also won:
MERIT AWARD
CONSUMER TELEVISION
:20 AND UNDER: SINGLE

BRONZE AWARD
CONSUMER TELEVISION
:30/:25 SINGLE

ART DIRECTOR
Randy Tatum

WRITERS
Tom Camp
Steve Casey

PRODUCTION COMPANY
Go Films

DIRECTOR
Gary McKendry

CREATIVE DIRECTOR
Jud Smith

CLIENT
IKEA

AGENCY
Carmichael Lynch/
Minneapolis

02074A

WOMAN: *(Looking through window.)* I wish we could be that organized.

MAN: People like that never have any fun. They're uptight.

(The woman next door appears in black leather. She spanks the couch playfully with a riding crop.)

WOMAN: They don't seem that uptight.

SUPER: You can't be too organized event. Now through April 8. Ikea.com.

GOLD AWARD
CONSUMER TELEVISION
:30/:25 CAMPAIGN

ART DIRECTOR
John Gellos

WRITER
Gregg Wasiak

AGENCY PRODUCERS
Rick Debbie
Will Morrison

PRODUCTION COMPANY
Production Farm

DIRECTORS
Gregg Wasiak
John Gellos

CREATIVE DIRECTORS
John Gellos
Gregg Wasiak

CLIENT
International Division of
The History Channel

AGENCY
The Concept Farm/New York

02075A

In case you missed it the first time

(During the historic 1938 title bout between Max Schmel and Joe Louis, something goes wrong with a photographer camera. The photographer turns the camera for closer inspection, when the flash accidentally goes off and blinds him momentarily. At this moment, Schmeling lays the famous knockout blow to Louis.)

SUPER: In case you missed it the first time. The History Channel logo.

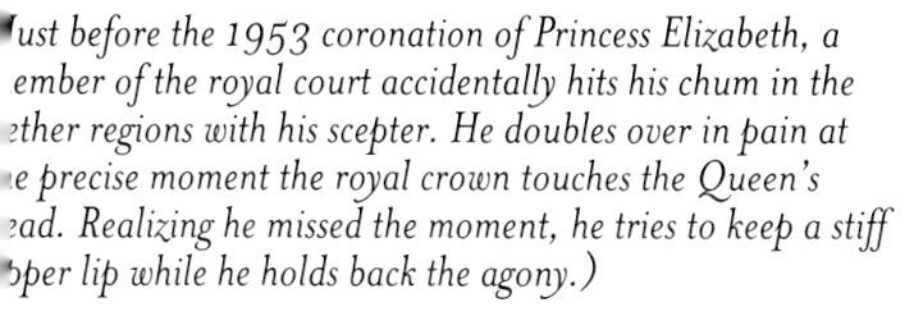

ust before the 1953 coronation of Princess Elizabeth, a ember of the royal court accidentally hits his chum in the ether regions with his scepter. He doubles over in pain at e precise moment the royal crown touches the Queen's ead. Realizing he missed the moment, he tries to keep a stiff pper lip while he holds back the agony.)

JPER: In case you missed it the first time.
The History Channel logo.

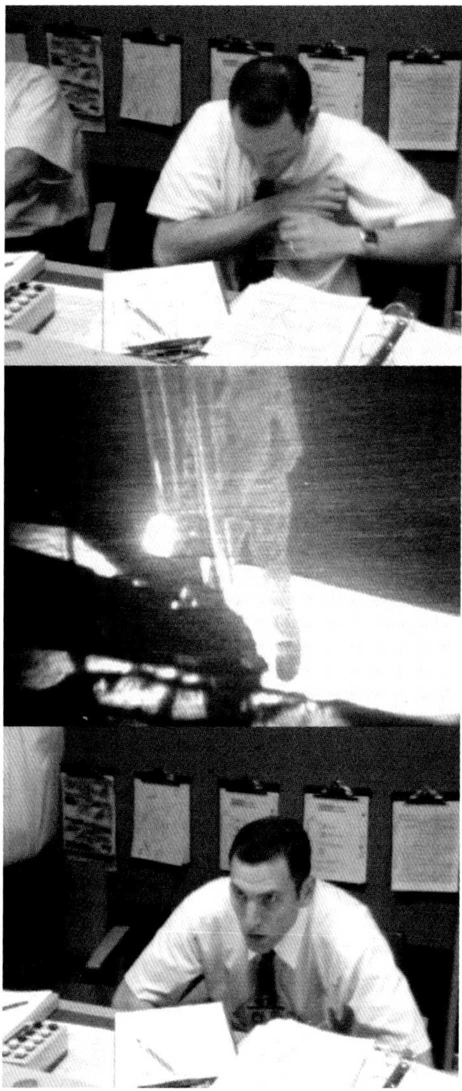

(At NASA mission control, engineers watch Neil Armstrong's 1967 descent from his capsule. A technician knocks over a cup of coffee onto his lap. While he's recovering, Neil recites his famous line, "That's one small step for man..." As the room erupts in joy, the technician realizes he has missed the "giant leap for mankind." He pretends to join in the celebratory mood, embarrassed that he has missed the moment of a lifetime.)

SUPER: In case you missed it the first time.
The History Channel logo.

SILVER AWARD
CONSUMER TELEVISION
:30/:25 CAMPAIGN

ART DIRECTORS
Jeff Labbe
Eric King

WRITERS
Jeff Labbe
Eric King
Scott Wild

AGENCY PRODUCER
Betsy Beale

PRODUCTION COMPANY
Harvest Productions

DIRECTOR
Baker Smith

CREATIVE DIRECTOR
Chuck McBride

CLIENT
Fox Sports

AGENCY
TBWA/Chiat/Day/
San Francisco

02077A

Also won:
MERIT AWARD
CONSUMER TELEVISION
:30/:25 SINGLE

Beware of things made in October.

MOM: Okay, new boat photo.

DAD: Okay.

(Dad puts the new boat in gear. The throttle comes off and the boat lurches, sending mom and daughter into the water. Dad tries to turn the boat away from a floating dock. The steering wheel breaks off the dashboard. Sunbathers dive off the dock, and dad leaps from the boat.)

SUPER: Beware of things made in October.

(At a factory, two distracted workers sloppily assemble the boat as they watch baseball.)

SUPER: MLB Playoffs are coming. Fox logo.

SILVER AWARD
CONSUMER TELEVISION
:30/:25 CAMPAIGN

ART DIRECTOR
Jeff Williams

WRITERS
Jeff Kling
Brant Mau

AGENCY PRODUCERS
Jeff Selis
Tieneke Pavesic

PRODUCTION COMPANY
@radical.media

DIRECTOR
Errol Morris

CREATIVE DIRECTORS
Susan Hoffman
Rob Palmer

CLIENT
Miller High Life

AGENCY
Wieden + Kennedy/Portland

02076A

Miller
HIGH LIFE

ANNOUNCER: Gobble, gobble. Hear that? Gobble gobble. You might have had your lion's share of that Thanksgiving dinner but you won't be able to sleep until you answer the siren call of that leftover turkey sandwich. That's right, now you're living the High Life.

SUPER: Miller High Life.

(A man waits alone in a lobby. The soundtrack is very sad orchestral music. A woman with beautiful legs enters. As the camera zooms in on her legs, the soundtrack suddenly goes out of tune. This happens again on the next close up of her legs. The camera reveals that we've been watching an orchestra attempting to record the scene's score. The musicians have been distracted by her legs in Aristoc tights.)

SUPER: Aristoc. For legs. For eyes.

BRONZE AWARD
CONSUMER TELEVISION
:30/:25 CAMPAIGN

ART DIRECTOR
Paul Briginshaw

WRITER
Malcolm Duffy

AGENCY PRODUCER
Fiona Marks

PRODUCTION COMPANY
Gorgeous Enterprises

DIRECTOR
Peter Thwaites

CREATIVE DIRECTORS
Malcolm Duffy
Paul Briginshaw

CLIENT
Aristoc

AGENCY
Miles Calcraft Briginshaw
Duffy/London

02078A

GOLD AWARD
CONSUMER TELEVISION
:20 AND UNDER: SINGLE

ART DIRECTOR
Shunichiro Miki

WRITER
Mitsuaki Imura

AGENCY PRODUCER
Yasuhito Nakae

PRODUCTION COMPANY
AOI Promotion

DIRECTOR
Shunichiro Miki

CREATIVE DIRECTOR
Yasuaki Iwamoto

CLIENT
Coca-Cola Japan

AGENCY
Hakuhodo/Tokyo

02079A

NURSE: 37 kilograms. Next please.

SFX: Ignition of jet pack on fat boy's back as he hovers just above the scale.

NURSE: Well, 20 kilograms. Next, please.

SUPER: Let's diet. Fanta.

A barking dog runs full speed toward a parked Celica. He ows no sign of slowing down. Finally, he hits the car.)

FX: Dog hitting car.

JPER: The Celica Action Package. Looks fast.

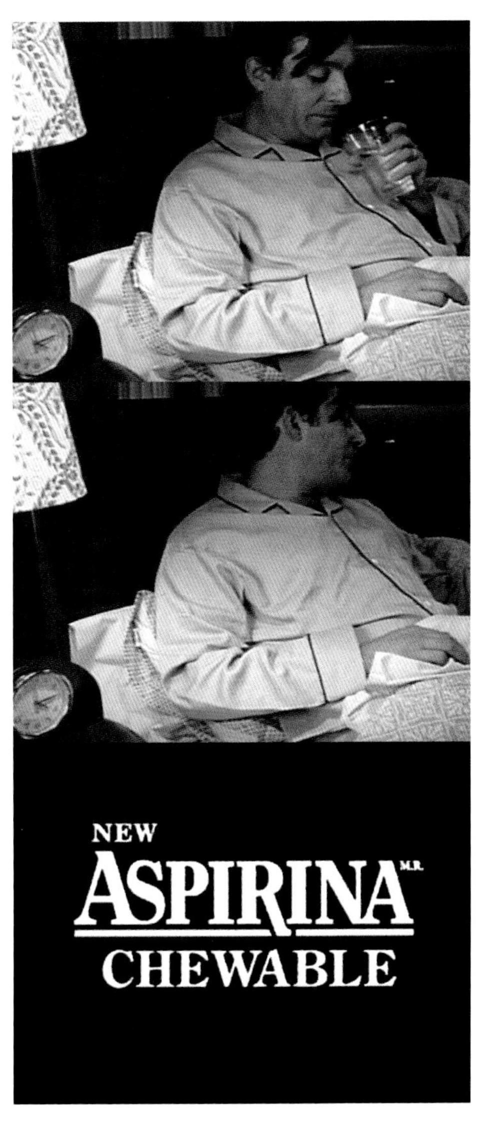

(A man can't sleep due to his headache. To make things worse, his wife is snoring. He grabs a chewable Aspirin from his night table, puts it in his mouth, and pours the water on his wife's face.)

SILVER AWARD
CONSUMER TELEVISION
:20 AND UNDER: SINGLE

ART DIRECTOR
Verner Soler

WRITER
Sherry Hawkins

AGENCY PRODUCER
Elaine Adachi

PRODUCTION COMPANY
Independent

DIRECTOR
Chris Smith

CREATIVE DIRECTORS
Neal Foard
Doug Van Andel

CLIENT
Toyota Motor Sales

AGENCY
Saatchi & Saatchi/Torrance

02080A

BRONZE AWARD
CONSUMER TELEVISION
:20 AND UNDER: SINGLE

ART DIRECTORS
Daniel Bravo
Ruben Rocha

WRITERS
Hector Fernandez
Miguel Moreno

AGENCY PRODUCER
Paco Muñoz

PRODUCTION COMPANY
La Tienda De La Imagen

DIRECTOR
Lorena Orraca

CREATIVE DIRECTORS
Hector Fernandez
Miguel Moreno

CLIENT
Bayer de Mexico

AGENCY
BBDO Mexico/Mexico City

02081A

GOLD AWARD
CONSUMER TELEVISION
:20 AND UNDER: CAMPAIGN

ART DIRECTOR
Dean Webb

WRITER
Dean Webb

AGENCY PRODUCER
Richard Chambers

PRODUCTION COMPANY
The Mill

CREATIVE DIRECTOR
Andrew Fraser

CLIENT
Guardian Film 4

AGENCY
BMP DDB/London

02082A

ANNOUNCER: In the movies, when you realize there's a car following you, there's really only one thing to say.

VOICE OF MOVIE ACTOR: Looks like we got company.

ANNOUNCER: Take a fresh look at film with the Guardian's Friday review.

ANNOUNCER: In the movies, in any jungle, anywhere in the world, you will always hear this bird.

SFX: The cry of a kooka burra.

ANNOUNCER: But you will never see it.

VOICEOVER: Take a fresh look at film with the Guardian's Friday review.

NNOUNCER: In the movies, there's always someone who isn't quite putting their heart into the battle.

In the footage of the battle scene, a circle appears around ıe warrior who looks slightly confused.)

OICEOVER: Take a fresh look at film with the Guardian's Friday review.

SFX: Laughter of a young couple as they play on the beach.

(The young man shakes up a can of Fanta, aims it at the young woman, and pops the top. The young woman ducks and the soda sprays over her head and blows up a nearby island.)

SUPER: Fun Time. Fanta.

SILVER AWARD
CONSUMER TELEVISION
:20 AND UNDER: CAMPAIGN

ART DIRECTOR
Shunichiro Miki

WRITER
Mitsuaki Imura

AGENCY PRODUCER
Yasuhito Nakae

PRODUCTION COMPANY
AOI Promotion

DIRECTOR
Shunichiro Miki

CREATIVE DIRECTOR
Yasuaki Iwamoto

CLIENT
Coca-Cola Japan

AGENCY
Hakuhodo/Tokyo

02083A

BRONZE AWARD
CONSUMER TELEVISION
:20 AND UNDER: CAMPAIGN

ART DIRECTOR
Dean Webb

WRITER
Dean Webb

AGENCY PRODUCER
Richard Chambers

PRODUCTION COMPANY
The Mill

CREATIVE DIRECTOR
Andrew Fraser

CLIENT
Guardian Film 4

AGENCY
BMP DDB/London

02084A

ANNOUNCER: In the movies, men always take it in turns to punch each other in the jaw.

(Footage from an old move shows two men in a fight. They take turns punching each other in the jaw.)

VOICEOVER: Take a fresh look at film with the Guardian's Friday review.

GOLD AWARD
CONSUMER TELEVISION
VARYING LENGTHS CAMPAIGN

ART DIRECTORS
Damon Pittman
Craig Adams

WRITERS
Hernán La Greca
Craig Adams
Steve Kuhn
Damon Pittman
Fernando Semenzato

AGENCY PRODUCERS
Damon Pittman
Craig Adams

PRODUCTION COMPANIES
Turner Studios
Spin Productions

DIRECTORS
Larry Robertson
Keith Adams

CREATIVE DIRECTOR
Fernando Semenzato

CLIENT
Cartoon Network
Latin America

AGENCY
Cartoon Network
Latin America/Atlanta

02085A

SEE ALSO 02088A AND 02089A

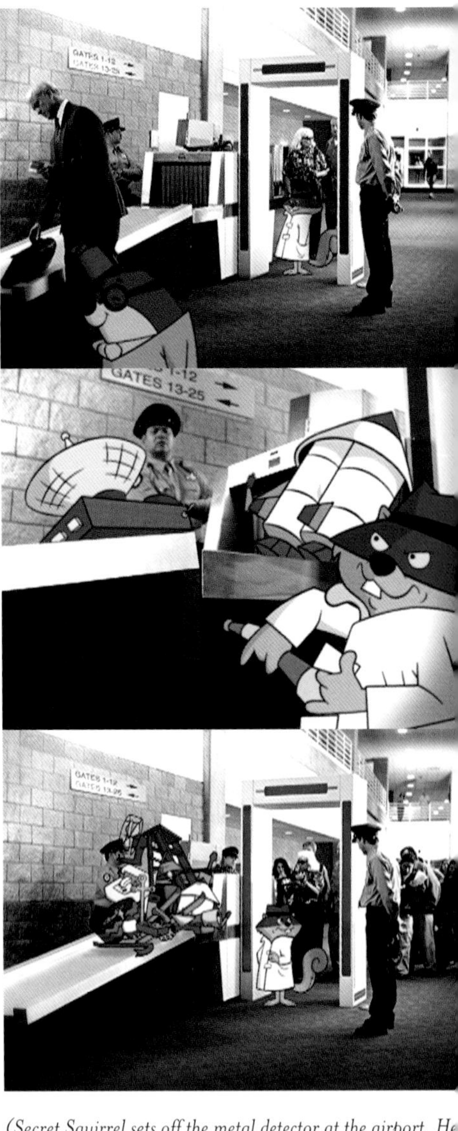

(Secret Squirrel sets off the metal detector at the airport. He takes a radar gun out of his trench coat and walks through again but the alarm still goes off. He pulls out a jet pack, a bazooka, television set, a boat; the alarm continues to go off.)

ANNOUNCER: Cartoon Network. Clearly, the best place for cartoons.

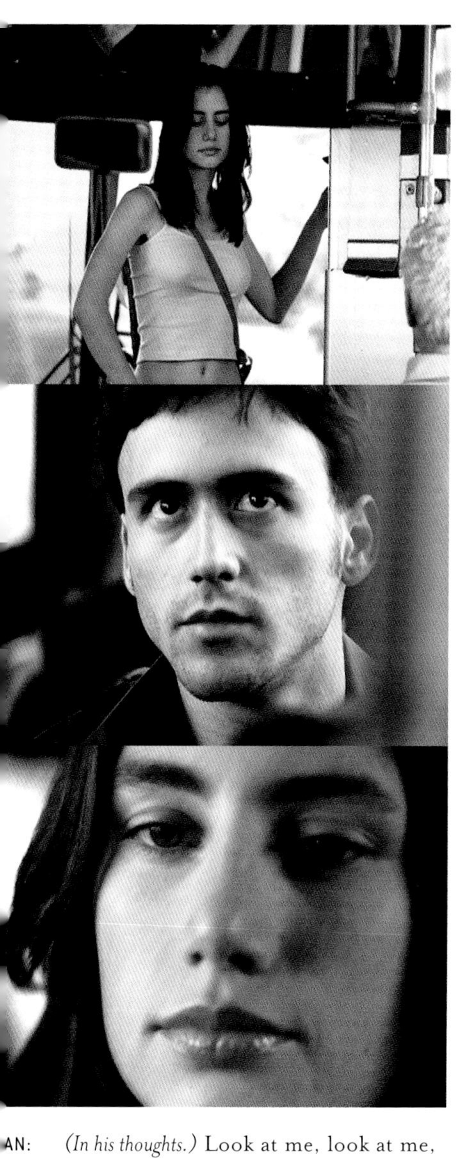

AN: *(In his thoughts.)* Look at me, look at me, look at me, look at me, look at me, look at me. Look at me, look at me, look at me.

Vhen the girl looks at him, the man, ashamed, turns his ad away, but soon begins staring again.)

AN: Look at me again, look at me again, look at me again, look at me again.

PER: Communicate, it's simple. Telecom logo.

(A man comes home from work to find his wife in bed. A cell phone rings. The man picks up his phone but realizes it wasn't his. The closet door opens and a naked man rushes out and picks up his cell phone from the bedside table.)

SUPER: A bonus for every call you receive. 2p per minute. Comviq logo.

SILVER AWARD
CONSUMER TELEVISION
VARYING LENGTHS CAMPAIGN

ART DIRECTORS
Maximiliano Anselmo
Santiago Chaumont
Juan Cabral

WRITERS
Sebastián Wilhelm
Alberto Ponte
Javier Mentasti
Christian Camean

AGENCY PRODUCER
Hernán Carnavale

PRODUCTION COMPANIES
La Doble A
Wassabi Films
Argentina Cine

DIRECTORS
Maximiliano Anselmo
Alberto Ponte
Sebastián Wilhelm
Diego Kaplan
Fabián Bielinski

CREATIVE DIRECTORS
Maximiliano Anselmo
Alberto Ponte
Sebastián Wilhelm

CLIENT
Telecom

AGENCY
Agulla & Baccetti/Buenos Aires

02086A

BRONZE AWARD
CONSUMER TELEVISION
VARYING LENGTHS CAMPAIGN

ART DIRECTOR
Kim Cramer

WRITER
Martin Ringqvist

AGENCY PRODUCER
Charlotte Most

PRODUCTION COMPANY
Thomas/Thomas

DIRECTOR
Kevin Thomas

CLIENT
Comviq

AGENCY
Forsman & Bodenfors/
Göthenburg

02087A

GOLD AWARD
CONSUMER TELEVISION
UNDER $50,000 BUDGET:
SINGLE

ART DIRECTOR
Craig Adams

WRITERS
Craig Adams
Steve Kuhn
Damon Pittman
Fernando Semenzato

AGENCY PRODUCER
Craig Adams

PRODUCTION COMPANIES
Turner Studios
Spin Productions

DIRECTOR
Keith Adams

CREATIVE DIRECTOR
Fernando Semenzato

CLIENT
Cartoon Network
Latin America

AGENCY
Cartoon Network
Latin America/Atlanta

02088A

(Fred and Barney try to figure out how a car works. They look at the floor, then back at each other. They start banging their feet on the floor, trying to make the car move.)

SUPER: Cartoon Network. Clearly, the best place for cartoons.

SILVER AWARD
CONSUMER TELEVISION
UNDER $50,000 BUDGET:
SINGLE

ART DIRECTOR
Craig Adams

WRITERS
Craig Adams
Steve Kuhn
Damon Pittman
Fernando Semenzato

AGENCY PRODUCER
Craig Adams

PRODUCTION COMPANIES
Turner Studios
Spin Productions

DIRECTOR
Keith Adams

CREATIVE DIRECTOR
Fernando Semenzato

CLIENT
Cartoon Network
Latin America

AGENCY
Cartoon Network
Latin America/Atlanta

02089A

JANE JETSON: One Pluto Burger, please. *(Nothing happens.)* One Pluto Burger, please.

(Nothing happens. Jane looks around in confusion.)

SUPER: Cartoon Network. Clearly, the best place for cartoons.

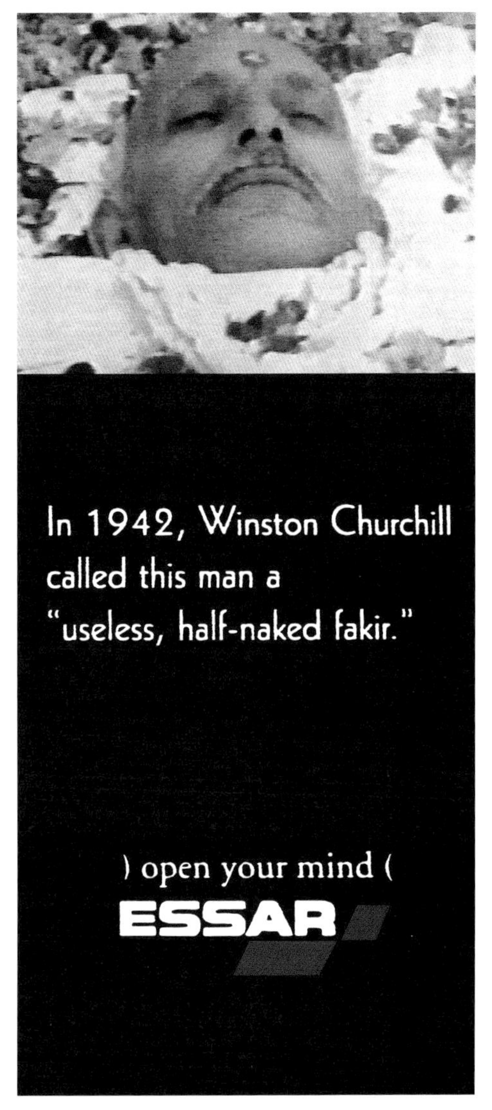

A woman pals around town with her best friend—who happens to be a mannequin. Throughout the various scenes, jingle plays.)

JINGLE: Cheryl n' me. Cheryl n' me. Shopping together, feeling so free. She knows fashion, she knows what's in. A friendship like ours will never, ever, ever, ever... Moveable arms, permanent smile. Life of the party, impeccable style. Carries herself with poise and class. You'd never know she's made of fiberglass, fiberglass, fiberglass. Cheryl n' me. Cheryl n' me. Shopping together. Feeling so free. Plastic and hard isn't so bad. I don't know if she's happy or sad. Yes, it's true she's a mannequin. Said it before and I'll say it again. My best friend is a mannequin, mannequin, mannequin.

SUPER: Lucky magazine. Your new shopping friend.

(Thousands of people march in Mahatma Gandhi's funeral procession. Scenes from the funeral are interspersed with the super.)

SUPER: In 1942, Winston Churchill....called this man a...."useless, half-naked fakir." Don't jump to conclusions.

(Thousands of people continue to march slowly in tribute.)

SUPER: Open your mind. Essar logo.

GOLD AWARD
NON BROADCAST
CINEMA

ART DIRECTOR
Phil Covitz

WRITERS
Dave Loew
Warren Cockrel

AGENCY PRODUCER
Stacey Higgins

PRODUCTION COMPANY
Tate & Partners

DIRECTOR
Baker Smith

CREATIVE DIRECTORS
Bob Kerstetter
Steve Stone

CLIENT
Lucky Magazine

AGENCY
Black Rocket/San Francisco

02090A

SILVER AWARD
NON BROADCAST
OUT-OF-HOME

ART DIRECTOR
Priya Pardiwalla

WRITERS
Vijay Kuruvilla
Josy Paul

AGENCY PRODUCER
Naren Multani

CREATIVE DIRECTORS
Josy Paul
Vijay Kuruvilla
Priya Pardiwalla

CLIENT
Essar

AGENCY
RMG David/Mumbai

02091A

GOLD AWARD
FOREIGN LANGUAGE TELEVISION

ART DIRECTOR
Sam Martin

WRITER
Jason Aspes

AGENCY PRODUCER
Jac Ho

PRODUCTION COMPANY
Renegade Films

DIRECTOR
Dogboy

CREATIVE DIRECTOR
Marc Lucas

CLIENT
Philips Lighting

AGENCY
D'Arcy/Hong Kong

02092A

(As a man videotapes the chain reaction of his very complex trail of dominoes, the light flickers and then goes out.)

SFX: Dominoes falling. A cry of despair.

SUPER: Extended Life Technology. Ecotone. The longer lasting light bulb.

ANNOUNCER: Choose the bulb with Extended Life Technology. Ecotone. The longer lasting light bulb, from Philips.

SILVER AWARD
FOREIGN LANGUAGE TELEVISION

ART DIRECTOR
Robin de Lestrade

WRITER
Olivier Camensuli

AGENCY PRODUCERS
Christine Bouffort
Géraldine Fau

PRODUCTION COMPANY
1/33 Productions

DIRECTOR
Neil Harris

CREATIVE DIRECTOR
Olivier Altmann

CLIENT
Le Cidem

AGENCY
BDDP et Fils/
Boulogne Billancourt

02093A

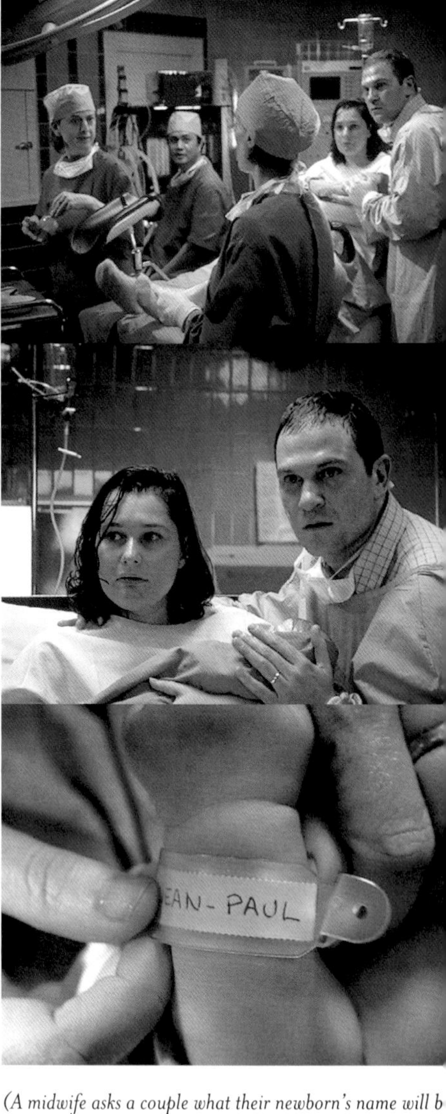

(A midwife asks a couple what their newborn's name will b Before the parents choose, each person gives their opinion. Jack! Jean! Paul! Jean-Paul!)

SUPER: Don't let others decide for you. Vote.

A young woman on a bus is holding a screaming baby. The aby's cries have the same rhythm as a car's engine turning over. man offers to help. The baby's cries change as he examines ie baby, tapping his tummy and pressing his feet. The cries ow mimic a smoothly running engine.)

NNOUNCER: A Midas man's work is never done.

UPER: Tune ups. 265 Francs.

(A young man in a store takes a sneaker off a display, puts it on, and darts out the door. Another man runs after him. They run at top speed, darting in and out of the crowd. The second man stops to catch his breath. The first man runs tirelessly. We pan out to see that he has a prosthetic leg.)

SUPER: The Disabled Sports Association would like to thank Adidas for their kind support. Sponsor logos.

BRONZE AWARD
FOREIGN LANGUAGE TELEVISION

WRITERS
Valérie Larrondo
Matthew Branning

AGENCY PRODUCER
Pierre Marcus

PRODUCTION COMPANY
Stink

DIRECTOR
Lawrence Hamburger

CREATIVE DIRECTOR
Anne de Maupeou

CLIENT
Midas

AGENCY
CLM/BBDO/
Issy des Moulineaux

02094A

SILVER AWARD
FOREIGN LANGUAGE CINEMA

ART DIRECTOR
Philip Borchardt

WRITER
Athanassios Stellatos

PRODUCTION COMPANY
Centrifuge Films

DIRECTOR
Marc Malze

CREATIVE DIRECTOR
Christoph Klingler

CLIENT
Behinderten-Sportverband/
Berlin

AGENCY
TBWA/Berlin

02095A

SILVER AWARD
INTEGRATED BRANDING

ART DIRECTOR
Philip Lord

WRITERS
Barton Corley
Sumiko Sato

PHOTOGRAPHER
Kazuyasu Hagane

PRODUCTION COMPANIES
Lost Planet
Megane Film
Sony PCL

DIRECTORS
Hank Corwin
Kumio Onaga
Hirotaka Takada

CREATIVE DIRECTOR
John C. Jay

CLIENT
Nike Japan

AGENCY
Wieden + Kennedy/Tokyo

02097A

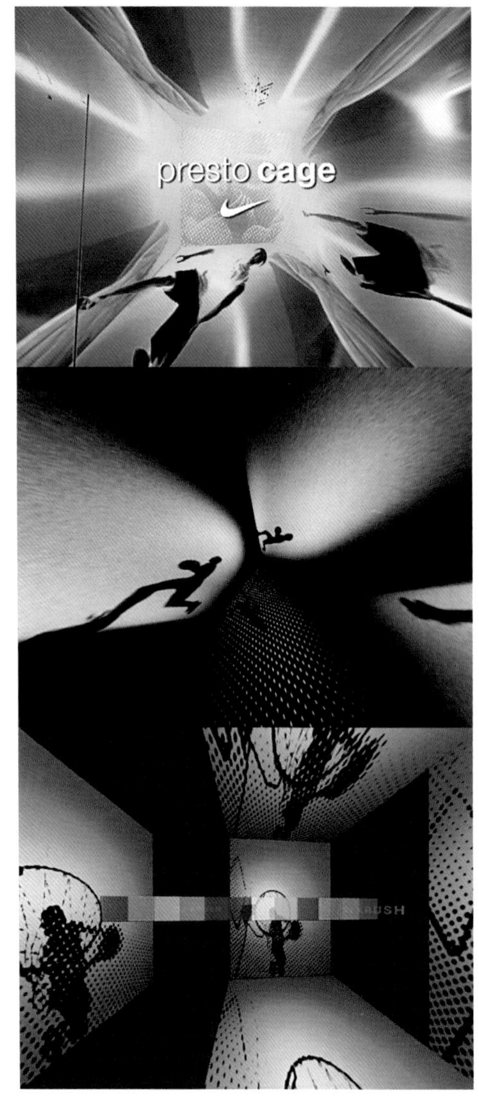

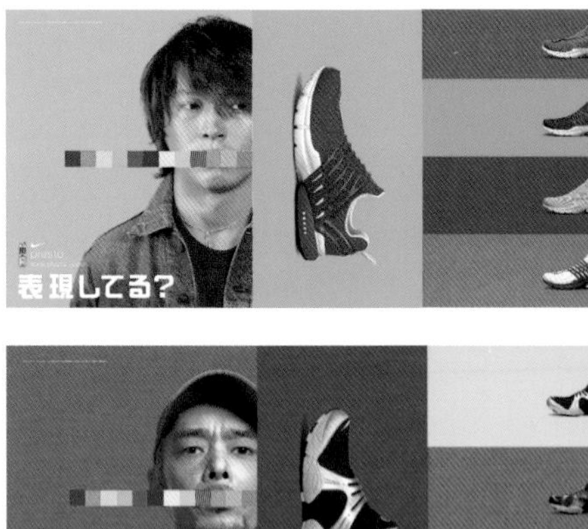

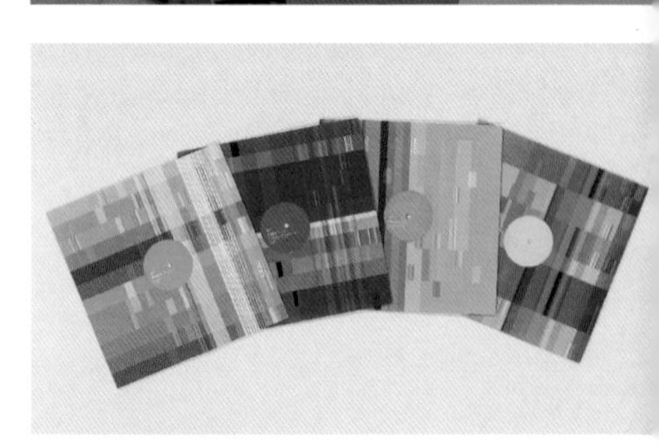

SUPER: With this DVD, you can be a DJ and VJ at the same time. You can create your own remix of the exclusive tracks of DJ Krush, Ken Ishii, Fumiya Tanaka and DJ Kenseii. We call it DVDJ. Swoosh.

BRONZE AWARD
INTEGRATED BRANDING

ART DIRECTORS
Philip Lord
Josh Berger

WRITER
Barton Corley

PHOTOGRAPHERS
John Huet
Kenji Aoki

AGENCY PRODUCER
Cherie Appleby

PRODUCTION COMPANY
@radical.media

DIRECTOR
Antony Hoffman

CREATIVE DIRECTORS
John C. Jay
Sumiko Sato

CLIENT
Nike Japan

AGENCY
Wieden + Kennedy/Tokyo

02098A

(This campaign begins with a "Big Brotheresque" voice commanding a cadre of youthful soccer players to "play boring soccer." They numbly obey until rescued by a crew of the world's top soccer players.)

GOLD AWARD
COLLEGE COMPETITION: ADVERTISING

ART DIRECTOR
Lindsay Shea

WRITER
John Neerland

SCHOOL
Brainco/Minneapolis

CC059

Your comments welcome
U.S. Department of State
00+1+800+647+4000
(toll-free)

Your comments welcome
U.S. Department of State
00+1+800+647+4000
(toll-free)

Your comments welcome
U.S. Department of State
00+1+800+647+4000
(toll-free)

Your comments welcome
U.S. Department of State
00+1+800+647+4000
(toll-free)

Your comments welcome
U.S. Department of State
00+1+800+647+4000
(toll-free)

Your comments welcome
U.S. Department of State
00+1+800+647+4000
(toll-free)

Your comments welcome
U.S. Department of State
00+1+800+647+4000
(toll-free)

Your comments welcome
U.S. Department of State
00+1+800+647+4000
(toll-free)

Your comments welcome
U.S. Department of State
00+1+800+647+4000
(toll-free)

Your comments welcome
U.S. Department of State
00+1+800+647+4000
(toll-free)

Your comments welcome
U.S. Department of State
00+1+800+647+4000
(toll-free)

Experience U.S. democracy

Experience U.S. democracy

Experience U.S. democracy

SILVER AWARD
COLLEGE COMPETITION: ADVERTISING

ART DIRECTOR
Brandon Sides

WRITER
Reuben Hower

SCHOOL
University of Colorado/
Boulder

CC024

BRONZE AWARD
COLLEGE COMPETITION: ADVERTISING

ART DIRECTOR
Mike Kelvin Lee

WRITER
Jen Robison

SCHOOL
Miami Ad School/
San Francisco

CC012

GOLD AWARD
COLLEGE COMPETITION: DESIGN

DESIGNER
Kaya Toyoshima

SCHOOL
Parsons School of Design/
New York

CCD005

SILVER AWARD
COLLEGE COMPETITION: DESIGN

DESIGNERS
Brad Gutting
Kyle Sorrell

SCHOOL
Portfolio Center/Atlanta

CCD008

BRONZE AWARD
COLLEGE COMPETITION: DESIGN

ART DIRECTOR
Stuart Jennings

WRITER
Tannen Campbell

SCHOOL
VCU Adcenter/Richmond

CCD026

In the mid 1800s, Henry Walter Bates observed a close resemblance in color patterns and even in superficial morphology between butterfly species that are palatable to bird predators and other butterfly species that birds find extremely unpleasant or even harmful to eat. By mimicking the noxious species, the harmless ones gained protection from predation despite their palatability.

Maxygen's technologies help us to improve positive genetic traits for commercial applications in protein pharmaceuticals, vaccines, chemicals and agriculture products. We seek to create therapeutics that are more effective against disease and have fewer side effects, chemical products that are more efficient and generate less waste, and agriculture products with higher yield and increased nutritional qualities.

GOLD AWARD
ONE SHOW DESIGN
ANNUAL REPORT

DESIGNER
Gary Williams

ART DIRECTOR
Bill Cahan

PHOTOGRAPHERS
Ann Giordano
Esther Henderson
Ray Manley
Robert Markow
John Sann

ILLUSTRATOR
Jason Holley

CREATIVE DIRECTOR
Bill Cahan

CLIENT
Maxygen

AGENCY
Cahan & Associates/
San Francisco

02003D

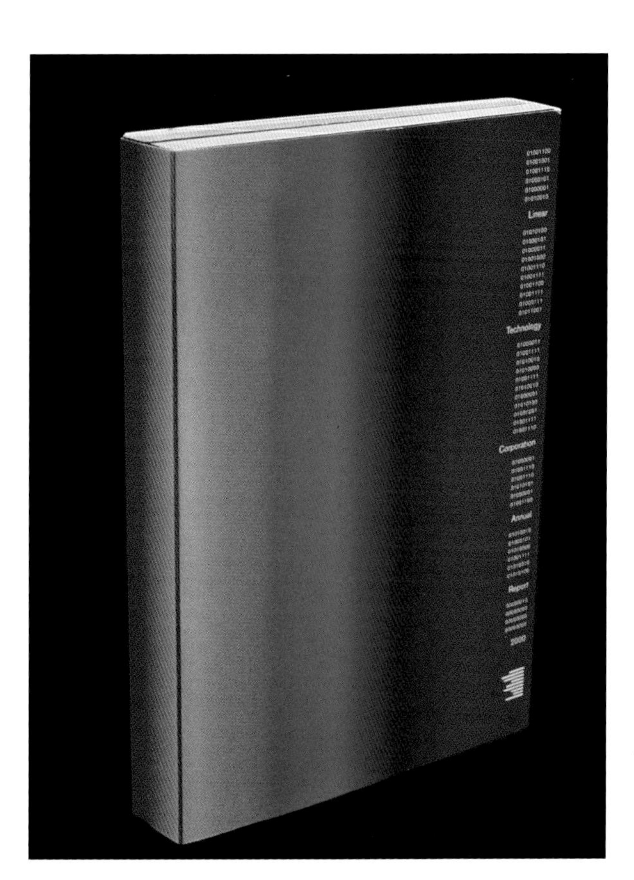

SILVER AWARD
ONE SHOW DESIGN
ANNUAL REPORT

DESIGNER
Todd Simmons

ART DIRECTOR
Bill Cahan

WRITERS
Thom Elkjer
Todd Simmons

PHOTOGRAPHER
Todd Hido

ILLUSTRATOR
Todd Simmons

CREATIVE DIRECTOR
Bill Cahan

CLIENT
Linear Technology

AGENCY
Cahan & Associates/
San Francisco

02002D

SILVER AWARD
ONE SHOW DESIGN
ANNUAL REPORT

DESIGNER
Wong Wai Han

WRITER
Jonathan Zax

PHOTOGRAPHER
Frank Pinckers

CREATIVE DIRECTOR
Edmund Wee

CLIENT
Sampoerna

AGENCY
Epigram/Singapore

02001D

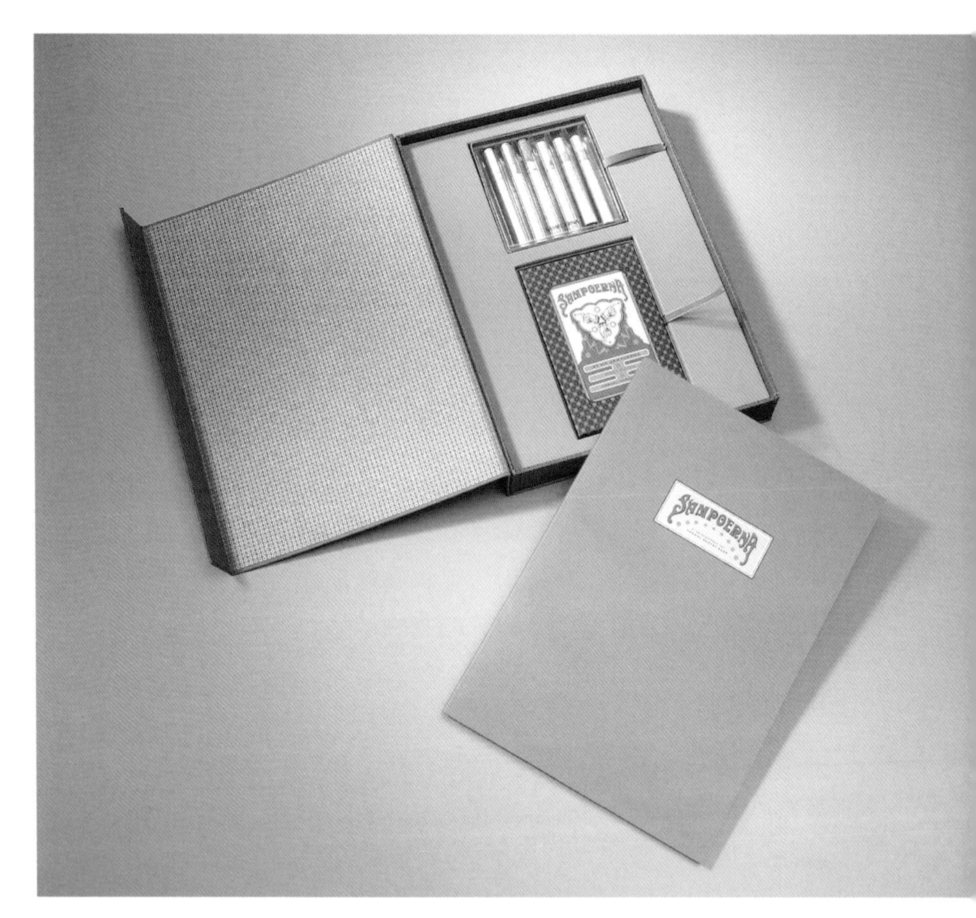

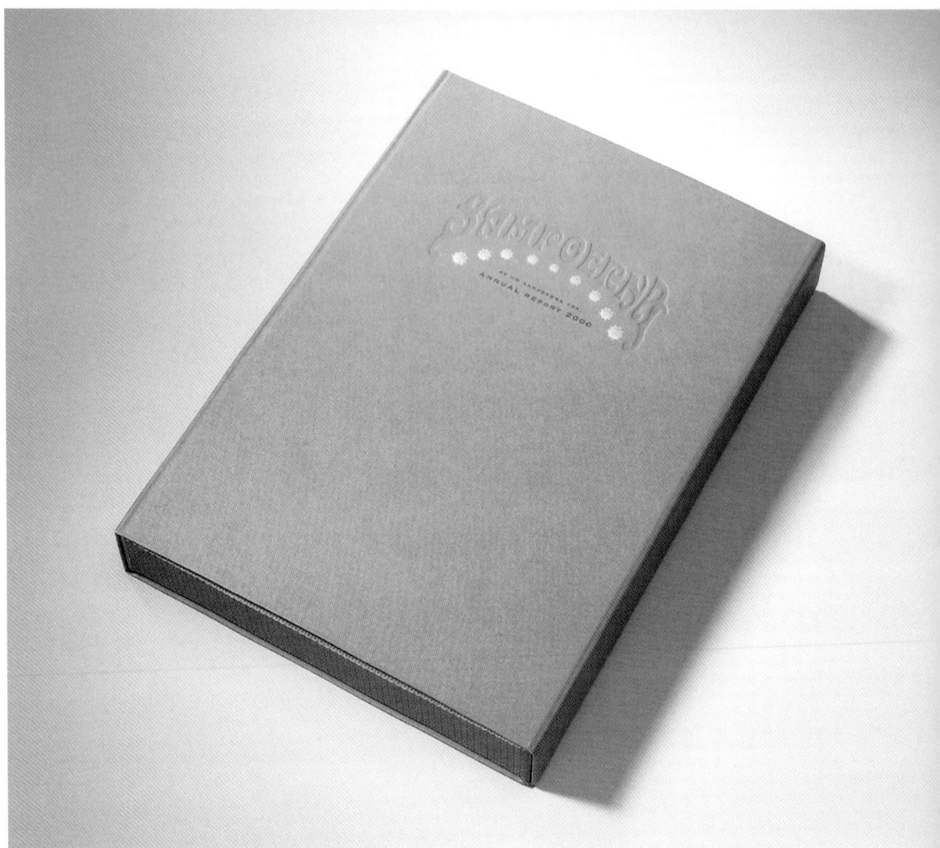

GOLD AWARD
ONE SHOW DESIGN
BOOKLET/BROCHURE

DESIGNERS
Anton Nordstierna
Gavin Smart

ART DIRECTOR
Lisa Careborg

WRITERS
Katja Grillner
Fredrik Nilsson

PHOTOGRAPHER
Mikael Olsson

CREATIVE DIRECTOR
Anders Kornestedt

CLIENT
White Arkitekter

AGENCY
Happy Forsman &
Bodenfors/Göthenburg

02005D

GOLD AWARD
ONE SHOW DESIGN
BOOKLET/BROCHURE

DESIGNER
Marion English Powers

ART DIRECTORS
Marion English Powers
Pat Powell

WRITERS
Dan Monroe
Dave Smith
Sarah Devine
Kristin Henson

PHOTOGRAPHERS
Don Harbor
Personal Archives
Blindspot

CLIENT
Alabama Vets

AGENCY
Slaughter Hanson/
Birmingham

02004D

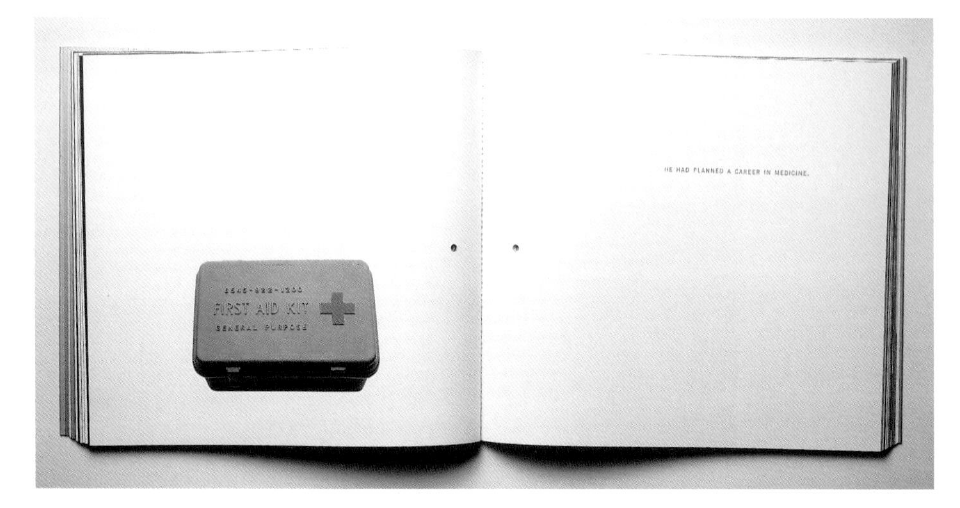

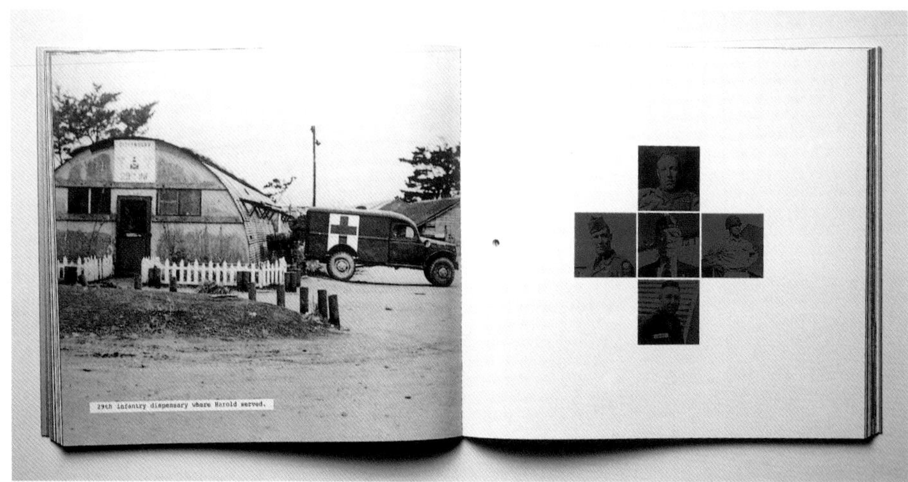

SILVER AWARD
ONE SHOW DESIGN
BOOKLET/BROCHURE

ART DIRECTORS
Reiner Hebe
Stefanie Wahl

WRITER
Reiner Hebe

PHOTOGRAPHERS
Niels Schubert
Werner Pawlok

ILLUSTRATOR
Dominik Zehle

CREATIVE DIRECTOR
Reiner Hebe

CLIENT
MAAS Goldsmith

AGENCY
HEBE. Werbung & Design/
Leonberg

02006D

BRONZE AWARD
ONE SHOW DESIGN
BOOKLET/BROCHURE

DESIGNER
Helmut Himmler

ART DIRECTOR
Minh Khai Doan

WRITERS
Dirk Galia
Jörg Petermann

ILLUSTRATOR
Patrick They

CREATIVE DIRECTORS
Helmut Himmler
Dirk Galia

CLIENT
Eckes Chantre Cognac

AGENCY
Ogilvy & Mather/Frankfurt

02007D

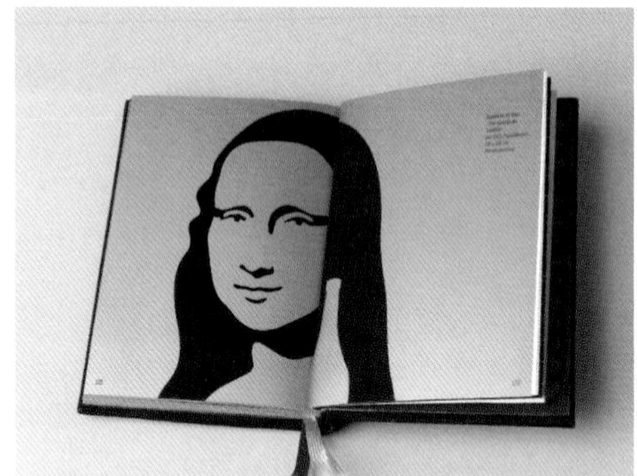

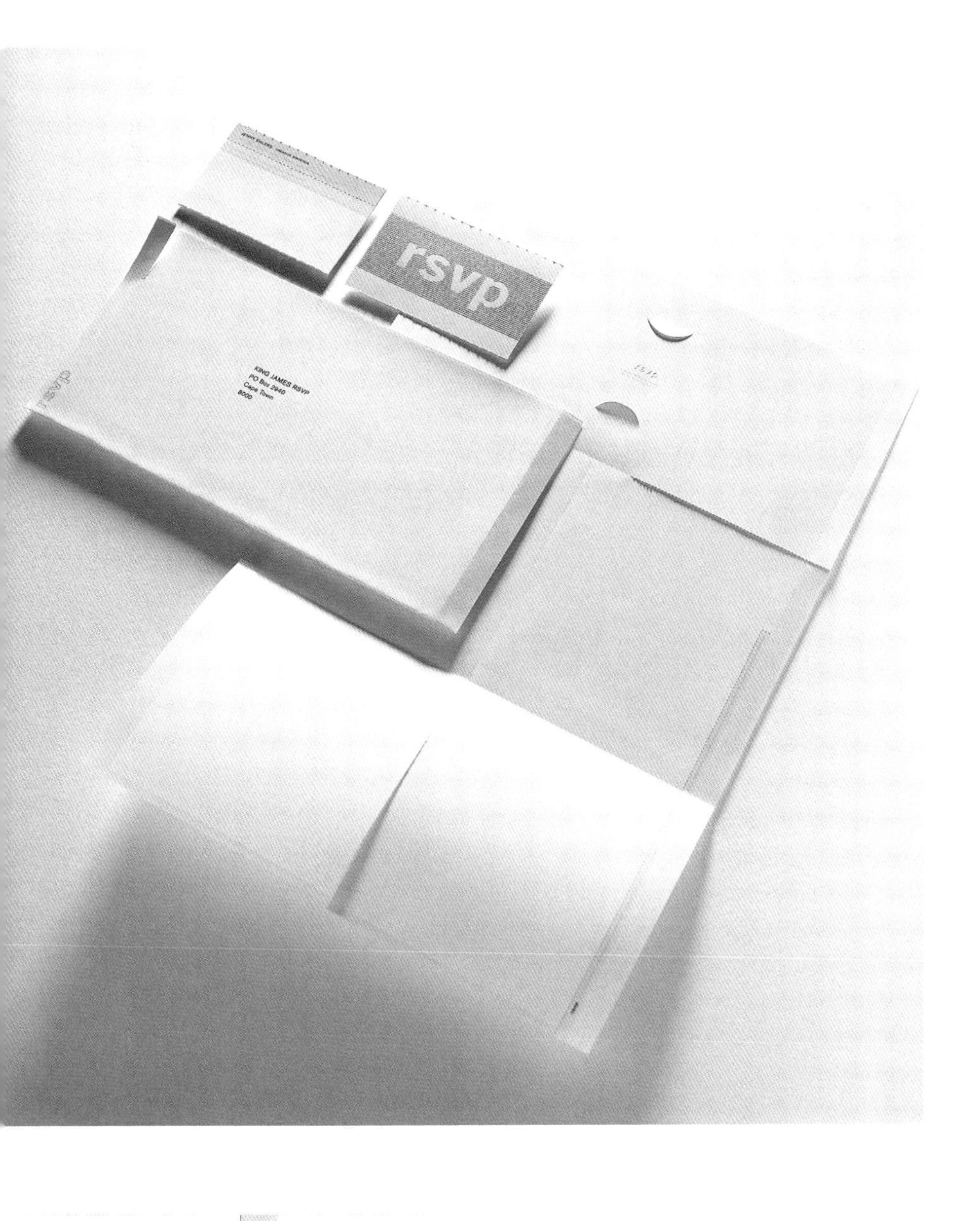

GOLD AWARD
ONE SHOW DESIGN
CORPORATE IDENTITY

DESIGNER
Ingrid Ling

ART DIRECTOR
Jenny Ehlers

CREATIVE DIRECTOR
Jenny Ehlers

CLIENT
King James RSVP

AGENCY
King James RSVP/Cape Town

02008D

s
KIDSWARE

SILVER AWARD
ONE SHOW DESIGN
CORPORATE IDENTITY

DESIGNER
Priti Arora

ART DIRECTOR
Priti Arora

WRITERS
Anisha Sarin
Priti Arora

ILLUSTRATOR
Sanjay Shetye

CREATIVE DIRECTORS
Sanjay Sipahimalani
Yayati Godbole

CLIENT
Premsons Bazaar

AGENCY
Grey Worldwide/Mumbai

02009D

BRONZE AWARD
ONE SHOW DESIGN
CORPORATE IDENTITY

DESIGNER
Andrew Randall

ART DIRECTOR
Steve Sandstrom

PHOTOGRAPHER
Steve Sandstrom

CREATIVE DIRECTOR
Steve Sandstrom

CLIENT
Food Chain Films

AGENCY
Sandstrom Design/Portland

02010D

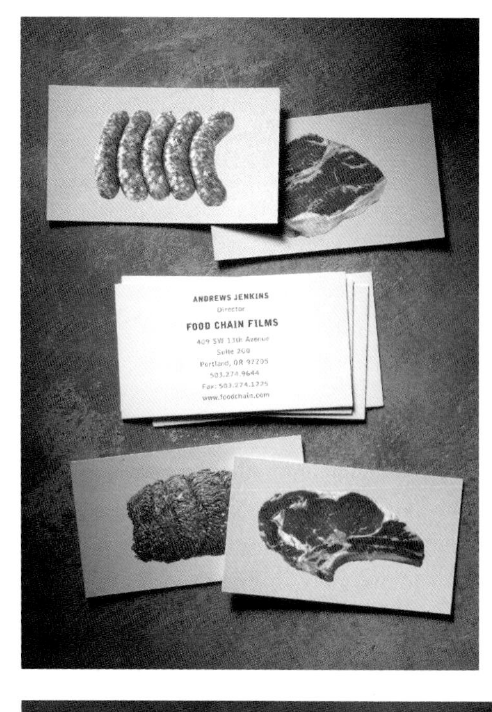

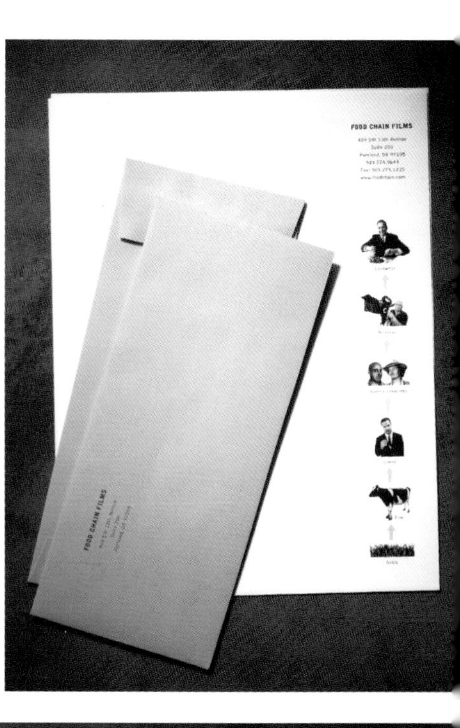

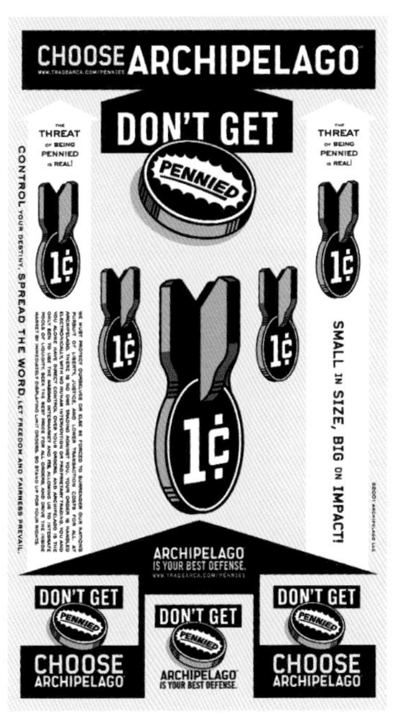

GOLD AWARD
ONE SHOW DESIGN
PROMOTIONAL AND POINT-OF PURCHASE POSTERS

DESIGNER
Alan Leusink

WRITER
Scott Vincent

ILLUSTRATOR
Alan Leusink

CREATIVE DIRECTOR
Alan Colvin

CLIENT
Archipelago

AGENCY
Duffy Design/Minneapolis

02011D

SILVER AWARD
ONE SHOW DESIGN
PROMOTIONAL AND
POINT-OF-PURCHASE POSTERS

DESIGNERS
Edan Bryant
Mike McIntyre
M. Fred
Casey Gill
Shannon Wright

ART DIRECTOR
Kevin Fitzgerald

CLIENT
Cartoon Network

AGENCY
Cartoon Network/Atlanta

02012D

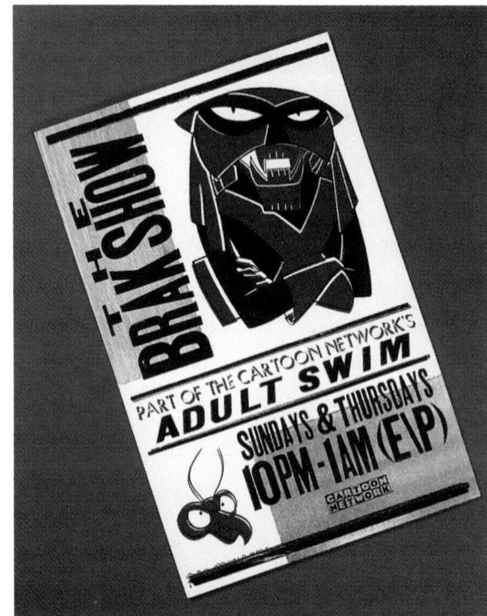

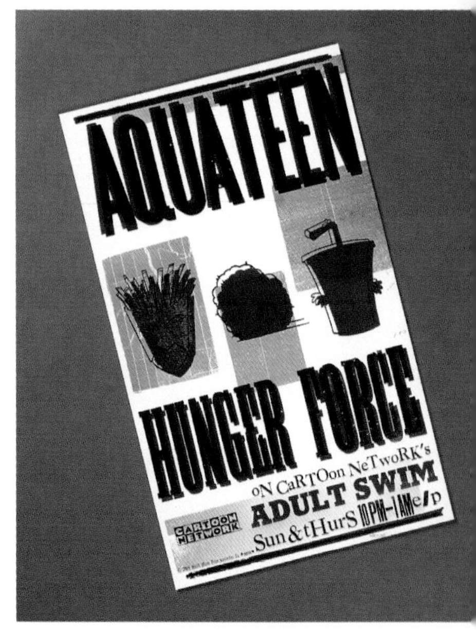

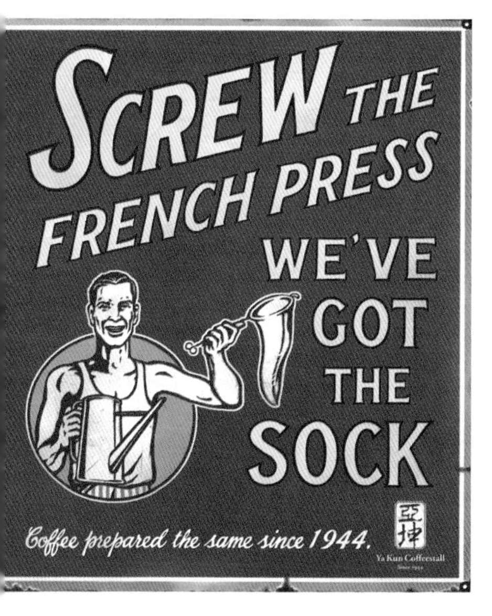

BRONZE AWARD
ONE SHOW DESIGN
PROMOTIONAL AND
POINT-OF-PURCHASE POSTERS

ART DIRECTORS
Eric Yeo
David Seah
Tay Guan Hin

WRITER
Jay Phua

ILLUSTRATORS
Pok Cheng Hai
Felix Wang

CREATIVE DIRECTORS
Linda Locke
Tay Guan Hin

CLIENT
Ya Kum Coffee Stall

AGENCY
Leo Burnett/Singapore

02013D

GOLD AWARD
ONE SHOW DESIGN
PUBLIC SERVICE POSTERS

DESIGNER
ShiWei Cai

ART DIRECTOR
ShiWei Cai

WRITER
ZhiHong Xu

CREATIVE DIRECTOR
ShiWei Cai

CLIENT
Nanjing Massacre Memorial

AGENCY
JST Design Consultants/
Beijing

02014D

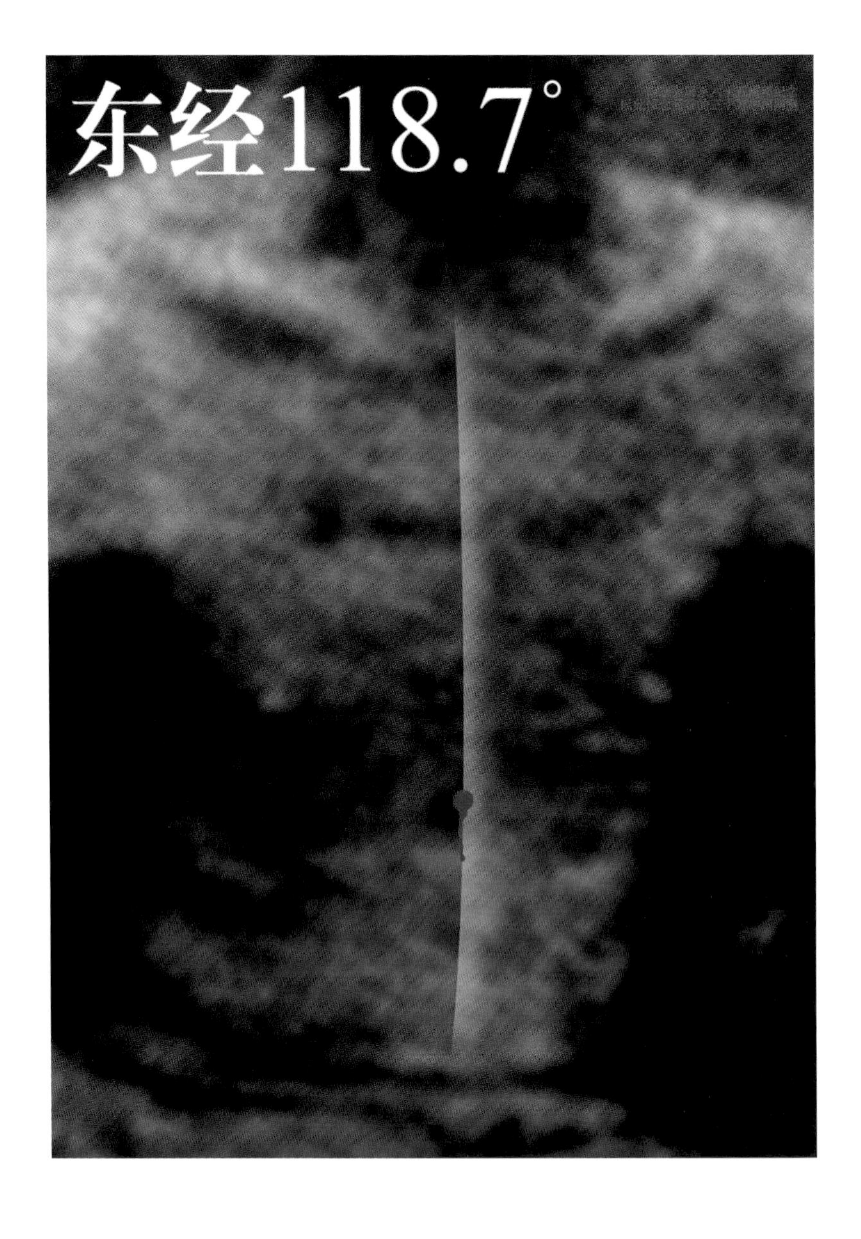

SILVER AWARD
ONE SHOW DESIGN
PUBLIC SERVICE POSTERS

DESIGNER
Patric Bolecek

WRITER
Charles Hall

PHOTOGRAPHER
Dan Hallman

ILLUSTRATOR
Kevin Lyons

CREATIVE DIRECTORS
Charles Hall
Brian Collins

CLIENT
Office of National Drug
Control Policy

AGENCY
Ogilvy & Mather/Brand
Integration Group/New York

02015D

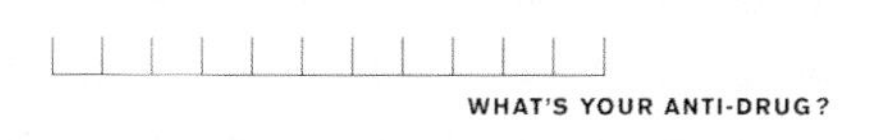

WHAT'S YOUR ANTI-DRUG?

www.whatsyourantidrug.com

BRONZE AWARD
ONE SHOW DESIGN
PUBLIC SERVICE POSTERS

ART DIRECTOR
Jon Grider

WRITER
Mark Henderson

CREATIVE DIRECTOR
Dave Hofmann

CLIENT
Milwaukee Urban League

AGENCY
Cramer-Krasselt/Milwaukee

02016D

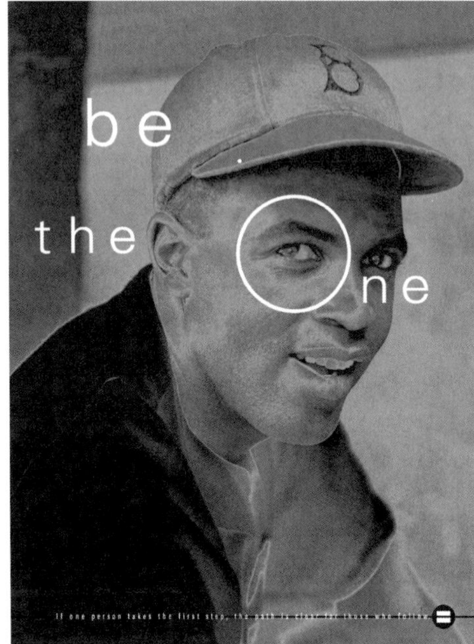

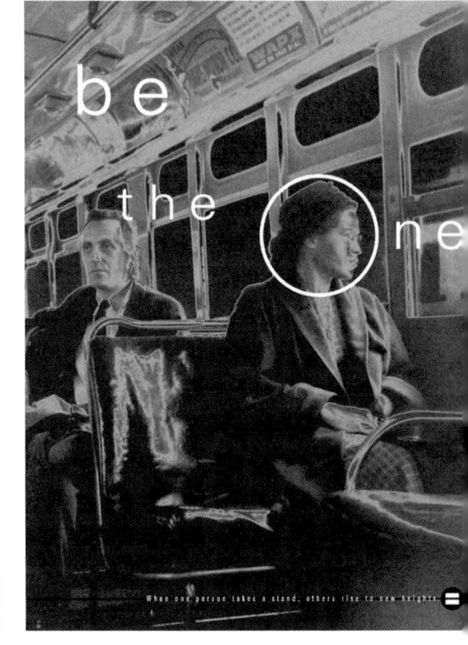

GOLD AWARD
ONE SHOW DESIGN
COMMERCIAL PRODUCT
PACKAGING

DESIGNER
Hjalti Karlsson

ART DIRECTOR
Stefan Sagmeister

WRITER
Karen Salmansohn

CREATIVE DIRECTOR
Stefan Sagmeister

CLIENT
Blue Q

AGENCY
Sagmeister/New York

02017D

SILVER AWARD
ONE SHOW DESIGN
COMMERCIAL PRODUCT
PACKAGING

DESIGNER
Joanne Thomas

ART DIRECTORS
Joanne Thomas
Graham Lang

ILLUSTRATOR
Joanne Thomas

CREATIVE DIRECTOR
Joanne Thomas

CLIENT
Foschini

AGENCY
The Jupiter Drawing Room/
Cape Town

02018D

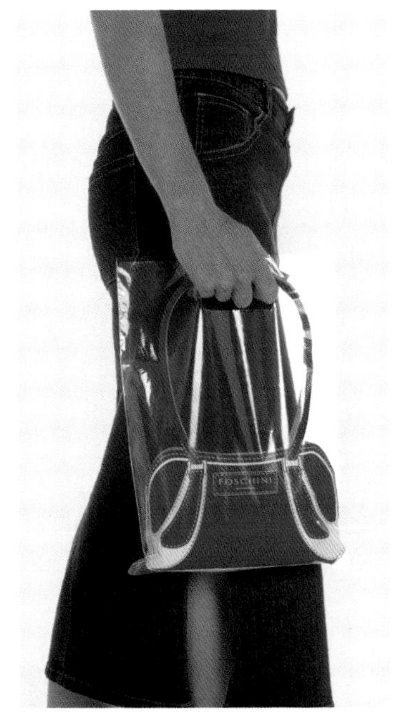

SILVER AWARD
ONE SHOW DESIGN
COMMERCIAL PRODUCT
PACKAGING

DESIGNERS
David Salanitro
Ted Bluey

ART DIRECTOR
David Salanitro

WRITERS
David Salanitro
Ted Bluey

PHOTOGRAPHER
Reservoir

ILLUSTRATORS
David Salanitro
Ted Bluey

CREATIVE DIRECTOR
David Salanitro

CLIENT
Reservoir

AGENCY
Reservoir/San Francisco

02019D

BRONZE AWARD
ONE SHOW DESIGN
COMMERCIAL PRODUCT
PACKAGING

DESIGNER
Steve Sandstrom

ART DIRECTOR
Steve Sandstrom

WRITERS
Steve Sandoz
Palmer Pettersen

CREATIVE DIRECTOR
Steve Sandstrom

CLIENT
Tazo

AGENCY
Sandstrom Design/Portland

02020D

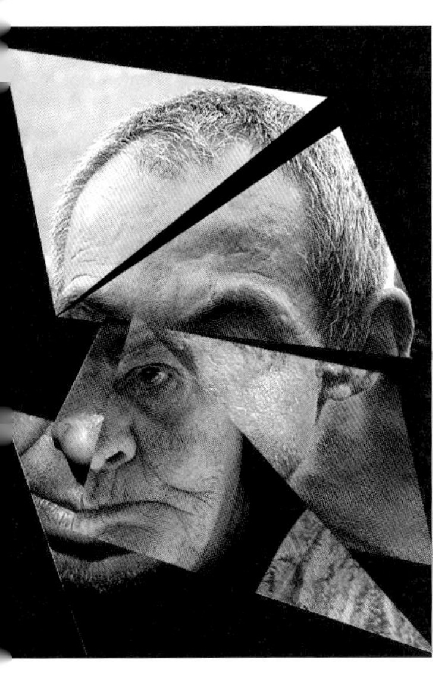

BRONZE AWARD
ONE SHOW DESIGN
ENVIRONMENT

DESIGNER
Flávio Wild

ART DIRECTOR
Flávio Wild

PHOTOGRAPHERS
Flávio Wild
Gustavo Demarchi

CLIENT
3rd Mercosur Visual
Arts Biennial

AGENCY
Wildstudio Design/
Porte Alegre

02021D

SILVER AWARD
ONE SHOW DESIGN
BOOK JACKET DESIGN

DESIGNERS
Michael Ian Kaye
Soohyen Park
Bill Darling
Roman Luba
Spencer Bagley
Mark Obriski
David Goldstein

WRITER
Tony Hendra

TYPOGRAPHER
Nigel Kent

CREATIVE DIRECTORS
Rick Boyko
Brian Collins

CLIENT
Brotherhood

AGENCY
Ogilvy & Mather/Brand Integration Group/New York

02023D

BROTHERHOOD

FRANK McCOURT

RUDOLPH W. GIULIANI MAYOR OF THE CITY OF NEW YORK

THOMAS VON ESSEN COMMISSIONER FIRE DEPARTMENT, CITY OF NEW YORK

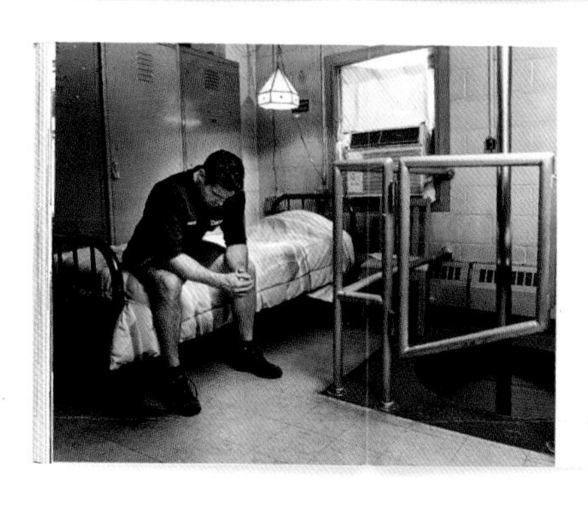

SILVER AWARD
ONE SHOW DESIGN
BOOK JACKET DESIGN

DESIGNER
Steve Sandstrom

ART DIRECTOR
Steve Sandstrom

WRITER
Steve Sandoz

PHOTOGRAPHERS
John Bohls
Stock

CREATIVE DIRECTOR
Steve Sandstrom

CLIENT
Sandstrom Design

AGENCY
Sandstrom Design/Portland

02024D

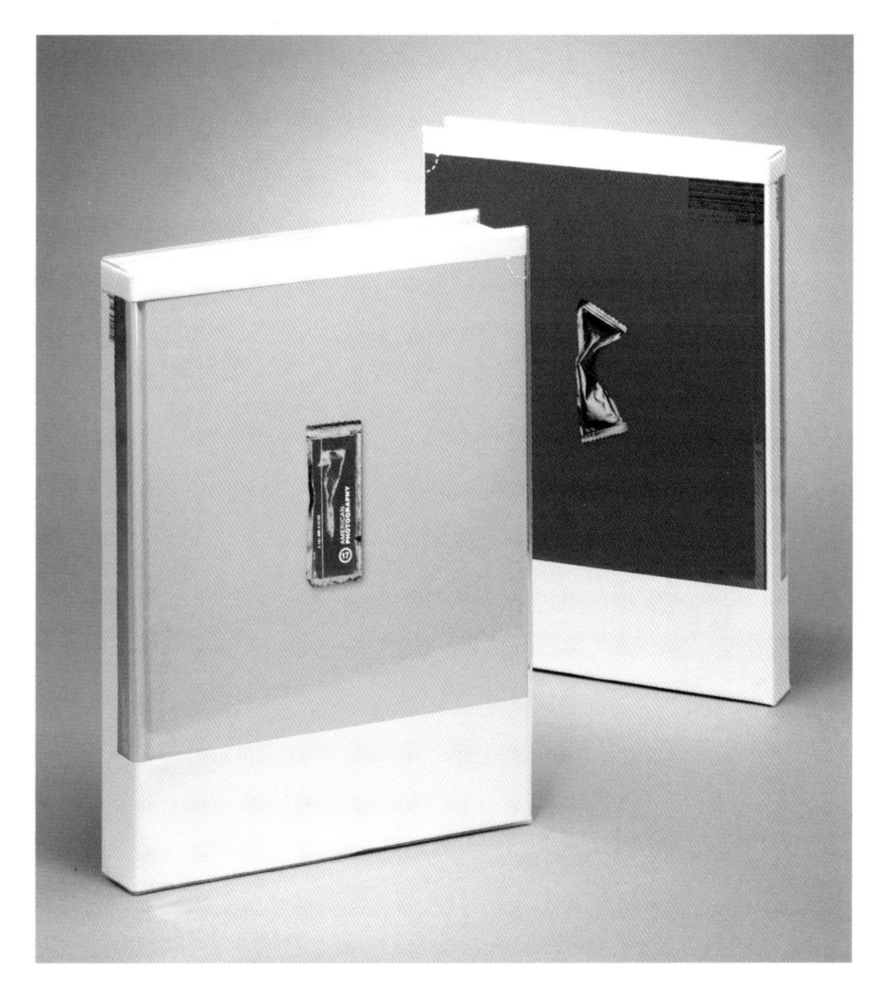

BRONZE AWARD
ONE SHOW DESIGN
BOOK JACKET DESIGN

DESIGNER
Stefan G. Bucher

ART DIRECTOR
Stefan G. Bucher

WRITERS
Alison Morley
Peggy Roalf

PHOTOGRAPHERS
Craig Cutler
Various

CLIENT
Amilus Inc.

AGENCY
344 Design LLC/Pasadena

02025D

BRONZE AWARD
ONE SHOW DESIGN
BOOK JACKET DESIGN

DESIGNER
Greger Ulf Nilson

ART DIRECTOR
Greger Ulf Nilson

PHOTOGRAPHER
Lars Tunbjörk

CREATIVE DIRECTOR
Greger Ulf Nilson

CLIENT
Journal

AGENCY
Schumacher Jersild Wessman & Enander/Stockholm

02026D

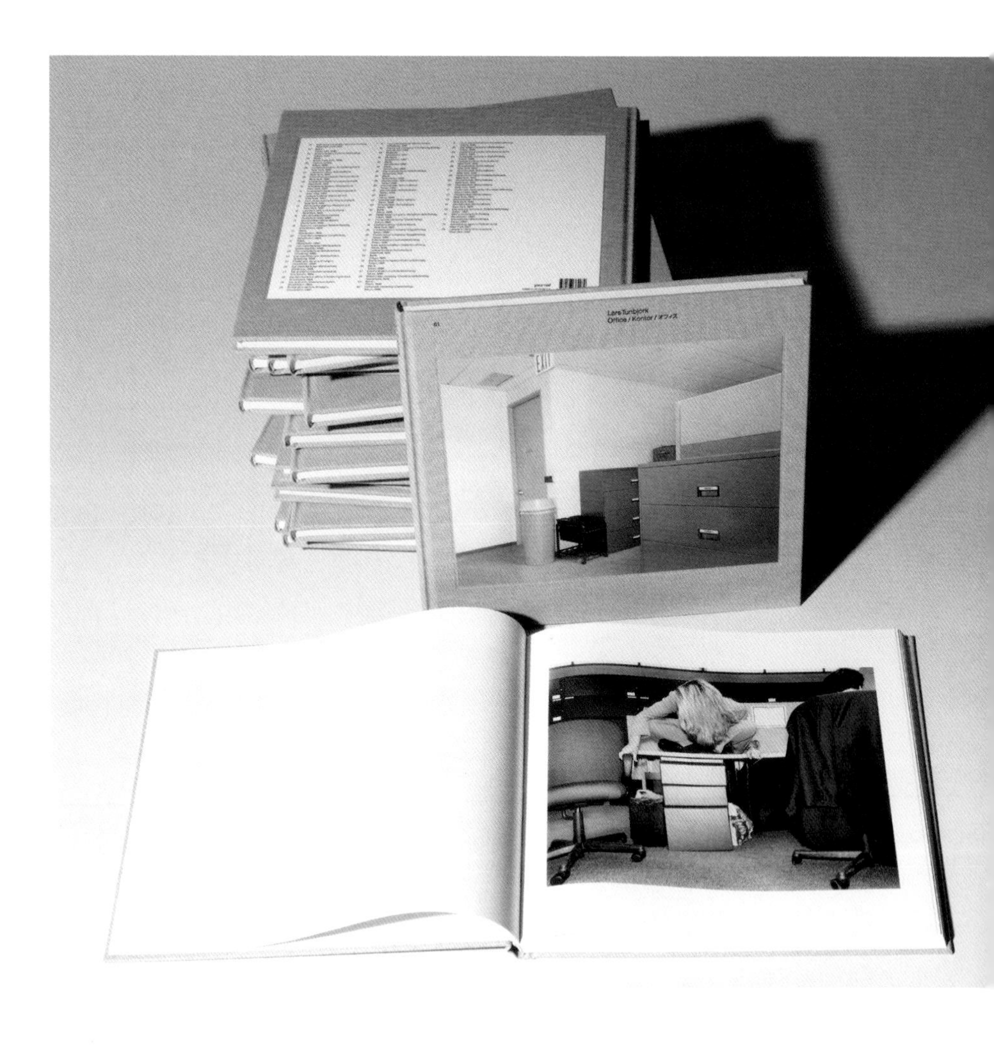

BRONZE AWARD
ONE SHOW DESIGN
TRADE MAGAZINE FULL ISSUE

DESIGNERS
David Israel
Diana Litchfield

WRITER
Tonice Sgrignoli

CREATIVE DIRECTORS
Rick Boyko
Brian Collins

CLIENT
Ogilvy & Mather

AGENCY
Ogilvy & Mather/Brand Integration Group/New York

02027D

BRONZE AWARD
ONE SHOW DESIGN
TRADE MAGAZINE FULL ISSUE

DESIGNERS
David Israel
Nathalie Hennequin
Diana Litchfield

WRITER
Tonice Sgrignoli

CREATIVE DIRECTORS
Rick Boyko
Brian Collins

CLIENT
Ogilvy & Mather

AGENCY
Ogilvy & Mather/Brand Integration Group/New York

02028D

GOLD AWARD
ONE SHOW DESIGN
DIRECT MAIL

ART DIRECTOR
Bertrand Fleuret

WRITER
Luca Grelli

ILLUSTRATOR
Danijel Zezelj

CREATIVE DIRECTORS
Glenn Cole
Paul Shearer

CLIENT
Nike Europe

AGENCY
Wieden + Kennedy/Amsterdam

02029D

SILVER AWARD
ONE SHOW DESIGN
DIRECT MAIL

DESIGNERS
Erik Vervroegen
Soo Mean Chang
Molly Sheahan

ART DIRECTORS
Erik Vervroegen
Soo Mean Chang
Molly Sheahan

WRITER
Kerry Keenan

PHOTOGRAPHER
Megan Maloy

CREATIVE DIRECTORS
Tony Granger
Kerry Keenan
Erik Vervroegen

CLIENT
Art Director's Club

AGENCY
Bozell/New York

02030D

Also won:
MERIT AWARDS
ONE SHOW DESIGN
DIRECT MAIL

MERIT

MERIT

MERIT

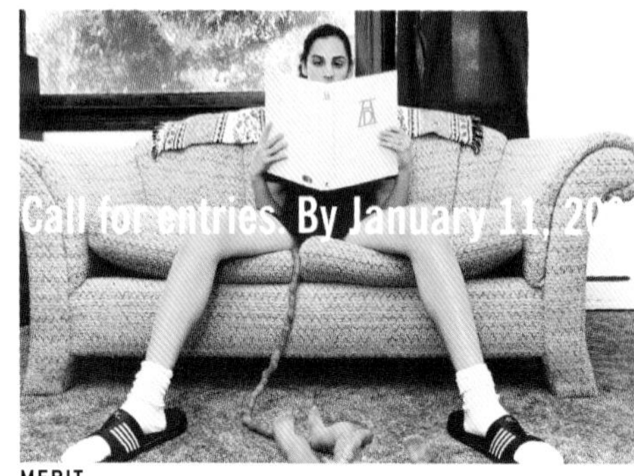

MERIT

BRONZE AWARD
ONE SHOW DESIGN
DIRECT MAIL

ART DIRECTORS
Jelly Helm
Tracey Morgan
Jon Bunning

WRITER
Jelly Helm

CLIENT
VCU Adcenter

AGENCY
VCU Adcenter/Richmond

02031D

Also won:
MERIT AWARD
ONE SHOW DESIGN
BOOKLET/BROCHURE

fig. A

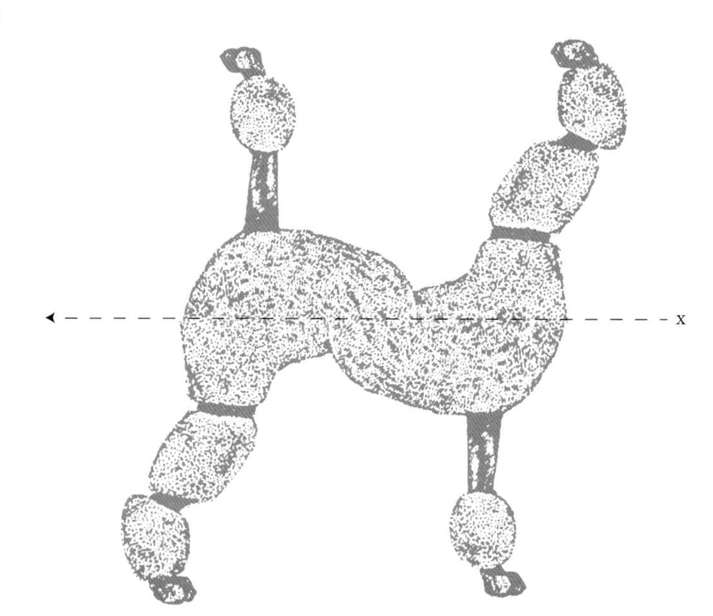

fig. B

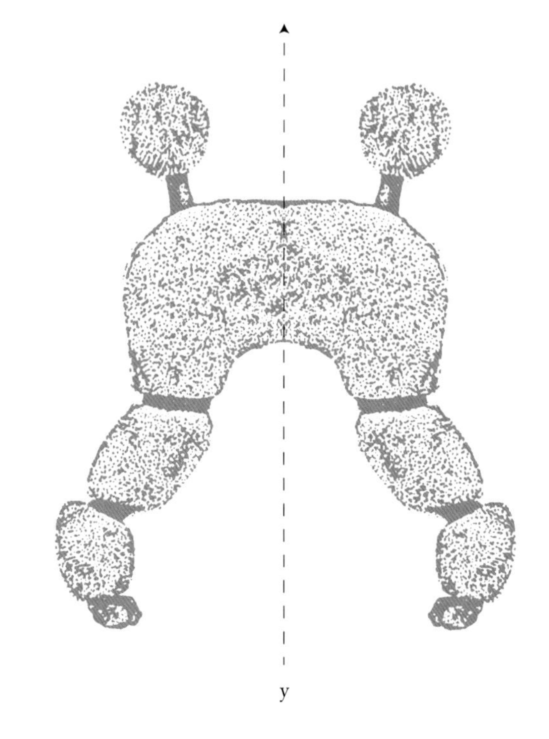

BEST *of* SHOW

" ________ is a very active, intelligent, and elegant-appearing ________ – squarely built, well proportioned, moving soundly and carrying him/herself proudly. Properly clipped in the traditional fashion and carefully groomed, the ________ has about him/her an air of distinction and dignity peculiar to him/herself."

ART DIRECTOR
David Carter

WRITER
Joe Sweet

DESIGNERS
Mark Sandau
Brooke Posard
Steve Sage
Tom Riddle

AGENCY PRODUCERS
Robyn Boardman
Robert van de Weteringe Buys

PRODUCTION COMPANY
Anonymous Content

DIRECTORS
John Frankenheimer
Wong Kar Wai
Ang Lee
Guy Ritchie
Alejandro Gonzalez Iñarrítu

CREATIVE DIRECTORS
David Lubars
Bruce Bildsten
Kevin Flatt

CLIENT
BMW North America

AGENCY
Fallon/Minneapolis

02096A

Also won:
GOLD AWARD
INTEGRATED BRANDING

DRIVER: She's a legend in her own lifetime. She's unrivalled in her world. She's a complete—

SUPER: From the director of Snatch.

STAR: Glenn!

GLENN: Right here, darlin'!

DRIVER: Hello?

GLENN: Hey, is she doin' okay?

DRIVER: Yeah, she's fine.

GLENN: Show her the sights—breakfast, lunch, and dinner.

DRIVER: Let me see what I can do.

SUPER: A film by Guy Ritchie.

DRIVER: Just hold on tight, sir.

SUPER: Star...now playing at bmwfilms.com.

PER: From Director Alejandro González Iñárritu. Powder keg. Only at bmwfilms.com.

MONK: At last...come.

SUPER: From the director of Crouching Tiger, Hidden Dragon.

MONK: Everything will be just fine.

SUPER: A film by Ang Lee. Chosen...now playing at bmwfilms.com.

ABOUT CHOSEN

The Driver meets a ship carrying an eight-year-old Tibetan boy at a dark, deserted New York shipyard. But he's not the only one waiting. Ang Lee, director of the Oscar-winning Crouching Tiger, Hidden Dragon and star Clive Owen create a thrilling, yet beautiful, tale filled with mystery.

Sign up now to experience *The Hire Film Series*, featuring directors Wong Kar-Wai, Guy Ritchie, and others

View the Film →

View the film with DVD-like features. BMW Film Player now available.

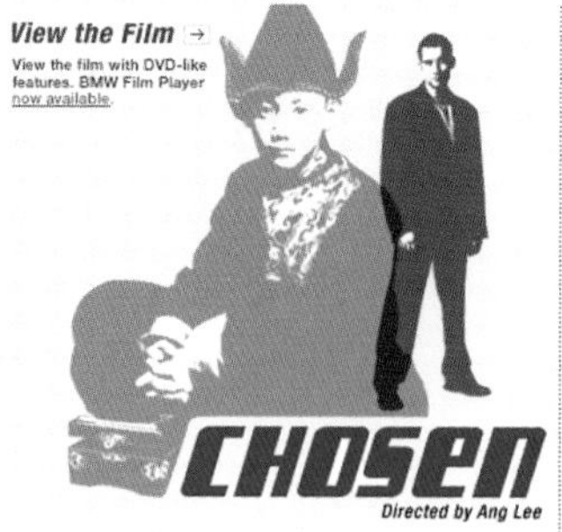

FILMS →

The Hire Film Series will include five films. Click here to view available films.

BMW INTERACTIVE FILM PLAYER →

For maximum enjoyment, we recommend the free BMW Player. It has DVD-like features and allows access to larger-format films, compelling Sub-Stories, Director Commentaries, and detailed highlights of the vehicles driven in the series. Download now.

DIRECTORS →

BMW Films feature the work of award-winning movie directors. Click here to learn more about the directors.

MACHINES →

The Machines section of the BMW Player provides photos and key information about the BMWs driven in the films. Click here to learn more about the machines.

Help | E-Mail a Friend | Sign-Up

Home | Current Film | Directors | BMW Interactive Film Player | Films | Machines
©2001 BMW of North America, LLC bmwusa.com Privacy Policy Content Rating

Home | Current Film | Directors | BMW Interactive Film Player | Films | Machines

CHOSEN

Synopsis
The Director
Featured Machine
Film Credits
On-Location Photos
Wallpaper
Required Software

Help | E-Mail a Friend | Sign-Up

©2001 BMW of North America, LLC bmwusa.com Privacy Policy Content Rating

Home | Current Film | Directors | BMW Inter ctive Film Player | Films | Machines

MACHINES

Learn why the BMWs driven in *The Hire* Digital Film Series were selected and explore their features and technology.

540i 6-speed

Help | E-Mail a Friend | Sign-Up

©2001 BMW of North America, LLC bmwusa.com Privacy Policy Content Rating

BEST OF SHOW

ONE SHOW DESIGN

DESIGNER
Hjalti Karlsson

ART DIRECTOR
Stefan Sagmeister

WRITER
Peter Hall

PHOTOGRAPHER
Kevin Knight

CREATIVE DIRECTOR
Stefan Sagmeister

CLIENT
Booth Clibborn

AGENCY
Sagmeister/New York

02022D

Also won:
GOLD AWARD
ONE SHOW DESIGN
BOOK JACKET DESIGN

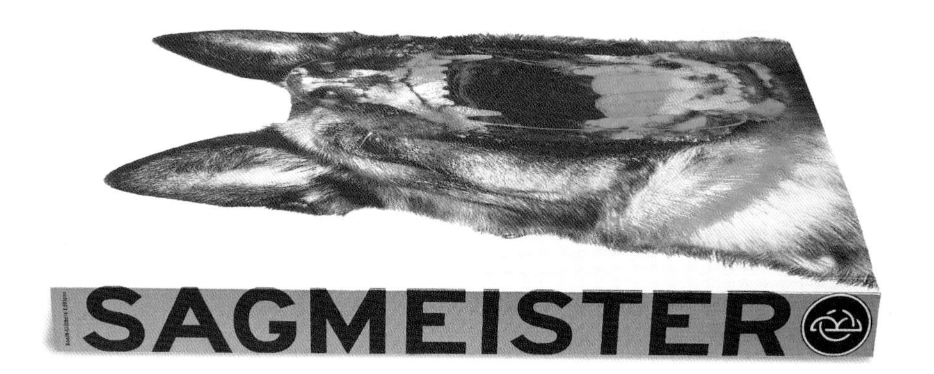

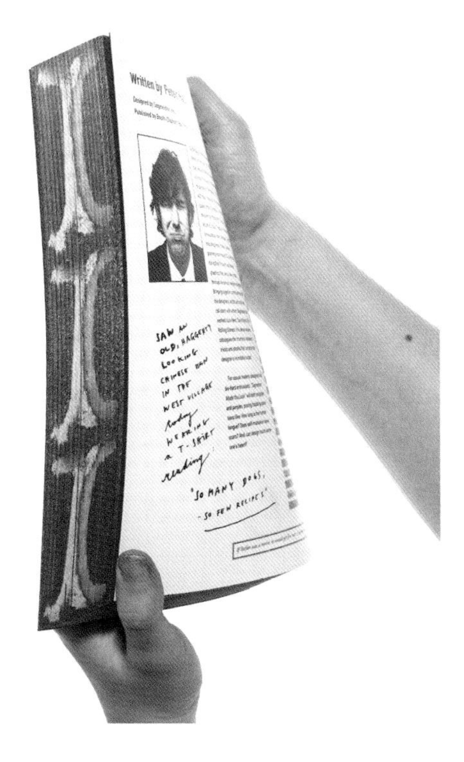

YOUR VENERABLE ADJUDICATORS, 2002:

Scott Aal, Arthur Bijur, Greg Bokor, Rossana Bardales, Roger Camp, Eugene Cheong, Marie Catherine Dupuy, Ryan Ebner, Michael Hart, Paul Hirsch, Lance Jensen, Mike Mazza, Raymond McKinney, Amy Nicholson, Liz Paradise, Michael Patti, Hank Perlman, Jeremy Postaer, Jean Robaire, Kirk Souder, Joe Duffy, Dana Arnett, Shepard Fairey, Rico Lins, Thom Middlebrook, Steve Sandstrom, Adam Chasnow, Wayne Best, Stephanie Crippen, Al Kelly, Carl Loeb, Chuck Meehan, Ari Merkin, Zak Mroueh, Mark Nardi, Eddie van Bloem, Bob Winter

JUDGES CHOICE

CLIENT
Polaroid

AGENCY
Leo Burnett/Chicago

KIRK SOUDER
FREELANCE/MARINA DEL RAY

It turns out my pick didn't make it into the book (well, I guess it did now), and so, with a hint of personal creative insecurity, let me describe what happens:

A young man is eating some fast food at an outdoor stand somewhere. An attractive dark-skinned woman sits down across from him who bears a bindiya on her forehead and proceeds to order and eat a meal. Throughout the meal she keeps noticing him sheepishly trying to steal glances at her and her bindiya. Finally, she takes out her Polaroid, takes a picture of her own bindiya, walks over to the young man, peels off the picture's backing, sticks the picture on the young man's forehead, walks back to her meal, sits down and smiles at him. He smiles back, the wall between them tumbled.

We give ourselves certain mandatories when we set out to make advertising. Usually they are these: It needs to communicate the brand strategy, demonstrate the product, stand out in its environment, be fresh and be great.

Every now and then, though, a spot comes along that reminds us that maybe our mandatories are too few, and we're making it too easy on ourselves. After all, a spot can adhere vehemently to all the above criteria and still feed the prevailing view of the world that advertising, its brands, and its practitioners, are a crass and self-centered gang, obsessed with our own tiny issues and either totally insensitive, or totally ignorant to the real issues of the real world.

This spot managed to put a check in the box of all the mandatories listed above, and then one more: Move the world along just a little bit. It didn't just demonstrate how great the product was, it demonstrated how cognizant the brand was of the world in which we live, and it demonstrated what we can do to fully appreciate the richness of that world.

In the end, Polaroid didn't just give us a picture, they gave us a big picture. And we see far too few of those.

JUDGES' CHOICE

CLIENT
Interbrew UK

AGENCY
Lowe/London

MY NICHOLSON
REELANCE/NEW YORK

Last year we had to wave goodbye to young dot-com clients who would gladly buy cool work to set their companies apart. Then everyone else went into a belt-tightening frenzy. It really made you think the work just had to suffer somehow.

It was so not true. There was so much work that I wish I had done. (Okay, there were a couple of things I was glad I didn't do.) But all of my favorite stuff was for major clients with real advertising problems and the solutions were elegant, hilarious, inspiring and inventive. That's the hardest stuff to do. And there was lots of it.

The History Channel did a campaign that was simple and seamless and made me want to watch the History Channel. There was a speeding campaign that made me think twice about buying a motorcycle. The campaign for Club 18-30 made me wish I was 23 again. I fell in love with Citibank and I already bank there. A pack of Guinness matches made me wish I still smoked. A brilliant McDonald's poster made me drool. And I'm saving up for a BMW, a Range Rover and any product that Motorola comes out with.

But my absolute favorite had to be a campaign for Heineken. It was a series of horrible spots that the company keeps threatening to run until sales increase. Then, when sales have exceeded expectations, the offending cast members are eaten by lions in a final spot that ends with the long-running tagline: "How Refreshing. How Heineken." It was amazing. You'd think any advertiser could have done it, but they didn't. And if it sounds annoying, it wasn't. It was entertaining, I felt like I was in on the joke the whole time, and it even made fun of advertising while it sold me something. I loved it. I'm gonna go drink a lot of beer now.

RAYMOND MCKINNEY
THE MARTIN AGENCY/RICHMOND

I absolutely loved the Cartoon Network commercials. While we were judging, I couldn't wait for a new one to come on. My favorite was the one where Aquaman was in a grocery store trying in vain to communicate with a dead fish at the butcher's counter and, later, with a stack of canned tuna. The absurdity of the whole idea captures exactly what it is that makes people who love cartoons love cartoons. And you couldn't help but feel a little sad when the fish didn't answer back.

MARIE CATHERINE DUPUY
TBWA/PARIS

My initial impression while watching this year's work was that despite the crisis in the US and the terrible events of September 11th, the quality of creative has held up well. There weren't as many stand-outs as in prior years. The "mega" brands are king, with marvelously produced spots. Thank you, Frank Budgen for Nike's "Tag" and "Shadow," Reebok for "Escape the Sofa," and the BBDO campaign, "New York."

Given the economic climate, we were expecting "low budget, great ideas." But aside from a few films (Toyota "School" or "West Side Story" reinterpreted by Cup O' Noodle), there was nothing new at all. On the contrary there was a plethora of epic ads (Fallon's BMW campaign). I also saw a tendency toward injecting strangeness (weird animals, animation, etc.) into the real (Cartoon Network). One of the most original campaigns was "Believe in Olive Fingers," for Musco Family Olives. It's not a leading brand, but I still remember it, having seen the commercial just once.

I thought there were few entries from European and South American countries, which is in fact not the case, since according to the awards won, the results were quite traditional: 50% American, 50% rest of the world. What does this mean? The Anglo-Saxon model has strongly influenced the rest of the world (apart from a few Asian countries such as Singapore, Thailand and Japan). The Latinos have lost their Latin-ness. This is a pity. There are other models to be invented. Let's get multi-cultural again.

JUDGES' CHOICE

CLIENT
Cartoon Network Latin America

AGENCY
Cartoon Network Latin America/Atlanta

CLIENT
The Economist

AGENCY
Abbott Mead Vickers.BBDO/London

EUGENE CHEONG
OGILVY/SINGAPORE

After wearing my retinas out from looking at several lifetimes' supply of advertising, here are a few things that became obvious: Long, filmic commercials seem to be extremely effective. I suppose in an ocean of :20 and :30 spots, three to six minute films tend to jut out like icebergs.

Simple, almost vacuous ads are still the way to go. (The drunk-driving TV commercial where nothing happens apart from a guy trying to button his shirt with his two good index fingers is a good example of this genre.) The judges (myself included) were 'too tired to notice' the more thoughtful work. This is a pity. I feel there should always be a place in the book for intelligent but 'slower' advertising.

An outdoor piece for *The Economist* is my personal pick for Best of Show. What a pure idea! No words. No logo. And technically, no picture. But the message couldn't be clearer: The picture's not quite complete without *The Economist*. What a clever idea it is, too. Puzzling in the beginning. Flattering, once you piece it together. Elaborately designed print ads with so-so headlines no longer fool the judges.

ARTHUR BIJUR
CLIFF FREEMAN AND PARTNERS/NEW YORK

In the final analysis, the BMW campaign went where others haven't. It was extremely ambitious, totally original, and deserves to be singled out. Even though some of the parts definitely weren't as good as the whole, the idea here was the thing and it really sold the hell out of the brand. Not only did all the ads and mini-movies reflect well on BMW, but so did the mere fact that this company would do something this complex, intelligent and unusual.

Overall, this year was good. Not great. The high notes just weren't as high as they've been in the past and there weren't as many of them. Why? You can't blame it on September 11. We could theorize about the end of all those years of economic optimism and excess and so forth but ultimately you just shrug and acknowledge that the work just wasn't as great.

Nevertheless, there were some gems. Nike did their thing again with a really good campaign in "Play." Dulux print was awesome, as was *Campaign Brief Magazine's* "Light Bulb" print. Toyota did a perfect spot about a dog chasing a stationary car that got the big laugh of the show, and there were other stand-outs.

There was more international work this year and I gained a new appreciation for how few clients do true branding. VW, Nike, Levi's and BMW are pretty much the same everywhere in the world, which is impressive It's remarkable that with so many global brands out there, those are the only ones doing it right. On the negative side, there was a surprising number of retreads and rip-offs, and I have to mention the now huge SUV category, which has positioned itself for worst commercials by an entire genre.

ROSSANA BARDALES
CLIFF FREEMAN AND PARTNERS/NEW YORK

My choice would have to be the integrated work done for BMW by Fallon. There's a lot to be said not only for the ingenuity but also for the amount of relentless effort it must have taken to get this kind of thinking into several produced pieces of effective advertising. This piece of work was really well thought out and well produced and it reaffirmed my belief in the effectiveness of integration and what can happen when great minds come together. It's also proof that there are still a lot of stones left unturned for the rest of us.

As for trends, what I seemed to find in a lot of the work was a pattern or formula. Most of the time the formulas have been beaten to death and no longer have the punch or impact they once did. Also, there was a lot of safe advertising, some ads that seemed to be trying really hard to get in under the radar. There was also the making of a new kind of "funny." It was based more on absurdity than violence. Some of the work did it very well and other ads were just absurd. But at the end of the day, there was always that one ad or that one campaign you wished you would have done. Ads and clients that restored my faith in asking the question "what if?" and getting results from it.

CLIENT
BMW North America

AGENCY
Fallon/Minneapolis

REG BOKOR
ULLEN/WENHAM

This year, I liked the print category overall better than TV. My favorite thing in the show may have been the absolutely perfect "matchbook" for Guinness, where the white tipped black matches were in the shape of the pint. I couldn't bring myself to award Best of Show to it, though, as a one off. For shear originality, the Levi's spots where the woman and man crash through walls in one spot, and the car full of friends who pull into a deserted gas station to play catch with their body parts in another, showed me something that I've never seen before (I'm not sure the idea was big enough to warrant Best of Show). My vote is for the BMW campaign as a whole—a big breakthrough idea that transcended advertising and was wonderfully executed and promoted.

CLIENT
Federal Express

AGENCY
BBDO/Bangkok

IKE MAZZA
JBLICIS & HAL RINEY/SAN FRANCISCO

For me, this ad is as good as it gets. Simple. Smart. Powerful in its subtlety. A brilliant solution off what I would imagine was a pretty dull brief. I could have easily picked one of the many terrific TV spots, but this humble little collateral poster stuck with me. Bravo to all involved.

CLIENT
Guinness

AGENCY
Abbott Mead Vickers.BBDO/
London

PAUL HIRSCH

GOODBY SILVERSTEIN & PARTNERS/SAN FRANCISCO

As we all know, last year was a tough year. And after spending a week looking at ads it certainly showed. Maybe clients were being too safe. Maybe agencies were a bit conservative. I don't know. But there was definitely one too many commercials with actors in T-shirts with words on them. (I blame my friend Roger Camp for starting this trend.) In the end, however, there was still plenty of work I wish I'd done. The Fox "October" stuff is as funny as spots with nail guns should be. There was a wonderful PBS commercial with Big Bird. BMW did groundbreaking long-form web movies. Wieden + Kennedy and Cliff Freeman are still pumping out the good stuff faster than people can copy them. And some special sort of congratulations, maybe a toaster oven, should go to Modernista! for their MTV and Gap work. We all should part with an account for doing that sort of thing.

Aside from the ads you might have seen, the foreign work was some of the best in the show. Look out for an insurance commercial from Buenos Aries with a Thelma and Louise like ending. A public service campaign from Portugal against speeding with a three minute lockdown shot that breaks your heart. A Japanese campaign for Converse that was the coolest looking print in the show. And, oh, those British Levi's spots. Kids running through walls. How the hell are we supposed to compete with that? Damn you, BBH.

As for a personal favorite, it would have to be Guinness' "Dreamer" from Abbott Mead Vickers. Shot by Jonathan Glazer, it's poetic and beautiful and strange. And it made me jealous. Congratulations to all who worked on it. It's tremendous. And it once again proves what everyone in advertising already knows. If you flip a horse on its back and put a squirrel and some dogs in a spot you know you'll have a winner.

JUDGES' CHOICE

CLIENT
Coca-Cola Japan

AGENCY
Hakuhodo/Tokyo

ANCE JENSEN
ODERNSITA!/BOSTON

Every awards show has its own unspoken code of aesthetics, and the One Show is no exception. In my opinion, the focus has always been on concept and idea, and less on visceral emotional resonance and feeling. It is hard to argue with logic, but personally, I am beginning to question if a clever idea, funny visual or amazing word play compels people to desire a product. Other judges would say yes, absolutely. Me, I'm not so sure. An example would be the Nike Swoosh campaign. Granted, not much of a headline, but those ads made me want that clothing. I'm fascinated with how to get people to not think and simply desire, and this was a good example of it.

I also loved the Fanta stuff from Asia. The TV spot where the guy shakes up his soda and aims it at his girlfriend who ducks so that the stream shoots across the bay and blows up an island is the best spot I have ever seen in my entire life. It is the only spot I remember after all these months. That would have to be my personal pick for Best of Show. A guilty pleasure.

Speaking of Asia, the art direction coming out of it is just amazing. Every print ad that I gravitated towards seemed to be from Singapore. Just beautiful, beautiful stuff. There was also a very cool poster campaign for The Samaritans of England that I thought was the coolest thing I had ever seen.

I am very happy that the BMW integrated campaign won Best of Show. There was a lot of talk about the TV commercials just being movie trailers, and not "great TV spots," but to me, that was never the point. The point was the bigger idea. And I am glad that that idea was rewarded. It shows that there are many, many ways to think about the craft of advertising. Often times, as creatives, we are our own worst enemy. The folks responsible for the BMW campaign freed their minds. And hopefully, all of ours as well. Congratulations.

CLIENT
Guardian Film 4

AGENCY
BMP DDB/London

MICHAEL HART
FALLON/MINNEAPOLIS

Not an easy choice. In print, the Club 18-30 campaign and the car lighter ad for VW stood out. And the optica illusions ad for TAM airlines ought to forever quiet any grumbling I might do about difficult assignments. It's fare ad. And it's brilliant.

But the work I keep thinking about, and keep wishing I'd done, was the charmingly simple spots for the Guardian. While not really the "big" and artfully produced spots it seems everyone is scrambling to create, these ads are a lot like my favorite people. Smart, funny and to the point. Plus, from now on, whenever I see a tired, cliched scene in a movie, I'll think of this campaign. Which, of course, virtually guarantees I'll remember the campaign for decades.

JUDGES' CHOICE

CLIENT
Procter & Gamble-Oil of Olay

AGENCY
Saatchi & Saatchi/Cape Town

Tock. Tick.

EAN ROBAIRE
K.A.ROBAIRE/LOS ANGELES

There were a few things that I loved enough to think of as "Best of Show worthy." When all is said and done, though, I'm a sucker for simplicity. Especially wait-a-second-(PAUSE)-oh-my-God-this-is-awesome, strategically-dead-nuts-on-brilliant, holy-shit-I-wish-I'd-done-that, man-I-hate-these-guys simplicity. "Tock, Tick." The only thing that would have been better is if they'd said it in fewer words. But that's just sour grapes.

ICHAEL PATTI
BDO/NEW YORK

My Best of Show? Oil of Olay: The "Tock, Tick" ad! Great.

RYAN EBNER
BUTLER SHINE & STERN/SAUSALITO

Judges' Pick: Levi's "Odyssey" from BBH/London.

Once in a while, I'll see something that makes me feel like everything I do is worthless. Usually it's a music video. Or a book. Or a feature length film.

This time it was a television commercial.

Simple idea. Awesome production. No drum and bass score.

SCOTT AAL
GRANT SCOTT & HURLEY/SAN FRANCISCO

Judging from the quantity of work, you wouldn't have guessed that it was a slow year for our business. I was glad to see judges passing over the really easy ads. I just can't reward a campaign for a professional wrestling school in the same way as a campaign for, say, Motorola, no matter how nice the art direction or writing. Blood, sweat and tears count for something, and I think other judges agreed.

I saw a couple of really, really nice things in the first round of judging that I thought would easily make the book, yet didn't even garner enough votes to make it to the second round. I was shocked. But I suppose everyone has their own opinion, and that's what keeps it interesting. Or maybe, just maybe, some of the judges were mistakenly pushing the wrong button on their hand-held, wireless voting units. That's how I'm rationalizing all the money *my* agency wasted this year.

There were plenty of things that made me envious. One campaign remained with me in a way that none of the other work did. It's a series of European spots to discourage speeding, in which people who have been crippled as a result of their reckless driving try to accomplish simple tasks. It takes one man two minutes to button a single shirt button. Ninety seconds for another man to take off a shoe. In so much public servi television, the cleverness of the idea overwhelms the message. You always feel so manipulated. Not so wi these spots. The agency and director didn't try to make the people seem sad or pathetic. Instead, we're simply given a window into the tragedy of their lives. Each spot ends with the old proverb, "More haste, les speed." (More familiar overseas than in the US, I believe). Move too fast, and you could end up wasting tim in the end. I have to say, I drive a little slower to meetings these days.

JUDGES' CHOICE

CLIENT
Levi Strauss

AGENCY
Bartle Bogle Hegarty/London

CLIENT
Portuguese Road Safety

AGENCY
BBDO Portugal/Lisbon

Z PARADISE
:KINNEY & SILVER/RICHMOND

My personal pick for Best of Show would have to be the Portuguese Road Safety TV campaign. It's rare when a public service idea that goes for the emotional dagger doesn't leave me somewhat cynical. This work just flat out moved me. Production-wise, I think they made a few brilliant moves. First, they made the spots painfully long. Painful in a way that was necessary to make a point. Second, they used locked down shots to keep them very simple and real. Third, the music was emotional but not disturbing or sappy. The end result was powerful work. I find myself thinking about these spots a lot.

Trends I noticed in this year's work were influenced by the fact that so much of it was international. Whether it was my intrigue with different production sensibilities or fresh approaches to humor, it all seemed amazingly bold. In fact, I wondered if most American clients would ever even buy work like that. At least it motivated me to try. And the really telling part of it was that it wasn't just Europe. It was everywhere. Africa, South America, Asia. I hate to say it, but I think we have some catching up to do.

HANK PERLMAN
HUNGRY MAN/NEW YORK

Whether or not advertising is art can be debated. I do know that when I watch a commercial, I judge it as I woulc a painting, a song, a movie, a book, or a joke. An ad either has an effect on me or it doesn't. I try to consider how many other people will connect with it as well, but ultimately it comes down to what it does to me.

When I first saw these spots for Otsuka Pharmaceutical, they resonated with me in the way a good book or movie does. The situations and characters were very authentic. They felt like a true reflection of real life tha I think advertising rarely achieves. It adds up to these spots selling a lot of fermented milk, which is a gooc thing. I enjoyed being sold to in this campaign. There were characters who I liked and who I wanted to watch explaining, in a very human-being (as opposed to an advertising) kind of way the benefits of the product. The relationships between the characters in these spots have several subtle layers and the comedy goes far beyond the typical jokes you would find in most ads or sit-coms. By the way I've been drinking a lot more soy milk since seeing these spots and it's not even the same thing. That's how good this campaign is

I really appreciated how the scenes were allowed to play out with no additional coverage. This helped the spots feel that much more real to me. (By the way, the word, "real," is probably overused in advertising, an I plead guilty.) In my favorite spot, a son and a father are discussing who should drink the milk that will mak them live a longer and healthier life. They both want the other to drink the milk. The son says, "You've got tc live long," and the father answers back, "What for?" and the son gets really annoyed and says, "I don't know, Dad!" To me that seems universal, that's real life, that's funny, and it's part of what I think is the smartest and best advertising I saw this year when judging the One Show.

Long live the Masai!

ROGER CAMP
WIEDEN + KENNEDY/PORTLAND

Given the economy and the state of advertising these days I was surprised to see as many great pieces as did. Glazer's Levi's wall spot, Guinness' "Dreamer" spot, Nike "Freestyle," and the PBS Big Bird spot, were ju some of the truly outstanding pieces we saw, but there was one spot that deserves to be mentioned because of the circumstances that surround it. Is it better than the previous ads I just mentioned? Maybe. Maybe not, but it is a hilarious piece of film that may become a casualty of the democratic process called a show judging. It is an ad for Masai milk and it was one of the most polarizing pieces we saw.

Each night at dinner the conversation would drift from people complaining about their clients to the work w saw earlier in the day. As we discussed the Masai milk campaign, judges tended to recall it with a hearty chuckle or a groan. In an informal poll, it seemed to get either a 10 (best score) or a 1 and not much in between. The campaign consisted of people in odd situations talking about the benefits of the milk through a hilarious dubbed translation into English. Some judges felt the dubbing was unintentional while others fe that because the situations were funny, the translation must be part of the concept. Personally, I had to/wanted to believe that the translation voiceover was intentional and genius. So rather than default to th list of usual suspects for my judges' pick, I wanted to point out a campaign, in a sea of 15,000 entries, that created a debate. By the way, if the creative team on this campaign could let me know if the dubbing was intentional I would appreciate it. I have some bets pending.

CLIENT
Otsuka Pharmaceutical

AGENCY
Dentsu/Japan

CLIENT
Campaign Brief Asia

AGENCY
Saatchi & Saatchi/Hong Kong

EREMY POSTAER
GSD&M/AUSTIN

I thought there was a lot of cool work. I can't stop thinking about the light bulbs that killed people, though.

ONE SHOW DESIGN

CLIENT
Guinness

AGENCY
BBDO/New York

STEVE SANDSTROM
SANDSTROM DESIGN/PORTLAND

It seems that selecting a personal Best of Show should be relatively easy. Find the best, most original idea that is executed with perfect sensibilities and there you have it. But it's not that simple. While the number o entries was not overwhelming, there was a lot of really good work.

A judge's selection can be splitting hairs. I judged the Clio Awards the week following One Show judging. It wa fascinating to see work that I gave some of my highest marks in One Show Design not even make the final cut in The Clios. The opinions of even the most celebrated and respected creative people in the field can be so varied that almost any recognition, be it Merit or Gold, is an accomplishment. The credibility of a show is built around the quality of the judges, and I think it should be. It is more important to get an honor from judges you admire than from judges you have no opinion of. But it can be amazing how different groups of judges respond to the same work.

As far as my personal favorite, well, it's a tough pick. I really liked Stefan Sagmeister's book. But that's easy because I like so much of his work and the book is a collection of it. So it would be like giving him Best of Show for years of great thinking and interesting design (some of which is better than the book). I think tha should be a different award.

My choice goes to another piece—a book of matches for Guinness. It has a simple black cover with a small gold harp. Inside, there are a few black matches clustered in the center with white tops. The cluster makes the shape of a pint of the dark brew, and the white tops represent the foamy head of the ale. This visual play may not be readily apparent to many. But once you get it, it's a brilliant little gem. A little inside humo for the Guinness drinker. The idea was great and the execution was perfect. There was other work with mor drama, more elaborate production, even higher degrees of difficulty. I feel badly to select one example as a Best of Show because of this. But it felt unique, true to the brand, and if I had done it, it would be one of those ideas I would have been most proud of.

JUDGES' CHOICE

ONE SHOW DESIGN

CLIENT
Archipelago

AGENCY
Duffy Design/Minneapolis

HEPARD FAIREY
LACK ROCKET/LOS ANGELES

The Archipelago pennies campaign is my choice for Best of Show because its no frills classic poster approach utilizes a combination of foolproof devices. The posters are simple enough to be digested quickly, but stylish enough to be memorable. The bold colors and typography with simple images communicate the messages very clearly. Even if the look is retro, a campaign like this is very refreshing as an alternative to the current glut of photo based "sexy" lifestyle ads. The poster's blue-collar style has a very "For the People," altruistic appeal—simple, but not too dry to have an emotional impact. I found myself more interested in the value of a penny after viewing these posters and their included metaphors than I had been since I kept money in a piggy bank.

CLIENT
Mensa Singapore

AGENCY
Gosh Advertising/Singapore

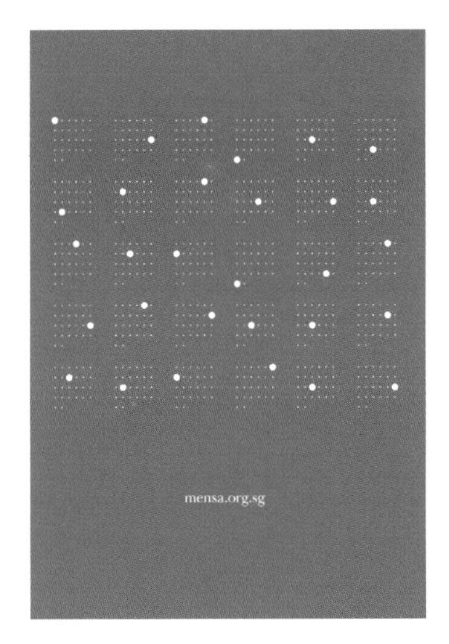

HOMAS MIDDLEBROOK
CKINNEY SILVER DESIGN/RALEIGH

I think Best of Show is best considered several weeks after the event to see what really stuck with you. In my case there were two posters of very similar technique but wildly differing aesthetic. The first was a one-color poster series for Mensa (the genius organization), which used an abstract series of graphic patterns that spelled out the phrase, "Are You The Prodigy We're Looking For?" The beauty of these posters was that they relied upon the viewers' curiosity, and they perfectly captured the ethos of Mensa. I think it's appropriate to note that I stood in front of one of the posters for several minutes, trying to de-code it. Then Duffy came up and pointed out that the answer was written on the entry. There's a reason why he's a giant in this business.

The second poster was also a one-color application of black ink on pink paper that advertised a Canadian leather shop. The imagery was of two "friends" engaged in some sort of bizarre sex act. To be honest I don't know what they were doing but it was so graphically strong and simply done that I would consider buying a pair of chaps. In both cases it was good design on a budget.

Was there a trend? There is a trend, and it is simply that being brilliant is the price of entry. With the glut of product design, packaging, collateral and environmental work, anything that isn't visually or conceptually engaging, anything that doesn't reinforce a strong brand message is simply invisible. I was impressed and encouraged by the amount of great work submitted and I left with that wonderful feeling of challenge and anxiety that you always get from the good stuff.

ONE SHOW DESIGN

CLIENT
Off Site

AGENCY
Core 77/New York

offsite
CORDY SWOPE
IS IN CHINATOWN!
HE OBSERVES AND FINDS INSIGHTS, AND THEN HE DELIVERS.
DECEMBER 12
At FUN lounge, 130 Madison Street, (Between Pike and Market)
6-9 pm. Presentation begins at 6:30
deepFry
BOMBAY SAPPHIRE

RICO LINS
RICO LINS + STUDIO/SÃO PAULO

Among a great deal of well designed, well produced work, I was looking for something that could make one think about good design in a slightly different way. The most outstanding entries had not a merely aesthetic but a strong conceptual approach. A fresh, gimmick-free attitude that could bring new thoughts to form/function/media discussion. As One Show Design is the baby of the originally ad-only One Show, I was looking for stand-alone design ideas that differentiated themselves from advertising. I narrowed down my choice to three entries, which stand out for their simplicity:

The book designed for White Arkitekter by Happy Forsman & Bodenfors/Göthenburg. It cleverly packs a social/aesthetic/functional issue (the quality of our contemporary visual netscape) in an expandable brochure. Beautifully designed, it is bound with removable hardware-store-like plastic screws. It is an invitation to interact: Pages can be added or removed, and a range of stickers are supplied to stimulate protest and personal statement. Great work.

A one-color letterpress-like flyer printed on reused Chinese take-out menu by Core 77. It has a very efficient direct and yet inexpensive, do-it-yourself quality, and it raises some good questions about design practice and people's communication needs.

The Cahan & Associates/San Francisco pocket-sized annual report. The report packs two witty interpretation of the same theme in a paper case. The first is a very clean, flat colored, text-only brochure. The second is its counterpart: a minimal, expressionistic translation into 1-0-1-0-1 binary code.

JUDGES' CHOICE

ONE SHOW DESIGN

CLIENT
Nike Italy

AGENCY
Wieden + Kennedy/
Amsterdam

OE DUFFY
UFFY DESIGN/MINNEAPOLIS

The Rome Street Football/SPQR brochure from Wieden + Kennedy/Amsterdam jumped off the table at me. I love when that happens, particularly when it's design that was done for a real client, with real marketing objectives and the balls to accept and embrace something breakthrough—a surprise. One more thing. This is just the latest in a constant string of design excellence from a client and agency in the US, Europe and Japan that refuse to rest on their laurels. Keep on surprising us, Nike and Wieden + Kennedy. You help make us proud to be designers.

CLIENT
Alabama Vets

AGENCY
Slaughter Hanson/
Birmingham

ANA ARNETT
SA PARTNERS/CHICAGO

"Identifying Courage," by Slaughter Hanson/Birmingham, a Gold Pencil winner, had particular resonance for me. While design played a role in the success of this piece, content manifested itself in a much more powerful way. In essence, design did its job by stepping back—letting the power of the story and photographs drive the emotion of the final presentation.

This is a book which celebrates the stories of war veterans who risked their lives in defense of our country. In some ways, the book actually made me feel good about patriotism. Having seen more than enough American flags over the last year, this story went beyond the typical devices of symbolism by emphasizing the importance of human life and sacrifice. I found this particularly powerful given the nature of what our nation has gone through these last 10 months. This work demonstrates that design can go beyond the service of making something look good. Design can also capture the emotion that can make a good work great.

For the most part, I was pleasantly surprised to find that many entries had returned to the classical elements of typography, writing and color. Having (hopefully) seen the end of the "Photoshop Era," designers seem to be paying more attention to the enduring ingredients that have, and will always, make the most difference. The work you see in this Annual will grab your attention through the masterful positioning of content, versus falsely using decoration to carry the message. So if there was any apparent trend, it was the regard for how classical form can still follow function—ultimately defining brilliant ways to solve new problems.

GOLD
ON GOLD

NAME: Mr.T
FORMER NAME: Laurence Turead
BIRTHDATE: May 21, 1952
HAIR: Black
EYES: Brown

HOBBIES: Relaxing
FAVORITE MUSIC: Gospel
FAVORITE FOOD: Steak
FAVORITE DRINK: Milk
FAVORITE TV SHOW: The A-Team

GOLD ON GOLD

BEST OF SHOW

GOLD AWARD
INTEGRATED BRANDING

CLIENT
BMW North America

AGENCY
Fallon/Minneapolis

02096A

DAVID CARTER

The brief called for a brand campaign. And that's what we did. We just did it a little differently. We had to. BMW's customers don't watch much TV, yet they do have computers with high-speed connections. There was also the problem of showing what a BMW can really do. In a typical car spot, if you show a car taking a corner a little too aggressively, you have to load the screen with disclaimers. Knowing the inherent challenges, BMW said, "Surprise us."

Well then, why not create something that could really show off the car? Why not put it in a place we know our customers are spending time? And why not make it entertaining enough that people will come to it on their own?

In the end, it took a brave client, more than a hundred people working in every department at Fallon and a great collaboration with our production partners at Anonymous Content to pull it off. Fortunately, it worked.

Some people have asked, "Is it an ad?" Maybe the better question is, "What is an ad?"

GOLD ON GOLD

GOLD AWARD
NEWSPAPER OVER 600 LINES
SINGLE

CLIENT
Procter & Gamble-Oil of Olay

AGENCY
Saatchi & Saatchi/Cape Town

02001A

Tock. Tick.

ARK MASON
LADE GILL

We spent a day thinking about how we arrived at the idea. We dissected. We analyzed. We post-rationalized. We conceptualized. We argued. We tried to be smart. Nothing stuck. Because the truth is simple ideas defy any real explanation.

GOLD AWARD
NEWSPAPER OVER 600 LINES
CAMPAIGN

CLIENT
Land Rover North America

AGENCY
GSD&M/Austin

02004A

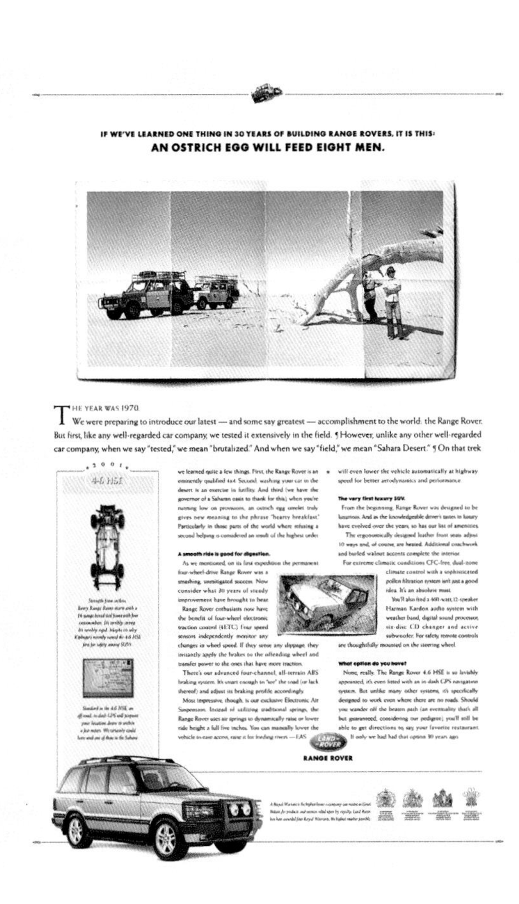

EREMY POSTAER
AVID CRAWFORD

Once in a while, being able to actually write copy and art direct a page comes in handy.

Thanks to Michael Buss, Rob Story, Cameron Day and Lou Flores for knowing about esoteric stuff like syntax and kerning.

GOLD AWARD
MAGAZINE COLOR
FULL PAGE OR SPREAD: SINGLE

CLIENT
Nike

AGENCY
Wieden + Kennedy/Portland

02009A

MARK FITZLOFF
SIMON MAINWARING
BILL KAROW
JAYANTA JENKINS

Ad Schedule	Daily rainfall Portland, OR
Creative team briefed March 13th	(.25 inches)
Internal presentation April 1st	(.32 inches)
Present to Nike April 8th	(.15 inches)
Photo shoot w/o April 15th	(.8 inches)
Ship mechanical May 3rd	(.76 inches)

GOLD AWARD
MAGAZINE COLOR
FULL PAGE OR SPREAD: SINGLE

CLIENT
Nike

AGENCY
Wieden + Kennedy/Portland

02010A

MARK FITZLOFF
SIMON MAINWARING
BILL KAROW
JAYANTA JENKINS

Ad Schedule cont'd	Daily rainfall Portland, OR
Write Gold on Gold blurb June 3rd	(.08 inches)

GOLD ON GOLD

GOLD AWARDS
MAGAZINE COLOR
FULL PAGE OR SPREAD: SINGLE

POSTERS: SINGLE

CLIENT
Club 18-30

AGENCY
Saatchi & Saatchi/London

02013A
02033A

IKE SUTHERLAND
NTONY NELSON

Most people go on holiday to relax and unwind. People who go on Club 18-30 holidays go to get drunk and to get laid. A dream brief from an honest client, although making the ads proved to be a bit of a nightmare. But after 10 months of budget hold-ups, 12 days in Ibiza (great if you're on holiday, not so great if you're shooting all day and trying to sleep at night), one tropical storm, two models arrested and beaten by the police, 2,500 photographs and three weeks solid in retouching, we finally got what we wanted.

After all that we needed a good holiday.

GOLD AWARD
MAGAZINE COLOR
FULL PAGE OR SPREAD:
CAMPAIGN

CLIENT
Dulux

AGENCY
Lowe Bull Calvert Pace/
Johannesburg

02014A

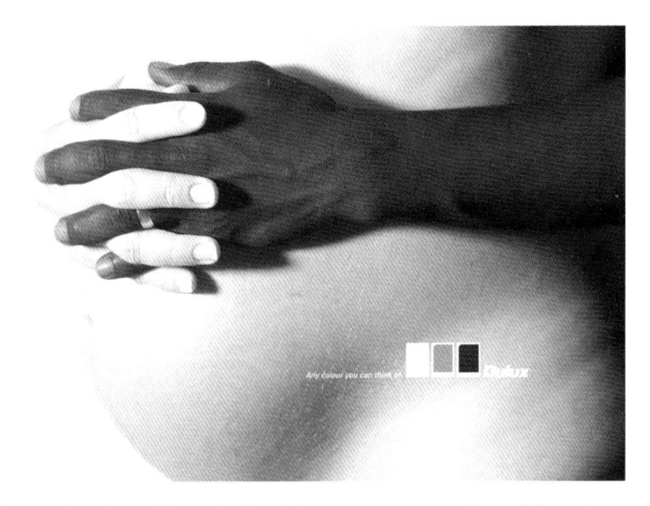

NDREW WHITEHOUSE
USTIN GOMES

The client briefed us to come up with something "out of the paint box," since consumers could not differentiate between the Dulux brand and their leading competitor Plascon. The paint category in South Africa has generally been extremely retail-driven in the past but we really believed the advertising should make an emotional connection with consumers. Color is, after all, a very emotional subject.

Initially the campaign drew criticism from a number of people within the industry who claimed it was "creativity for creativity's sake." The client was under pressure to pull the work, but to her credit, she stood her ground. Thank goodness for brave clients.

Once again, the results have proved that creativity pays. The Dulux profit margin has increased by 30% so far. The AdTrack results have also been staggering. The campaign has a prompted noting score of 79% amongst all adults (expect 24% in this category). The liking score amongst our core target audience, 25 to 34 years old, was 8 out of 10. Finally, the campaign also tested very well in the black market—the prompted noting figure was 86% with verified noting (where they can describe the ad) at 55%. Interestingly, in this market, the multi-racial pregnant ad was the most well-liked, with a score of 7.4 out of 10. A minority of the population was not as enthusiastic about the ad, however, condemning us to "the fiery lakes of hell" for suggesting that white women sleep with black men. Well, we've survived the fiery lakes of hell relatively unsinged and are now looking forward to rolling out the rest of the campaign.

GOLD AWARD
OUTDOOR: SINGLE

CLIENT
Absolut Vodka

AGENCY
TBWA/Chiat/Day/New York

02017A

JOSEPH MAZZAFERRO

Absolut has a 22 year history of inspiring creativity through its advertising. This billboard pays homage to the greatest creative community of Los Angeles: actors. On Sunset Boulevard, standing 60 feet tall, it is located next door to the Mondrian Hotel, home of the Sky Bar, a popular nightspot for actors, directors, and movie producers.

The billboard plays on the idea that Los Angeles is a town full of actors, and they all promote themselves aggressively with headshots. In a way, headshots are considered the local currency. We worked with the Sheila Manning Casting Agency to procure 1,000 actual headshot of Los Angeles actors, from which we received 500 "auditions." Each is an 8 by 10 black and white glossy and attached to the board by pushpins. On the launch day, several radio and morning television shows arrived by helicopter to document a live casting call beneath the billboard. Hundreds of eager actors lined up on Sunset to submit their headshot for future posting.

GOLD ON GOLD

GOLD AWARD
TRADE ANY SIZE
B/W OR COLOR: CAMPAIGN

CLIENT
Campaign Brief Asia

AGENCY
Saatchi & Saatchi/Hong Kong

02025A

AURICE WEE
ENEE LIM

No good idea is complete without that Great Pillar of Hong Kong advertising—the focus group. So naturally, to make sure our ads were right on the money, we got in a bunch of advertising people, gave them each a copy of *Campaign Brief Asia,* demonstrated the idea by dropping giant light bulbs on them while they thumbed through the magazine, then asked them what they thought of it.

We got the following results:

25% said "Aaaaaaaaaaaaaaaaaaaaaaaaaaaaaahhhh," followed by a few minutes of guttural noises, blood sputtering and violent twitching, then silence.

15% said "Aaaaaaaaaaaaaaaaaaaaaaaaaaaaaahhhh," and repeatedly commented, "Oh [name of religious deity]," for the next few minutes.

55% did not make any comments.

Only one person, a 35-year-old Group Account Director, didn't get it. We had to drop a second light bulb on her.

GOLD AWARD
COLLATERAL: POINT OF PURCHASE AND IN-STORE

CLIENT
Guinness

AGENCY
BBDO/New York

02028A

RANK ANSELMO
YSON ATIENZA

We didn't do a Superbowl spot.
We didn't shoot with a big name director.
We didn't work with famous celebrities.
We didn't have a multi-million dollar budget.
We didn't stay at the Four Seasons.
We didn't expense any hookers.

But damn that Gold Pencil sure is shiny!

GOLD ON GOLD

GOLD AWARD
COLLATERAL: SELF-PROMOTION

CLIENT
Mother

AGENCY
Mother/London

02031A

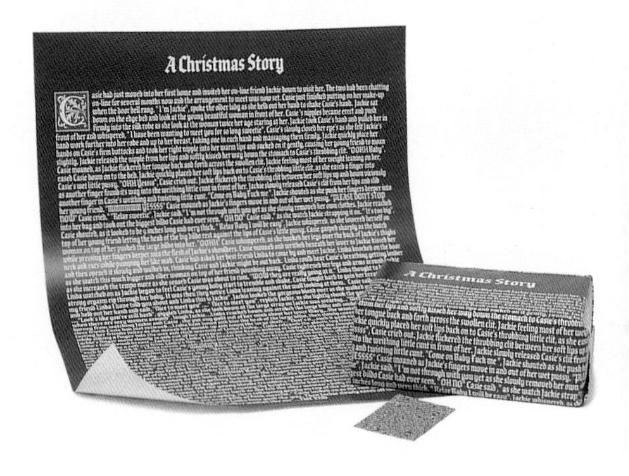

BEN MOOGE
LUKE WILLIAMSON
THOMAS HILLAND

Egypt. December, 3000 B.C.
Pharaoh is faced with his usual visible gift dilemma. He can never think of anything good to get the queen and to make things worse, she can always see what's coming.

Pharaoh commands that a paper-like substance is made to cover his gifts. Young Effendi takes Pharaoh's brief rather too liberally.

Queen hates her presents as usual, but loves the ingenious soaked papyrus sheets with the amusing hieroglyphics that cover them.

London. November, 2001 A.D.
Mother are faced with their usual Xmas mailer dilemma. Inspired by a relatively fresh, 5,000-year-old idea they decide against a gift and concentrate on the paper.

Tired of cherubs, trees, angels, and snowmen, a gap in the wrapping paper market appears—including the ever-seasonal Mushroom Cloud, the traditional Knitting Patterns, the Xmas-comes-but-once-a-year Oil Rig and Air Conditioning Units, festive Lesbo-Porn and the brutally honest Closing Down Sale (Everything Must Go

Paris. December, 2001 A.D.
Colette exhibits thousands of sheets of the Mother Xmas wrapping paper as part of an Xmas installation. The paper is gone by the end of the fourth day. Many Parisians have strangely wrapped Xmas presents.

GOLD AWARD
POSTERS: CAMPAIGN

CLIENT
Mattel Southeast Asia

AGENCY
Ogilvy & Mather/
Kuala Lumpur

02036A

GAVIN SIMPSON
PAUL LIM
BRIAN CAPEL
CASE DEENADAYALAN
EDDIE AZADI
NGOW FEI FEI
LYDIA LIM
JAMES WONG
SONAL DABRAL
THAM KHAI MENG
NEIL FRENCH

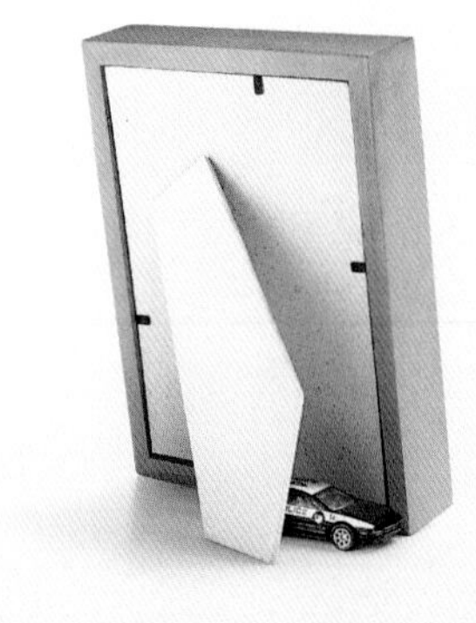

Here's a gentle reminder for those who like to work alone. Gavin Simpson, Paul Lim, Brian Capel, Case Deenadayalan, Eddie Azadi, Ngow Fei Fei, Lydia Lim, James Wong, Sonal Dabral, Tham Khai Meng, Neil French.

☐ Newspaper
☐ Blanket
Please call 0800 248 964 to make a don tion because some people don't have the choice.
AUCKLAND CITY MISSION
WINTER APPEAL

GOLD ON GOLD

GOLD AWARD
PUBLIC SERVICE/POLITICAL
NEWSPAPER OR MAGAZINE
SINGLE

CLIENT
Auckland City Mission

AGENCY
Publicis Mojo/Auckland

02039A

UY DENNISTON

Doing great work for any client is rewarding. But when you do great work for a charity the rewards are magnified.

ARL FLEET

Creating public service ads requires you to be selfless and giving. Entering them into awards balances that out quite nicely.

GOLD AWARD
PUBLIC SERVICE/POLITICAL NEWSPAPER OR MAGAZINE CAMPAIGN

CLIENT
Misericordia

AGENCY
Young & Rubicam/Chicago

02042A

CIGARS WEREN'T HANDED OUT THE
DAY PETER WAS BORN
MISERICORDIA

KEN ERKE
JON WYVILLE

We were reading through a Misericordia brochure and found a quote from Sister Rosemary, a nun who's been with the home for over 30 years: "We try to make their birthdays especially fun, since the actual day they were born was generally not a happy one."

We hoped if we presented thoughts as honest and powerful as Sister Rosemary's, our ads might move some people.

If you would like more information about Misericordia or if you would like to offer your support, please call 773.273.4166.

GOLD AWARD
PUBLIC SERVICE/POLITICAL RADIO: SINGLE

CLIENT
American Legacy Foundation

AGENCY
Arnold Worldwide/Crispin Porter & Bogusky/Boston and Miami

ROGER BALDACCI

Every single day, tobacco kills 1,200 people. The tobacco companies spend over $26 million a day to market their products. Bar promotions. Giveaways. You'd think just having an addictive substance in your product would be enough to keep people "brand loyal." Apparently not.

GOLD AWARD
PUBLIC SERVICE/POLITICAL RADIO: CAMPAIGN

CLIENT
American Legacy Foundation

AGENCY
Arnold Worldwide/Crispin Porter & Bogusky/Boston and Miami

ROGER BALDACCI
MIKE MARTIN
RICH MACHIN

The tobacco companies make a product that kills 400,000 Americans each year.

Think about that for six seconds please.

Done? Okay, with the Truth campaign, we hope to open some eyes, and this case, ears, and expose teens to the marketing practices of the tobacco companies and their seemingly defective product.

GOLD ON GOLD

GOLD AWARD
PUBLIC SERVICE/POLITICAL
TELEVISION: SINGLE

CLIENT
DETR

AGENCY
Abbott Mead Vickers.BBDO/
London

02054A

ICK WORTHINGTON
AUL BRAZIER

Three things stand out as memorable on the shoot.

One funny. Two not.

The sound of a car hitting a child (albeit a dummy child). Not funny.

Shooting 12,000 feet of film through a high-speed camera that can't be stopped mid-roll, take after take to get the perfect timing, the perfect frame. Shooting the plates of the kid running out into the road without the car. Plates of the kid in the air. Plates of the kid on the ground. Watching it all on playback and going home extremely happy only to find out the following day that every inch of the negative had been ruined.

Not funny.

Watching a guy who'd just robbed the newsagent burst out of the shop directly in front of the camera, look both ways then take off, not knowing that we'd caught him at 1,200 frames per second, or that we had 20 security guards and police on hand. It wasn't his day. But he made ours.

GOLD AWARD
PUBLIC SERVICE/POLITICAL
TELEVISION: CAMPAIGN

CLIENT
Portuguese Road Safety

AGENCY
BBDO Portugal/Lisbon

02057A

OGO ANAHORY
SE BONTEMPO
DRO BIDARRA

No pro-bono-let's-do-some-good-n-grab-some-prizes motivation. There was a client, a pitch, a brief, and everybody got paid. Just the truth. No metaphors, no fantasy, no extra drama, no over dramatization. Just the truth. No camera moves, no cutting and editing. Just action and cut. Just the truth. No black and white, no fancy telecine. No gimmicks. No post-production. Just the truth. No dramatic voiceover with fatherly advice, no creepy sound effects. Just the truth. No actors. Just Helder, Teresa, and Henrique.

GOLD AWARD
CONSUMER RADIO: SINGLE

CLIENT
Hollywood Video

AGENCY
Cliff Freeman and Partners/
New York

SEE 02058A

IAN REICHENTHAL
ADAM CHASNOW

Remember at the end of "Silence of the Lambs," when Hannibal Lecter calls Clarice after he escapes? Clarice asks him where he is, and he replies, "I can't say—but I'm about to have an old friend for dinner."

Sure, it's a play on words. And not a particularly good one. But most people, including us, just overlooked it and left the theater thinking Dr. Lecter was a diabolical genius.

In "Hannibal," (the sequel to "Silence of the Lambs") it's harder to overlook the bad wordplays because there are so many more of them. Before eating each and every one of his victims, Lecter drops a hint. Hints like, "Oh, Maureen, you look positively DELICIOUS in that dress," and "Carl, stand there for a moment with your back turned to me while I DIGEST what you're saying. (Slurrrrrrrrrrrrp-p-p-p.)"

Okay, those are made-up examples because we were too lazy to go back and watch the movie again. But the point is: There were a lot more bad wordplays in "Hannibal" than in "Silence of the Lambs." And it made Dr. Lecter seem like less like a diabolical genius and more like a bad borsht-belt comic.

It's just something that we noticed. And joked about. And then we wrote our script and beat that joke into the ground.

GOLD AWARD
CONSUMER RADIO: CAMPAIGN

CLIENT
Hollywood Video

AGENCY
Cliff Freeman and Partners/
New York

SEE 02061A

IAN REICHENTHAL
ADAM CHASNOW
GREG GERSTNER

As expected as it may be to write a Gold on Gold thanking our client, we'd like to say thank you to our client, Hollywood Video.

For sticking with this campaign for five years.

For turning down co-op money from the movie studios so they wouldn't have to forfeit any creative control

And for not only letting us do these commercials, but for thanking us afterwards.

We're really lucky.

GOLD AWARD
CONSUMER TELEVISION
OVER :30: SINGLE

CLIENT
HSBC La Buenos Aires

AGENCY
Agulla & Baccetti/
Buenos Aires

02064A

SEBASTIAN WILHELM
JUAN CABRAL
SEBASTIAN BLEZOWSKI
MARCELO VERGARA
RAFAEL DALVIA
ALBERTO PONTE
SEBASTIAN STAGNO

Argentina is immersed in the worst economic and social crisis in history. Riots and public protests are a part of everyday life. Violence rates are increasing and people's trust in the country is at an all-time low.

In that context, winning a One Show Gold Pencil made all Argentineans immensely happy. Everybody came out on the streets in a huge parade, cheering, bearing Argentinean flags as we sat in a Cadillac, waving our hands to the exhilarated crowd. Children's first choice when they grow up is to be advertising creatives, ar monuments of the creative team on horses are being sculpted as you read.

On the back of this success, we hope to build the foundations of a better tomorrow for our republic.

GOLD ON GOLD

GOLD AWARD
CONSUMER TELEVISION
OVER :30: SINGLE

CLIENT
Levi Strauss

AGENCY
Bartle Bogle Hegarty/London

02065A

NTONY GOLDSTEIN
AVIN LESTER

This brief seems almost harder to crack than the one that sat on our desk all those months ago for Levi's Engineered Jeans. It raises some rather serious ethical questions. What is one supposed to say?

Does one bask in the blinding spotlight of glory? Or do the decent thing and play the modest card? Point out that it was a team effort that made this possible. Without which we would not be accepting this award. And that the team was exceptional. A brave client, a visionary director, unyielding account men and women, tireless producers and post producers to name but a few. And should we single out the individual who worked (as did his colleagues) so tirelessly in post that he collapsed from exhaustion?

No, sod it. Let's bask. We won a Gold at the One Show. Did we mention WE won a Gold at the One Show.

GOLD AWARD
CONSUMER TELEVISION
OVER :30: CAMPAIGN

CLIENT
Nike

AGENCY
Wieden + Kennedy/Portland

02069A

ASH SREE
ONICA TAYLOR
IKE BYRNE
NDY FACKRELL

People like to play. It's something we have hardwired into our DNA. But something we as a society seem to have forgotten. There's something innately pleasing and educational about playing. For instance when I take this pencil and let's say, beat Andy Fackrell around the head with it. It makes me smile. It's fun.

Let's see if it's just as much fun with Monica? It is.

Mike, Mike—Come back, I want to play.

We really got on as a team.

GOLD AWARD
CONSUMER TELEVISION
:30/:25: SINGLE

CLIENT
Toyota GB

AGENCY
Saatchi & Saatchi/London

02072A

JO STAFFORD
BRETT SALMONS

So, this is where we're supposed to share with you our creative process. Or recount some behind-the-scenes story or a witty anecdote. Well the truth is, the shoot really wasn't all that exciting and neither are we. We'r just proud of our ad, pleased that it was liked and glad that it was—oh, just shut up.

GOLD AWARD
CONSUMER TELEVISION
:30/:25: CAMPAIGN

CLIENT
International Division of the History Channel

AGENCY
The Concept Farm/New York

02075A

GREGG WASIAK
JOHN GELLOS

Alright, we're coming clean. This campaign wasn't our recommendation.

We had our hearts set on another one, but it was slightly over budget. We grumbled and moped for days and then shot the back-up.

Sometimes, even despite yourself, the planets just align and you find yourself in the rare and humbled position of writing one of these.

Thanks for listening.

GOLD AWARD
CONSUMER TELEVISION
:20 AND UNDER: SINGLE

CLIENT
Coca-Cola Japan

AGENCY
Hakuhodo/Tokyo

02079A

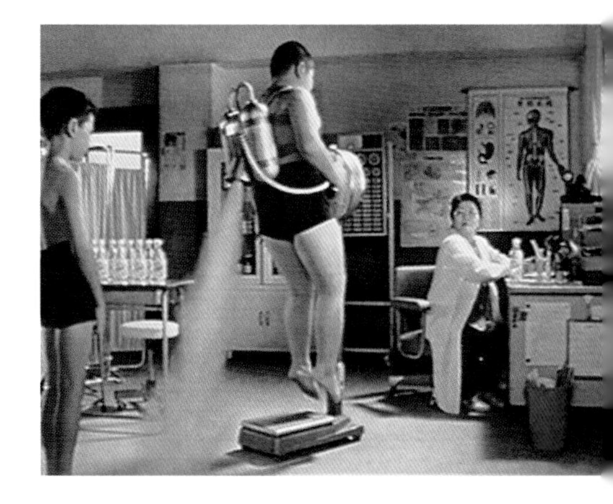

YASUAKA IWAMOTO

Fanta is a refreshing beverage that has been out on the market for many years. It was a well-known and established brand even before the target age group—junior high through high schoolers—was born. This is where the problem lies. The target consumer acknowledged the existence of Fanta, but not enough to prefe it over other brands. In other words, Fanta did not have a bond with the target age group. One of their characteristics is that they simply want to have a good time and share fun with their friends. That is how w started the "Fun Time Series," a series of silly, comical unexpected happenings. The difficult part was bringi out the twist, and making an ordinary daily scene very funny. Our meetings would last for hours trying to see who could come up with the most absurd ideas. After they had aired, the Fanta series was talked abou everywhere. Fanta regained a new appeal through the series, and as a result, succeeded in building a stronger relationship with the young target group.

GOLD ON GOLD

GOLD AWARD
CONSUMER TELEVISION
:20 AND UNDER: CAMPAIGN

CLIENT
Guardian Film 4

AGENCY
BMP DDB/London

02082A

DEAN WEBB

In the movies, admen are always shallow, conceited individuals who can't resist blowing their own trumpets.

—Dean 'Gold' Webb

GOLD AWARD
CONSUMER TELEVISION
VARYING LENGTHS CAMPAIGN

CLIENT
Cartoon Network Latin America

AGENCY
Cartoon Network Latin America/Atlanta

02085A

AMON PITTMAN

My fellow creatives and I set out on a mission: Come up with phase 2 of our "Clearly The Best Place For Cartoons" campaign. Our mission led us to a bar, and then to several pitchers of beer...which (of course) led to ideas. Finally we realized that the ideas probably should have something to do with the campaign we were "conceptualizing." We focused our attention (somewhat) on the dramatic differences between the cartoon world and our world, and why cartoon characters couldn't (and shouldn't) make it in ours. One of us threw out a character, then we'd imagine them in a terribly out-of-place situation, and finally create various scenarios that we'd like to watch unfold. Someone scribbled down the ideas, and phase 2 of our campaign was born...at the expense of several million brain cells, which died.

GOLD AWARD
CONSUMER TELEVISION
UNDER $50,000 BUDGET
SINGLE

CLIENT
Cartoon Network Latin America

AGENCY
Cartoon Network Latin America/Atlanta

02088A

RAIG ADAMS
AMON PITTMAN
ERNAN LAGRECA
TEVE KUHN
ERNANDO SEMENZATO

This campaign arose from the need to give real meaning to Cartoon Network's brand umbrella of "the best place for cartoons." We sought to illustrate this brand image on air by placing the cartoon characters in real-world environments. We chose Fred and Barney because they are loveable, familiar characters, and we didn't have to pay them scale. By tapping into one of their most recognizable traits, we executed our concept while staying true to our product. When the two begin to pound their feet on the floorboard of the car (which we ended up having to pay for, thank you very much), the viewer is witness to their inability to function in our world, thus showing that Cartoon Network is "clearly, the best place for cartoons." The process of producing this campaign also proved that most of the creatives in our department are unable to function in the real world either. But we'll save that for another campaign.

GOLD AWARD
NON-BROADCAST CINEMA

CLIENT
Lucky Magazine

AGENCY
Black Rocket/San Francisco

02090A

PHIL COVITZ
WARREN COCKREL
DAVE LOEW

"Just shoot it and show us when you're done."

—James Truman and Kim France, Clients

Hail James and Kim.

GOLD AWARD
FOREIGN LANGUAGE TELEVISION

CLIENT
Philips Lighting

AGENCY
D'Arcy/Hong Kong

02092A

JASON ASPES
SAM MARTIN

This is such a shock. Neither one of us ever dreamed that we would win this award. And I'm not talking about a Gold Pencil. We've always dreamed of that. I'm talking about this particular award: foreign language television commercial. I mean, what are the chances? Neither one of us can speak a foreign language. Hell, between the two of us, we've spent over 20 years studying four different languages and we still can't count to 10 in any of them. But I suppose a simple idea executed well will always cut through the clutter no matter what language you're speaking.

Special thanks to Marc Lucas, Peter Milne, Guillaume Roux, Sam Silverwood-Cope and Su Yin Tan.

GOLD AWARD
COLLEGE COMPETITION
ADVERTISING

SCHOOL
Brainco/Minneapolis

CC059

OHN NEERLAND
INDSAY SHEA

One of our early concepts was a set of post cards that would be sent to everyone outside of the United States. The cards promoted the cultures, ethnicities and values that America has in common with the rest of the world. After hitting a few sturdy brick walls, we stepped back and thought about what would truly resonate with, say, a cattle herder in rural Nigeria. We figured that the best way for him to appreciate the United States was to experience firsthand one of the freedoms enjoyed here. We also just liked the idea of government agencies and leaders being inundated with millions or even billions of post cards, phone calls and emails from abroad. We're curious about how the client would react.

GOLD AWARD
COLLEGE COMPETITION
DESIGN

SCHOOL
Parsons School of Design/
New York

CCD019

AYA TOYOSHIMA

When I started this project, I thought of taking snapshots of crowds on the streets of New York to portray one of the strengths of America—diversity. I wanted to convey America, with all kinds of people, from all over the world, with all sorts of backgrounds and cultures.

The idea for the main copy: "This is America," came from my mother, when she came to visit me in America from Japan. Her first words were: "This is America!" I thought that statement was pretty strong, and it must be the words of the many people who come to America for the first time.

GOLD ON GOLD

ONE SHOW DESIGN
BEST OF SHOW

GOLD AWARD
BOOK JACKET DESIGN

CLIENT
Booth Clibborn

AGENCY
Sagmeister/New York

02022D

STEFAN SAGMEISTER

"Made You Look" contains practically all the work we ever designed, including the bad stuff.

Removing the book from the red-tinted, transparent slip case causes the mood of the dog to worsen considerably; bending it over results in the title "Made You Look" (or in the other direction: dog food) showing up on the fore edge. Peter Hall wrote a very detailed text (for a design book). I included hand written excerpts from my diary and many comments from our dear clients.

GOLD ON GOLD

BILL CAHAN
GARY WILLIAMS
ANN GIORDANO
ESTHER HENDERSON
RAY MANLEY
ROBERT MARKOW
JOHN SANN
JASON HOLLEY

GOLD AWARD
ONE SHOW DESIGN
ANNUAL REPORT

CLIENT
Maxygen

AGENCY
Cahan & Associates/
San Francisco

02003D

Maxygen wanted to focus on their products this year. My first thought was to create a book/journal that felt like something found in the 19th century. A scientific journal of a sort. Visually, the theme of the book rested on the idea of nature as a metaphor. The size and scope of the book emphasized the credibility of Maxygen as the leader in their industry.

MARION ENGLISH

GOLD AWARD
ONE SHOW DESIGN
BOOKLET/BROCHURE

CLIENT
Alabama Vets

AGENCY
Slaughter Hanson/
Birmingham

02004D

The Alabama Veterans Memorial Foundation had received a grant to proceed with the building of a memorial to honor all veterans of wars from the 20th century. Very little of that money was earmarked for a brochure/book to be sold at the memorial. In other words, all the pre-press work would have to be donated—the research, the photography, the color separations, you get the picture. And yet, it seemed somehow fitting. Most of the people who volunteered their stories were from impoverished counties, where finding even a minimum wage job is difficult, and in many cases "working the land" is the only option. Some stories came from families that didn't own a map—couldn't so much as locate the country where their sons' bodies were buried. Others came from families for whom the only thing left of their sons were medals and faded uniforms.

For many of these men, a military career was a way out—a noble alternative to the same backbreaking life their fathers and grandfathers had led before them. And, while these kids initially might not have been worth much on paper, their contributions to our state and to our country were heroic. And their sacrifices were great. Some gave up their youth, others—their lives.

So our mission was to honor men we came to know through their stories as deeply as they had honored us. A drill sergeant who volunteered for Vietnam because his boys were dying "as quickly as you strike a match, and blow it out," a 19-year-old kid who would have avoided the draft had he made the college baseball team, a Coca-Cola delivery man whose dream of being a pilot cost him his life.

And so, our charge was to use our minds to create a brochure—a memorial not only to these men and the seven others whose stories we share with the reader, but to the rest of Alabama's Veterans. In comparison to their sacrifices, ours were paltry. We hope we did them right.

GOLD AWARD
ONE SHOW DESIGN
BOOKLET/BROCHURE

CLIENT
White Arkitekter

AGENCY
Happy Forsman & Bodenfors/Göthenburg

02005D

ANDERS KORNESTEDT
LISA CAREBORG
GAVIN SMART

Keen to rejuvenate their reputation, White Architects, the largest architecture firm in Sweden, wanted us to create something special as part of their 50th anniversary celebration. We agreed to concentrate on the future and the coming 50 years, rather than the past. The company has a history of strong ethic and humanistic values. In a society where architecture often equals luxury buildings for the elite, this was an opportunity to look at architecture from a different perspective and discuss issues like the homeless, segregation and new working methods.

We decided that a book would give us space enough to discuss the different issues thoroughly. A book with a purpose to get people to react, debate and make their own opinion. Design-wise it was important to inspire the reader. We included post cards addressed to people with whom architects should get in contact, fold-outs with drive-by pictures presenting new ways of looking at architecture, a spray stencil saying, "Demolish!", stickers that say "nice" and "ugly" with pictures of buildings to practice sticking them on, heac lines sprayed on buildings designed by White Architects, and so on. All on 14 different types of material!

Because there were a lot of people involved, we had a hectic time collecting all the information. However, w managed to complete almost 500 pages in just a few months, mainly thanks to a brave client and a patien printer. (The book seems to do the job it was set out to do. On the way to work a few days ago we saw an "ugly" sticker placed eye-catchingly on a building of questionable design.)

GOLD AWARD
ONE SHOW DESIGN
CORPORATE IDENTITY

CLIENT
King James RSVP

AGENCY
King James RSVP/Cape Town

02008D

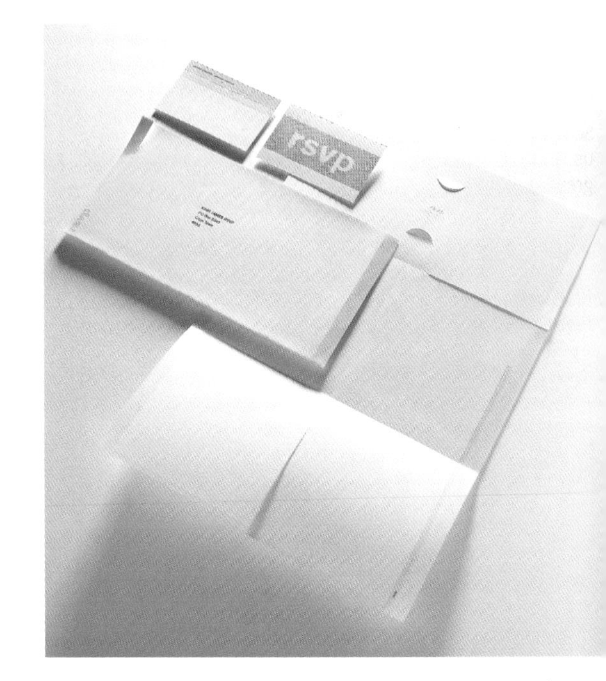

JENNY EHLERS
INGRID LING

It took 18 months for us to produce a corporate identity for RSVP, not because we didn't have a good idea, but because we never could get it down on paper. It's the same old story, never enough time to do any wor of our own. When we did eventually get down to it, with two Virgos working on the project we became the epitome of anal—a testing time for us all. We got anal about the paper stock, anal about the size of the perforations, anal about the depth of the embossing, anal about the compliment slips all being the same size, anal about the color and anal about the size of the type (especially). We drove our production manager craz we drove ourselves crazy, and the printer doesn't really come round to the agency for drinks anymore. Ther we decided we should carry our identity through into our offices, so we painted everything white. We got an about the desks, anal about the walls, anal about the shade of white. There's a lot of white, even our floors are white, which is the subject of great debate back here. Ah, perfectionism. Well, it seems it paid off this time

GOLD ON GOLD

GOLD AWARD
ONE SHOW DESIGN
PROMOTIONAL AND POINT OF PURCHASE POSTERS

CLIENT
Archipelago

AGENCY
Duffy Design/Minneapolis

02011D

COTT VINCENT

The new business people are roaming down the hall looking for a team to pitch a new account. Who wants to work on this new financial services thing...some sort of electronic communication network...has to do with...um...stock exchanges...something...we'll figure it out. Everyone scatters. At that exact moment I wander out of the bathroom. And I see a group of new business people standing in front of me with sinister smiles slowly washing across their faces. We go meet them. The CEO, Jerry Putnam, is terrifyingly smart, loves good ideas and has a great sense of humor. We find out how great when we present the work. Thinking we're going to have to push him a little we bring some pretty crazy boards. We leave in shock. Mumbling something to the effect of, "Jerry, we don't think you can do that on TV. But we'll check with the attorneys." Turns out Jerry hates wasting his marketing budget on work that no one's going to notice. Clients like this don't come along that often.

So the stock market changes from fractions to decimals. And now traders can jump ahead of each other's trades by increasing their bid by a penny. It's really throwing a wrench into the way trades are executed. Using Archipelago can help stop this from happening. Jerry wants to do stuff like teepee the New York Stock Exchange with rolls of toilet paper with the Archipelago logo on it. And drop pennies on the traders as they leave for the day. We're all set to go until we find out that for various reasons, these are both felonies.

So Alan Leusink at Duffy comes up with this campaign instead. Traders love it. It works like crazy. None of us land in jail. Unfortunately, now I'm spoiled. Every time I wander out of the bathroom I think something great is going to happen. Sadly, it almost never does.

GOLD AWARD
ONE SHOW DESIGN
PUBLIC SERVICE POSTERS

CLIENT
Nanjing Massacre Memorial

AGENCY
JST Design Consultants/
Beijing

02014D

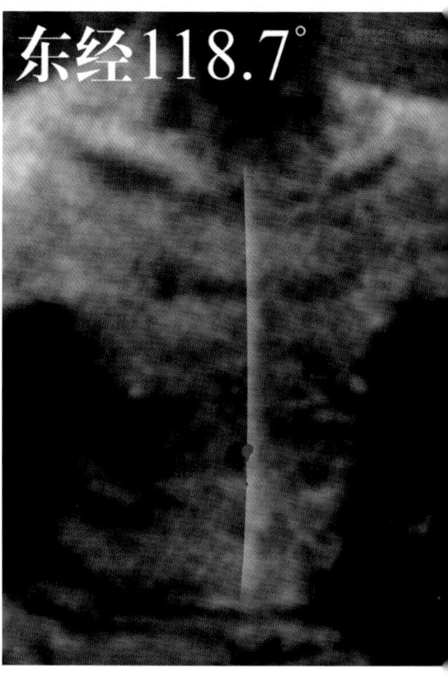

SHIWEI CAI
ZHIHONG XU

The nightmare visions of blood, death, and terror could not be forgotten over the past 65 years. What we could do is rescue the victims from oblivion. Sixty-five years later, the air is still full with the memory of the Nanjing Massacre. Facing the memory, our breath becomes heavy. We wanted to arouse public consciousness with this piece. Time will never allow us to understand it, but we could not face the event with reticence. Thanks to the One Show, which gave us courage to expose this scar.

GOLD AWARD
ONE SHOW DESIGN
COMMERCIAL PRODUCT
PACKAGING

CLIENT
Blue Q

AGENCY
Sagmeister/New York

02017D

STEFAN SAGMEISTER

Mitch Nash from Blue Q came into the studio with the idea for a perfume called Unavailable. The concept, developed by writer Karen Salmansohn, was that they would sell a perfume with a separate attached little book talking about the philosophy of Unavailable: the idea being that you might be more desirable when unavailable (don't fake orgasm but do fake call waiting).

Since so many perfumes are sold in gift packs where the customer gets a little bullshit item like a vanity case or a shower scrubber or a whatnot extra, I was very wary of the attached little book, thinking it would only become another throwaway item. Ten years prior I was involved in a project in Hong Kong involving hidden, custom-made glass eyeballs in a die-cut of a notebook, that idea came to mind again. It allowed us not only to combine book and bottle tightly, but have the book become the packaging, the philosophy wrapping the scent tightly.

The black bar over the type was a rather obvious choice, influenced by censorship bars—information that is not available. We printed the words themselves only on the back of the bottle so the viewer has to tilt it for to become available. In designing the layout, we tried different, more elaborate schemes only to return to the simple stuff again. The bottle itself is a classic stock bottle (we neither had the budget nor the required minimum to design a custom bottle). The soap was an easy solution, printing the entire book inside the cardboard box. Again the philosophy wraps the scent.

The "Un" of Unavailable is only embossed half as deep as the rest of the word, making sure the user does become, with repeated use, available (a sweet idea our intern Stephan Haas came up with).

GOLD ON GOLD

GOLD AWARD
ONE SHOW DESIGN
DIRECT MAIL

CLIENT
Nike Europe

AGENCY
Wieden + Kennedy/
Amsterdam

02029D

AUL SHEARER

The brief: Go conquer Rome.

Well, football made parts of it. So off we went and hung out with street football players in Rome, and dug deep, looking for some unique insight. After some hard, grueling work sitting around the cool parts of Rome, one popped up.

In the past, Rome was divided into two sides primarily by wealth. This divide still exists and is fiercely competitive through its football teams. So our campaign was born (well, everyone loves a good story).

It grew into a healthy, young 60-second MTV series, a strong exciting football tournament, and eventually this handsome football comic book that all the parents were proud of.

It is a credit to Nike that we are given the chance to reach deep into individuals and their sporting communities. "Just Do It," as we hope they now say on the football pitches of Rome.

"I think that I shall never see a billboard lovely as a tree.
Indeed, unless the billboards fall, I'll never see a tree at all."
Ogden Nash, SONG OF THE OPEN ROAD, 1945

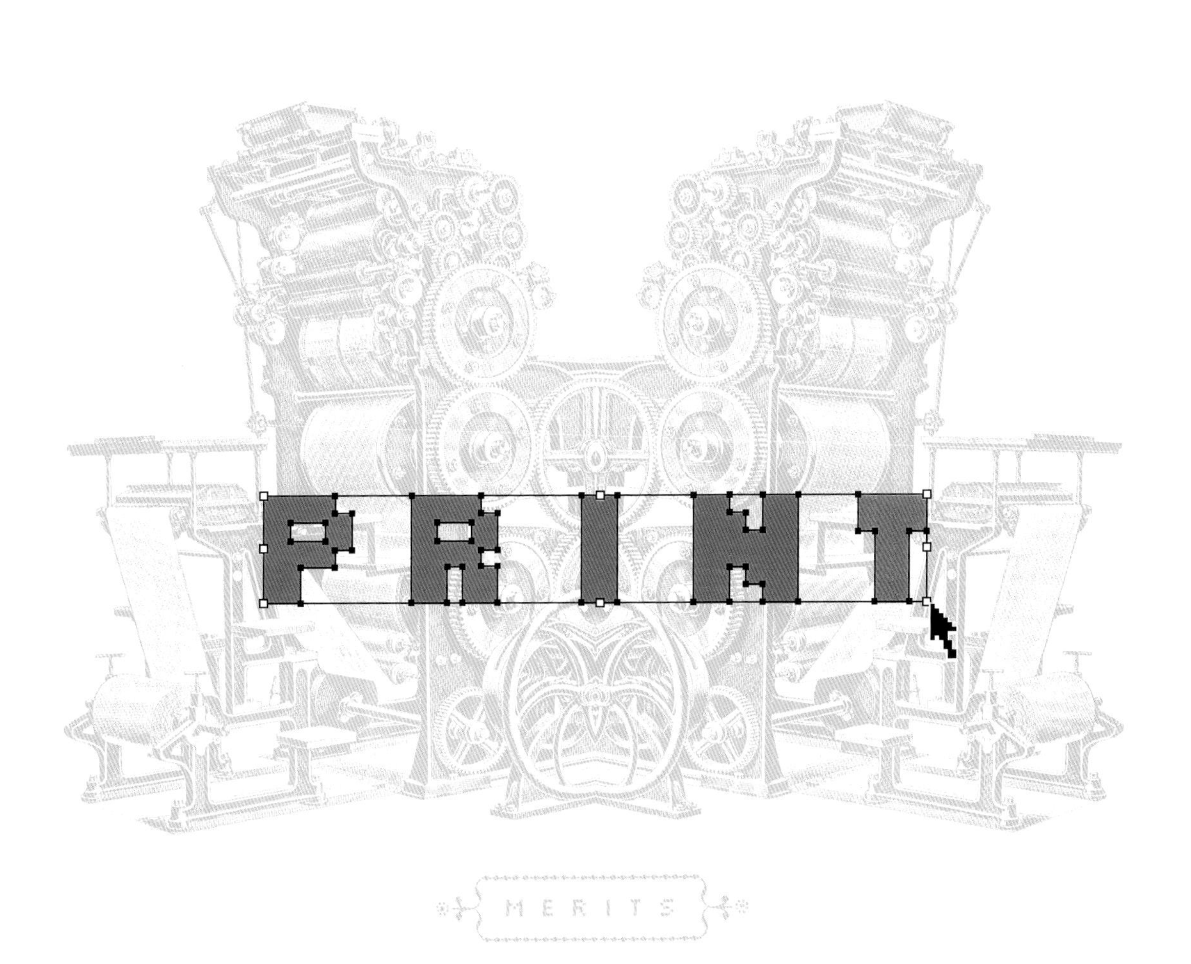
PRINT
MERITS

MERIT AWARD
NEWSPAPER OVER 600 LINES
SINGLE

ART DIRECTOR
Dave Dye

WRITER
Sean Doyle

TYPOGRAPHER
David Wakefield

CREATIVE DIRECTORS
Dave Dye
Sean Doyle

CLIENT
The Economist

AGENCY
Abbott Mead Vickers.BBDO/
London

02105A

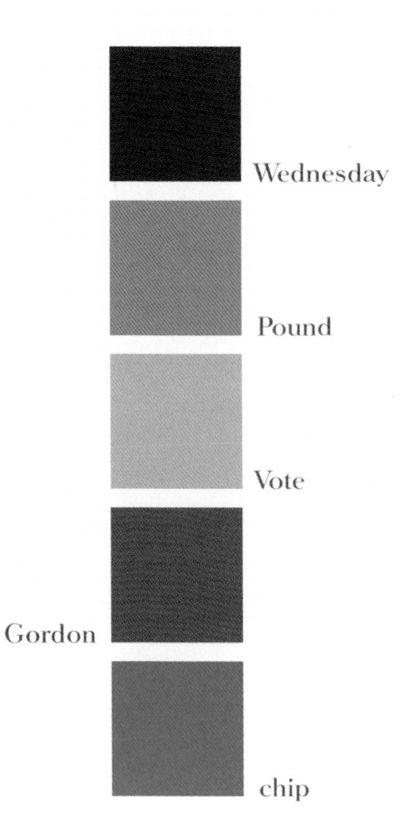

MERIT AWARD
NEWSPAPER OVER 600 LINES
SINGLE

ART DIRECTOR
Dave Dye

WRITER
Sean Doyle

TYPOGRAPHER
David Wakefield

CREATIVE DIRECTORS
Dave Dye
Sean Doyle

CLIENT
The Economist

AGENCY
Abbott Mead Vickers.BBDO/
London

02106A

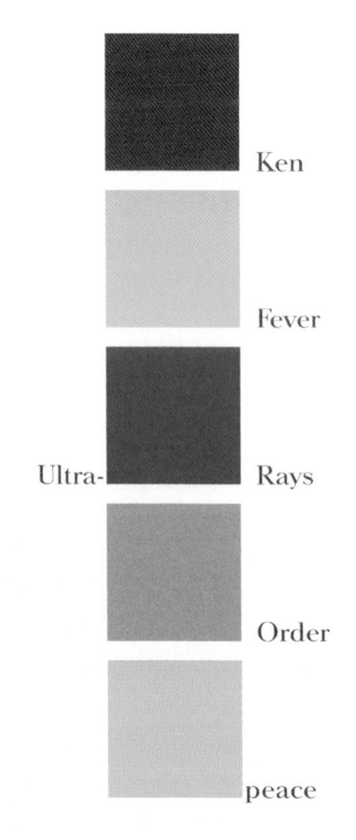

PRINT MERIT

MERIT AWARD
NEWSPAPER OVER 600 LINES
SINGLE

ART DIRECTOR
Simon Langley

WRITER
Richard Morgan

PHOTOGRAPHER
Robert Wilson

CREATIVE DIRECTORS
Peter Souter
Tony Cox

CLIENT
Guinness

AGENCY
Abbott Mead Vickers.BBDO/
London

02099A

Also won:
MERIT AWARD
MAGAZINE COLOR
FULL PAGE OR SPREAD: SINGLE

REGIONAL news

HSBC to freeze salaries of 14,000 workers next year

Thailand may triple visa fees

Has Thaksin turned against liberalisation?

NOTEBook

The S-Class.

Hair2day Hair2morrow

REGIONAL news

Beleaguered Hong Kong turns to Beijing for help

China gives nod to HK-based broadcaster Phoenix

China seen as No 1 tourist draw by 2020

HK developers rush to clear stocks

Business leaders make intelligent choice for the future

CEO inspired by attractive investment opportunity

MERIT AWARD
NEWSPAPER OVER 600 LINES
SINGLE

ART DIRECTOR
Kirsten Ackland

WRITER
Justin White

ILLUSTRATOR
Fedtrick Chua

PHOTOGRAPHER
Jonathan Tay

CREATIVE DIRECTOR
Peter Callaghan

CLIENT
Daimler Chrysler

AGENCY
Batey/Singapore

02100A

MERIT AWARD
NEWSPAPER OVER 600 LINES
SINGLE

ART DIRECTOR
Scott Dube

WRITER
Ian MacKellar

ILLUSTRATORS
Pon Lau
Scott Dube

CREATIVE DIRECTORS
Michael McLaughlin
Jack Neary
Scott Dube
Ian MacKellar

CLIENT
Federal Express Canada

AGENCY
BBDO Canada/Toronto

02101A

Before
FedEx Express
After
FedEx Express
We now offer later pick-up times.
For information on FedEx® Extra Hours call 1 800 Go FedEx. Or visit www.fedex.ca

MERIT AWARD
NEWSPAPER OVER 600 LINES
SINGLE

ART DIRECTOR
Ivan Johnson

WRITER
Kyle Cockeran

PHOTOGRAPHER
Steve Goldberg

CREATIVE DIRECTOR
Errol Denman

CLIENT
Isuzu

AGENCY
Berry Bush BBDO/Cape Town

02102A

PRINT MERIT

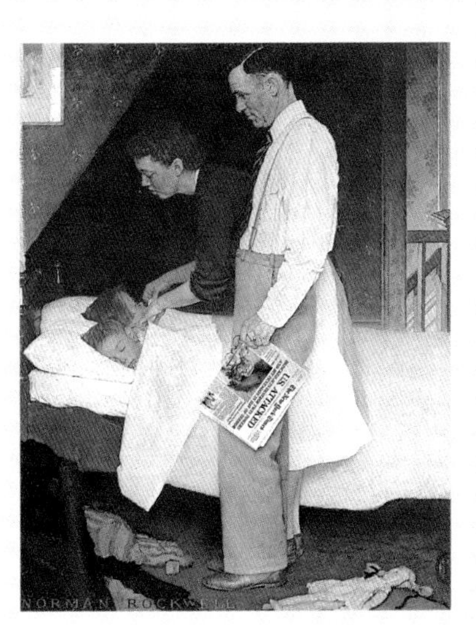

Make sense of our times.

The New York Times

MERIT AWARD
NEWSPAPER OVER 600 LINES
SINGLE

ART DIRECTOR
Jan Jacobs

WRITER
Dave Holloway

PHOTOGRAPHER
Simon Harsent

CREATIVE DIRECTORS
Tony Granger
Kerry Keenan
Erik Vervroegen

CLIENT
New York Times

AGENCY
Bozell/New York

02104A

MERIT AWARD
NEWSPAPER OVER 600 LINES
SINGLE

ART DIRECTORS
Marco Ceo
Matt Spett

ILLUSTRATOR
Image Tap

PHOTOGRAPHER
Phillip Esparza

CREATIVE DIRECTOR
Carl Warner

CLIENT
McIlhenny Co.

AGENCY
DDB/Dallas

02107A

MERIT AWARD
NEWSPAPER OVER 600 LINES
SINGLE

ART DIRECTORS
Toh Han Ming
Patrick Low

WRITER
Mark Fong

ILLUSTRATOR
Shinta

PHOTOGRAPHER
Hon

CREATIVE DIRECTORS
Patrick Low
Mark Fong

CLIENT
Class 95FM

AGENCY
Dentsu Young & Rubicam/
Singapore

02108A

CLASS 95FM

MERIT AWARD
NEWSPAPER OVER 600 LINES
SINGLE

ART DIRECTOR
Steve Sage

WRITER
Greg Hahn

CREATIVE DIRECTOR
Bob Moore

CLIENT
United Airlines

AGENCY
Fallon/Minneapolis

02110A

Monday, September 10.

On Monday, a hose in my sink broke just when I needed to rush out the door, and I thought life was being unfair.

On Monday, when you asked people how they were doing, without much thought, or much contemplation, they replied "fine" or "good."

On Monday, the papers and the news magazines were filled with stories about the new fall TV schedule.

On Monday, there were not many people in the religious section at the bookstore.

On Monday, the American flag hung, for the most part, unnoticed at government buildings and at schools.

On Monday, we passed strangers without much regard.

On Tuesday, September 11, all that changed.

On Tuesday, September 11, different things seemed important.

On Tuesday, September 11, blissful naiveté was lost. Sanctity was mercilessly shaken.

On Tuesday, September 11, somebody tried to take America apart.

On Tuesday, September 11, America came together.

On Tuesday, there were no Republicans, Democrats, yuppies, blue collars, or any other labels. There were only Americans.

On Tuesday, September 11, strangers died for each other.

On Tuesday, September 11, the best of the human spirit spit back into the eye of the worst.

On Tuesday, September 11, America was knocked to its knees.
On Tuesday, September 11, America got back up again.

We'd like to acknowledge the bravery and selflessness of the rescue workers, medical personnel, and extraordinary citizens of this country. Your acts of heroism and compassion have touched all our hearts. We'd also like to thank our employees for their caring professionalism in the wake of last week's horrible tragedy. We join you in mourning. As we join you in strength.

UNITED

PRINT MERIT

The kind of pain
we feel once in a lifetime.
Or twice.
Four at the most.

A tribute to George Harrison (1943-2001)

MERIT AWARD
NEWSPAPER OVER 600 LINES
SINGLE

ART DIRECTOR
Federico Callegari

WRITER
Leo Prat

CREATIVE DIRECTORS
Joaquín Mollá
José Mollá

CLIENT
Rolling Stone

AGENCY
La Comunidad/Buenos Aires

02116A

MERIT AWARD
NEWSPAPER OVER 600 LINES
SINGLE

ART DIRECTOR
Gumpon Laksanajinda

WRITER
Saravut Sasananund

ILLUSTRATOR
Surachai Putikulangkul

PHOTOGRAPHER
Kiradee Ketakinta

CREATIVE DIRECTOR
Wisit Lumsiricharoenchoke

CLIENT
Red Bull Beverage

AGENCY
Ogilvy/Bangkok

02120A

MERIT AWARD
NEWSPAPER OVER 600 LINES
SINGLE

ART DIRECTORS
Gavin Simpson
Sonal Dabral

WRITERS
Paul Lim
Sonal Dabral

PHOTOGRAPHER
Edmund/Barney Studio

CREATIVE DIRECTOR
Sonal Dabral

CLIENT
Guinness Anchor Berhad

AGENCY
Ogilvy & Mather/
Kuala Lumpur

02117A

MERIT AWARD
NEWSPAPER OVER 600 LINES
SINGLE

ART DIRECTORS
Brian Capel
Sonal Dabral

WRITERS
Case Deenadayalan
Sonal Dabral

ILLUSTRATOR
Pako/Image Form

PHOTOGRAPHERS
Fai/IFL Studio
Corbis Images

CREATIVE DIRECTOR
Sonal Dabral

CLIENT
Mattel Southeast Asia

AGENCY
Ogilvy & Mather/
Kuala Lumpur

02118A

MERIT AWARD
NEWSPAPER OVER 600 LINES
SINGLE

ART DIRECTORS
Brian Capel
Sonal Dabral

WRITERS
Case Deenadayalan
Sonal Dabral

ILLUSTRATOR
Pako/Image Form

PHOTOGRAPHERS
Fai/IFL Studio
Corbis Images

CREATIVE DIRECTOR
Sonal Dabral

CLIENT
Mattel Southeast Asia

AGENCY
Ogilvy & Mather/
Kuala Lumpur

02119A

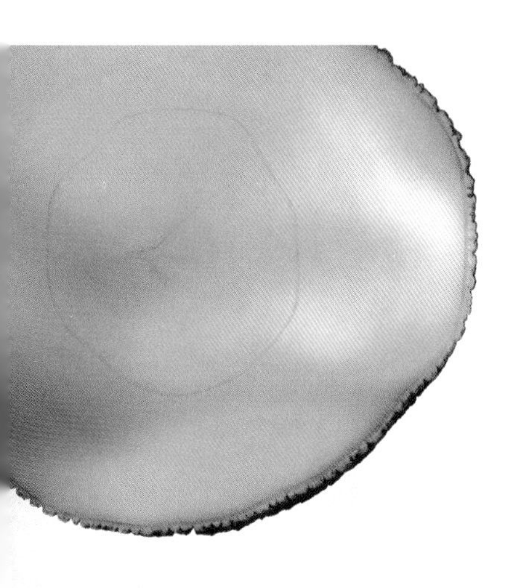

Growing older without ageing.

MERIT AWARD
NEWSPAPER OVER 600 LINES
SINGLE

ART DIRECTOR
Anneke Nieuwoudt

WRITERS
Anneke Nieuwoudt
Brett Wild

ILLUSTRATOR
Grant Linton

PHOTOGRAPHER
Stock

CREATIVE DIRECTOR
Brett Wild

CLIENT
Procter & Gamble-Oil of Olay

AGENCY
Saatchi & Saatchi/
Johannesburg

02122A

PRINT MERIT

MERIT AWARD
NEWSPAPER OVER 600 LINES
SINGLE

ART DIRECTOR
Ikuo Toyama

WRITERS
Kensui Arao
John Merrifield

PHOTOGRAPHER
Kensaku Nagao

CREATIVE DIRECTOR
John Merrifield

CLIENT
Adidas

AGENCY
Saatchi & Saatchi/Tokyo

02121A

MERIT AWARD
NEWSPAPER OVER 600 LINES
SINGLE

ART DIRECTOR
Arnie Presiado

WRITER
Bob Rickert

CREATIVE DIRECTOR
Steve Rabosky

CLIENT
Oregon Sports Hall of Fame

AGENCY
Saatchi & Saatchi/Torrance

02123A

STORIES BASED ON EVIDENCE FROM STEVE PREFONTAINE'S RUNNING SHORTS:

They were there at the beginning. A pair of nylon maroon shorts with gold trim waiting for the start of Steve's first race. At the time nobody cared about the guy and running was something people did only when they were in a hurry. The fading on the left thigh of Steve's shorts indicates that as a kid Steve got up before daylight in the town of Coos Bay, Oregon to go for what he used to call "a little run." It was often very cold in fact. Absolutely freezing and this maniac wouldn't stop running. His shorts tried to keep him as warm as they could and he'd see the faces of those he called "my people." The deliverymen, the construction workers, the guys who worked at the mill. He'd pass those blue-collar guys and Pre would wave and they'd wave back. Pre related to those guys. And sometimes it would be raining or almost below freezing in the morning, so the shorts would try to use their nylon seam or the hem to itch him as he ran to make him want to turn around and go home but he just wouldn't. Because it was cold out there and apparently the shorts just wanted to go home and jump in the nice warm dryer. But no, no way. Pre would just keep going. It was the first indicator that Pre was special. A research study completed recently by a major eastern school indicates this tactic has been used successfully on virtually thousands of other high school kids before and since. The tactic is simple: The shorts take that scratchy part on the seam and rub it on the guy's leg and he can't take it so he turns around. But with Pre, it's like he enjoyed the pain or something. You couldn't stop him. A deep fold in his shorts indicated that once they even did their best to avoid going out by hiding at the bottom of Pre's drawer in his dresser. Evidence indicates he spent just over five minutes and they were put on and forced to go. Tom Jordan wrote in his book about how one Coos Bay resident described Pre's training. "I used to see Pre training while on my way to work. He used to run through Mingus Park, past the swimming pool and then up the steep 10th Street hill. It's an odd thing, but although I saw him running the streets and trails of Coos Bay hundreds of times, I don't think I ever saw him running downhill. He was always going up." Of course, The shorts he wore in those days were usually a nylon/cotton blend. Washed the night before by his mom Elfriede, who used Bold detergent a lot to maximize their softness. In fact, when you consider what Pre stood for, Bold was the perfect name for the detergent that washed them. Pre's mom was a really supportive woman. She washed his shorts after every practice and every meet and never complained as long as he threw them in the hamper. There's also a tiny stitch that's come loose that appears to have been repaired. One theory is that Pre was running way out in the country somewhere and as he came over a hill he was chased by a pack of wild leopards. We researched quite a few leopard migrating patterns and discovered that there are no leopards in Oregon. At first glance this seems to prove the probability that Pre outran the leopards as false. However, there are no travel records for Pre during that time, so we can't be 100% conclusive. Another possibility is that Pre was sleeping one night and one of his opponents snuck into his room very very quietly. Tiptoed over to his dresser and got his shorts out. He could've pulled them out because Steve was a very hard sleeper. Maybe he took them back to his place and very scientifically pulled the string out of the shorts. Why would he go to all this trouble? Lots of reasons. First, remember nobody could beat this guy. You ever try to run while you got an itch on your leg? Not easy. Also, they might have tried to just use it as a distraction. Say the guy's running along and he's right behind Pre and he's probably not gonna win the race. All he'd have to do is just yell out, "Don't you hate it when you get an itch on your leg? Man! I hate it when I get an itch on my leg. Say right up there on your right thigh when you're trying to win a big race. I would hate that. Wouldn't you, Pre?" Seems like a lot of work to go through just to try to beat Pre. Plus there's the possibility of the first-degree burglary charge and all. So that's probably not it. All those may be wrong though. Maybe he just snagged it on a door hinge or something. We also couldn't help but notice that the maroon color of the shorts had faded. No big deal to the untrained eye without forensic help. But consider this: It never sunshines long enough in Oregon for it to fade a pair of high-quality shorts like these, now does it? No, it doesn't. So the only possible conclusion is that he traveled with these babies and took them to Europe with him when he ran there. Or that they just went to Los Angeles with him when he ran there in early 1975. See, even without exact travel records we're able to follow the footsteps of one of track's greatest legends. Sorta like a scientific GPS system or something. We also found a small tear just inside the lining of the elastic band near the back of the shorts next to the tag. This could have happened in a variety of ways. The first conclusion drawn was that Pre was involved in a scuffle of some kind. But after checking with the records department at the Eugene Police, we found that Steve was never involved in anything of the sort. Subsequent checks in Portland, Los Angeles, Salem and in fifteen different police stations also turned up negative. After that we turned our attention to another possibility. That Pre was using a cyclone fence in his backyard to practice for the steeplechase event. We know, Steve never ran the steeplechase event, but we have to check out every possibility. We looked at the fence and examined the diagnostics of the shorts against the metallic flecking on the fence itself and were able to conclusively determine that it was impossible for Steve's shorts to have been torn on that fence. Finally, we got a tip from a Mrs. Janet Avery in Norman, Oklahoma, who said that in early 1971 she saw Pre running along the Willamette River near Autzen Stadium (on the trails that are now known as Pre's trail, coincidentally). He said he was jogging toward Pre along the trail when Pre stuck his left hand up as if to nonverbally say hello. As he did, he underestimated his distance from a thick branch of thistle bush that stuck out over the trail. Pre turned at the last second but it was too late, and the thistle got the back of his shorts, snagging it as he blew past Mrs. Avery. This would explain the tear perfectly. Or it might have happened at the 1971 NCAA cross-country championships in Knoxville, Tennessee. When you see Pre's shorts, just be glad you can. Because they almost didn't make it to the case. In fact, they almost didn't even make it back to the U.S. At one point Pre was headed to Europe for a big international meet and his luggage was lost by Pan Am on his connecting flight from Idlewild (now known as JFK International). He went to Paris. His luggage to Havana. For two full weeks Pre went without these shorts, not to mention his toothbrush. Not coincidentally it's been well-documented that Pre's efforts during that span were more than sub-par. The "official" explanation from the USA Track and Field was that he had a "blister." A ridiculous thing for them to even try to get by with considering Pre's incredible tolerance for pain. The real story was probably more like this. The shorts wind up in Havana. Pre opens his bag somewhere in Germany. His shorts aren't there. He goes to open his second bag only to realize his second bag isn't there. Panic sets in and a frantic Pre calls USA Track and Field for assistance. They in turn begin making calls and are first stonewalled by a new customer service representative at Pan Am. Meanwhile at the Havana airport an unclaimed bag had raised suspicion. A bomb squad had been called in and to their dismay the closest thing to a bomb they found were Pre's damp nylon shorts and a semi-fresh Granny Smith apple. Fortunately for Pre a "high government official" was a fan of his and expedited the process. Shortly after returning to the U.S., Pre's bag arrived in Eugene by diplomatic pouch. The bag had been searched and the shorts appeared unharmed. However, due to Department of Agriculture regulations, the apple was unable to make it. Keep in mind, this is just the evidence we found on his shorts. We've also got his letterman's jacket from the University of Oregon, a pair of his shoes, a sweatshirt and some other stuff we haven't even had time to examine yet. Our man Ken who runs the front desk can tell you more if you're interested. The letterman's jacket looks really really worn. Like he might have slept in the thing on a bus one too many times. We did everything we could to get the wrinkles out but in the end, well, you'll just have to see for yourself. The crease in the back we think is from Steve's bus ride from Marshfield High to one of his away meets in Eugene or Corvallis. Probably against South Eugene. The shorts were folded over and over and over until one day they just broke down and stayed that way. Here's a neat tip. If you put your ear up really close to them you can almost hear the rambunctious kids on the bus and the crowd cheering as he rounds the last bend and heads for home and then the gasp of the crowd as he breaks the tape. It's a little eerie and we're not sure how it works, but about the closest thing we can compare it to is one of those seashells you put your ear up to and listen to the waves of the ocean with. All of this is something the casual observer won't see. They'll probably just look up at the shorts and think to themselves, "Hmmm, a pair of shorts." But you'll see them in a completely different way. To learn even more about Pre, come see his shorts at the Oregon Sports Hall of Fame. They're here along with Pre's letterman's jacket, and artifacts from all over the state. We're located at 3rd and Salmon. Actually 321 S.W. Salmon in downtown Portland, Oregon. To visit, just head downtown and find yourself some parking anywhere near Pioneer Courthouse Square. From there, it's a really easy walk to our front door. Or if you'd prefer, a little run.

WAY MORE THAN YOU NEED TO KNOW. THE OREGON SPORTS HALL OF FAME.

We're open every day except holidays at 321 S.W. Salmon. Across from the big elk statue in the park. Admission is $4.

Osama Bin Laden, Bonnie & Clyde, Unabomber, Darth Vader, O. J. Simpson, Charles Manson, Timothy Mc Veigh, Jason, Norman Bates, Dr. Evil & Mini-Me, Pablo Escobar, Ramon Eduardo Arellano, Lex Luthor, Al Capone, Darth Maul, Medusa, Buu, James Watson, Anastasia and Drizella, Goldfinger, Dr. No, Commodus, Apocalypse, The Doorbell Killer, The Interstate Killer, Igor Giorgadze, Mr. Smee, Jean-Thierry Mathurian, Riddler, John Reginald Christie, Queen of Hearts, Klingons, The Torture Mother, Sulejman Gracanin, Nora Clavicle, The Bloody Benders, Louise Pette, Marsha, Donald Harvey, Johann Hoch, The Hillside Stranglers, Maleficent, Butcher of Hannover, Kane, Brooklyn Lue, The, Ali Abu Bakr Ali Saleh, Edmund Kemper III, Governor Ratcliffe, Henri Landru, Raymond Shao, Lord Ffogg & Lady, The Thrill Killer, Peasoup, King Tut, John Williams, Kamal Beyrouti, The Bloody Countess, Callisto, Agent Smith, Cheetah, Sivershankar Pottu Amman, Dracula, Fre, Capitan Huck, Mohammad Ali Agka, Poison Hera, The Monster of the Andes, Lee H. Oswald, Hopeton Eric Brown, Grant Harry Bergsli, Victor Creed, Vandal Savage, A. Pinochet,

Gorilla Murderer, Christie Bruce Charlton, Jaire Lopez, Thomas Piper, Winston Leroy Hall, The Boston Strangler, Serge Pierre Fernand Lardin, Dr. Cassandra, Gilles de Rais, Gianfranco Marcelli, The Singing Strangler, The Educated Murderer, Tamiami Strangler, Ronald Joseph Paul MC Guire, Anthonie Horst, Momcilo Gruban, The Beast of the Black Forest, Dr. Thomas Cream, Habib Mokni, Jeffrey Dahmer, Heylel Cruz, Marius Perron, Gerald Schaefer, Jose Antonio Solorzano, Elizabeth Bathory, Salvatore Ventura, Gaston, Pogo the Clown, Nicolae Ion, Lucian Staniak, Daniel Clement Chafe, Carlton Gary, Charles Arthur Floyd, Ali Lamouti, The Tourist from Hell, Moussa Abdo Farahat Alnawi, Albert Fish, Richard Floyd MacCoy Jr., Adrian Ripburger, Peter Sutcliffe, The Moors Murderers, Albert De Salvo, Egghead, Lucian Staniak, Larry Eyler, Yorkshire Ripper, The Gay Slayer, Joker, Lord Voldemort, Eddie The Head, Jim Jones, Mun-Ha, Butch, Satan Goss, Chuckie, James Miller,

Strip Slayer, Stephen Richards, Heinz Kehrli, Alfred Cline, The Harry Powers, Bobba Fett, Thierry Paulin, Darkseid, Mohamed Atef, Adolfo De Jesus Constanzo, Kalibak, Machete Murderer, The Joseph Victor Fernandes, Charles Raymond Feduccia, Dean Corll, The Ripper, Melvin David Rees, Mrs. Lestrange, Albert Johnson Walker, Theresa Cross, Earle Nelson, Darren Irvin Cohen, Wartime Jack the Ripper, Charles Schmid, John Scripps, The Buttermilk Bluebeard, The Milwaukee Monster, Mahmood Ghodsi, Baron Adelbert Gruner, Bobby Joe Long, John Dillinger, Magneto, The Mass Murderer of Munstberg, Anatoly Onoprienko, The Original Bluebeard, Purple Tentacle, Patricia Joan O' Byrne, Albert DeSalvo, The Pied Piper of Phoenix, Queen of Diamonds, The Giggling Granny, Oualid Bannani, Theodore Durrant, Shan Yu, The Angel of Death, Mickey & Mallory Knox, Boris The Blade, Billy The Kid, Michael Meyers, Jack the Ripper, Kaiser Soze,

Paim, Senator Palpatine, The Mad Biter, Ali Ramadan Abou Za Kouk, The Lipstick Murderer, The Old Ladies Killer, Iago, Professor Zodiak, William McDonald, Nebraska Fiend, The Mad Bomber, The Campus Killer, Taieb Hamidi, Mohammad Ahmad, Joseph Mumfre, Abu, New Orleans Axeman, Ravan, Ted Bundy, Mr. MXYZPTLK, Paul Cosner, Abdul Aziz Salem, Carl Panzram, Jeff Rhoades, The Rostov Ripper, Black Barax, John Wayne Glover, The Monster of Montmarte, Mongi Fatnassi, Gordon Cummins, Frollo, Marcel Petiot, Vernon Butts, Cell, Rory Conde, Jimmie Knorr, The Boston Belfry Murderer, Vitalii Anohin, Charles Ng, Jamel Aoui, Godfather of Matamoros, The Night Stalker, The Archer, Herman Mudgett, Mohammad Ibrahim, The Killer Cop, Nannie Doss, Clock King, Joseph Smith, The Demon of the Belfry, Elouise Marie Corbin, The Brides in the Bath Murderer, Victor Manuel Gerena, Samir Georges Rabbat, Catwoman, The Terminator, Emanuel Zorg, Hans Grüeber, Ramirez Night Prowler, Jesse James, Penguin, Abimael Guzmán, Carlos The Jackal, Dr. Freeze, Mr. Pink, H.H. Holmes, Henri Hill, Dr. Hannibal Lecter - The Cannibal, Lucifer, Spawn, Iceman, Brothers Fratello, Cleo Green, Andrei Chikatilo,

Cindy, Billy, Pam and I.

Freddie Krueger, Pinhead, Mr. Blonde, Francis Drake, Be-Bop & Rocksteadye, The Doubles Killer, Jabba the Hutt, Clayton Lee Waagner, Lucius Malfoy, The Trash Bag Murderer, Arthur Bishop, Lord Droon, Jab Allah Hamed Al Zawi, Dr. Clever, Want-Ad Killer, Ted Kaczynski, Vasili Komaroff, The Classified Ad Rapist, Charles Augustus, Harvey Carnigan, Angel of Death, Marc Remillard, Goran Borovnica, Venon, Carol Eugene Watts, Monocle, Knodar, Cincinnati Strangler, The Vampire of Sacramento, Richard Ramirez, Black Manta, Ernst Stavro Blofeld, Tyler Durden, "Deacon" Jim, Nicolas Claux, Scarecrow, Eliahu Tzror, Milverton, The Sex Beast, Bizarro, The Sydney Mutilator, Jaws, James Robert Leydic, Douglas Clark, The Archer, The Death Maker, Jean-Bautiste, Archie McCafferty, The Trailside Killer, Freeza, David & Judith Wulkan, Tiamat, Salah Karkar, Nikolai Dzumagalies, Heinrich Pommerencke, Captain Cold, Youssef Abbas, The Mad Dog, Inoun Haddad, Joseph Anderson, Carmelo Barbera, Monster of Rillington Place, Henri Valery, Mario Felipe Batista, Richard Cottingham, J. Worthington, John Collins, Willian Maxwell Brodie, Coed Murderer, The

Marcellus Wallace, Brutus, The Cannibal, Sauron, Captain Hook, Gertrude Baniszewski, Dr. Wily, Peter Kurten, The Vampire of Paris, Lady Tremaine, Richard Angelo, Patrick Kearney, Vaughn Greenwood, Joe Ball, Colin Ireland, The Alligator Man, Evil Queen, Bluebeard, Archibald Hall, Sandman, Bluebeard, The Bender Family, Cavalier, William Heirens, Ouajifa Ben Ouajifa, The .44 Caliber Killer, Jafar, The Co-Ed Killer, The Ratcliffe Highway Murderer, Kenneth Bianchi, Hades, Jean Yves Tremblay, Abou Alqassim Younes, Andreas Bichel, The Vampire of Dusseldorf, The Bavarian Ripper, Judge Claude Frollo, The Lambeth Poisoner, Keith Hunter Jesperson, Lotfi Tounsi, Jake Bird, Mr. Who, Salomon Grundy, Tacoma Axe Killer, Alexander Rodionov, The French, William Bonin, Mohamed Ben Rahal, Werner Boost, Isadora Klein, Ian Brady, Gregory Philip Raji Abdo, Myra Hindley, Giganta, The Shoe-Fetish Slayer, Willie Sutton, Professor Moriarty, Freeway Killer, Rudolf Pleil, The Monster of Czinkota, The Brainiac, David Carpenter, The I-5 Killer, Richard Macek, Imhopted, Richard Chase, Khaled Ajawid, Herman Drenth, Posteal Laskey, Ahmad Abou Damgh, The Sunset

Mark Chapman, Ronald Biggs, John Wilkes Boot, Al Hasi, Vicent Vega, The Candy Man, Cruella de Vil, Timothy William Spencer, John Wayne Gacy, The French Ripper, The Plainfield Ghoul, Donald Eugene Webb, Raymond Fernandez, Dr. Psycho, The Granny Killer, Angelo Buono, The Red Demon, Prince John and Sir Wiss, The Southside Slayer, The Skid Row Slasher, Metal Fang, Richard Biegenwald, Antonio Angles, Al Hadi Ali Al Omrani, Vicytor Szczepinski, The Berlin Butcher, Zelda Prankster, Jack Gilbert Graham, Chandell, Toyman, The Monster Butler, Eugene Chesley Symonette, Prince Vegeta, The Stockyard Bluebeard, The Sunday Morning Slasher, Abdul Salam Salem, The Happy Face Killer, Dr. Funfrock, Mustafa Ali Khalifa Al Maghribi, Minstrel, Ed Gein, Bela Kiss, Billie Austin Bryant, Puzzler, Paul Knowles, The Casanova Killer, Clayface, Randall Woodfield, The Ruhr Hunter, Michael Bernard Knowles, Leonard Lake, Iceman, Robin Stapley, Jerry Brudos, Emilio Largo, Foulfellow, Edward Leonski, The Freeway Killer, Rattlesnake Lissemba, Black Widow, Edward Rulloff, Master, Pedro Lopez, Ursula, The Stocking Strangler, Antonio Walter Derosa

Pedro Noscoso, Karl Denke, Fabrice Chatellier, Adam Ezerski, The Red Spider, Gregory Allan Pictou, Joseph Vacher, Bartemius Crouch Jr, The Sheriff of Northingham, Gerhard Arthur Puff, John Haigh, Joshep Edward Earlywine, Eric Robert Rudolph, Wayne Williams, Joachim Kroll, Akuma, Shefki Ritsch, George "Machine Gun" Kelly, Hamed Saleh Salem James J. Bulger, Al Kimaja, Dr. Zachary Smith, The Vampire Rapist, Ashor Husian Soliaman Quniaber, John Elgin Johnson, Fritz Haarmann, Ivica Rajic, The Atlanta Child Murderer, Ezeddine Rihane, Nikolay Soltys, The Dutchess of Death, Major Ray Lisemba, Shodan, Wayne Boden, Olafur Bragi Bragason, Solomon Grundy, Martha Beck, The Acid Bath Murderer, Peter Pettigrew, Enver Tosca, Thornton, Roger Downs, Sinestro, George Metesky, The Guardian, Lotfi Goddi, Glen Steward Godwin, Don Lester Macdonald, David Berkowitz, Desaad, Ahmed Hadjeri, Vlad the Impaler, Georg Karl Grossman,

WENDLER
armoured cars

MERIT AWARD
NEWSPAPER OVER 600 LINES SINGLE

ART DIRECTOR
Max Geraldo

WRITER
Daniela Ribeiro

CREATIVE DIRECTOR
Atila Francucci

CLIENT
Wendler

AGENCY
TBWA/Capsula/São Paulo

02124A

MERIT AWARD
NEWSPAPER OVER 600 LINES SINGLE

ART DIRECTOR
Gareth Lessing

PHOTOGRAPHER
Clive Stewart

CREATIVE DIRECTOR
Chris Garbutt

CLIENT
Colman's Spray & Cook

AGENCY
TBWA Hunt Lascaris/
Johannesburg

02125A

MERIT AWARD
NEWSPAPER OVER 600 LINES
SINGLE

ART DIRECTOR
Gareth Lessing

WRITER
Benjamin Abramowitz

PHOTOGRAPHER
Clive Stewart

CREATIVE DIRECTORS
Frances Luckin
Sandra de Witt

CLIENT
Playstation

AGENCY
TBWA Hunt Lascaris/
Johannesburg

02126A

PRINT MERIT

MERIT AWARD
NEWSPAPER OVER 600 LINES
CAMPAIGN

ART DIRECTOR
Shahrukh Irani

WRITER
Amitabh Agnihotri

PHOTOGRAPHER
Tejal Patni

CREATIVE DIRECTOR
Elsie Nanji

CLIENT
Marico Industries

AGENCY
Ambience D'Arcy/Mumbai

02127A

MERIT AWARD
NEWSPAPER OVER 600 LINES
CAMPAIGN

ART DIRECTOR
Steve Mitsch

WRITER
Richard Wallace

PHOTOGRAPHER
Andy Spreitzer

CREATIVE DIRECTORS
Tony Granger
David Nobay

CLIENT
Datek

AGENCY
Bozell/New York

02128A

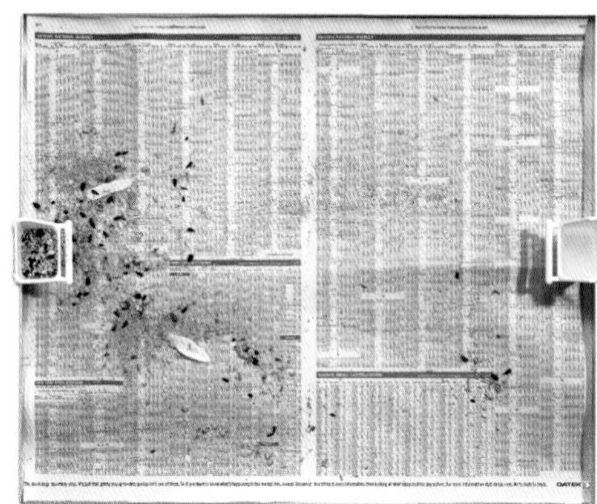

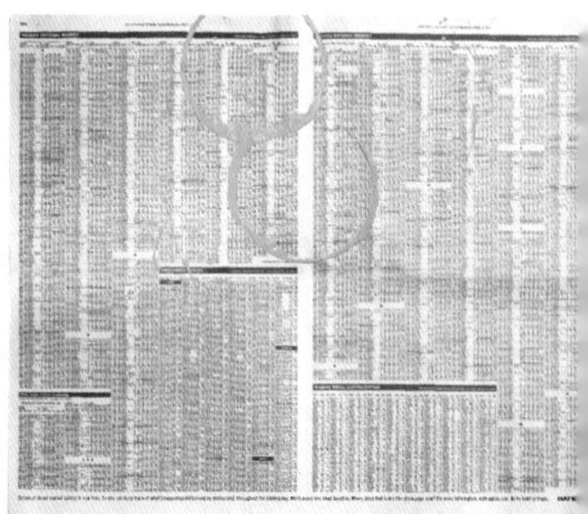

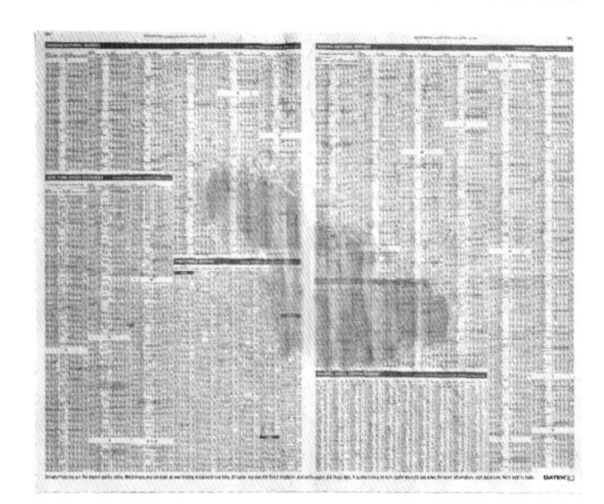

PRINT MERIT

MERIT AWARD
NEWSPAPER OVER 600 LINES
CAMPAIGN

ART DIRECTOR
Montse Pastor

WRITERS
Marta del Río
Daniel Acosta

ILLUSTRATOR
Alfonso Abad

CREATIVE DIRECTOR
Antonio Montero

CLIENT
Smart

AGENCY
Contrapunto/Madrid

02129A

MERIT AWARD
NEWSPAPER OVER 600 LINES
CAMPAIGN

ART DIRECTOR
Supachai Toemtechatpong

WRITER
Ken Trevor

PHOTOGRAPHER
Kiradee Ketakinta

CREATIVE DIRECTOR
Ken Trevor

CLIENT
Yontrakit Intersales

AGENCY
Far East Public
Company/Bangkok

02130A

Honey,
I'm home.

The more powerful new Passat 2.3

Careful,
they're still hot.

The more powerful new Passat 2.3

Sorry,
I'm early.

The more powerful new Passat 2.3

MERIT AWARD
NEWSPAPER OVER 600 LINES
CAMPAIGN

ART DIRECTORS
Lou Flores
Steve Newton
David Crawford

WRITERS
Cameron Day
Mark Ray
Jeremy Postaer

ILLUSTRATOR
Kevin Peake

CREATIVE DIRECTORS
David Crawford
Jeremy Postaer

CLIENT
Land Rover North America

AGENCY
GSD&M/Austin

02131A

Also won:
MERIT AWARDS
NEWSPAPER OVER 600 LINES
SINGLE

LAND ROVERS HAVE ALWAYS PERFORMED ADMIRABLY IN COLLISIONS.
EVEN WHEN IT'S NATIONS COLLIDING.

SINCE THEIR INCEPTION IN 1948, LAND ROVERS HAVE BEEN CALLED INTO BATTLE FOR OPERATIONS TOO NUMEROUS to divulge. What we can tell you, however, is this: Over the past 50 years, our four-wheel-drive vehicles have seen active duty as everything from UN ambulances and minesweepers to mobile satellite tracking stations and armored personnel carriers. To be sure, there are a lot of people who owe their lives to Land Rovers. We'd like to think that says something about the way we build them.

In 1970, an internal conflict erupted.

Before going to war for others, our original Range Rover had to survive a battle that threatened its own existence. You see, 30 years ago, many of our own employees felt that building a more luxurious Land Rover ran counter to the functional, purposeful, no-frills values we stood for. Others, conversely, believed no company was better suited to create a more accommodating type of all-terrain vehicle. Ironically, both camps were right. So after much deliberation, it was ultimately decided that the project would only proceed under one stipulation: Range Rover would never surrender an iota of capability in exchange for creature comforts. It didn't then. It doesn't now. And it's not about to.

Luxury and utility magnificently collide.

As far as we're concerned, creating the world's most luxurious four-wheel-drive vehicle is not the sort of thing that happens by accident.

Nor, for that matter, does it happen overnight.

Each detail is painstakingly thought out. Every feature skillfully incorporated. Only the finest select leathers and exotic woods suffice. Sophisticated technology is seamlessly integrated and made easy to use.

A 30-year evolution that continues to this very day. Within our 2001 Range Rover 4.6 HSE, you'll discover a 460-watt, 12-speaker Harman Kardon sound system. An off-road navigation system that leaves others at a complete loss. Dual-zone climate controls with built-in pollen filters. And numerous other refinements that render Range Rover the gold standard of luxury SUVs.

Accidents never happen in a perfect world.

In a perfect world, we wouldn't need to utilize heavier, 14-gauge boxed steel ladder frames in our vehicles.

But it isn't exactly a perfect world, now is it? From day one, we've combined our durable, purpose-built frames with lighter aluminum body panels that are extremely corrosion resistant. The result? A lower, more advantageous center of gravity. Which, in turn, amounts to a better handling vehicle that not only lasts longer, but is also ultimately safer.

Perhaps that begins to explain why *Kiplinger's* rated the 2001 Range Rover 4.6 HSE first for safety among SUVs.

Accidents are part of what it means to be human. Surviving them is part of what it means to be a Land Rover.

Rally the troops.

We hereby invite you to visit a Land Rover Centre, where you can find out firsthand how our Range Rover has benefited from over 30 years of hard-fought battles. Many of which took place within our own company.

2001
4.6 HSE

Even in our present-day models we continue to utilize a battle-proven 14-gauge boxed steel frame, torque-laden V8 engine and permanent four-wheel drive. Civilians never had it so good.

With the touch of a button, Sport mode allows the transmission to downshift sooner and upshift later. Ideal for outrunning renegade shopping carts.

LAND-ROVER
RANGE ROVER

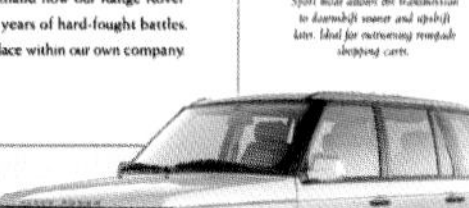

A Royal Warrant is the highest honor a company can receive in Great Britain for products and services relied upon by royalty. Land Rover has been awarded four Royal Warrants, the highest number possible.

MERIT

WHEN HE SET OUT TO BUILD THE FIRST LAND ROVER, MAURICE WILKS HAD NO SHORTAGE OF
TALENT, DEDICATION OR VISION.
THERE WAS, HOWEVER, A SHORTAGE OF STEEL.

IT WAS 1945. WORLD WAR II'S AFTERMATH FOUND Great Britain both economically depressed and in the midst of a crippling steel shortage. Alas, the once bustling assembly lines at Rover Car Company were now at a complete standstill. Only a miracle could save the company from certain financial collapse. And a miracle was just what happened when Rover company engineer and eccentric thinker Maurice Wilks hit on a stroke of genius. A notion so bold and audacious that it would single-handedly

HOW A VEHICLE DESIGNED FOR THE GREAT OUTDOORS
ENDED UP IN THE LOUVRE.

IT IS BELIEVED THAT DAVINCI'S *MONA LISA* TOOK THREE YEARS TO COMPLETE. ANDREA MANTEGNA LABORED OVER HIS *Calvary* altarpiece for nearly five years. And the white marble of Bouchardon's *Cupid Making a Bow from the Mace of Hercules* required more than a decade to take its final shape. So it only seems right that when our first-generation Range Rover

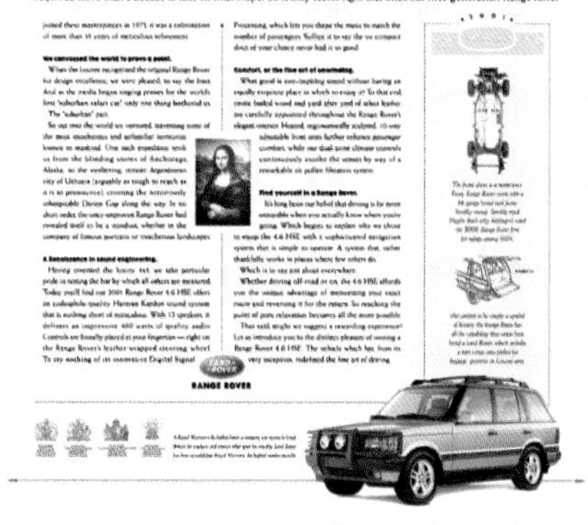

RIT

MERIT AWARD
NEWSPAPER OVER 600 LINES
CAMPAIGN

ART DIRECTOR
Alex Lim Thye Aun

WRITER
Alex Kuo

ILLUSTRATOR
Procolor

PHOTOGRAPHER
Tommy Kang Photography

CREATIVE DIRECTOR
Chris Chiu

CLIENT
Giant Hypermart

AGENCY
Impiric/Singapore

02132A

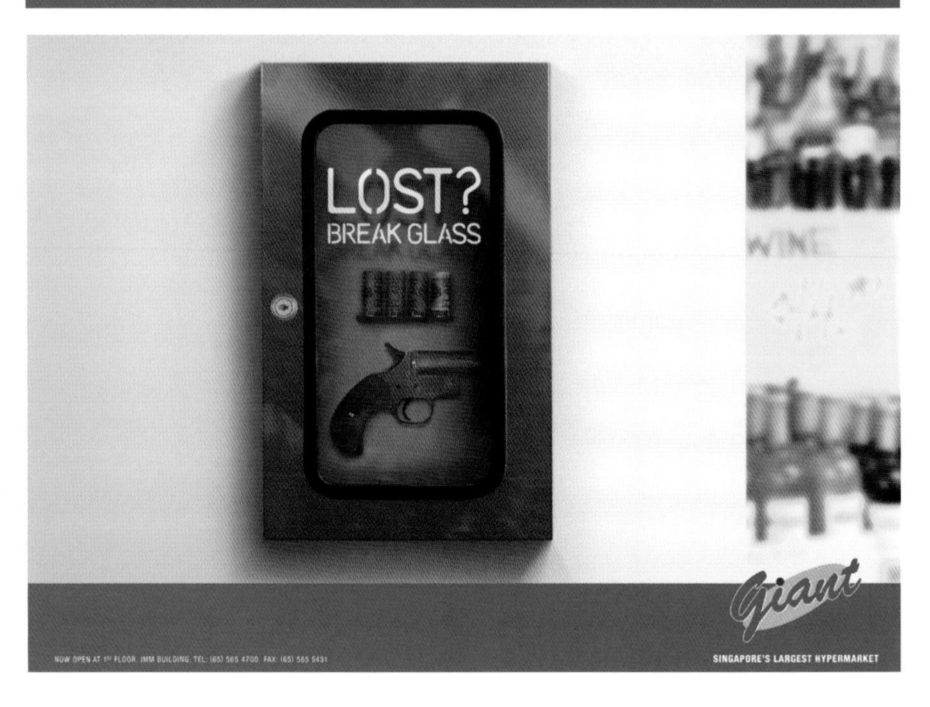

THE SHOES WERE

DESIGNED FOR JUMPING.

But millions use them to walk tall.

Phil Knight doesn't sell sneakers. He makes millions of people who run or throw or hike or climb believe they are athletes too.

His shoes make people feel better about themselves.

No wonder, when Michael Jordan jumped, so did the Nike stocks.

Or when McEnroe screamed that his favourite four-letter word was Nike, an entire generation lapped it up.

In fact, Nike has converted marketing into the refined art of tapping people's dreams and frustrations. Their biases and eccentricities.

Taking great care to always, always, always harness only a true emotion.

It all began in Phil's car. Which he drove across campuses in Oregon to sell "waffle sole" running shoes adorned with a $35 swoosh logo (yes, that's how much he paid for the design).

Next came the management team. Former athletes, coaches and Ekins (Nike spelt backwards). Sales guys who swore loyalty by tattooing swooshes on their ankles.

One of the first pieces of communication from the company. This ad can still be found in bedrooms and boardrooms across the globe.

All believed they weren't marketing shoes but working for a higher goal. That of improving athletic performance.

This wasn't a company. It was a cult. And yet, Adidas remained the market leader by far.

Then, one balmy September morning in 1988, talking to Nike employees, an ad man blurted out, "You Nike guys, you just do it."

That outburst became a war cry.

Bill Bowerman, co-founder, was later to recall "It invited dreams. It was a call to action. A refusal to hear excuses and a license to be mad, courageous and exceptional."

It was Nike.

In four short years sales crossed $10 billion. The ad man was listed among the ten most influential men in America by Time. And kids from the Bronx to the mean streets of Bangkok were out to kill for a pair of Nikes.

That for you, is a small example of the financial and psychological power businesses today wield.

Consider this: Two trillion dollars in trade flow around the globe. Every day.

Half of the hundred largest budgets in the world now belong to corporations. Not nations.

More than one million people move to the city of Mumbai for better prospects. Every year.

Nike's slogans have moved beyond advertising into folklore and popular expression.

And Rupert Murdoch's communication empire encompasses more of the earth than any political empire ever.

Clearly, business deserves to be recognised as the lifeblood of our times.

And business leaders, the moving force behind a fast-changing world.

Come August, do join us in making some very deserving people walk tall.

presents

THE ECONOMIC TIMES AWARDS FOR CORPORATE EXCELLENCE

ABOUT MINOR HICCUPS.

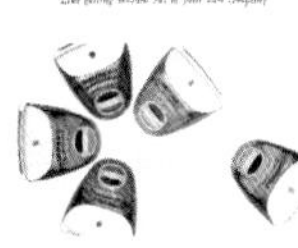

MEET THE MOST SUCCESSFUL CONSULTANTS IN THE BEAUTY & SKINCARE BUSINESS.

SELL YOUR PRODUCT

MERIT AWARD
NEWSPAPER OVER 600 LINES
CAMPAIGN

ART DIRECTORS
Sagar Mahabaleshwarkar
Kunal Naik

WRITERS
Pushpinder Singh
Venkatagiri Rao

CREATIVE DIRECTOR
Piyush Pandey

CLIENT
Bennett Coleman & Co.

AGENCY
Ogilvy & Mather/Mumbai

02134A

MERIT AWARD
NEWSPAPER OVER 600 LINES
CAMPAIGN

ART DIRECTOR
Arab Iqbal

WRITER
Abhijit Avasthi

PHOTOGRAPHER
Raj Mistry

CREATIVE DIRECTOR
Piyush Pandey

CLIENT
Pidilite Industries

AGENCY
Ogilvy & Mather/Mumbai

02135A

MERIT AWARD
NEWSPAPER OVER 600 LINES
CAMPAIGN

ART DIRECTORS
Ian Gabaldoni
Brett Salmons
Chris Bleackley

WRITERS
Richard Baynham
Jo Stafford
John Pallant

TYPOGRAPHER
Tim Quest

PHOTOGRAPHER
Max Forsythe

CREATIVE DIRECTOR
David Droga

CLIENT
Toyota Corolla

AGENCY
Saatchi & Saatchi/London

02136A

MERIT AWARD
NEWSPAPER OVER 600 LINES
CAMPAIGN

ART DIRECTORS
Christina Yu
Lance Martin

WRITER
Christina Yu

ILLUSTRATORS
Christian Borstlap
Christina Yu

CREATIVE DIRECTORS
Zak Mroueh
Paul Lavoie

CLIENT
Milestone

AGENCY
Taxi/Toronto

02137A

MERIT AWARD
NEWSPAPER OVER 600 LINES
CAMPAIGN

ART DIRECTOR
Gareth Lessing

WRITER
Cindy Lee

ILLUSTRATOR
Gareth Lessing

PHOTOGRAPHER
Michael Meyersfeld

CREATIVE DIRECTORS
Frances Luckin
Sandra de Witt

CLIENT
Interflora

AGENCY
TBWA Hunt Lascaris/
Johannesburg

02138A

MERIT AWARD
NEWSPAPER 600 LINES OR LESS
SINGLE

ART DIRECTOR
David Ferrer

WRITER
David Guerrero

ILLUSTRATOR
Oliver Brillantes

PHOTOGRAPHER
Albert Labrador

CREATIVE DIRECTOR
David Guerrero

CLIENT
Adidas Philippines

AGENCY
BBDO/Guerrero Ortega/
Makati City

02140A

MERIT AWARD
NEWSPAPER 600 LINES OR LESS
SINGLE

ART DIRECTOR
Jim Amadeo

WRITER
Lawson Clarke

CREATIVE DIRECTOR
Jim Amadeo

CLIENT
Ragged Mountain

AGENCY
Clarke Goward/Boston

02141A

Vincent
WE'VE PACKED ALL THE GOODNESS OF SUNFLOWERS INTO VITALITE SPREAD.

MERIT AWARD
NEWSPAPER 600 LINES OR LESS
SINGLE

ART DIRECTOR
Nick Tan

WRITER
Elena Fletcher

ILLUSTRATOR
D.I. Joe

PHOTOGRAPHER
Teo Studio

CREATIVE DIRECTOR
Chris Kyme

CLIENT
Shin Chin Distributors

AGENCY
Foote Cone & Belding/
Singapore

02143A

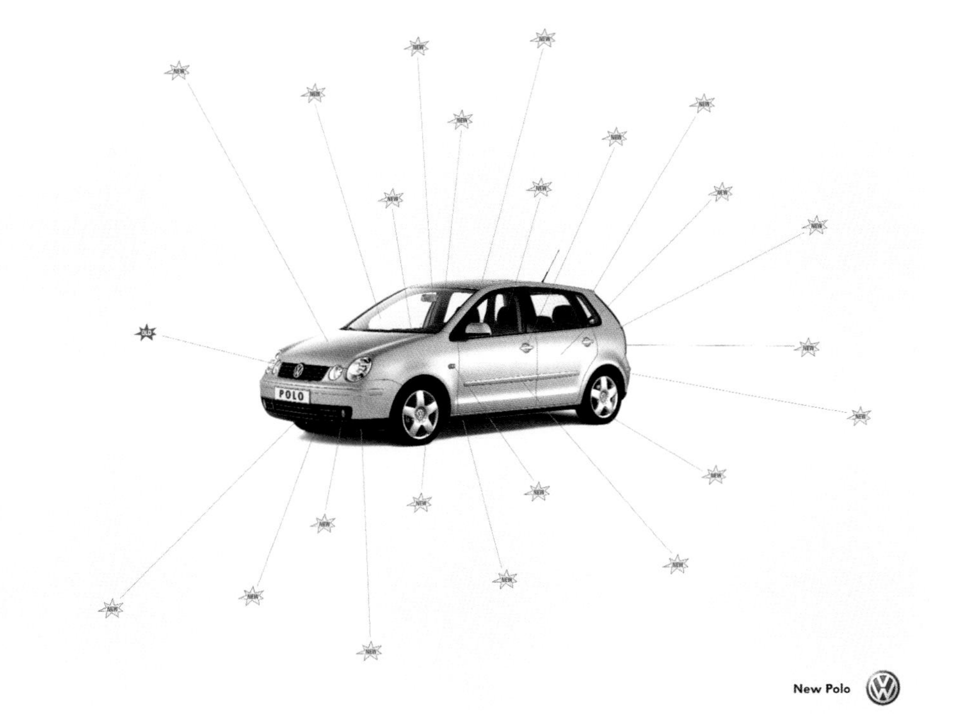

MERIT AWARD
NEWSPAPER 600 LINES OR LESS
SINGLE

ART DIRECTORS
Alfred Burkard
Philipp Straeuli

WRITER
Lukas Schmid

ILLUSTRATORS
Philipp Kropf
Sebastian Hugelshofer

CREATIVE DIRECTOR
Mark Stahel

CLIENT
AMAG Volkswagen

AGENCY
Lowe Lintas GGK AG/Zurich

02144A

MERIT AWARD
NEWSPAPER 600 LINES OR LESS SINGLE

ART DIRECTOR
Alexander Heil

WRITER
Christian Seifert

PHOTOGRAPHER
Joachim Bacherl

CREATIVE DIRECTOR
Christian Seifert

CLIENT
IBM Germany

AGENCY
Ogilvy & Mather/Frankfurt

02149A

Official sponsor of the Mercedes Benz Truck Racing Team
IBM

MERIT AWARD
NEWSPAPER 600 LINES OR LESS SINGLE

ART DIRECTORS
Ashidiq Ghazali
Claire Chen

WRITER
Audra Tan

ILLUSTRATOR
Yau Digital

PHOTOGRAPHER
Roy Zhang

CREATIVE DIRECTOR
Andy Greenaway

CLIENT
Glaxo Smithkline

AGENCY
Ogilvy & Mather/Singapore

02148A

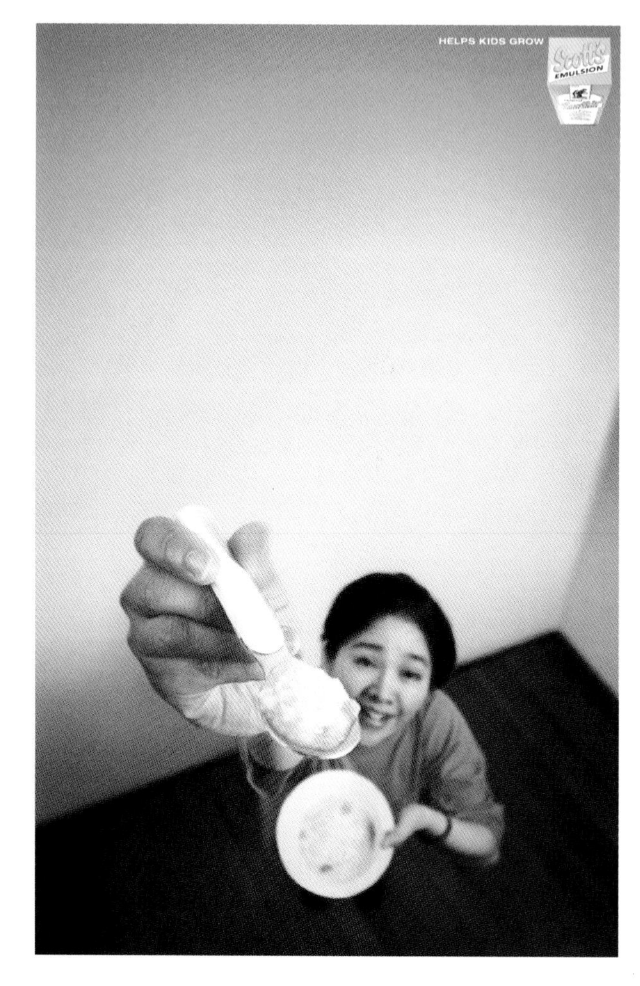

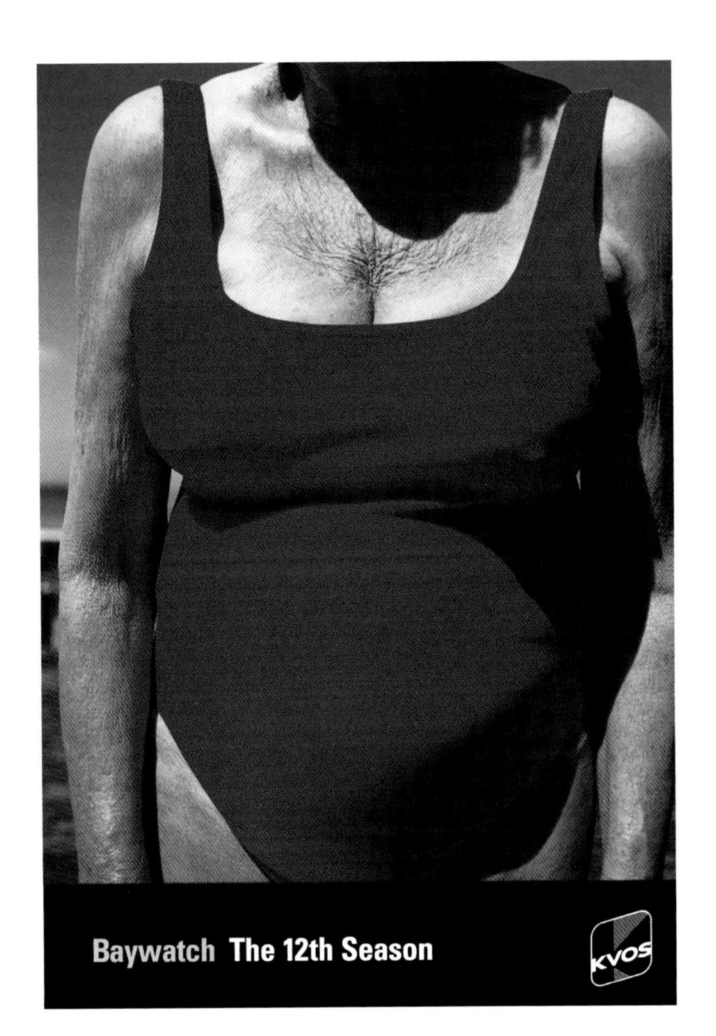

MERIT AWARD
NEWSPAPER 600 LINES OR LESS
SINGLE

ART DIRECTOR
Cosmo Campbell

WRITER
Alan Russell

PHOTOGRAPHER
Robert Kenney

CREATIVE DIRECTOR
Randy Stein

CLIENT
KVOS TV

AGENCY
Palmer Jarvis DDB/Vancouver

02151A

Also won:
MERIT AWARD
MAGAZINE B/W OR COLOR
LESS THAN A PAGE: SINGLE

GUEST PARKING
STUDIO F - LOT 2
Jerry Springer
Weekdays 3 pm
KVOS

MERIT AWARD
NEWSPAPER 600 LINES OR LESS
SINGLE

ART DIRECTOR
Cosmo Campbell

WRITER
Alan Russell

PHOTOGRAPHER
Robert Kenney

CREATIVE DIRECTOR
Randy Stein

CLIENT
KVOS TV

AGENCY
Palmer Jarvis DDB/Vancouver

02150A

Also won:
MERIT AWARD
MAGAZINE B/W OR COLOR
LESS THAN A PAGE: SINGLE

MERIT AWARD
NEWSPAPER 600 LINES OR LESS
SINGLE

ART DIRECTOR
William Hammond

WRITER
Steve Straw

ILLUSTRATOR
Grant Linton

PHOTOGRAPHER
Gerard Turnley

CREATIVE DIRECTOR
Brett Wild

CLIENT
Engen

AGENCY
Saatchi & Saatchi/
Johannesburg

02152A

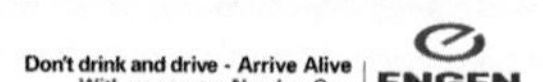

Don't drink and drive - Arrive Alive
With us you are Number One
ENGEN

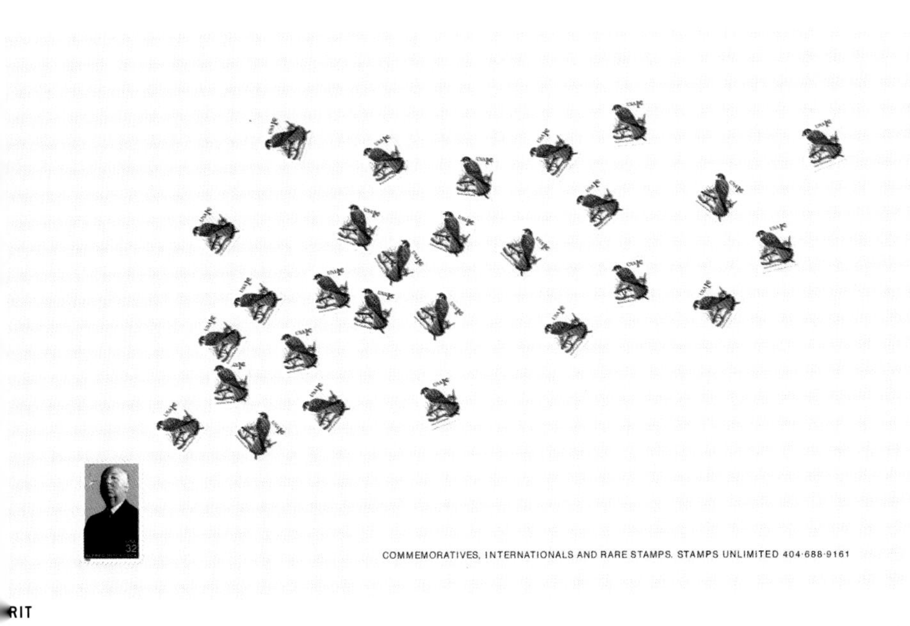

COMMEMORATIVES, INTERNATIONALS AND RARE STAMPS. STAMPS UNLIMITED 404·688·9161

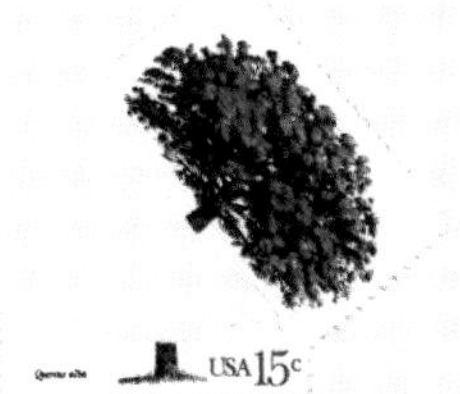

COMMEMORATIVES, INTERNATIONALS AND RARE STAMPS. STAMPS UNLIMITED 404·688·9161

PRINT MERIT

MERIT AWARD
NEWSPAPER 600 LINES OR LESS
CAMPAIGN

ART DIRECTOR
Lee Dayvault

WRITER
Brad Mislow

CREATIVE DIRECTOR
Jim Noble

CLIENT
Stamps Unlimited

AGENCY
BBDO/Atlanta

02154A

Also won:
MERIT AWARD
NEWSPAPER 600 LINES OR LESS
SINGLE

MERIT AWARD
NEWSPAPER 600 LINES OR LESS
CAMPAIGN

ART DIRECTOR
Ari Merkin

WRITER
Ari Merkin

CREATIVE DIRECTOR
Alex Bogusky

CLIENT
Fifth Avenue Stamp Gallery

AGENCY
Crispin Porter & Bogusky/
Miami

02155A

Also won:
MERIT AWARD
NEWSPAPER 600 LINES OR LESS
SINGLE

Antigua Barbuda 50¢
Antigua Barbuda 30¢
$6
St. Vincent & The Grenadines
Antigua Barbuda 15¢
FIFTH AVENUE STAMP GALLERY
For millions of years, prehistoric creatures ruled the earth.
In some places, they still do. So why not honor their longevity
with a Queen Mother souvenir stamp? Each sheet is just $9.95.
To order, call us at 1(800)607-2799. Dinosaurs sold separately.

MERIT

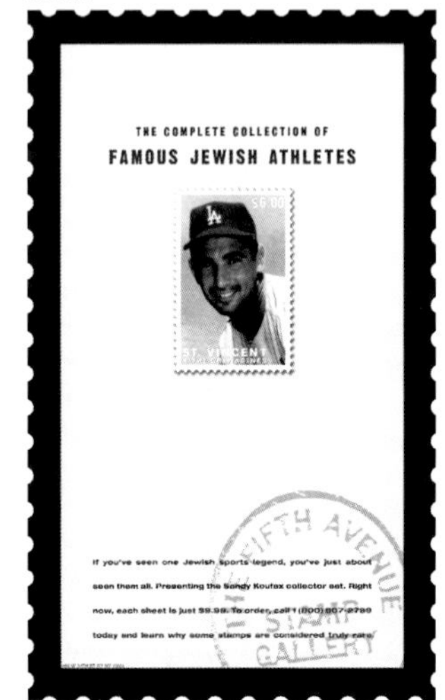

PRINT MERIT

MERIT AWARD
NEWSPAPER 600 LINES OR LESS
CAMPAIGN

ART DIRECTORS
Manas Nanda
Rashmi Yadav

WRITER
Janmenjoy Mohanty

PHOTOGRAPHER
Gurinder Osan

CLIENT
Dabur India

AGENCY
Leo Burnett/New Delhi

02156A

Stop back pain. Before it stops you.
Back-aid

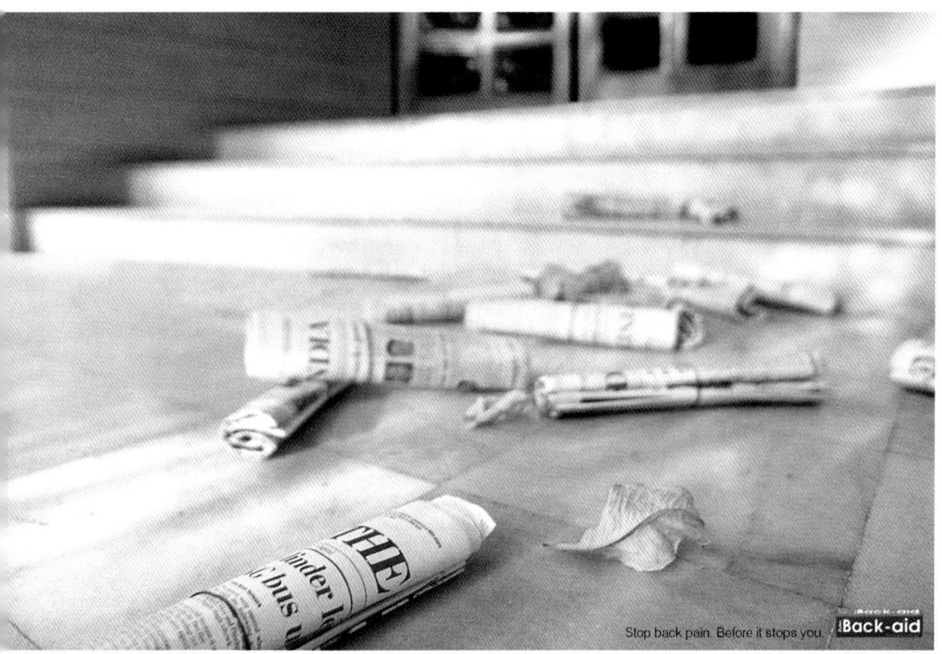
Stop back pain. Before it stops you.
Back-aid

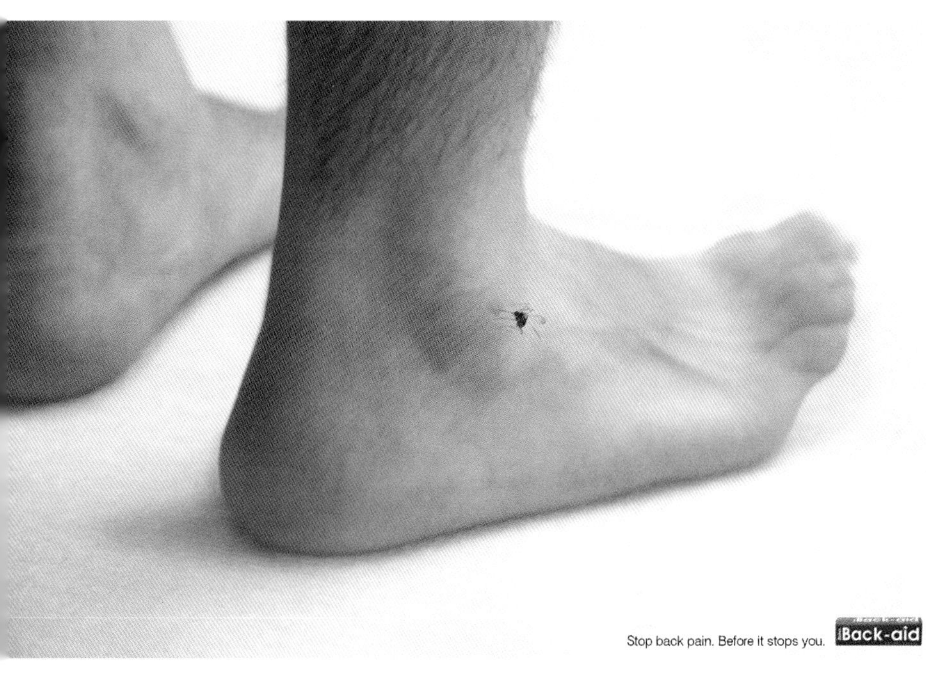
Stop back pain. Before it stops you.
Back-aid

MERIT AWARD
NEWSPAPER 600 LINES OR LESS
CAMPAIGN

ART DIRECTOR
Paul Laffy

WRITER
Brian Hayes

ILLUSTRATOR
Dave Nadeau

PHOTOGRAPHER
Dan Nourie

CREATIVE DIRECTOR
Jim Hagar

CLIENT
American Heritage Dictionary

AGENCY
Mullen/Wenham

02157A

Also won:
MERIT AWARDS
NEWSPAPER 600 LINES OR LESS
SINGLE

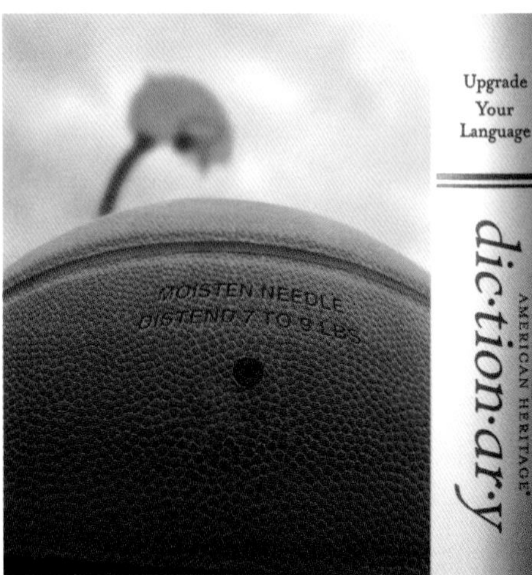

MERIT AWARD
NEWSPAPER 600 LINES OR LESS
CAMPAIGN

ART DIRECTOR
Debbie Gyngell

WRITER
Bridget O'Donoghue

PHOTOGRAPHER
David Prior

CREATIVE DIRECTOR
Mike Schalit

CLIENT
Delta Motor Corporation

AGENCY
NET#WORK BBDO/
Johannesburg

02158A

MERIT AWARD
MAGAZINE B/W
FULL PAGE OR SPREAD: SINGLE

ART DIRECTORS
Diane Magid
Theo Rocha

WRITER
Mike Ward

PHOTOGRAPHER
Dave Emmite

CREATIVE DIRECTOR
Terry Schneider

CLIENT
Duncan Yo-Yo

AGENCY
Borders Perrin Norrander/
Portland

02545A

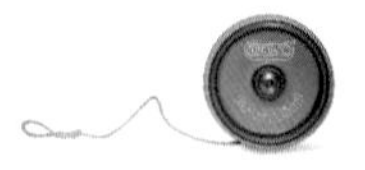

MERIT AWARD
MAGAZINE B/W
FULL PAGE OR SPREAD: SINGLE

ART DIRECTOR
Graham Johnson

WRITER
Oliver Devaris

PHOTOGRAPHER
Brett Odgers

CREATIVE DIRECTOR
Tom McFarlane

CLIENT
Sydney Aquarium

AGENCY
M&C Saatchi/Sydney

02161A

PRINT MERIT

MERIT AWARD
MAGAZINE B/W
FULL PAGE OR SPREAD: SINGLE

ART DIRECTORS
Annie Wong
Karen Lai

WRITER
Simon Handford

CREATIVE DIRECTORS
Gary Tranter
Matt Cullen

CLIENT
Kimberly-Clark Corporation

AGENCY
Ogilvy & Mather/Hong Kong

02162A

MERIT AWARD
MAGAZINE COLOR
FULL PAGE OR SPREAD: SINGLE

ART DIRECTOR
Dave Dye

WRITER
Sean Doyle

TYPOGRAPHER
David Wakefield

CREATIVE DIRECTORS
Dave Dye
Sean Doyle

CLIENT
The Economist

AGENCY
Abbott Mead Vickers.BBDO/
London

02175A

MERIT AWARD
MAGAZINE COLOR
FULL PAGE OR SPREAD: SINGLE

ART DIRECTOR
Alexandre Rato Pagano

WRITERS
Marcelo Nogueira
Rafael Artissian

PHOTOGRAPHER
Fernanda Tricoli

CREATIVE DIRECTORS
Marcello Serpa
Eugenio Mohallem

CLIENT
Tintas Coral

AGENCY
Almap BBDO Comunicacoes/
São Paulo

02164A

MERIT AWARD
MAGAZINE COLOR
FULL PAGE OR SPREAD: SINGLE

ART DIRECTOR
Melanie Lloyd

WRITER
Susan Ebling Corbo

PHOTOGRAPHER
William Huber

CREATIVE DIRECTORS
Alan Pafenbach
Ron Lawner

CLIENT
Volkswagen of America

AGENCY
Arnold Worldwide/Boston

02169A

MERIT AWARD
MAGAZINE COLOR
FULL PAGE OR SPREAD: SINGLE

ART DIRECTOR
Paul Renner

WRITER
Tim Gillingham

PHOTOGRAPHER
Russ Quackenbush

CREATIVE DIRECTORS
Alan Pafenbach
Ron Lawner

CLIENT
Volkswagen of America

AGENCY
Arnold Worldwide/Boston

02170A

MERIT AWARD
MAGAZINE COLOR
FULL PAGE OR SPREAD: SINGLE

ART DIRECTORS
Anurux Jansanjai
Thirasak Thanapatanakul

WRITER
Suthisak Sucharittanonta

ILLUSTRATOR
Anuchai Sricharunputong

PHOTOGRAPHER
Anuchai Sricharunputong

CREATIVE DIRECTOR
Suthisak Sucharittanonta

CLIENT
Pepsi-Cola

AGENCY
BBDO/Bangkok

02171A

MERIT AWARD
MAGAZINE COLOR
FULL PAGE OR SPREAD: SINGLE

ART DIRECTOR
Xavier Beauregard

WRITER
Vincent Pedrocchi

PHOTOGRAPHER
Vincent Dixon

CREATIVE DIRECTOR
Olivier Altmann

CLIENT
BMW France

AGENCY
BDDP et Fils/
Boulogne Billancourt

02172A

MERIT AWARD
MAGAZINE COLOR
FULL PAGE OR SPREAD: SINGLE

ART DIRECTOR
Grant Parker

WRITER
Patrick McClelland

PHOTOGRAPHER
Nick Meeks

CREATIVE DIRECTORS
Joanna Wenley
Jeremy Craigen

CLIENT
Volkswagen

AGENCY
BMP DDB/London

02174A

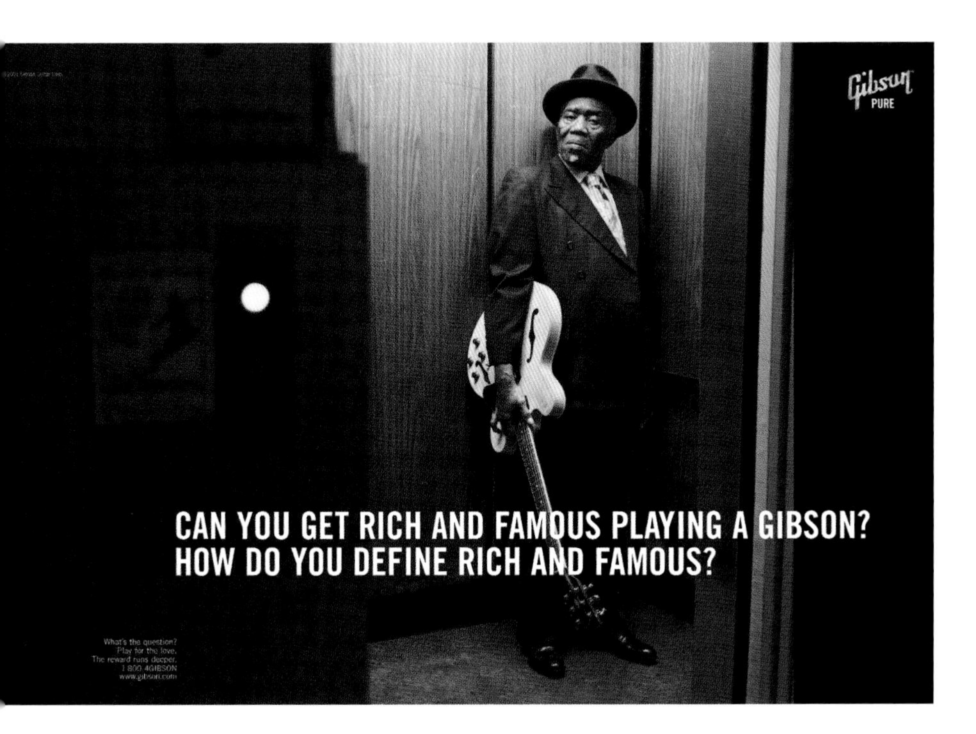

MERIT AWARD
MAGAZINE COLOR
FULL PAGE OR SPREAD: SINGLE

ART DIRECTOR
Randy Hughes

WRITER
Glen Wachowiak

PHOTOGRAPHER
Shawn Michienzi

CREATIVE DIRECTOR
Brian Kroening

CLIENT
Gibson Guitars

AGENCY
Carmichael Lynch/
Minneapolis

02176A

MERIT AWARD
MAGAZINE COLOR
FULL PAGE OR SPREAD: SINGLE

ART DIRECTORS
Hans Hansen
Jeff Terwilliger

WRITERS
Eric Sorensen
Sheldon Clay

PHOTOGRAPHER
Peter Lavery

CREATIVE DIRECTOR
Jud Smith

CLIENT
Porsche Cars of North
America

AGENCY
Carmichael Lynch/
Minneapolis

02179A

MERIT AWARD
MAGAZINE COLOR
FULL PAGE OR SPREAD: SINGLE

ART DIRECTOR
Josh Lancaster

WRITER
Jamie Hitchcock

PHOTOGRAPHER
Grant Maiden

CREATIVE DIRECTOR
Philip Andrew

CLIENT
South Pacific Tyres

AGENCY
Clemenger BBDO/Wellington

02180A

STICK WITH DUNLOP
0800 DUNLOP (0800 386 567)

MERIT AWARD
MAGAZINE COLOR
FULL PAGE OR SPREAD: SINGLE

ART DIRECTORS
Larry Ong
Key Guan

WRITER
Larry Ong

PHOTOGRAPHER
Raymond Tan

CREATIVE DIRECTOR
Larry Ong

CLIENT
Shanghai Toothpaste Company

AGENCY
Individual/Shanghai

02183A

MERIT AWARD
MAGAZINE COLOR
FULL PAGE OR SPREAD: SINGLE

ART DIRECTOR
Gaston Castañares

WRITER
Santiago Sendon

ILLUSTRATOR
Victor Bustos

PHOTOGRAPHER
Sergio Belintende

CREATIVE DIRECTORS
Santiago Sendon
Gaston Castañares

CLIENT
Volkswagen

AGENCY
DDB Argentina/Buenos Aires

02184A

MERIT AWARD
MAGAZINE COLOR
FULL PAGE OR SPREAD: SINGLE

ART DIRECTORS
Roberto Fernandez
Erh Ray

CREATIVE DIRECTORS
Erh Ray
Jáder Rossetto

WRITERS
Flavio Casarotti
Fabio Victoria

PHOTOGRAPHER
Alexandre Catan

CLIENT
Moto Honda da Amazonia

AGENCY
DM9 DDB Publicidade/
São Paulo

02185A

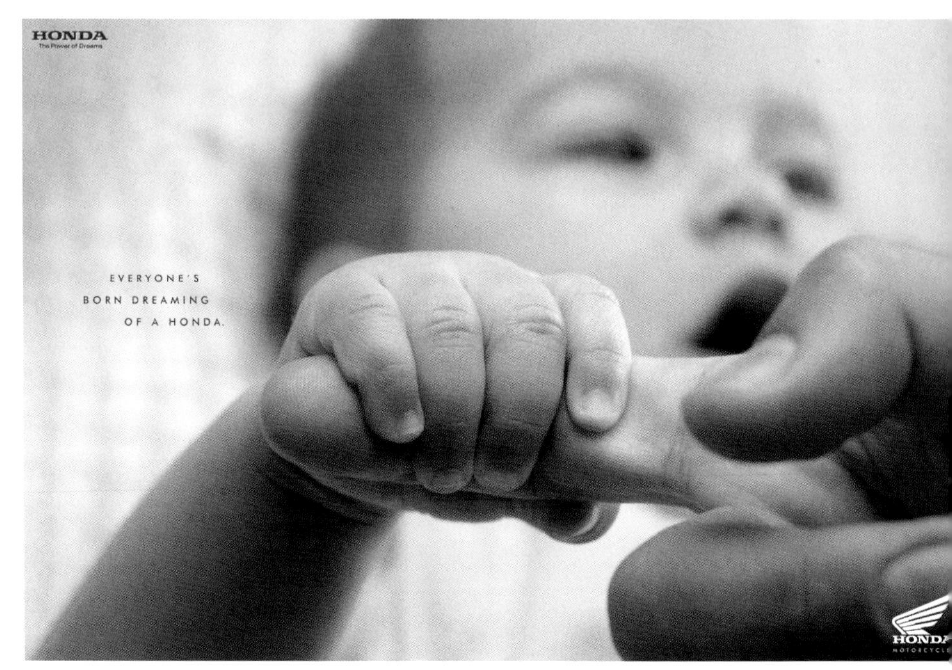

PRINT MERIT

MERIT AWARD
MAGAZINE COLOR
FULL PAGE OR SPREAD: SINGLE

(fig.1)
All the lines are parallel.

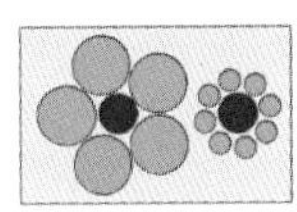

(fig.2)
Both circles in the middle are identical.

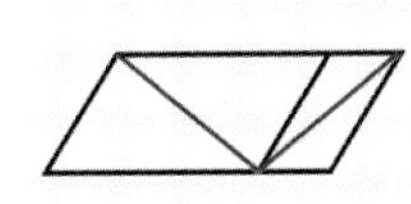

(fig.3)
The red lines are the same size.

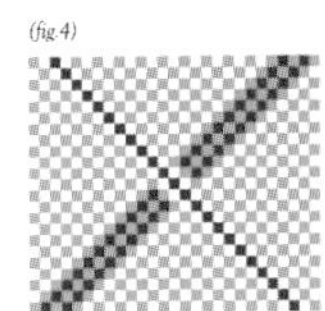

(fig.4)
All the pink is exactly the same.

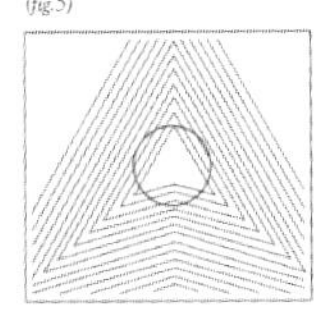

(fig.5)
The circle in the middle is perfect.

(fig.6)
TAM
just $49
Rio de Janeiro-São Paulo
This is the price of a ticket on TAM Airlines.

(fig.7)
The blue and the yellow figures are the same size.

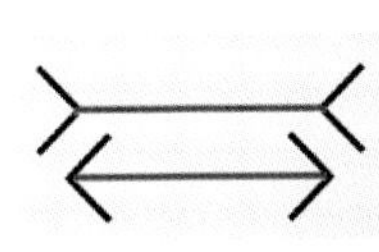

(fig.8)
The two red lines have the same length.

ART DIRECTOR
Roberto Fernandez

WRITER
Flavio Casarotti

ILLUSTRATOR
Roberto Fernandez

CREATIVE DIRECTORS
Erh Ray
Jader Rossetto
Pedro Cappeletti

CLIENT
TAM Airlines

AGENCY
DM9 DDB Publicidade/
São Paulo

02186A

MERIT AWARD
MAGAZINE COLOR
FULL PAGE OR SPREAD: SINGLE

ART DIRECTOR
Robson Oliveira

ILLUSTRATOR
Pineapple Digital Studio

CREATIVE DIRECTORS
José Zaragoza
Javier Talavera
Sidney Braz

CLIENT
Johnson & Johnson

AGENCY
DPZ/São Paulo

02187A

MERIT AWARD
MAGAZINE COLOR
FULL PAGE OR SPREAD: SINGLE

ART DIRECTOR
Alexandre Lage

WRITER
Icaro Doria

PHOTOGRAPHER
Fernando Moussalli

CREATIVE DIRECTORS
José Zaragoza
Carlos Rocca

CLIENT
Timberland

AGENCY
DPZ/São Paulo

02188A

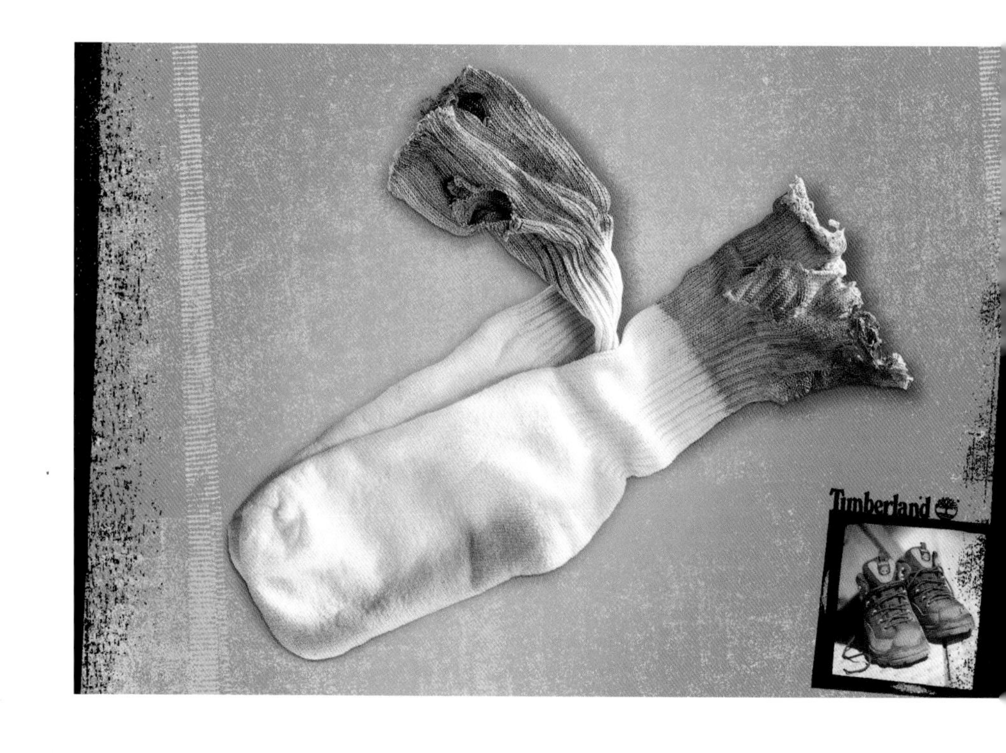

MERIT AWARD
MAGAZINE COLOR
FULL PAGE OR SPREAD: SINGLE

ART DIRECTOR
Quintes Venter

WRITER
Wingwing Mdlulwa

ILLUSTRATOR
Paul Vermeulen

PHOTOGRAPHER
Quintes Venter

CREATIVE DIRECTORS
Ashley Bacon
Eoin Welsh

CLIENT
SC Johnson/Rally Car Wax

AGENCY
Foote Cone & Belding/
Sandton

02189A

MERIT AWARD
MAGAZINE COLOR
FULL PAGE OR SPREAD: SINGLE

ART DIRECTORS
Anders Eklind
Mikko Timonen
Andreas Malm

WRITERS
Filip Nilsson
Johan Olivero

PHOTOGRAPHER
Henrik Bonnevier

CLIENT
Volvo Cars Sweden

AGENCY
Forsman & Bodenfors/
Göthenburg

02190A

MERIT AWARD
MAGAZINE COLOR
FULL PAGE OR SPREAD: SINGLE

ART DIRECTORS
Anders Eklind
Mikko Timonen
Andreas Malm

WRITERS
Filip Nilsson
Johan Olivero

PHOTOGRAPHER
Jesper Brandt

CLIENT
Volvo Cars Sweden

AGENCY
Forsman & Bodenfors/
Göthenburg

02191A

MERIT AWARD
MAGAZINE COLOR
FULL PAGE OR SPREAD: SINGLE

ART DIRECTORS
Anders Eklind
Mikko Timonen
Andreas Malm

WRITERS
Filip Nilsson
Johan Olivero

PHOTOGRAPHER
Sjöberg Classic Picture Library

CLIENT
Volvo Cars Sweden

AGENCY
Forsman & Bodenfors/
Göthenburg

02192A

MERIT AWARD
MAGAZINE COLOR
FULL PAGE OR SPREAD: SINGLE

ART DIRECTOR
Kok Keong

WRITER
Carol Huang

ILLUSTRATORS
D.I. Joe
Savian Fan

PHOTOGRAPHER
Teo Studio

CREATIVE DIRECTORS
Kok Keong
Carol Huang

CLIENT
Belluzio Footwear

AGENCY
Frog Advertising/Singapore

02193A

MERIT AWARD
MAGAZINE COLOR
FULL PAGE OR SPREAD: SINGLE

ART DIRECTOR
Kok Keong

WRITER
Carol Huang

ILLUSTRATORS
D.I. Joe
Savian Fan

PHOTOGRAPHERS
Jonathan Tay Studio
Leslie Sim

CREATIVE DIRECTORS
Kok Keong
Carol Huang

CLIENT
Denim Cartel

AGENCY
Frog Advertising/Singapore

02194A

MERIT AWARD
MAGAZINE COLOR
FULL PAGE OR SPREAD: SINGLE

ART DIRECTOR
Marcos Medeiros

PHOTOGRAPHERS
Eduardo Girao
Fabio Ribeiro

CREATIVE DIRECTORS
Valdir Bianchi
Ricardo Chester

CLIENT
Chrysler Brasil

AGENCY
Giovanni Foote Cone &
Belding/São Paulo

02196A

MERIT AWARD
MAGAZINE COLOR
FULL PAGE OR SPREAD: SINGLE

ART DIRECTOR
Bob Kincey

WRITER
Lorine Solomonescu

PHOTOGRAPHER
Danny Yin

CREATIVE DIRECTORS
Valdir Bianchi
Ricardo Chester

CLIENT
Chrysler Brasil

AGENCY
Giovanni Foote Cone &
Belding/São Paulo

02197A

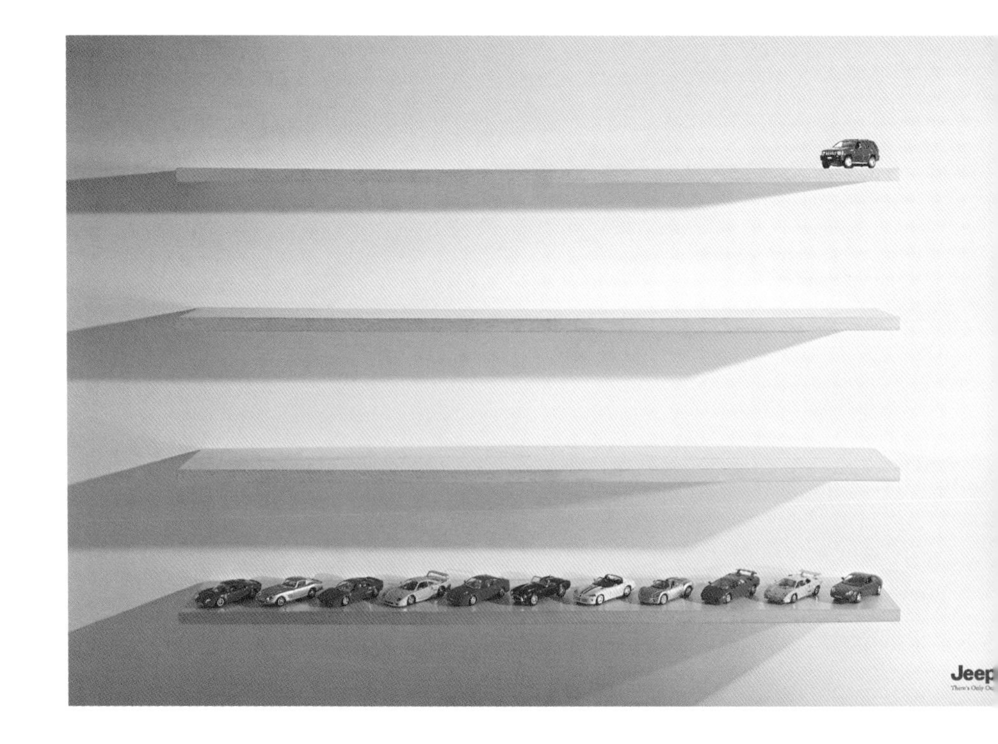

MERIT AWARD
MAGAZINE COLOR
FULL PAGE OR SPREAD: SINGLE

ART DIRECTOR
Marcos Medeiros

WRITER
Olavo Tokutake

PHOTOGRAPHER
Fabio Ribeiro

CREATIVE DIRECTOR
Valdir Bianchi

CLIENT
Izzo Motors

AGENCY
Giovanni Foote Cone &
Belding/São Paulo

02195A

MERIT AWARD
MAGAZINE COLOR
FULL PAGE OR SPREAD: SINGLE

ART DIRECTORS
E. Rodriguez
A. Avila
A. Arteaga
L. Garcia

WRITERS
J.M.Gallardo
A. Jara
V. Gonzalez

PHOTOGRAPHER
Enrique Covarrubias

CREATIVE DIRECTORS
L. Lamasney
G. Gutierrez
A. Vazquez
R. Valdez

CLIENT
Glaxo Smithkline Beecham

AGENCY
Grey Mexico/Mexico City

02198A

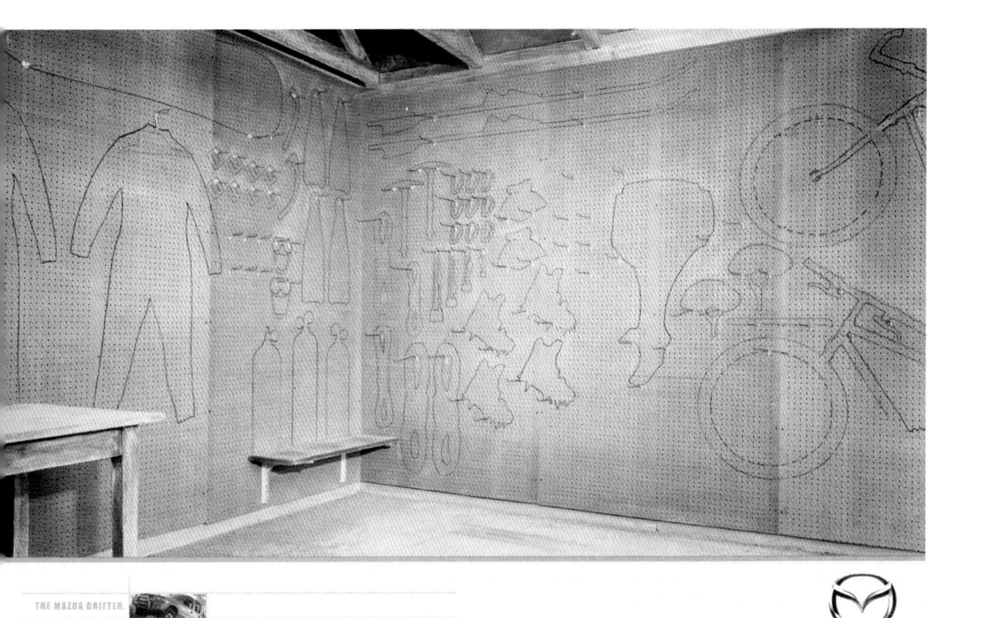

MERIT AWARD
MAGAZINE COLOR
FULL PAGE OR SPREAD: SINGLE

ART DIRECTOR
Grant Jacobsen

WRITER
Haidee Nel

PHOTOGRAPHER
Michael Meyersfeld

CREATIVE DIRECTOR
Alan Irvin

CLIENT
Mazda

AGENCY
Grey Worldwide/Johannesburg

02199A

MERIT AWARD
MAGAZINE COLOR
FULL PAGE OR SPREAD: SINGLE

ART DIRECTOR
John Trahar

WRITER
Tripp Westbrook

CREATIVE DIRECTORS
Jeremy Postaer
David Crawford

CLIENT
Land Rover North America

AGENCY
GSD&M/Austin

02200A

The world is full of things that we, as mere mortals, can neither control nor predict. To that end, we present the Discovery Series II. Standard features include permanent four-wheel drive, a boxed steel frame and an uncanny knack for returning from truly unforgiving places. Something the people who regularly test our vehicles seem to appreciate. For your very own Discovery (minus the stickers and orange paint) visit a Land Rover Centre or www.landrover.com. Starting at just $33,995.

LAND ROVER
DISCOVERY

MERIT AWARD
MAGAZINE COLOR
FULL PAGE OR SPREAD: SINGLE

ART DIRECTOR
Sam Bonds

WRITER
Kristen Livolsi

CREATIVE DIRECTORS
Derek Pletch
Scott MacGregor

CLIENT
United Healthcare

AGENCY
GSD&M/Austin

02201A

HOW TO PREVENT MEDICAL ERRORS

MAJOR CAUSES OF DEATH IN THE UNITED STATES:

No one wants to hear that their appendix operation was a success when it was their gallbladder that needed to be removed. The fact is, errors in the health care system are a growing concern. Fortunately, most errors are preventable, especially when people become active and informed participants in their own health. This is why UnitedHealth Foundation is providing information from medical and patient safety experts* that can help keep you and your family safe. By following the tips below, you can limit the chance of getting a medicine that will clear up your acne when you need one to relax your muscles.

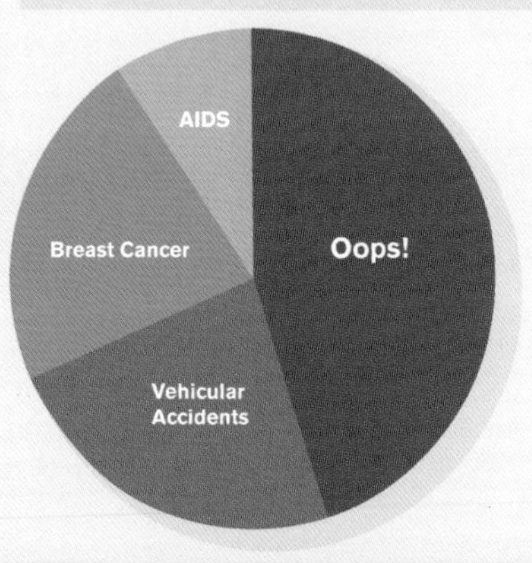

1. Make sure you and every member of your health care team knows about every prescription, over-the-counter medication, herbal product or supplement you may be taking. Be sure your doctor knows about any allergies or adverse reactions you have to any medicine.

2. When your doctor writes a prescription, make sure you can read it and that you fully understand what it's for. Be sure you know exactly when and how to take it and that you are aware of any potential side effects your medication may cause.

3. When you pick up your medicine from the pharmacy, ask the pharmacist to confirm that it is the medicine and the dosage that your doctor prescribed.

4. If you have a test, be sure to call and get the results. No news is not necessarily good news.

5. If you need to stay at a hospital and you have a choice, choose one where many patients have had the procedure or surgery you need.

6. If you're having surgery, be sure that your health care team agrees on exactly what will be done to exactly which part of your body. Having the surgeon mark the site to be operated on is a good idea.

7. When being discharged from a hospital, ask your doctor or health professional to thoroughly explain the treatment plan you will use at home, review your medications and coordinate your follow-up visit.

8. Speak up if you have questions or concerns and don't be shy about asking your doctor or nurse for more information from reliable sources. Good health professionals value the relationships they have with their patients.

We believe that the more you know about your health, the healthier you'll be. Keep this information and share it with your family and your health care team. For more information on preventing medical errors and other health care-related topics, visit us at www.unitedhealthfoundation.org.

UnitedHealth
Foundation

*Agency for Healthcare Research and Quality and the National Patient Safety Foundation

PRINT MERIT

MERIT AWARD
MAGAZINE COLOR
FULL PAGE OR SPREAD: SINGLE

ART DIRECTOR
Noel Haan

WRITER
Andrew Meyer

ILLUSTRATOR
H.A. Rey

CREATIVE DIRECTORS
Andrew Meyer
Noel Haan
Steffan Postaer
Mark Faulkner

CLIENT
Altoids

AGENCY
Leo Burnett/Chicago

02202A

SUBARU
ALL-WHEEL DRIVE

MERIT AWARD
MAGAZINE COLOR
FULL PAGE OR SPREAD: SINGLE

ART DIRECTOR
Michael Miller

WRITER
David Westgate

CREATIVE DIRECTOR
Nick Souter

CLIENT
Subaru Australia

AGENCY
Leo Burnett/Sydney

02206A

MERIT AWARD
MAGAZINE COLOR
FULL PAGE OR SPREAD: SINGLE

ART DIRECTOR
Doug Pedersen

WRITER
Curtis Smith

PHOTOGRAPHER
Stuart Hall

CREATIVE DIRECTOR
Jim Mountjoy

CLIENT
North Carolina Travel & Tourism

AGENCY
Loeffler Ketchum Mountjoy/ Charlotte

02207A

Also won:
MERIT AWARDS
MAGAZINE B/W OR COLOR
LESS THAN A PAGE: SINGLE

COLLATERAL: POSTERS
SINGLE

MERIT AWARD
MAGAZINE COLOR
FULL PAGE OR SPREAD: SINGLE

ART DIRECTOR
Doug Pedersen

WRITER
Curtis Smith

PHOTOGRAPHER
Stuart Hall

CREATIVE DIRECTOR
Jim Mountjoy

CLIENT
North Carolina Travel & Tourism

AGENCY
Loeffler Ketchum Mountjoy/ Charlotte

02208A

PRINT MERIT

MERIT AWARD
MAGAZINE COLOR
FULL PAGE OR SPREAD: SINGLE

ART DIRECTOR
Vancelee Teng

WRITER
Subun Khow

PHOTOGRAPHER
Yin-Yang

CREATIVE DIRECTOR
Jeffrey Curtis

CLIENT
Nestle Kit Kat

AGENCY
Lowe/Bangkok

02209A

MERIT AWARD
MAGAZINE COLOR
FULL PAGE OR SPREAD: SINGLE

ART DIRECTOR
Paulo Augusto César-Pepê

WRITER
Alexandre Gama

PHOTOGRAPHERS
Photonica
Gustavo Lacerda

CREATIVE DIRECTOR
Alexandre Gama

CLIENT
Umbro

AGENCY
Neogama/São Paulo

02212A

MERIT AWARD
MAGAZINE COLOR
FULL PAGE OR SPREAD: SINGLE

ART DIRECTORS
Alfred Wee
Ashidiq Ghazali

WRITER
Audra Tan

ILLUSTRATOR
Procolor

PHOTOGRAPHER
Jonathan Tay

CREATIVE DIRECTOR
Andy Greenaway

CLIENT
Glaxo Smithkline

AGENCY
Ogilvy & Mather/Singapore

02213A

MERIT AWARD
MAGAZINE COLOR
FULL PAGE OR SPREAD: SINGLE

ART DIRECTORS
Alfred Wee
Ashidiq Ghazali

WRITER
Audra Tan

ILLUSTRATOR
Procolor

PHOTOGRAPHER
Jonathan Tay

CREATIVE DIRECTOR
Andy Greenaway

CLIENT
Glaxo Smithkline

AGENCY
Ogilvy & Mather/Singapore

02214A

MERIT AWARD
MAGAZINE COLOR
FULL PAGE OR SPREAD: SINGLE

ART DIRECTORS
Alfred Wee
Ashidiq Ghazali

WRITER
Audra Tan

ILLUSTRATOR
Procolor

PHOTOGRAPHER
Jonathan Tay

CREATIVE DIRECTOR
Andy Greenaway

CLIENT
Glaxo Smithkline

AGENCY
Ogilvy & Mather/Singapore

02215A

MERIT AWARD
MAGAZINE COLOR
FULL PAGE OR SPREAD: SINGLE

ART DIRECTOR
Rich Pryce-Jones

WRITER
Neil McOstrich

PHOTOGRAPHER
Ian Campbell

CREATIVE DIRECTOR
Neil McOstrich

CLIENT
Clorox Canada

AGENCY
Palmer Jarvis DDB/Toronto

02218A

MERIT AWARD
MAGAZINE COLOR
FULL PAGE OR SPREAD: SINGLE

ART DIRECTOR
Anneke Nieuwoudt

WRITER
Maria Van Wyk

TYPOGRAPHER
Grant Linton

PHOTOGRAPHER
Gerard Turnley

CREATIVE DIRECTOR
Brett Wild

CLIENT
Procter & Gamble-Oil of Olay

AGENCY
Saatchi & Saatchi/
Johannesburg

02221A

MERIT AWARD
MAGAZINE COLOR
FULL PAGE OR SPREAD: SINGLE

ART DIRECTORS
Mike Martin
Rajesh Ranchod

WRITER
Mike Yee

CLIENT
Daimler Chrysler South Africa

AGENCY
Sonnenberg Murphy Leo
Burnett/Johannesburg

02223A

PRINT MERIT

MERIT AWARD
MAGAZINE COLOR
FULL PAGE OR SPREAD: SINGLE

ART DIRECTORS
Mark Bamfield
Marcus Rebeschini

WRITER
Robert Kleman

ILLUSTRATOR
Edward Loh

PHOTOGRAPHER
Sam Tan

CREATIVE DIRECTOR
Mark Bamfield

CLIENT
Samsonite Asia

AGENCY
TBWA/Singapore

02226A

Also won:
MERIT AWARD
COLLATERAL: POINT OF
PURCHASE AND IN-STORE

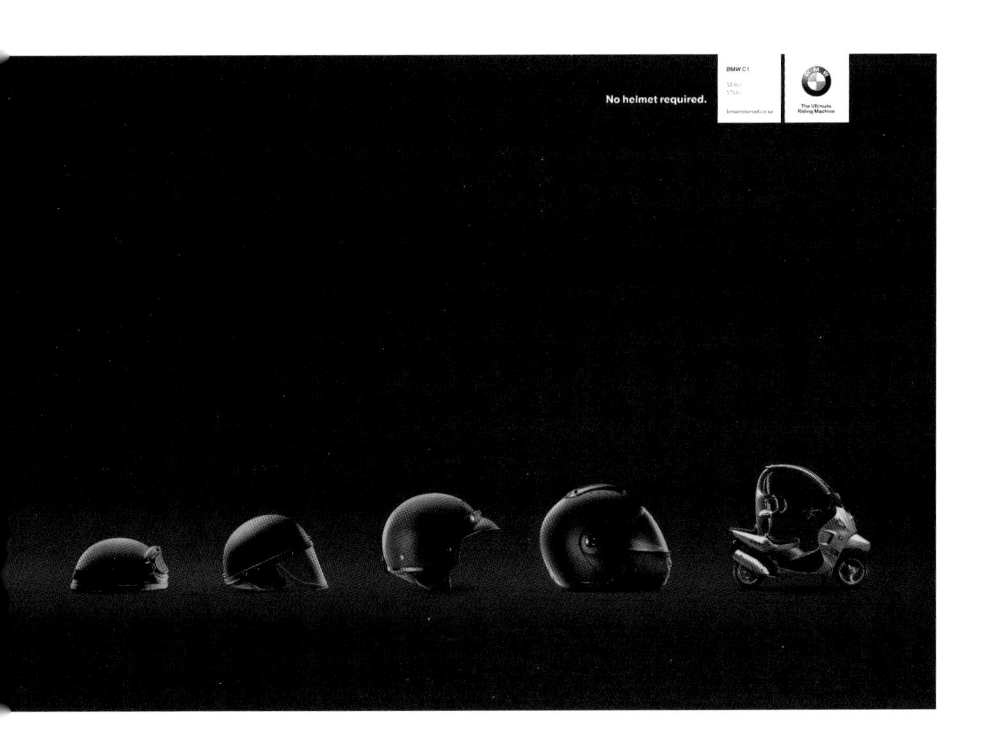

MERIT AWARD
MAGAZINE COLOR
FULL PAGE OR SPREAD: SINGLE

ART DIRECTOR
Rupert Allcock

WRITER
Jacques Massardo

PHOTOGRAPHER
Michael Meyersfeld

CREATIVE DIRECTOR
Chris Garbutt

CLIENT
BMW C1

AGENCY
TBWA Hunt Lascaris/
Johannesburg

02225A

Also won:
MERIT AWARD
COLLATERAL: POSTERS
SINGLE

MERIT AWARD
MAGAZINE COLOR
FULL PAGE OR SPREAD: SINGLE

ART DIRECTOR
Camilla Herberstein

WRITER
Gary du Toit

PHOTOGRAPHER
Michael Meyersfeld

CREATIVE DIRECTOR
Sandra de Witt

CLIENT
BMW C1

AGENCY
TBWA Hunt Lascaris/
Johannesburg

02224A

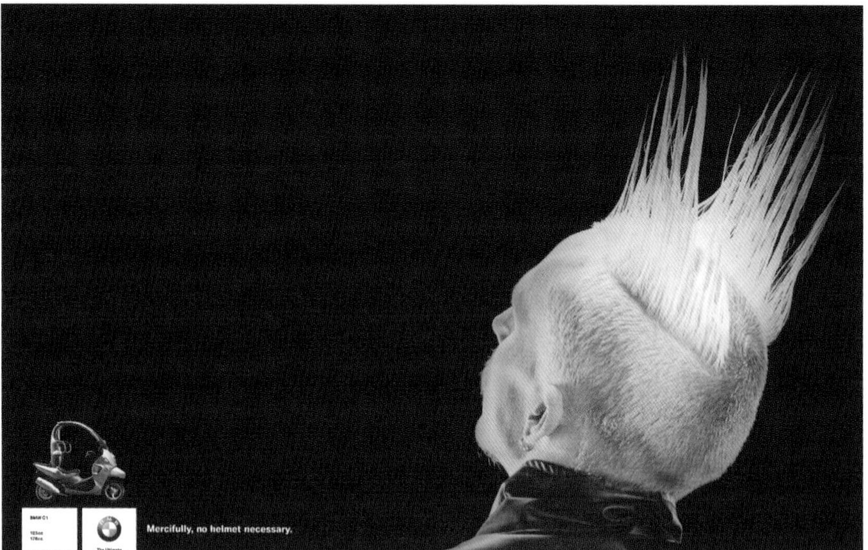

MERIT AWARD
MAGAZINE COLOR
FULL PAGE OR SPREAD: SINGLE

ART DIRECTORS
Muntsa Dachs
David Garriga

WRITER
Mauricio Alarcon

PHOTOGRAPHER
Tony Stone

CREATIVE DIRECTOR
Muntsa Dachs

CLIENT
Swatch

AGENCY
Vinizius Young & Rubicam/
Barcelona

02230A

Also won:
MERIT AWARD
COLLATERAL: POSTERS
SINGLE

PRINT MERIT

MERIT AWARD
MAGAZINE COLOR
FULL PAGE OR SPREAD: CAMPAIGN

ART DIRECTOR
Simon McQueen

WRITER
Antonia Clayton

PHOTOGRAPHER
Coppi Barbieri

CREATIVE DIRECTOR
Peter Souter

CLIENT
Campbell

AGENCY
Abbott Mead Vickers.BBDO/
London

02232A

MERIT AWARD
MAGAZINE COLOR
FULL PAGE OR SPREAD: CAMPAIGN

ART DIRECTOR
Martin Casson

WRITER
Matthew Abbott

PHOTOGRAPHERS
Ian Berry
Justin Leighton
Tom Stoddart

CREATIVE DIRECTOR
Peter Souter

CLIENT
The Economist

AGENCY
Abbott Mead Vickers.BBDO/
London

02233A

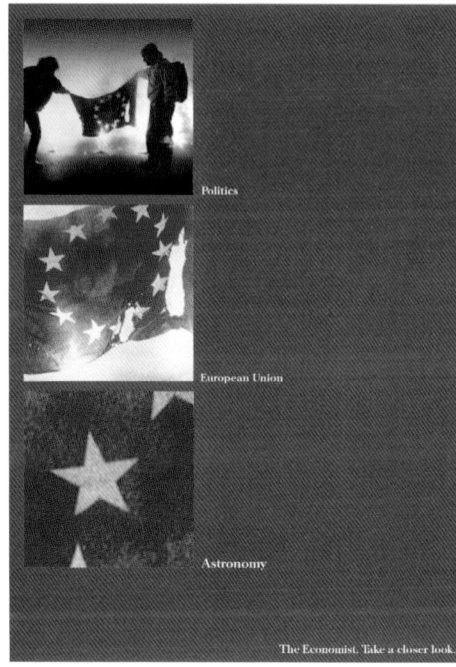

PRINT MERIT

MERIT AWARD MAGAZINE COLOR FULL PAGE OR SPREAD: CAMPAIGN

ART DIRECTOR
John Treacey

WRITER
Jean Fox Robertson

PHOTOGRAPHER
Peer Lindgreen

CREATIVE DIRECTOR
Stephen Stretton

CLIENT
Metropolis

AGENCY
Archibald Ingall Stretton/ London

02234A

MERIT AWARD
MAGAZINE COLOR
FULL PAGE OR SPREAD: CAMPAIGN

ART DIRECTOR
Paul Renner

WRITER
Dave Weist

PHOTOGRAPHER
Raul Penner

CREATIVE DIRECTORS
Alan Pafenbach
Ron Lawner

CLIENT
Volkswagen of America

AGENCY
Arnold Worldwide/Boston

02235A

Also won:
MERIT AWARDS
MAGAZINE COLOR
FULL PAGE OR SPREAD: SINGLE

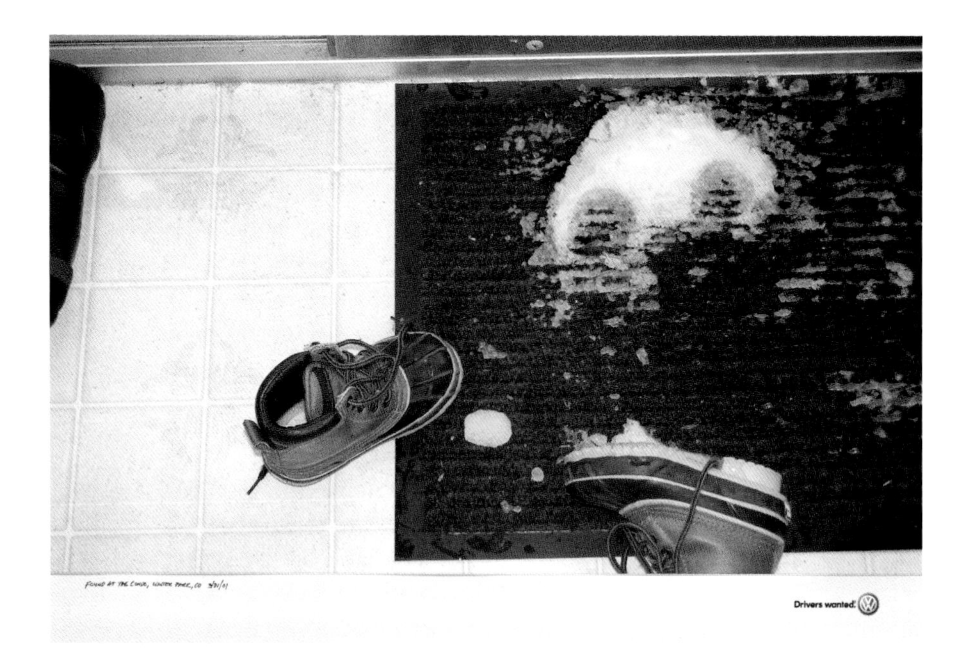

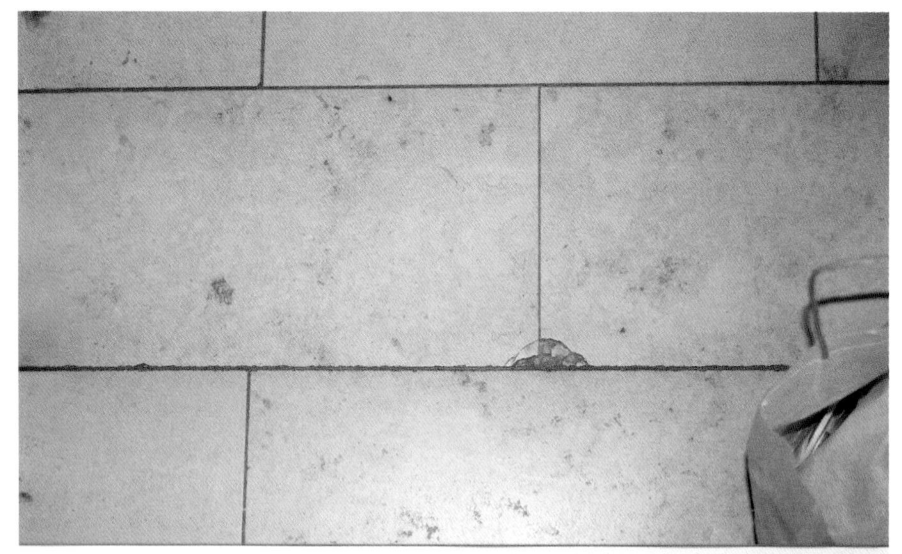

PRINT MERIT

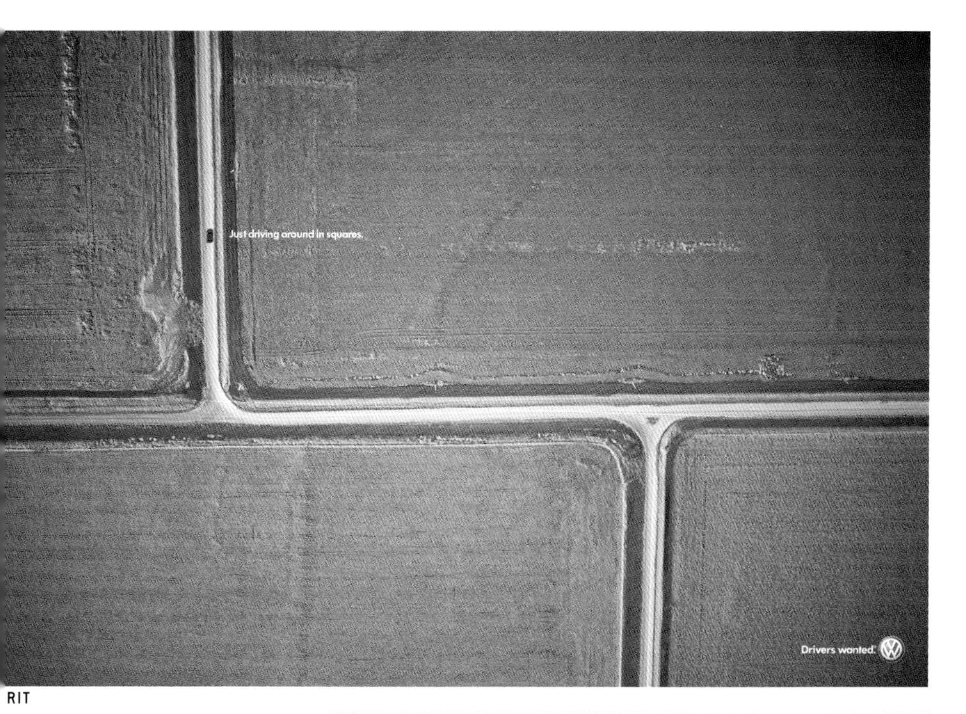

RIT

MERIT AWARD
MAGAZINE COLOR
FULL PAGE OR SPREAD:
CAMPAIGN

ART DIRECTOR
Adele Ellis

WRITER
Carl Loeb

PHOTOGRAPHER
Stock

CREATIVE DIRECTORS
Alan Pafenbach
Ron Lawner

CLIENT
Volkswagen of America

AGENCY
Arnold Worldwide/Boston

02236A

Also won:
MERIT AWARD
MAGAZINE COLOR
FULL PAGE OR SPREAD: SINGLE

MERIT AWARD
MAGAZINE COLOR
FULL PAGE OR SPREAD:
CAMPAIGN

ART DIRECTORS
Beat Keller
Francesco Talamino
Carles Patris

WRITERS
Camil Roca
Javier Inglés

PHOTOGRAPHER
Joan Garrigosa

CREATIVE DIRECTORS
Camil Roca
Beat Keller

CLIENT
Grauvell

AGENCY
Bassat Ogilvy/Barcelona

02237A

MERIT AWARD
MAGAZINE COLOR
FULL PAGE OR SPREAD:
CAMPAIGN

ART DIRECTOR
David Szabo

WRITER
Jonathan Bain

PHOTOGRAPHER
Poon@
Studio One-Twenty-One

CREATIVE DIRECTOR
David Szabo

CLIENT
Samsonite

AGENCY
Beast/Hong Kong

02238A

Also won:
MERIT AWARD
MAGAZINE COLOR
FULL PAGE OR SPREAD: SINGLE

MERIT AWARD
MAGAZINE COLOR
FULL PAGE OR SPREAD: CAMPAIGN

ART DIRECTOR
Ivan Johnson

WRITER
Kyle Cockeran

ILLUSTRATOR
Ivan Johnson

PHOTOGRAPHER
I.N.P.R.A.

CREATIVE DIRECTOR
Errol Denman

CLIENT
News 24

AGENCY
Berry Bush BBDO/Cape Town

02239A

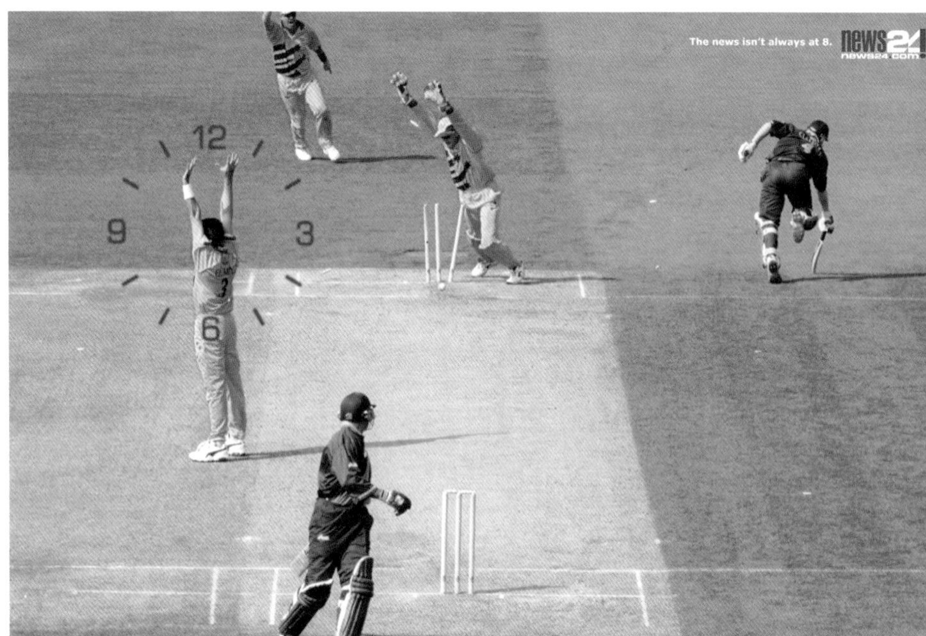

PRINT MERIT

MERIT AWARD
MAGAZINE COLOR
FULL PAGE OR SPREAD:
CAMPAIGN

ART DIRECTORS
Dejan Rasic
Steve Back

WRITER
Matthew Keon

PHOTOGRAPHER
Alan Myles

CREATIVE DIRECTOR
Tim Mellors

CLIENT
Pedigree Dog Food

AGENCY
BMF/Sydney

02240A

#Make your own rules.

When at large family gatherings try passing wind. Position yourself under the table and wait until the meal is being served. Let it out slowly then retreat to the kitchen where you can sit back and watch the action.

#Make your own rules.

When playing fetch with your owner don't always bring the stick back. Make them go and chase it for a while.

#Make your own rules.

When out for a walk, pick the busiest most visible spot to do your number two's. Wait for a large crowd to gather then take your time and make sure everyone watches.

MERIT AWARD
MAGAZINE COLOR
FULL PAGE OR SPREAD:
CAMPAIGN

ART DIRECTORS
Justin Tindall
Feargal Balance
Dylan Harrison
Dan Hine

WRITERS
Feargal Balance
Dylan Harrison
Amber Casey
Adam Tucker

PHOTOGRAPHER
Antonio Riello

CREATIVE DIRECTORS
Joanna Wenley
Jeremy Craigen
Andrew Fraser

CLIENT
Guardian

AGENCY
BMP DDB/London

02241A

Also won:
MERIT AWARD
NEWSPAPER OVER 600 LINES
SINGLE

MERIT

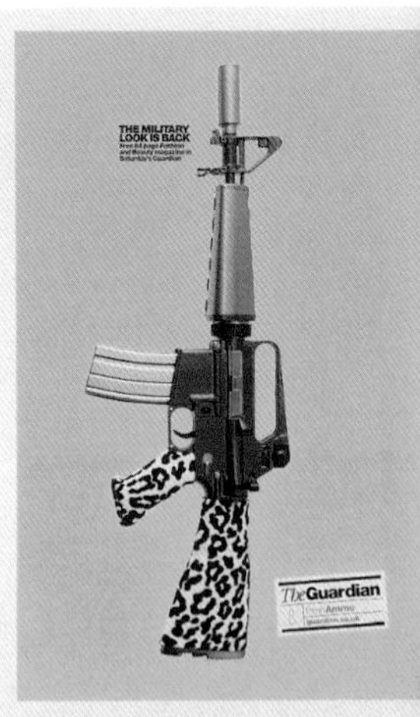

DO GLOSSY MAGAZINES SELL NEWSPAPERS?
WE FIND OUT THIS SATURDAY

PPRINT MERIT

MERIT AWARD
MAGAZINE COLOR
FULL PAGE OR SPREAD: CAMPAIGN

ART DIRECTORS
Ewan Patterson
Rob Jack

WRITERS
Ewan Patterson
Rob Jack

PHOTOGRAPHER
Ashton Keiditsch

CREATIVE DIRECTORS
Mike Hannett
Dave Buchanan

CLIENT
Volkswagen Passat

AGENCY
BMP DDB/London

02242A

The beautifully crafted Passat W8. You'll want to keep it that way.

The beautifully crafted new Passat. You'll want to keep it that way.

The beautifully crafted new Passat. You'll want to keep it that way.

MERIT AWARD
MAGAZINE COLOR
FULL PAGE OR SPREAD:
CAMPAIGN

ART DIRECTOR
Jason Smith

WRITERS
Sheldon Clay
Jim Nelson

PHOTOGRAPHER
Chris Wimpey

CREATIVE DIRECTOR
Jim Nelson

CLIENT
Harley-Davidson

AGENCY
Carmichael Lynch/
Minneapolis

02243A

Also won:
MERIT AWARDS
MAGAZINE COLOR
FULL PAGE OR SPREAD: SINGLE

SOMEWHERE ON AN AIRPLANE A MAN IS TRYING TO RIP OPEN A SMALL BAG OF PEANUTS.

Give us life at ground level, rolling along the endless highway on a Harley-Davidson. 100% depressurized. Just sunlight on chrome. The voice of a V-Twin ripping the open air. And elbow room, stretching all the way to the horizon. Maybe you too think this is the way life ought to be lived. Time to spread some wings. 1-800-443-2153 or www.harley-davidson.com. **The Legend Rolls On.**

MERIT

NO. I'VE DECIDED TO OPT FOR A SMALL AND RATHER UNEVENTFUL LIFE.

You could eat up a lifetime pondering what to do with your days on earth. Or you could take one look at a machine like the Wide Glide. And let gut instinct take it from there. Get a load of the high handlebar and stretched-out profile. We didn't hold anything back in building this ride. So what's holding you back? 1-800-443-2153 or www.harley-davidson.com. **The Legend Rolls On.**

MERIT

MAY ALL YOUR ENCOUNTERS WITH THE LAW START WITH THE WORDS "NICE HARLEY."

Be forewarned. There'll be no keeping a low profile on this one. Raw Sportster muscle, with a look last seen mixing it up at the local dirt track. Orange and black racing paint job. Wide flat-track handlebar. Curvaceous 2-into-1 exhaust. The new Sportster 883R. Lucky thing there's no law against having a little fun. 1-800-443-2153 or www.harley-davidson.com. **The Legend Rolls On.**

RIT

HYATT
AMEN
TO BEING AT THE TOP OF
FOOD
CHAIN

MERIT AWARD
MAGAZINE COLOR
FULL PAGE OR SPREAD:
CAMPAIGN

ART DIRECTORS
David Yang
Sonya Grewal
Ed Tajon

WRITERS
Lee Gonzalez
Christine Montaquila
Kate Levin

PHOTOGRAPHERS
Andy Anderson
Susie Cushner
John McCallum

CREATIVE DIRECTORS
Kate Levin
Marshall Ross

CLIENT
Hyatt

AGENCY
Cramer-Krasselt/Chicago

02244A

Also won:
MERIT AWARD
TRADE COLOR
FULL PAGE OR SPREAD: SINGLE

MERIT AWARD
MAGAZINE COLOR
FULL PAGE OR SPREAD: CAMPAIGN

ART DIRECTOR
Yoichi Komatsu

WRITER
Ken Fukunishi

ILLUSTRATOR
Keiji Ito

PHOTOGRAPHER
Hiroshi Noguchi

CREATIVE DIRECTORS
Masahisa Nakamura
Yoichi Komatsu

CLIENT
Converse Sales Promotion/
Moonstar Chemical

AGENCY
Dentsu/Tokyo

02245A

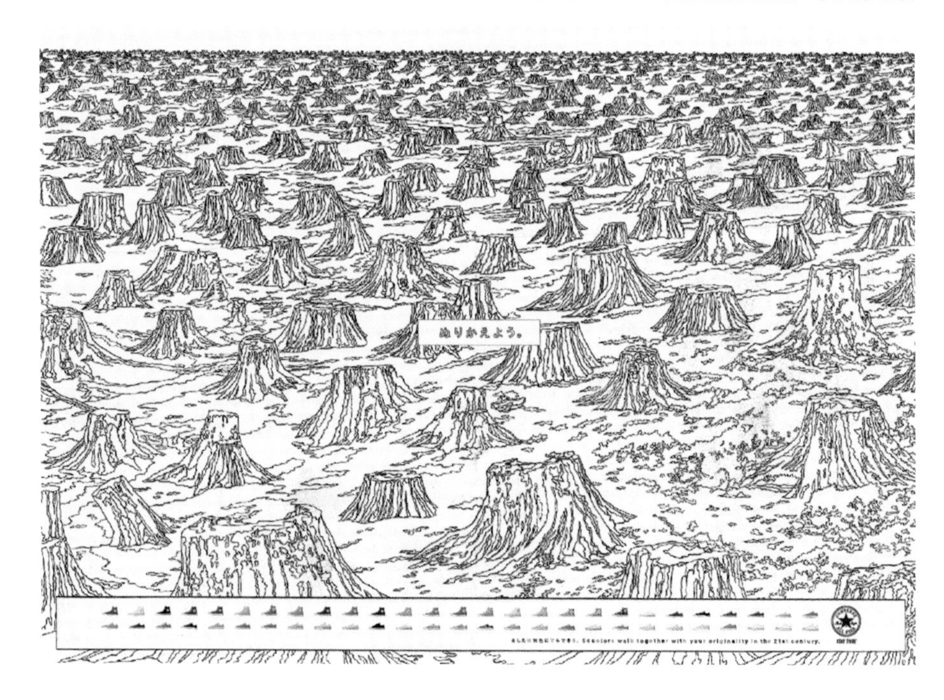

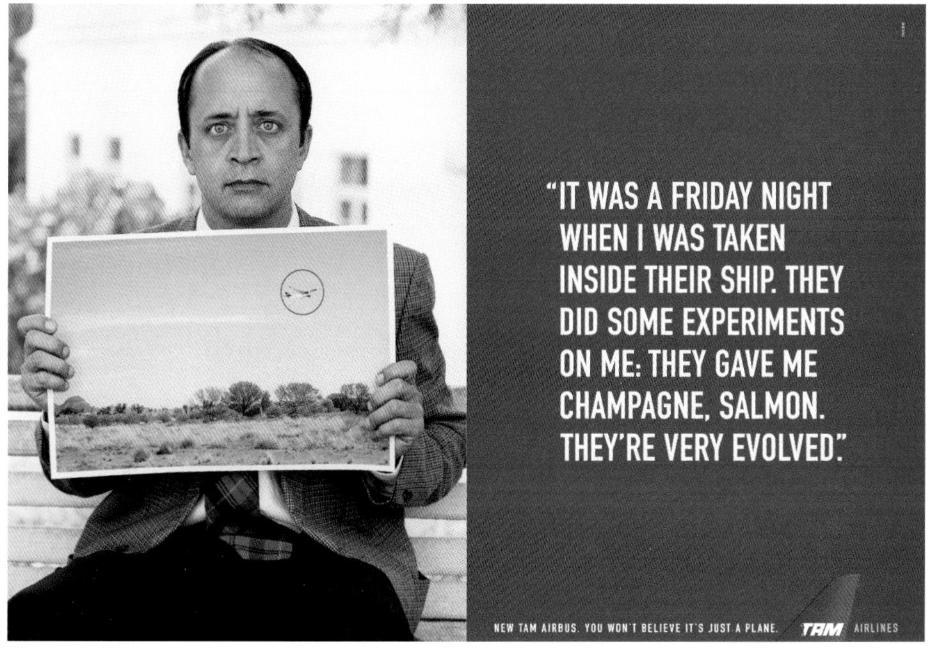

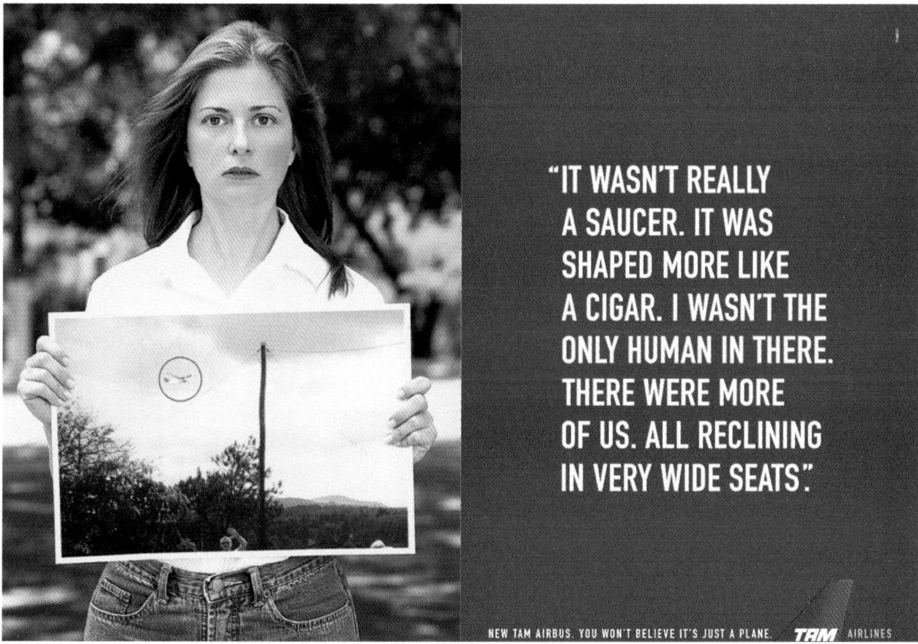

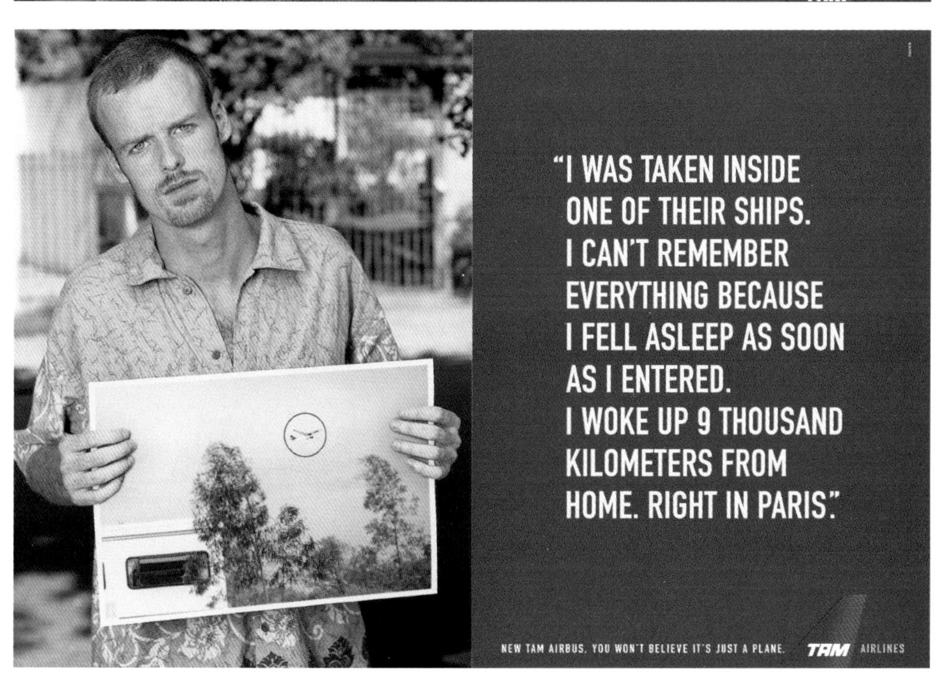

MERIT AWARD
MAGAZINE COLOR
FULL PAGE OR SPREAD:
CAMPAIGN

ART DIRECTOR
Mariana Sá

WRITER
Manir Fadel

PHOTOGRAPHER
Manolo Moran

CREATIVE DIRECTORS
Erh Ray
Jáder Rossetto
Pedro Cappeletti

CLIENT
TAM Airlines

AGENCY
DM9 DDB Publicidade/
São Paulo

02246A

**MERIT AWARD
MAGAZINE COLOR
FULL PAGE OR SPREAD:
CAMPAIGN**

ART DIRECTOR
Derek Chia

WRITER
Simon Wong

ILLUSTRATOR
Derek Chia

CLIENT
Dunlop Tyres

AGENCY
Doris Soh & Associates/
Singapore

02247A

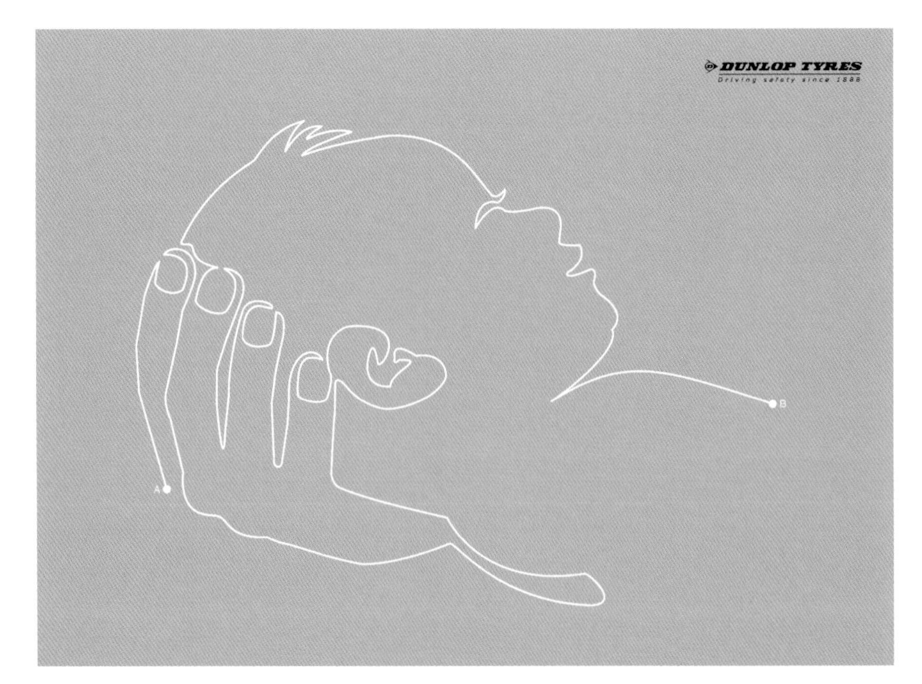

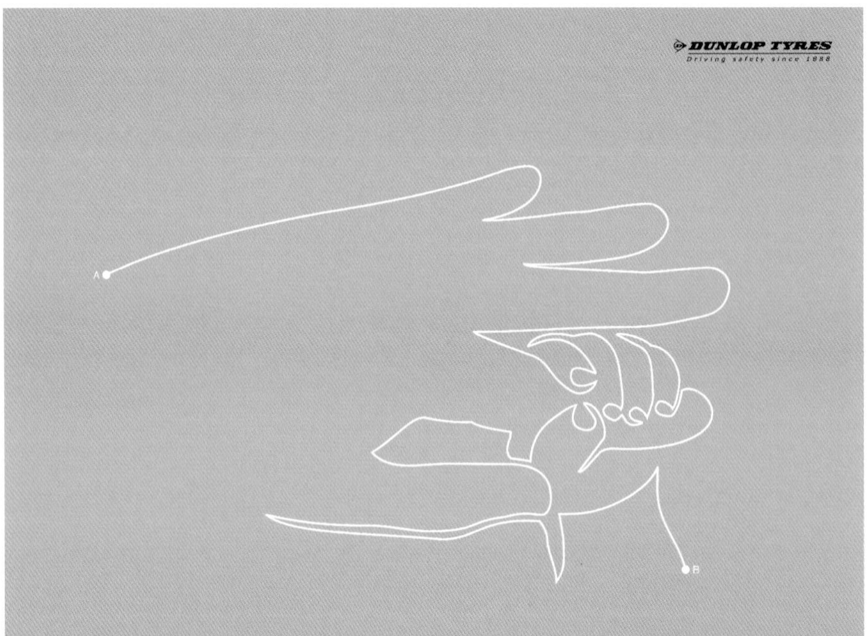

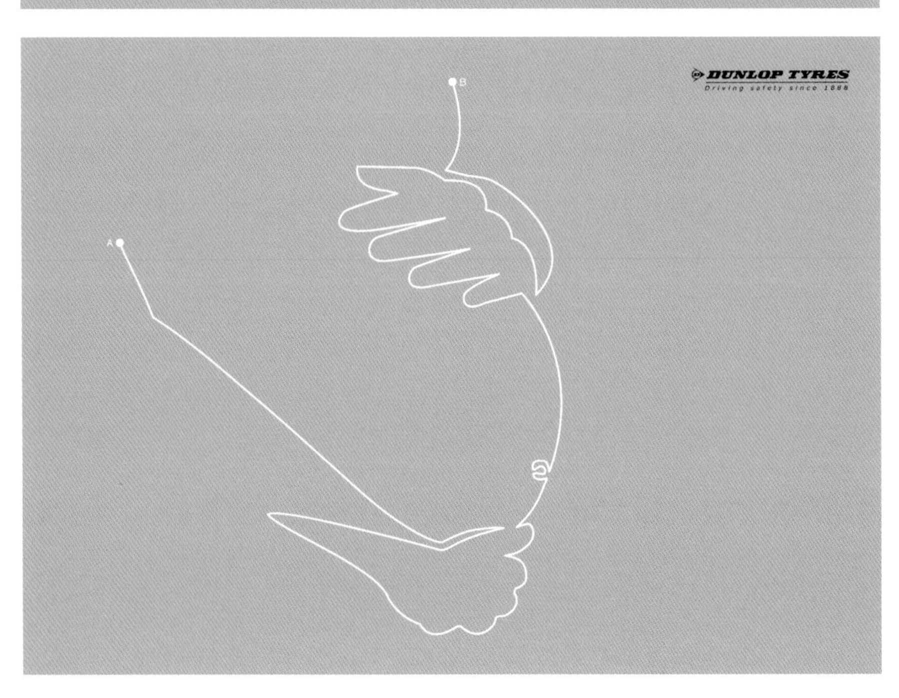

PRINT MERIT

MERIT AWARD
MAGAZINE COLOR
FULL PAGE OR SPREAD:
CAMPAIGN

ART DIRECTOR
Andre Kirkelis

WRITER
Carlos Schleder

PHOTOGRAPHER
Rogerio Miranda

CREATIVE DIRECTORS
Jose Zaragoza
Sidney Braz

CLIENT
Johnson & Johnson

AGENCY
DPZ/São Paulo

02248A

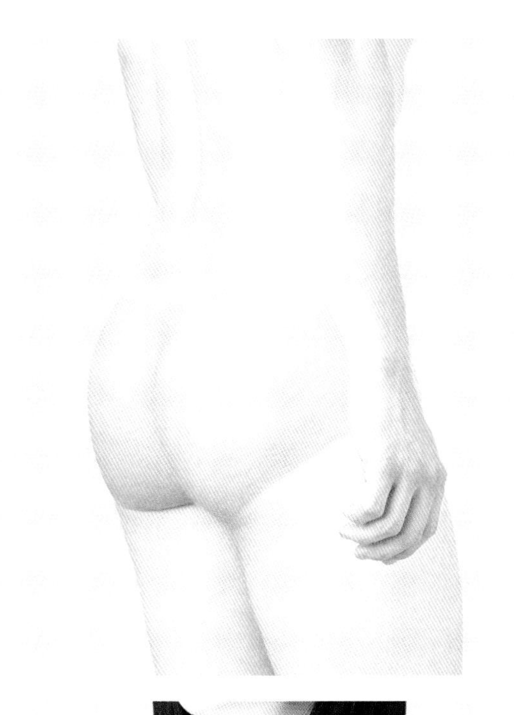

Sundown sunblock.
Maximum protection.

MERIT AWARD
MAGAZINE COLOR
FULL PAGE OR SPREAD: CAMPAIGN

ART DIRECTOR
Sidney Araujo

WRITER
Eduardo Lima

PHOTOGRAPHER
Fabio Bataglia

CREATIVE DIRECTORS
Fabio Fernandes
Eduardo Lima

CLIENT
Natan

AGENCY
f/nazca Saatchi & Saatchi/
São Paulo

02249A

NATAN
JEWELRY
The power of carats.

NATAN
JEWELRY
The power of carats.

NATAN
JEWELRY
The power of carats.

PRINT MERIT

MERIT AWARD
MAGAZINE COLOR
FULL PAGE OR SPREAD:
CAMPAIGN

ART DIRECTORS
Dan Bryant
Bob Barrie

WRITERS
Dean Buckhorn
Scott Cooney

PHOTOGRAPHERS
John Gipe
Mark LaFavor Pictures

CREATIVE DIRECTORS
David Lubars
Dean Hanson

CLIENT
Nikon

AGENCY
Fallon/Minneapolis

02250A

THE GUY AT THE PHOTO LAB
MAY SUDDENLY START VACATIONING THE SAME PLACES YOU DO.
Nikon
Is it the scenery? Or is it the N65? This remarkable Nikon, with its legendary Nikkor lenses, delivers the stunning quality of an SLR without sacrificing simplicity. Let the camera automatically focus and set exposure and flash. Or use manual control, interchangeable lenses, and experiment. Either way, you'll consistently get pictures you can't wait to see. That is, if the guy at the lab ever gets back from vacation.

IT MAY BE TIME TO MOVE THE PHOTO ALBUM
TO THE COFFEE TABLE.

A CAMERA WITH DOZENS OF FEATURES
INCLUDING ONE THAT LETS YOU IGNORE DOZENS OF FEATURES

MERIT AWARD
MAGAZINE COLOR
FULL PAGE OR SPREAD:
CAMPAIGN

ART DIRECTOR
Eric Yeo

WRITER
Robert Gaxiola

ILLUSTRATOR
Procolor

PHOTOGRAPHERS
Stock
Hannibal Barca

CREATIVE DIRECTOR
Chris Kyme

CLIENT
Stuttgart Auto

AGENCY
Foote Cone & Belding/
Singapore

02251A

911 Turbo. 420 bhp.

911 Turbo. 420 bhp.

911 Turbo. 420 bhp.

PRINT MERIT

MERIT AWARD
MAGAZINE COLOR
FULL PAGE OR SPREAD: CAMPAIGN

ART DIRECTOR
Marcos Medeiros

WRITER
Erick Rosa

PHOTOGRAPHER
Fabio Ribeiro

CREATIVE DIRECTORS
Valdir Bianchi
Ricardo Chester

CLIENT
Chrysler Brasil

AGENCY
Giovanni Foote Cone & Belding/São Paulo

02252A

Jeep

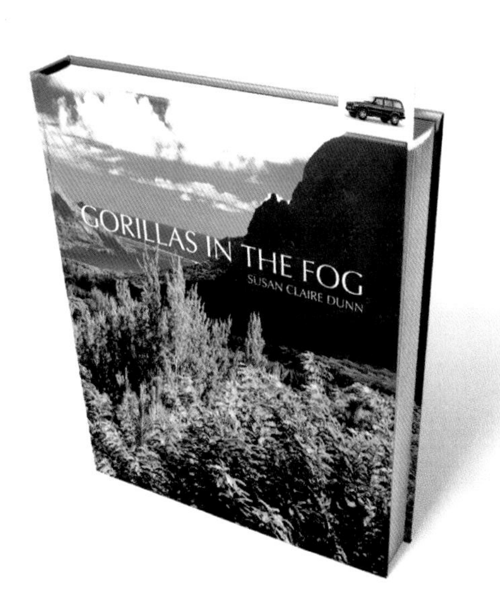

Jeep

MERIT AWARD
MAGAZINE COLOR
FULL PAGE OR SPREAD:
CAMPAIGN

ART DIRECTOR
Jacklyn Rogers

WRITER
Paula Lang

ILLUSTRATOR
Jacklyn Rogers

CREATIVE DIRECTOR
Graham Warsop

CLIENT
Prodec Paints

AGENCY
The Jupiter Drawing Room/
Johannesburg

02262A

Also won:
MERIT AWARDS
COLLATERAL: POSTERS
CAMPAIGN

MAGAZINE COLOR
FULL PAGE OR SPREAD: SINGLE

MERIT

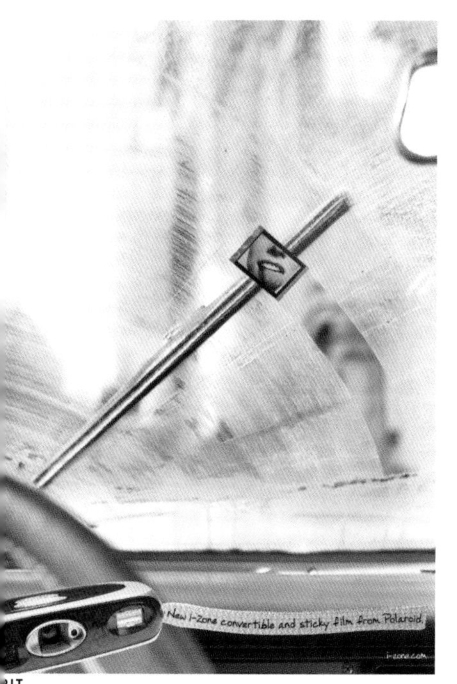

RIT

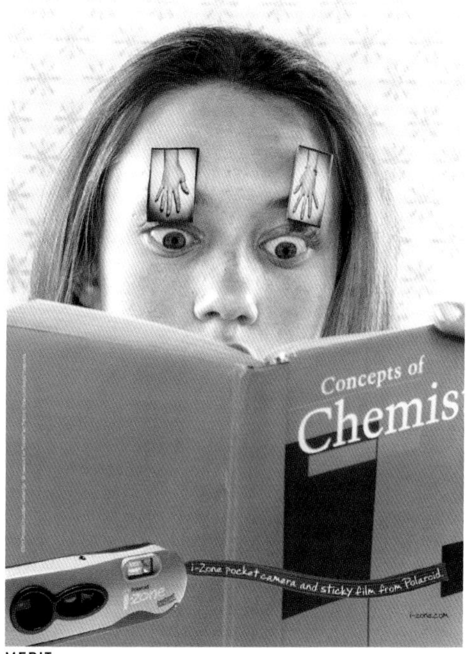

MERIT

MERIT

MERIT AWARD
MAGAZINE COLOR
FULL PAGE OR SPREAD: CAMPAIGN

ART DIRECTORS
Lisa Leone
Per Jacobson

WRITERS
Matt Horton
John Condon

PHOTOGRAPHER
Johan Fowelin

CREATIVE DIRECTORS
Matt Horton
Kerry Keenan
Jonathan Hoffman

CLIENT
Polaroid

AGENCY
Leo Burnett/Chicago

02253A

Also won:
MERIT AWARDS
MAGAZINE COLOR
FULL PAGE OR SPREAD: SINGLE

MERIT AWARD
MAGAZINE COLOR
FULL PAGE OR SPREAD:
CAMPAIGN

ART DIRECTORS
Amy Haddad
Michael Long

WRITER
Kerry Keenan

PHOTOGRAPHER
Nadav Kander

CREATIVE DIRECTORS
Kerry Keenan
Jonathan Hoffman

CLIENT
Polaroid Joycam

AGENCY
Leo Burnett/Chicago

02254A

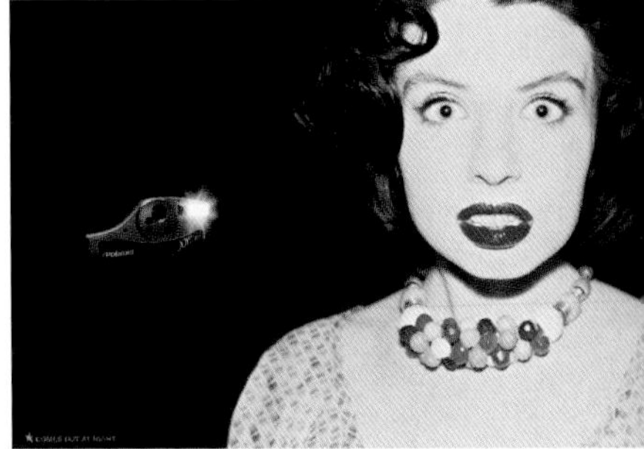

:RIT

RIT

MERIT AWARD
MAGAZINE COLOR
FULL PAGE OR SPREAD:
CAMPAIGN

ART DIRECTOR
Sidney Araújo

WRITER
Alexandre Gama

PHOTOGRAPHERS
Superstock
Fototeca
Stock
Zena
Keystock

CREATIVE DIRECTOR
Alexandre Gama

CLIENT
Swatch

AGENCY
Neogama/São Paulo

02255A

Also won:
MERIT AWARDS
MAGAZINE COLOR
FULL PAGE OR SPREAD:
SINGLE

MERIT AWARD
MAGAZINE COLOR
FULL PAGE OR SPREAD:
CAMPAIGN

ART DIRECTOR
Peter Wilkens

WRITER
Peter Huegel

PHOTOGRAPHERS
Dirk Pudwell

CREATIVE DIRECTORS
Christian Franke
Paul Armbruster

CLIENT
Pagelli Guitars

AGENCY
Ogilvy & Mather/Frankfurt

02257A

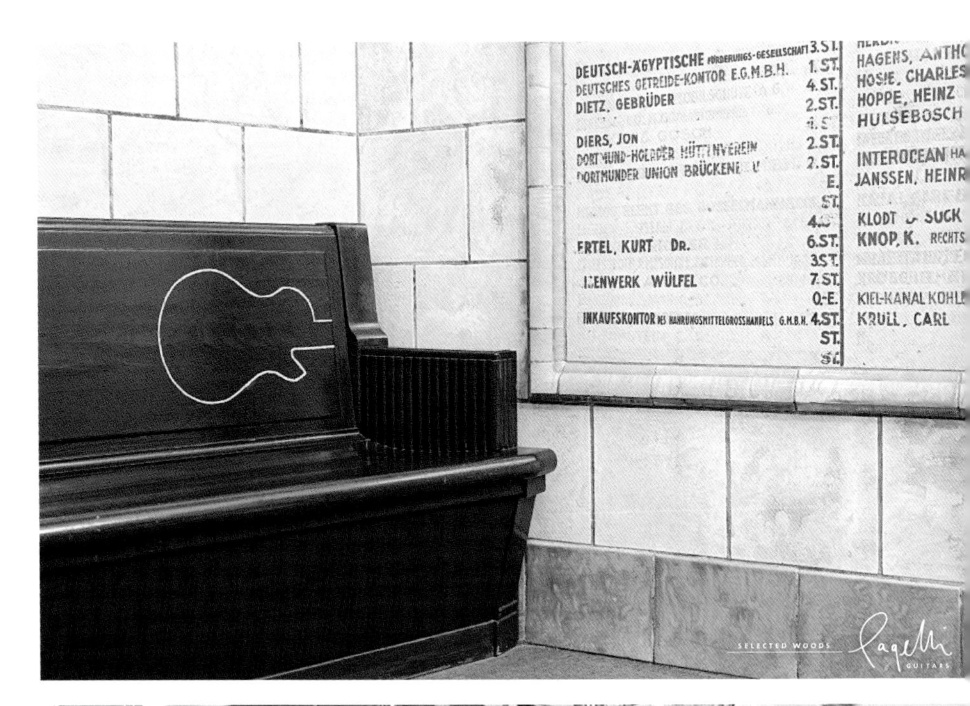

MERIT AWARD
MAGAZINE COLOR
FULL PAGE OR SPREAD:
CAMPAIGN

ART DIRECTOR
Annie Wong

WRITER
Simon Handford

CREATIVE DIRECTORS
Gary Tranter
Matt Cullen

CLIENT
The Economist

AGENCY
Ogilvy & Mather/Hong Kong

02256A

Also won:
MERIT AWARDS
MAGAZINE COLOR
FULL PAGE OR SPREAD: SINGLE

MERIT

MERIT

MERIT AWARD
MAGAZINE COLOR
FULL PAGE OR SPREAD:
CAMPAIGN

ART DIRECTORS
John LaMacchia
Jeff Curry

WRITERS
Andrea Sinert
Jeff O'Keefe

CREATIVE DIRECTORS
Dan Burrier
Peter Wood

CLIENT
Motorola

AGENCY
Ogilvy & Mather/New York

02258A

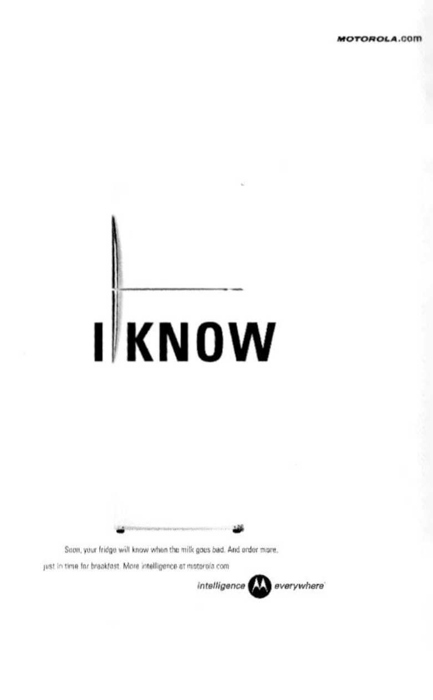

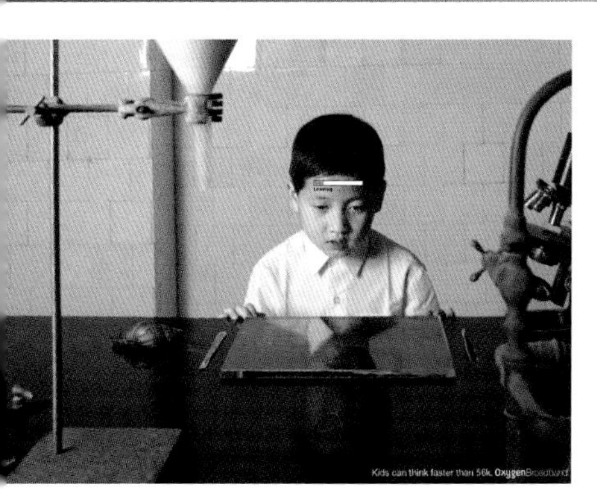

MERIT AWARD
MAGAZINE COLOR
FULL PAGE OR SPREAD: CAMPAIGN

ART DIRECTORS
Maurice Wee
Francis Wee

WRITERS
Craig Davis
Renee Lim
Daniel Lim

PHOTOGRAPHER
Stanley Wong

CREATIVE DIRECTOR
Craig Davis

CLIENT
China Light & Power/Oxygen Broadband

AGENCY
Saatchi & Saatchi/Hong Kong

02259A

MERIT AWARD
MAGAZINE COLOR
FULL PAGE OR SPREAD:
CAMPAIGN

ART DIRECTOR
Amabel Minchan

WRITER
Samuel Vazquez

ILLUSTRATOR
Alexandra Pitzolu

PHOTOGRAPHER
Alfonso Perez

CREATIVE DIRECTORS
Cesar Garcia
Miguel Roig

CLIENT
Queserias Bel Espania

AGENCY
Saatchi & Saatchi/Madrid

02260A

RIT

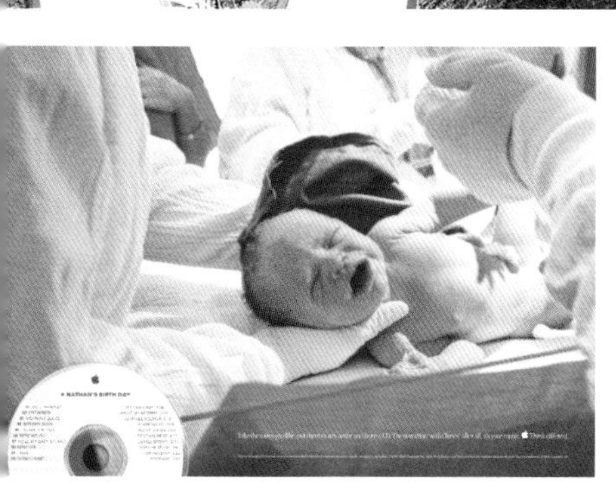

MERIT AWARD
MAGAZINE COLOR
FULL PAGE OR SPREAD:
CAMPAIGN

ART DIRECTORS
Margaret Midgett-Keene
Chuck Monn

WRITER
Jeff Maki

PHOTOGRAPHERS
Laura Crosta
Lauren Greenfield
Stock-Tony Stone
Peter Roger

CREATIVE DIRECTORS
Lee Clow
Duncan Milner

CLIENT
Apple iTunes

AGENCY
TBWA/Chiat/Day/
Los Angeles

02261A

Also won:
MERIT AWARD
MAGAZINE COLOR
FULL PAGE OR SPREAD: SINGLE

**MERIT AWARD
MAGAZINE COLOR
FULL PAGE OR SPREAD:
CAMPAIGN**

ART DIRECTOR
Frank Hahn

WRITER
Tim Wolfe

ILLUSTRATOR
David Foldvari

PHOTOGRAPHER
Trevor Graves

CREATIVE DIRECTORS
Glenn Cole
Paul Shearer

CLIENT
Nike Europe

AGENCY
Wieden + Kennedy/
Amsterdam

02263A

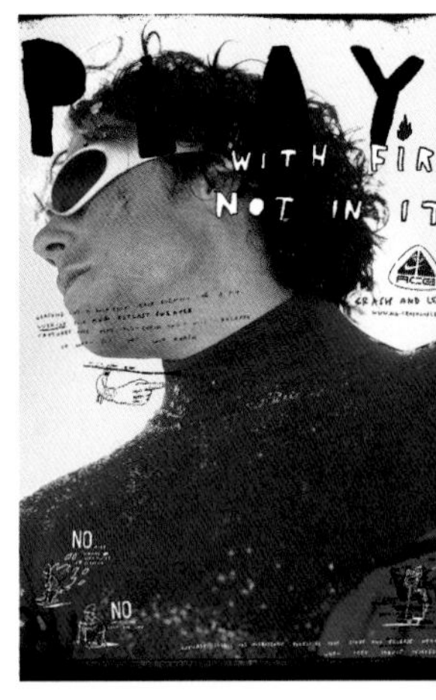

PRINT MERIT

WHILE MAINSTREAM NEWS WAS BUSY COVERING "SURVIVOR" THE TV SHOW, THE WOMEN OF BURKINA FASO WERE PLAYING IT FOR REAL.

With celebrity fluff and infotainment often masquerading as "news," you're less likely to hear about desperate places like Burkina Faso, a West African nation where more than 60% of the people live in poverty.

Unable to afford cottonseed oil or other ingredients, soap makers have turned to a most unnatural resource: waste spewed into a swamp by an oil refinery. These entrepreneurs wade through the toxic muck, skimming oily residue that they make into soap. Despite numerous drownings and exposure to noxious chemicals, mothers teach the craft to their daughters. They have little choice. Without soap to sell, the family doesn't eat.

This story was reported in the pages of Mother Jones, the non-profit, independent magazine dedicated to bringing you news that matters. For preferred rates on introductory subscriptions, call 1-800-GET-MOJO or visit motherjones.com.

Photography by Herve Cortinat

Mother Jones

ERIT

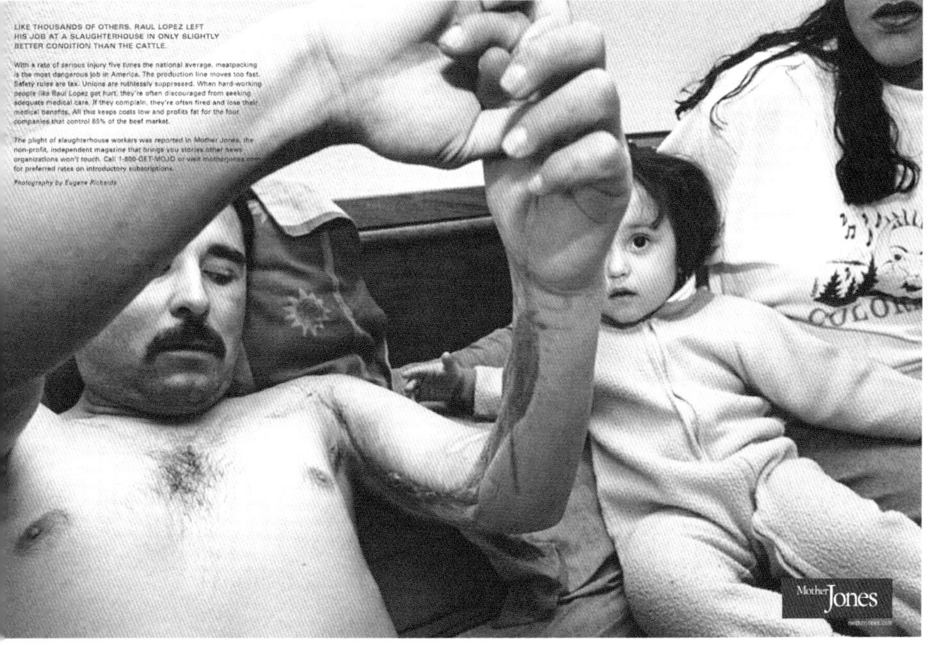

MERIT AWARD
MAGAZINE COLOR
FULL PAGE OR SPREAD: CAMPAIGN

ART DIRECTOR
Jon Wyville

WRITER
Dave Loew

PHOTOGRAPHERS
Herve Cortinat
Eugene Richards
Michio Hoshino

CREATIVE DIRECTORS
Dave Loew
Jon Wyville

CLIENT
Mother Jones

AGENCY
Young & Rubicam/Chicago

02264A

Also won:
MERIT AWARD
MAGAZINE COLOR
FULL PAGE OR SPREAD: SINGLE

MERIT AWARD
MAGAZINE B/W OR COLOR
LESS THAN A PAGE: SINGLE

ART DIRECTOR
Shelley Stout

WRITER
Mike Ward

PHOTOGRAPHER
Dave Emmite

CREATIVE DIRECTOR
Terry Schneider

CLIENT
Columbia Sportswear

AGENCY
Borders Perrin Norrander/
Portland

02265A

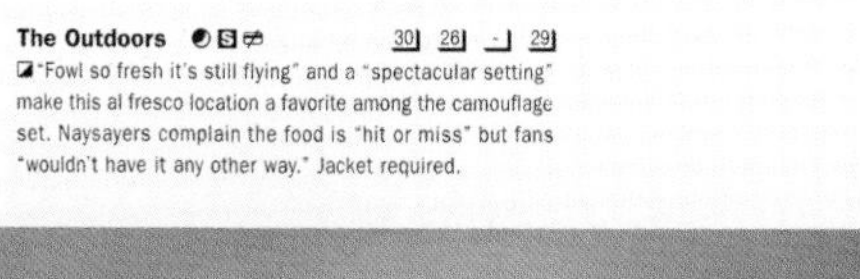

MERIT AWARD
MAGAZINE B/W OR COLOR
LESS THAN A PAGE: SINGLE

ART DIRECTOR
Andy Azula

WRITER
Mike McKay

PHOTOGRAPHER
Hunter Freeman

CREATIVE DIRECTORS
Jeffrey Goodby
Rich Silverstein

CLIENT
The Wall Street Journal

AGENCY
Goodby Silverstein & Partners/
San Francisco

02266A

MERIT AWARD
MAGAZINE B/W OR COLOR
LESS THAN A PAGE: SINGLE

ART DIRECTORS
Ketchai Parponsilp
Jon Chalermwong

WRITER
Panusard Tanashindawong

PHOTOGRAPHER
Niphon Baiyen

CREATIVE DIRECTOR
Jureeporn Thaidumrong

CLIENT
Procter & Gamble

AGENCY
Saatchi & Saatchi/Bangkok

02270A

MERIT AWARD
MAGAZINE B/W OR COLOR
LESS THAN A PAGE: CAMPAIGN

ART DIRECTOR
Dean Lee

WRITER
James Lee

PHOTOGRAPHER
Frank Vena

CREATIVE DIRECTOR
Randy Stein

CLIENT
Lastminutelodgings.com

AGENCY
Palmer Jarvis DDB/Vancouver

02271A

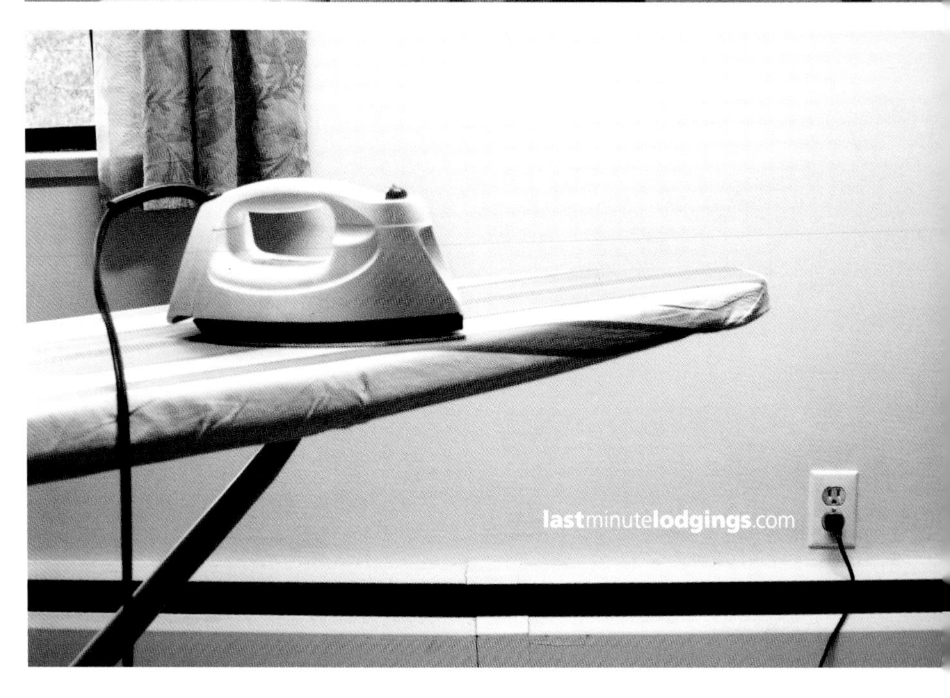

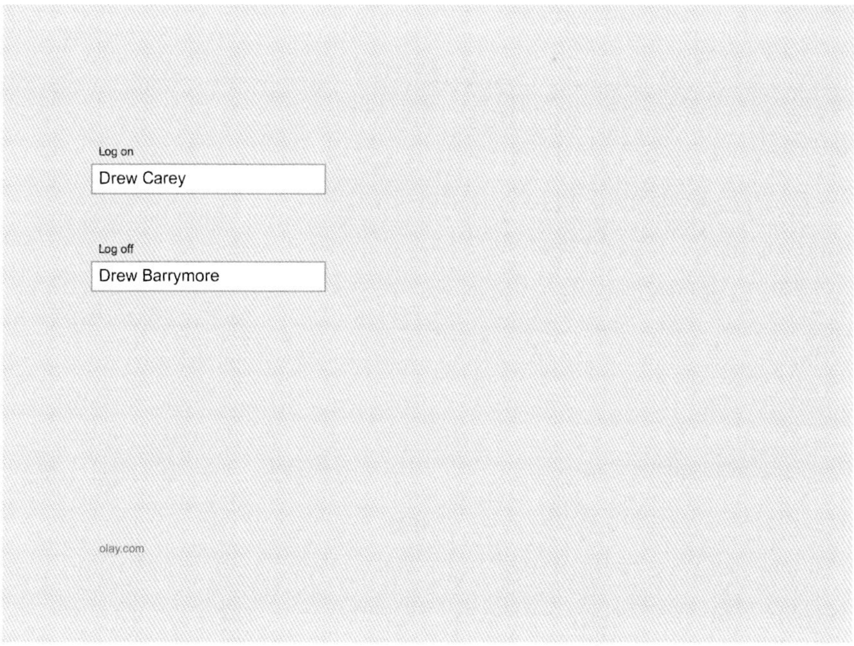

Log on

Drew Carey

Log off

Drew Barrymore

olay.com

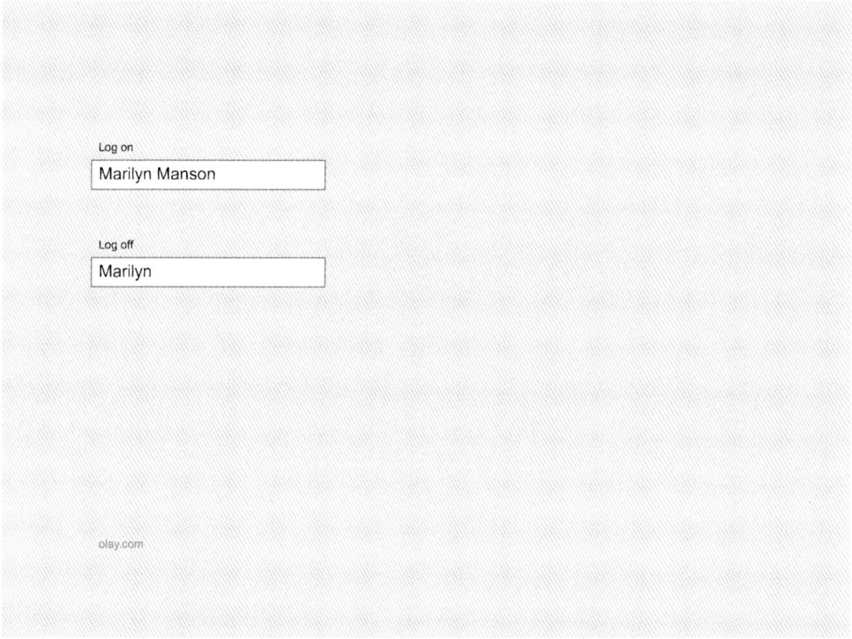

Log on

Marilyn Manson

Log off

Marilyn

olay.com

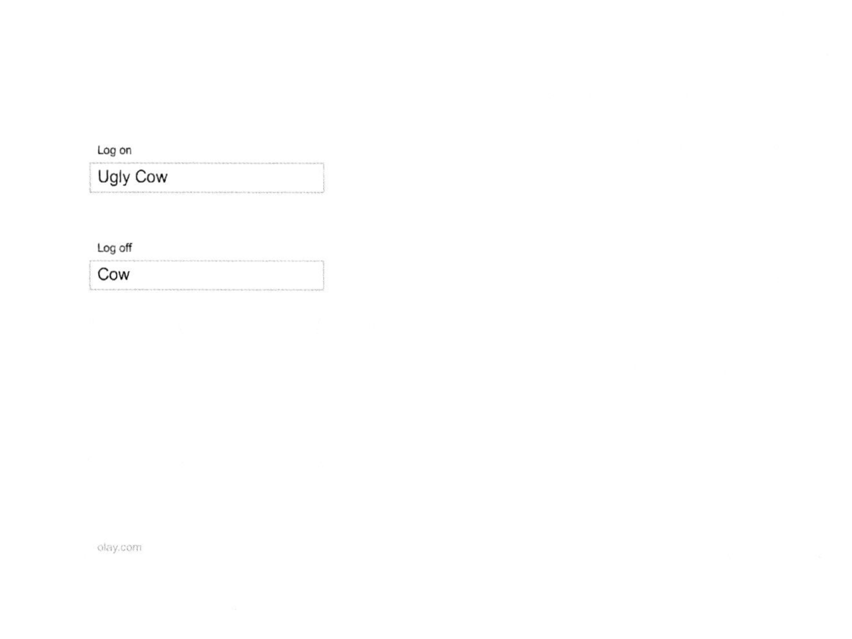

Log on

Ugly Cow

Log off

Cow

olay.com

PRINT MERIT

MERIT AWARD
MAGAZINE B/W OR COLOR
LESS THAN A PAGE: CAMPAIGN

ART DIRECTOR
Maurice Wee

WRITER
Renee Lim

CREATIVE DIRECTOR
Francis Wee

CLIENT
Procter & Gamble-Oil of Olay

AGENCY
Saatchi & Saatchi/Hong Kong

02272A

MERIT AWARD
MAGAZINE B/W OR COLOR
LESS THAN A PAGE: CAMPAIGN

ART DIRECTORS
Jay Russell
Scott Brewer

WRITERS
Wade Alger
Hayden Gilbert

PHOTOGRAPHER
Scott Harben

CREATIVE DIRECTORS
Kevin Sutton
Tim Murphy

CLIENT
Urban Home

AGENCY
Square One/Dallas

02273A

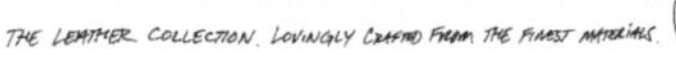

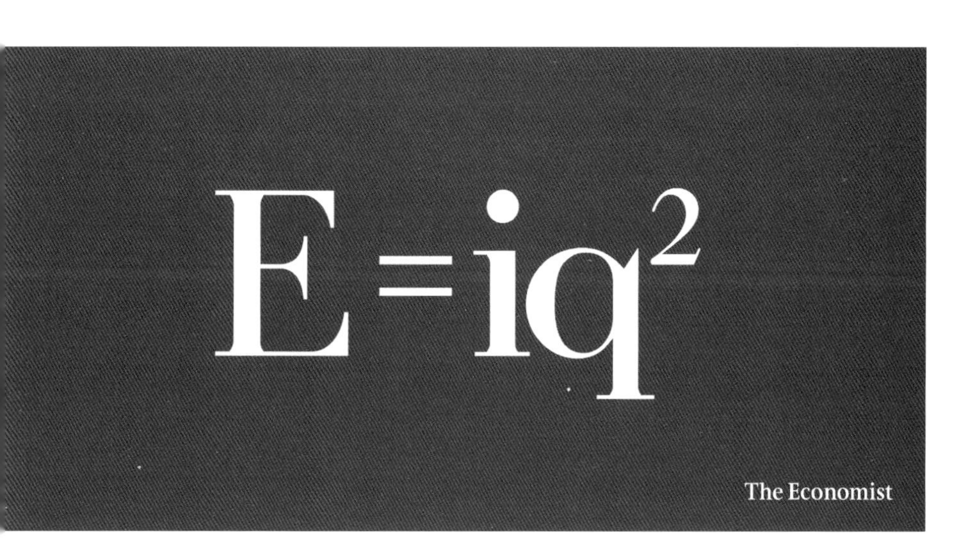

MERIT AWARD
OUTDOOR: SINGLE

ART DIRECTOR
Dave Dye

WRITER
Sean Doyle

CREATIVE DIRECTOR
Peter Souter

CLIENT
The Economist

AGENCY
Abbott Mead Vickers.BBDO/
London

02274A

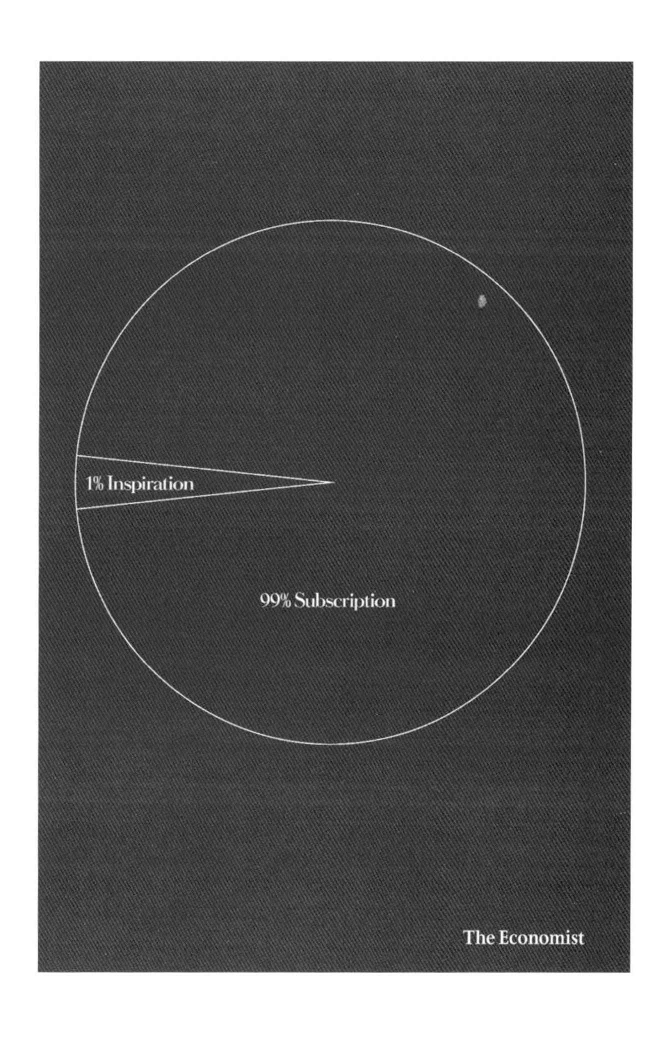

MERIT AWARD
OUTDOOR: SINGLE

ART DIRECTOR
Paul Young

WRITER
Ben Kay

CREATIVE DIRECTOR
Peter Souter

CLIENT
The Economist

AGENCY
Abbott Mead Vickers.BBDO/
London

02275A

MERIT AWARD
OUTDOOR: SINGLE

ART DIRECTORS
Drew Lees
Thomas Kerk

WRITERS
Justin White
Niranjan Kaushik

ILLUSTRATOR
Drew Lees

CREATIVE DIRECTOR
Peter Callaghan

CLIENT
Singapore Zoological Gardens

AGENCY
Batey/Singapore

02276A

Also won:
MERIT AWARD
COLLATERAL: POSTERS
SINGLE

MERIT AWARD
OUTDOOR: SINGLE

ART DIRECTOR
Darren Pitt

WRITER
Rohan Lancaster

CREATIVE DIRECTOR
Paul Taylor

CLIENT
Public Transport Corporation

AGENCY
M&C Saatchi/Melbourne

02277A

MERIT AWARD OUTDOOR: SINGLE

ART DIRECTOR
Dorky Mallare

WRITERS
Rosene Santos
Raoul Floresca
Peachy Todino Pacquing

PHOTOGRAPHER
Elly Puyat

CREATIVE DIRECTOR
Peachy Todino Pacquing

CLIENT
The Economist

AGENCY
OgilvyOne worldwide/
Makati City

02278A

MERIT AWARD OUTDOOR: SINGLE

ART DIRECTOR
George Boutilier

WRITER
George Boutilier

CREATIVE DIRECTOR
Kevin Kehoe

CLIENT
Washington State Lottery

AGENCY
Publicis in the West/Seattle

02279A

MERIT AWARD
OUTDOOR: SINGLE

ART DIRECTOR
Joseph Mazzaferro

WRITERS
Pete Lewtas
Larry Gies

CREATIVE DIRECTORS
Dallas Itzen
Patrick O'Neill

CLIENT
Absolut Vodka

AGENCY
TBWA/Chiat/Day/New York

02281A

PRINT MERIT

MERIT AWARD
OUTDOOR: CAMPAIGN

ART DIRECTOR
Ralph Watson

WRITER
Ken Marcus

ILLUSTRATOR
Evan Hecox

PHOTOGRAPHER
Hans Gissinger

CREATIVE DIRECTORS
Marty Weiss
Ralph Watson
Rick Condos

CLIENT
The Economist

AGENCY
Brand Architecture
International/New York

02282A

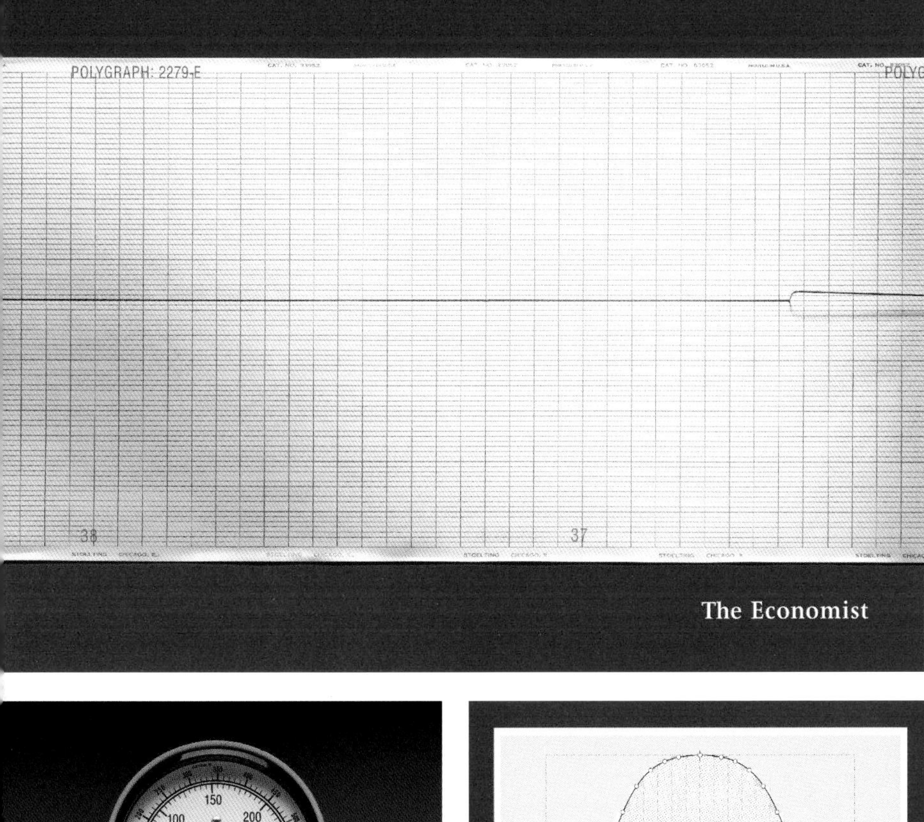

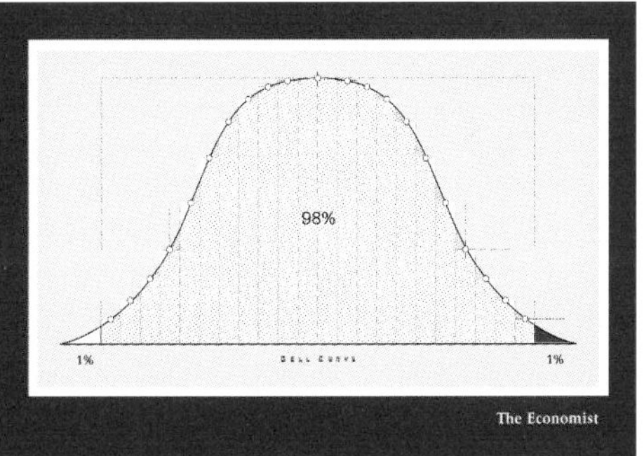

MERIT AWARD
OUTDOOR: CAMPAIGN

ART DIRECTORS
Staffan Håkanson
Staffan Forsman

WRITERS
Martin Ringqvist
Björn Engström
Emma Zetterholm

PHOTOGRAPHER
Lennart Sjöberg

CLIENT
Göteborgs Posten

AGENCY
Forsman & Bodenfors/
Göthenburg

02283A

MERIT AWARD
OUTDOOR: CAMPAIGN

ART DIRECTORS
Andreas Malm
Mikko Timonen
Anders Eklind

WRITERS
Filip Nilsson
Johan Olivero

PHOTOGRAPHER
Jesper Brandt

CLIENT
Volvo of Sweden

AGENCY
Forsman & Bodenfors/
Göthenburg

02284A

MERIT AWARD
OUTDOOR: CAMPAIGN

ART DIRECTORS
Morten Kristiansen
Katrine Bervell

WRITERS
Morten Kristiansen
Katrine Bervell

CREATIVE DIRECTOR
Erik Heisholt

CLIENT
SAS

AGENCY
Leo Burnett/Oslo

02285A

MERIT AWARD
OUTDOOR: CAMPAIGN

ART DIRECTORS
Will Uronis
Michael Langone

WRITER
Shane Hutton

PHOTOGRAPHER
Alexi Hay

CREATIVE DIRECTORS
Lance Jensen
Gary Koepke

CLIENT
MTV

AGENCY
Modernista!/Boston

02286A

MERIT AWARD
OUTDOOR: CAMPAIGN

ART DIRECTORS
Will Uronis
Michael Langone

WRITER
Shane Hutton

PHOTOGRAPHER
Alexi Hay

CREATIVE DIRECTORS
Lance Jensen
Gary Koepke

CLIENT
MTV

AGENCY
Modernista!/Boston

02287A

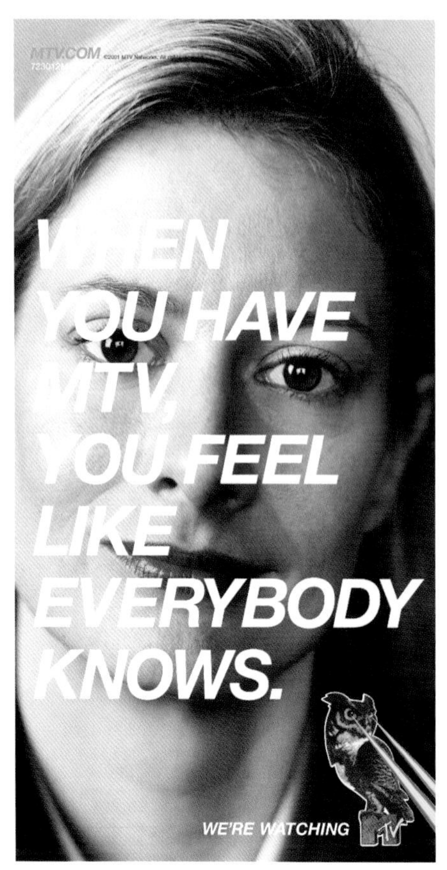

MERIT AWARD
OUTDOOR: CAMPAIGN

ART DIRECTOR
George Boutilier

WRITER
George Boutilier

PHOTOGRAPHER
Bob Peterson

CREATIVE DIRECTOR
Kevin Kehoe

CLIENT
Washington State Lottery

AGENCY
Publicis in the West/Seattle

02288A

MERIT AWARD
OUTDOOR: CAMPAIGN

ART DIRECTORS
Moe VerBrugge
Maya Rao Frey

WRITERS
Maya Rao Frey
Moe VerBrugge

PHOTOGRAPHER
Axel Forno

CREATIVE DIRECTOR
Lee Clow

CLIENT
MOCA

AGENCY
TBWA/Chiat/Day/Los Angeles

02290A

MERIT AWARD
GUERILLA ADVERTISING

ART DIRECTOR
Carolyn Davis

WRITER
Matthew Page

CREATIVE DIRECTOR
Barry Robinson

CLIENT
BMW Group-MINI

AGENCY
BADJAR Advertising/
Melbourne

02291A

MERIT AWARD
GUERILLA ADVERTISING

ART DIRECTOR
David Hughes

WRITER
Bill Garrison

PHOTOGRAPHER
Bill Dutkovic

CREATIVE DIRECTOR
Rodney Underwood

CLIENT
Zippo

AGENCY
Blattner Brunner/Pittsburgh

02292A

MERIT AWARD
GUERILLA ADVERTISING

ART DIRECTOR
Dali Meskam

WRITER
Raymond Quah

PHOTOGRAPHERS
Fred's Foto
Cedric Lim

CREATIVE DIRECTOR
Chris Kyme

CLIENT
Adidas Singapore

AGENCY
Foote Cone & Belding/
Singapore

02293A

MERIT AWARD
GUERILLA ADVERTISING

ART DIRECTOR
Perry Goh

WRITER
Hari Ramanathan

ILLUSTRATOR
Wei Ming

PHOTOGRAPHER
Wei Ming

CREATIVE DIRECTORS
Hari Ramanathan
Perry Goh

CLIENT
Hush Puppies

AGENCY
Goh Ramanathan/Singapore

02294A

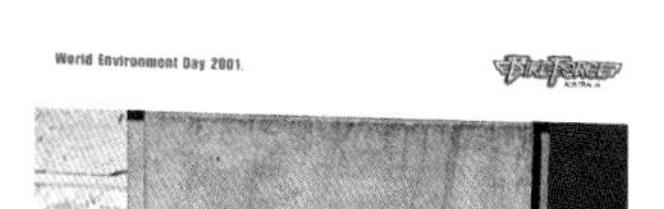

MERIT AWARD
GUERILLA ADVERTISING

ART DIRECTORS
Jana Benjafield
Mick Colliss

WRITERS
Mick Colliss
Jana Benjafield

CREATIVE DIRECTOR
Ron Samuel

CLIENT
Bikeforce Australia

AGENCY
JDA/Perth

02295A

MERIT AWARD
GUERILLA ADVERTISING

ART DIRECTOR
Greg Sheppard

PHOTOGRAPHER
Janyon Boschoff

CREATIVE DIRECTOR
Chris Garbutt

CLIENT
Dunlop

AGENCY
TBWA Hunt Lascaris/
Johannesburg

02296A

These coasters were placed in sports bars around the country. The coasters are coated with an adhesive substance that, when wet, sticks to the bottom of your glass.

MERIT AWARD
GUERILLA ADVERTISING

ART DIRECTOR
Peter Khoury

WRITER
Avital Pinchevsky

PHOTOGRAPHER
Merwalene van der Merwe

CREATIVE DIRECTORS
Sandra de Witt
Frances Luckin

CLIENT
Nashua

AGENCY
TBWA Hunt Lascaris/
Johannesburg

02297A

A special edition of magazine sent by direct mail to homes of media professionals.

MERIT AWARD
GUERILLA ADVERTISING

ART DIRECTOR
Pedro Pletitsch

WRITER
Marcelo Sato

PHOTOGRAPHERS
Getty Images
Ale Ermel

CREATIVE DIRECTORS
Tiao Bernardi
Rita Corradi
J.R. D'Elboux

CLIENT
Editoria Simbolo

AGENCY
Young & Rubicam/São Paulo

02298A

MERIT AWARD
TRADE B/W
FULL PAGE OR SPREAD: SINGLE

ART DIRECTORS
Kevin Dailor
Julian Newman

WRITER
Dana Satterwhite

PHOTOGRAPHER
Craig Cutler

CREATIVE DIRECTORS
Ron Lawner
Alan Pafenbach

CLIENT
Volkswagen of America

AGENCY
Arnold Worldwide/Boston

02299A

MERIT AWARD
TRADE B/W
FULL PAGE OR SPREAD: SINGLE

ART DIRECTOR
Doug Pedersen

WRITER
Curtis Smith

ILLUSTRATOR
Floyd Coffey

CREATIVE DIRECTOR
Jim Mountjoy

CLIENT
Velux America

AGENCY
Loeffler Ketchum Mountjoy/
Charlotte

02300A

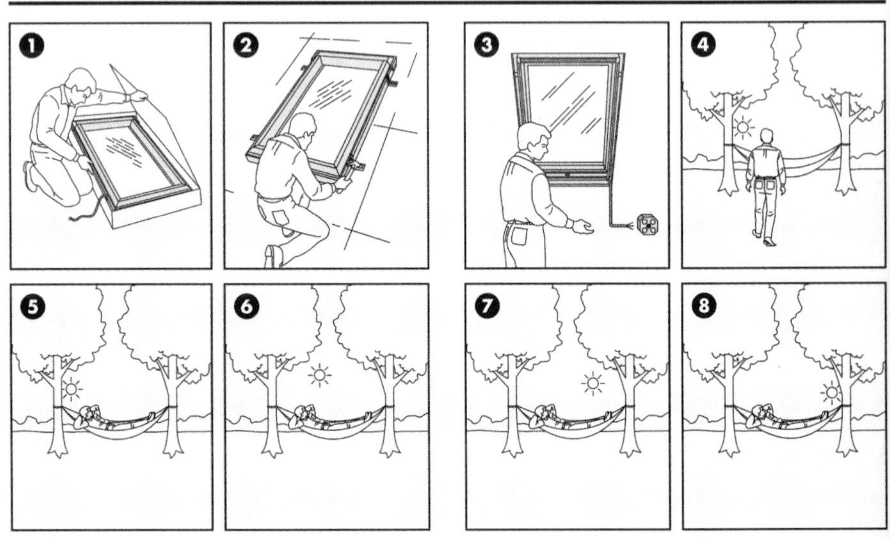

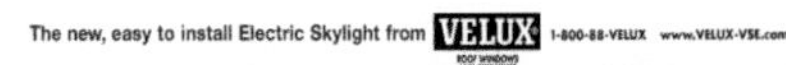

“Committed to excellenc

PUBLICIS & HAL RIN

PRINT MERIT

MERIT AWARD
TRADE B/W
FULL PAGE OR SPREAD: SINGLE

ART DIRECTOR
Aaron Allen

WRITER
Aaron Allen

CREATIVE DIRECTORS
Steve Luker
Kevin Jones

CLIENT
Publicis & Hal Riney

AGENCY
Publicis & Hal Riney/
San Francisco

02301A

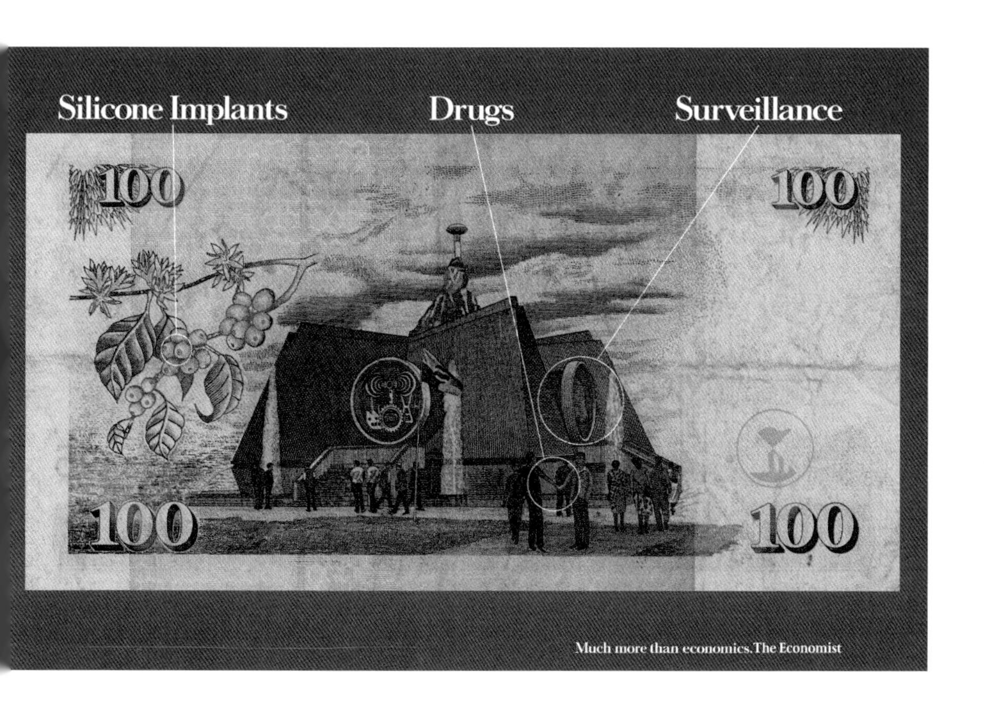

MERIT AWARD
TRADE COLOR
FULL PAGE OR SPREAD: SINGLE

ART DIRECTOR
Dave Dye

WRITER
Sean Doyle

TYPOGRAPHER
"Jelly" Hammond

CREATIVE DIRECTORS
Dave Dye
Sean Doyle

CLIENT
The Economist

AGENCY
Abbott Mead Vickers.BBDO/
London

02303A

MERIT AWARD
TRADE COLOR
FULL PAGE OR SPREAD: SINGLE

ART DIRECTOR
Steve Andrews

WRITER
Mike Weidner

PHOTOGRAPHER
Lee Dayvault

CREATIVE DIRECTORS
Dave Stanton
Jackie Hathiramani

CLIENT
Georgia World Congress Center

AGENCY
BBDO/Atlanta

02302A

MERIT AWARD
TRADE COLOR
FULL PAGE OR SPREAD: SINGLE

ART DIRECTOR
James Clunie

WRITER
Michael Atkinson

PHOTOGRAPHER
Steve Henke

CREATIVE DIRECTOR
Brian Kroening

CLIENT
American Standard

AGENCY
Carmichael Lynch/
Minneapolis

02305A

One of the things we're fighting for is

the right to protest that we're fighting.

Freedom of speech is a fundamental part of our society. TIME is there to help us understand every word. **TIME.**

MERIT AWARD
TRADE COLOR
FULL PAGE OR SPREAD: SINGLE

ART DIRECTOR
Con Williamson

WRITER
Dan Rollman

PHOTOGRAPHER
Stock

CREATIVE DIRECTOR
Kevin Roddy

CLIENT
Time

AGENCY
Fallon/New York

02307A

Definitive proof that our country is united.

No matter what our differences may be, we're all Americans. And TIME is there to help us understand that. **TIME.**

MERIT AWARD
TRADE COLOR
FULL PAGE OR SPREAD: SINGLE

ART DIRECTOR
Con Williamson

WRITER
Dan Rollman

PHOTOGRAPHER
Stock

CREATIVE DIRECTOR
Kevin Roddy

CLIENT
Time

AGENCY
Fallon/New York

02308A

MERIT AWARD
TRADE COLOR
FULL PAGE OR SPREAD: SINGLE

ART DIRECTOR
Matt Vescovo

WRITER
Kevin Roddy

PHOTOGRAPHER
Stock

CREATIVE DIRECTOR
Kevin Roddy

CLIENT
Time

AGENCY
Fallon/New York

02309A

God, Allah, Krishna, Buddha, Jehovah bless America.

America's diversity is united under one ideal. And TIME is there to help people understand it. **TIME.**

MERIT AWARD
TRADE COLOR
FULL PAGE OR SPREAD: SINGLE

ART DIRECTOR
Matt Vescovo

WRITER
Kevin Roddy

PHOTOGRAPHER
Stock

CREATIVE DIRECTOR
Kevin Roddy

CLIENT
Time

AGENCY
Fallon/New York

02310A

The mayor that never sleeps.

In these trying times, what America needs most is leadership. It certainly has it. And TIME is there. **TIME.**

The contents of this magazine

are coming to your front door.

Whether you subscribe to it or not.

In uncertain times, it's one thing people rely on. **TIME.**

MERIT AWARD
TRADE COLOR
FULL PAGE OR SPREAD: SINGLE

ART DIRECTOR
Bobby Applby

WRITER
Scott Cooney

PHOTOGRAPHER
Stock

CREATIVE DIRECTOR
Kevin Roddy

CLIENT
Time

AGENCY
Fallon/New York

02311A

Remodelling office work since 1981. Happy birthday. IBM PC.

IBM

MERIT AWARD
TRADE COLOR
FULL PAGE OR SPREAD: SINGLE

ART DIRECTOR
Marc Zinnecker

WRITER
Peter Strauss

CREATIVE DIRECTOR
Stephan Junghanns

CLIENT
IBM Germany

AGENCY
Ogilvy & Mather/Frankfurt

02312A

MERIT AWARD
TRADE COLOR
FULL PAGE OR SPREAD: SINGLE

ART DIRECTOR
Ian Grais

WRITER
Ian Grais

PHOTOGRAPHER
Dave Robertson

CREATIVE DIRECTORS
Chris Staples
Ian Grais

CLIENT
Maclean's

AGENCY
Rethink/Vancouver

02314A

MERIT AWARD
TRADE COLOR
FULL PAGE OR SPREAD: SINGLE

ART DIRECTOR
Rose Sauquillo

WRITER
Jane Murray

PHOTOGRAPHER
Shin Sugino

CREATIVE DIRECTORS
Zak Mroueh
Paul Lavoie

CLIENT
Association of Universities and Colleges of Canada

AGENCY
Taxi/Toronto

02319A

PRINT MERIT

MERIT AWARD
TRADE COLOR
FULL PAGE OR SPREAD: SINGLE

ART DIRECTOR
Hayden Pasco

WRITER
John Robertson

ILLUSTRATORS
Charles Anderson
Hayden Pasco

CREATIVE DIRECTORS
John Vitro
John Robertson

CLIENT
Taylor Guitars

AGENCY
VitroRobertson/San Diego

02320A

MERIT AWARD
TRADE COLOR
FULL PAGE OR SPREAD: SINGLE

ART DIRECTOR
Hayden Pasco

WRITER
John Robertson

ILLUSTRATORS
Charles Anderson
Hayden Pasco

CREATIVE DIRECTORS
John Vitro
John Robertson

CLIENT
Taylor Guitars

AGENCY
VitroRobertson/San Diego

02321A

MERIT AWARD
TRADE COLOR
FULL PAGE OR SPREAD: SINGLE

ART DIRECTOR
Hayden Pasco

WRITER
John Robertson

ILLUSTRATORS
Charles Anderson
Hayden Pasco

CREATIVE DIRECTORS
John Vitro
John Robertson

CLIENT
Taylor Guitars

AGENCY
VitroRobertson/San Diego

02322A

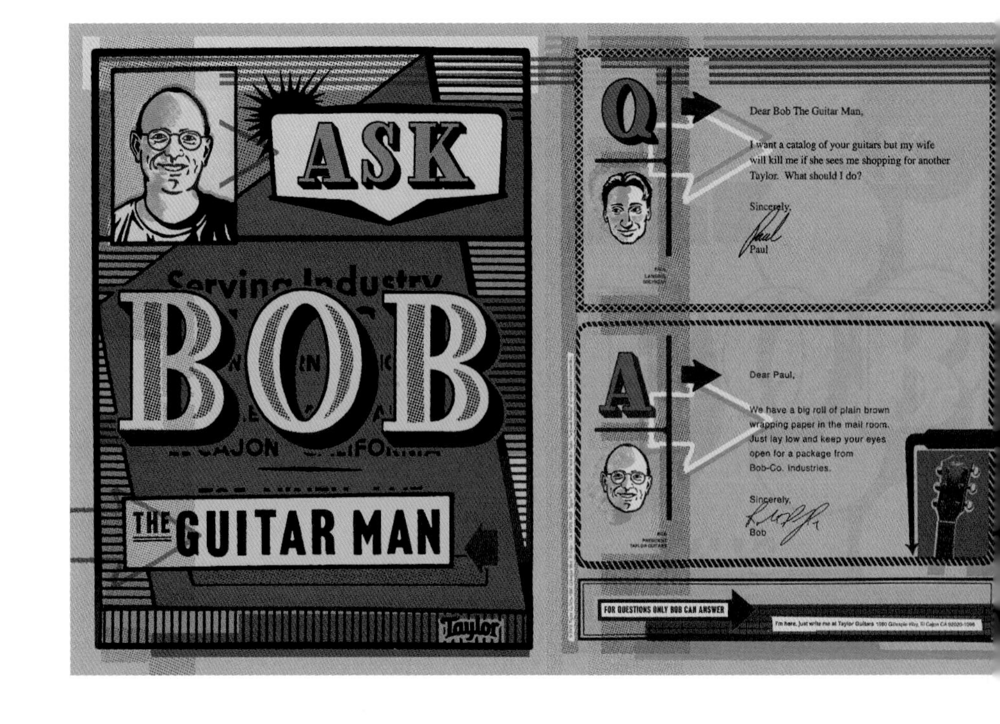

PRINT MERIT

MERIT AWARD
TRADE B/W OR COLOR
ANY SIZE: CAMPAIGN

ART DIRECTOR
James Clunie

WRITER
Michael Atkinson

PHOTOGRAPHER
Ron Crofoot

CREATIVE DIRECTOR
Brian Kroening

CLIENT
American Standard

AGENCY
Carmichael Lynch/
Minneapolis

02324A

Also won:
MERIT AWARD
TRADE COLOR
FULL PAGE OR SPREAD: SINGLE

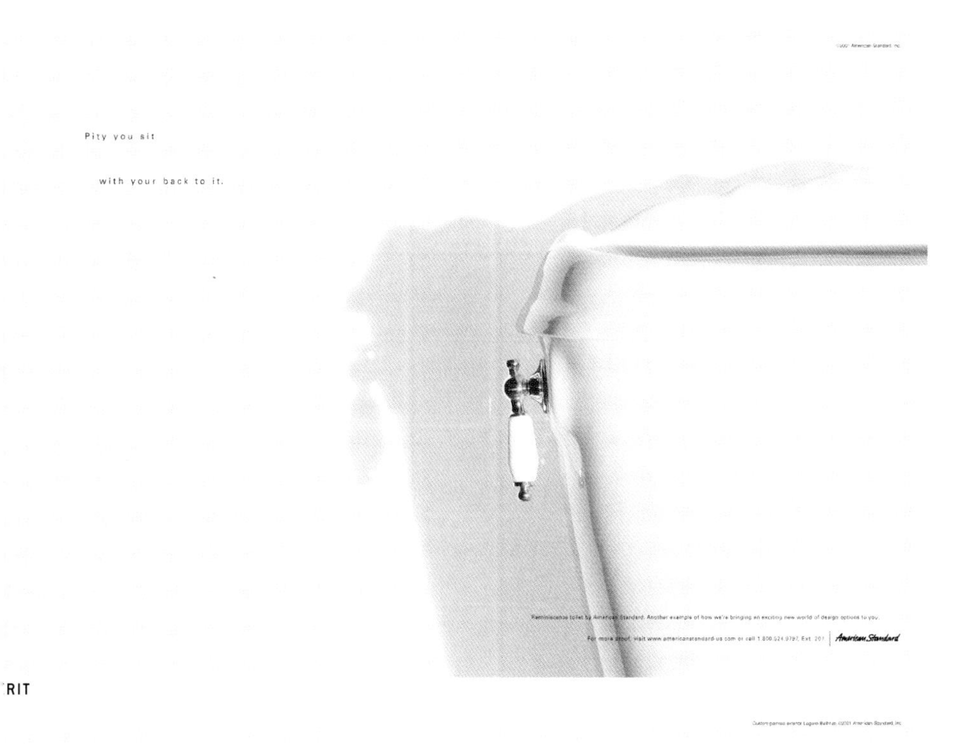

RIT

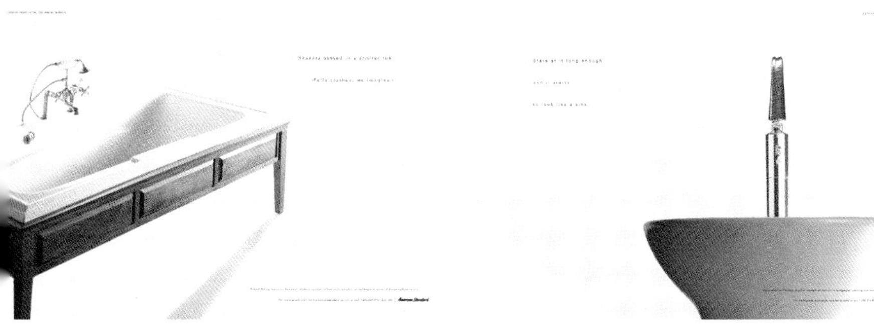

PRINT MERIT

MERIT AWARD
TRADE B/W OR COLOR
ANY SIZE: CAMPAIGN

ART DIRECTOR
David Damman

WRITERS
Linus Karlsson
Ryan Peck

PHOTOGRAPHER
Shawn Michienzi

CREATIVE DIRECTOR
Bob Moore

CLIENT
The Hockey School

AGENCY
Fallon/Minneapolis

02326A

MERIT AWARD
TRADE B/W OR COLOR
ANY SIZE: CAMPAIGN

ART DIRECTOR
Dan Bryant

WRITERS
Roger Baldacci
Franklin Tipton

PHOTOGRAPHER
R.J. Muna

CREATIVE DIRECTORS
David Lubars
Bob Moore

CLIENT
International

AGENCY
Fallon/Minneapolis

02325A

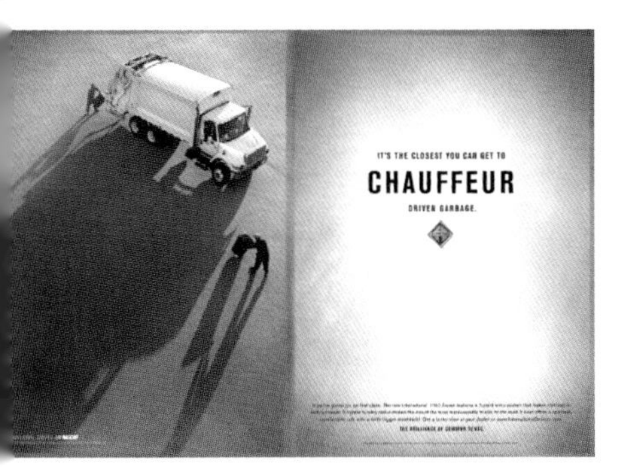

MERIT AWARD
TRADE B/W OR COLOR
ANY SIZE: CAMPAIGN

ART DIRECTOR
Brian Murphy

WRITER
Jamie Barrett

PHOTOGRAPHER
Stock

CREATIVE DIRECTOR
Jamie Barrett

CLIENT
Time

AGENCY
Fallon/New York

02327A

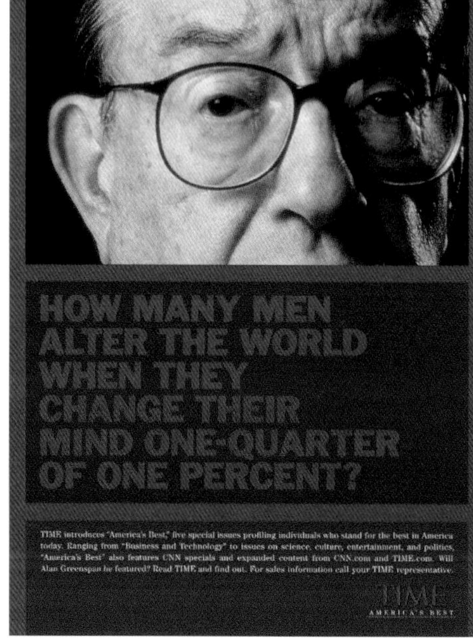

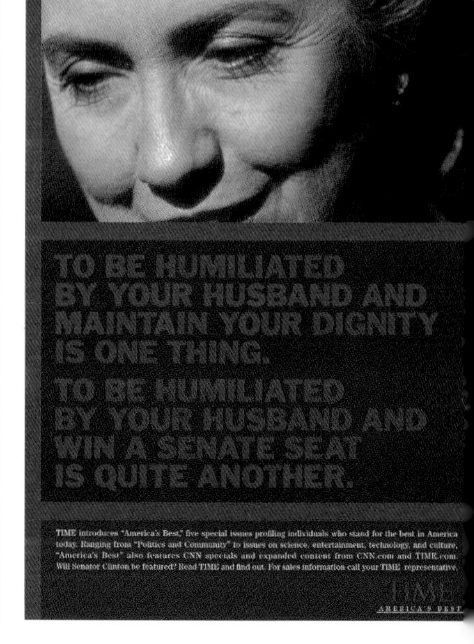

PRINT MERIT

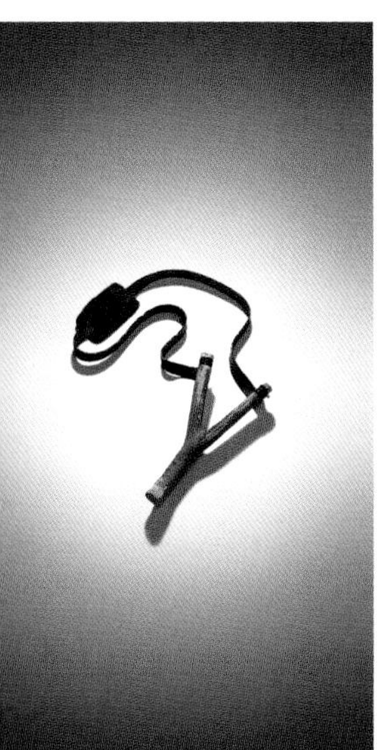

MERIT AWARD
TRADE B/W OR COLOR
ANY SIZE: CAMPAIGN

ART DIRECTORS
Paulo Pretti
Daniel Venticinque

WRITERS
Sérgio Scarpelli
Edgard Gianesi

TYPOGRAPHER
Burti

PHOTOGRAPHERS
Ricardo de Vicq
Keystone
Contexto
Image Bank
Stock

CREATIVE DIRECTOR
Paulo Pretti

CLIENT
Fischer America

AGENCY
Fischer America/São Paulo

02328A

MERIT AWARD
TRADE B/W OR COLOR
ANY SIZE: CAMPAIGN

ART DIRECTOR
Doug Pedersen

WRITER
Curtis Smith

ILLUSTRATOR
Floyd Coffey

CREATIVE DIRECTOR
Jim Mountjoy

CLIENT
Velux America

AGENCY
Loeffler Ketchum Mountjoy/
Charlotte

02329A

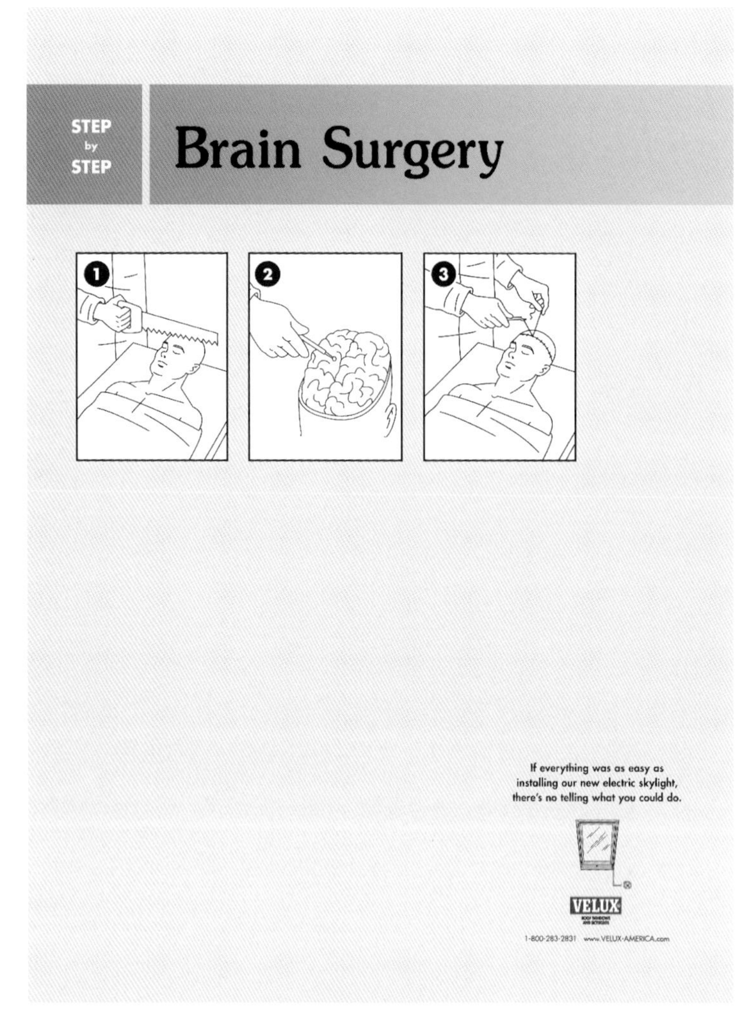

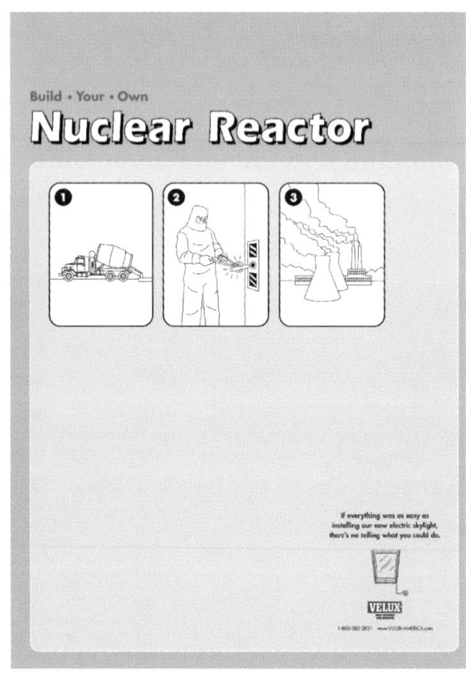

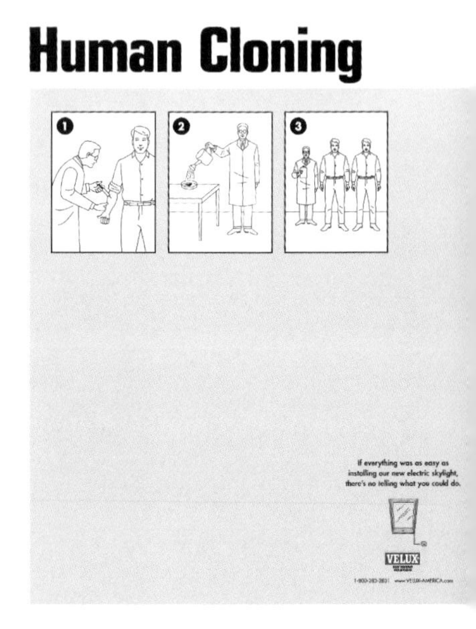

PRINT MERIT

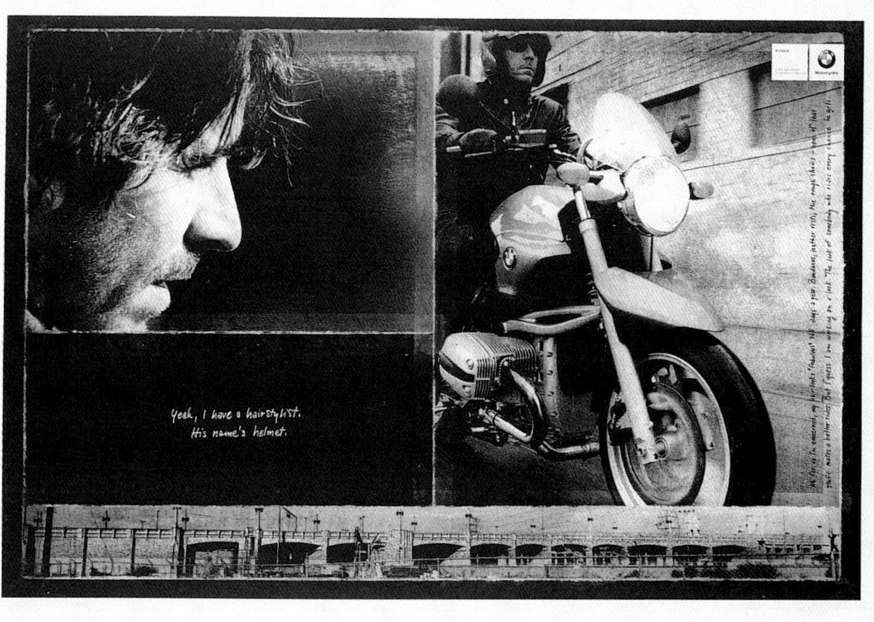

MERIT AWARD
TRADE B/W OR COLOR
ANY SIZE: CAMPAIGN

ART DIRECTOR
Cameron Webb

WRITER
Mark Lowe

PHOTOGRAPHER
Steve Bonini

CREATIVE DIRECTOR
Rick Rabe

CLIENT
BMW Motorcycles

AGENCY
Merkley Newman Harty/
New York

02330A

MERIT AWARD
TRADE B/W OR COLOR
ANY SIZE: CAMPAIGN

ART DIRECTOR
Michael Ancevic

WRITER
Stephen Mietelski

PHOTOGRAPHERS
David Burnett
Greg Miller
Axel Koester

CREATIVE DIRECTOR
Edward Boches

CLIENT
Fortune Magazine

AGENCY
Mullen/Wenham

02331A

Rule #1
Do unto others until they can do no more.
FORTUNE
Business rules
fortune.com

Rule #7

Pay attention to the man behind the curtain.

Rule #5

Be your biggest fan.

MERIT AWARD
TRADE B/W OR COLOR
ANY SIZE: CAMPAIGN

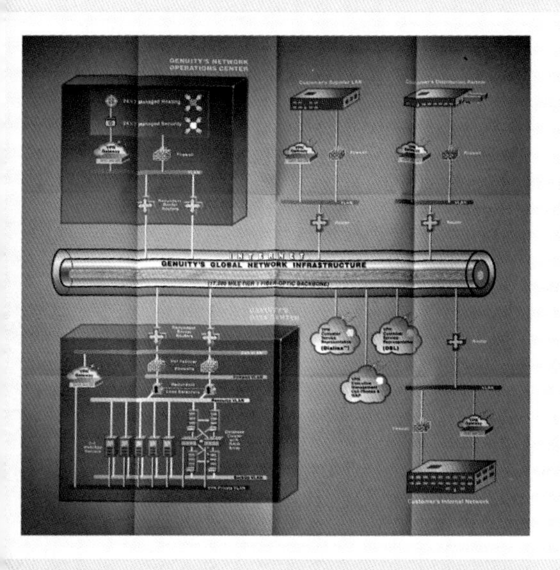

BOY, *is this going to need*
A CATCHY NAME.

Genuity's *Black Rocket*™ is a revolutionary eBusiness Network Platform that combines critical network services with our own high-speed, Tier 1, fiber-optic global network into a single, secure, scalable foundation on which to run your applications. It integrates Managed Web Hosting, Access, Transport and Security into one ready-to-launch package. Reducing the complexity, time and cost of building and deploying your eBusiness initiatives.

But if you checked out the schematic to the left, you probably already know that.

Genuity's *Black Rocket*™ also gives you single-source accountability. Once your eBusiness is up and running, Black Rocket™ provides a secure, managed and resilient environment with 24/7 technical support and proactive monitoring in Genuity's state-of-the-art Network Operations Center. All backed by a comprehensive Service Level Agreement assuring uptime.

Of course, there are some things you can't see in a schematic. Like our "Rocket Engineers" who can provide a strategic plan for launching your eBusiness initiatives, so that your project runs smoothly from the start. And by partnering with industry powerhouses for best-of-breed applications, systems integration and technologies, Genuity can deliver turnkey managed solutions to meet your needs.

Put this kind of thinking to work on your eBusiness. Visit genuity.com/blackrocket or call 1-800-GENUITY.

Black Rocket™ is Genuity's eBusiness Network Platform

A BRIEF HISTORY

BBN

In 1969, BBN was hired by the U.S. government to develop the ARPAnet, the forerunner of the Internet.

GTE

In 1997, BBN was acquired by GTE, the company that created our high-speed, 17,500-mile, Tier 1, fiber-optic network.

GENUITY

In 2000, GTE Internetworking became an independent company, renaming itself Genuity. Today, we offer a vast array of managed Internet services, including Black Rocket™

We have a
17,500-mile, TIER 1 NETWORK,
billion-dollar partners and something else you wouldn't expect from an Internet company.

A HISTORY.

Leading suppliers of managed Internet infrastructure and services don't just spring up overnight. So where did we come from?

Initially, we were known as a research and development company called BBN. As BBN, we developed what would become the Internet, then went on to establish a number of other firsts. The first router, the first e-mail message sent over a network, the first packet network encryption technology and more.

Years later, GTE acquired BBN and invested billions of dollars to expand their existing infrastructure into a 17,500-mile, Tier 1, fiber-optic global network.

This powerhouse of Internet services was spun off from GTE last year, and today we're a billion-dollar company known as Genuity.

Innovation is in our blood. And now we've combined our expertise in Web Hosting, Internet Access, Transport and Security into a scalable and secure, ready-to-launch eBusiness Network Platform called *Black Rocket*.™ Our team of "Rocket Engineers" can ensure your project runs smoothly from the start, allowing you to reduce the time, cost and complexity of building and deploying eBusiness.

Put our 30 years of experience to work on your eBusiness. Visit www.genuity.com/blackrocket or call 1-800-GENUITY.

Black Rocket™ is Genuity's eBusiness Network Platform

A BRIEF HISTORY

BBN

In 1969, BBN was hired by the U.S. government to develop the ARPAnet, the forerunner of the Internet.

GTE

In 1997, BBN was acquired by GTE, the company that created our high-speed, 17,500-mile, Tier 1, fiber-optic network.

GENUITY

In 2000, GTE Internetworking became an independent company, renaming itself Genuity. Today, we offer a vast array of managed Internet services, including Black Rocket.™

GENUITY™

In 1969, we worked on a
SECRET GOVERNMENT PROJECT
that became the Internet.

OHHH, SO THAT'S WHY NOBODY KNOWS WHO WE ARE!

Back in the '60s a small band of computer whizzes was hired by the Department of Defense to work on the ARPAnet. Or what is commonly known as the forerunner to the Internet. These visionaries came from the legendary research and development company, BBN.

Government work being what it is, there wasn't a lot of publicity.

Their work did, however, yield many firsts. The first router. The first sent e-mail message. The first network packet encryption technology and more.

Years later GTE acquired BBN and invested billions to expand their existing infrastructure into a 17,500-mile, Tier 1, fiber-optic global network.

Spun off from GTE last year, this powerhouse of Internet services is known today as Genuity. With Data Centers located around the world and Network Operations Centers continually monitoring security and bandwidth for serious eBusinesses everywhere.

Innovation is in our blood. And now we've combined our expertise in Web Hosting, Internet Access, Transport and Security into an integrated eBusiness Network Platform called *Black Rocket*.™ Our "Rocket Engineers" can ensure your project runs smoothly from the start, allowing you to reduce the cost and complexity of building and deploying eBusiness.

To put our 30 years of experience to work on your eBusiness, visit www.genuity.com/blackrocket or call 1-800-GENUITY.

Black Rocket™ is Genuity's eBusiness Network Platform

A BRIEF HISTORY

BBN

In 1969, BBN was hired by the U.S. government to develop the ARPAnet, the forerunner of the Internet.

GTE

In 1997, BBN was acquired by GTE, the company that created our high-speed, 17,500-mile, Tier 1, fiber-optic network.

GENUITY

In 2000, GTE Internetworking became an independent company, renaming itself Genuity. Today, we offer a vast array of managed Internet services, including Black Rocket™

GENUITY™

ART DIRECTORS
Toygar Bazarkaya
Chris Poulin

WRITERS
Ted Jendrysik
George Goetz

PHOTOGRAPHERS
Mark Hooper
Bruce Peterson
Stock

CREATIVE DIRECTORS
Chris Poulin
George Goetz

CLIENT
Genuity

AGENCY
Mullen/Wenham

02332A

MERIT AWARD
TRADE B/W OR COLOR
ANY SIZE: CAMPAIGN

ART DIRECTOR
Daryl Gardiner

WRITER
Kevin Rathgeber

PHOTOGRAPHER
Mark Montizambert

CREATIVE DIRECTOR
Randy Stein

CLIENT
Docusystems

AGENCY
Palmer Jarvis DDB/Vancouver

02333A

Also won:
MERIT AWARD
TRADE COLOR
FULL PAGE OR SPREAD: SINGLE

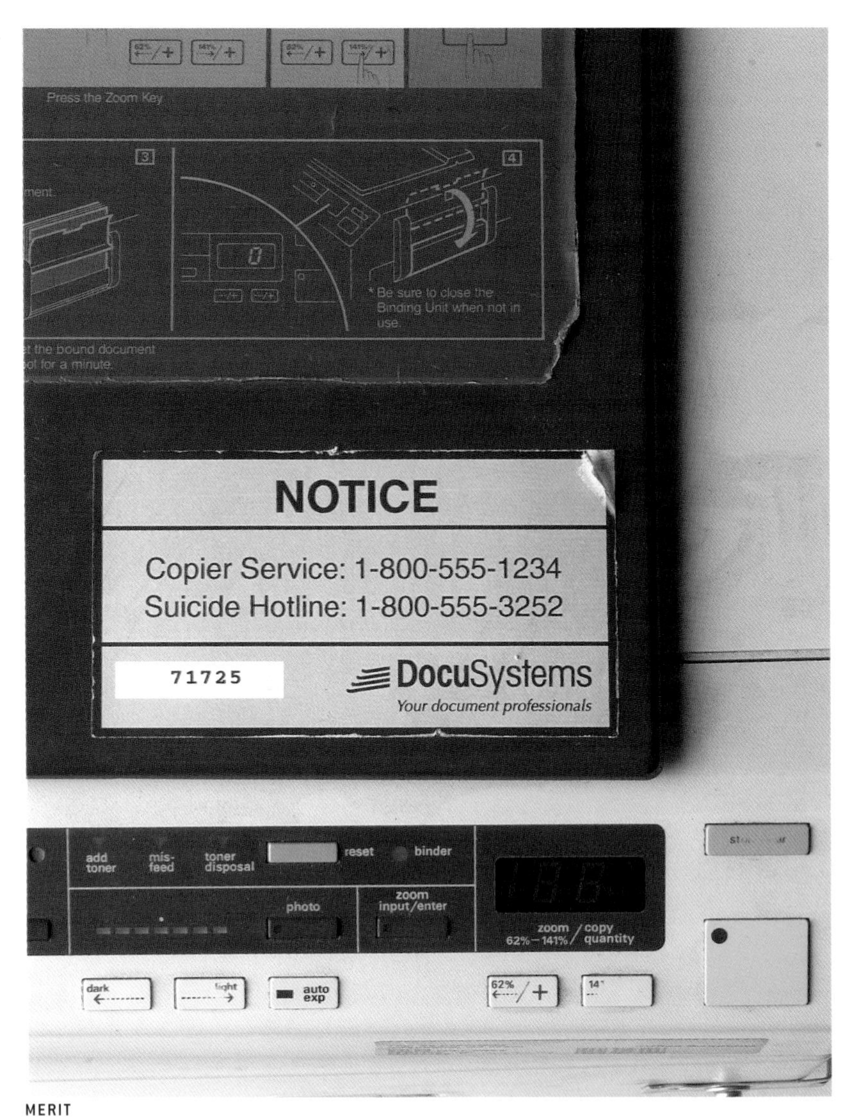

MERIT

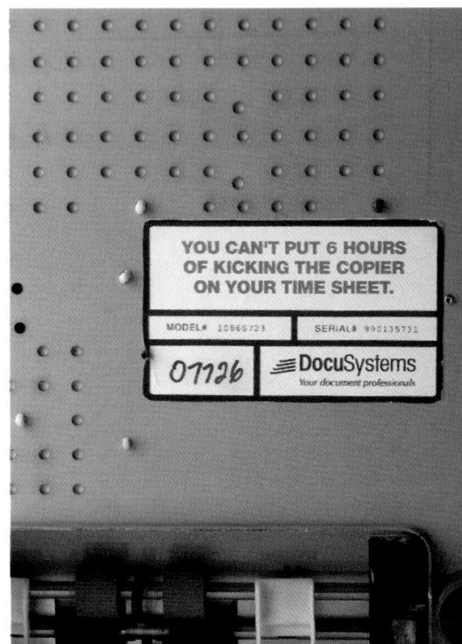

PRINT MERIT

MERIT AWARD
TRADE B/W OR COLOR
ANY SIZE: CAMPAIGN

ART DIRECTOR
Kyle Mitchell

WRITER
Robin Fitzgerald

PHOTOGRAPHER
Michael Ruppert

CREATIVE DIRECTORS
Jean Robaire
Sally Hogshead

CLIENT
Michael Ruppert Studios

AGENCY
Robaire and Hogshead/
Los Angeles

02323A

MERIT AWARD
TRADE B/W OR COLOR
ANY SIZE: CAMPAIGN

ART DIRECTOR
Simon Yeo

WRITER
Srinath Mogeri

ILLUSTRATOR
Invy Ng

PHOTOGRAPHER
Eric Seow

CREATIVE DIRECTOR
Sion Scott-Wilson

CLIENT
Civil Aviation
Authority of Singapore

AGENCY
Saatchi & Saatchi/Singapore

02334A

Also won:
MERIT AWARD
TRADE COLOR
FULL PAGE OR SPREAD: SINGLE

MERIT

MERIT AWARD
TRADE B/W OR COLOR
ANY SIZE: CAMPAIGN

ART DIRECTOR
Lance Martin

WRITER
Michael Mayes

PHOTOGRAPHER
Shin Sugino

CREATIVE DIRECTORS
Zak Mroueh
Paul Lavoie

CLIENT
Marketing Awards

AGENCY
Taxi/Toronto

02335A

MERIT AWARD
TRADE B/W OR COLOR
ANY SIZE: CAMPAIGN

ART DIRECTOR
Denis Kakazu Kushiyama

WRITERS
Carlos Fonseca
Luiz Antonio Fleury

PHOTOGRAPHER
Ale Ermel

CREATIVE DIRECTORS
Tiao Bernardi
Rita Corradi
J.R. D'Elboux

CLIENT
About

AGENCY
Young & Rubicam/São Paulo

02336A

MERIT AWARD
COLLATERAL: POINT OF PURCHASE AND IN-STORE

ART DIRECTOR
Joseph Tay

WRITERS
James Lim
Ali Shabaz

PHOTOGRAPHERS
Teo Studio
Procolor

CLIENT
Bayer S.E.A

AGENCY
BBDO/Singapore

02337A

Baygon Ant Bait Station

Today I thought about
all I had achieved in life.
It wasn't much.
A hard day calls for a hard lemonade.
mike's hard lemonade
MAKE IT MIKE'S.

MERIT AWARD
COLLATERAL: POINT OF PURCHASE AND IN-STORE

ART DIRECTOR
Taras Wayner

WRITER
Richard Bullock

CREATIVE DIRECTOR
Eric Silver

CLIENT
Mike's Hard Lemonade

AGENCY
Cliff Freeman and Partners/
New York

02338A

MERIT AWARD
COLLATERAL: POINT OF PURCHASE AND IN-STORE

ART DIRECTOR
Clare Lim

WRITER
Raymond Ng

PHOTOGRAPHERS
Raymond Sih
IFL Studio

CREATIVE DIRECTOR
Edwin Leong

CLIENT
Nike

AGENCY
Grey Worldwide/
Kuala Lumpur

02340A

MERIT AWARD
COLLATERAL: POINT OF PURCHASE AND IN-STORE

ART DIRECTOR
Clare Lim

WRITER
Raymond Ng

PHOTOGRAPHERS
Raymond Sih
IFL Studio

CREATIVE DIRECTOR
Edwin Leong

CLIENT
Nike

AGENCY
Grey Worldwide/
Kuala Lumpur

02341A

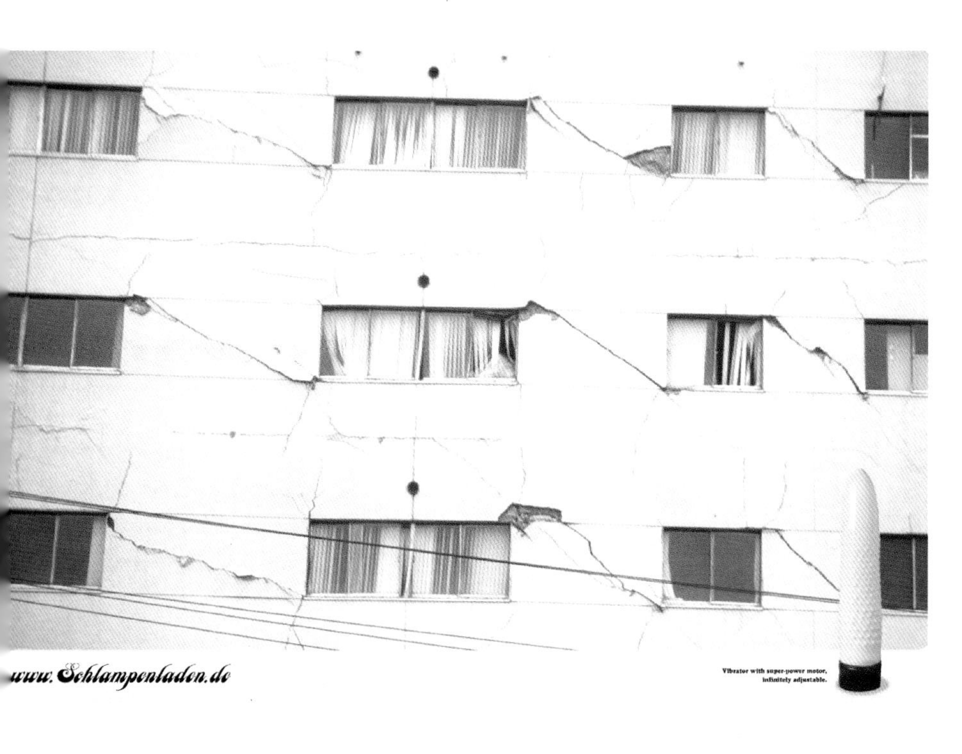

MERIT AWARD
COLLATERAL: POINT OF PURCHASE AND IN-STORE

ART DIRECTOR
Evi Nern

WRITER
Anna Kohlhaupt

PHOTOGRAPHERS
Stock
Joachim Bacherl

CREATIVE DIRECTORS
Anna Kohlhaupt
Patrick They

CLIENT
Schlampenladen

AGENCY
Ogilvy & Mather/Frankfurt

02342A

**MERIT AWARD
COLLATERAL: POINT OF
PURCHASE AND IN-STORE**

ART DIRECTOR
Himanshu Save

WRITER
K.S. Gopal

ILLUSTRATOR
Himanshu Save

CREATIVE DIRECTOR
K.S. Gopal

CLIENT
Toshiba India

AGENCY
Quadrant Communications/
Mumbai

02343A

**MERIT AWARD
COLLATERAL: POINT OF
PURCHASE AND IN-STORE**

ART DIRECTOR
Laura Hauseman

WRITER
Al Jackson

PHOTOGRAPHER
Parrish Kohanim

CREATIVE DIRECTOR
Bart Cleveland

CLIENT
Ellicott City Infiniti

AGENCY
Sawyer Riley Compton/Atlanta

02344A

MERIT AWARD
COLLATERAL: POINT OF PURCHASE AND IN-STORE

ART DIRECTOR
Greg Sheppard

ILLUSTRATOR
Greg Sheppard

PHOTOGRAPHER
Janyon Boschoff

CREATIVE DIRECTORS
Sandra de Witt
Chris Garbutt

CLIENT
BMW X5

AGENCY
TBWA Hunt Lascaris/
Johannesburg

02345A

MERIT AWARD
COLLATERAL: POINT OF PURCHASE AND IN-STORE

ART DIRECTOR
Jeremy Pippenger

WRITER
Jeremy Pippenger

CREATIVE DIRECTOR
Tom Gianfagna

CLIENT
Blue Note Music

AGENCY
Tom Gianfagna Inc./New York

02339A

MERIT AWARD
COLLATERAL: SELF-PROMOTION

ART DIRECTOR
Jean Robaire

WRITER
Robin Fitzgerald

PHOTOGRAPHER
Michael Ruppert

CREATIVE DIRECTOR
Jean Robaire

CLIENT
a.k.a.Robaire

AGENCY
a.k.a.Robaire/Los Angeles

02348A

MERIT AWARD
COLLATERAL: SELF-PROMOTION

ART DIRECTOR
Xavier Beauregard

WRITER
Vincent Pedrocchi

PHOTOGRAPHER
Thibault Montanat

CREATIVE DIRECTOR
Olivier Altmann

CLIENT
BDDP et Fils

AGENCY
BDDP et Fils/
Boulogne Billancourt

02350A

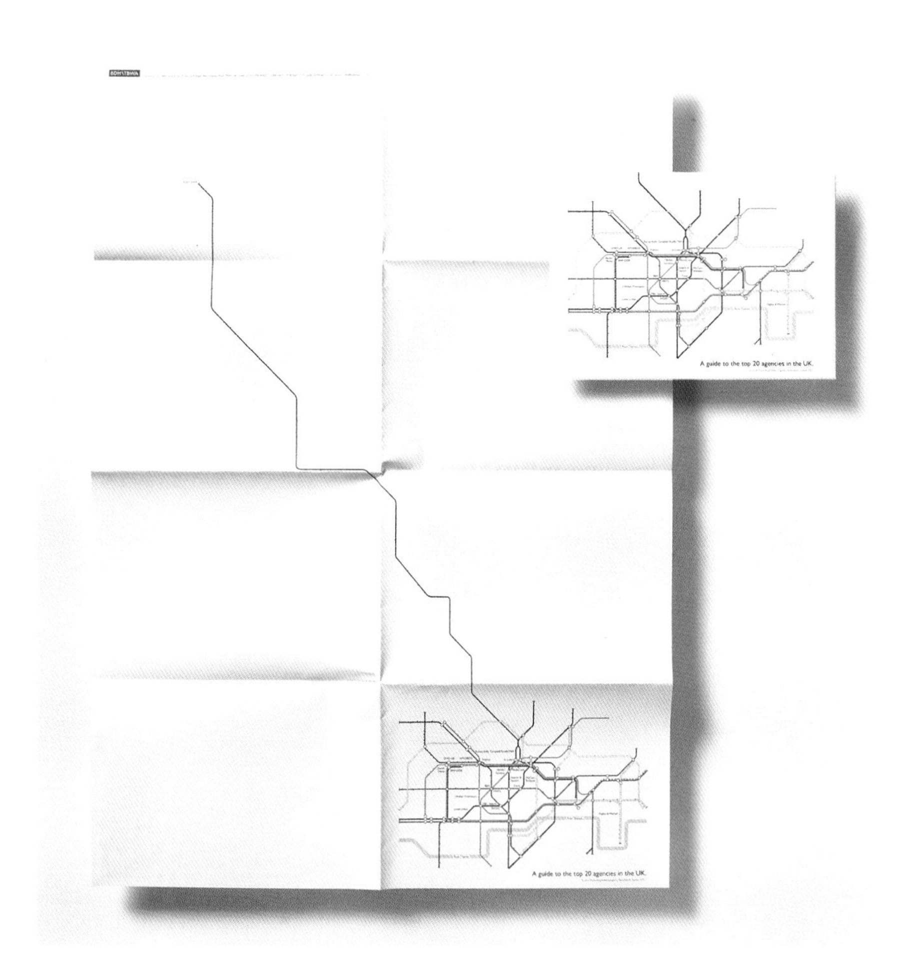

MERIT AWARD
COLLATERAL: SELF-PROMOTION

ART DIRECTOR
Lynton Hemsley

WRITER
Jeremy Clark

ILLUSTRATOR
Debra Leeson

CREATIVE DIRECTOR
Danny Brooke-Taylor

CLIENT
BDH\TBWA

AGENCY
BDH\TBWA/Manchester

02351A

MERIT AWARD
COLLATERAL: SELF-PROMOTION

ART DIRECTOR
Stephen Goldblatt

WRITER
Ryan Ebner

PHOTOGRAPHER
Brian Mahaney

CREATIVE DIRECTORS
John Butler
Mike Shine

CLIENT
Butler Shine & Stern

AGENCY
Butler Shine & Stern/Sausalito

02352A

MERIT AWARD
COLLATERAL: SELF-PROMOTION

ART DIRECTOR
David Stone

WRITER
David Stone

CREATIVE DIRECTOR
David Stone

CLIENT
David Stone

AGENCY
David Stone Copywriting/
Broomfield

02353A

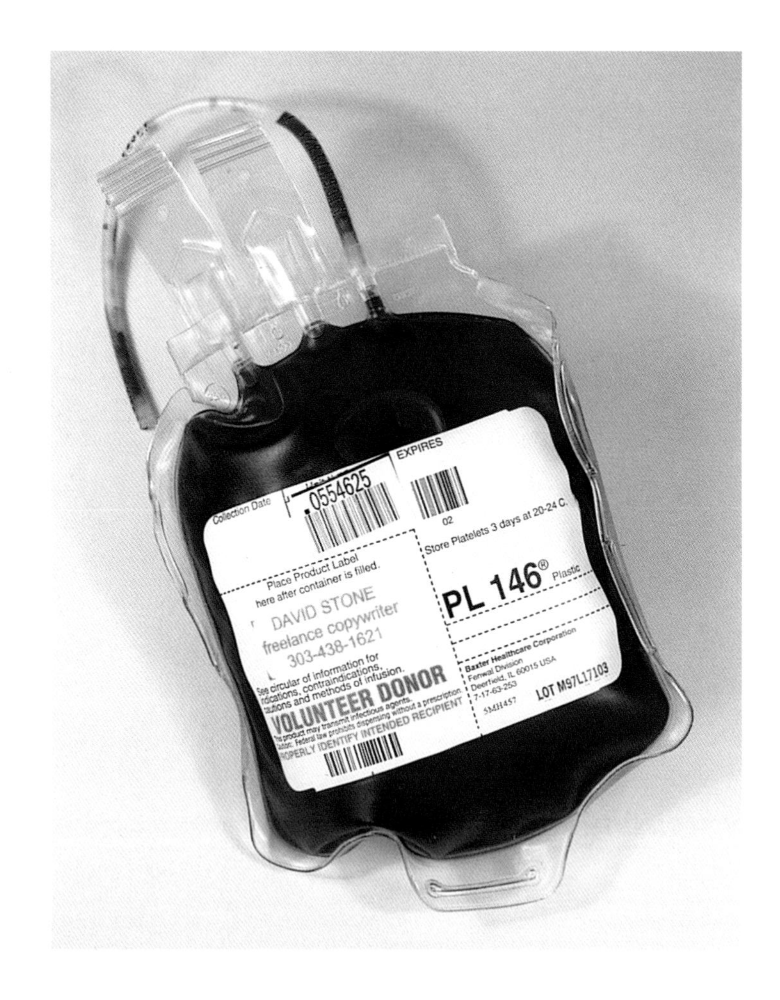

MERIT AWARD
COLLATERAL: SELF-PROMOTION

ART DIRECTOR
Jon Loke

WRITER
Victor Ng

CLIENT
Victor Ng

AGENCY
Leo Burnett/Singapore

02357A

ONE SHOW ENTRY LABEL

For Office Use Only

Please complete labels in duplicate. Tape one to the back of your entry. Attach the other so it can be easily removed. All information should be typed. Credits will be listed in both our Awards Program and One Show Annual exactly as they appear here.

Category 5B (Self-Promotion)
Include Category Number, Letter and Title

Contact Victor Ng

Agency

Address 33 Pekin Street, #03-01 Far East Square

City Singapore State - Zip 048763

Phone (65) 236 1855

Fax (65) 532 2090

Email victor_ng_copywriter@yahoo.com

Client Victor Ng

Title of Commercial(s) Victor Ng

This was sent to creative directors of top agencies two weeks before the One Show deadline.

TAKE YOUR CHILDREN TO WORK DAY
LOWE LINTAS & PARTNERS, THURSDAY, APRIL 26

MERIT AWARD
COLLATERAL: SELF-PROMOTION

ART DIRECTOR
Rebecca Peterson

WRITER
Stephen Lundberg

PHOTOGRAPHER
Rebecca Peterson

CREATIVE DIRECTORS
Gary Goldsmith
Dean Hacohen

CLIENT
Lowe Lintas & Partners

AGENCY
Lowe/New York

02354A

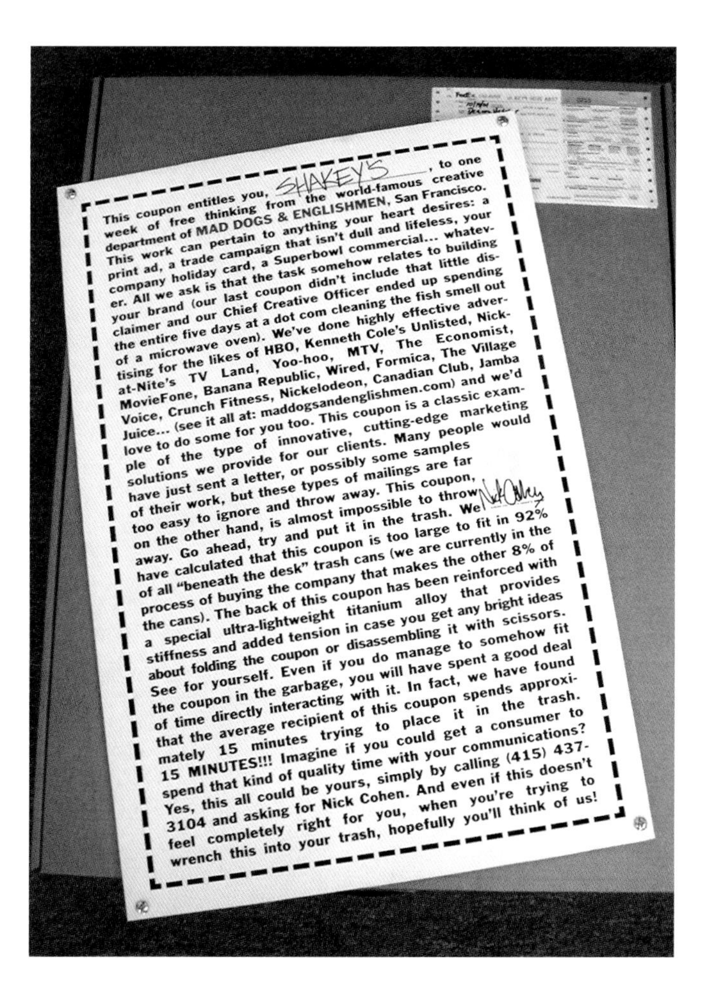

MERIT AWARD
COLLATERAL: SELF-PROMOTION

ART DIRECTOR
Nick Cohen

WRITER
Deacon Webster

CREATIVE DIRECTOR
Nick Cohen

CLIENT
Mad Dogs & Englishmen/
San Francisco

AGENCY
Mad Dogs & Englishmen/
San Francisco

02355A

MERIT AWARD
COLLATERAL: SELF-PROMOTION

ART DIRECTOR
Bob Gates

WRITER
Jim Hagar

CREATIVE DIRECTOR
Jim Hagar

CLIENT
Mullen

AGENCY
Mullen/Wenham

02356A

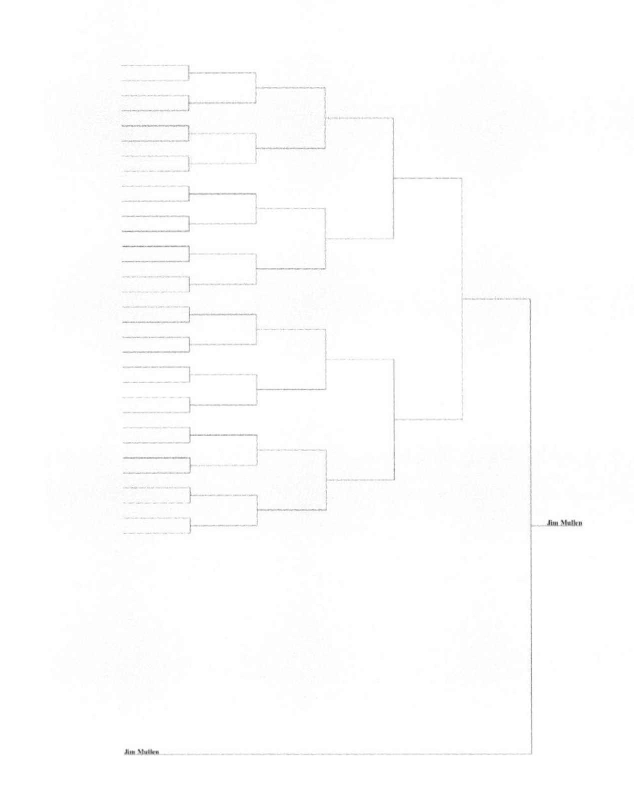

MERIT AWARD
COLLATERAL: SELF-PROMOTION

ART DIRECTORS
Kyle Mitchell
Jean Robaire

WRITERS
Robin Fitzgerald
Sally Hogshead

CREATIVE DIRECTORS
Jean Robaire
Sally Hogshead

CLIENT
Robaire and Hogshead

AGENCY
Robaire and Hogshead/
Los Angeles

02349A

MERIT AWARD
COLLATERAL: SELF-PROMOTION

ART DIRECTORS
Nick Hunziker
Rodrigo Butori
Kimberly Wright
Bret Ridgeway

WRITER
Andrew Simon

CREATIVE DIRECTORS
Matt Bogen
Bret Ridgeway
Damon Webster

CLIENT
Saatchi & Saatchi

AGENCY
Saatchi & Saatchi/Torrance

02358A

MERIT AWARD
COLLATERAL: POSTERS
SINGLE

ART DIRECTOR
Eric Goldstein

WRITER
Tor Myhren

PHOTOGRAPHER
Wendy Lynch

CREATIVE DIRECTOR
Tracy Wong

CLIENT
Belding Awards

AGENCY
WONGDOODY/Seattle

02359A

Also won:
MERIT AWARD
ONE SHOW DESIGN
DIRECT MAIL

MERIT AWARD
COLLATERAL: POSTERS
SINGLE

ART DIRECTORS
Ron Smrczek
Mark Scott

WRITER
Brian Howlett

PHOTOGRAPHER
Stock

CREATIVE DIRECTOR
Brian Howlett

CLIENT
Labatt Breweries

AGENCY
Axmith McIntyre Wicht/
Toronto

02360A

MERIT AWARD
COLLATERAL: POSTERS
SINGLE

ART DIRECTOR
Kevin Thoem

WRITER
Al Jackson

PHOTOGRAPHER
Mark Wiens

CREATIVE DIRECTORS
Kevin Thoem
Al Jackson

CLIENT
Go With the Flow

AGENCY
Bubba's Deli/Roswell

02362A

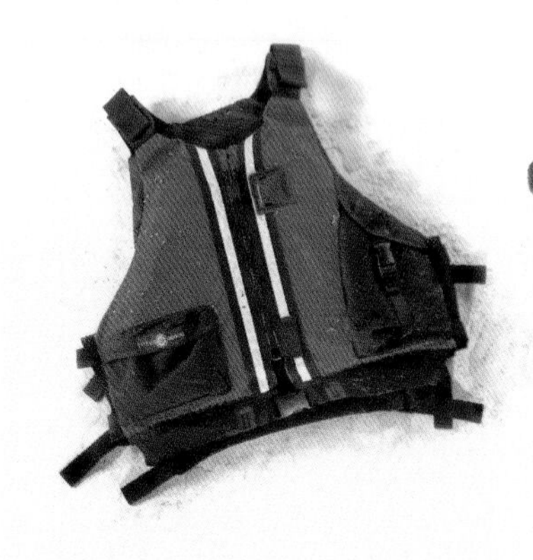

MERIT AWARD
COLLATERAL: POSTERS
SINGLE

ART DIRECTOR
Mariana Sá

WRITER
Manir Fadel

PHOTOGRAPHER
Richard Kohout

CLIENT
Antarctica/Malzbier

AGENCY
DM9 DDB Publicidade/
São Paulo

02363A

MERIT AWARD
COLLATERAL: POSTERS
SINGLE

ART DIRECTOR
Steve Driggs

WRITER
Greg Hahn

PHOTOGRAPHER
Lou Capozzola

CREATIVE DIRECTOR
David Lubars

CLIENT
Sports Illustrated

AGENCY
Fallon/Minneapolis

02364A

MERIT AWARD
COLLATERAL: POSTERS
SINGLE

ART DIRECTORS
Gavin Simpson
Sonal Dabral

WRITERS
Paul Lim
Sonal Dabral

PHOTOGRAPHER
Thomas/Barney Studio

CREATIVE DIRECTOR
Sonal Dabral

CLIENT
Guinness Anchor Berhad

AGENCY
Ogilvy & Mather/
Kuala Lumpur

02368A

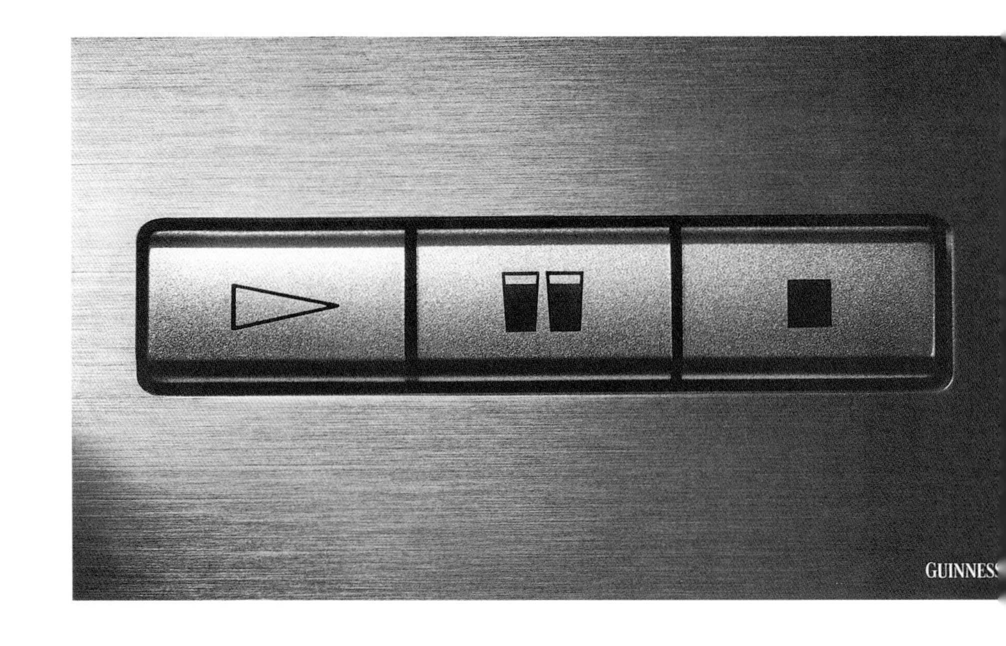

MERIT AWARD
COLLATERAL: POSTERS
SINGLE

ART DIRECTOR
Marcos Reyes

WRITER
Holguer Ortiz

PHOTOGRAPHER
Flavio Bizzarri

CREATIVE DIRECTOR
Carlos Tornell

CLIENT
Mattel Matchbox

AGENCY
Ogilvy & Mather/Mexico City

02367A

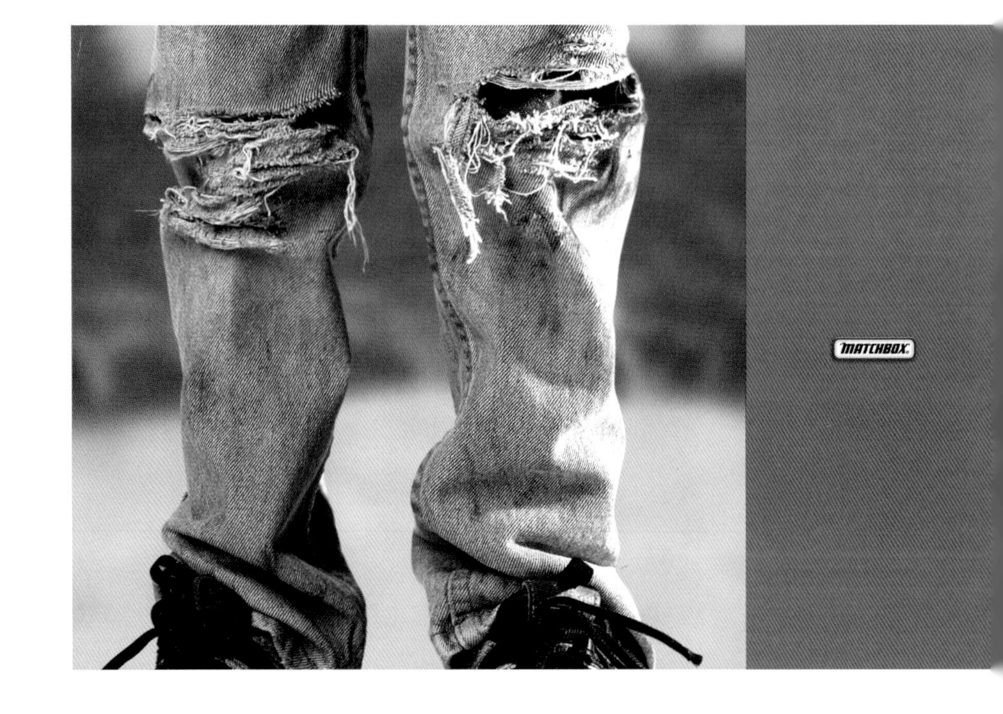

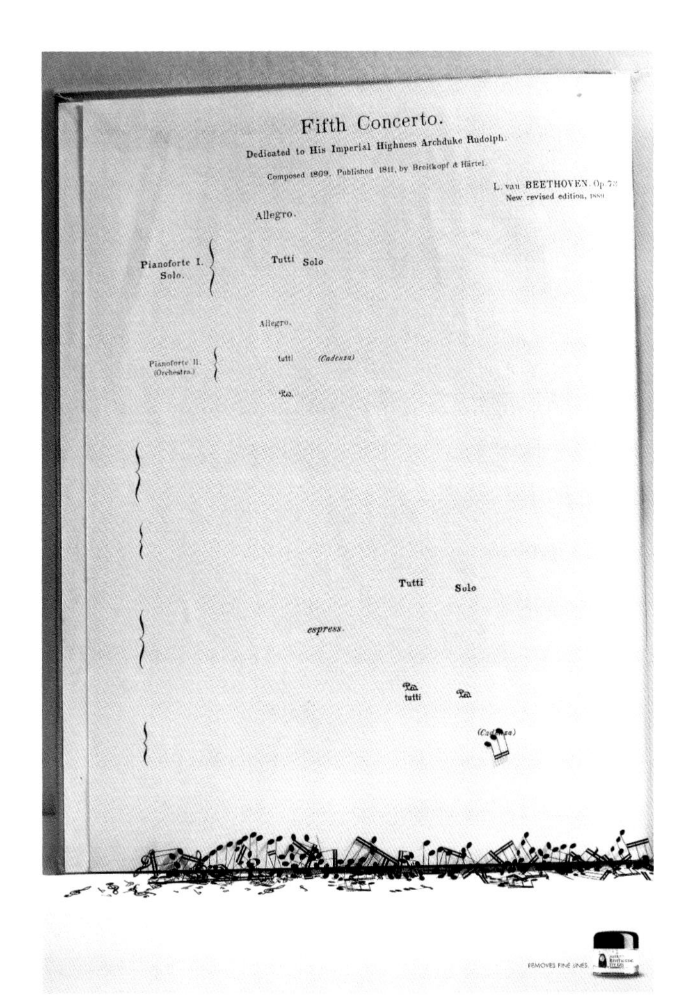

MERIT AWARD
COLLATERAL: POSTERS
SINGLE

ART DIRECTOR
Loh Chan Wai

WRITER
Loh Chan Wai

PHOTOGRAPHERS
Edmund Leong
Barney Studio

CREATIVE DIRECTOR
Edmund Choe

CLIENT
Procter & Gamble Malaysia

AGENCY
Saatchi & Saatchi/Petaling Jaya

02372A

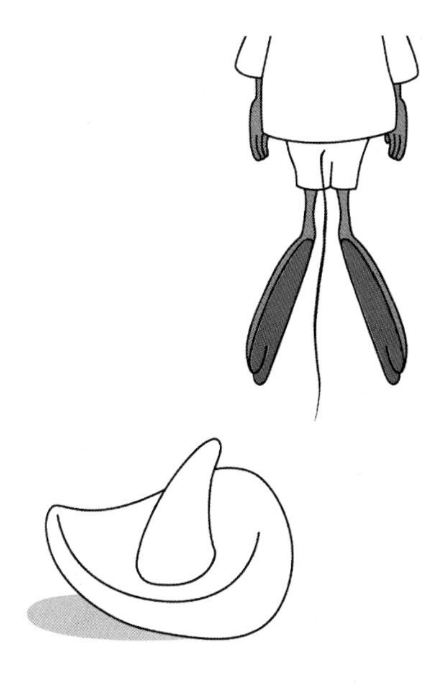

MERIT AWARD
COLLATERAL: POSTERS
SINGLE

ART DIRECTOR
Boris Schwiedrzik

WRITER
Helge Bloeck

CREATIVE DIRECTOR
Christoph Klingler

CLIENT
Kawasaki Motoren GmbH

AGENCY
TBWA/Berlin

02373A

PRINT MERIT

MERIT AWARD
COLLATERAL: POSTERS
CAMPAIGN

ART DIRECTOR
Tom Cheevers

WRITER
Erik Johnson

PHOTOGRAPHER
Jon Deshler

CREATIVE DIRECTORS
Tom Cheevers
Erik Johnson

CLIENT
NEVCO

AGENCY
Cheevers/Portland

02378A

PRINT MERIT

MERIT AWARD
COLLATERAL: POSTERS
CAMPAIGN

ART DIRECTORS
Dave Heytman
Mandy Kennedy

WRITERS
Oliver Devaris
Charlie Cook

PHOTOGRAPHER
Julian Wolkenstein

CREATIVE DIRECTOR
Tom McFarlane

CLIENT
National Gallery

AGENCY
M&C Saatchi/Sydney

02380A

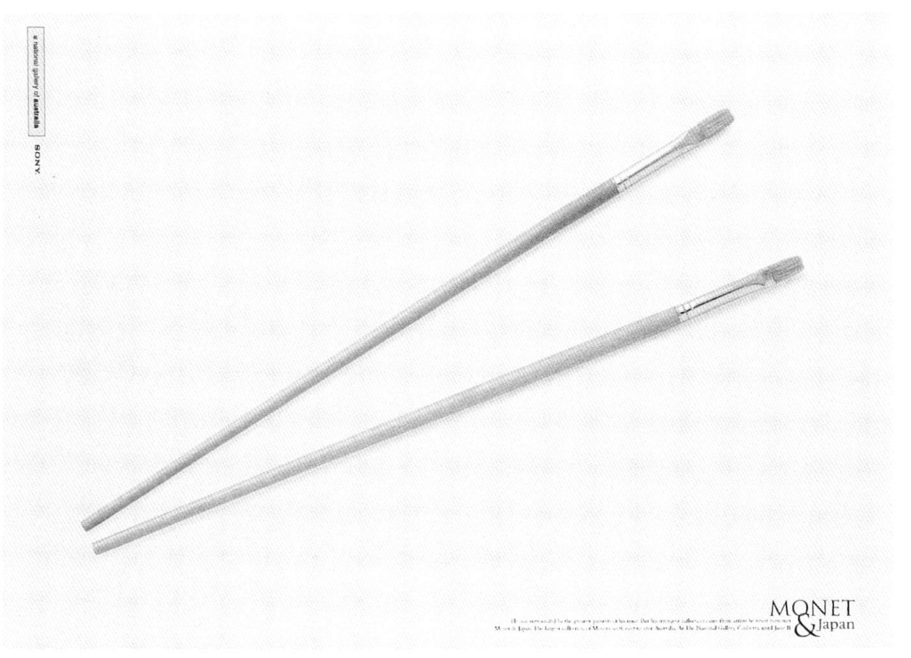

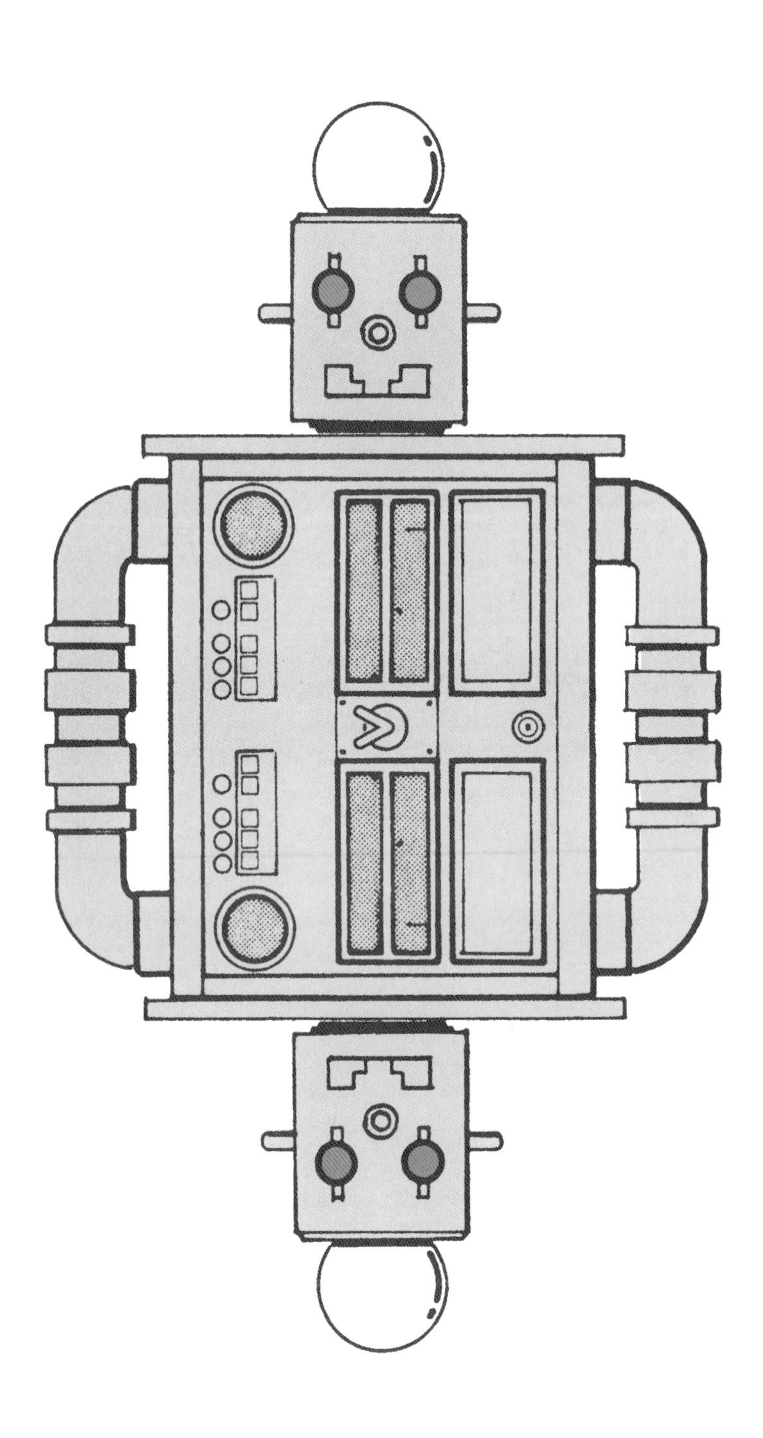

DESIGN MERITS

a. The word *robot* comes from the Czech *robota* which means obligatory work or servitude.
b. The term was coined by Karel Capek in 1917, it was first used in his short story "Opilec".
c. In March 2001, Sandia Laboratories engineered a robot that jumped 29.5 feet in the air.
d. At Cynthia's Cyberbar in London, England, two 7-ft. robots named Cynthia and Rastus can mix 75 different cocktails. They can even choose the glass and pour the drink.
e. In 1999, Mitsubishi Heavy Industries of Japan developed a series of robotic fish.
f. The world's smallest robot is the Monsieur microbot, at .06 in. high it weighs only .05 oz.

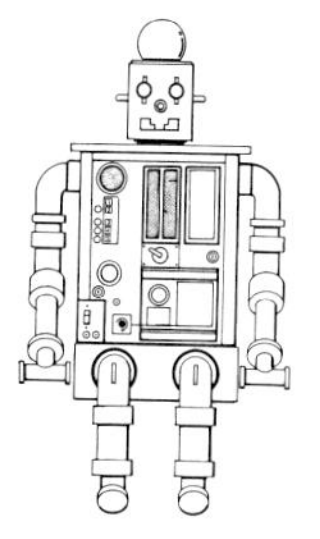

MERIT AWARD
ANNUAL REPORT

DESIGNER
Dawn Selg

WRITER
Gayle Thorsen

ILLUSTRATOR
Lisa Franke

CREATIVE DIRECTOR
David Whitman

CLIENT
The McKnight Foundation

AGENCY
Agency Eleven/Minneapolis

02032D

MERIT AWARD
ANNUAL REPORT

DESIGNER
Bob Dinetz

ART DIRECTORS
Bill Cahan
Bob Dinetz

WRITER
Frank Schwere

PHOTOGRAPHERS
David Stolberg
Bob Dinetz

CREATIVE DIRECTOR
Bill Cahan

CLIENT
Gartner

AGENCY
Cahan & Associates/
San Francisco

02033D

DICK BECK
Senior Vice President
& CFO

リチャードP.ベック
上級副社長
最高財務責任者
970/407-6204

www.advanced-energy.com

AE ADVANCED ENERGY®

Advanced Energy Industries.Inc.
米国コロラド州フォートコリンズ市
シャープポイント1625番地〒80525
代表番号：970/221-4670
ファックス：970/407-5204

It's like having the wind at your back.

MERIT AWARD
ANNUAL REPORT

DESIGNER
Michael Braley

ART DIRECTORS
Bill Cahan
Michael Braley

WRITERS
Thom Elkjer
Michael Braley

PHOTOGRAPHERS
Jock McDonald
Graham MacIndoe

CREATIVE DIRECTOR
Bill Cahan

CLIENT
Silicon Valley National Bank

AGENCY
Cahan & Associates/
San Francisco

02034D

MERIT AWARD
ANNUAL REPORT

DESIGNER
Robert Kastigar

ART DIRECTOR
Robert Kastigar

WRITER
Rob Price

PHOTOGRAPHER
William Abranowicz

CREATIVE DIRECTORS
Paul Curtin
Rob Price

CLIENT
Williams Sonoma

AGENCY
Eleven/San Francisco

02035D

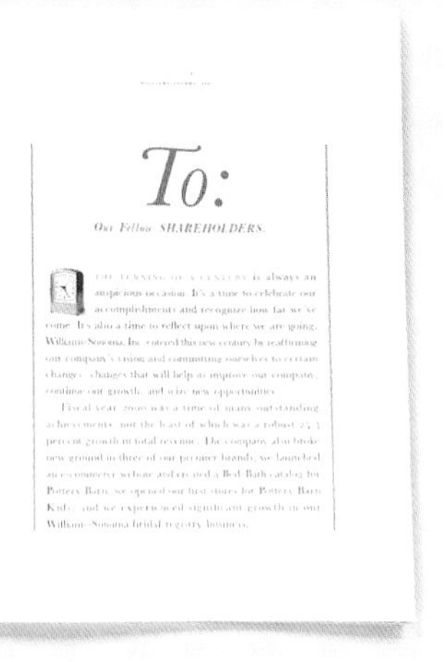

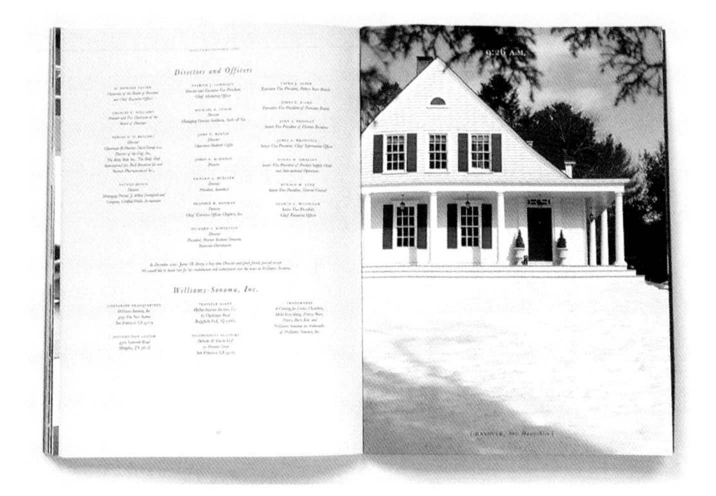

DESIGN MERIT

MERIT AWARD
ANNUAL REPORT

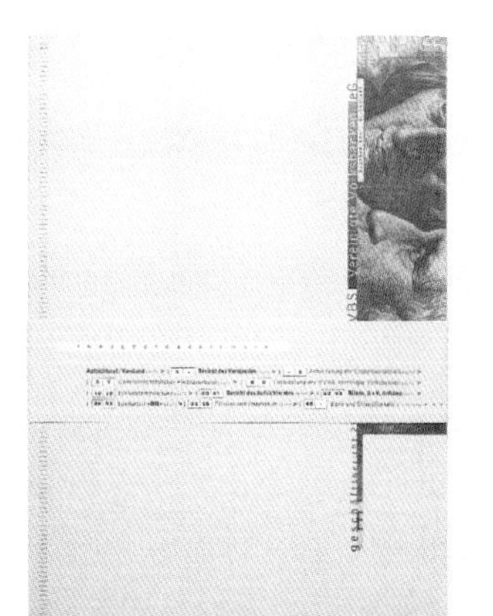

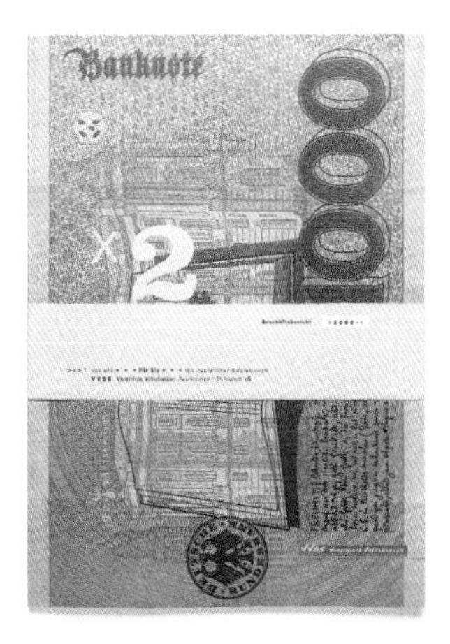

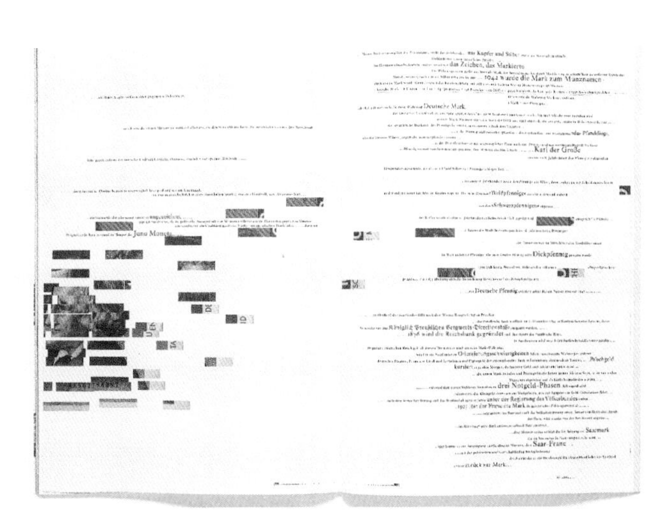

DESIGNER
Patrick Bittner

ART DIRECTOR
Patrick Bittner

WRITER
Germaine Paulus

PHOTOGRAPHERS
Andrew Wakeford
Patrick Bittner

CREATIVE DIRECTOR
Ivica Maksimovic

CLIENT
Vereinigte Volksbanken VVBS

AGENCY
Maksimovic & Partners/
Saarbrucken

02036D

MERIT AWARD
BOOKLET/BROCHURE

DESIGNER
Bob Goebel

WRITER
HoJo Willenzik

PHOTOGRAPHER
Victor John Penner

CREATIVE DIRECTORS
Carol Mack
David Whitman

CLIENT
Gage

AGENCY
Agency Eleven/Minneapolis

02037D

MERIT AWARD
BOOKLET/BROCHURE

DESIGNER
Kevin Grady

ART DIRECTOR
Kevin Grady

WRITERS
Rich Mackin
Kevin Grady

ILLUSTRATORS
Bates
Rich Mackin
Kevin Grady

CREATIVE DIRECTORS
Pete Favat
Alex Bogusky
Ron Lawner

CLIENT
American Legacy Foundation

AGENCY
Arnold Worldwide/Boston
and Crispin Porter & Bogusky/
Miami

02038D

DESIGN MERIT

MERIT AWARD BOOKLET/BROCHURE

DESIGNER
Gianfranco Cerro

ART DIRECTOR
Gianfranco Cerro

WRITER
Paula Gasparotto Chande

ILLUSTRATOR
Robson Romão

CREATIVE DIRECTOR
José Luiz Tavares

CLIENT
Coca-Cola

AGENCY
Bates Brasil/São Paulo

02039D

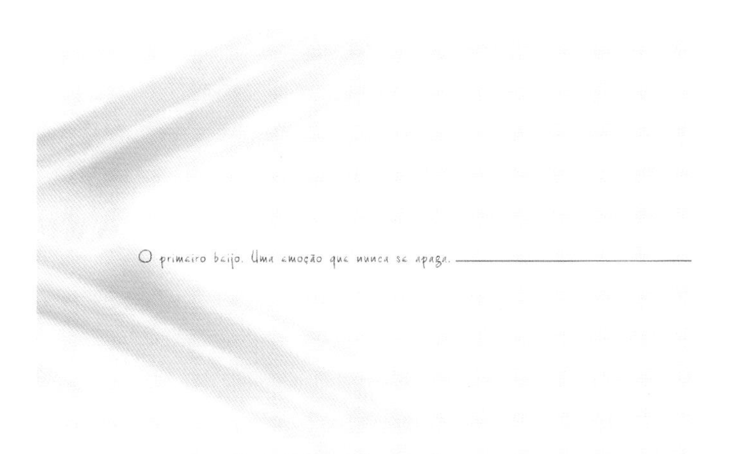

O primeiro beijo. Uma emoção que nunca se apaga.

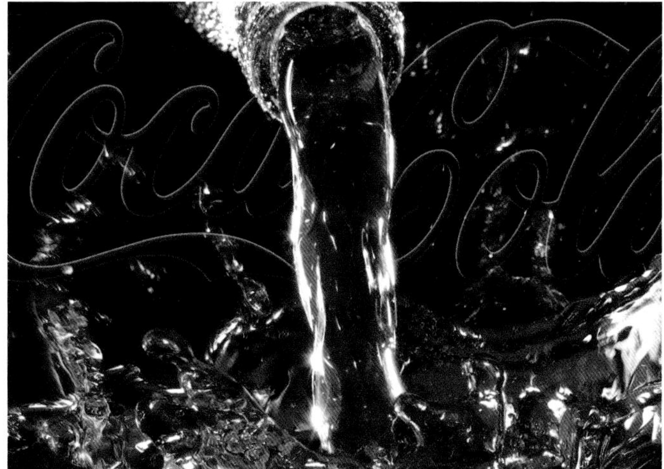

Lenny
Kravitz
Pela 1ª vez no Brasil exclusivo para você
A festa toda é um espetáculo.
Mas, nada melhor do que fechar
essa noite tão especial com um grande show.
Um encontro magico, liderado pela maior
revelação pop do cenário musical internacional.
Coca-Cola

MERIT AWARD
BOOKLET/BROCHURE

DESIGNER
Henry Yap

ART DIRECTOR
Henry Yap

WRITER
Szu-Hung Lee

CREATIVE DIRECTORS
Ean-Hwa Huang
Szu-Hung Lee

CLIENT
BBDO Malaysia

AGENCY
BBDO/Kuala Lumpur

02040D

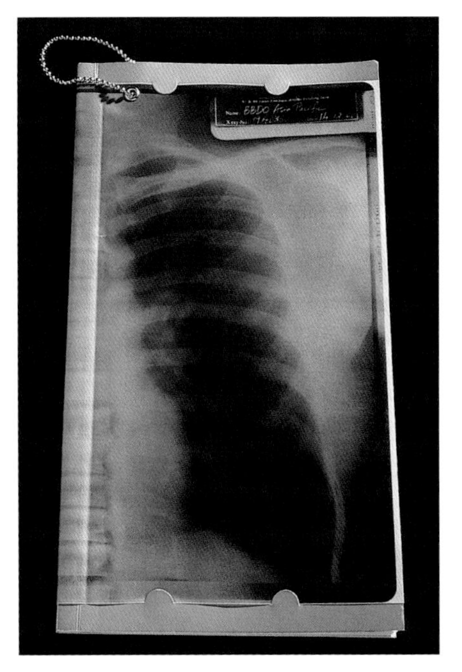

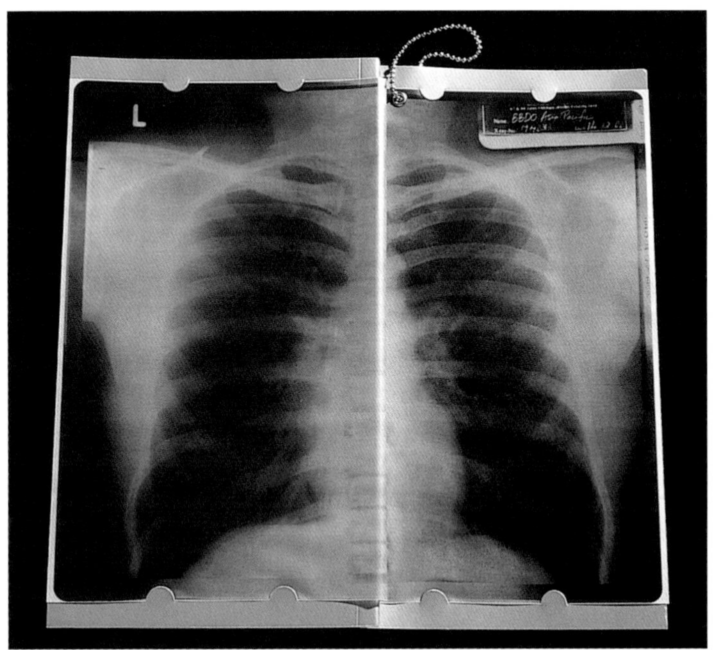

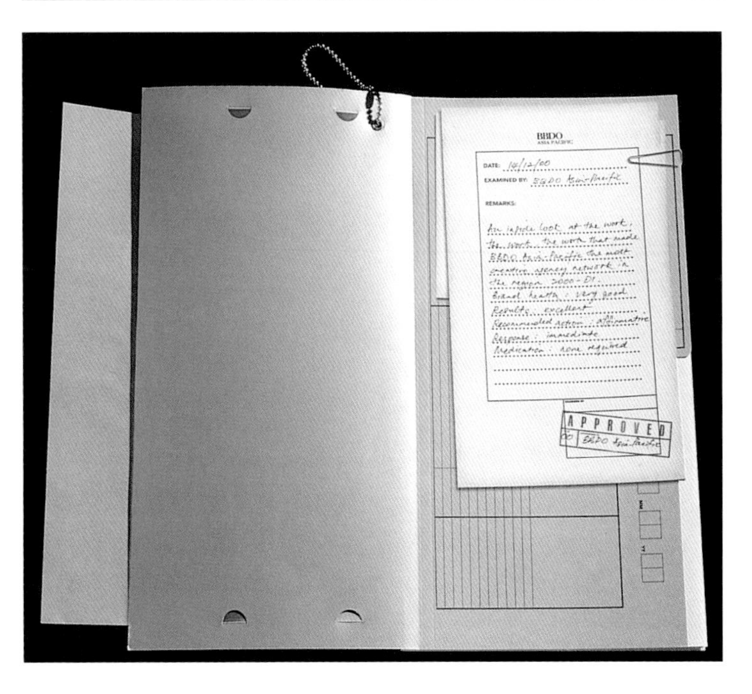

DESIGN MERIT

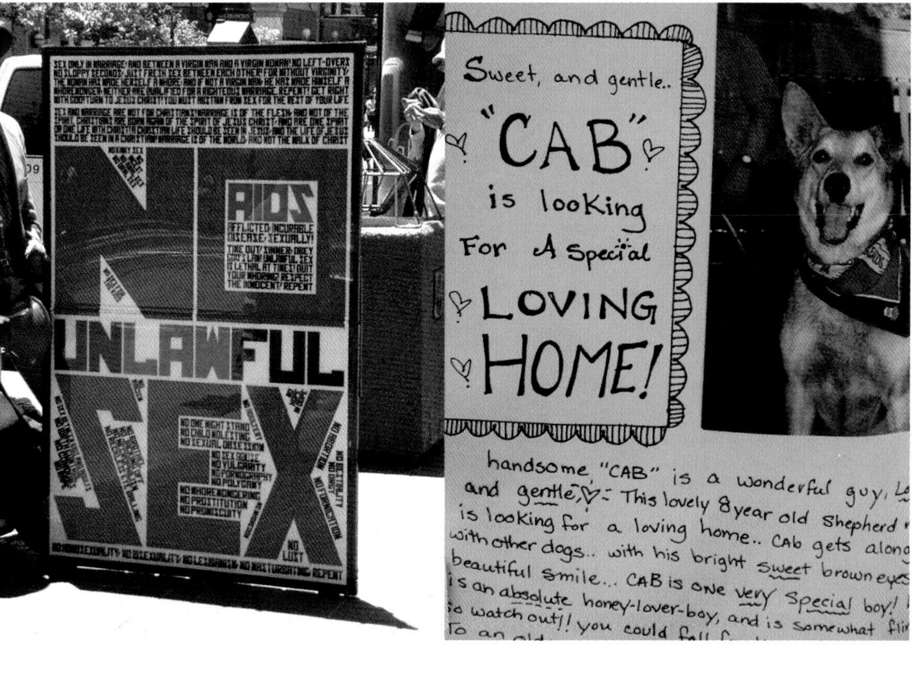

MERIT AWARD
BOOKLET/BROCHURE

DESIGNERS
Bob Dinetz
Michael Braley
Kevin Roberson
Sharrie Brooks
Gary Williams

ART DIRECTORS
Bill Cahan
Bob Dinetz
Michael Braley
Kevin Roberson
Sharrie Brooks
Gary Williams

WRITERS
Kevin Roberson
Bob Dinetz
Gary Williams

ILLUSTRATORS
Gary Williams
Bob Dinetz

PHOTOGRAPHERS
Bob Dinetz
Kevin Roberson
Sharrie Brooks

CREATIVE DIRECTOR
Bill Cahan

CLIENT
AIGA

AGENCY
Cahan & Associates/
San Francisco

02041D

MERIT AWARD
BOOKLET/BROCHURE

DESIGNER
Michael Braley

ART DIRECTORS
Bill Cahan
Michael Braley

WRITERS
David Stolberg
Suzanne Young

PHOTOGRAPHERS
Jock McDonald
Alan Powers

CREATIVE DIRECTOR
Bill Cahan

CLIENT
Stroock & Stroock & Lavan

AGENCY
Cahan & Associates/
San Francisco

02042D

MERIT AWARD
BOOKLET/BROCHURE

DESIGNER
Alyssa D'Arienzo Toro

ART DIRECTOR
Alyssa D'Arienzo Toro

WRITER
Steve Connelly

PHOTOGRAPHER
Paul Clancy

CREATIVE DIRECTOR
Alyssa D'Arienzo Toro

CLIENT
Druker A505

AGENCY
Connelly Partners/Boston

02043D

MERIT AWARD
BOOKLET/BROCHURE

DESIGNERS
Yael Eisele
Allison Williams

ART DIRECTOR
Allison Williams

WRITER
Laura Silverman

PHOTOGRAPHER
Gentyl and Hyers

CREATIVE DIRECTOR
Allison Williams

CLIENT
Takashimaya New York

AGENCY
Design: MW/New York

02044D

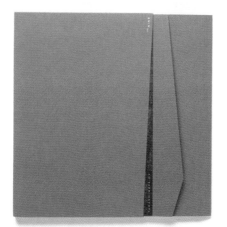

MERIT AWARD BOOKLET/BROCHURE

ART DIRECTOR
Jörg Bruns

PHOTOGRAPHER
René Staud Studios

CREATIVE DIRECTORS
Andreas Thomsen
Martin Breuer

CLIENT
Sony

AGENCY
Euro RSCG Thomsen Roehle/
Dusseldorf

02045D

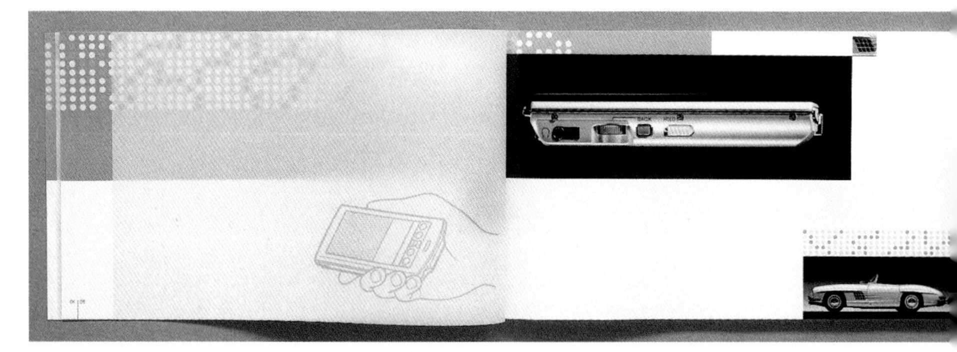

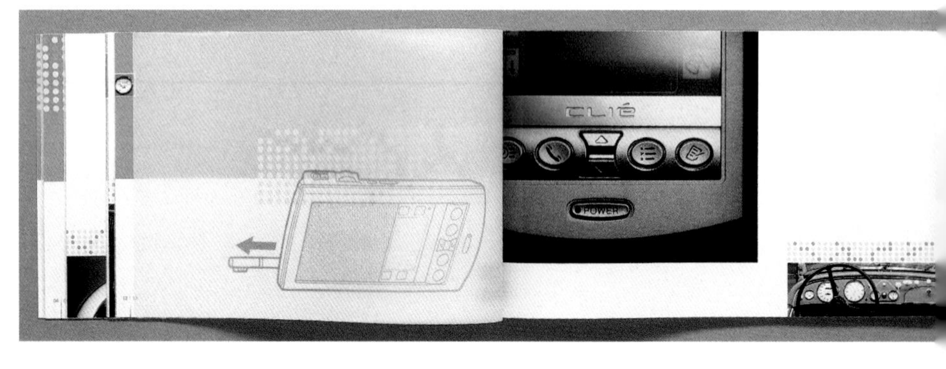

DESIGN MERIT

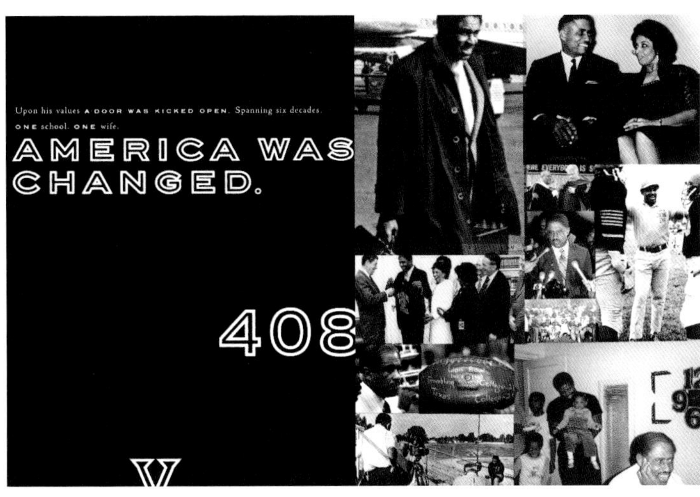

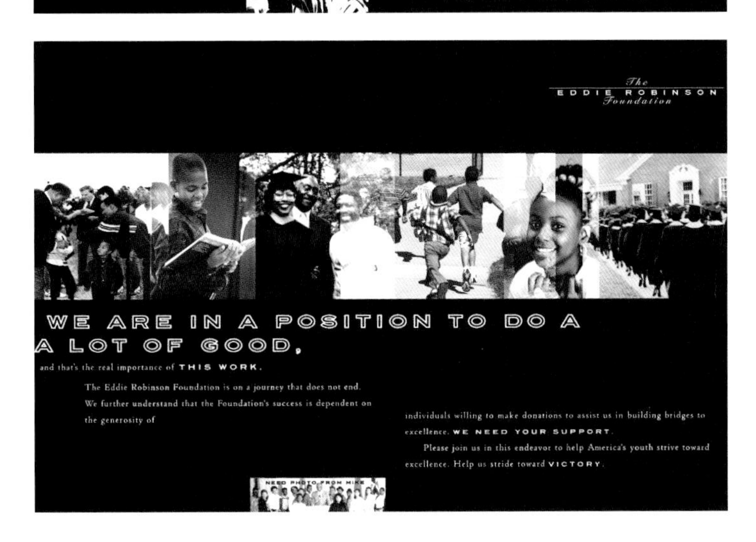

MERIT AWARD
BOOKLET/BROCHURE

ART DIRECTORS
Mike Franklin
Mark Arnold

WRITERS
Mike Franklin
Clifford Franklin

PHOTOGRAPHER
The Eddie Robinson Foundation

CREATIVE DIRECTOR
Mike Franklin

CLIENT
The Eddie Robinson Foundation

AGENCY
Fuse/St. Louis

02046D

MERIT AWARD
BOOKLET/BROCHURE

DESIGNERS
Cheryl Watson
Sharon McKendry

ART DIRECTOR
Cheryl Watson

WRITERS
Jeff Mueller
Jeff Speigel

PHOTOGRAPHER
Twist Film

DIRECTOR
Rich Michell

CREATIVE DIRECTOR
Minda Gralnek

CLIENT
Target Corporation

AGENCY
Graphiculture/Minneapolis

02054D

MERIT AWARD
BOOKLET/BROCHURE

DESIGNER
Andreas Kittel

ART DIRECTOR
Andreas Kittel

WRITERS
Ulf Beckman
Ingrid Sommar

PHOTOGRAPHERS
Joakim Bergström
Åke Eson Lindman
Björn Keller
Lasse Kärkkäinen
Jonas Linell
Mathias Pettersson

CREATIVE DIRECTOR
Anders Kornestedt

CLIENT
Rohsska Museet

AGENCY
Happy Forsman & Bodenfors/
Göthenburg

02047D

MERIT AWARD
BOOKLET/BROCHURE

ART DIRECTOR
Andreas Kittel

WRITERS
Monroe Blair
Stephanie Brown
Lillemor Petersson
Paul Scott
Elsebeth Welander-Berggren

PHOTOGRAPHER
Tord Lund

CLIENT
Rohsska Museet

AGENCY
Happy Forsman & Bodenfors/
Göthenburg

02048D

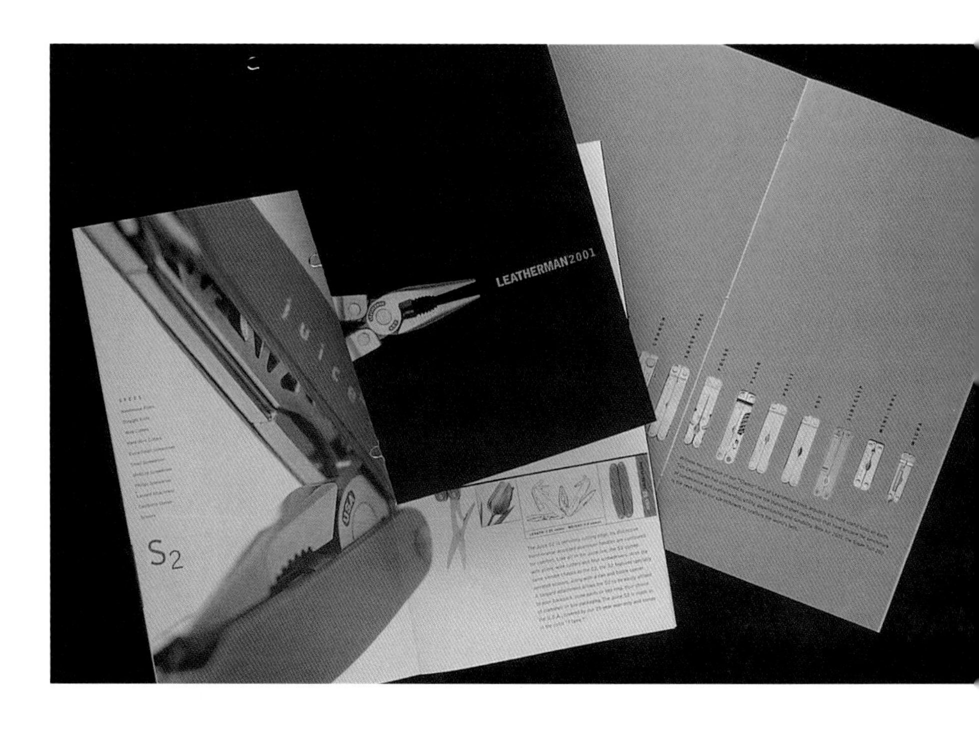

MERIT AWARD
BOOKLET/BROCHURE

DESIGNERS
Lisa Cerveny
Andrew Smith
Andrew Wicklund
Don Stayner

ART DIRECTORS
Jack Anderson
Lisa Cerveny

PHOTOGRAPHERS
Jeff Condit
Studio Three
Stock

CLIENT
Leatherman Tool Group

AGENCY
Hornall Anderson Design Works/Seattle

02049D

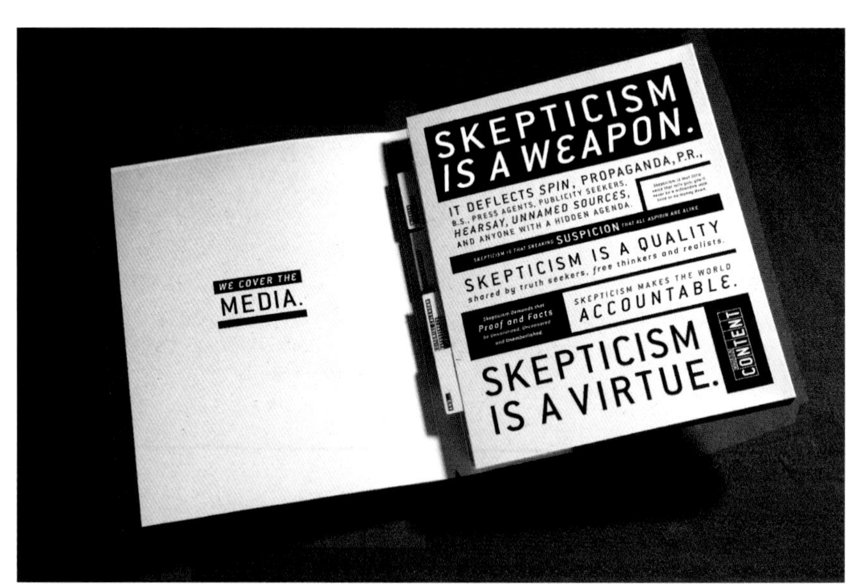

MERIT AWARD
BOOKLET/BROCHURE

DESIGNER
Edward Chiquitucto

ART DIRECTOR
John McNeil

WRITER
Josh Tavlin

CREATIVE DIRECTORS
Luke Hayman
Brian Collins

CLIENT
Brill's Content

AGENCY
Ogilvy & Mather/Brand Integration Group/New York

02050D

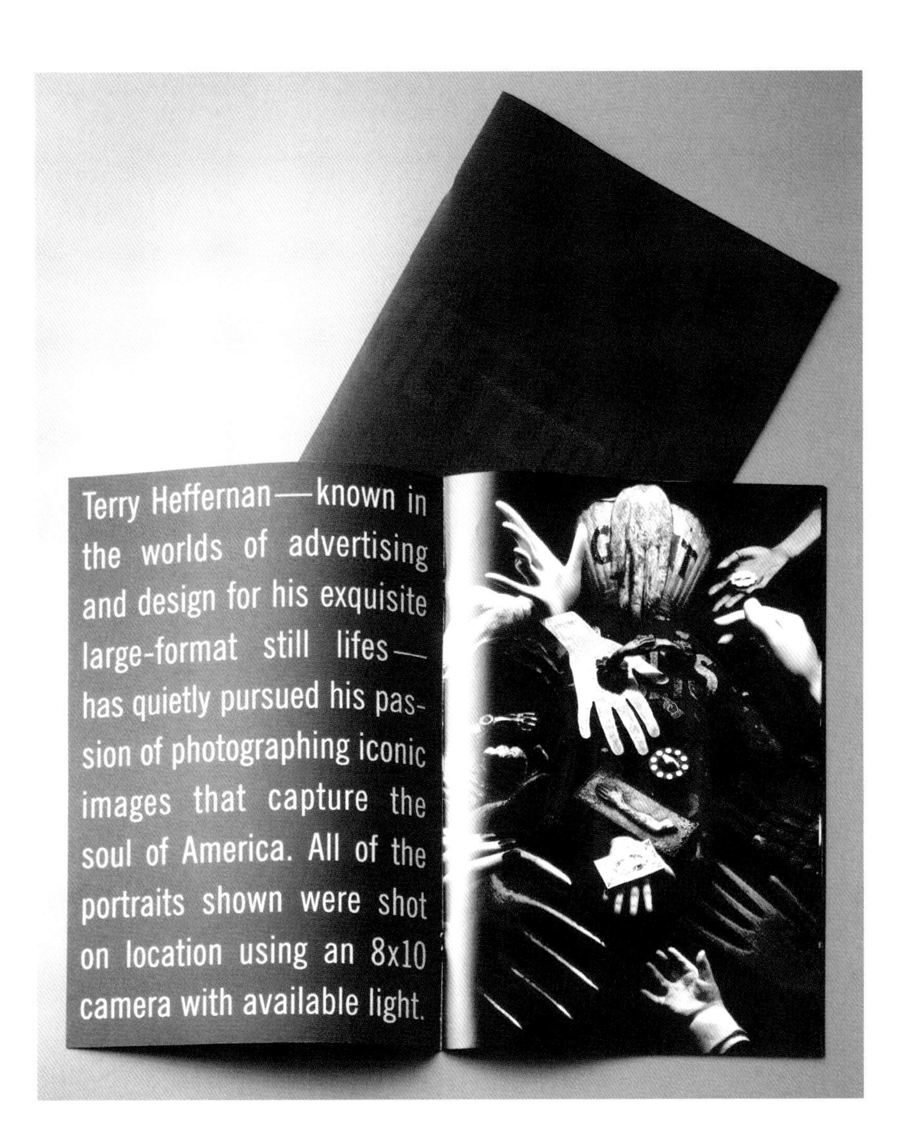

DESIGN MERIT

DESIGN MERIT

MERIT AWARD
BOOKLET/BROCHURE

DESIGNER
David Asari

ART DIRECTOR
David Asari

WRITER
Delphine Hirasuna

PHOTOGRAPHER
Terry Heffernan

CREATIVE DIRECTOR
Kit Hinrichs

CLIENT
Terry Heffernan

AGENCY
Pentagram Design/
San Francisco

02051D

DESIGN MERIT

MERIT AWARD
BOOKLET/BROCHURE

DESIGNERS
Kevin Finn
Julian Melhuish

ART DIRECTORS
Julian Melhuish
Kevin Finn

WRITERS
Julian Melhuish
Kevin Finn

PHOTOGRAPHER
Ingvar Kenne

CREATIVE DIRECTOR
Malcolm Poynton

CLIENT
Spicers Paper

AGENCY
Saatchi & Saatchi/Sydney

02052D

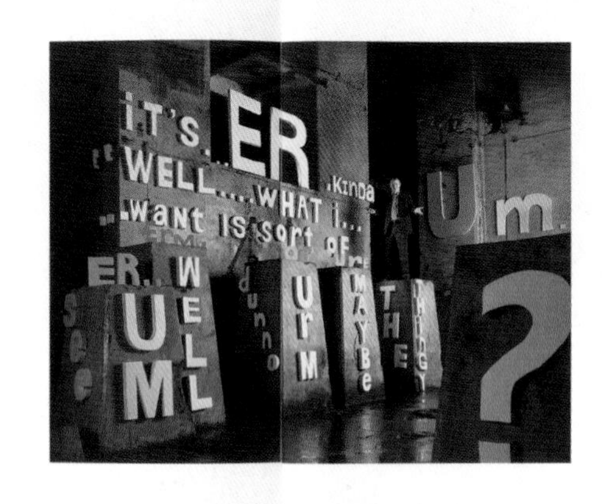

DESIGN MERIT

MERIT AWARD
BOOKLET/BROCHURE

DESIGNER
Steve Sandstrom

ART DIRECTOR
Steve Sandstrom

WRITER
Peter Wegner

ILLUSTRATOR
Ward Schumacher

PHOTOGRAPHERS
Garry Winogrand
Chris Mueller

CREATIVE DIRECTORS
Steve Sandstrom
Peter Wegner

CLIENT
Waggener Edstrom

AGENCY
Sandstrom Design/Portland

02053D

MERIT AWARD
BOOKLET/BROCHURE

PHOTOGRAPHER
Richard Phibbs

CREATIVE DIRECTOR
Joanne Reeves

CLIENT
John Varvatos

AGENCY
Toth Brand Imaging/Concord

02055D

MERIT AWARD
BOOKLET/BROCHURE

DESIGNERS
Sarah Moffat
Mike Harris

CREATIVE DIRECTORS
Bruce Duckworth
David Turner

CLIENT
Virgin Atlantic

AGENCY
Turner Duckworth/
San Francisco

02056D

MERIT AWARD
BOOKLET/BROCHURE

DESIGNER
France Simard

ART DIRECTOR
Frank Viva

WRITER
Doug Dolan

PHOTOGRAPHER
Various

CREATIVE DIRECTOR
Frank Viva

CLIENT
Butterfield & Robinson

AGENCY
Viva Dolan/Toronto

02058D

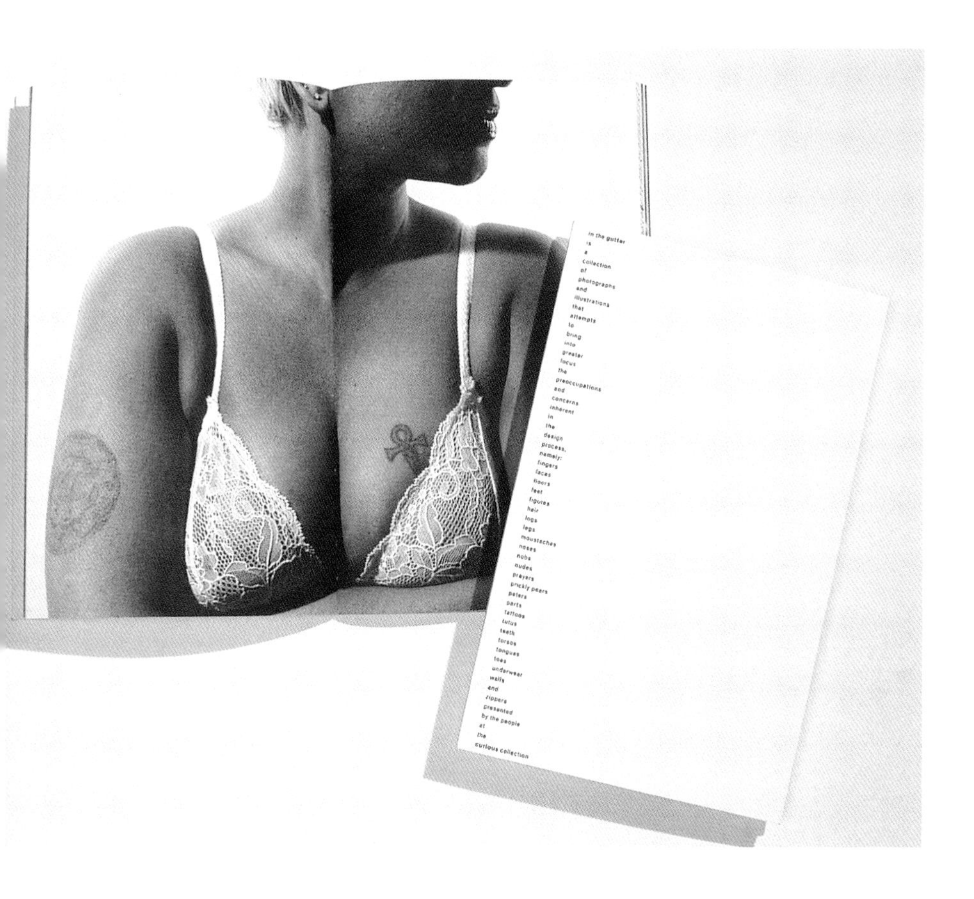

MERIT AWARD
BOOKLET/BROCHURE

DESIGNER
Frank Viva

WRITER
Frank Viva

ILLUSTRATOR
Frank Viva

PHOTOGRAPHER
Ron Baxter Smith

CREATIVE DIRECTOR
Frank Viva

CLIENT
Curious Collection-
Arjo Wiggins

AGENCY
Viva Dolan/Toronto

02059D

MERIT AWARD
BOOKLET/BROCHURE

DESIGNER
Frank Viva

ART DIRECTOR
Frank Viva

WRITER
Doug Dolan

PHOTOGRAPHER
Ron Baxter Smith

CREATIVE DIRECTOR
Frank Viva

CLIENT
Curious Collection-
Arjo Wiggins

AGENCY
Viva Dolan/Toronto

02060D

MERIT AWARD
BOOKLET/BROCHURE

DESIGNER
Hans Seeger

ART DIRECTOR
Thomas Wolfe

WRITER
John Naresky

ILLUSTRATOR
Art Paul

CREATIVE DIRECTOR
Dana Arnett

CLIENT
Fox River Paper

AGENCY
VSA Partners/Chicago

02061D

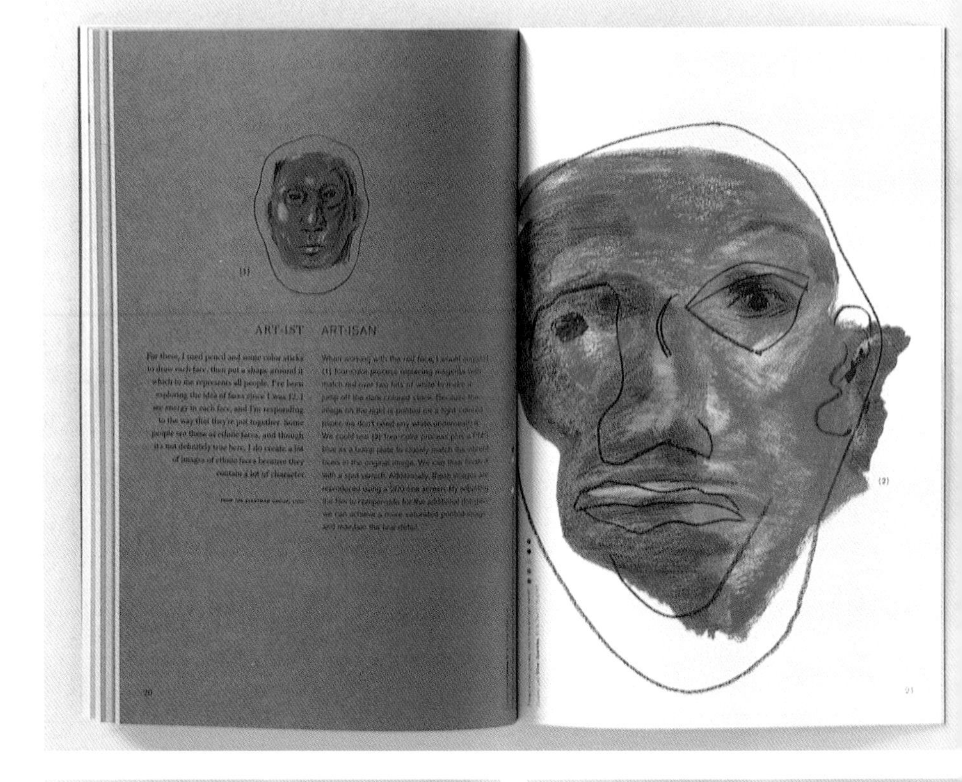

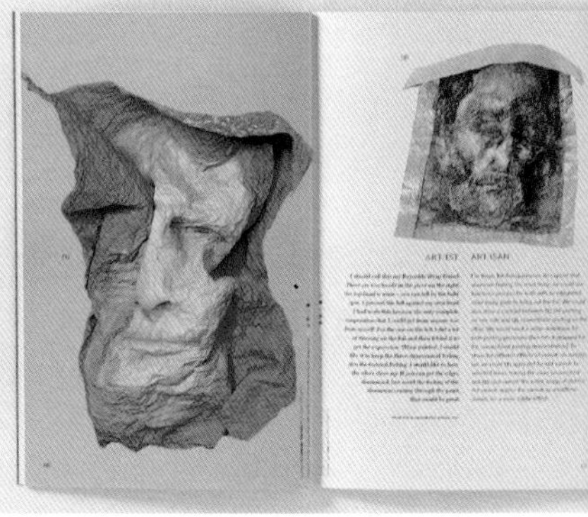

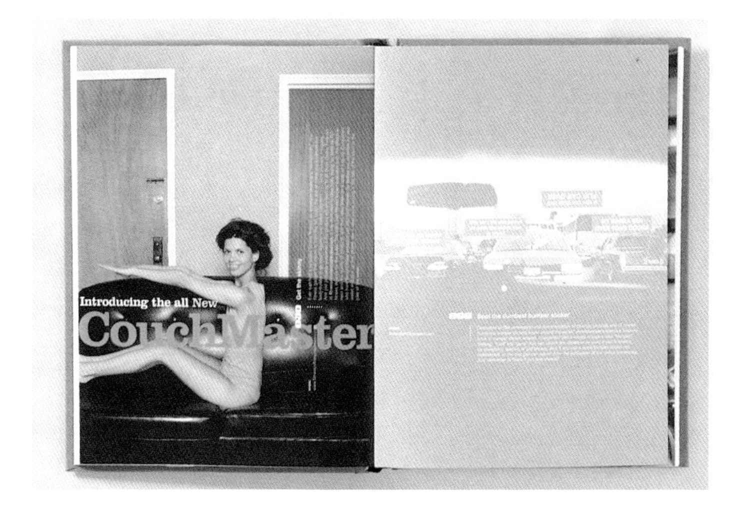

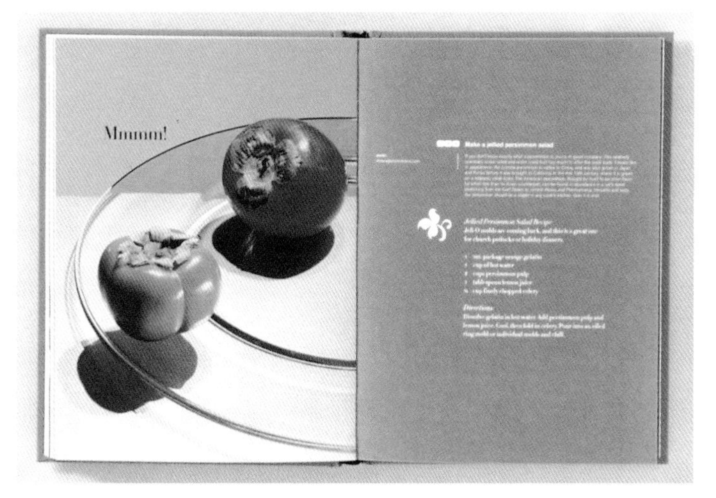

DESIGN MERIT

MERIT AWARD
BOOKLET/BROCHURE

DESIGNER
Thomas Wolfe

ART DIRECTOR
Thomas Wolfe

WRITER
Reid Armbruster

ILLUSTRATORS
Elvis Swift
Irene Rofheart Piggot
Carlos Aponte
Thomas Wolfe

PHOTOGRAPHERS
Masao Ota
Guido Vitti
Kyoko Hamada
Nick Clements
Yellow Dog Productions
Fredrik Broden
Thomas Hannich
Sven Banziger
Alyce Smith
Mark Smalling
Barry Harris

CREATIVE DIRECTOR
Thomas Wolfe

CLIENT
Fox River Paper

AGENCY
VSA Partners/Chicago

02062D

MERIT AWARD
BOOKLET/BROCHURE

DESIGNER
Judith Francisco

ART DIRECTOR
Judith Francisco

WRITER
Jessica Lehrer

ILLUSTRATOR
Jason Brooks

PHOTOGRAPHERS
Robert Wyatt
Marc de Groot

CREATIVE DIRECTORS
Paul Shearer
Glenn Cole

CLIENT
Nike Europe

AGENCY
Wieden + Kennedy/
Amsterdam

02063D

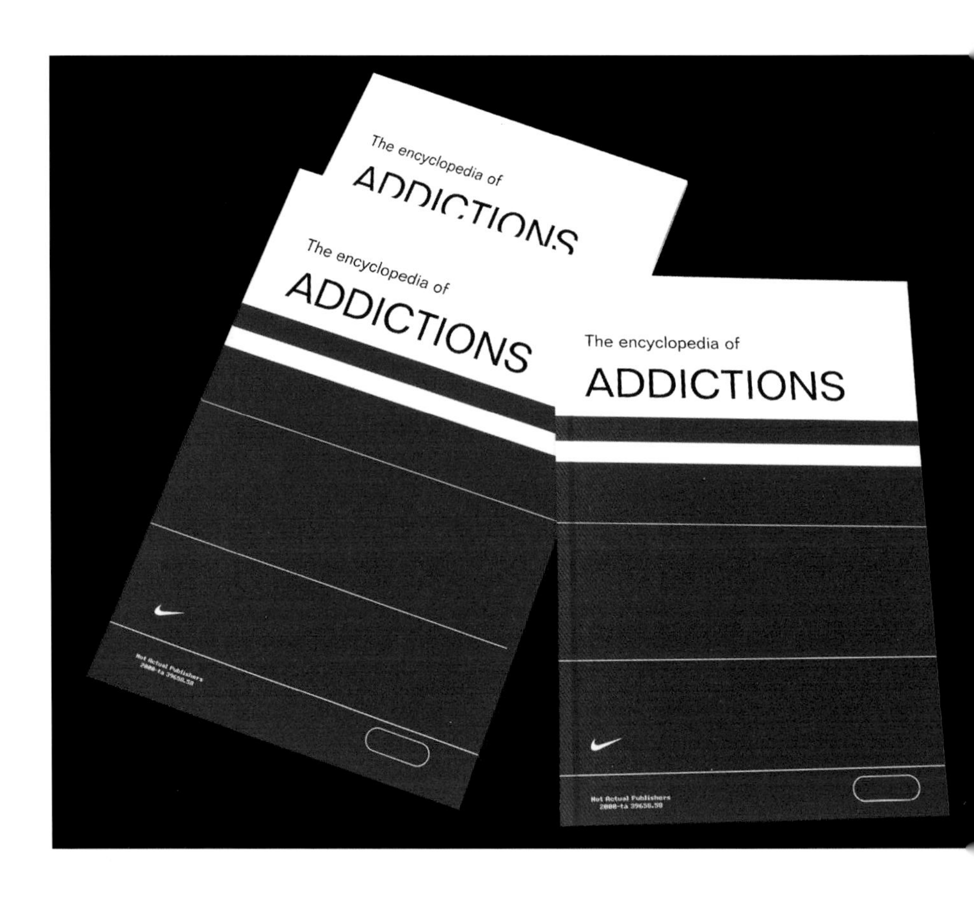

MERIT AWARD
BOOKLET/BROCHURE

DESIGNER
Mario Guay

ART DIRECTOR
Mario Guay

WRITER
Jessica Lehrer

PHOTOGRAPHER
Elaine Constantine

CREATIVE DIRECTORS
Paul Shearer
Glenn Cole

CLIENT
Nike Europe

AGENCY
Wieden + Kennedy/
Amsterdam

02064D

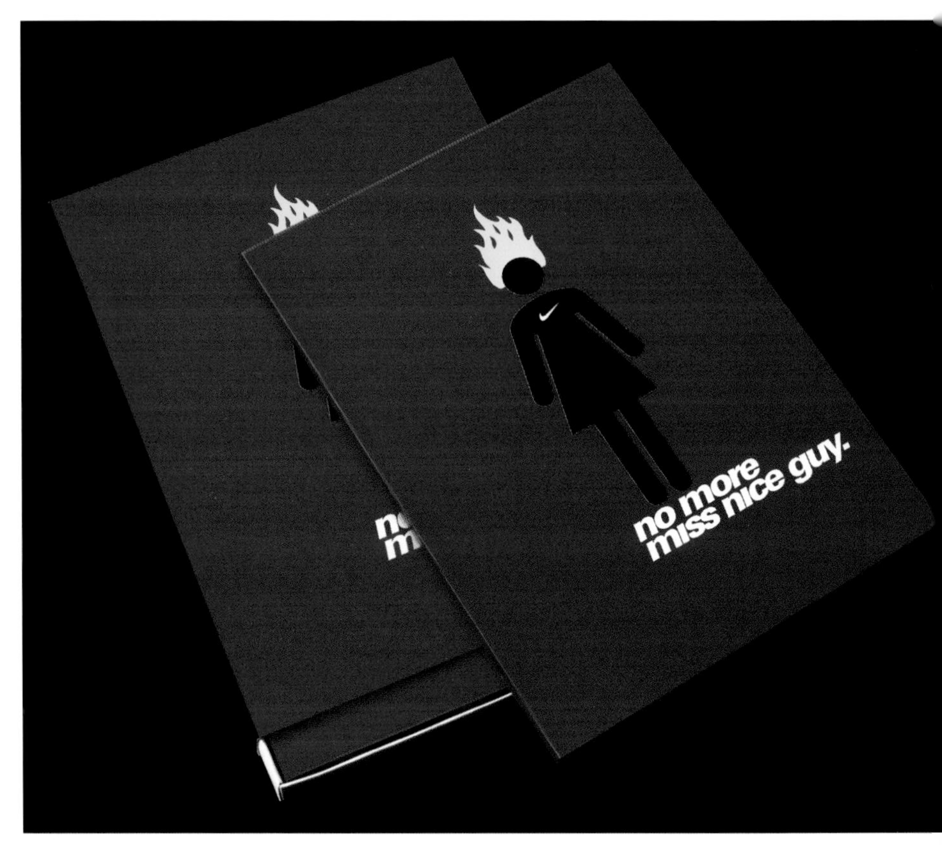

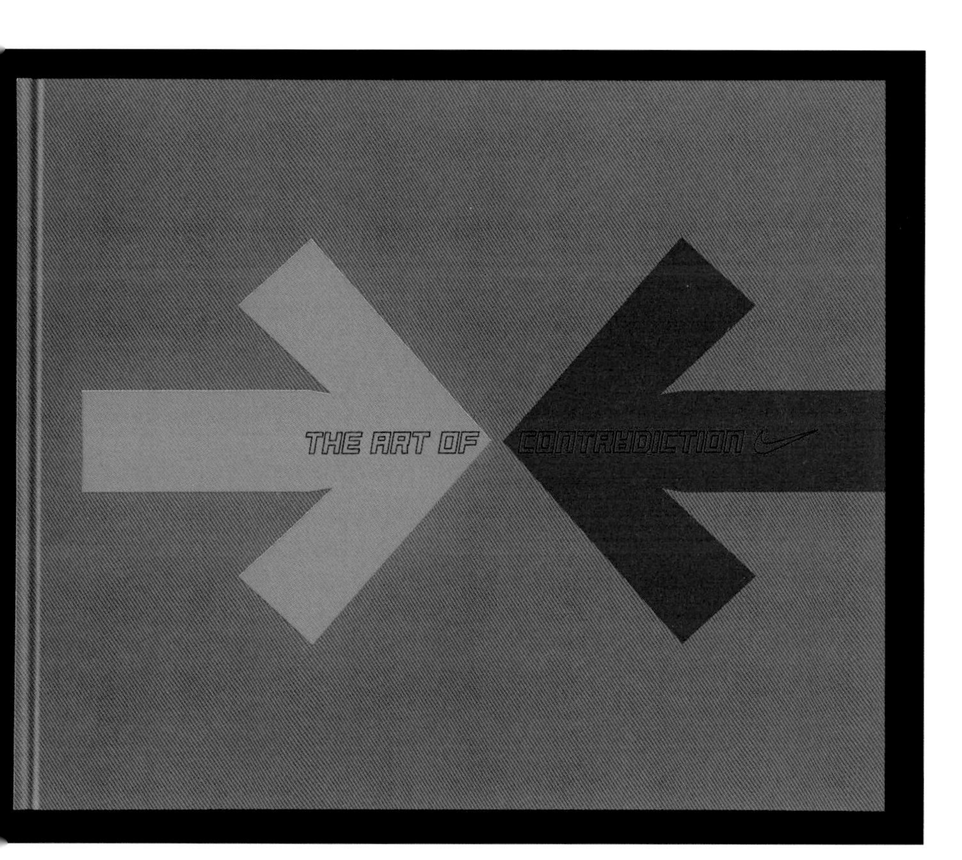

MERIT AWARD
BOOKLET/BROCHURE

DESIGNER
Judith Francisco

ART DIRECTOR
Judith Francisco

WRITER
Jessica Lehrer

ILLUSTRATORS
Ian Bilbey
Fiona Hewitt

PHOTOGRAPHER
Lee Jenkins

CREATIVE DIRECTORS
Paul Shearer
Glenn Cole

CLIENT
Nike Europe

AGENCY
Wieden + Kennedy/
Amsterdam

02065D

MERIT AWARD
BOOKLET/BROCHURE

DESIGNER
Judith Francisco

ART DIRECTOR
Judith Francisco

WRITER
Jessica Lehrer

ILLUSTRATOR
Paul Davis

PHOTOGRAPHER
Annette Aurell

CREATIVE DIRECTORS
Paul Shearer
Glenn Cole

CLIENT
Nike Europe

AGENCY
Wieden + Kennedy/
Amsterdam

02066D

MERIT AWARD
BOOKLET/BROCHURE

ART DIRECTORS
Robert Nakata
Marc Shillum

WRITER
Michael Russoff

PHOTOGRAPHER
Various

CREATIVE DIRECTORS
Jon Matthews
John Boiler

CLIENT
Siemens AG

AGENCY
Wieden + Kennedy/
Amsterdam

02067D

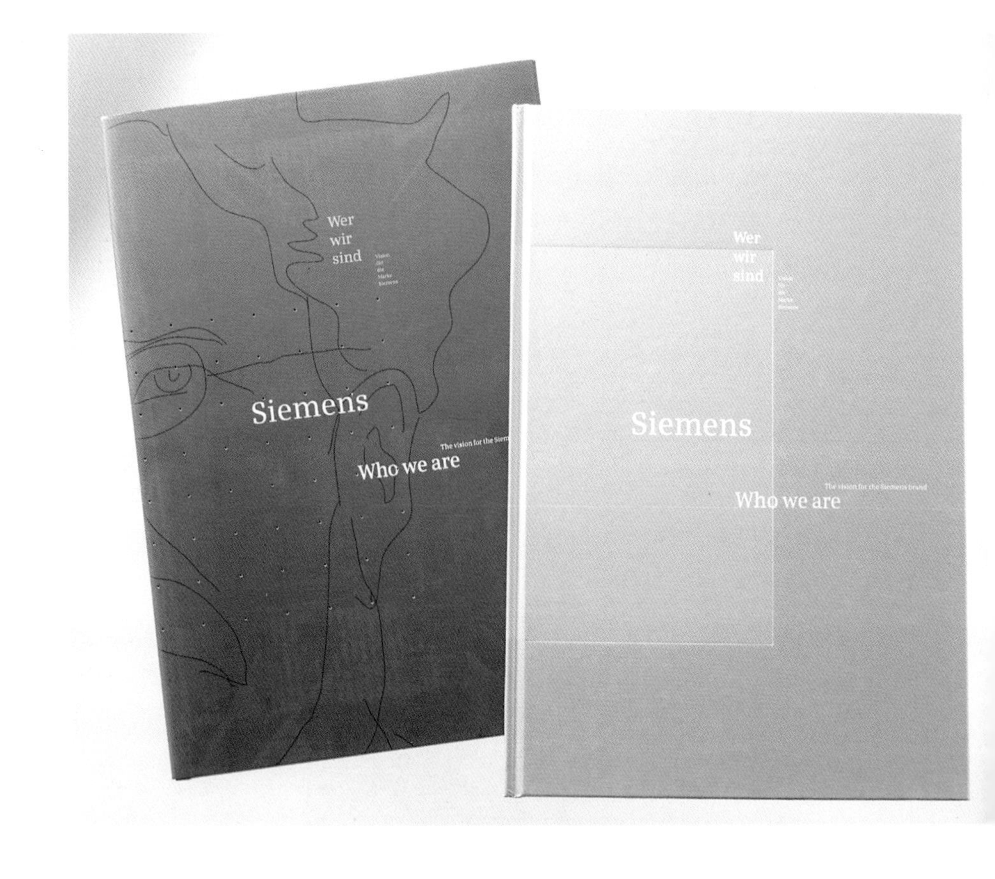

MERIT AWARD
BOOKLET/BROCHURE

ART DIRECTOR
Todd Schulz

WRITERS
Ralf Zilligen
Jon Matthews

CREATIVE DIRECTORS
Jon Matthews
John Boiler

CLIENT
Siemens AG

AGENCY
Wieden + Kennedy/
Amsterdam

02068D

Fact (n). an event or thing that is known to have happened or to be true or to exist. Faction (n). small united group within a larger one, but differing from it in aims and ideas. Factor (n). fact or circumstance or force that helps to produce a result. Factory (n). building in which goods are manufactured. Film Factory (n). a faction of people working under certain factors to produce a fact on film. The Film Factory. 110-114 Tung Lo Wan Road, 1/F Flat A&B Wing Hing Court, Hong Kong. Tel (852) 2570 8267 or fax (852) 2807 1244 or email filmfact@filmfactory.net

Louis Ng. Director. My job is to make fun. Make fun of writers. Make fun of art directors. Make fun of creative directors. Make fun of account service people. Make fun of big potatoes. Make fun of small potatoes. Make fun of audiences. Make fun of trends. Make fun of history. Make fun of knowledge. Make fun of technology. Make fun of authority. Make fun of establishment. Make fun of society. Make fun of life. Make fun of myself. The more fun I make, the better I do my job. Seriously. Come and make fun of me at The Film Factory. 110-114 Tung Lo Wan Road, 1/F Flat A&B Wing Hing Court. Hong Kong. Call (852) 2570 8267 or fax (852) 2807 1244 instead. Email me at louis@filmfactory.net

Oceanic Chan. Director. I believe in giving. Giving milk to tea. Giving fried dace with black beans to noodles. Giving incense to ancestors. Giving jokes to conversation. Giving money to beggars. Giving comfort to relatives. Giving help to friends. Giving love to women. Giving logic to nonsense. Giving solutions to problems. Giving craft to effect. Giving tricks to shooting. And I give some part of myself to every commercial I make. Come and share in my giving at The Film Factory. 110-114 Tung Lo Wan Road, 1/F Flat A&B Wing Hing Court, Hong Kong. Call (852) 2570 8267 or fax (852) 2807 1244 instead. Email me at oceanic@filmfactory.net

Wicky Wong. Director. Value: Defining value. Walking around Central, Wanchai, Mongkok, Sam Shui Po, St. Germain, Patpong and Jatujak. Searching and bargaining. From the value of a slice of cheese to a chunk of property. From the value of chicken feet to an hour with a prostitute. From the value of a pile of garbage to a piece of art. From the value of a fleeting smile to everlasting happiness. From the value of a blink of an eye to film that captures time. Come and join my search for the true value of film at The Film Factory. 110-114 Tung Lo Wan Road, 1/F Flat A&B Wing Hing Court. Hong Kong. Call (852) 2570 8267 or fax (852) 2807 1244 instead. Email me at wicky@filmfactory.net

Man Chung. Director. I'm only one year old. Yet my hair-style is two years old. My common sense is five years old. My literacy level is eight years old. My taste is ten years old. My concept of fun is twelve years old. My sense of humor is fifteen years old. My body build is eighteen years old. My ass is twenty years old. My hand is fifty years old. My filthy mind is one hundred years old. My passion with directing even older. To see how old I really am, look me up at The Film Factory. 110-114 Tung Lo Wan Road, 1/F Flat A&B Wing Hing Court, Hong Kong. Call (852) 2570 8267 or fax (852) 2807 1244 instead. Email me at manchung@filmfactory.net

May Tang. Executive Producer. BUDDHISM advises to give up worldly possessions. Regretfully, there is one vice I cannot surrender. Chatting to my cats. At home, I have three to talk to. Outside, I chat with stray cats. At the office I chat with agency cats (most of them are producers). Chatting with cats is my expertise. To find the truth about all kinds of cats and their secrets, chat with me at The Film Factory. 110-114 Tung Lo Wan Road, 1/F Flat A&B Wing Hing Court, Hong Kong. Call (852) 2570 8267 / 9029 3828 or fax (852) 2807 1244 instead. Email me at may@filmfactory.net

Winnie Tang. Executive Producer. Dai Shan is my real name. My nickname is Winnie. I love to eat but I'm constantly on diet. I love sports but my leg constantly lets me down. I love film but I cannot act. That's why I'm a producer. I can always talk and let the director do the rest. Let's talk. Look me up at The Film Factory. 110-114 Tung Lo Wan Road, 1/F Flat A&B Wing Hing Court, Hong Kong. Call (852) 2570 8267 / 9106 6811 or fax (852) 2807 1244 instead. Email me at winnie@filmfactory.net

Amy Leung. Casting Director. My job is to observe and judge. Different faces. Different races. Different ages. Each individual has a unique story. And it's all in their voices. Their faces. Their walking styles. You might find me looking at you in a strange way. But it's for a good reason. Trust me. You'll believe it when you see me working at The Film Factory. 110-114 Tung Lo Wan Road, 1/F Flat A&B Wing Hing Court, Hong Kong. Call (852) 2570 8267 / 9800 8117 or fax (852) 2807 1244 instead. Email me at casting@filmfactory.net

Kris Lo. Cameraman. My job is to catch the light. That's why I'm always in a hurry. Light never waits. I try to run in front of him to see his face. But most of the time, I can only glimpse his back. Instead of trying to see his face, you're more than welcome see mine first. It's easy. Just visit me at The Film Factory. 110-114 Tung Lo Wan Road, 1/F Flat A&B Wing Hing Court, Hong Kong. You can also call (852) 2570 8267 / 9276 1167 or fax (852) 2807 1244 instead. Email me at kris@filmfactory.net Unlike the light, I'll wait.

Wong Wing Tat. Head of camera department. 168cm. 65kg. Curly hair. I don't know how to handle my hair so I often wear a cap to cover my head. I also wear a lot of caps in my company, and you can find me helping heads of other departments. Want to see how all my caps fit? Head to The Film Factory. 110-114 Tung Lo Wan Road, 1/F Flat A&B Wing Hing Court, Hong Kong. Call (852) 2570 8267 / 9800 8839 or fax (852) 2807 1244 instead. Email me at tat@filmfactory.net

KK Szeto. Production Manager. I have walked a hundred and twenty-nine thousand two hundred and forty-one point three kilometers. I have driven over eight hundred and eighty-one thousand twenty-four point nine hours. I fiddle with my glasses one thousand one hundred and ten times per day. I use only nineteen to twenty words a year. I have one brain, two legs, and several hundred hands. If this fits the description of the man you're looking for, you can find me at The Film Factory. 110-114 Tung Lo Wan Road, 1/F Flat A&B Wing Hing Court, Hong Kong. Call (852) 2570 8267 / 9195 7430 or fax (852) 2807 1244 instead. Email me at kk@filmfactory.net

Calvin Hui. Production manager. Time is everything. Time to understand the script. Time to prepare a budget. Time to find props. Time to build a set. Time to find a location. Time of the transportation. Time to make up. Time of lighting. Time of shooting. Time to eat. Time of wrapping up. It's my job to manage time. Find time to visit me at The Film Factory. 110-114 Tung Lo Wan Road, 1/F Flat A&B Wing Hing Court, Hong Kong. Call (852) 2570 8267 / 9095 2205 or fax (852) 2807 1244 instead. Email me at calvin@filmfactory.net

Ng Shun Tak. Production co-ordinator. You might find my face familiar. I was the taxi driver in the SUNDAY "Ghost" commercial. Whatever my directors ask me to do, I do. It's this kind of commitment that has earned me my title. Don't be surprised if you find me dressed as a woman in another commercial. Blame it on commitment. And you can find this rare kind of commitment at The Film Factory. 110-114 Tung Lo Wan Road, 1/F Flat A&B Wing Hing Court, Hong Kong. Call (852) 2570 8267 / 9642 4104 or fax (852) 2807 1244 instead. Email me at prod@filmfactory.net

Kent Chiu. Production Co-coordinator. 1 girlfriend, 2 cats, 50 toy guns, 100 action figures, 200 X rated films, 300 questions, 500 solutions, 700 strands of hair lost daily, 1000 things to do (today!) and 1 overwhelming, all-consuming, totally [illegible]sorbing passion: Film Making. Find my passion in action a[illegible] The Film Factory. 110-114 Tung Lo Wan Road, 1/F Flat A&B [illegible]ing Hing Court, Hong Kong. Call (852) 2570 8267 / 9234 30[illegible]2 or fax (852) 2807 1244 instead. Email me at prod@filmf[illegible]tory.net

Joann Chow. Manager. I love dogs. I eat with them. I talk with them. I play with them. I sleep with them. Managing the office is like managing a bunch of wild dogs. They bite, they pee. That's why I spend so much time at work. And find peace with my dogs at home. That's a pretty good balance don't you think? But don't take my word for it. See me and my dogs at The Film Factory. 110-114 Tung Lo Wan Road, 1/F Flat A&B Wing Hing Court, Hong Kong. Call (852) 2570 8267 / 9195 8428 or fax (852) 2807 1244 instead. Email me at joann@filmfactory.net

Fact (n). an event or thing that is known to have happened or to be true or to exist. Faction (n). small united group within a larger one, but differing from it in aims and ideas. Factor (n). fact or circumstance or force that helps to produce a result. Factory (n). building in which goods are manufactured. Film Factory (n). a faction of people working under certain factors to produce a fact on film. The Film Factory. 110-114 Tung Lo Wan Road, 1/F Flat A&B Wing Hing Court, Hong Kong. Tel (852) 2570 8267 or fax (852) 2807 1244 or email filmfact@filmfactory.net

DESIGN MERIT

MERIT AWARD
CORPORATE IDENTITY

DESIGNER
Willis Wong

ART DIRECTOR
Willis Wong

WRITERS
K.C. Tsang
Christopher Thong

CREATIVE DIRECTOR
Willis Wong

CLIENT
The Film Factory Limited

AGENCY
BBDO/Hong Kong

02069D

DESIGN MERIT

MERIT AWARD
CORPORATE IDENTITY

DESIGNERS
Vanessa Eckstein
Frances Chen
Stephanie Yung

ART DIRECTOR
Vanessa Eckstein

PHOTOGRAPHER
Ernesto Di Pietro

CREATIVE DIRECTOR
Vanessa Eckstein

CLIENT
El Zanjon

AGENCY
Blok Design/Toronto

02070D

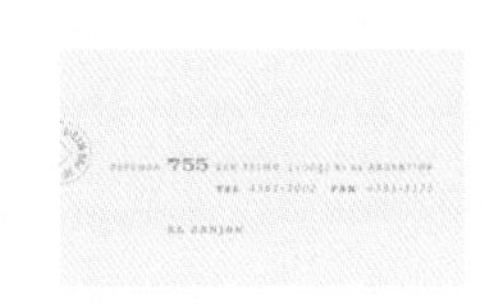

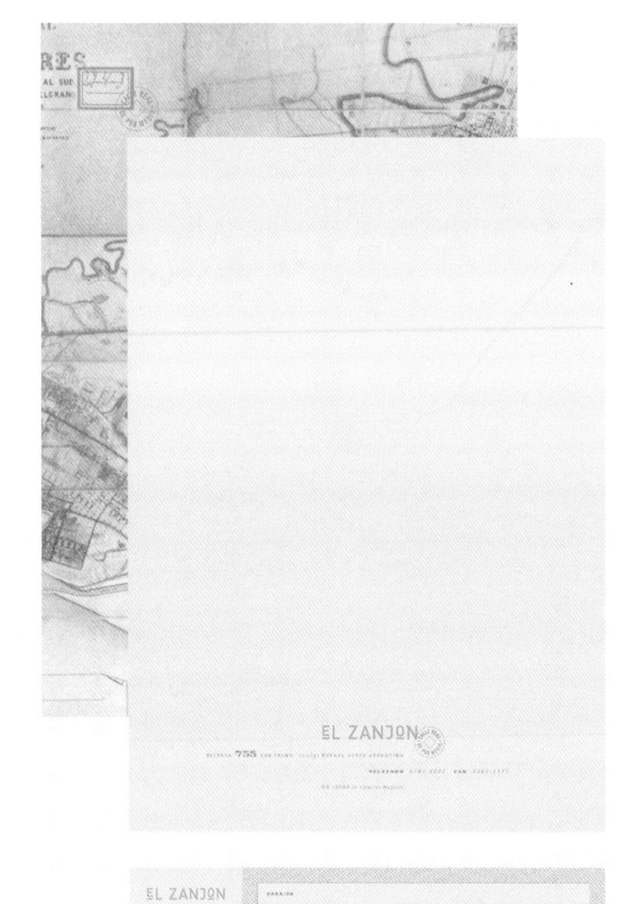

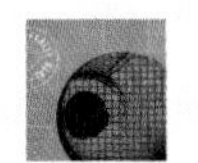

DESIGN MERIT

MERIT AWARD
CORPORATE IDENTITY

DESIGNERS
Vanessa Eckstein
Frances Chen
Stephanie Yung

ART DIRECTOR
Vanessa Eckstein

CREATIVE DIRECTOR
Vanessa Eckstein

CLIENT
Steam Films

AGENCY
Blok Design/Toronto

02071D

MERIT AWARD
CORPORATE IDENTITY

DESIGNERS
Ed Bennett
Pierre Loo

CREATIVE DIRECTOR
John Jarvis

CLIENT
Colle + McVoy

AGENCY
Colle + McVoy/Minneapolis

02074D

MERIT AWARD
CORPORATE IDENTITY

DESIGNERS
Mike White
Paul Bastyr
Charlie Ross

ILLUSTRATORS
Paul Bastyr
Mike White

CREATIVE DIRECTOR
Kobe Suvongse

CLIENT
Sub Zero

AGENCY
Duffy Design/Minneapolis

02075D

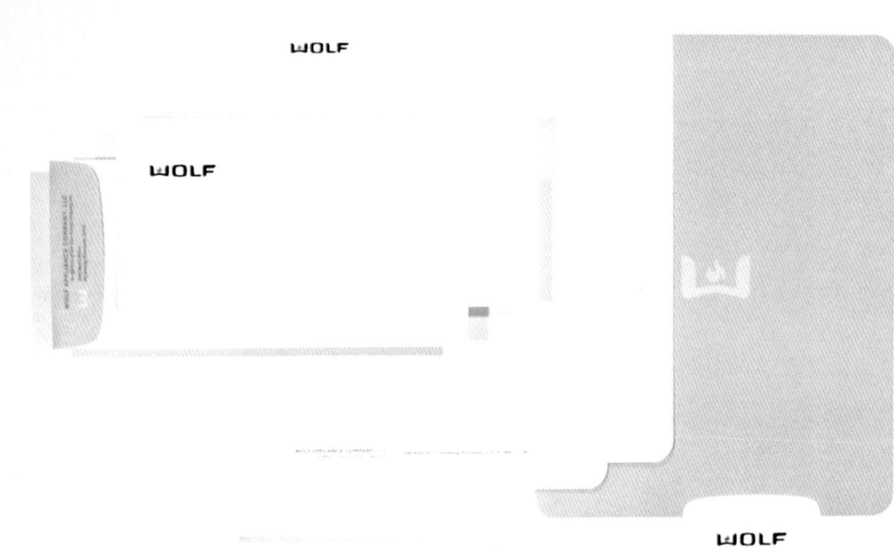

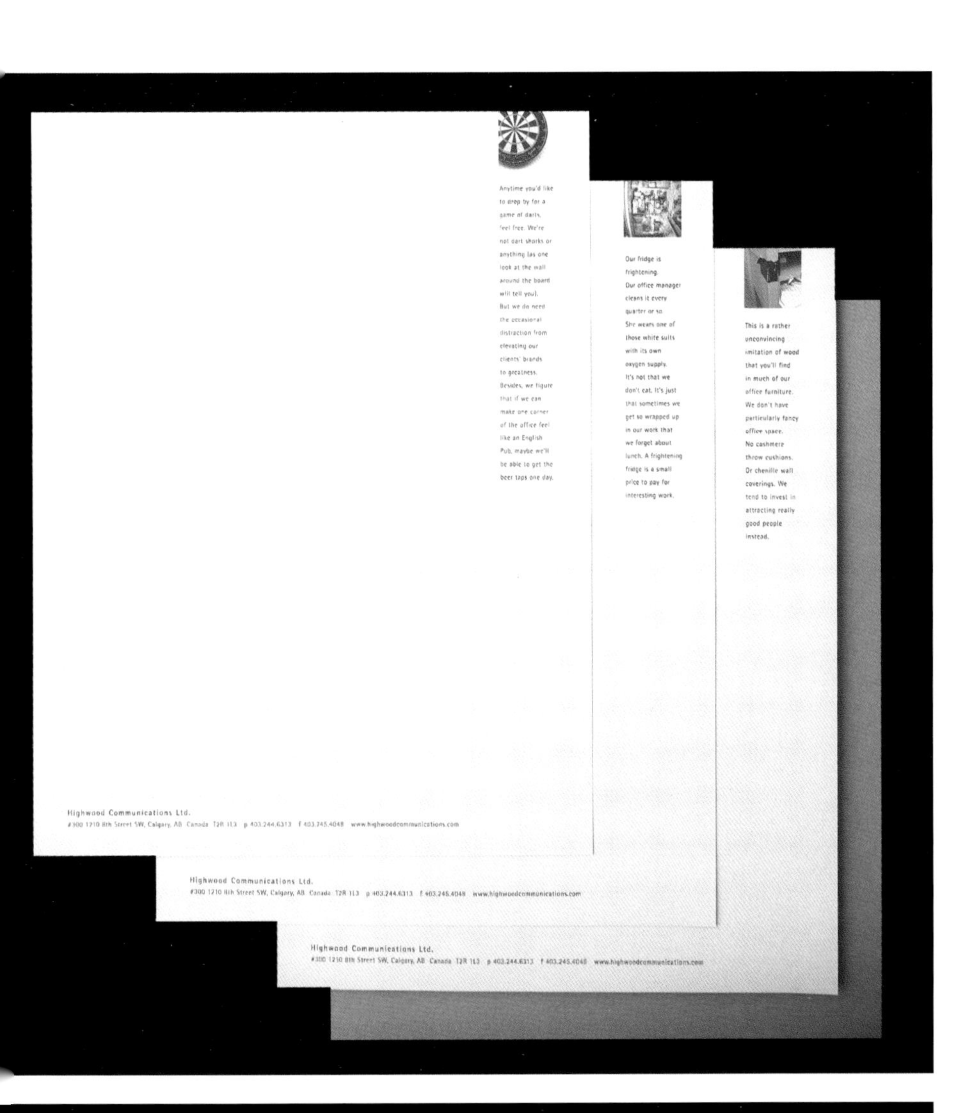

MERIT AWARD
CORPORATE IDENTITY

DESIGNER
Jimi Scherer

ART DIRECTOR
Jimi Scherer

WRITERS
Steve Williams
Dan King

PHOTOGRAPHER
Beau Lark

CREATIVE DIRECTORS
Steve Williams
Jimi Scherer
Keli Pollock
Dan King

CLIENT
Highwood Communications

AGENCY
Highwood Communications/
Calgary

02076D

MERIT AWARD
CORPORATE IDENTITY

DESIGNER
Pann Lim

ART DIRECTORS
Pann Lim
Roy Poh

WRITER
Pann Lim

ILLUSTRATOR
Pann Lim

CLIENT
Yellowbox Studios

AGENCY
Kinetic Interactive/Singapore

02077D

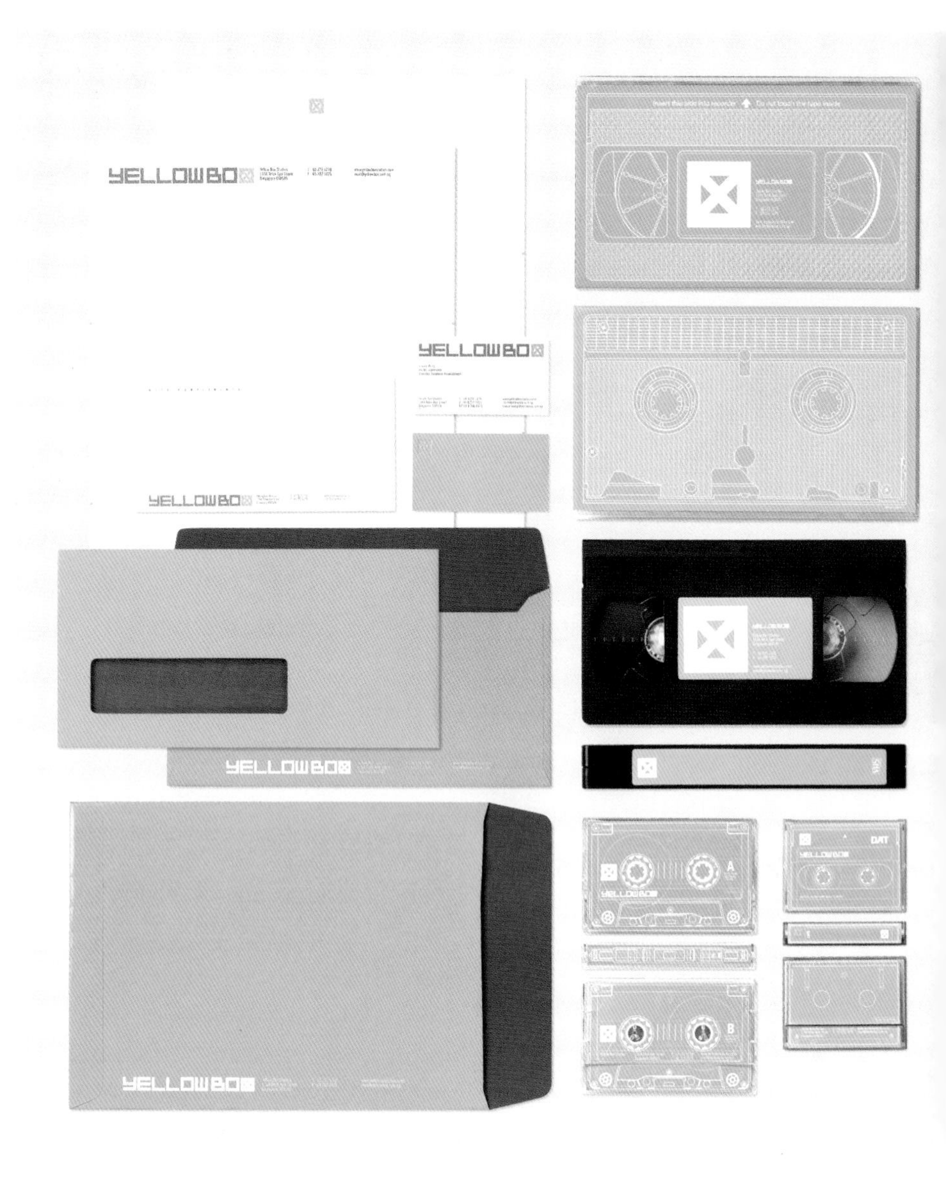

DESIGN MERIT

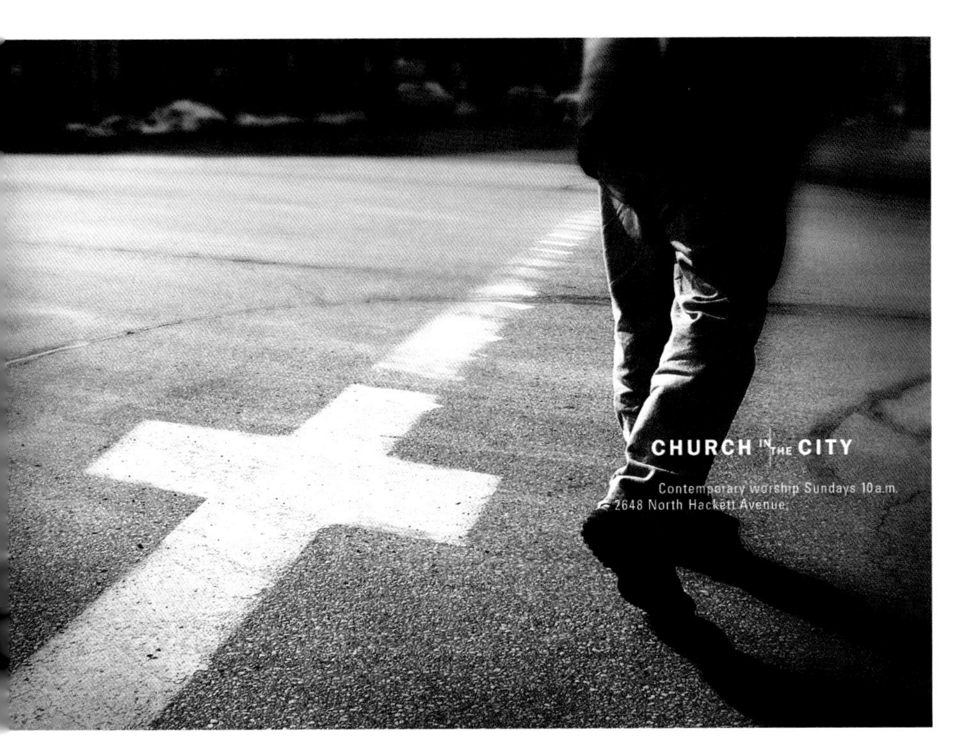

CHURCH IN THE CITY
Contemporary worship Sundays 10 a.m.
2648 North Hackett Avenue

MERIT AWARD
CORPORATE IDENTITY

DESIGNER
Rich Kohnke

ART DIRECTOR
Rich Kohnke

WRITERS
Dave Hanneken
Denise Kohnke

ILLUSTRATOR
Jim McDonald

PHOTOGRAPHER
Rich Kohnke

CREATIVE DIRECTORS
Rich Kohnke
Dave Hanneken

CLIENT
Church in the City

AGENCY
Kohnke Hanneken/Milwaukee

02078D

MERIT AWARD
CORPORATE IDENTITY

DESIGNER
Luis Peña

ART DIRECTOR
Luis Peña

ILLUSTRATOR
Luis Peña

CREATIVE DIRECTOR
Luis Peña

CLIENT
Catherine Bowen

AGENCY
PeñaBrand/Butler Shine & Stern/Sausalito

02072D

MERIT AWARD
CORPORATE IDENTITY

DESIGNER
Luis Peña

ART DIRECTOR
Luis Peña

ILLUSTRATOR
Luis Peña

CREATIVE DIRECTOR
Luis Peña

CLIENT
PeñaBrand

AGENCY
PeñaBrand/Butler Shine & Stern/Sausalito

02073D

MERIT AWARD
CORPORATE IDENTITY

DESIGNER
Neil Powell

CREATIVE DIRECTOR
Neil Powell

CLIENT
Brooklyn Woods

AGENCY
Powell/New York

02079D

MERIT AWARD
CORPORATE IDENTITY

DESIGNER
Neil Powell

CREATIVE DIRECTOR
Neil Powell

CLIENT
Powell

AGENCY
Powell/New York

02080D

MERIT AWARD
CORPORATE IDENTITY

ART DIRECTOR
Ian Grais

CREATIVE DIRECTORS
Chris Staples
Ian Grais

CLIENT
Rethink

AGENCY
Rethink/Vancouver

02081D

MERIT AWARD
CORPORATE IDENTITY

DESIGNER
Tim McGrath

CLIENT
Crusty Underwear

AGENCY
Rick Johnson & Company/
Albuquerque

02082D

MERIT AWARD
CORPORATE IDENTITY

DESIGNER
Michele Melandri

ART DIRECTOR
Michele Melandri

WRITER
Craig Simpson

CREATIVE DIRECTOR
Steve Sandstrom

CLIENT
Kombucha Wonder Drink

AGENCY
Sandstrom Design/Portland

02083D

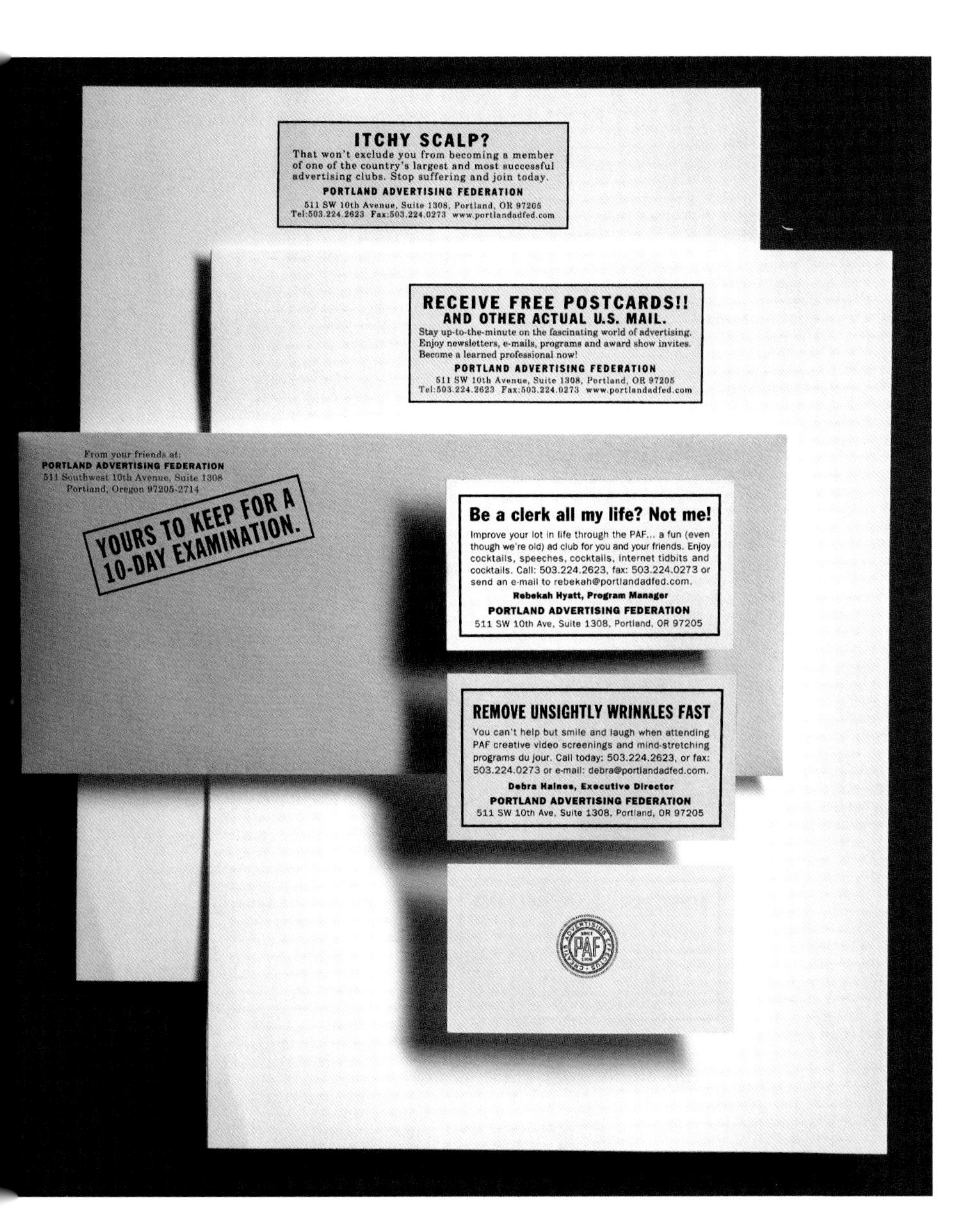

MERIT AWARD
CORPORATE IDENTITY

DESIGNER
Steve Sandstrom

ART DIRECTOR
Steve Sandstrom

WRITERS
Greg Eiden
Steve Sandstrom

CREATIVE DIRECTOR
Steve Sandstrom

CLIENT
Portland Advertising Federation

AGENCY
Sandstrom Design/Portland

02084D

MERIT AWARD
CORPORATE IDENTITY

DESIGNER
Dan Richards

ART DIRECTOR
Dan Richards

CREATIVE DIRECTOR
Steve Sandstrom

CLIENT
Surround Collaborative Architects

AGENCY
Sandstrom Design/Portland

02085D

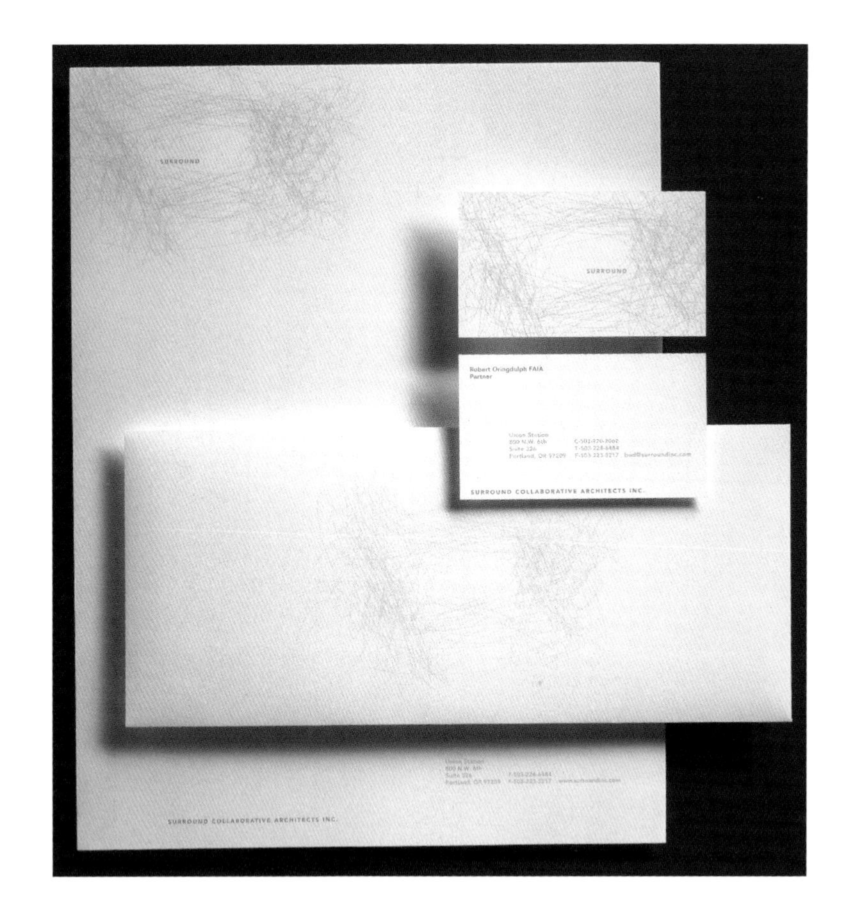

MERIT AWARD
CORPORATE IDENTITY

DESIGNER
Megan Futter

ART DIRECTOR
Megan Futter

WRITER
Louis Gavin

ILLUSTRATOR
Andrew Brink

CREATIVE DIRECTOR
Nathan Reddy

CLIENT
GR8 Design

AGENCY
TBWA Gavin/Reddy/Houghton

02086D

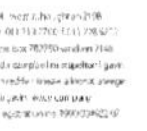

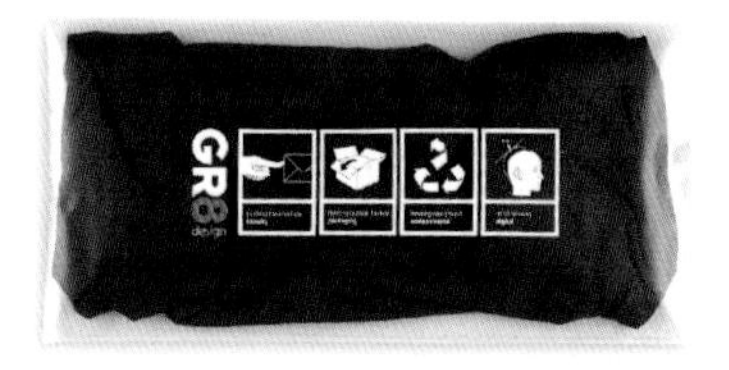

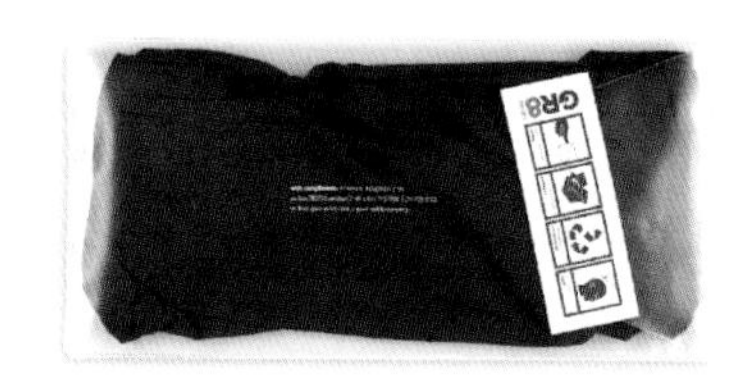

MERIT AWARD
LOGO/TRADEMARK

DESIGNERS
Bromley Creative Team

ART DIRECTORS
Bromley Creative Team

CREATIVE DIRECTORS
Bromley Creative Team

CLIENT
San Antonio Convention & Visitors Bureau

AGENCY
Bromley Communications/ San Antonio

02087D

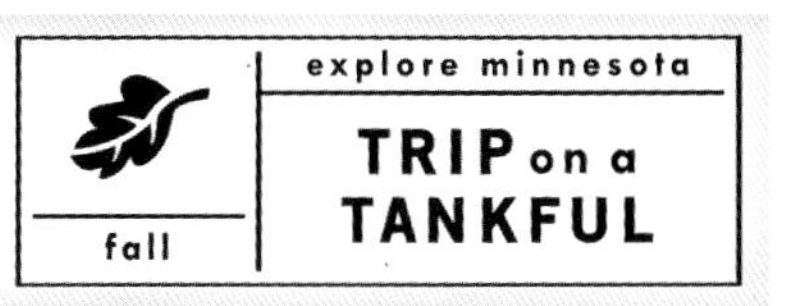

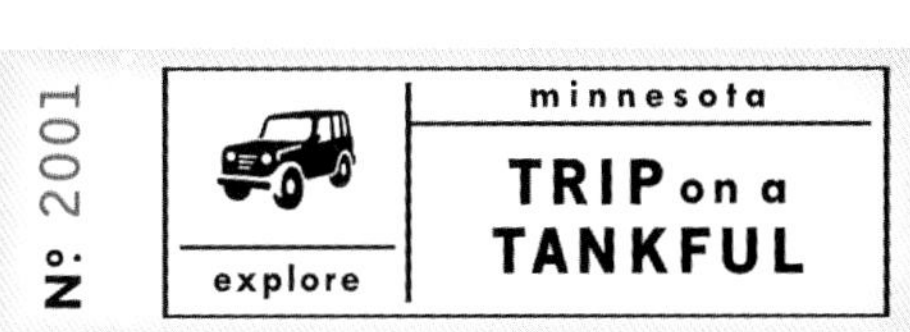

MERIT AWARD
LOGO/TRADEMARK

DESIGNER
Barry Townsend

ILLUSTRATOR
Barry Townsend

CREATIVE DIRECTORS
John Jarvis
Ed Bennett

CLIENT
Minnesota Office of Tourism

AGENCY
Colle + McVoy/Minneapolis

02089D

MERIT AWARD
LOGO/TRADEMARK

DESIGNER
Alan Leusink

ART DIRECTOR
Alan Leusink

ILLUSTRATOR
Alan Leusink

CREATIVE DIRECTOR
Alan Colvin

CLIENT
Archipelago

AGENCY
Duffy Design/Minneapolis

02090D

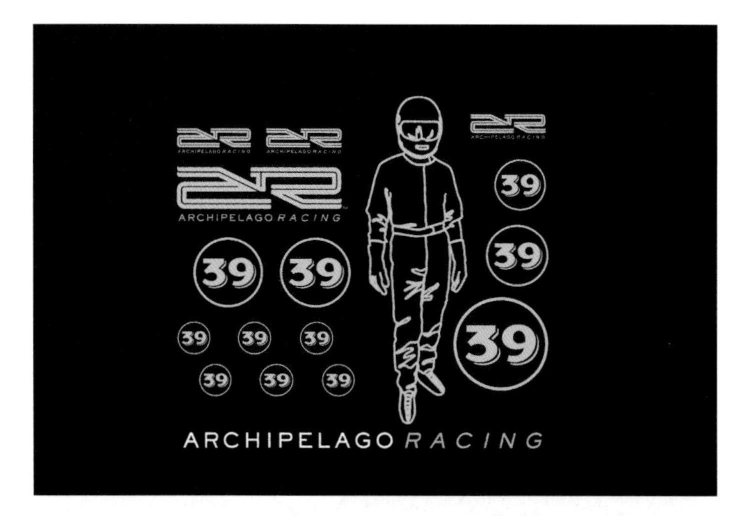

MERIT AWARD
LOGO/TRADEMARK

DESIGNER
Luis Peña

ART DIRECTOR
Luis Peña

ILLUSTRATOR
Luis Peña

CREATIVE DIRECTOR
Luis Peña

CLIENT
Amino

AGENCY
PeñaBrand/Butler Shine & Stern/Sausalito

02088D

MERIT AWARD
LOGO/TRADEMARK

DESIGNERS
Luke Partridge
Kris Wright

ILLUSTRATORS
Luke Partridge
Kris Wright

CREATIVE DIRECTOR
Tom Hudder

CLIENT
Bob Reuter

AGENCY
Rodgers Townsend/St. Louis

02091D

MERIT AWARD
PROMOTIONAL AND POINT-OF-PURCHASE POSTERS

ART DIRECTOR
Alexander Reiss

PHOTOGRAPHERS
Thorsten Kaspar
Fritz Brunier
David Hiepler

ILLUSTRATOR
Tim Belser

WRITERS
Oliver Frank
Judy Horney

CREATIVE DIRECTORS
Lars Oehlschlaeger
André Aimaq

CLIENT
Nike International

AGENCY
Aimaq Rapp Stolle/Berlin

02092D

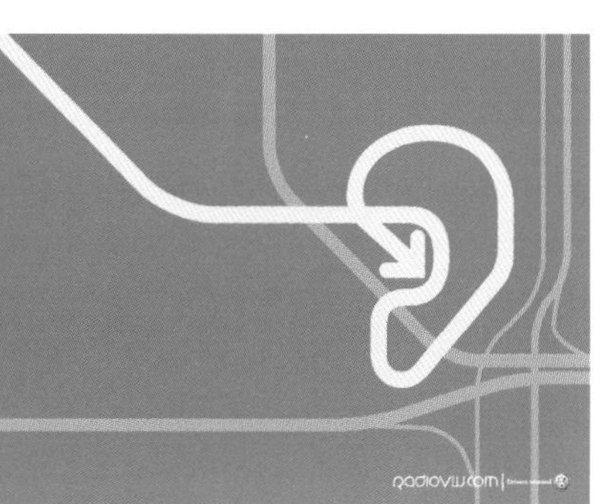

MERIT AWARD
PROMOTIONAL AND POINT-OF-PURCHASE POSTERS

ART DIRECTOR
Chris Bradley

WRITER
Carl Loeb

ILLUSTRATORS
Estero
Kid Acne
Oscar
Fred Deacin
Jago

CREATIVE DIRECTORS
Ron Lawner
Alan Pafenbach

CLIENT
Volkswagen of America

AGENCY
Arnold Worldwide/Boston

02094D

MERIT AWARD
PROMOTIONAL AND POINT-OF-PURCHASE POSTERS

ART DIRECTOR
Chris Bradley

WRITER
Carl Loeb

ILLUSTRATOR
Oscar

CREATIVE DIRECTORS
Ron Lawner
Alan Pafenbach

CLIENT
Volkswagen of America

AGENCY
Arnold Worldwide/Boston

02095D

MERIT AWARD
PROMOTIONAL AND POINT-OF-PURCHASE POSTERS

DESIGNER
Pann Lim

ART DIRECTORS
Pann Lim
Andrew Lok

WRITERS
Andrew Lok
Pann Lim

ILLUSTRATOR
Pann Lim

CREATIVE DIRECTORS
Gary Tranter
Matt Cullen

CLIENT
Singapore Airlines

AGENCY
Batey/Singapore

02093D

DESIGN MERIT

MERIT AWARD
PROMOTIONAL AND POINT-OF-PURCHASE POSTERS

DESIGNER
Travis Olson

ILLUSTRATOR
Travis Olson

CREATIVE DIRECTOR
Bill Thorburn

CLIENT
Children's Theater

AGENCY
Carmichael Lynch/
Minneapolis

02096D

MERIT AWARD
PROMOTIONAL AND POINT-OF-PURCHASE POSTERS

ART DIRECTOR
Jonathan Nah

WRITER
Noel Yeo

CREATIVE DIRECTOR
Lim Soon Huat

CLIENT
Mensa Singapore

AGENCY
Gosh Advertising/Singapore

02097D

Zqd xnt sgd oqnchfx
vd'qd knnjhmf enq?
mensa.org.sg

1.18.5 25.15.21 20.8.5
16.18.15.4.9.7.25 23.5'18.5
12.15.15.11.9.14.7 6.15.18?

mensa.org.sg

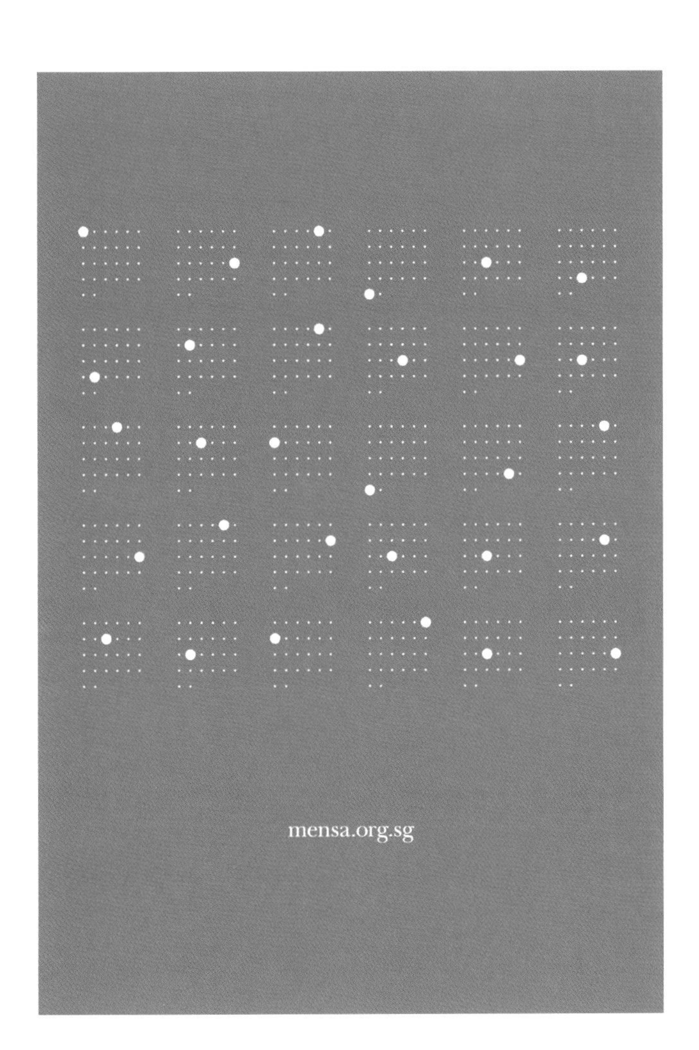

MERIT AWARD
PROMOTIONAL AND POINT-OF-PURCHASE POSTERS

ART DIRECTOR
Jonathan Nah

WRITER
Noel Yeo

CREATIVE DIRECTOR
Lim Soon Huat

CLIENT
Mensa Singapore

AGENCY
Gosh Advertising/Singapore

02098D

MERIT AWARD
PROMOTIONAL AND POINT-OF-PURCHASE POSTERS

DESIGNER
Simon Fairweather

ART DIRECTOR
Melanie Forster

WRITERS
Rob Reilly
Larry Goldstein
Laura Grabe

CREATIVE DIRECTORS
Melanie Forster
Rob Reilly

CLIENT
Popeyes

AGENCY
Hill Holliday/New York

02099D

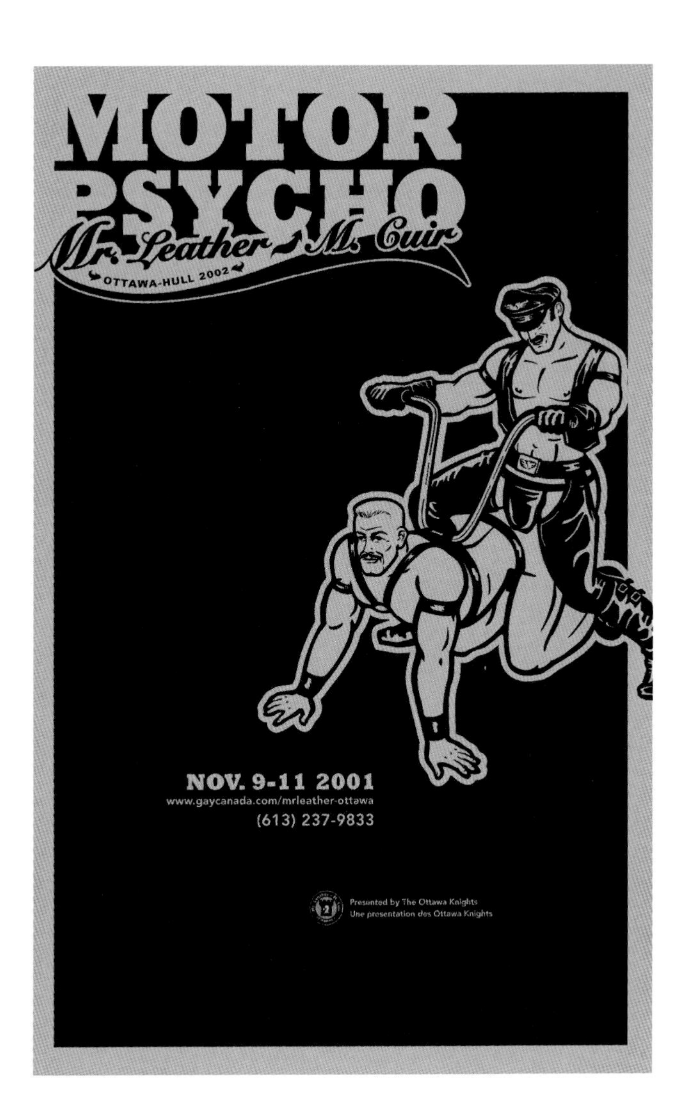

DESIGN MERIT

MERIT AWARD
PROMOTIONAL AND POINT-OF-PURCHASE POSTERS

DESIGNER
Gaëtan Albert

ART DIRECTOR
Jean-Luc Denat

WRITER
Stephen Hards

ILLUSTRATOR
Bérangère Bouffard

CREATIVE DIRECTORS
Mario L'Écuyer
Gaëtan Albert

CLIENT
Ottawa Knights

AGENCY
Iridium Design/Ottawa

02100D

MERIT AWARD
PROMOTIONAL AND POINT-OF-PURCHASE POSTERS

DESIGNER
Heloise Jacobs

WRITERS
Graham Warsop
Brendan Jack

ART DIRECTOR
Heloise Jacobs

ILLUSTRATOR
John Rush

CREATIVE DIRECTOR
Graham Warsop

CLIENT
Discovery Health

AGENCY
The Jupiter Drawing Room/
Johannesburg

02109D

DESIGN MERIT

MERIT AWARD
PROMOTIONAL AND POINT-OF-PURCHASE POSTERS

DESIGNERS
Roy Poh
Pann Lim

ART DIRECTORS
Roy Poh
Pann Lim

WRITERS
Roy Poh
Pann Lim

ILLUSTRATORS
Roy Poh
Pann Lim

PHOTOGRAPHER
Jimmy Fok

CLIENT
Lorgan's The Retro Store

AGENCY
Kinetic Interactive/Singapore

02101D

MERIT AWARD
PROMOTIONAL AND POINT-OF-PURCHASE POSTERS

DESIGNER
Mike Bass

ART DIRECTOR
Mike Bass

WRITER
Bryan Judkins

CLIENT
Bach Dancing & Dynamite Society

AGENCY
Lindsay Stone & Briggs/ Madison

02102D

MERIT AWARD
PROMOTIONAL AND POINT-OF-PURCHASE POSTERS

DESIGNER
Mike Bass

ART DIRECTOR
Mike Bass

WRITER
Bryan Judkins

CLIENT
Bach Dancing & Dynamite Society

AGENCY
Lindsay Stone & Briggs/ Madison

02103D

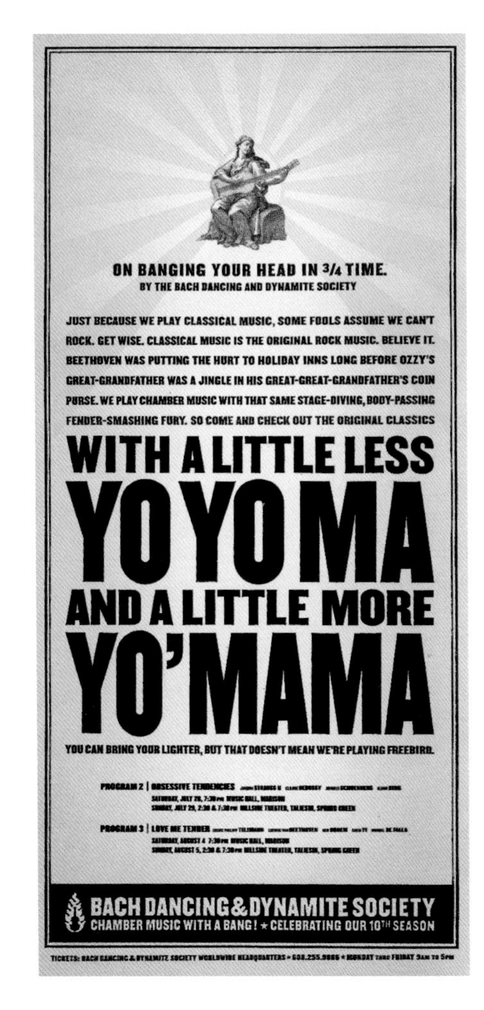

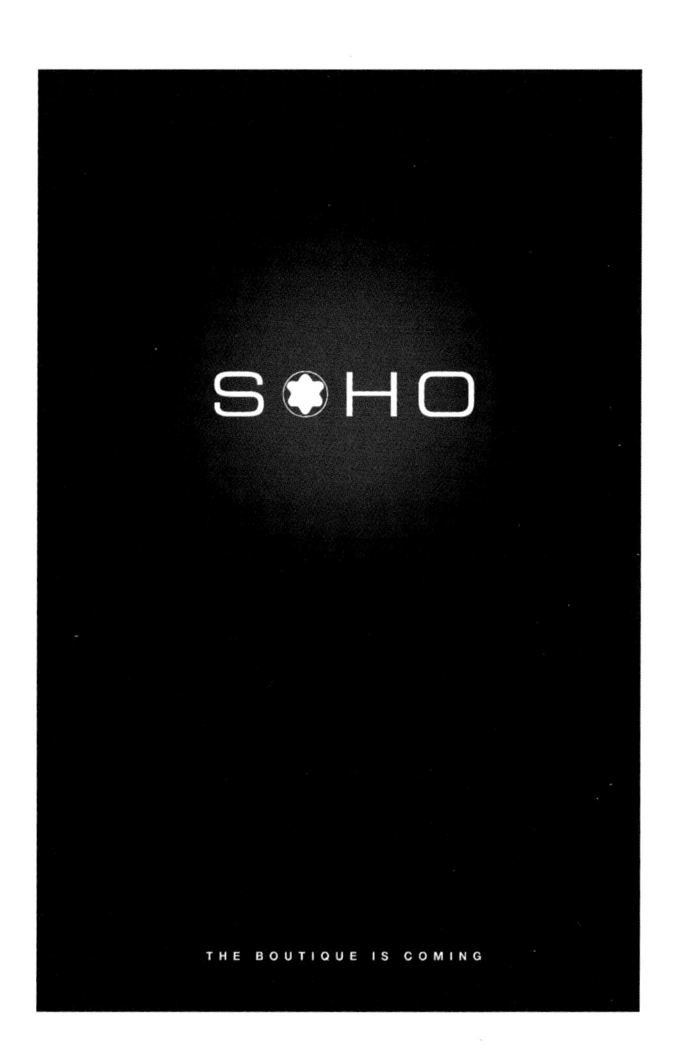

MERIT AWARD
PROMOTIONAL AND POINT-OF-PURCHASE POSTERS

ART DIRECTORS
John Cheung
Elizabeth Maertens

WRITER
Bob Cohen

CREATIVE DIRECTORS
Gary Goldsmith
Dean Hacohen
Lisa Bransom

CLIENT
Montblanc

AGENCY
Lowe/New York

02104D

MERIT AWARD
PROMOTIONAL AND POINT-OF-PURCHASE POSTERS

DESIGNER
Becca Morton

ART DIRECTORS
Becca Morton
Jera Austin

WRITER
Gage Clegg

PHOTOGRAPHER
Gary Jenson

CREATIVE DIRECTORS
Ron Lopez
Randy Snow

CLIENT
Las Vegas Convention and Visitors Authority

AGENCY
R&R Partners/Las Vegas

02105D

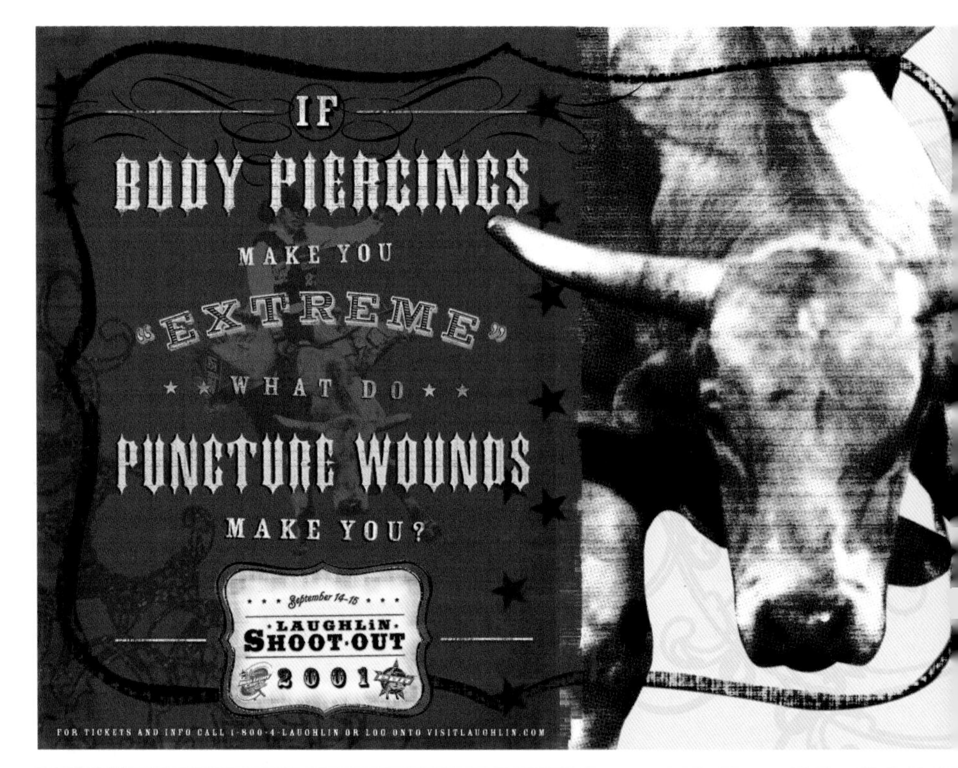

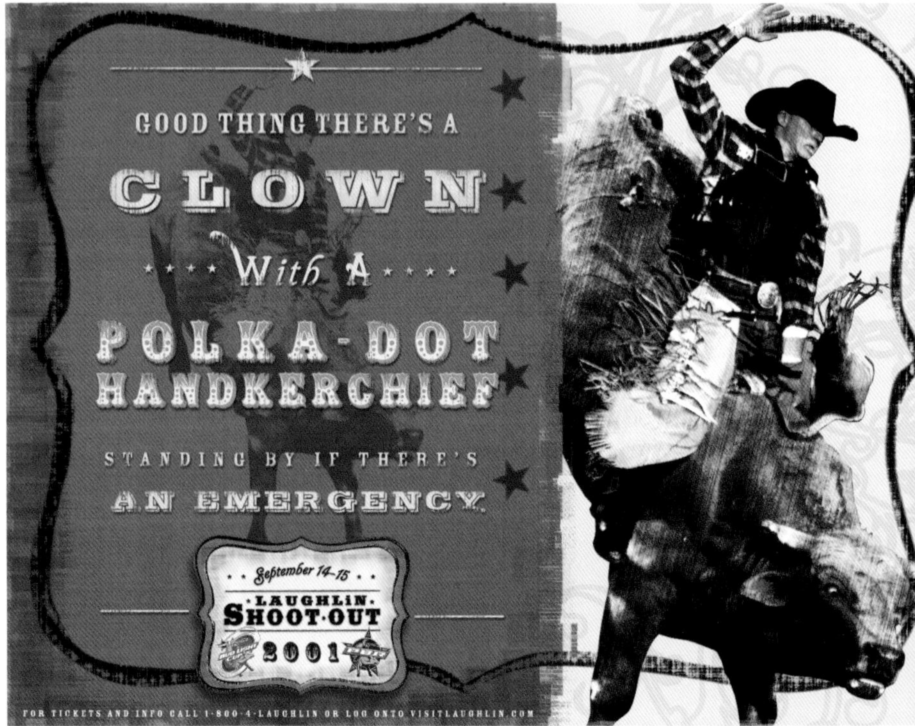

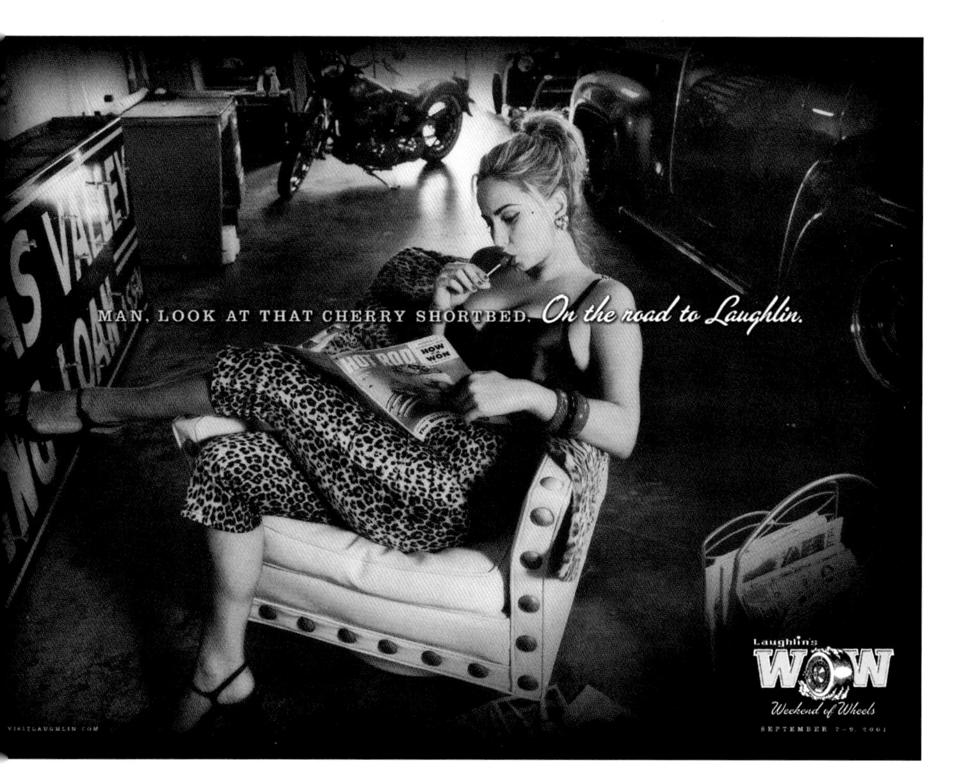

DESIGN MERIT

MERIT AWARD
PROMOTIONAL AND POINT-OF-PURCHASE POSTERS

DESIGNER
Becca Morton

ART DIRECTOR
Becca Morton

WRITER
Gage Clegg

PHOTOGRAPHER
David Perry

CREATIVE DIRECTORS
Ron Lopez
Randy Snow

CLIENT
Las Vegas Convention and Visitors Authority

AGENCY
R&R Partners/Las Vegas

02106D

MERIT AWARD
PROMOTIONAL AND POINT-OF-PURCHASE POSTERS

DESIGNER
Hylton Mann

ART DIRECTOR
Hylton Mann

WRITER
George Low

CREATIVE DIRECTOR
Brett Wild

CLIENT
Petervale

AGENCY
Saatchi & Saatchi/
Johannesburg

02107D

PETERVALE HARDWARE
2001
CALENDAR

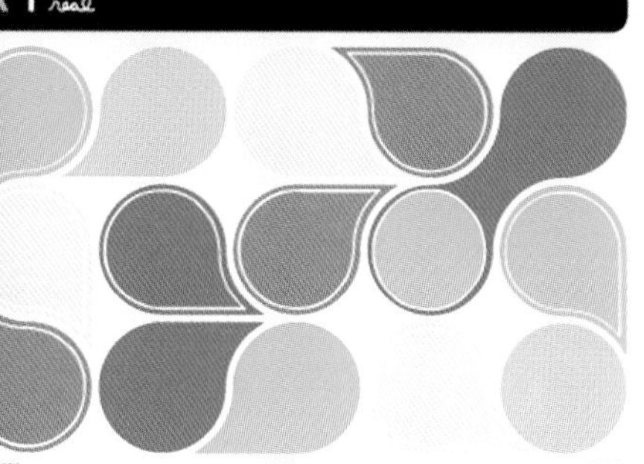

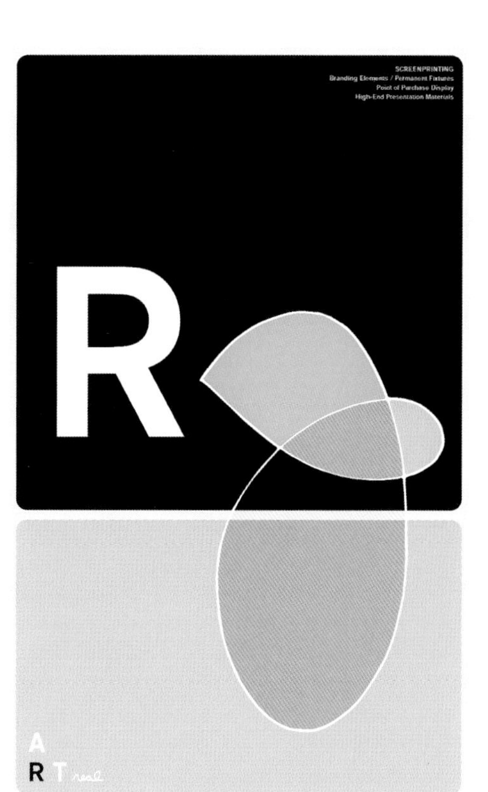

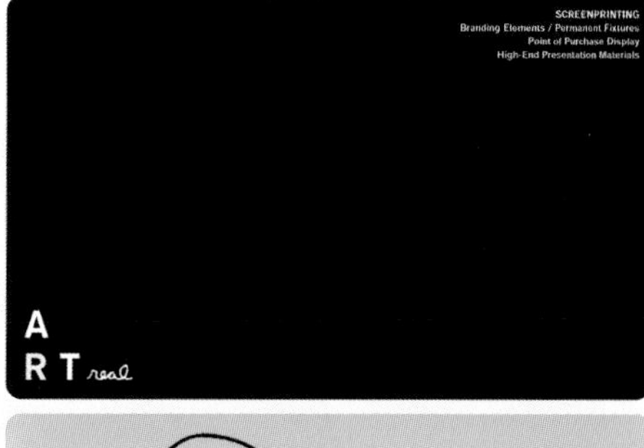

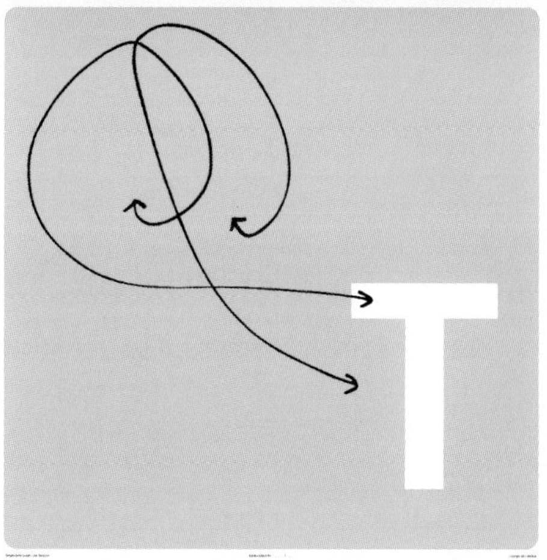

MERIT AWARD
PROMOTIONAL AND POINT-OF-PURCHASE POSTERS

DESIGNER
Brian Gunderson

CREATIVE DIRECTORS
Joel Templin
Gaby Brink

CLIENT
Art Real Screen Printers

AGENCY
Templin Brink Design/
San Francisco

02108D

MERIT AWARD
PUBLIC SERVICE POSTERS

DESIGNERS
Randall Myers
Allen Boe

ART DIRECTOR
Randall Myers

WRITER
Caleb Jensen

ILLUSTRATOR
Greg Paprocki

CREATIVE DIRECTOR
Clint! Runge

CLIENT
Homestead of America

AGENCY
Archrival/Lincoln

02110D

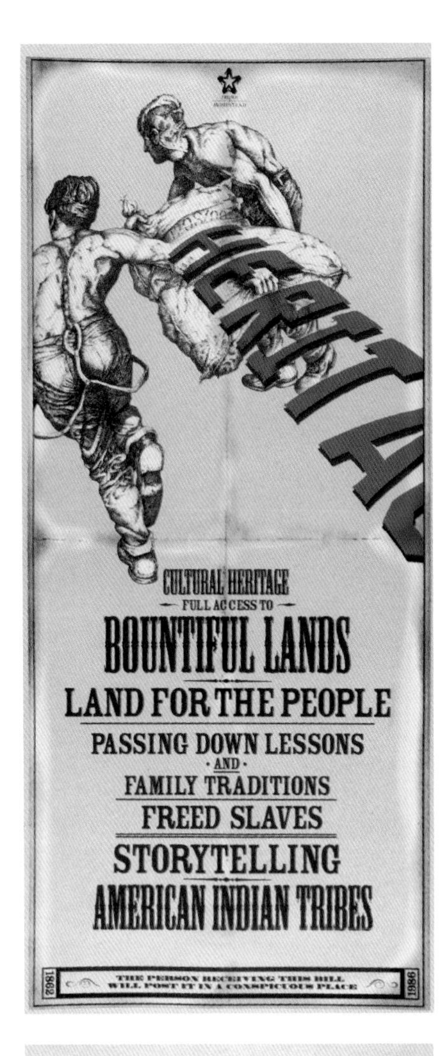

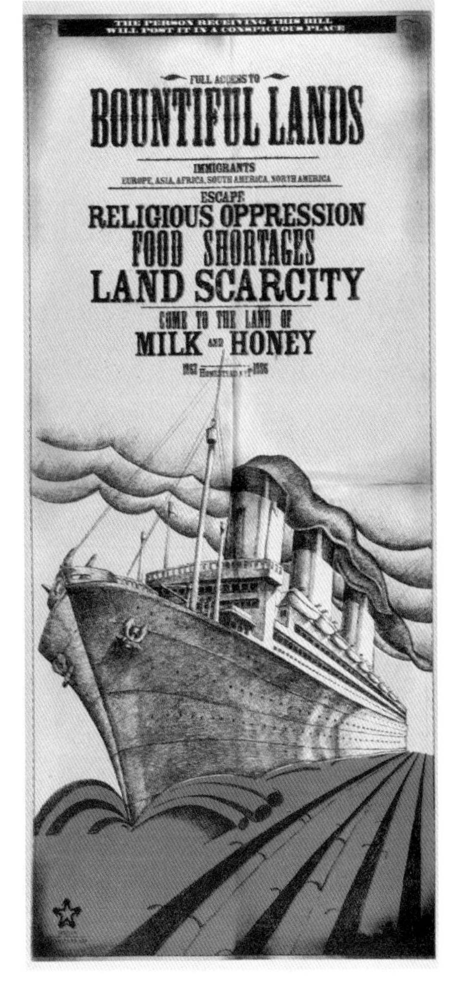

DESIGN MERIT

MERIT AWARD
PUBLIC SERVICE POSTERS

DESIGNER
Katsue Kikita

ART DIRECTORS
Marcus Woolcott
Katsue Kikita

WRITER
Aya Murakoshi

ILLUSTRATOR
Katsue Kikita

CREATIVE DIRECTORS
Alejandro Lopez
Marcus Woolcott

CLIENT
Beacon Communications

AGENCY
Beacon Communications/
Tokyo

02111D

MERIT AWARD
PUBLIC SERVICE POSTERS

DESIGNER
Alan Leusink

ART DIRECTOR
Alan Leusink

ILLUSTRATOR
Alan Leusink

CREATIVE DIRECTOR
Alan Leusink

CLIENT
Art and Architecture

AGENCY
Duffy Design/Minneapolis

02113D

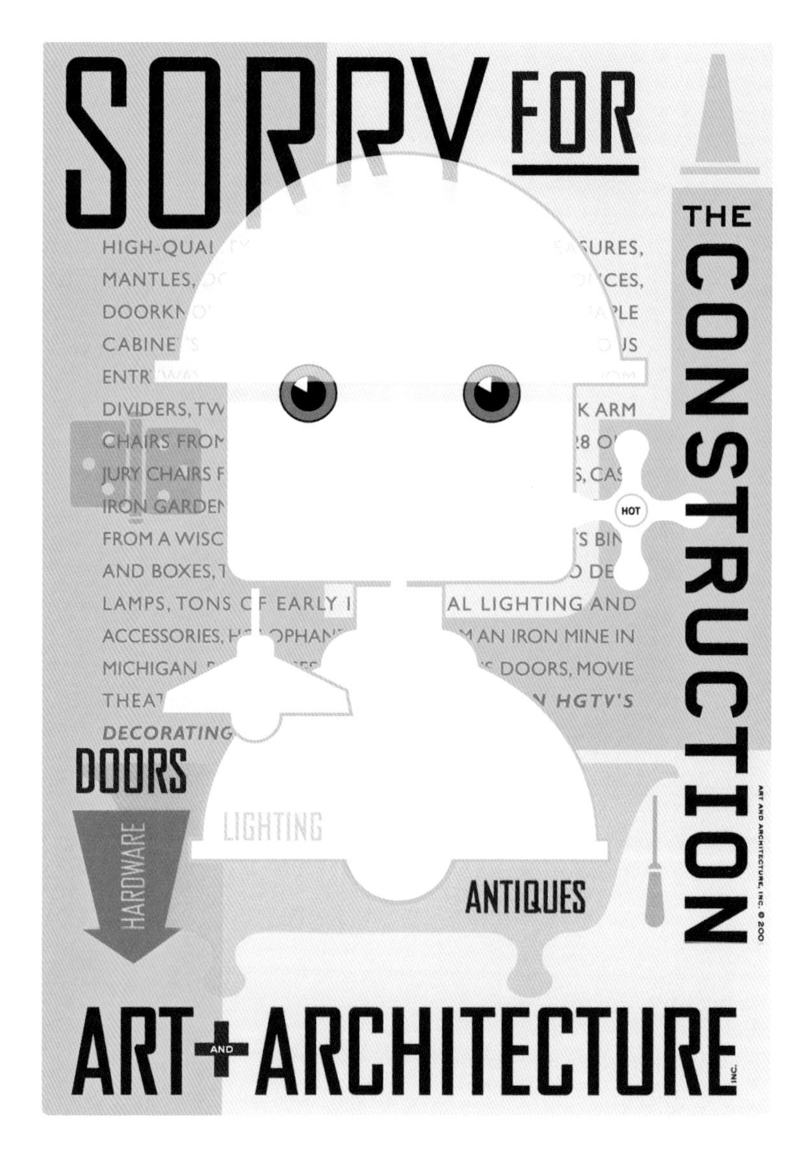

DESIGN MERIT

MERIT AWARD
PUBLIC SERVICE POSTERS

DESIGNERS
Rich Snyder
Paul Curtin

ART DIRECTOR
Paul Curtin

WRITER
Jay Rendon

ILLUSTRATOR
Christopher Wormell

CREATIVE DIRECTOR
Paul Curtin

CLIENT
California Coastal Commission

AGENCY
Eleven/San Francisco

02114D

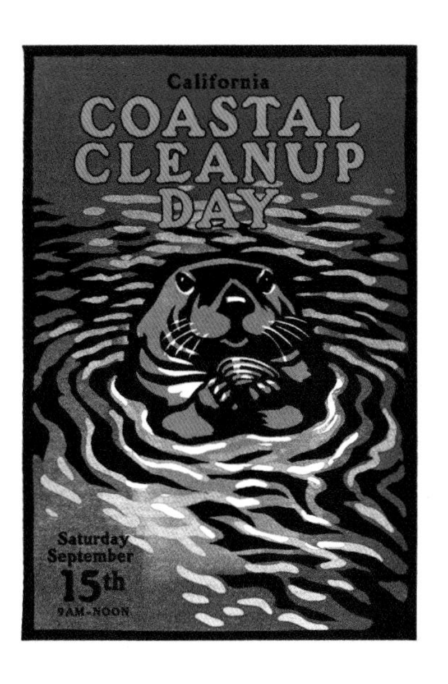

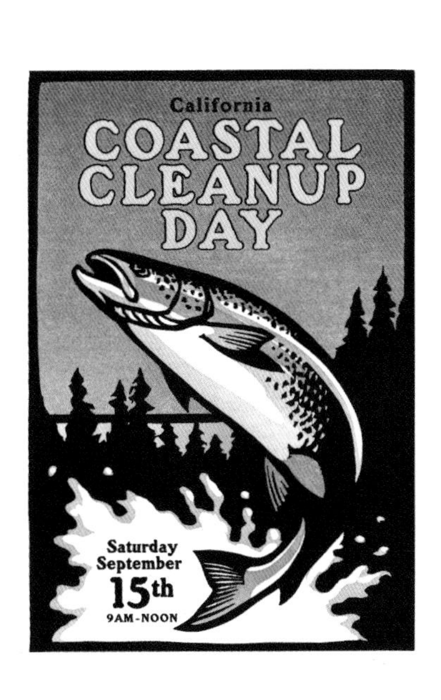

MERIT AWARD
PUBLIC SERVICE POSTERS

DESIGNERS
Rich Silverstein
Shui Wong

ART DIRECTOR
Rich Silverstein

ILLUSTRATOR
Michael Schwab

CREATIVE DIRECTOR
Rich Silverstein

CLIENT
Golden Gate National Parks

AGENCY
Goodby Silverstein &
Partners/San Francisco

02115D

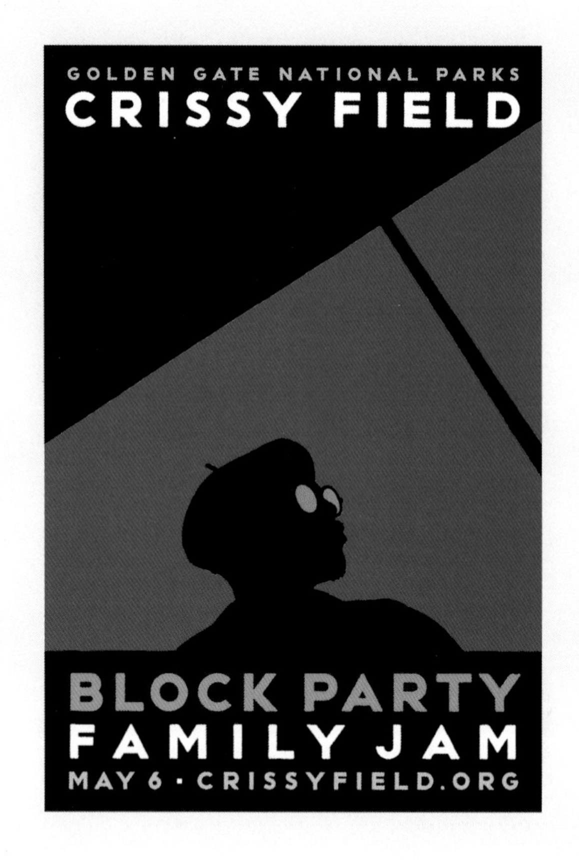

MERIT AWARD
PUBLIC SERVICE POSTERS

DESIGNERS
Rich Silverstein
Shui Wong

ART DIRECTOR
Rich Silverstein

ILLUSTRATOR
Michael Schwab

CREATIVE DIRECTOR
Rich Silverstein

CLIENT
Golden Gate National Parks

AGENCY
Goodby Silverstein &
Partners/San Francisco

02117D

MERIT AWARD
PUBLIC SERVICE POSTERS

DESIGNERS
Rich Silverstein
Shui Wong

ART DIRECTOR
Rich Silverstein

ILLUSTRATOR
R. Kenton Nelson

CREATIVE DIRECTOR
Rich Silverstein

CLIENT
Golden Gate National Parks

AGENCY
Goodby Silverstein &
Partners/San Francisco

02118D

MERIT AWARD
PUBLIC SERVICE POSTERS

DESIGNERS
Rich Silverstein
Shui Wong

ART DIRECTOR
Rich Silverstein

ILLUSTRATOR
Craig Frazier

CREATIVE DIRECTOR
Rich Silverstein

CLIENT
Golden Gate National Parks

AGENCY
Goodby Silverstein &
Partners/San Francisco

02119D

MERIT AWARD
PUBLIC SERVICE POSTERS

DESIGNER
Graham Clifford

ART DIRECTOR
Graham Clifford

WRITER
Graham Clifford

CLIENT
Residents of New York City

AGENCY
Graham Clifford Design/
New York

02120D

Thank you to the Red Cross, FDNY, NYPD and all the rescue workers for their tireless efforts on behalf of all the residents of New York City.

MERIT AWARD
PUBLIC SERVICE POSTERS

ILLUSTRATOR
Brian Niemann

CREATIVE DIRECTOR
Brian Niemann

CLIENT
Salvation Army of Texas

AGENCY
Griffith Phillips Creative/
Dallas

02121D

MERIT AWARD
PUBLIC SERVICE POSTERS

DESIGNER
Gavin Smart

ART DIRECTOR
Anders Kornestedt

WRITER
Björn Engström

CLIENT
Arkitektur Museet

AGENCY
Happy Forsman & Bodenfors/
Göthenburg

02122D

MERIT AWARD
PUBLIC SERVICE POSTERS

DESIGNER
Gavin Smart

ART DIRECTOR
Anders Kornestedt

WRITER
Björn Engström

CLIENT
Arkitektur Museet

AGENCY
Happy Forsman & Bodenfors/
Göthenburg

02123D

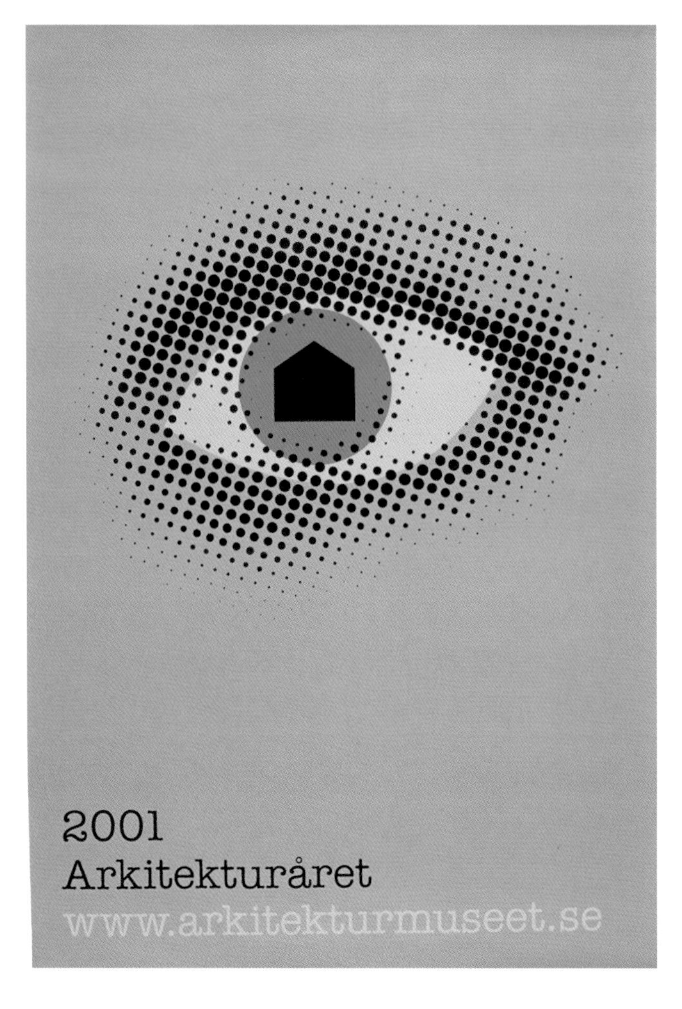

MERIT AWARD
PUBLIC SERVICE POSTERS

DESIGNER
Andreas Kittel

ART DIRECTOR
Andreas Kittel

PHOTOGRAPHERS
Joakim Bergström
Åke Eson Lindman
Björn Keller
Lasse Kärkkäinen
Jonas Linell
Mathias Pettersson

CREATIVE DIRECTOR
Anders Kornestedt

CLIENT
Rohsska Museet

AGENCY
Happy Forsman & Bodenfors/
Göthenburg

02124D

SITT VACKERT
WATER CLOSET WORKSHOP
GUSTAVSBERG 2000
RÖHSSKA MUSEET
9.6–12.8 2001
VASAGATAN 37–39
GÖTEBORG, SVERIGE
WWW.DESIGNMUSEUM.SE

MERIT AWARD
PUBLIC SERVICE POSTERS

DESIGNER
Andreas Kittel

ART DIRECTOR
Andreas Kittel

PHOTOGRAPHER
Jesper Sundelin

CLIENT
Rohsska Museet

AGENCY
Happy Forsman & Bodenfors/
Göthenburg

02125D

MERIT AWARD
PUBLIC SERVICE POSTERS

DESIGNERS
Pann Lim
Roy Poh

ART DIRECTORS
Pann Lim
Roy Poh

WRITERS
Andrew Lok
Kok Hong

ILLUSTRATORS
Pann Lim
Roy Poh

PHOTOGRAPHER
Jimmy Fok

CLIENT
Residents' Committee

AGENCY
Kinetic Interactive/Singapore

02126D

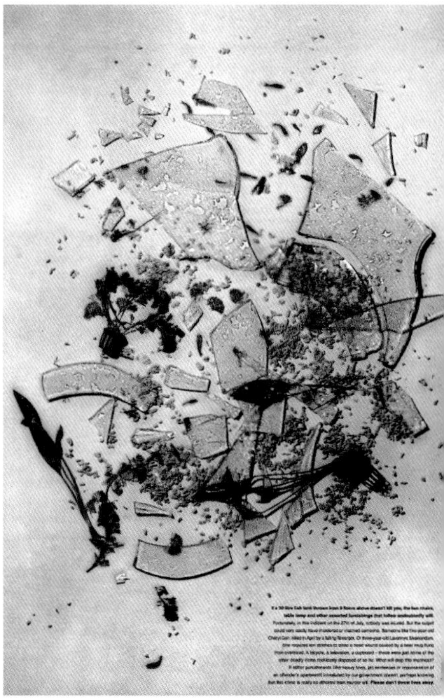

MERIT AWARD
PUBLIC SERVICE POSTERS

DESIGNERS
Pann Lim
Roy Poh

ART DIRECTORS
Pann Lim
Roy Poh

WRITERS
Alex Goh
Pann Lim
Roy Poh

ILLUSTRATOR
Edward Loh

PHOTOGRAPHER
Edward Loh

CLIENT
Singapore Cancer Society

AGENCY
Kinetic Interactive/Singapore

02127D

MERIT AWARD
PUBLIC SERVICE POSTERS

DESIGNERS
Pann Lim
Roy Poh

ART DIRECTORS
Pann Lim
Roy Poh

WRITERS
Pann Lim
Roy Poh

ILLUSTRATORS
Pann Lim
Roy Poh

PHOTOGRAPHER
Jimmy Fok

CLIENT
Singapore Petroleum Limited

AGENCY
Kinetic Interactive/Singapore

02128D

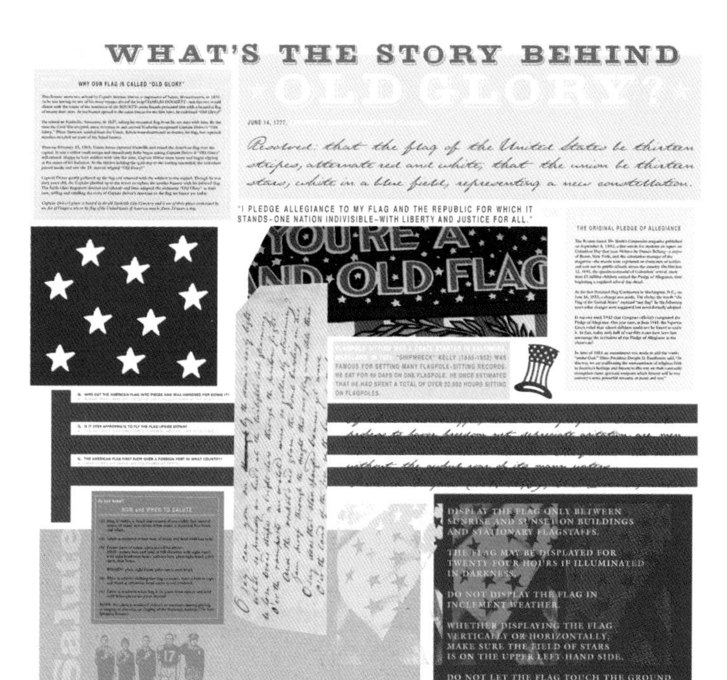

DESIGN MERIT

MERIT AWARD
PUBLIC SERVICE POSTERS

DESIGNER
Karen Hostetter Kilpatrick

ART DIRECTOR
Karen Hostetter Kilpatrick

CREATIVE DIRECTOR
Joel McWhorter

CLIENT
McWhorter Design

AGENCY
McWhorter Design/Decatur

02129D

MERIT AWARD
PUBLIC SERVICE POSTERS

ART DIRECTOR
Alexander Heil

WRITER
Cora Walker

PHOTOGRAPHER
Stock

CLIENT
Frankfurter Museum

AGENCY
Ogilvy & Mather/Frankfurt

02130D

MERIT AWARD
PUBLIC SERVICE POSTERS

DESIGNER
Luis Peña

ART DIRECTOR
Luis Peña

ILLUSTRATOR
Luis Peña

CREATIVE DIRECTOR
Luis Peña

CLIENT
Amnesty International

AGENCY
PeñaBrand/Butler Shine & Stern/Sausalito

02112D

DESIGN MERIT

MERIT AWARD
PUBLIC SERVICE POSTERS

DESIGNER
Don Emery

WRITER
Mike Noble

CREATIVE DIRECTOR
Brock Haldeman

CLIENT
AIGA

AGENCY
Pivot Design/Chicago

02131D

Thursday, June 14, 5:30–9:30pm
AIGA Chicago 2001 Annual Members Meeting
A Backyard Barbecue with

Milton Glaser

Sponsored by:
Appleton Coated • Aquent • Beckett/Strathmore Papers • Digital Logic • Domtar Papers • Dupli-Graphic • Fine Arts Engraving • Fox River Paper Company • The Fox Company • Fraser Papers
Gilbert Paper • Graphic Packaging/Arrow Gold • Jet Lithocolor Inc. • Lake County Press, Inc. • Mead Corporation • Mohawk Paper Mills • Potlatch Corporation • Quantum Color Graphics
Rohrer Letterpress • RPP Printing Enterprises, Inc. • Unique Printers • Unisource • Wickander Printing Corporation

UNDER
GRADUATE
SUMMER
RESEARCH IN
NANOTECHNOLOGY
NORTHWESTERN UNIVERSITY
TWO PROGRAMS. UNLIMITED POSSIBILITIES.

Minority
Internships in
Nanotechnology
(MIN)

Develop your potential, increase your knowledge, and gain valuable experience in the exciting new field of nanotechnology.

Nanotechnology is widely viewed as the most significant technological frontier currently being explored. Materials and devices at the nanoscale (a nanometer is one billionth of one meter) hold vast promise for innovation in virtually every industry.

At the Nanoscale Science and Engineering Center (NSEC) head-quartered at Northwestern University, researchers are addressing the myriad of challenges in nanotechnology. One of only six such centers established in the country, the NU-NSEC focuses on pioneering research in chemical and biological sensors that could change our world.

Through the REU and MIN programs, the NU-NSEC offers opportunities for undergraduates to engage in hands-on research for a 9-week period over the summer.

Undergraduates who are U.S. citizens or permanent residents, majoring in the physical sciences or engineering, with at least one year remaining to complete their degree are welcomed to apply. Applicants to the MIN program must also be of African-American, Latino, or Hispanic descent.

Participants receive a total stipend of $4,000 for the 9-week program.

Applications are available on line at www.nsec.northwestern.edu or call 847.491.5784

MERIT AWARD
PUBLIC SERVICE POSTERS

DESIGNER
Don Emery

CREATIVE DIRECTOR
Brock Haldeman

CLIENT
Institute for Nanotechnology

AGENCY
Pivot Design/Chicago

02132D

DESIGN MERIT

MERIT AWARD
PUBLIC SERVICE POSTERS

ART DIRECTOR
Marco Howell

WRITER
Kay Cochran

CREATIVE DIRECTOR
Tom Hudder

CLIENT
Black World History Museum

AGENCY
Rodgers Townsend/St. Louis

02133D

MERIT AWARD
PUBLIC SERVICE POSTERS

ART DIRECTORS
Rob Semos
Jefferson Rall

ILLUSTRATOR
Gary Baseman

CREATIVE DIRECTOR
Bruce Broder

CLIENT
Much Ado About Books

AGENCY
St. John & Partners/
Jacksonville

02134D

MERIT AWARD
PUBLIC SERVICE POSTERS

DESIGNER
Anna Qiu

ART DIRECTOR
Helen Dou

WRITER
Lilian Shen

PHOTOGRAPHER
Yi Yan

CREATIVE DIRECTOR
Wendy Cheung

CLIENT
Shenzen Social Protection Governor

AGENCY
TBWA/Shanghai

02135D

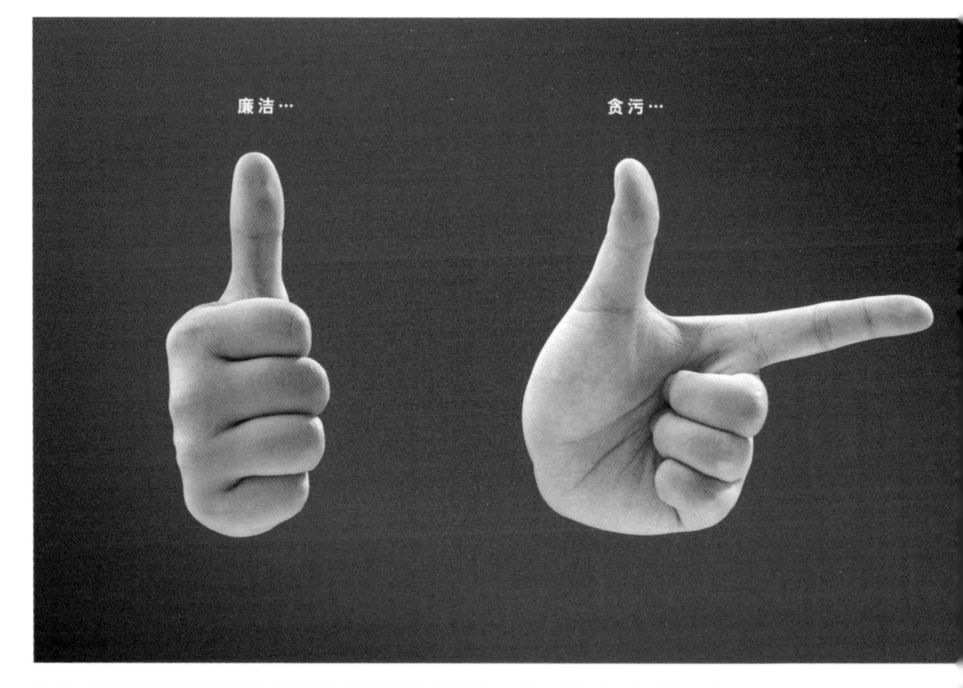

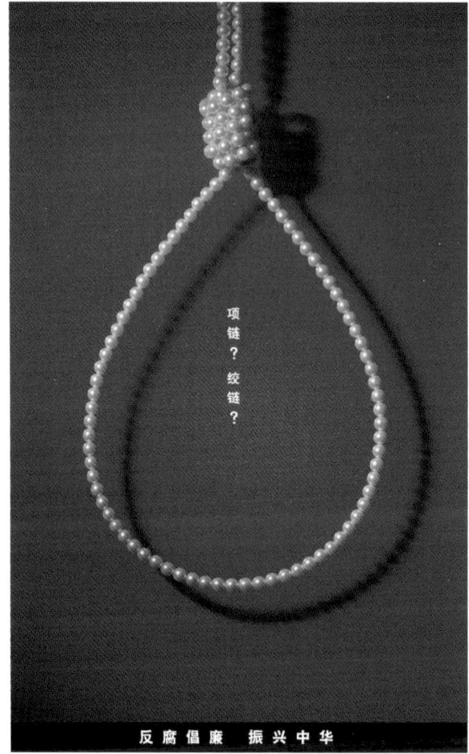

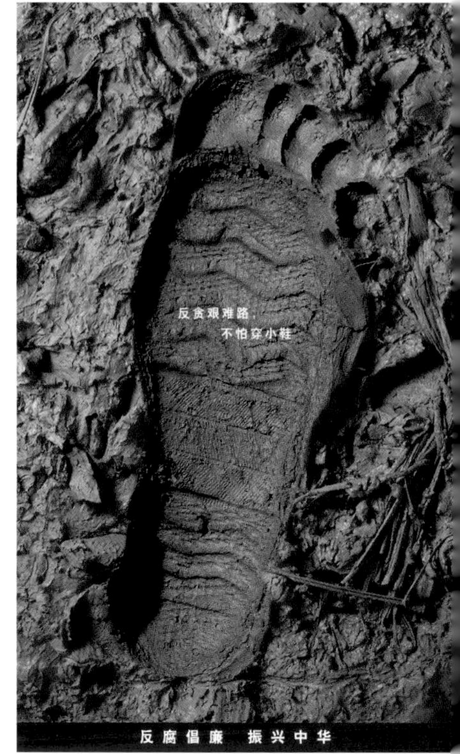

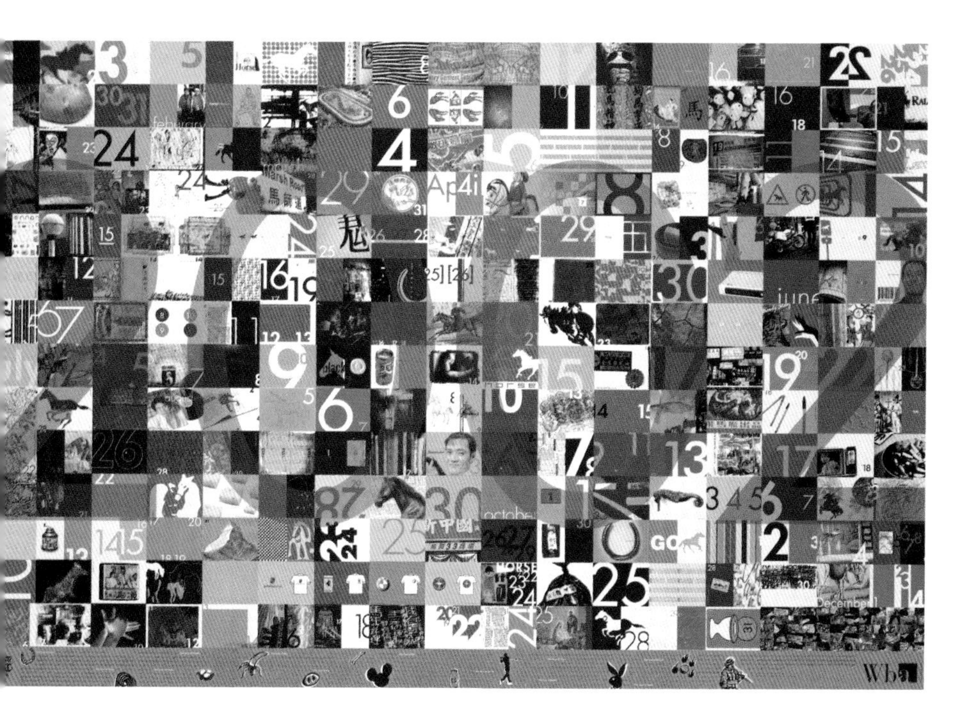

DESIGN MERIT

MERIT AWARD
PUBLIC SERVICE POSTERS

DESIGNERS
Charine Chan
Liver Ng
Tommy Chung
Manfred Chung

ART DIRECTORS
David Lo
Dennis Ou
Ringo Hui

WRITER
Ophelia Lau

ILLUSTRATORS
David Lo
Ringo Hui

CREATIVE DIRECTOR
David Lo

CLIENT
WBA HK Limited

AGENCY
WBA HK Limited/Hong Kong

02136D

MERIT AWARD
COMMERCIAL PRODUCT PACKAGING

DESIGNER
Alex Lea

ART DIRECTOR
Kevin Brady

WRITER
Kevin Brady

CLIENT
Kevin Brady

AGENCY
Bozell/New York

02137D

MERIT AWARD
COMMERCIAL PRODUCT PACKAGING

DESIGNER
David Schrimpf

WRITER
Zaar Taha

CREATIVE DIRECTOR
Bill Thorburn

CLIENT
Potlatch

AGENCY
Carmichael Lynch/
Minneapolis

02138D

DESIGN MERIT

MERIT AWARD
COMMERCIAL PRODUCT PACKAGING

DESIGNERS
Todd Piper-Hauswirth
Kyle Hames

ART DIRECTORS
Charles S. Anderson
Todd Piper-Hauswirth

WRITERS
Lisa Pemrick
Charles S. Anderson
John Gross

ILLUSTRATOR
CSA Images

CLIENT
CSA Images

AGENCY
Charles S. Anderson Design/
Minneapolis

02139D

MERIT AWARD
COMMERCIAL PRODUCT PACKAGING

DESIGNER
Chris Pinkham

ART DIRECTOR
Chris Pinkham

WRITERS
Tom Kelly
Lawson Clarke

CREATIVE DIRECTOR
Jim Amadeo

CLIENT
Tealuxe

AGENCY
Clarke Goward/Boston

02140D

MERIT AWARD
COMMERCIAL PRODUCT PACKAGING

DESIGNER
Carlos Gabriel

ART DIRECTOR
Carlos Gabriel

WRITER
Carlos Gabriel

CREATIVE DIRECTORS
Peter Harle
Dave Woods

CLIENT
UDV

AGENCY
Claydonheeleyjonesmason/London

02141D

MERIT AWARD
COMMERCIAL PRODUCT PACKAGING

DESIGNER
Suzanne Langley

PHOTOGRAPHER
Joseph Hunwick

CREATIVE DIRECTORS
Shaun Dew
Steve Gibbons

CLIENT
Procter & Gamble

AGENCY
Dew Gibbons/London

02142D

MERIT AWARD
COMMERCIAL PRODUCT PACKAGING

DESIGNER
Matthew Clark

ART DIRECTOR
Matthew Clark

CREATIVE DIRECTOR
Maria Kennedy

CLIENT
CC Beverage Corporation

AGENCY
Karacters Design Group/
Vancouver

02143D

MERIT AWARD
COMMERCIAL PRODUCT PACKAGING

DESIGNER
Cheryl Meyer

WRITER
Eugene Fuller

CREATIVE DIRECTOR
Charlie Callahan

CLIENT
Buffalo Wild Wings

AGENCY
Periscope/Minneapolis

02144D

**MERIT AWARD
COMMERCIAL PRODUCT
PACKAGING**

DESIGNER
Steve Sandstrom

ART DIRECTOR
Steve Sandstrom

WRITERS
Candace Gonzales
Dave Scott
Dennis Constantine

CREATIVE DIRECTOR
Steve Sandstrom

CLIENT
Kink fm102

AGENCY
Sandstrom Design/Portland

02146D

MERIT AWARD
COMMERCIAL PRODUCT PACKAGING

DESIGNERS
Steve Sandstrom
Michele Melandri

ART DIRECTORS
Steve Sandstrom
Michele Melandri

WRITER
Craig Simpson

CREATIVE DIRECTOR
Steve Sandstrom

CLIENT
Kombucha Wonder Drink

AGENCY
Sandstrom Design/Portland

02147D

MERIT AWARD
COMMERCIAL PRODUCT PACKAGING

DESIGNER
Steve Sandstrom

ART DIRECTOR
Steve Sandstrom

WRITERS
Steve Sandoz
Palmer Pettersen

CREATIVE DIRECTOR
Steve Sandstrom

CLIENT
Tazo

AGENCY
Sandstrom Design/Portland

02148D

**MERIT AWARD
COMMERCIAL PRODUCT
PACKAGING**

DESIGNER
Oscar Snidare

ART DIRECTOR
Ann-Marie Wessman

WRITER
Mattias Jersild

PHOTOGRAPHER
Mikael Jansson

CLIENT
Vin & Spirit/Amfora Vinhus

AGENCY
Schumacher Jersild Wessman
& Enander/Stockholm

02149D

**MERIT AWARD
COMMERCIAL PRODUCT
PACKAGING**

DESIGNER
Oscar Snidare

ART DIRECTOR
Ann-Marie Wessman

CLIENT
R.O.O.M.

AGENCY
Schumacher Jersild Wessman
& Enander/Stockholm

02150D

DESIGN MERIT

MERIT AWARD COMMERCIAL PRODUCT PACKAGING

ART DIRECTOR
Andy Gass

WRITER
Scott Shalles

CREATIVE DIRECTOR
Vincent LoPresti

CLIENT
Supre

AGENCY
Signal/Addison

02151D

MERIT AWARD COMMERCIAL PRODUCT PACKAGING

DESIGNERS
Clare McGoldrick
Michelle Donnelly
Dave Watson

WRITER
Jane Murray

ILLUSTRATOR
Michelle Donnelly

CREATIVE DIRECTOR
Jane Hope

CLIENT
Corel

AGENCY
Taxi/Toronto

02152D

DESIGN MERIT

MERIT AWARD
COMMERCIAL PRODUCT
PACKAGING

DESIGNER
David Turner

CREATIVE DIRECTORS
David Turner
Bruce Duckworth

CLIENT
McKenzie River Corporation

AGENCY
Turner Duckworth/
San Francisco

02153D

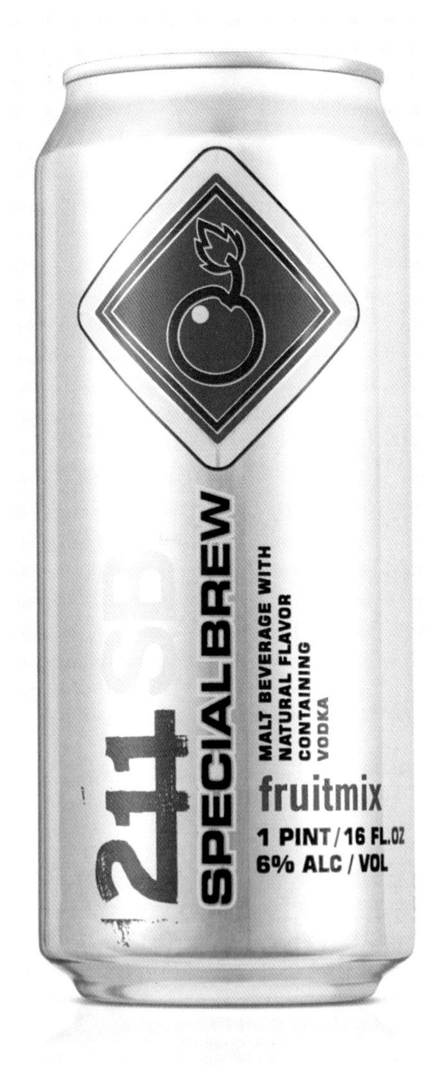

MERIT AWARD
ENVIRONMENT

DESIGNERS
John Nordon
Peter Maxwell

CREATIVE DIRECTOR
Kathryn Findlay

CLIENT
Claydonheeleyjonesmason

AGENCY
Claydonheeleyjonesmason/
London

02154D

MERIT AWARD
DIRECT MAIL

DESIGNER
Dawn Selg

WRITER
Tim Alevizos

CLIENT
Gage

AGENCY
Agency Eleven/Minneapolis

02155D

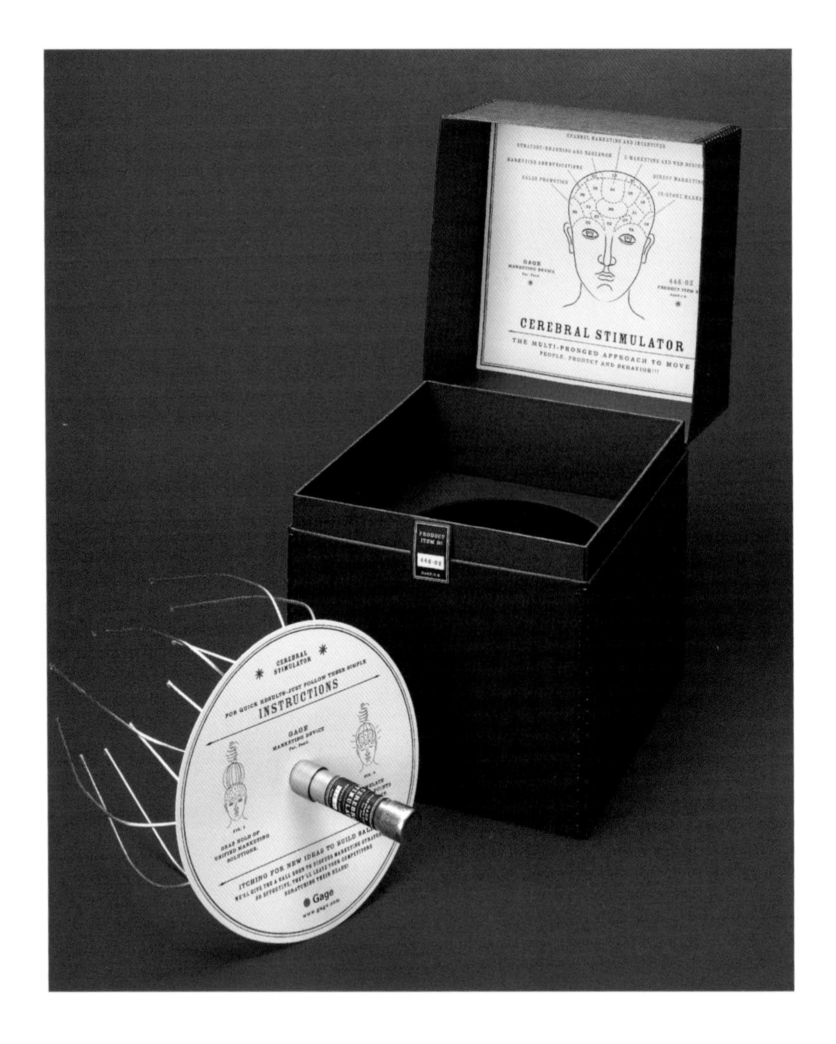

MERIT AWARD
DIRECT MAIL

DESIGNER
Jennifer O'Brien

WRITER
HoJo Willenzik

CLIENT
UPM

AGENCY
Agency Eleven/Minneapolis

02156D

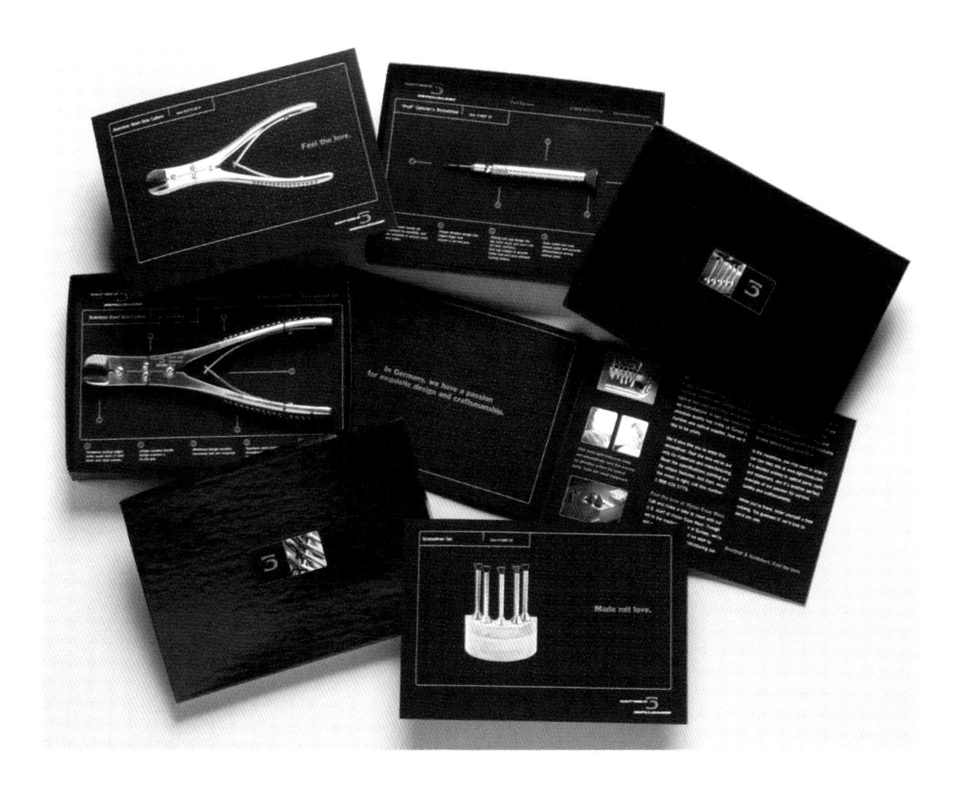

DESIGN MERIT

MERIT AWARD DIRECT MAIL

DESIGNERS
Paul Howell
Rene Molina

ART DIRECTOR
Paul Howell

WRITER
Arlyn Stotts

PHOTOGRAPHERS
Gerd George
Stefan Lindauer
Fred Kopke
Anil Chanrai

CREATIVE DIRECTOR
Paul Howell

CLIENT
Breitfeld & Schliekert

AGENCY
Alpern Lehman/Scottsdale

02157D

THE MARTIN AGENCY

October 8, 2001

Bill Jones
4035 Piedmont Parkway
High Point, NC 27265

Dear Bill,

Thank you for your interest in The Martin Agency. Unfortunately, your qualifications don't match our needs at this time.

Allow me to offer this suggestion: take some pointers from eminent headhunter Guy Tucker. If you'd followed Guy's advice, by now you'd be working right down the hall from me, and perhaps even calling me by my affectionate nickname, "Sparky."

As luck would have it, Guy is presenting his career-boosting wisdom at the Ad Club of the Triad on Thursday, October 25. I suggest you call 316-5144 to RSVP, or visit adclubofthetriad.com.

If our needs change in the future, I'll have your resume on file.

Sincerely,

Mike Hughes
President

CLIFF FREEMAN AND PARTNERS

October 8, 2001

Bob Smith
210 South Cherry Street
Winston-Salem, NC 27101

Dear Bob,

Thank you for your interest in Cliff Freeman and Partners. I regret to inform you that your qualifications do not meet our needs at this time.

In the spirit of offering you helpful advice, I suggest you learn what you can from prominent headhunter Guy Tucker. Had you followed Guy's career counsel, you'd have been here long ago, and by now built a little log cabin out of One Show pencils.

Fortunately for you, Guy is presenting his career-boosting wisdom at the Ad Club of the Triad on Thursday, October 25. I suggest you call 316-5144 to RSVP, or visit adclubofthetriad.com.

In the meantime, we will file your resume should an appropriate position become available.

Sincerely,

Cliff Freeman
Chairman/Chief Creative Officer

375 HUDSON STREET NEW YORK CITY 10014 212 463 3200

Fallon | Minneapolis

October 8, 2001

Jane Williams
212 South Elm Street
Greensboro, NC 27401

Dear Jane,

Thank you for your interest in Fallon. At this time, we have no requirements for a person with your qualifications.

Your inquiry might have met with a more positive response had you been fortunate enough to receive guidance from astute headhunter Guy Tucker. If you'd followed Guy's career advice, by now you'd probably have a lifetime pass to the executive hot tub here at Fallon.

As it happens, Guy is presenting his career-boosting wisdom at the Ad Club of the Triad on Thursday, October 25. I suggest you call 316-5144 to RSVP, or visit adclubofthetriad.com.

In the meantime, we will file your resume. Again, thank you for your interest.

Sincerely,

David Lubars
President/Executive Creative Director

MERIT AWARD DIRECT MAIL

DESIGNER
Mark Brown

ART DIRECTOR
Mark Brown

WRITER
Mike Turner

CREATIVE DIRECTORS
Mark Brown
Mike Turner

CLIENT
Ad Club of the Triad

AGENCY
Bouvier Kelly/Greensboro

02158D

MERIT AWARD
DIRECT MAIL

DESIGNER
Suzanne Shade

ART DIRECTOR
Suzanne Shade

WRITER
Nicole Michels

CREATIVE DIRECTORS
John Butler
Mike Shine

CLIENT
Nuance Communications

AGENCY
Butler Shine & Stern/Sausalito

02163D

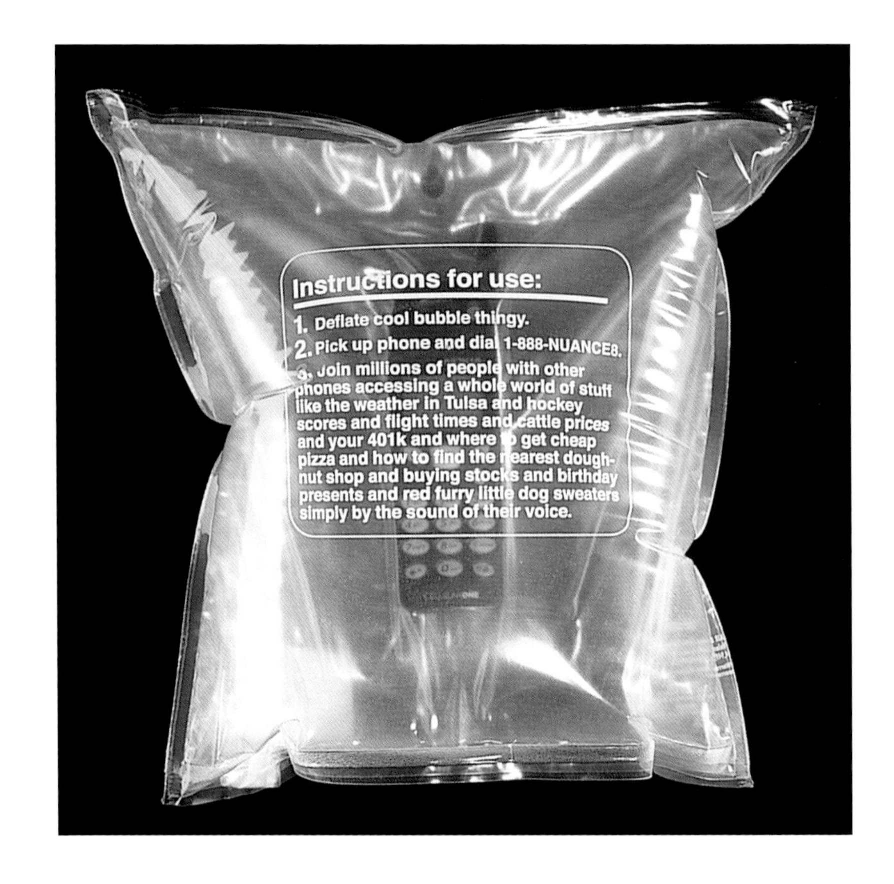

MERIT AWARD
DIRECT MAIL

DESIGNERS
Matthew Crouch
Kevin Fitzgerald
Jacob Escobedo
Bob Fisher
Jay Rogers
Annie Liebert
Joe Williams
Ryan Summers

ART DIRECTORS
Bob Fisher
Kevin Fitzgerald

WRITER
Merrill Hagan

CREATIVE DIRECTOR
Gary Albright

CLIENT
Cartoon Network

AGENCY
Cartoon Network/Atlanta

02165D

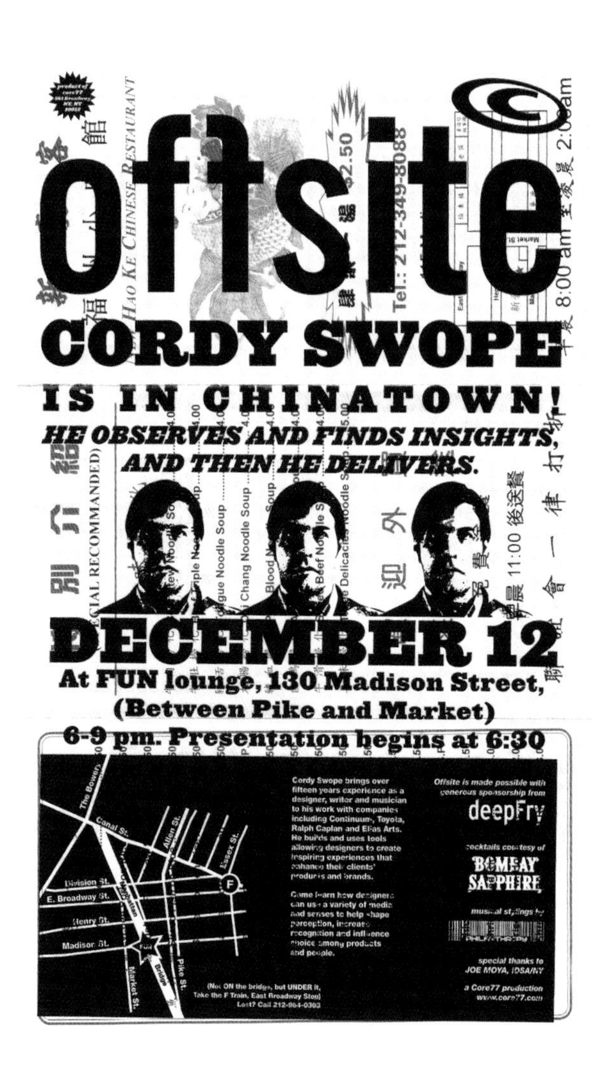

MERIT AWARD
DIRECT MAIL

DESIGNER
Frank Bonomo

ART DIRECTOR
Eric Ludlum

WRITER
Allan Chochinov

CREATIVE DIRECTOR
Eric Ludlum

CLIENT
Off Site

AGENCY
Core 77/New York

02166D

MERIT AWARD
DIRECT MAIL

DESIGNER
Mike del Marmol

ART DIRECTOR
Mike del Marmol

WRITER
Tom Adams

PHOTOGRAPHER
Sebastian Gray

CREATIVE DIRECTOR
Alex Bogusky

CLIENT
Florida Department of Health

AGENCY
Crispin Porter & Bogusky/
Miami

02167D

MERIT AWARD
DIRECT MAIL

ART DIRECTORS
Tony Calcao
Andrew Keller

WRITERS
Steve O'Connell
Ari Merkin

PHOTOGRAPHERS
Sebastian Gray
Tony Calcao

CREATIVE DIRECTOR
Alex Bogusky

CLIENT
MINI

AGENCY
Crispin Porter & Bogusky/
Miami

02168D

DESIGN MERIT

MERIT AWARD
DIRECT MAIL

DESIGNER
Alan Leusink

ART DIRECTOR
Alan Leusink

WRITER
Scott Vincent

ILLUSTRATOR
Alan Leusink

CREATIVE DIRECTOR
Alan Colvin

CLIENT
Archipelago

AGENCY
Duffy Design/Minneapolis

02169D

MERIT AWARD
DIRECT MAIL

DESIGNERS
Alan Leusink
Nate Hinz

ART DIRECTOR
Alan Leusink

WRITER
Mark Wirt

ILLUSTRATOR
Alan Leusink

CREATIVE DIRECTOR
Alan Colvin

CLIENT
Archipelago

AGENCY
Duffy Design/Minneapolis

02170D

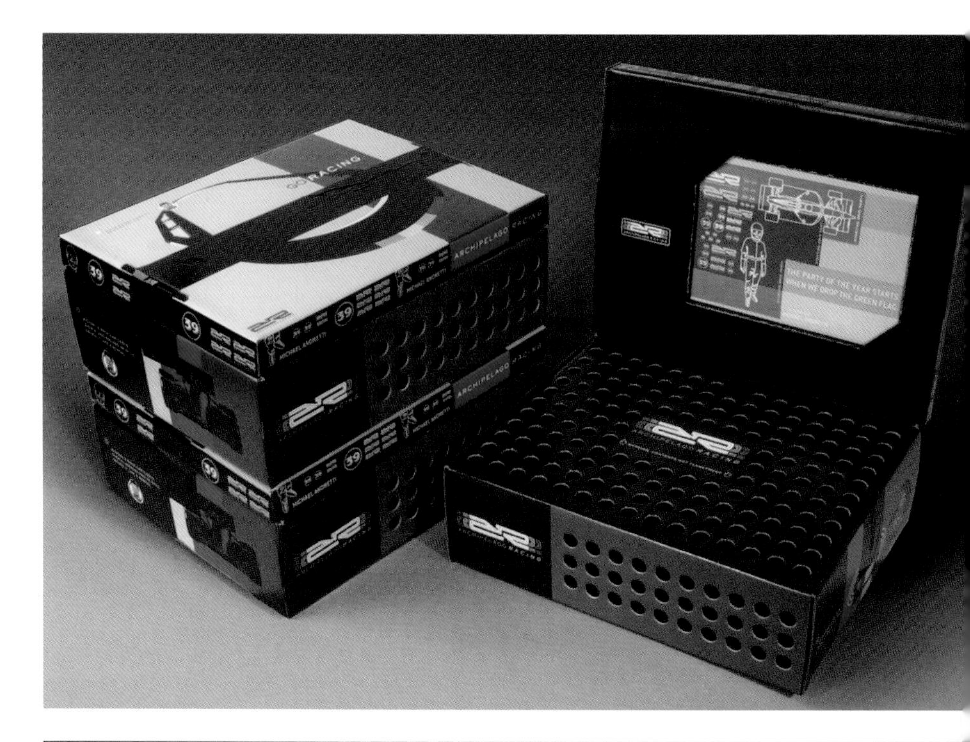

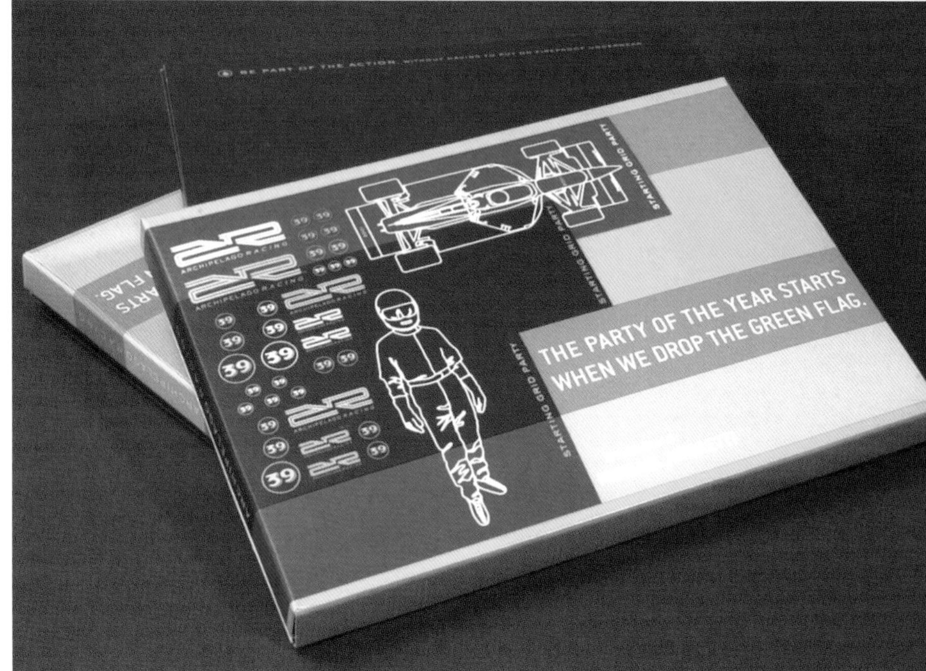

DESIGN MERIT

MERIT AWARD
DIRECT MAIL

DESIGNER
Greg Motylenski

ART DIRECTOR
Greg Motylenski

WRITER
Craig Strydom

ILLUSTRATORS
Adam McCauley
Mark Matcho

CREATIVE DIRECTOR
Stephen Etzine

CLIENT
Farmers & Mechanics Bank

AGENCY
Eisner Communications/
Baltimore

02172D

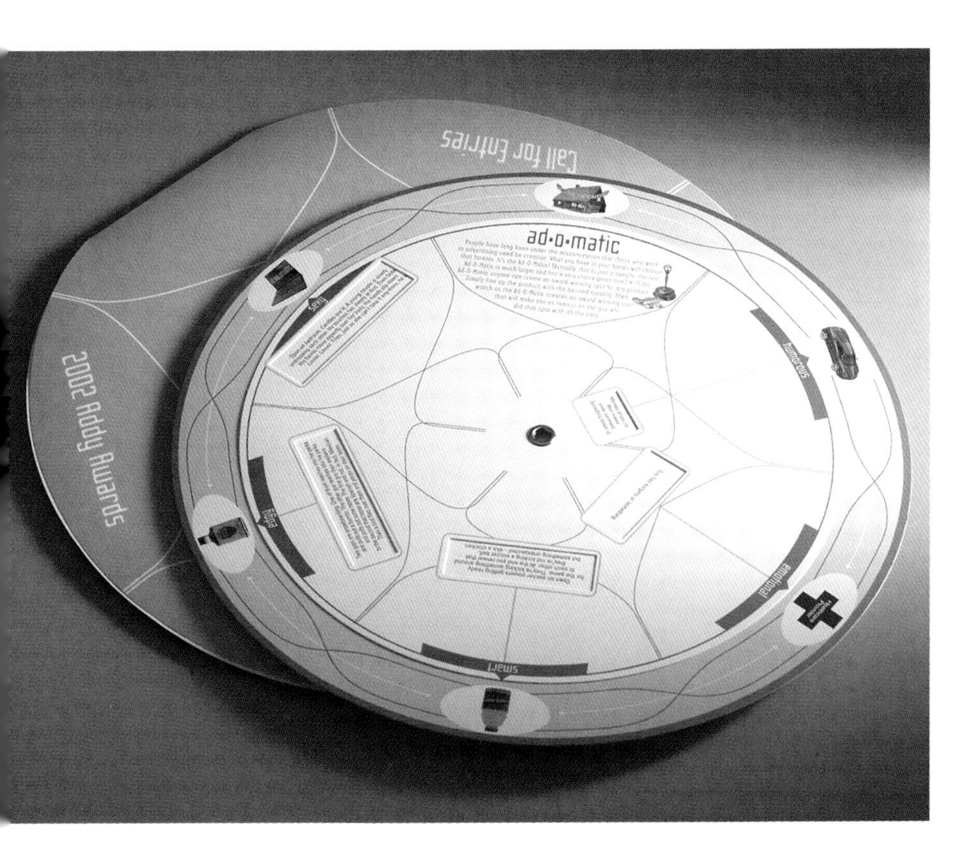

MERIT AWARD
DIRECT MAIL

DESIGNER
Greg Motylenski

ART DIRECTOR
Greg Motylenski

WRITERS
Jeff Siegel
Eric Hartsock

PHOTOGRAPHER
Stock

CREATIVE DIRECTORS
Eric Hartsock
Jeff Siegel

CLIENT
Advertising Association of
Baltimore

AGENCY
Eisner Underground/
Baltimore

02171D

MERIT AWARD
DIRECT MAIL

DESIGNER
Jason Wood

ART DIRECTOR
Jason Wood

WRITER
Mike Roe

CREATIVE DIRECTOR
Mary Knight

CLIENT
Precor

AGENCY
Foote Cone & Belding/Seattle

02173D

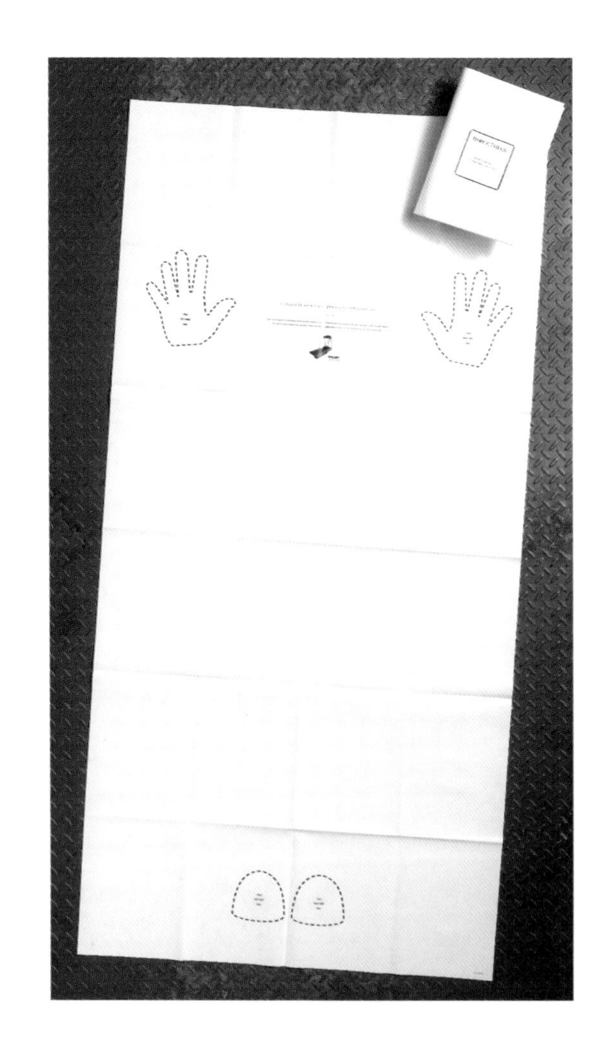

MERIT AWARD
DIRECT MAIL

ART DIRECTOR
Vincent Lee

WRITER
Lim Soon Huat

CREATIVE DIRECTOR
Lim Soon Huat

CLIENT
Stonesoft Singapore

AGENCY
Gosh Advertising/Singapore

02174D

DESIGN MERIT

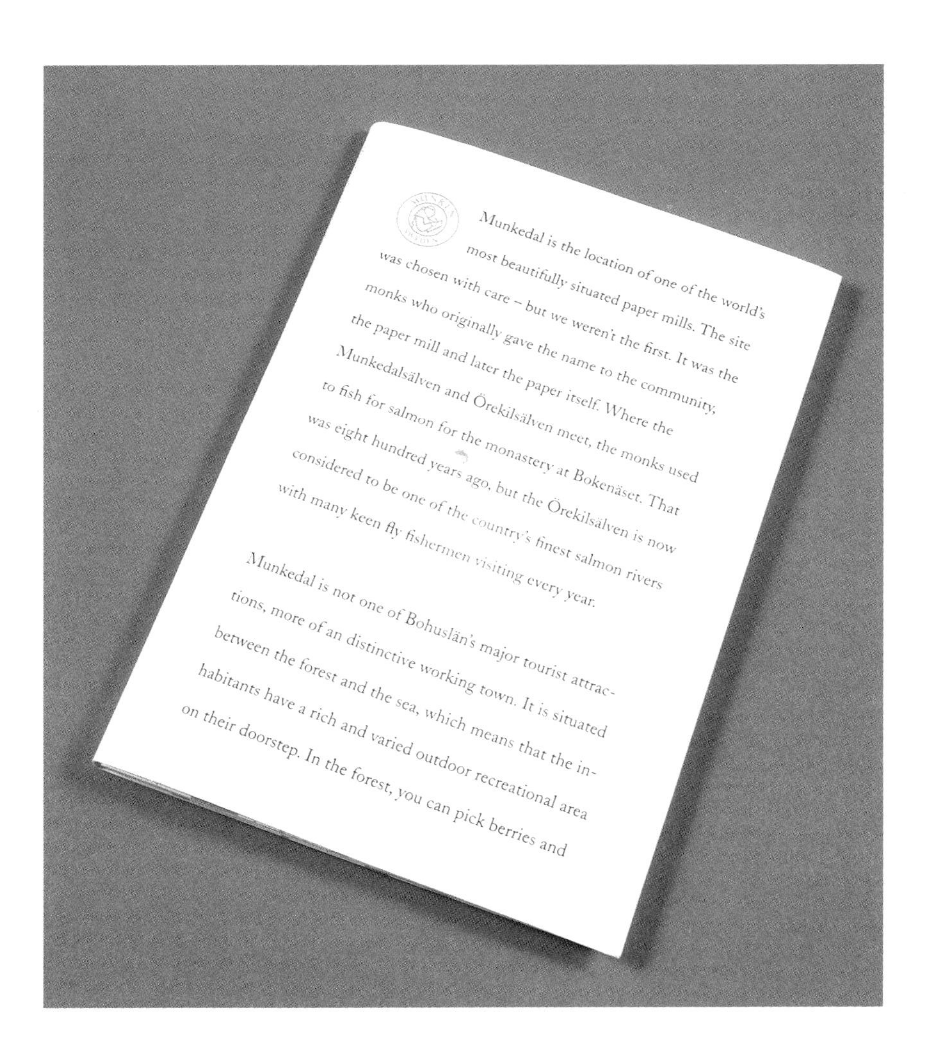

MERIT AWARD
DIRECT MAIL

ART DIRECTOR
Andreas Kittel

WRITER
Anders Westgårdh Story

ILLUSTRATOR
Gavin Smart

CREATIVE DIRECTOR
Anders Kornestedt

CLIENT
Munkedals AB

AGENCY
Happy Forsman & Bodenfors/
Göthenburg

02175D

MERIT AWARD
DIRECT MAIL

ART DIRECTOR
Anders Kornestedt

WRITER
Björn Engström

ILLUSTRATOR
Anna Kask

CLIENT
Munkedals AB

AGENCY
Happy Forsman & Bodenfors/
Göthenburg

02176D

MERIT AWARD
DIRECT MAIL

ART DIRECTORS
Andreas Kittel
Anders Kornestedt

WRITER
Björn Engström

CLIENT
Munkedals AB

AGENCY
Happy Forsman & Bodenfors/
Göthenburg

02177D

MERIT AWARD
DIRECT MAIL

ART DIRECTOR
Luke Oeth

DESIGNER
Luke Oeth

CREATIVE DIRECTORS
Steve Mitchell
Doug Adkins

WRITER
Rob Franks

CLIENT
Hunt Adkins

AGENCY
Hunt Adkins/Minneapolis

02178D

DESIGN MERIT

MERIT AWARD
DIRECT MAIL

DESIGNERS
Linda Meek
Bruno Hohmann

WRITER
Elizabeth Browning

ART DIRECTOR
Linda Meek

ILLUSTRATOR
Various

PHOTOGRAPHERS
Ron Strong
Eric Perry
Peggy Day
Tom Burkhart
Tim Damon
John Roe

CREATIVE DIRECTORS
Bruce Rooke
Lauren Crane

CLIENT
Ford Motor Company

AGENCY
J. Walter Thompson/Detroit

02179D

MERIT AWARD
DIRECT MAIL

ART DIRECTORS
Murphy Yeung
Sam Lau

WRITER
Timothy Lau

CREATIVE DIRECTOR
Andrew Ho

CLIENT
Jaguar X-Type

AGENCY
J. Walter Thompson/
Hong Kong

02180D

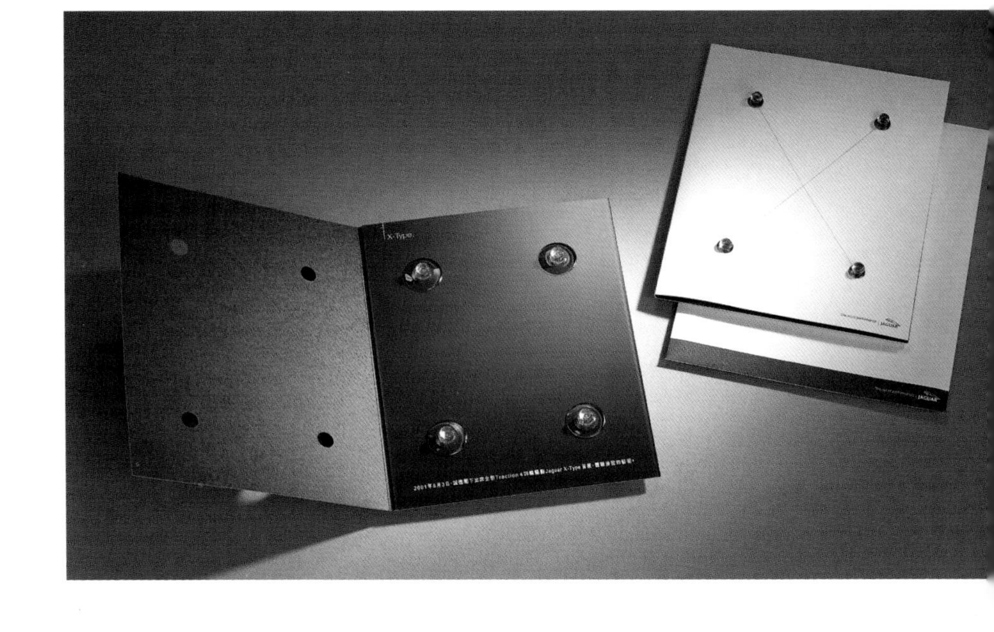

MERIT AWARD
DIRECT MAIL

ART DIRECTOR
Janay Blazejewski

WRITER
Michael Polovsky

PHOTOGRAPHER
Jim Huibregtse

CREATIVE DIRECTORS
Gary Goldsmith
Dean Hacohen
Patrick Hanlon

CLIENT
Montblanc

AGENCY
Lowe/New York

02181D

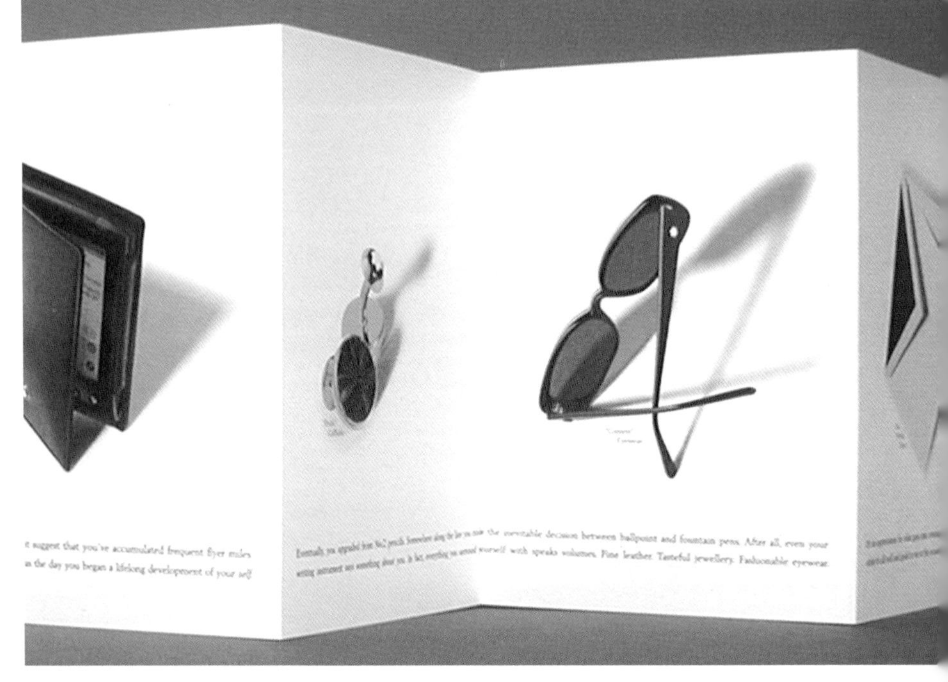

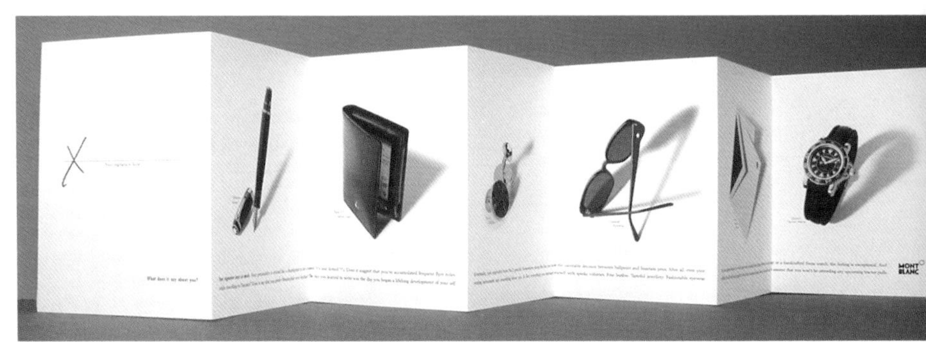

DESIGN MERIT

MERIT AWARD
DIRECT MAIL

DESIGNER
Shayne Pooley

ART DIRECTOR
Shayne Pooley

WRITER
Shane Weaver

ILLUSTRATOR
Michael Lui

CREATIVE DIRECTOR
Shane Weaver

CLIENT
OgilvyOne worldwide

AGENCY
OgilvyOne worldwide/
Singapore

02182D

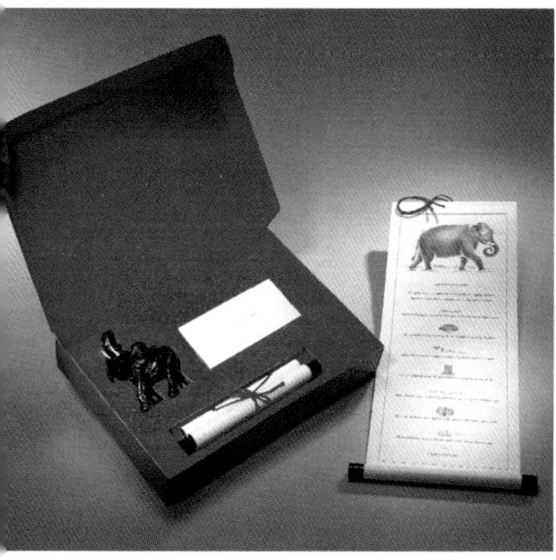

MERIT AWARD
DIRECT MAIL

DESIGNER
Luis Peña

ART DIRECTOR
Luis Peña

ILLUSTRATOR
Luis Peña

CREATIVE DIRECTOR
Luis Peña

CLIENT
PeñaBrand

AGENCY
PeñaBrand/Butler Shine & Stern/Sausalito

02164D

MERIT AWARD
DIRECT MAIL

ART DIRECTOR
Lotus Child

WRITER
Toria Emery

CREATIVE DIRECTOR
Jonathan Butts

CLIENT
Hewlett-Packard

AGENCY
Publicis Dialog/San Francisco

02183D

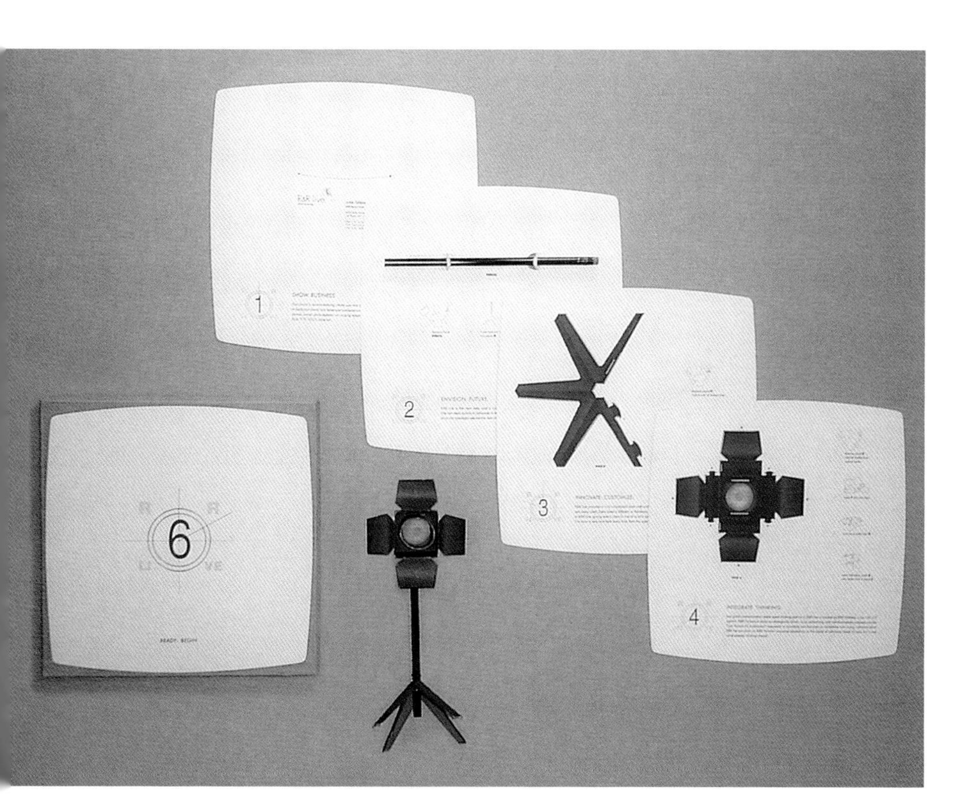

MERIT AWARD
DIRECT MAIL

DESIGNER
Matt Jones

ART DIRECTOR
Matt Jones

WRITERS
Arnie DiGeorge
Erik Dileo

ILLUSTRATORS
8-Fish
Matt Jones

CREATIVE DIRECTORS
Arnie DiGeorge
Randy Snow

CLIENT
R&R Live

AGENCY
R&R Partners/Las Vegas

02184D

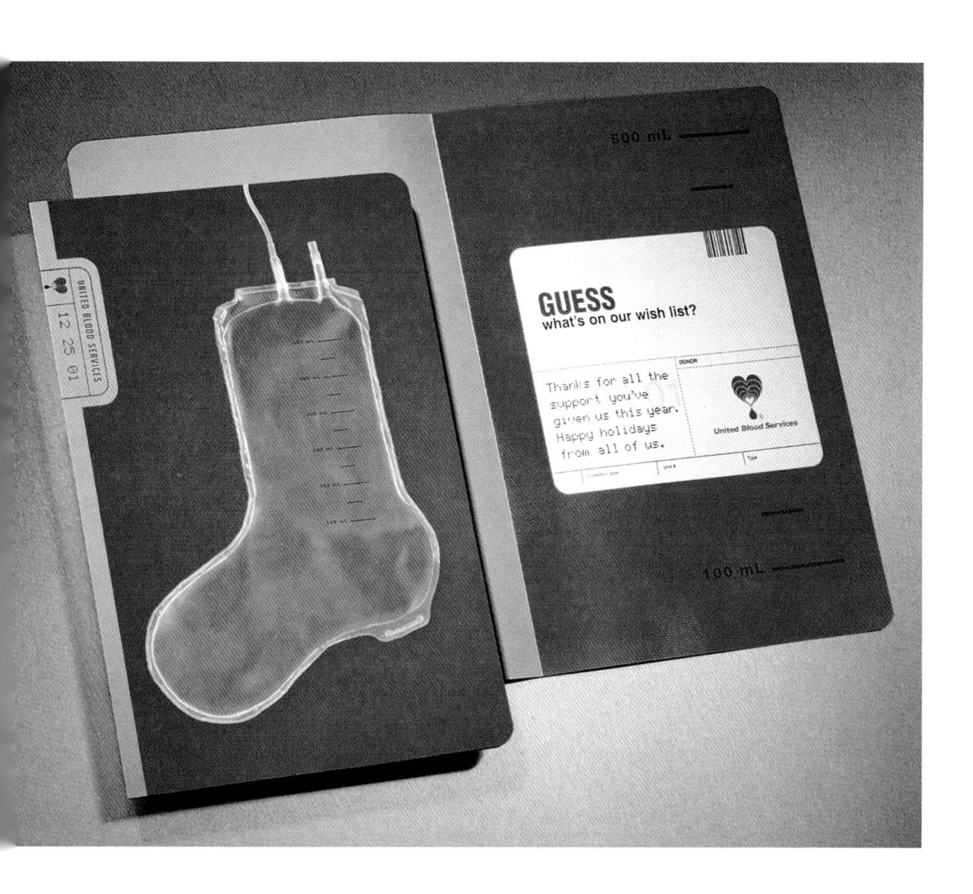

MERIT AWARD
DIRECT MAIL

DESIGNER
Lisa Graff

ART DIRECTOR
Mark Chamberlain

WRITER
Sam Maclay

PHOTOGRAPHER
Norm Johnson

CREATIVE DIRECTORS
Scott Johnson
Sam Maclay

CLIENT
United Blood Services

AGENCY
Rick Johnson & Company/
Albuquerque

02185D

MERIT AWARD
DIRECT MAIL

DESIGNER
Catherine Blomkamp

ART DIRECTORS
Catherine Blomkamp
Brett Wild

WRITER
Catherine Blomkamp

CREATIVE DIRECTOR
Brett Wild

CLIENT
Saatchi & Saatchi

AGENCY
Saatchi & Saatchi/
Johannesburg

02186D

MERIT AWARD
DIRECT MAIL

DESIGNER
Steve Sandstrom

ART DIRECTOR
Steve Sandstrom

PHOTOGRAPHER
Mark Hooper

CREATIVE DIRECTOR
Steve Sandstrom

CLIENT
Mark Hooper Photography

AGENCY
Sandstrom Design/Portland

02187D

MERIT AWARD
DIRECT MAIL

DESIGNERS
Joel Templin
Gaby Brink

PHOTOGRAPHERS
Neal Brown
Ann Cutting
Hugh Kretschmer
Lise Metzger
Jamey Stillings
Eric Tucker
Everard Williams

CREATIVE DIRECTORS
Joel Templin
Gaby Brink

CLIENT
Sharpe & Associates

AGENCY
Templin Brink Design/
San Francisco

02188D

MERIT AWARD
DIRECT MAIL

DESIGNER
Joel Templin

WRITER
Lisa Pemrick

CREATIVE DIRECTOR
Joel Templin

CLIENT
Turner Classic Movies

AGENCY
Templin Brink Design/
San Francisco

02189D

MERIT AWARD
BROADCAST DESIGN

DESIGNER
David Schrimpf

WRITER
Dan Ruppert Kan

CREATIVE DIRECTOR
Bill Thorburn

CLIENT
Potlatch

AGENCY
Carmichael Lynch/
Minneapolis

02191D

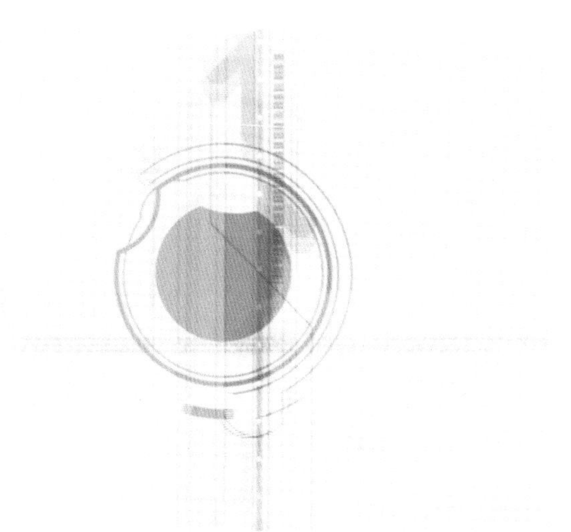

MERIT AWARD
BROADCAST DESIGN

DESIGNER
Carlos Bêla

CREATIVE DIRECTORS
Mateus de Paula Santos
Luciano Cury

CLIENT
Band News

AGENCY
Lobo Filmes/São Paulo

02192D

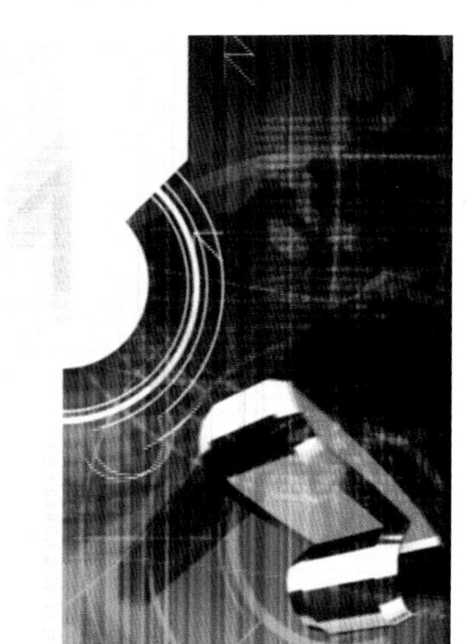

MERIT AWARD
BROADCAST DESIGN

DESIGNER
Carlos Bêla

CREATIVE DIRECTORS
Mateus de Paula Santos
Luciano Cury

CLIENT
Band News

AGENCY
Lobo Filmes/São Paulo

02193D

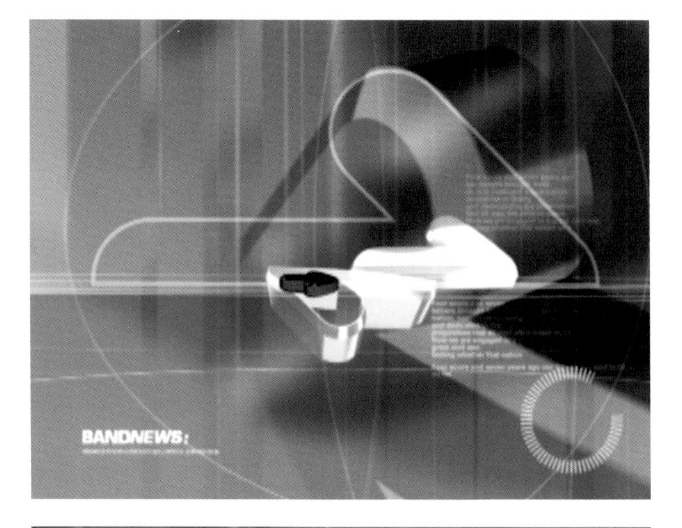

DESIGN MERIT

MERIT AWARD
BROADCAST DESIGN

DESIGNERS
Mario Sader
Mateus de Paula Santos

CREATIVE DIRECTOR
Mateus de Paula Santos

CLIENT
MTV Brasil

AGENCY
Lobo Filmes/São Paulo

02195D

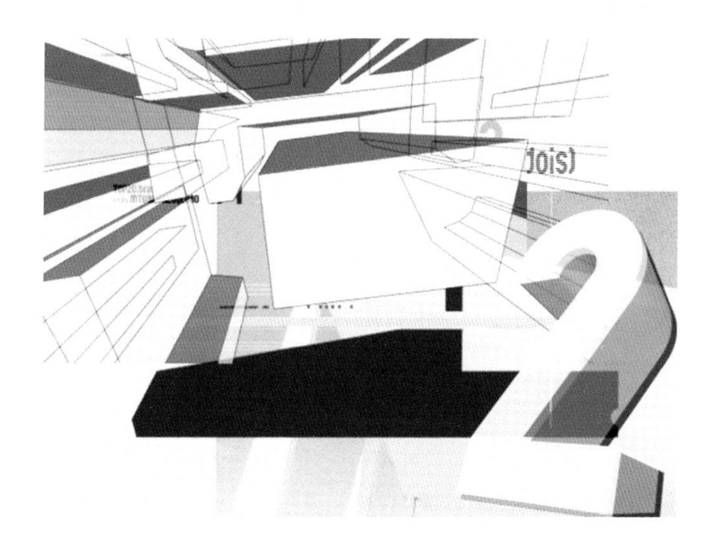

MERIT AWARD
BROADCAST DESIGN

DESIGNERS
Carlos Bêla
Denis Kamioka
Mario Sader
Mateus de Paula Santos

CREATIVE DIRECTOR
Mateus de Paula Santos

CLIENT
TV Globo

AGENCY
Lobo Filmes/São Paulo

02194D

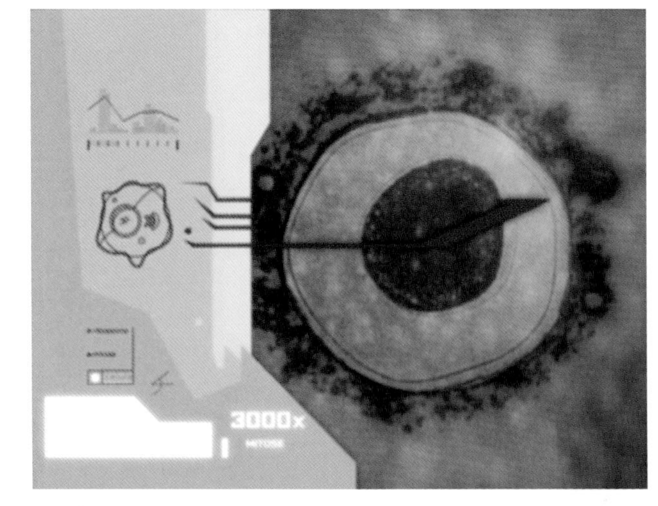

MERIT AWARD
BROADCAST DESIGN

DESIGNER
Jonathan Eva

ART DIRECTOR
Rafael Esquer

ANIMATOR
Tim Wilder

CLIENT
ESPN

AGENCY
@radical.media/New York

02196D

PUBLIC SERVICE

"The recognition of God as the ruling and leading power in the universe and the grateful acknowledgment of His favors and blessings are necessary to the best type of citizenship."
Boy Scouts of America, MEMBERSHIP POLICY, ESTABLISHED 1970

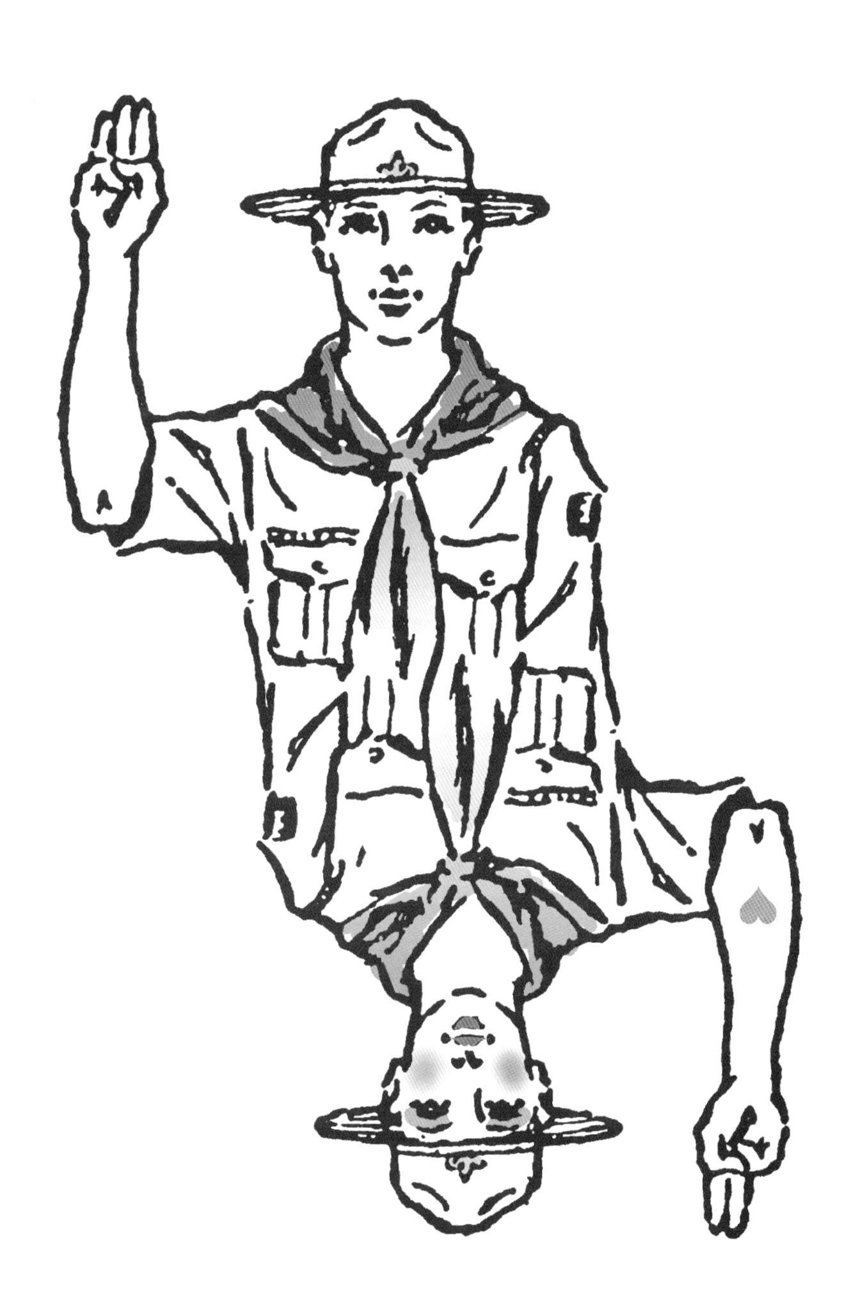

MERIT AWARD
PUBLIC SERVICE/POLITICAL
NEWSPAPER OR MAGAZINE
SINGLE

ART DIRECTORS
Rich Wakefield
Jackie Hathiramani

WRITERS
Jackie Hathiramani
Rich Wakefield

CREATIVE DIRECTOR
Jim Noble

CLIENT
Georgia Breast Cancer Coalition

AGENCY
BBDO/Atlanta

02385A

Also won:
MERIT AWARD
PUBLIC SERVICE/POLITICAL
OUTDOOR AND POSTERS

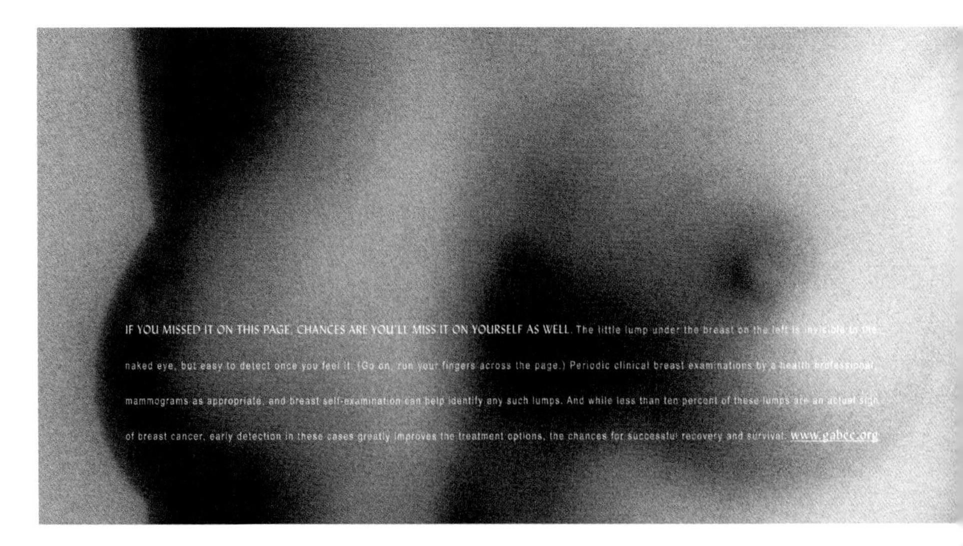

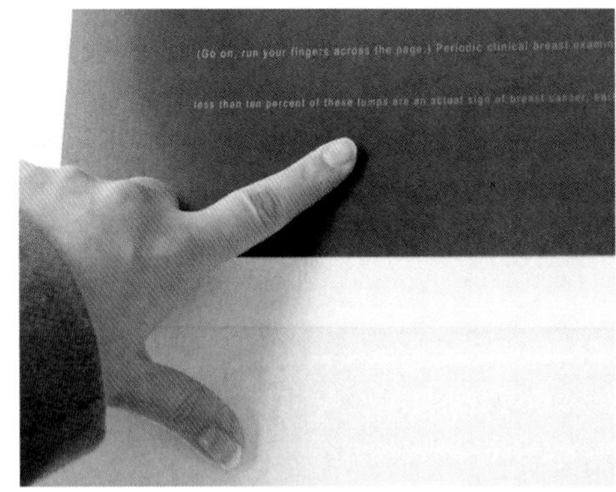

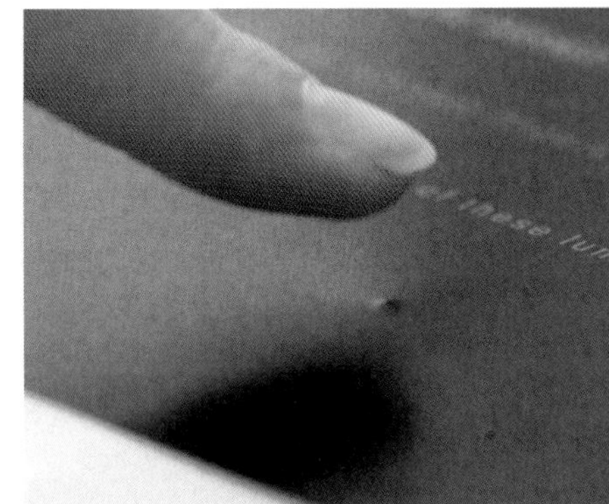

MERIT AWARD
PUBLIC SERVICE/POLITICAL
NEWSPAPER OR MAGAZINE
SINGLE

ART DIRECTOR
Taylor Smith

WRITER
Chris Jacobs

CREATIVE DIRECTOR
Chris Jacobs

CLIENT
Dahlonega Film Festival

AGENCY
Cole Henderson Drake/Atlanta

02386A

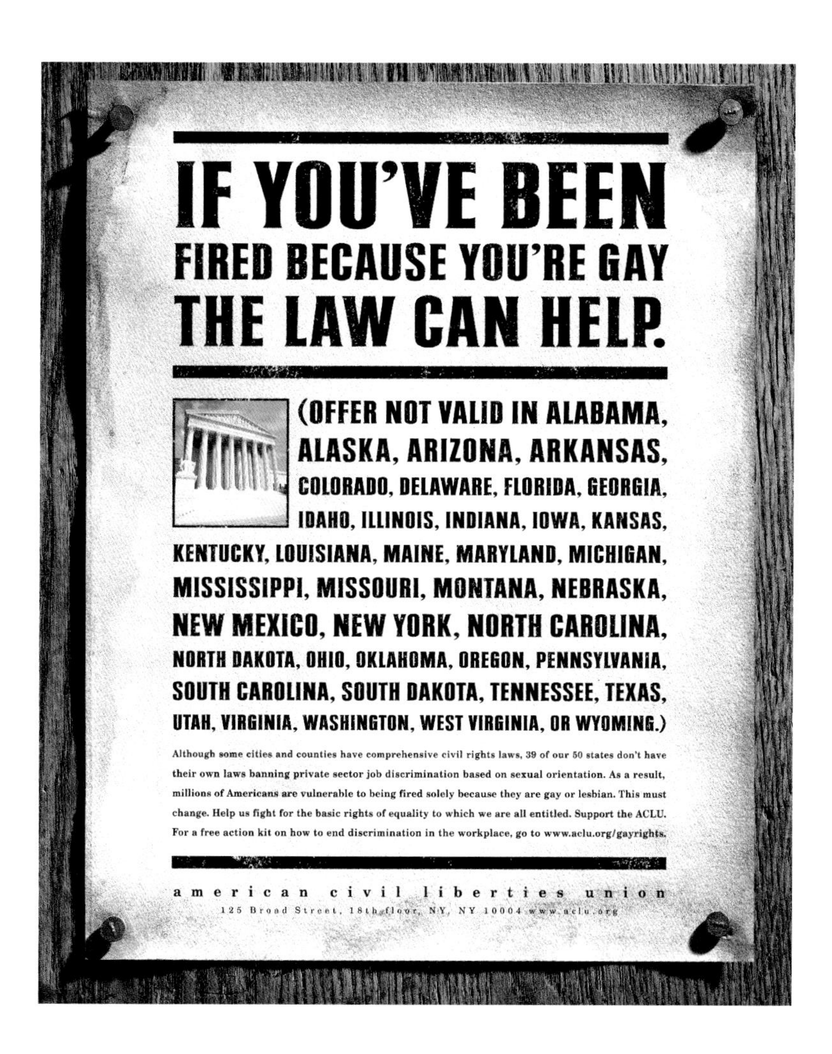

MERIT AWARD
PUBLIC SERVICE/POLITICAL
NEWSPAPER OR MAGAZINE
SINGLE

ART DIRECTORS
Eric Schutte
Barbara Eibel

WRITER
Pierre Lipton

PHOTOGRAPHER
Robert Ammirati

CREATIVE DIRECTOR
Sal DeVito

CLIENT
American Civil Liberties Union

AGENCY
DeVito/Verdi/New York

02387A

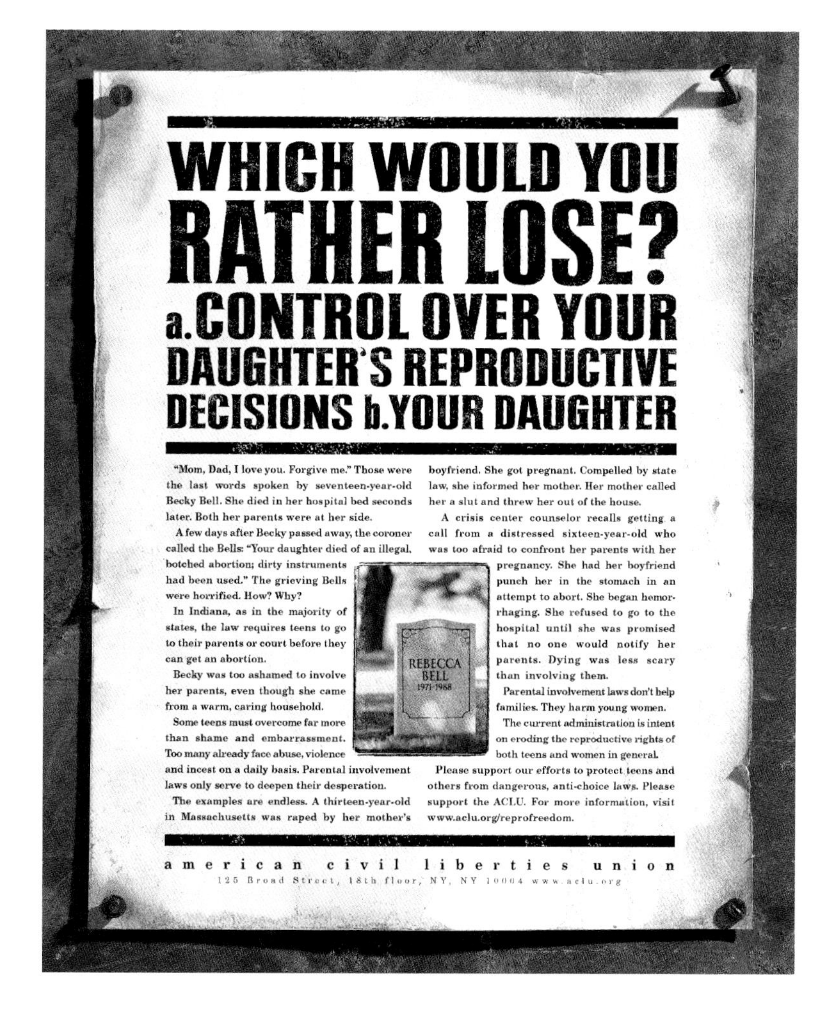

MERIT AWARD
PUBLIC SERVICE/POLITICAL
NEWSPAPER OR MAGAZINE
SINGLE

ART DIRECTOR
Barbara Eibel

WRITER
Mark Teringo

PHOTOGRAPHER
Robert Ammirati

CREATIVE DIRECTOR
Sal DeVito

CLIENT
American Civil Liberties Union

AGENCY
DeVito/Verdi/New York

02388A

MERIT AWARD
PUBLIC SERVICE/POLITICAL
NEWSPAPER OR MAGAZINE
SINGLE

ART DIRECTOR
Marcos Medeiros

WRITER
Luciana Cardoso

PHOTOGRAPHER
Jairo Goldflus

CREATIVE DIRECTORS
Jáder Rossetto
Pedro Cappeletti
Erh Ray

CLIENT
Project Take Part/
Iguatemi Mall

AGENCY
DM9 DDB Publicidade/
São Paulo

02389A

MERIT AWARD
PUBLIC SERVICE/POLITICAL
NEWSPAPER OR MAGAZINE
SINGLE

ART DIRECTOR
Marcos Medeiros

WRITER
Luciana Cardoso

PHOTOGRAPHER
Jairo Goldflus

ILLUSTRATOR
Marco Cézar

CREATIVE DIRECTORS
Jáder Rossetto
Pedro Cappeletti
Erh Ray

CLIENT
Project Take Part/
Iguatemi Mall

AGENCY
DM9 DDB Publicidade/
São Paulo

02390A

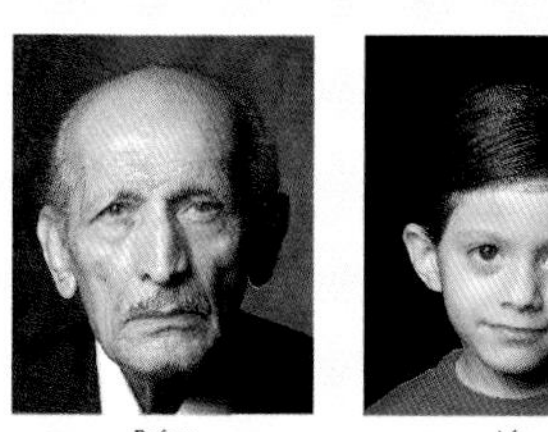

Before *After*

To pass on your vision to the next generation, call Tarun Mitra Mandal: Yuvraj Eye Donation Movement at 1919 or 022-4922897.

MERIT AWARD PUBLIC SERVICE/POLITICAL NEWSPAPER OR MAGAZINE SINGLE

ART DIRECTOR
C.H. Shyamsunder Goud

WRITER
Kaushik Mitra

PHOTOGRAPHER
Shekhar Supari

CREATIVE DIRECTORS
Agnello Dias
Vikram Gaikwad

CLIENT
Tarun Mitra Mandal Eye Donation Movement

AGENCY
Leo Burnett/Mumbai

02392A

MERIT AWARD PUBLIC SERVICE/POLITICAL NEWSPAPER OR MAGAZINE SINGLE

ART DIRECTORS
Jan Bjørkløf
Øivind Eide
Erik Heisholt

WRITER
Erik Heisholt

CREATIVE DIRECTOR
Erik Heisholt

CLIENT
Save the Children

AGENCY
Leo Burnett/Oslo

02391A

MERIT AWARD
PUBLIC SERVICE/POLITICAL
NEWSPAPER OR MAGAZINE
SINGLE

ART DIRECTOR
Doug Pedersen

WRITER
Curtis Smith

PHOTOGRAPHERS
Pat Staub
Stock

CREATIVE DIRECTOR
Jim Mountjoy

CLIENT
North Carolina First Flight
Centennial Commission

AGENCY
Loeffler Ketchum Mountjoy/
Charlotte

02394A

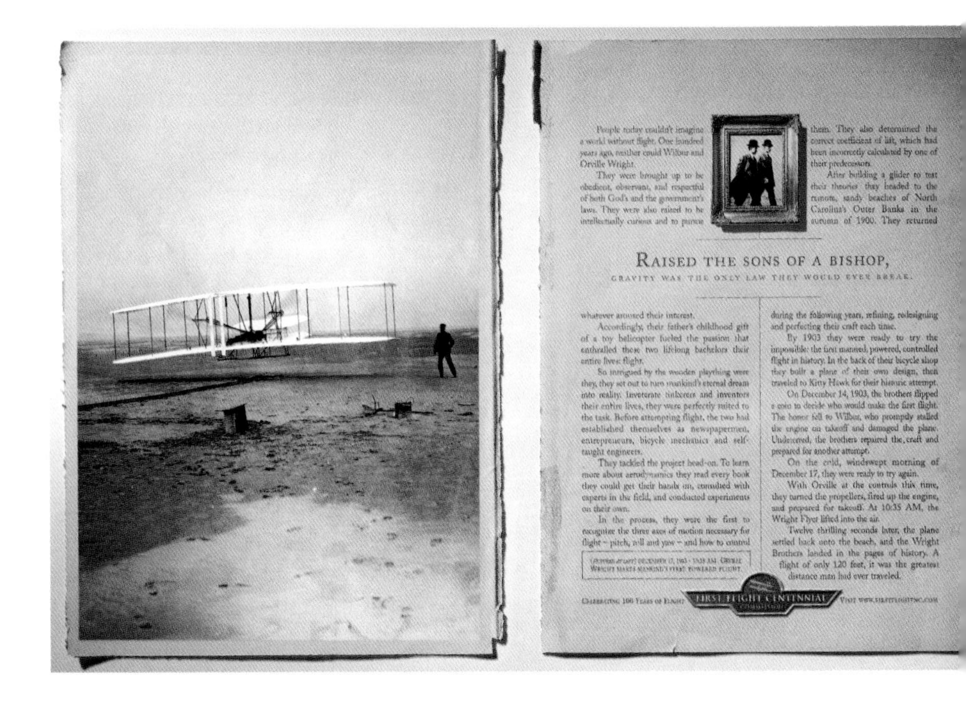

MERIT AWARD
PUBLIC SERVICE/POLITICAL
NEWSPAPER OR MAGAZINE
SINGLE

ART DIRECTOR
Brian Gross

WRITER
Alec Beckett

CREATIVE DIRECTORS
Brian Gross
Alec Beckett

CLIENT
United Way

AGENCY
Nail Communications/
Providence

02395A

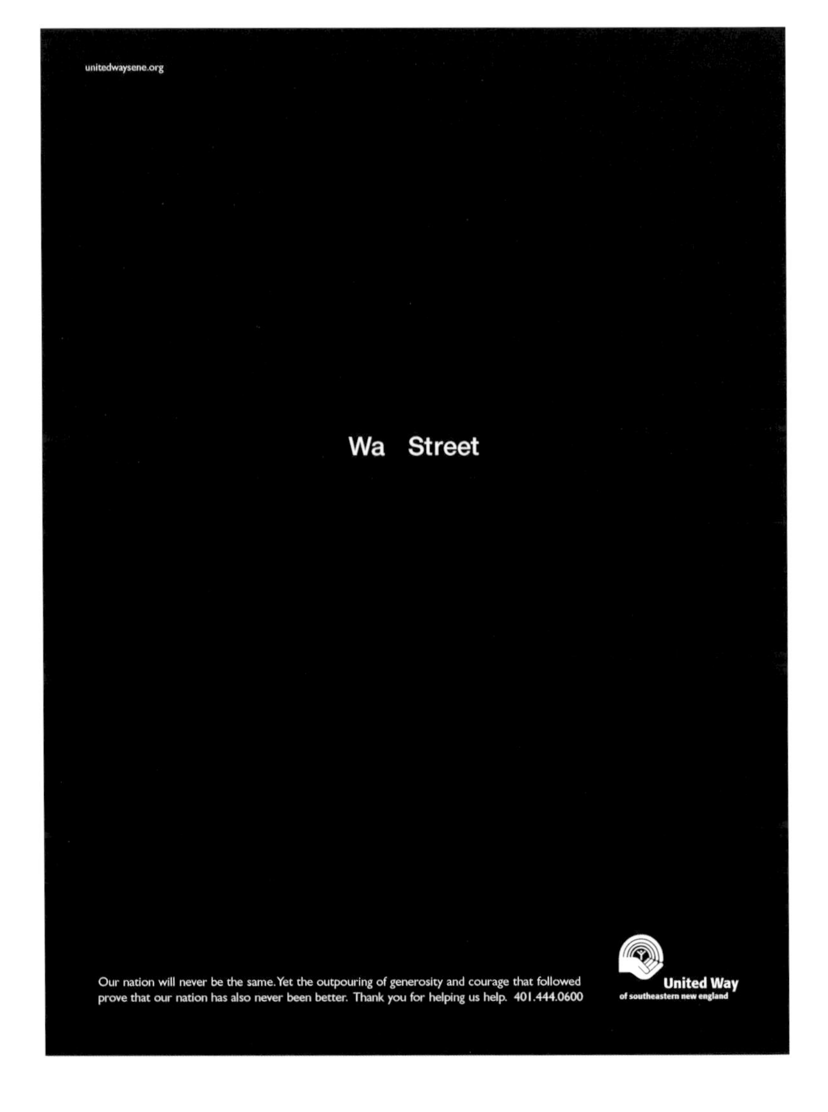

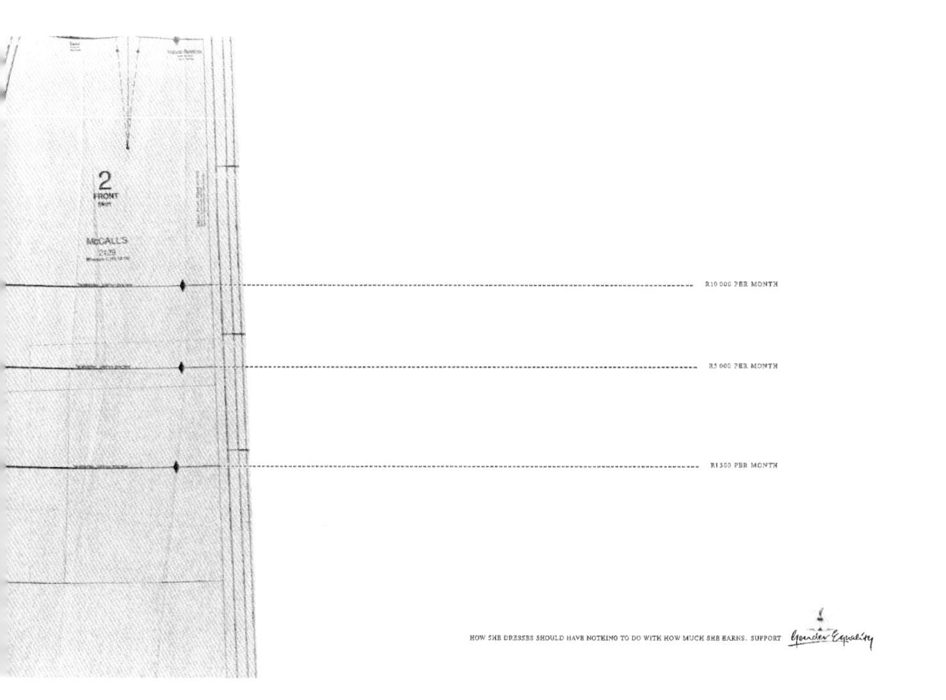

MERIT AWARD
PUBLIC SERVICE/POLITICAL
NEWSPAPER OR MAGAZINE
SINGLE

ART DIRECTOR
William Hammond

WRITER
Steve Straw

PHOTOGRAPHER
Mike Meyersfeld

CREATIVE DIRECTOR
Brett Wild

CLIENT
Gender Equality

AGENCY
Saatchi & Saatchi/
Johannesburg

02399A

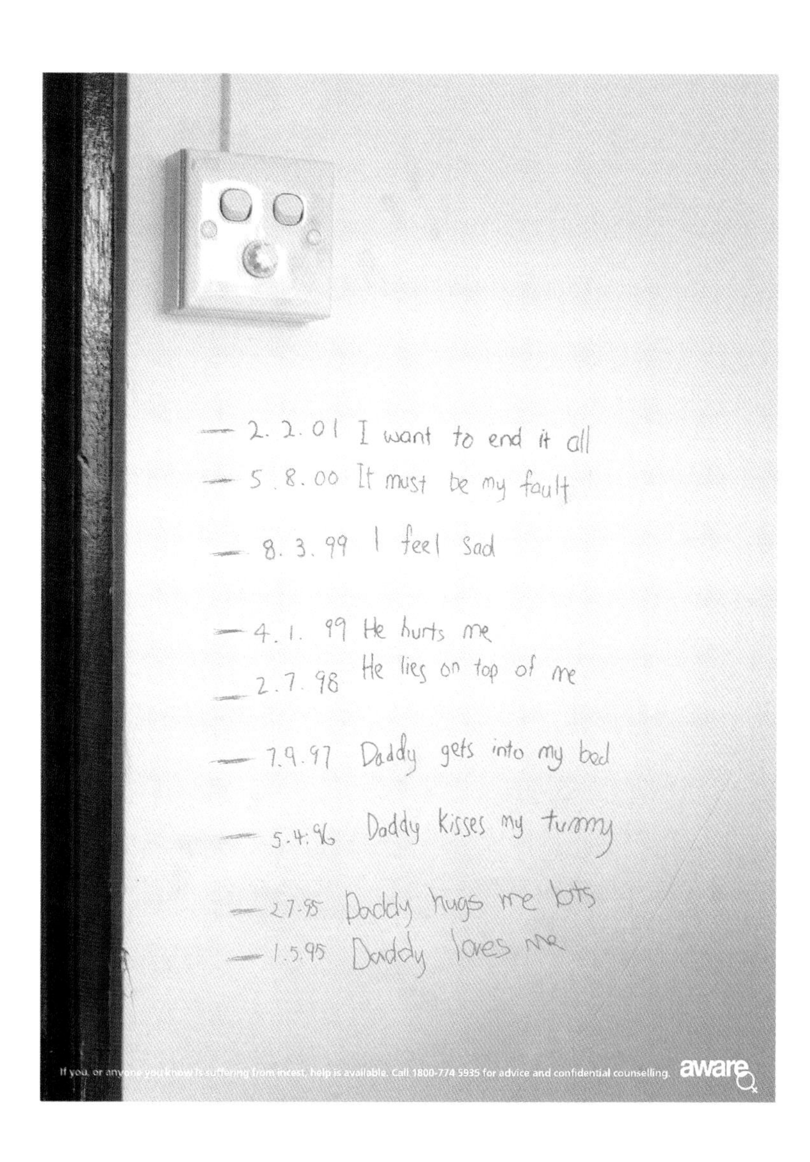

MERIT AWARD
PUBLIC SERVICE/POLITICAL
NEWSPAPER OR MAGAZINE
SINGLE

ART DIRECTOR
John Foster

WRITER
David Thackray

PHOTOGRAPHER
Edward Loh

ILLUSTRATOR
Aaron Tan

CREATIVE DIRECTOR
Sion Scott-Wilson

CLIENT
Aware

AGENCY
Saatchi & Saatchi/Singapore

02401A

MERIT AWARD
PUBLIC SERVICE/POLITICAL
NEWSPAPER OR MAGAZINE
SINGLE

ART DIRECTOR
Simon Cox

WRITER
Jagdish Ramakrishnan

PHOTOGRAPHER
Hon

CREATIVE DIRECTOR
Sion Scott-Wilson

CLIENT
Sea Shepherd
Conservation Society

AGENCY
Saatchi & Saatchi/Singapore

02402A

MERIT AWARD
PUBLIC SERVICE/POLITICAL
NEWSPAPER OR MAGAZINE
SINGLE

ART DIRECTOR
Kevin Thoem

WRITERS
Kevin Thoem
Ari Weiss

ILLUSTRATOR
Stock

CREATIVE DIRECTOR
Bart Cleveland

CLIENT
Atlanta Ballet

AGENCY
Sawyer Riley Compton/Atlanta

02153A

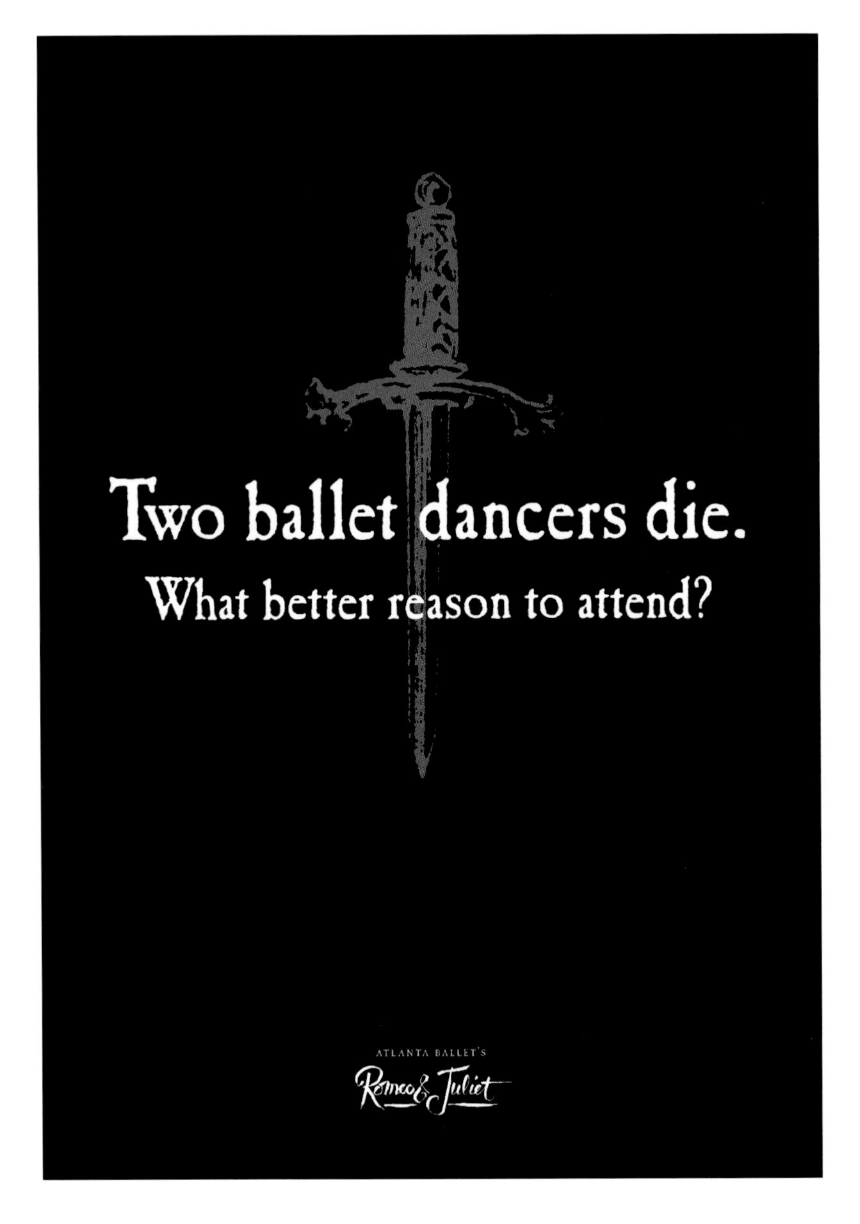

MERIT AWARD
PUBLIC SERVICE/POLITICAL
NEWSPAPER OR MAGAZINE
SINGLE

ART DIRECTOR
Kevin Thoem

WRITER
Brett Compton

PHOTOGRAPHER
Chris Davis

CREATIVE DIRECTORS
Bart Cleveland
Al Jackson

CLIENT
Georgia Tech

AGENCY
Sawyer Riley Compton/Atlanta

02403A

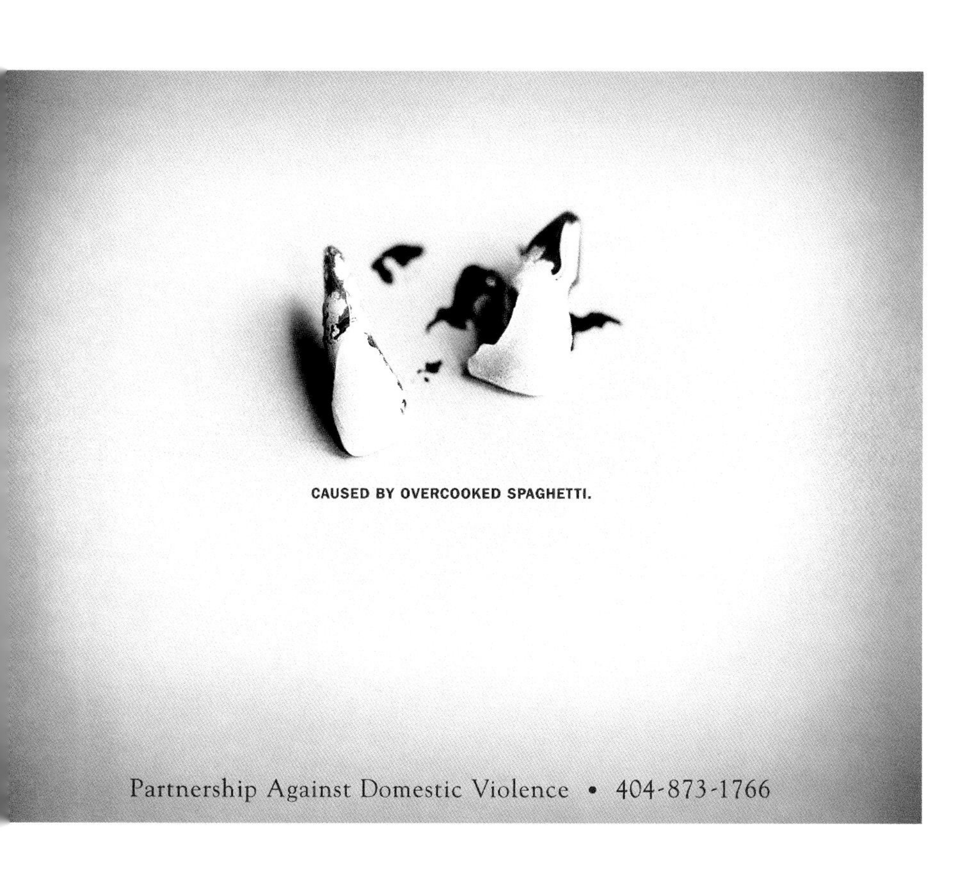

CAUSED BY OVERCOOKED SPAGHETTI.
Partnership Against Domestic Violence • 404-873-1766

MERIT AWARD
PUBLIC SERVICE/POLITICAL
NEWSPAPER OR MAGAZINE
SINGLE

ART DIRECTOR
Bart Cleveland

WRITER
Al Jackson

PHOTOGRAPHER
Tibor Nemeth

CREATIVE DIRECTOR
Bart Cleveland

CLIENT
The Partnership Against
Domestic Violence

AGENCY
Sawyer Riley Compton/Atlanta

02404A

MERIT AWARD
PUBLIC SERVICE/POLITICAL
NEWSPAPER OR MAGAZINE
CAMPAIGN

ART DIRECTOR
Josh Lancaster

WRITER
Jamie Hitchcock

CREATIVE DIRECTOR
Philip Andrew

CLIENT
Land Transport Safety Authority

AGENCY
Clemenger BBDO/Wellington

02405A

DODGE VAN 1988. Electric blue, great people mover, seats 12, 6 of which were killed after driver left road at 75kph trying to beat the holiday rush. **The Faster You Go, The Bigger The Mess** NACP-980-79

HONDA CRX 1986. Auto, suit boy racer, hit parked car doing 70 in a 50kph zone, girlfriend seriously injured, must sell quickly. Due to reckless driving charge, owner won't be driving this or any other vehicle for 9 months. **The Faster You Go, The Bigger The Mess** NACP-980-70

p.980a

PRIVATE ADVERTISERS

HONDA CRX 1986. Auto, suit boy racer, hit parked car doing 70 in a 50kph zone, girlfriend seriously injured, must sell quickly. Due to reckless driving charge, owner won't be driving this or any other vehicle for 9 months. **The Faster You Go, The Bigger The Mess** NACP-980-70

HONDA PRELUDE 1992. 5 speed manual, 2.2 VTec, 71,000 kms, climate, air cond, all electrics, DSP stereo system, cruise control, clean genuine car. $8,700. Phone Ivor: (09) 418-5441 or 025-276-7740. NACP-980-01

1994 TOYOTA TOWNACE 2.2L. 4x4, colour white, 5 seater, 104,000 kms, excellent condition, willing to negotiate price as owner is going overseas, if phone unattended, leave message. $15,800 ono. Phone (09) 817-1445 or (09) 363-6262 work NACP-980-02*

JAGUAR MK2. 3.4 litre, Dec 1962, manual, overdrive, wire wheels, excellent condition. $18,750 ono. Phone (09) 521-0039. NACP-980-03*

1995 MITSUBISHI PAJERO V6 SWB. 5 speed, 100 km, air cond, electrics, excellent condition. $17,500. Phone (09) 534-2417. NACP-980-04*

DODGE VAN 1988. Electric blue, great people mover, seats 12, 6 of which were killed after driver left road at 75kph trying to beat the holiday rush. **The Faster You Go, The Bigger The Mess** NACP-980-79

PORSCHE 911 CARRERA 2 1993. 45 kms, tiptronic, black leather. $78,000. For more details, phone Brent: 021-754-464. NACP-980-05

MITSUBISHI RVR XZ SPORTSGEAR, 1998, 1800 GDI motor, 17,000 kms, CD, Tiptronic, ABS, airbags, full electrics, rear seats foldable and slideable making it extremely spacious, great to drive, $24,500. Phone (03) 337-1753 or 025 228-5317 NACP-980-19*

Page 6 Ed 980 AUTO TRADER MAGAZINE autopoint.co.nz Phone 09 308-2833

MERIT AWARD
PUBLIC SERVICE/POLITICAL
NEWSPAPER OR MAGAZINE
CAMPAIGN

ART DIRECTOR
Zaidi Awang

WRITER
Iska Hashim

PHOTOGRAPHER
David Lok

CREATIVE DIRECTORS
Ali Mohamed
Yasmin Ahmad

CLIENT
Malaysian Nature Society

AGENCY
Leo Burnett/Kuala Lumpur

02406A

MERIT AWARD
PUBLIC SERVICE/POLITICAL
NEWSPAPER OR MAGAZINE
CAMPAIGN

ART DIRECTORS
Tay Guan Hin
Felix Wang

WRITER
Alex Shipley

PHOTOGRAPHERS
Ong Kai Sin
Alex Kai Keong Studio

ILLUSTRATOR
Felix Wang

CREATIVE DIRECTORS
Tay Guan Hin
Alex Shipley

CLIENT
Ocean Environment

AGENCY
Leo Burnett/Singapore

02407A

Also won:
MERIT AWARD
PUBLIC SERVICE/POLITICAL
NEWSPAPER OR MAGAZINE
SINGLE

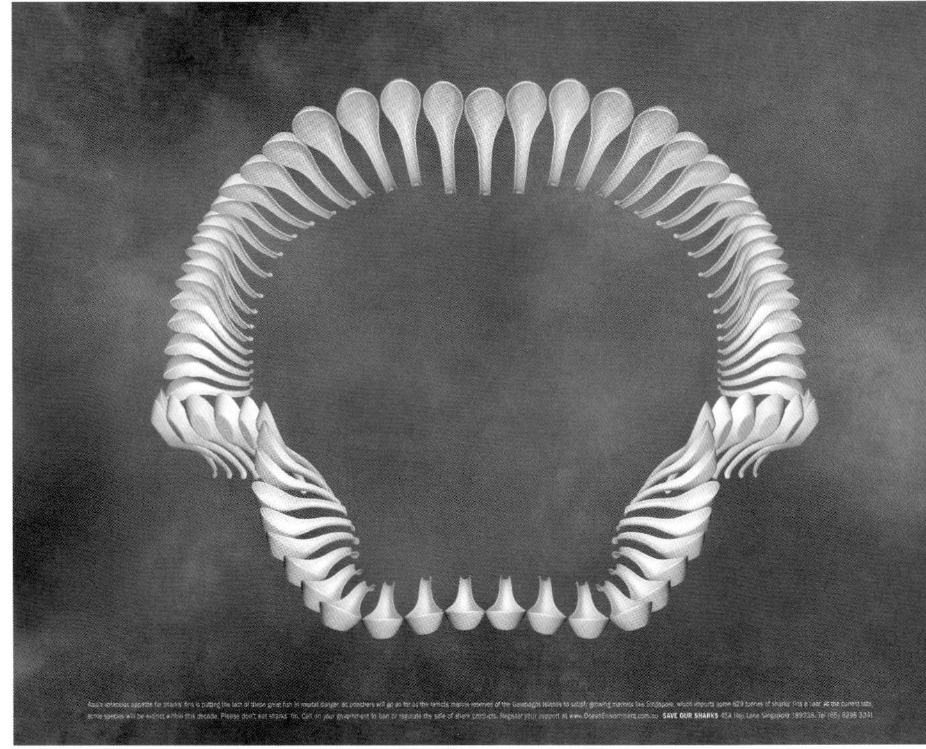

MERIT

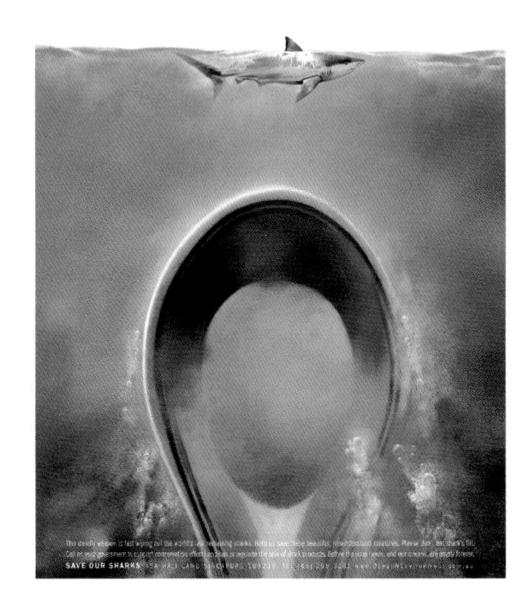

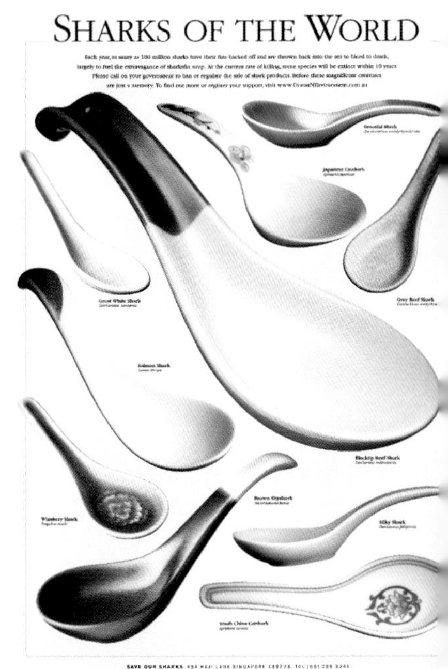

MERIT NEWSPAPER/MAGAZINE

MERIT OUTDOOR/POSTERS

MERIT AWARD
PUBLIC SERVICE/POLITICAL
NEWSPAPER OR MAGAZINE
CAMPAIGN

ART DIRECTORS
Gregory Yeo
Steve Hough

WRITERS
Steve Hough
Gregory Yeo

PHOTOGRAPHER
Museum Archive

ILLUSTRATORS
Alice Lee
Gary Choo
Lay Ling

CREATIVE DIRECTORS
Andy Greenaway
Craig Smith

CLIENT
Changi Museum

AGENCY
Ogilvy & Mather/Singapore

02408A

Also won:
MERIT AWARDS
PUBLIC SERVICE/POLITICAL
NEWSPAPER OR MAGAZINE
SINGLE

PUBLIC SERVICE/POLITICAL
OUTDOOR AND POSTERS

MERIT AWARD
PUBLIC SERVICE/POLITICAL
NEWSPAPER OR MAGAZINE
CAMPAIGN

ART DIRECTOR
Simon Cox

WRITER
Jagdish Ramakrishnan

CREATIVE DIRECTOR
Sion Scott-Wilson

CLIENT
Acres

AGENCY
Saatchi & Saatchi/Singapore

02410A

Also won:
MERIT AWARD
PUBLIC SERVICE/POLITICAL
NEWSPAPER OR MAGAZINE
SINGLE

MERIT

THERE'S A BEAR IN CHINA
SUFFERING FROM
YOUR HEMORRHOID
PROBLEM.

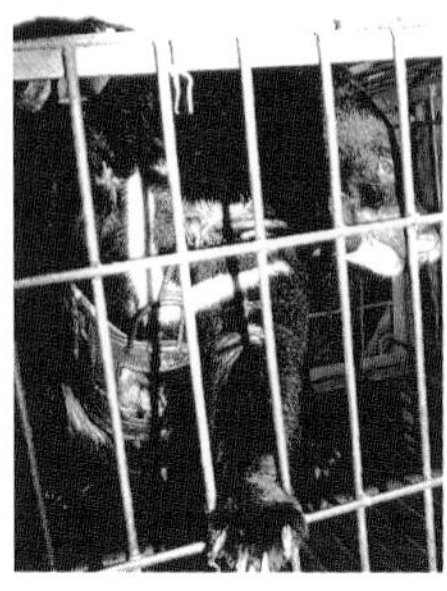

BEFORE THEY KILL THEM,
THEY MAKE THEM
WISH THEY
WERE DEAD.

THE BEARS ARE BEHIND BARS.
THE BEAR-BILE TRADERS
ARE ROAMING FREE.

SHOULDN'T THIS BE THE OTHER
WAY ROUND?

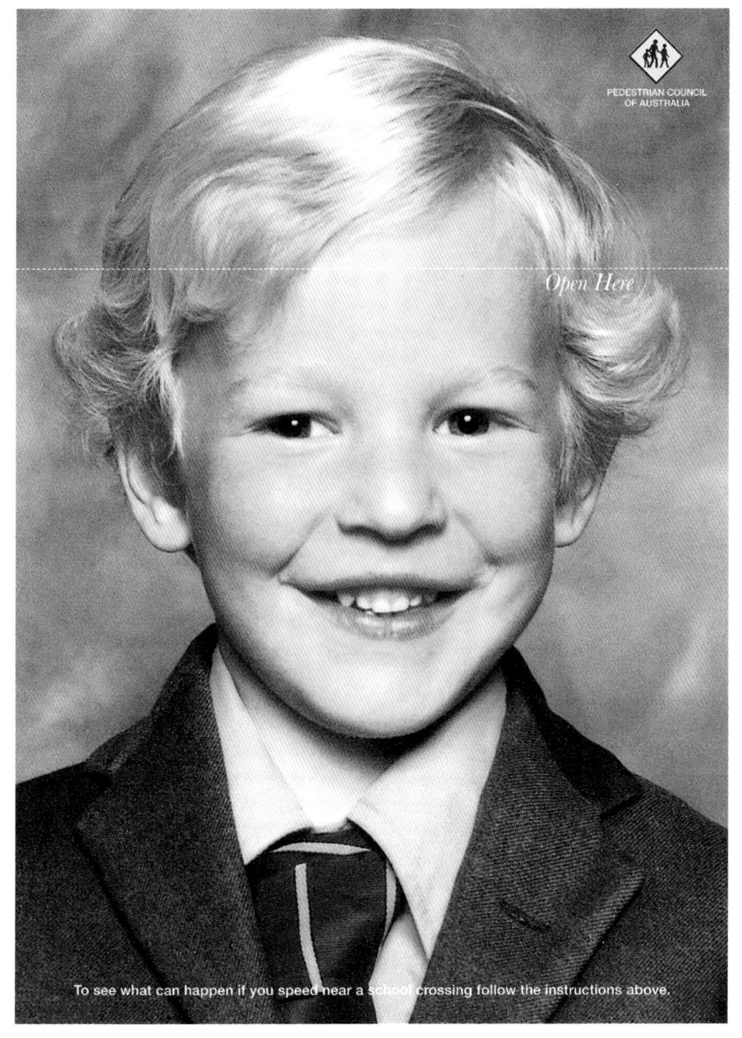

PEDESTRIAN COUNCIL
OF AUSTRALIA
Open Here
To see what can happen if you speed near a school crossing follow the instructions above.

Tear Out Here
To see what a bull-bar can do follow the instructions above.

To see what a drowsy driver can do follow the instructions above.

MERIT AWARD
PUBLIC SERVICE/POLITICAL NEWSPAPER OR MAGAZINE CAMPAIGN

ART DIRECTOR
Jay Furby

WRITER
Jay Furby

CLIENT
Pedestrian Council

AGENCY
Saatchi & Saatchi/Sydney

02409A

MERIT AWARD
PUBLIC SERVICE/POLITICAL
OUTDOOR AND POSTERS

ART DIRECTORS
André Nassar
Bruno Prosperi

WRITER
Renato Simões

PHOTOGRAPHER
Márcia Ramalho

CREATIVE DIRECTORS
José Henrique Borghi
Bruno Prosperi

CLIENT
Ação da Cidadania

AGENCY
Leo Burnett/São Paulo

02412A

MERIT AWARD
PUBLIC SERVICE/POLITICAL
OUTDOOR AND POSTERS

ART DIRECTOR
Melissa Johnson

WRITER
Vince Beggin

PHOTOGRAPHERS
Curtis Johnson
World Vision

ILLUSTRATOR
Brad Palm

CREATIVE DIRECTOR
Tom Kelly

CLIENT
Amnesty International

AGENCY
Martin|Williams/Minneapolis

02413A

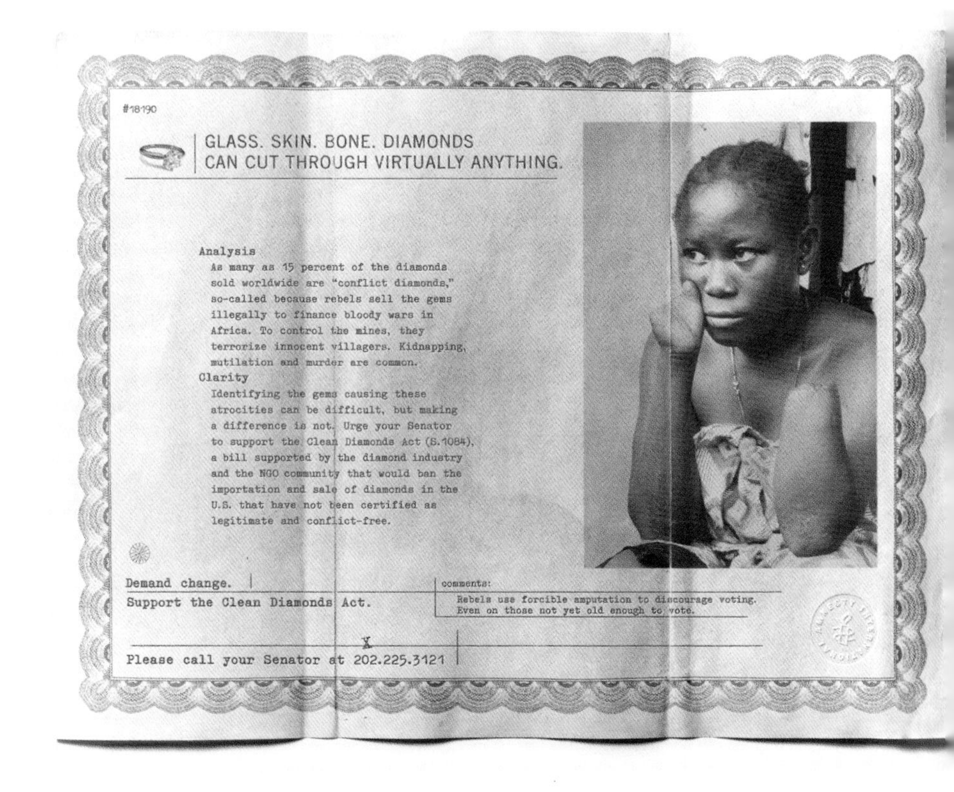

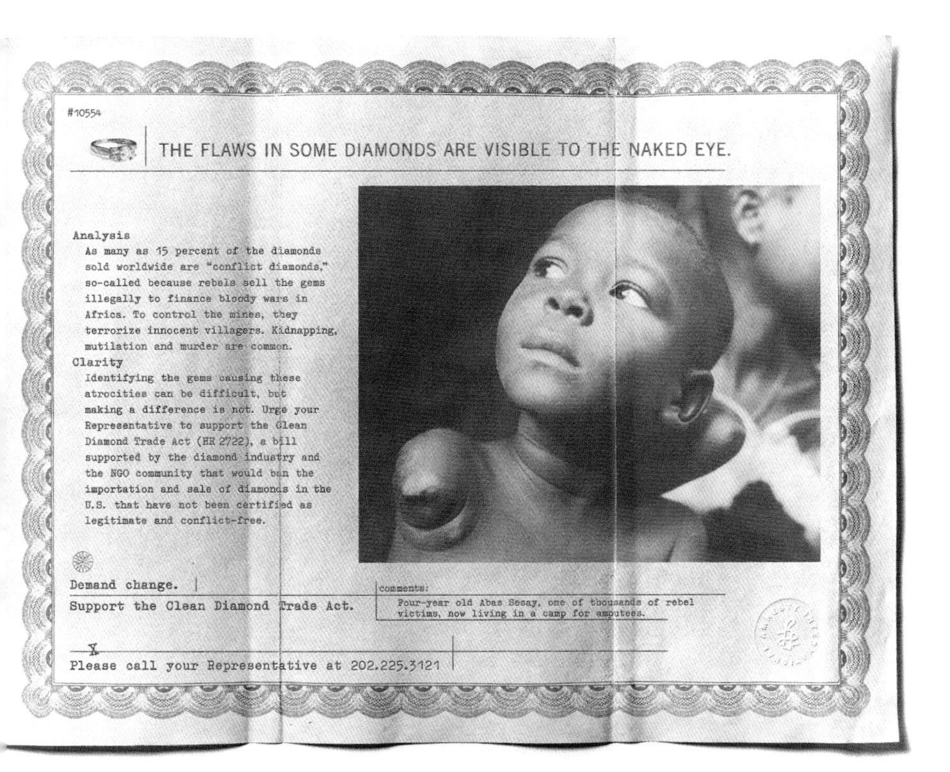

MERIT AWARD
PUBLIC SERVICE/POLITICAL
OUTDOOR AND POSTERS

ART DIRECTOR
Melissa Johnson

WRITER
Vince Beggin

PHOTOGRAPHERS
Curtis Johnson
Stock

ILLUSTRATOR
Brad Palm

CREATIVE DIRECTOR
Tom Kelly

CLIENT
Amnesty International

AGENCY
Martin|Williams/Minneapolis

02414A

MERIT AWARD
PUBLIC SERVICE/POLITICAL
OUTDOOR AND POSTERS

ART DIRECTOR
Peipei Ng

WRITER
Eugene Cheong

PHOTOGRAPHER
Roy Zhang

ILLUSTRATOR
Procolor

CREATIVE DIRECTORS
Andy Greenaway
Neil French

CLIENT
Churches of the Love
Singapore Movement

AGENCY
Ogilvy & Mather/Singapore

02418A

MERIT AWARD
PUBLIC SERVICE/POLITICAL
OUTDOOR AND POSTERS

ART DIRECTORS
Peter Robertson
Susan Hosking

WRITERS
Susan Hosking
Peter Robertson

PHOTOGRAPHER
Jono Rotman

CREATIVE DIRECTOR
Gavin Bradley

CLIENT
Women's Refuge

AGENCY
Saatchi & Saatchi/Wellington

02419A

MERIT AWARD
PUBLIC SERVICE/POLITICAL
OUTDOOR AND POSTERS

ART DIRECTORS
Peter Robertson
Susan Hosking

WRITERS
Susan Hosking
Peter Robertson

PHOTOGRAPHER
Jono Rotman

CREATIVE DIRECTOR
Gavin Bradley

CLIENT
Women's Refuge

AGENCY
Saatchi & Saatchi/Wellington

02420A

MERIT AWARD
PUBLIC SERVICE/POLITICAL
OUTDOOR AND POSTERS

ART DIRECTORS
Trevallyn Hall
Cal Bruns

WRITER
Trevallyn Hall

CLIENT
Salvation Army

AGENCY
Sonnenberg Murphy Leo Burnett/Johannesburg

02421A

MERIT AWARD
PUBLIC SERVICE/POLITICAL
OUTDOOR AND POSTERS

ART DIRECTOR
Philip Bonnery

WRITER
Anselmo Ramos

PHOTOGRAPHER
Public Domain

CREATIVE DIRECTOR
Armando Hernandez

CLIENT
Amnesty International

AGENCY
Young & Rubicam/Miami

02422A

RONALD WAYNE FRYE IS ON DEATH ROW BECAUSE OF A DRINKING RELATED PROBLEM. HIS DEFENSE LAWYER WAS AN ALCOHOLIC.

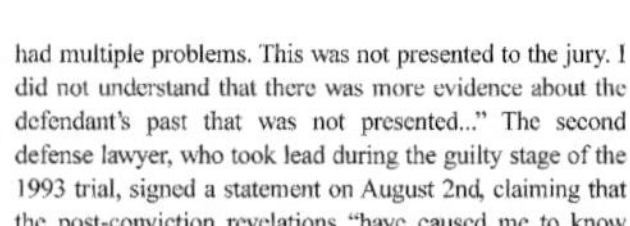

URGENT ACTION 50/01: North Carolina, USA. Ronald Wayne Frye, age 42, is scheduled to die by injection on August 31, 2001 in Raleigh Central Prison. He was sentenced to death on November 1993, for the murder of his landlord, 70 year old Ralph Childress, who was stabbed to death on January 2001. During the sentencing phase of the trial, the defense presented only two witnesses. The chief officer of the local jail testified that Frye did not cause any problems while in custody awaiting trial. The appointed psychologist gave a brief account of how Frye had been abused as a child, lived in foster care, dropped out of school, and abused drugs and alcohol as a teenager. The prosecution attacked the credibility of the expert testimony, claiming that the information came from the defendant himself and therefore likely to be self-serving. The jury sentenced Frye to death. The lawyer responsible for preparing Frye's sentencing defense was an alcoholic, who routinely drank, rather than work on his client's case. At a 1997 hearing, the lawyer (who went into a rehabilitation program in 1996 after being dismissed from a capital case due to his substance abuse), affirmed that during his 7 months on Frye's case, drank 375 millimeters of 80 proof rum every day. Moreover, he hired the psychologist only 11 days prior to the trial. At the 1997 hearing, the psychologist established that the defense did not submit school records, occupational records, medical records, witness statements, interviews or affidavits relevant to the case. If this evidence had been submitted, it would reflect a past history of severe childhood abuse and neglect. When Ronnie Frye was just 4 years old, he and his brother were given away to strangers. Frye's mother gave her two boys to a couple who were filling their car with petrol at a nearby gas station. They met Frye's mother in a restaurant where she handed them her children. There was no paperwork or official involvement. Their new father was an alcoholic, who routinely beat the boys over the next five years, sometimes with a bullwhip, leaving bloody welts. The boys were taken from the couple after the authorities discovered the abuse. Nine year-old Ronnie's scars and wounds were so striking that the photographic evidence was used for police training sessions about abuse. Social services then put the boys in the care of their biological father and his new wife. The father, who was often drunk, routinely beat his wife in front of the boys. Three years later, after a particularly violent beating, she left. As a result, the children were left to fend for themselves. They lived in squalor and were forced to beg for food on the streets. The jury heard only a minimal account of Ronnie Frye's tragic history. One juror recently signed an affidavit stating that this "background of abuse and neglect would have changed my decision and my vote." A second juror's affidavit states that "it would have made a difference in the way that I voted at the sentencing if I could have heard from Ronnie or a member of Ronnie's family. It would have made a great difference to know that Ronnie was criminally abused as a child and that his family had multiple problems. This was not presented to the jury. I did not understand that there was more evidence about the defendant's past that was not presented..." The second defense lawyer, who took lead during the guilty stage of the 1993 trial, signed a statement on August 2nd, claiming that the post-conviction revelations "have caused me to know that Ronnie was neither adequately nor properly represented at each phase of his trial. At the time of his trial, I was not aware of critical facts concerning Ronnie's childhood and upbringing, nor was I fully aware of the extent of the subsequently admitted alcoholic condition of my co-counsel... Were these and other later discovered matters known to me at the time, I am satisfied to a moral certainty that Ronnie Frye would have received a sentence of life in prison without the possibility of parole, instead of the death sentence."

RECOMMENDED ACTION: Please send appeals, as quickly as possible, in your own words; expressing sympathy for the family and friends of Ralph Childress; concerning that the jury heard only minimal evidence regarding Ronald Frye's background of abuse and neglect by noting that two jurors have stated they would have voted differently if all pertinent evidence had been submitted; questioning whether Ronald Frye was represented by an alcoholic lawyer who drank rather than prepare readily available, mitigating evidence; noting that in his co-counsel's August statement, Frye's second lawyer admits that the defense of Ronald Frye was indeed inadequate; arguing that the jury's verdict cannot be relied upon, by pointing out that the power of executive clemency exists to compensate for such cases; urging the Governor to grant clemency thereby breaking the cycle of violence.

PLEASE SEND APPEALS IMMEDIATELY: Governor Michael F. Easley, Office of the Governor, 20301 Mail Service Center, Raleigh, NC 27699-030, fax 1-919-715-3175 or 1-919-733-2120. Salutation: Dear Governor. You may also write, in not more than 250 words, to "Letters to the Editor": Raleigh News and Observer, PO Box 191, Raleigh, NC 27602, USA, fax 1-919-829-4872, e-mail forum @nando .com. Charlotte Observer, PO Box 20848, Charlotte, NC 28230, USA, fax 1-704-377-6214, e-mail opinion@charlotteobserver.com. Jacksonville News, PO Box 196, Jacksonville, NC 28541, USA, fax 1-910-353-7316, e-mail letters@jdnews.com. Winston-Salem Journal, PO Box 3159, Winston-Salem, NC 27102, USA, fax 1-336-727-7402, e-mail letters@wsjournal.com.

AMNESTY INTERNATIONAL 

TOO YOUNG TO VOTE. TOO YOUNG TO DRINK. TOO YOUNG TO HAVE SEX. OLD ENOUGH TO BE EXECUTED.

URGENT ACTION 220/01: Texas, USA. Gerald Lee Mitchell, black male, age 33, is scheduled to be executed on October 22, 2001, for a murder he committed when he was 17 years old. International law prohibits the death penalty against people who are under 18 at the time of their crime. Gerald Mitchell was sentenced to death in 1986 for the murder of Charles Angelo Mario, a white male shot dead in Houston on June 1985. Mitchell was convicted and sentenced by an all-white jury in a county where the population is approximately 20 percent African American. After the original jury pool was selected, the state removed all seven African Americans from the remaining group, citing "peremptory strikes," the right to dismiss jurors without giving a reason. Many blacks have been sentenced to death in the United States by all-white juries selected on the premise of *peremptory strikes*. After the prosecutor was challenged on his apparent discriminatory use of *peremptory strikes*, he argued that he used a basic standard when selecting jurors, "I was looking for someone who's a solid citizen, who had a background in the community, had a stake in the community..." He said that he did not want jurors who could view youth as such a mitigating factor that they would not vote for the death sentence. He also stated he did not want jurors who could look at the defendant as if he were their son. The trial court ruled that the prosecutor's use of Peremptory challenges had been racially neutral, emphasizing the removal of prospective black jurors who were categorized as either having friends or family in prison and those who had teenage children. Interestingly, some of the selected white jurors fell into these categories.

BACKGROUND INFORMATION: The International Covenant on Civil and Political Rights (ICCPR) prohibits the use of the death penalty against those who were under 18 at the time of the crime. When the USA ratified the ICCPR in 1992, it entered a "reservation," reserving the right to execute juvenile offenders. This reservation has been widely condemned as invalid, even by the Human Rights Committee, the expert body which monitors compliance with the ICCPR. Recognizing a young person's immaturity and potential for rehabilitation, the Convention on the Rights of the Child also prohibits the use of the death penalty against those under 18 years of age. This treaty has been ratified in 191 countries–excluding the United States and Somalia. The USA has signed the treaty, thereby obligating itself to respect its principles in good faith, pending its decision on whether to ratify it. The ban on the death penalty against children is so widely respected, that it has become a principle of customary international law, binding in all countries regardless of which treaties they have or have not ratified. The USA leads a tiny group of countries which have carried out such executions in the past decade. The only known executions worldwide in the past for years where in Iran (3), Democratic Republic of Congo (1), and the USA (8–4 in Texas). Over 80 prisoners are on death row in the USA for crimes committed when they were 16 or 17. Thirty-one of them are in Texas. More than 730 people have been executed in the USA since it resumed executions in 1977. In over 80 percent of cases, the original crime involved a white murder victim. Yet blacks and whites are the victims of murder in almost equal numbers in the USA. In Texas, which accounts for a third of US executions, over 20 percent of the executions have been of black defendants convicted of killing whites. In juvenile cases, the figure is 33 percent. Out of over 250 Texas executions, not one white defendant has been executed for the murder of a black. On August 14, 2001, in its report on the USA, the UN Committee on the Elimination of Racial Discrimination noted the "disturbing correlation between race, both of the victim and the defendant, and the imposition of the death penalty..." The Committee urged the USA to ensure that "no death penalty is imposed as a result of racial bias on the part of prosecutors, judges, juries and lawyers…"

RECOMMENDED ACTION: Please send appeals as quickly as possible, in your own words, to the Board expressing sympathy for the family of Charles Angelo Marino; expressing concern that, in violation of international law and standards of decency recognized around the world, Texas has scheduled the execution of Gerald Mitchell, who was under 18 at the time of the crime; expressing concern that this is another case of an African American tried by an all-white jury after all blacks had been removed by the state; urging the board, in the name of international law, commonly-held standards of decency, and the reputation of the State of Texas, to call on the Governor to commute Gerald Mitchell's death sentence; to the President: urging him to meet his obligation, under international law, to intervene in order to prevent this violation of international law, by calling on the Texas authorities to commute Gerald Mitchell's death sentence.

PLEASE SEND APPEALS IMMEDIATELY: Gerald Garrett, Chairperson Texas Board of Pardons and Paroles, P.O. Box 13401, Austin, Texas 78711-3401, fax 1-512-463-8120. Salutation: Dear Mr Chairperson. Your appeals should ask Mr Garrett to relay your message to all the Board members. If possible, and if resources permit, you may fax an appeal directly to them instead (Salutation: Dear Board Member [last name]). Alvin Shaw, Gerald Garrett, and Paddy Burwell, San Antonio Board Office, fax 1-210-226-1114. President George W. Bush c/o Albert R. Gonzales, Counsel to the President, The White House, 1600 Pennsylvania Avenue, Washington, DC 20500, fax 1-202-456-6279 (Counsel's fax) or 1-202-456-2461 (President's fax). Salutation: Dear Mr President. Copies to: Governor Rick Perry c/o Bill Jones, General Counsel, P.O. Box 12428, Austin, Texas 78711, fax 1-512-463-1932 (General Counsel's Fax), or 1-512-463-1849 (Governor's fax).

AMNESTY INTERNATIONAL 

MERIT AWARD
PUBLIC SERVICE/POLITICAL
OUTDOOR AND POSTERS

ART DIRECTOR
Philip Bonnery

WRITER
Anselmo Ramos

PHOTOGRAPHER
Public Domain

CREATIVE DIRECTOR
Armando Hernandez

CLIENT
Amnesty International

AGENCY
Young & Rubicam/Miami

02423A

SAFETY
BELTS
KEEP
FAMILIES
OGETHER
SAFE

MERIT AWARD
PUBLIC SERVICE/POLITICAL
OUTDOOR AND POSTERS

ART DIRECTORS
Regan Grafton
Haydn Morris

WRITER
Dan Moth

PHOTOGRAPHER
Robert Jackson-Mee

ILLUSTRATOR
Duncan Munro

CREATIVE DIRECTOR
Gordon Clarke

CLIENT
Waitakere City Council

AGENCY
young&rubicam.thinking/
Auckland

02424A

MERIT AWARD
PUBLIC SERVICE/POLITICAL
COLLATERAL: BROCHURES AND DIRECT MAIL

ART DIRECTOR
Mark Tan

WRITER
Neil Johnson

CREATIVE DIRECTOR
Neil Johnson

CLIENT
Volvo Cars East Asia

AGENCY
DDB/Singapore

02425A

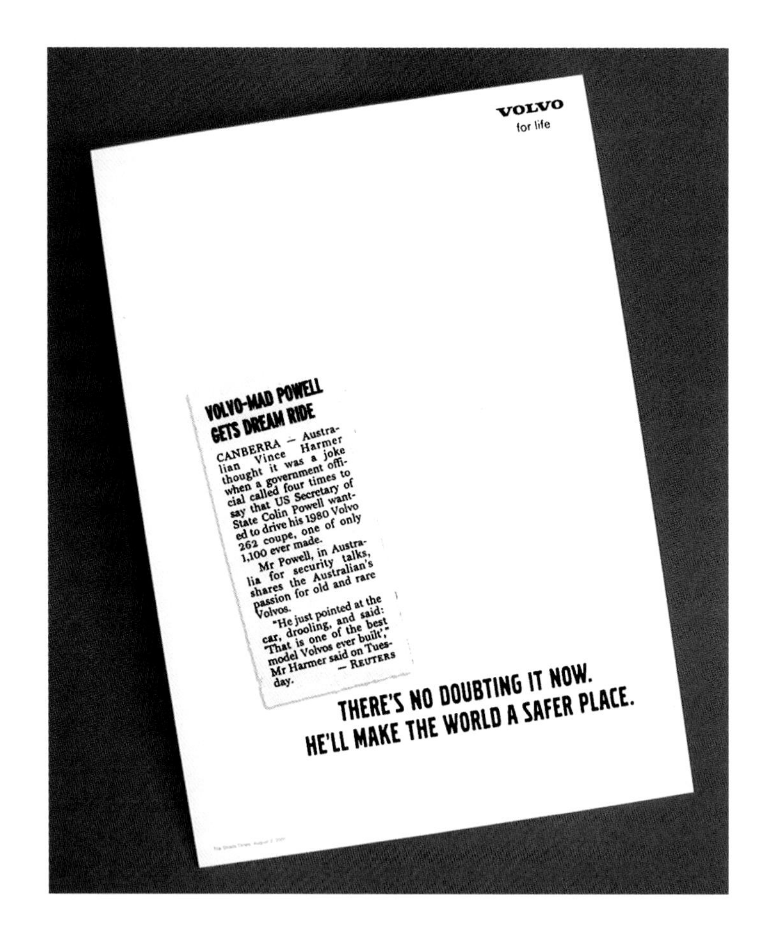

MERIT AWARD
PUBLIC SERVICE/POLITICAL
COLLATERAL: BROCHURES AND DIRECT MAIL

ART DIRECTOR
Melissa Johnson

WRITER
Vince Beggin

PHOTOGRAPHERS
Curtis Johnson
Stock

ILLUSTRATOR
Brad Palm

CREATIVE DIRECTOR
Tom Kelly

CLIENT
Amnesty International

AGENCY
Martin|Williams/Minneapolis

02426A

Also won:
MERIT AWARD
PUBLIC SERVICE/POLITICAL
OUTDOOR AND POSTERS

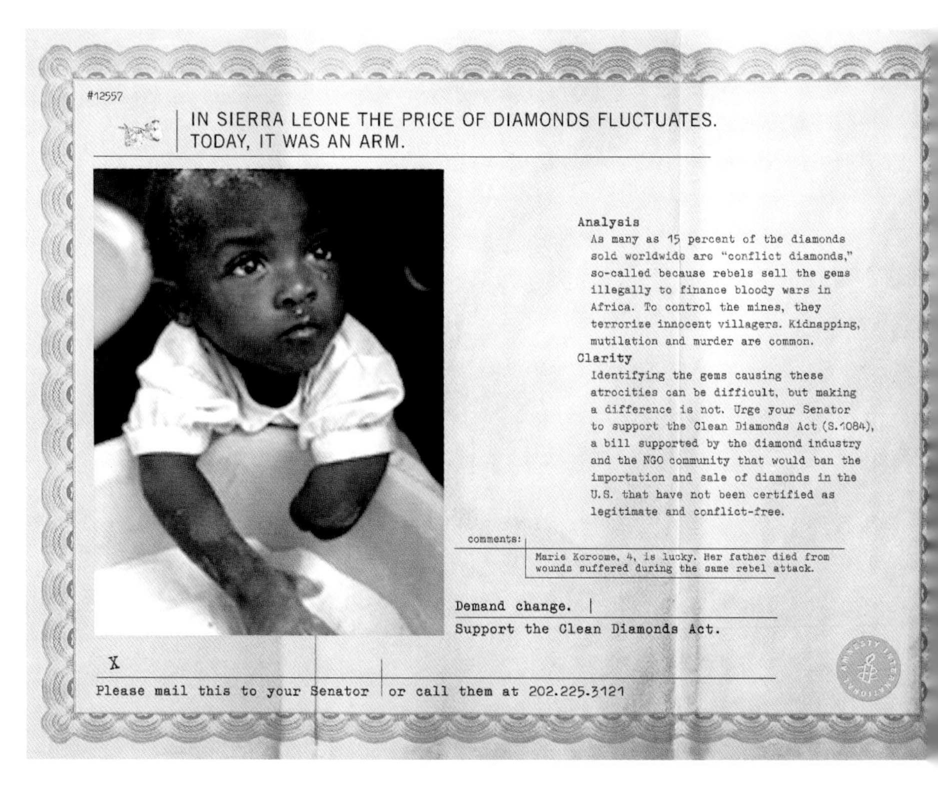

ANNOUNCER: If you've ever underestimated the power of advertising, may we suggest you get off your Sealy Posturpedic mattress, hop in the shower to get "Zestfully clean," wash your hair with Pert Plus—rinse and repeat—use some Paul Mitchell mousse, put on your Jockeys, a pair of Levi's, an Abrocrombie shirt, your Nike shoes, pour yourself a bowl of those "Greeeeat Kelloggs Frosted Flakes"—get milk—slice a Dole banana, maybe even cook up an incredible, edible egg, wash it all down with the best part of waking up, Folgers in your cup. Then brush your teeth with MFP fluoride, put on your Eddie Bauer jacket with Thinsolate, clap twice to turn off the lights, climb into your Volkswagen Beetle, drive your engine clean when you fill up the tank with Amoco Ultimate—and then pay a visit to the William F. Eisner Museum of Advertising & Design. Here, you'll learn how advertising can move and motivate not just consumers, but an entire culture. If what you see here doesn't convince you that advertising has a powerful impact on our society, well, may we suggest you move to Cuba. Flying the friendly skies, of course. Stop by and see program-free commercials for a change, as well as classic billboards, radio and print ads, even jingles. The William F. Eisner Museum of Advertising & Design, located in Milwaukee's Historic Third Ward.

MERIT AWARD
PUBLIC SERVICE/POLITICAL
RADIO: SINGLE

WRITER
Dave Hanneken

AGENCY PRODUCER
Darlene Stimac

PRODUCTION COMPANY
Independent Studios

CREATIVE DIRECTORS
Dave Hanneken
Rich Kohnke

CLIENT
William F. Eisner Museum of Advertising & Design

AGENCY
Kohnke Hanneken/Milwaukee

02428A

VOICE OF A 13-YEAR-OLD GIRL: I like to play football, which is unusual for a girl, I think...but, yeah, I like to play football...and do homework if I have any. I used to do a bit of horseback riding, but I gave that up...um, and like, I can't run that well, can't run at all, can't run fast...but I like a bit of tennis as well, bits and bobs, really, depends. I have a baby sister who's about four now, yeah, four, and she always lets me do her hair and I just I love it 'cause I enjoy doing hair and I do my own hair...and I just dunno and I love putting makeup on my little sister and so she's sort of like my guinea pig thing that you practice on.

(As she talks, her voice changes to that of a middle-aged man, then back to the girl's.)

ANNOUNCER: People online may not be who they say they are. Pedophiles use the Internet. Don't give out your email, mobile or other personal details. For more information visit thinkuknow.co.uk

MERIT AWARD
PUBLIC SERVICE/POLITICAL
RADIO: SINGLE

WRITERS
Nigel Roberts
Paul Belford

PRODUCTION COMPANY
COI

CREATIVE DIRECTORS
Nigel Roberts
Paul Belford

CLIENT
COI/Child Protection

AGENCY
Ogilvy/London

02429A

MERIT AWARD
PUBLIC SERVICE/POLITICAL
TELEVISION: SINGLE

ART DIRECTOR
Lee Einhorn

WRITER
Bill Hollister

AGENCY PRODUCER
Amy Feenan

PRODUCTION COMPANY
Playback

DIRECTOR
Pete Favat

CREATIVE DIRECTORS
Roger Baldacci
Pete Favat
Alex Bogusky
Ron Lawner

CLIENT
American Legacy Foundation

AGENCIES
Arnold Worldwide/Boston and
Crispin Porter & Bogusky/
Miami

02430A

FITZGERALD: Hello.

SUPER: Robert Fitzgerald. Tobacco Industry Chairman. April 1, 2001.

FITZGERALD: With the mounting evidence linking cigarettes to cancer, addiction, emphysema, heart disease and premature death, I want you, the American public, to hear directly from me what the tobacco industry is doing to take responsibility for this very serious problem. Effective immediately, we are issuing a cigarette recall. Every single cigarette in America is being pulled off the shelf, and will remain off until we can, with a clear conscious, offer the American public a cigarette that poses absolutely no health risk. Because if there are two things the tobacco industry cares about, it's your health and your trust. Thank you.

SUPER/VOICEOVER: April fools.

SUPER: Truth. Sponsored by truth. Thetruth.com

MERIT AWARD
PUBLIC SERVICE/POLITICAL
TELEVISION: SINGLE

ART DIRECTOR
Gerry Graf

WRITER
Gerry Graf

AGENCY PRODUCER
Gerry Graf

PRODUCTION COMPANY
hungry man

DIRECTOR
Bryan Buckley

CREATIVE DIRECTOR
Gerry Graf

CLIENT
Citizens Against Terrorism

AGENCY
BBDO/New York

02433A

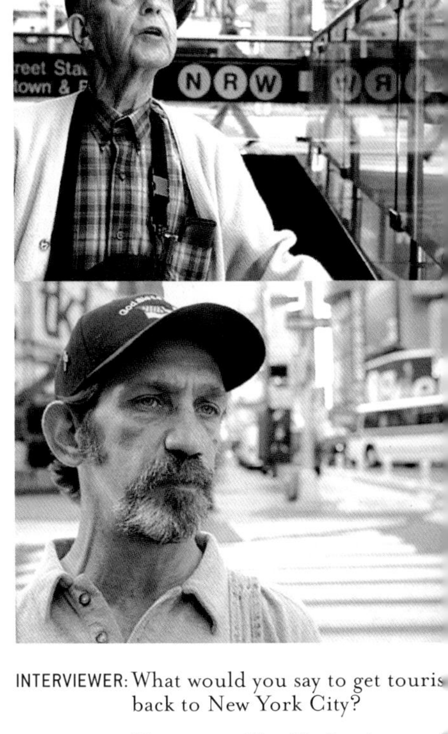

INTERVIEWER: What would you say to get touris back to New York City?

GUY 1: Tourists in New York, who need 'em?

GUY 2: You don't see people like this, like they're looking at a monste

GUY 3: The dance floors are actually breathable. I don't have anyone from Kansas or Wyoming knock me down.

GUY 4: I can get any donut I want.

GUY 5: *(Yelling at tourists on double decker bus.)* Yo, go home!

GUY 6: We're doing fine, you know. It' easier for me to park my truck; I can get into restaurants. I don care if people come to the city. *(Yells at horn honker.)* Shut up! Yo whadda you lookin' at?

SUPER: It's nice to see NY getting back to normal. Paid for by Citizens Against Terrorism.

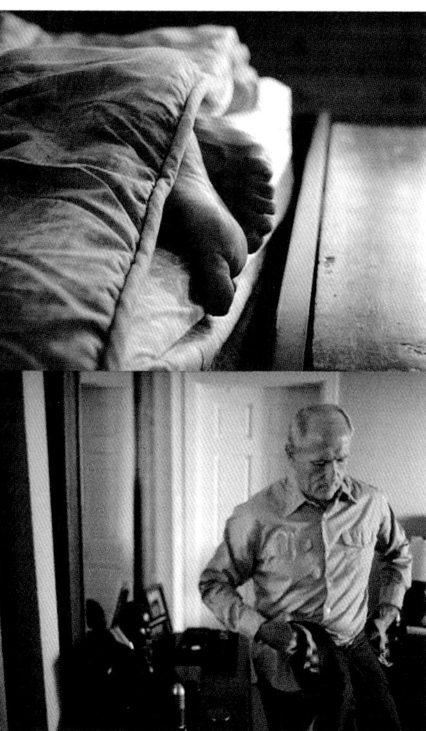

older, dignified, tough-looking gentleman is shown in ries of shots putting on a starched, immaculate military orm.)

ER: Freedom.

e last medal he pins on his coat is the gay pride rainbow ngle.)

ER: To differ. ACLU. Freedom to differ.

Picasso at the São Paulo Museum of Art.
No one should miss it.

(A guy is making faces. He takes the hand of his friend and passes it over his own face. His friend is blind. A cubist Picasso painting is next to them. We realize that by making those faces he's trying to get his blind friend to "see" the painting.)

SUPER: Picasso at the São Paulo Museum of Art. No one should miss it.

MERIT AWARD
PUBLIC SERVICE/POLITICAL
TELEVISION: SINGLE

ART DIRECTOR
Greg Wyatt

WRITER
Jim Elliott

AGENCY PRODUCER
Maleah Jacobs

PRODUCTION COMPANY
Moxie Pictures

DIRECTOR
Bob Purman

CREATIVE DIRECTOR
Jim Elliott

CLIENT
American Civil Liberties Union

AGENCY
Cole & Weber/Red Cell/Seattle

02435A

MERIT AWARD
PUBLIC SERVICE/POLITICAL
TELEVISION: SINGLE

ART DIRECTORS
Paulo Bemfica
Paulo Diehl

WRITER
Miguel Bemfica

AGENCY PRODUCER
Nivio De Souza

PRODUCTION COMPANY
Vertical Filmes

DIRECTOR
Carlos Manga Junior

CREATIVE DIRECTORS
Erh Ray
Jáder Rossetto
Pedro Cappeletti

CLIENT
MASP São Paulo Museum of Art

AGENCY
DM9 DDB Publicidade/São Paulo

02431A

MERIT AWARD
PUBLIC SERVICE/POLITICAL
TELEVISION: SINGLE

ART DIRECTOR
Clive Yaxley

WRITER
Jerry Gallaher

AGENCY PRODUCER
Kayt Magrobi

PRODUCTION COMPANY
Gorgeous Enterprises

DIRECTOR
Chris Palmer

CLIENT
Kick Racism Out of Football

AGENCY
M&C Saatchi/London

02432A

BABY (VOICE OF BENJAMIN ZEPHENIAH): Dear white fella. Couple things you should know. When I born, I black. When I grow up, I black. When I go in sun, I black. When I cold, I black. When I scared, I black. When I sick, I black. And when I die, I still black. You white fella. When you born, you pink. When you grow up, you white. When you go in sun, you red. When you cold, you blue. When you scared, you yellow. When you sick, you green. And when you die, you gray. And you have the cheek to call me colored.

SUPER: Let's kick racism out of football.

MERIT AWARD
PUBLIC SERVICE/POLITICAL
TELEVISION: SINGLE

ART DIRECTOR
Agostino Toscana

WRITER
Guido Cornara

AGENCY PRODUCER
Daniela Gasparotto

PRODUCTION COMPANY
BRW & Partners

CREATIVE DIRECTORS
Guido Cornara
Agostino Toscana

CLIENT
MTV

AGENCY
Saatchi & Saatchi/Milan

02436A

SUPER: Based on a true story.

LEONEL HERRERA: *(In Spanish with English subtitles.)* I wa to tell you my story. My name is Leo Herrera. I'm 53 years old, and in 19 was sentenced to death for murder c police officer in Los Fresnos, Texas. September 29, Enrique Carrisalez w killed by a single gunshot. David Ruck another police officer, who was stand a few meters away, was wounded. Ruck testimony framed me, and the fact t I was dead drunk when they found m became proof of my guilt. At the time the trial my face still bore the marks the "conversations" I had with the pol The wounded police officer's descript could have matched the majority of population of southern Texas, but t jury had no doubts. They said I was murderer, and I was sentenced to de It was only many years later that a sta ment written by my nephew came to light. Here's what it says: "In Septem 1981, when I was 9 years old, I saw n father Raul Herrera, the condemne man's brother, kill the police office Carrisalez, and a short time later sh at patrolman Rucker while fleeing t scene." After hearing all of this, do y think I'm innocent or guilty? I know innocent, but you'll have drawn your c conclusion now, won't you? Whatev your answer may be, come and tell m person. You can find me here, whe they buried me eight years ago, after sentence was carried out.

SUPER: The death penalty. The only injusti that can't be put right.

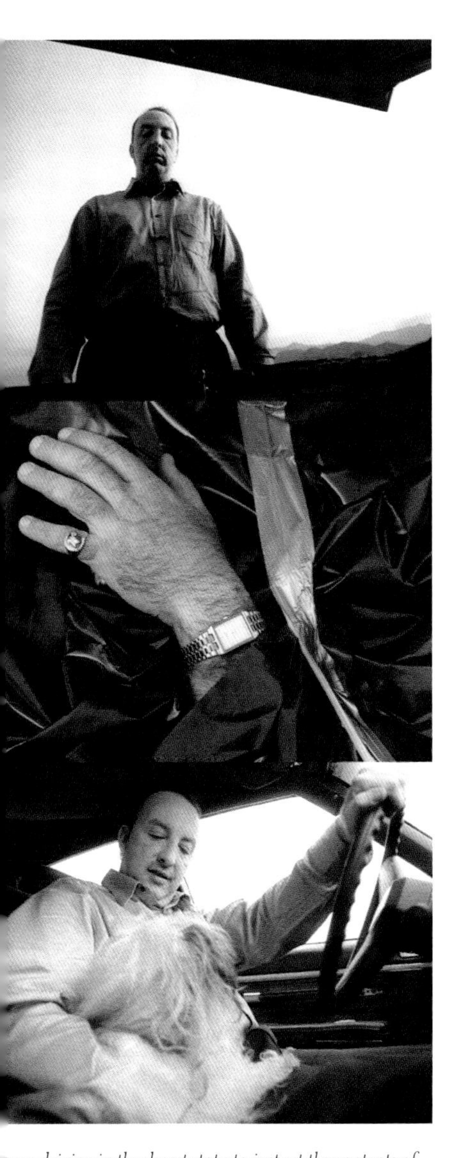

Call Toll Free
1-866-RING-CAM
They're your breasts.
You do it.

ɹan driving in the desert stops to inspect the contents of ɹrunk. Seeing that what he's placed in there is still alive, ˈnishes the job and tosses the results into a ravine, while ˌound gazes longingly out the window.)*

ER: That's the great thing about pets. They really don't care. Adopt today. Companion Animal Placement. www.rescue-a-pet.com.

CAM: Are you too busy to do your monthly breast self exam? Unsure of the right technique? My name is Cam and I'd like to help. Let me examine your breasts for you—absolutely free. I'm highly trained and highly motivated, so call the number on your screen.

SUPER: Call toll free 1-800-RING-CAM.

CAM: Call takers are standing by.

(Three of his teenaged friends sit around a phone.)

CAM: So put your breasts in my hands. Let Cam do your breast exam.

SUPER: They're your breasts. You do it. Examine yourself monthly. Breast Cancer Society logo.

MERIT AWARD
PUBLIC SERVICE/POLITICAL
TELEVISION: SINGLE

ART DIRECTOR
Dave Laden

WRITERS
Eric Aronin
Jim Jenkins

AGENCY PRODUCER
Ralph Laucella

PRODUCTION COMPANY
hungry man

DIRECTOR
Jim Jenkins

CREATIVE DIRECTOR
Eric Aronin

CLIENT
Companion Animal Placement

AGENCY
Suburban/New York

02434A

MERIT AWARD
PUBLIC SERVICE/POLITICAL
TELEVISION: SINGLE

ART DIRECTOR
Elspeth Lynn

WRITER
Lorraine Tao

AGENCY PRODUCERS
Janet Woods
James Davis

PRODUCTION COMPANY
Untitled

DIRECTOR
John Mastromonaco

CREATIVE DIRECTORS
Elspeth Lynn
Lorraine Tao

CLIENT
Breast Cancer Society

AGENCY
ZiG/Toronto

02437A

MERIT AWARD
PUBLIC SERVICE/POLITICAL
TELEVISION: CAMPAIGN

ART DIRECTOR
Steve Tom

AGENCY PRODUCERS
Jim Vaughan
Bill Weems

PRODUCTION COMPANY
Redtree Productions

DIRECTOR
Michael Moore

CREATIVE DIRECTORS
Pete Favat
Ron Lawner
Stu Cooperrider

CLIENT
Massachusetts Department of Public Health

AGENCY
Arnold Worldwide/Boston

02438A

ANNOUNCER: What do you do here?

TIM: I work out in the field cleaning up chemical spills, working with hazardous materials. Benzene.

ANNOUNCER: Benzene.

TIM: Benzene.

ANNOUNCER: Dangerous stuff.

TIM: It is very dangerous.

ANNOUNCER: What can it do to yah?

TIM: Causes cancer.

ANNOUNCER: When do you use this device?

TIM: On chemical spills.

ANNOUNCER: What's it show?

TIM: Volatile organics, which is probably Benzene, Toluene.

ANNOUNCER: What's it read?

TIM: 20,20PPM.

ANNOUNCER: Do you find that on a chemical spill?

TIM: Yes, you would.

ANNOUNCER: That kind of level?

TIM: Yep.

ANNOUNCER: Are you worried?

TIM: I'm worried now.

MERIT AWARD
PUBLIC SERVICE/POLITICAL
TELEVISION: CAMPAIGN

CREATIVE TEAM
Phil Dusenberry
Ted Sann
Charlie Miesmer
Michael Patti
Gerry Graf
David Johnson
John Leu

AGENCY PRODUCERS
Regina Ebel
Alexadra Sterlin
Lisa Petroni
Hyatt Choate

PRODUCTION COMPANIES
hungry man
Pytka

DIRECTORS
Barry Levinson
Bob Emerson
Joe Pytka
Santiago Suarez

CLIENT
Office of the Mayor

AGENCY
BBDO/New York

02439A

DIRECTOR: Thank you. Next. Name?

WALTERS: Ahh...Barbara Walters. *(Singing.)* Come and meet those dancing fee On the avenue I'm taking you to forty-second street.

SUPER: Everyone has a New York dream.

WALTERS: Hear the beat...

DIRECTOR: Next.

WALTERS: I, I can do something from Cats.

DIRECTOR: That's nice.

GULIANI: The New York miracle. Be a part o

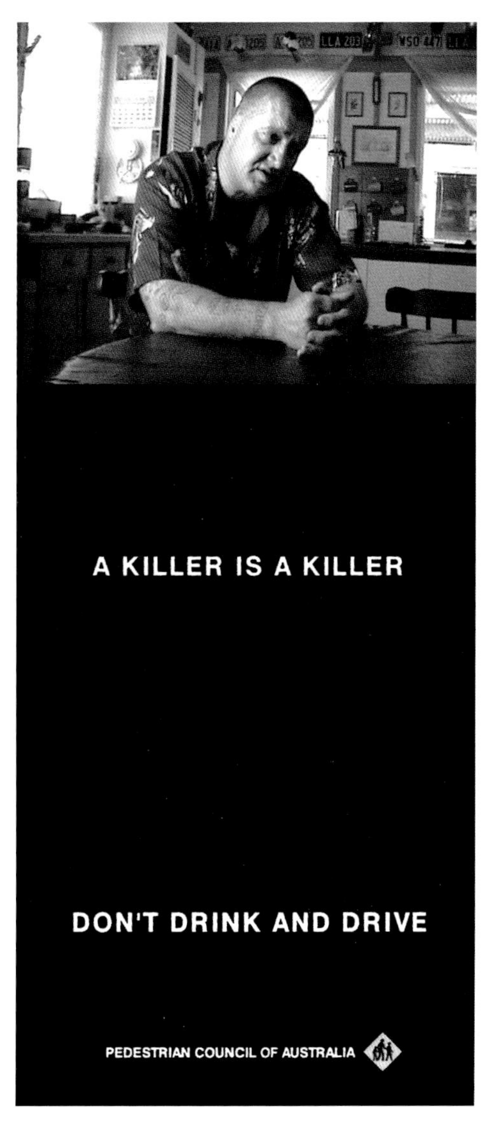
A KILLER IS A KILLER
DON'T DRINK AND DRIVE
PEDESTRIAN COUNCIL OF AUSTRALIA

CHOPPER: My name is Mark Brandon Read. A lot of people call me Chopper. Years ago I used to be a hit man. I know most of you out there may hate my guts. I'm not a very popular person. But you drink and you drive and you're going down the road and you kill a little kid, an old lady, an old person, some young mother pushing a pram across the road and you go skittle. You wipe them all up. You still hate me? Yeah, you still hate me, but you're no different than I am. You're the same as me. You're a murdering maggot just the same as I am.

SUPER: A killer is a killer. Don't drink and drive. Pedestrian Council of Australia logo.

MERIT AWARD
PUBLIC SERVICE/POLITICAL
TELEVISION: CAMPAIGN

ART DIRECTOR
Jay Furby

WRITER
Jay Furby

AGENCY PRODUCER
Scott McBurnie

PRODUCTION COMPANY
Silverscreen

DIRECTOR
David Gaddie

CLIENT
Pedestrian Council

AGENCY
Saatchi & Saatchi/Sydney

02440A

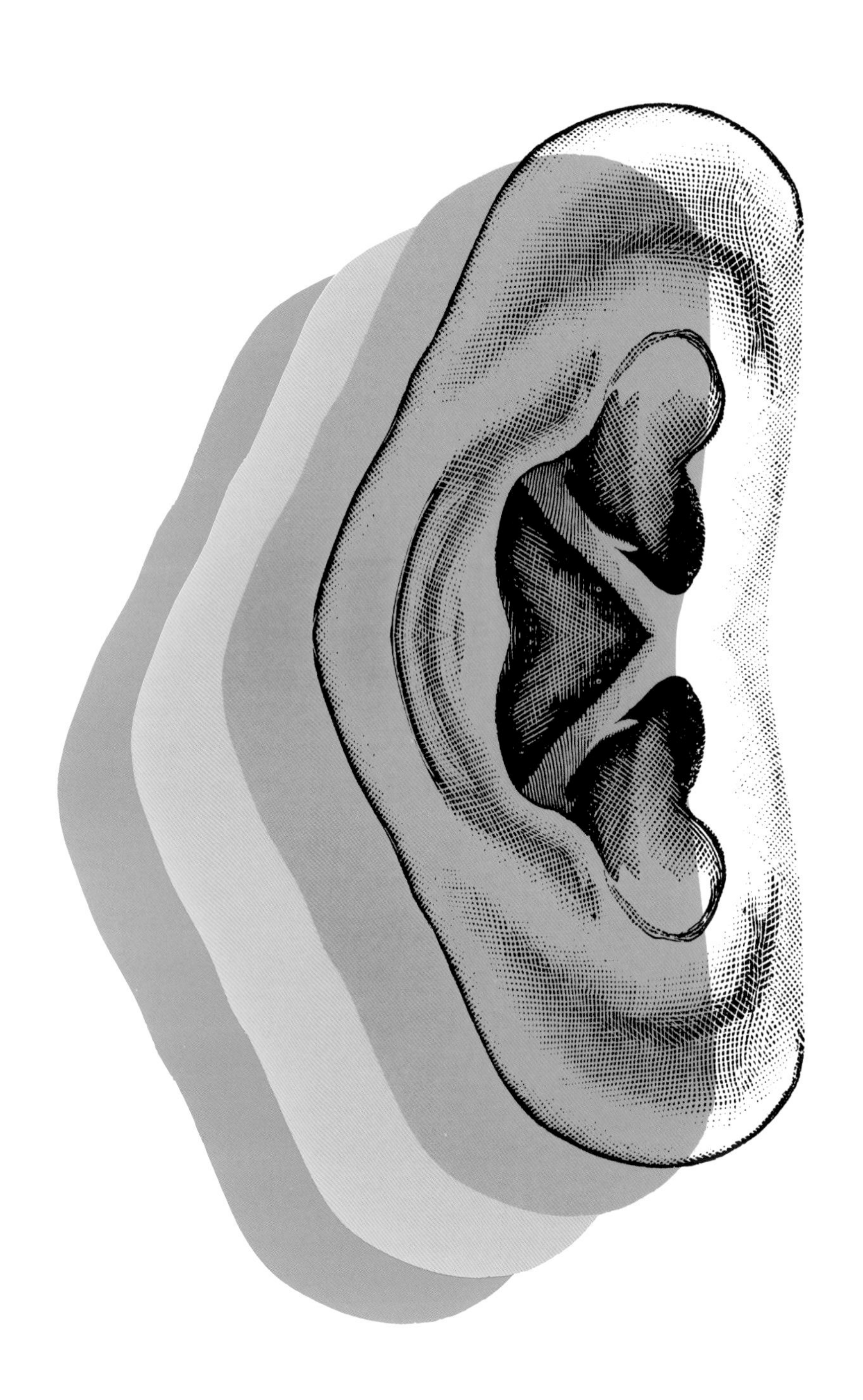

" ...as men busied themselves about their various concerns they were scrutinised and studied, perhaps almost as narrowly as a man with a microscope might scrutinise the transient creatures that swarm and multiply in a drop of water. With infinite complacency men went to and fro over this globe about their little affairs, serene in their assurance of their empire over matter. It is possible that the infusoria under the microscope do the same."
Orson Wells, OCT. 31, 1938 (from his famous radio broadcast of *H.G. Wells'* WAR OF THE WORLDS).

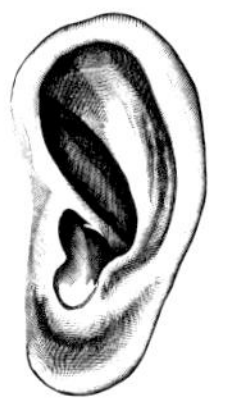

MERIT AWARD
CONSUMER RADIO: SINGLE

WRITERS
Denise Rossetto
Robert Kingston

AGENCY PRODUCER
Beatrice Bodogh

PRODUCTION COMPANY
Pirate Radio & Television

CREATIVE DIRECTORS
Doug Robinson
Angus Tucker
Steven Jurisic

CLIENT
Labatt Breweries of Canada

AGENCY
Ammirati Puris/Toronto

02441A

GUY 1: You know, sitting here with you boys makes me think back to all the great times we've had over a Blue Light.

GANG: Yeah, yeah.

GUY 2: You guys remember back a few minutes ago, when I couldn't find the remote?

GANG: Yeah.

GUY 3: Oh, wait. Remember the time when Jimmy brought in the chilidogs?

GUY 4: Yeah, I'm on my third.

GUY 1: Yeah, yeah, those sure were good times.

GUY 2: Remember when Al here said, "yeah, yeah, those sure were good times?" They were great times.

ANNOUNCER: Really new to the Maritimes. Blue Light, a beer with no history. Yet.

MERIT AWARD
CONSUMER RADIO: SINGLE

WRITERS
Denise Rossetto
Robert Kingston

AGENCY PRODUCER
Beatrice Bodogh

PRODUCTION COMPANY
Pirate Radio & Television

CREATIVE DIRECTORS
Doug Robinson
Angus Tucker
Steven Jurisic

CLIENT
Labatt Breweries of Canada

AGENCY
Ammirati Puris/Toronto

02442A

GUY 1: Ah, sitting in the pub having a Blue Light with you boys brings back a lot of memories.

GUY 2: Oh, yeah, like when the waitress just asked what we wanted to order and Robby here said the nachos.

GUY 3: Oh, remember the time when Stevie asked for more napkins? Classic.

GUY 1: Hey, here comes Pete.

GUY 4: Hey, guys.

GUY 1: Hey, Pete, we're just talking about Blue Light and the good old times.

GUY 4: Right on.

GUY 1: You guys remember the time when Pete just came in?

GANG: Yeah, that was a good time. That was cool man.

ANNOUNCER: Really new to the Maritimes. Blue Light, a beer with no history. Yet.

ANNOUNCER: Hollywood Video presents "60 Second Theatre," where we try (unsuccessfully) to pack a two-hour Hollywood production into 60 seconds. Today's presentation, *Shrek.*

FARQUAAD: Shrek, you must rescue a princess for me.

SHREK: Where is she, your highness?

FARQUAAD: In the lair of a vicious fire-breathing dragon.

SHREK: Why don't you rescue her?

FARQUAAD: What part of vicious fire-breathing dragon didn't you understand?

SHREK: The first part. It's a little ambiguous.

FARQUAAD: Just get going!

SHREK: I'm here to rescue you, fair princess. *(Thinking.)* Wow, she's pretty.

PRINCESS: Why, thank you, fair ogre. *(Thinking.)* Wow, he's ugly.

SHREK: It's getting dark, we'd better camp.

PRINCESS: I'll sleep in this cave.

SHREK: I'll sleep outside.

BOTH: Goodnight.

SHREK: *(Campfire.)* The princess could never fall in love with an ugly beast like me.

PRINCESS: *(Cave echo.)* I think I'm falling in love with that ugly beast. I must tell him the truth about me. Shrek, there's something I have to tell you.

SHREK: What is it?

PRINCESS: I'm...ugly.

SHREK: Nobody looks good in the morning.

PRINCESS: No, I mean I'm really ugly.

SHREK: Oh, that's just bed head.

PRINCESS: Kiss me, you'll see. *(They kiss.)* What do you think?

SHREK: Well, we're going to have ugly babies.

ANNOUNCER: If this doesn't satisfy your urge to see *Shrek* (and we can't say we blame you), then rent it today at Hollywood Video. Where every rental is yours for five days, and where *Shrek* is guaranteed to be in stock or next time it's free. Hollywood Video. Celebrity voices impersonated.

MERIT AWARD
CONSUMER RADIO: SINGLE

WRITERS
Ari Weiss
Aaron Adler

AGENCY PRODUCER
Katherine Cheng

PRODUCTION COMPANY
Kamen Entertainment Group

CREATIVE DIRECTOR
Arthur Bijur

CLIENT
Hollywood Video

AGENCY
Cliff Freeman and Partners/New York

02443A

MERIT AWARD
CONSUMER RADIO: SINGLE

WRITER
John Immesoete

AGENCY PRODUCER
Chris Bing

PRODUCTION COMPANY
CRC Chicago Recording Company

CREATIVE DIRECTORS
Bill Cimino
Mark Gross

CLIENT
Anheuser-Busch

AGENCY
DDB/Chicago

02446A

ANNOUNCER: Bud Light Presents...Real. American. Heroes.

SINGER: Real American Heroes.

ANNOUNCER: Today we salute you...Mr. Golf Ball Washer Inventor.

SINGER: Mr. Golf Ball Washer Inventor!

ANNOUNCER: The time-honored game of golf is the sport of kings and kings don't play with dirty balls.

SINGER: Don't play dirty!

ANNOUNCER: Because of you, we can give our balls a sudsy tumble at every tee. The result? Clean, shiny balls every time we whack 'em.

SINGER: Flying high!

ANNOUNCER: Drive after drive, putt after putt, hole after hole. Our dimpled balls stay clubhouse clean.

SINGER: Keep on drivin'.

ANNOUNCER: So crack open an ice cold Bud Light, Mr. Launder on the Links. You are in our thoughts every time we jiggle our balls.

SINGER: Mr. Golf Ball Washer Inventor.

ANNOUNCER: Bud Light Beer. Anheuser-Busch. St. Louis Missouri.

MERIT AWARD
CONSUMER RADIO: SINGLE

WRITER
Bob Winter

AGENCY PRODUCER
Chris Bing

PRODUCTION COMPANY
CRC Chicago Recording Company

CREATIVE DIRECTORS
Bill Cimino
Mark Gross

CLIENT
Anheuser-Busch

AGENCY
DDB/Chicago

02447A

ANNOUNCER: Bud Light Presents...Real Men of Genius.

SINGER: Real Men of Genius.

ANNOUNCER: Today we salute you, Mr. Horse Drawn Carriage Driver.

SINGER: Mr. Horse Drawn Carriage Driver!

ANNOUNCER: You start your day with a tip, tip! And a cheerio! Which is odd because you're from Brooklyn.

SINGER: Jolly Old Brooklyn!

ANNOUNCER: While most people sit behind a desk, you proudly sit two feet behind a four-legged manure factory.

SINGER: Oooh!

ANNOUNCER: No one knows the guts it takes to ride the subway to work dressed as a foppish dandy from the 18th century.

SINGER: Hey, foppish dandy!

ANNOUNCER: Blaring horns, profanity, vicious insults all met with a courtly tip of your stovepipe hat.

SINGER: Cheerio!

ANNOUNCER: So crack open an ice cold Bud Light, Buggy Boy. Because the way you say giddy-up makes us say whoa.

SINGER: Whoa! Whoa! Whoa!

ANNOUNCER: Bud Light Beer. Anheuser-Busch. St. Louis Missouri.

ANNOUNCER: Bud Light Presents...Real Men of Genius.

SINGER: Real Men of Genius.

ANNOUNCER: Today we salute you, Mr. Male Fur Coat Wearer.

SINGER: Mr. Male Fur Coat Wearer!

ANNOUNCER: Perhaps fashion's greatest mystery, what makes a big strong man say, "I think I need a new fur coat."

SINGER: I don't know.

ANNOUNCER: The very height of political incorrectness, nothing says, "I could give a rat's rear end" like a man in a floor-length chinchilla.

SINGER: Taking no prisoners.

ANNOUNCER: A look that's half street pimp, half Aunt Esther and full-on "fur-tastic." Sure it's goash but you don't spend more on your coat than your car not to be noticed.

SINGER: Look at me!

ANNOUNCER: So crack open an ice cold Bud Light, Mr. Male Fur Coat Wearer. Because it takes a real man to wear a lady's coat.

SINGER: Mr. Male Fur Coat Wearer.

ANNOUNCER: Bud Light Beer. Anheuser-Busch. St. Louis Missouri.

MERIT AWARD
CONSUMER RADIO: SINGLE

WRITER
John Immesoete

AGENCY PRODUCER
Chris Bing

PRODUCTION COMPANY
CRC Chicago Recording Company

CREATIVE DIRECTORS
John Immesoete
Bill Cimino
Mark Gross

CLIENT
Anheuser-Busch

AGENCY
DDB/Chicago

02448A

ANNOUNCER: Bud Light Presents...Real. American. Heroes.

SINGER: Real American Heroes.

ANNOUNCER: Today we salute you, Mr. Restroom Toilet Paper Refiller.

SINGER: Mr. Restroom Toilet Paper Refiller.

ANNOUNCER: Without your undying commitment, we might find ourselves trapped in a stall armed only with our newspaper.

SINGER: Oh, I need you now!

ANNOUNCER: Like a brave soldier you storm hostile territory delivering much needed supplies to your men.

SINGER: Oh!

ANNOUNCER: Should you leave one roll or two? Or perhaps that giant 10 pound super roll.

SINGER: Keep rolling!

ANNOUNCER: While others rest. You can't. Because somewhere there's a guy with his pants around his ankles doing the bunny hop in search of a fresh roll.

SINGER: Hop, hop, hop!

ANNOUNCER: So crack open an ice cold Bud Light. Master of the men's room. Because if you don't do your business. We can't do ours.

SINGER: Is there anybody out there?

ANNOUNCER: Bud Light Beer. Anheuser-Busch. St. Louis Missouri.

MERIT AWARD
CONSUMER RADIO: SINGLE

WRITERS
Bill Cimino
Mark Gross

AGENCY PRODUCER
Chris Bing

PRODUCTION COMPANY
CRC Chicago Recording Company

CREATIVE DIRECTORS
John Immesoete
Bill Cimino
Mark Gross

CLIENT
Anheuser-Busch

AGENCY
DDB/Chicago

02449A

MERIT AWARD
CONSUMER RADIO: SINGLE

WRITER
John Immesoete

AGENCY PRODUCER
Chris Bing

PRODUCTION COMPANY
CRC Chicago Recording Company

CREATIVE DIRECTORS
John Immesoete
Bill Cimino
Mark Gross

CLIENT
Anheuser-Busch

AGENCY
DDB/Chicago

02450A

ANNOUNCER: Bud Light Presents...Real Men of Genius.

SINGER: Real Men of Genius.

ANNOUNCER: Today we salute you, Mr. Supermarket Free Sample Guy.

SINGER: Mr. Supermarket Free Sample Guy!

ANNOUNCER: Though man dreads few things more than a trip to the supermarket, you offer us hope and sometimes a free mini-weenie.

SINGER: Love that freebie weenie!

ANNOUNCER: What exactly do you have? Aerosol cheese products, deep-fried morsels? Who cares? If it's on a toothpick and it's free, it could be plutonium and we'd eat it!

SINGER: It's all good, baby!

ANNOUNCER: For a guy wearing oven mitts and an apron, you're alright.

SINGER: You're a star.

ANNOUNCER: So crack open an ice cold Bud Light, titan of the toothpick. Because you put the free in freedom.

SINGER: Let it be free.

ANNOUNCER: Bud Light Beer. Anheuser-Busch. St. Louis Missouri.

MERIT AWARD
CONSUMER RADIO: SINGLE

WRITERS
Mark Gross
Bill Cimino

AGENCY PRODUCER
Sam Pillsbury

PRODUCTION COMPANY
CRC Chicago Recording Company

CREATIVE DIRECTORS
John Immesoete
Bill Cimino
Mark Gross

CLIENT
Anheuser-Busch

AGENCY
DDB/Chicago

02451A

ANNOUNCER: Bud Light Presents...Real. American. Heroes.

SINGER: Real American Heroes.

ANNOUNCER: Today we salute you, Mr. Wedding Band Guitar Player.

SINGER: Mr. Wedding Band Guitar Player!

ANNOUNCER: Any guitar player can rock a packed stadium, but it takes real talent to keep the Washinsky reception going all night long.

SINGER: Mazeltov!

ANNOUNCER: Perched on the stage in your undersized tuxedo you tirelessly churn out tunes from the 50s, 60s, 70s, 80s and 90s.

SINGER: Keep on rockin'!

ANNOUNCER: Sound check? You don't need no stinkin' sound check.

SINGER: No!

ANNOUNCER: And even though you've never had groupies, you have bagged the occasional bridesmaid.

SINGER: Never forget you!

ANNOUNCER: So crack open an ice cold Bud Light, guitar guy. Because every wedding you go to, you're the real best man. Bud Light Beer. Anheuser-Busch. St. Louis Missouri.

MERIT AWARD
CONSUMER RADIO: SINGLE

WRITERS
Pierre Lipton
Brad Emmett

AGENCY PRODUCER
Barbara Michelson

PRODUCTION COMPANY
McHale Barone

CREATIVE DIRECTOR
Sal DeVito

CLIENT
For Eyes

AGENCY
DeVito/Verdi/New York

02452A

NNOUNCER: If you want to get designer eyewear, you could go to one of our competitors.

RAZY CAL: This is Crazy Cal, from Crazy Cal's Optical. I'm crazy!

NNOUNCER: Of course, you'd probably want to wait for a sale. Like, maybe, Christmas.

RAZY CAL: Ho! Ho! Holy Cow! These prices are crazy!

FX: Reverb.

NNOUNCER: Halloween.

RAZY CAL: It's not a trick. It's a treat. These prices are crazy!

NNOUNCER: Memorial Day.

RAZY CAL: Come on down, and visit the Tomb of The Unknown Crazy!

NNOUNCER: Cinco de Mayo.

RAZY CAL: These prices esta loco!

NNOUNCER: Or, maybe, April Fool's Day.

RAZY CAL: These prices are totally sane. April Fools! They crazy!

NNOUNCER: But even if you did wait for a sale, you wouldn't get your glasses for less than you'd pay at For Eyes. Because we offer designer eyewear for 40 to 60% off every day. Not just on holidays. For Eyes. The store for people who can't see paying a lot for glasses.

MERIT AWARD
CONSUMER RADIO: SINGLE

WRITERS
Pierre Lipton
Brad Emmett

AGENCY PRODUCER
Barbara Michelson

PRODUCTION COMPANY
McHale Barone

CREATIVE DIRECTOR
Sal DeVito

CLIENT
For Eyes

AGENCY
DeVito/Verdi/New York

02453A

NNOUNCER: There are some things you shouldn't pay 40 to 60% less for. Like sushi, for example. *(Vomiting sound.)* Or, say, parachutes. *(Sound of fabric flapping and thud.)* Shotguns.

AN: Pull. *(Shotgun blast.)* My face!

NNOUNCER: Pit bulls. *(Dogs barking.)* Condoms. *(Baby crying.)* Mail-order brides. *(Pig squealing.)* A prosthetic leg. *(Wood breaking and a thud.)* A brain surgeon.

OCTOR: How many fingers am I holding up?

ATIENT: Thursday.

NNOUNCER: Smoke detectors. *(Crackling fire, snoring, and an approaching siren.)* Shower radios. *(Radio station being changed, a zap, then screaming.)* But when it comes to glasses, you should pay 40 to 60% less. Because at For Eyes, you get the same designer eyewear you get at other stores, just for less. For Eyes. The store for people who can't see paying a lot for glasses.

MERIT AWARD
CONSUMER RADIO: SINGLE

WRITERS
Alec Beckett
Brian Gross

PRODUCTION COMPANY
Bart Radio

CREATIVE DIRECTORS
Brian Gross
Alec Beckett

CLIENT
Sublime Juices & Beverages

AGENCY
Nail Communications/
Providence

02454A

FARMER: We've got those new Manning Vacuum machines over there. We milk mostly Holsteins. Some Jerseys. Like this beauty here. She's a good milker. She'll tense up sometimes—flow dries up, you know. You gotta put her at ease. Speak real soft. Gently stroke the udder. Hey there, girl, relax. You look nice this morning. Real nice. Yeah, I've been thinking about you. Uh-huh. Oh, I know, I'm going to touch your teats now. Oh, is that how you like it? You want me to squeeze 'em? Do you, do you? You dirty, dirty girl.

ANNOUNCER: That's not natural. Not like Sublime juiced beverages. All natural Raspberry, Tangeria and Lemonade. Real fruit. Real hard. Sublime juiced beverages. Not unnatural.

FARMER: One for you. *(Fwoop sound.)* And one for me. *(Fwoop sound.)*

MERIT AWARD
CONSUMER RADIO: CAMPAIGN

WRITERS
Adam Chasnow
Ian Reichenthal
Scott Vitrone

AGENCY PRODUCER
Katherine Cheng

PRODUCTION COMPANY
Kamen Entertainment Group

CREATIVE DIRECTOR
Eric Silver

CLIENT
Mike's Hard Lemonade

AGENCY
Cliff Freeman and Partners/
New York

02455A

Also won:
MERIT AWARD
CONSUMER RADIO: SINGLE

ANNOUNCER: Creating a drink as delicious as New Mike's Hard Iced Tea took the hard work of every employee. From the master craftsmen who perfected the recipe to the men who clean the tanks, everyone contributed. Except for Matt Bijarski in accounts receivable. He didn't really do that much. Unless you count sitting on your ass all day making personal phone calls. Which we don't.

SINGERS: Make it Mike's.

ANNOUNCER: Mike's Hard Iced Tea. Registered trademark of Mike's Hard Lemonade Company, Lakewood, Colorado. Lemon clear malt beverage with other natural flavors and caramel color.

LOUIE: Hey, Frank.

FRANK: Yeah, Louie.

LOUIE: I've got the new Budweiser catch phrase for summer 2001.

FRANK: What are you talking about?

LOUIE: Well, first they said, "Whassup."

FRANK: Yeah, that was good.

LOUIE: But then they posed the question, "What are you doing?"

FRANK: That was catchy.

LOUIE: Ah, but then they creatively morphed to "how are you doing?"

FRANK: And a great morph it was.

LOUIE: Okay, so now, all summer long, the new Budweiser catch phrase will be....

FRANK: Yeah?

LOUIE: Hi.

FRANK: Hi?

LOUIE: The simplicity is profound. It says nothing while saying everything.

FRANK: It says nothing, period.

LOUIE: Yeah, well, Budweiser loves it. They're making T-shirts, blimps, they have talking beer mugs.

FRANK: Yeah, what do they say?

LOUIE: Hi. And it sounds better with repetition. Hi. Hi. Hi. Hi. Hi.

FRANK: Yeah, stop it, that's annoying.

LOUIE: Frankie?

FRANK: What?

LOUIE: Hi.

FRANK: Stop, Louie.

LOUIE: Hi.

ANNOUNCER: Anheuser-Busch. St. Louis Missouri.

MERIT AWARD
CONSUMER RADIO: CAMPAIGN

WRITER
Steve Dildarian

AGENCY PRODUCER
Jennie Lindstrom

PRODUCTION COMPANY
Crescendo Studios

CREATIVE DIRECTORS
Jeffrey Goodby
Rich Silverstein

CLIENT
Anheuser-Busch

AGENCY
Goodby Silverstein & Partners/San Francisco

02456A

Age by which children develop brand loyalty: **2**
Percentage of children ages 8-16 who have a TV in their bedroom: **56**
Number of TV commercials viewed by American children a year: **20,000**
Number of violent acts the average American child sees on TV by age 18: **200,000**
Percentage of Americans who believe TV is responsible for juvenile crime: **73**
Hours per year the average American youth watches television: **1,023**
Hours per year the average American youth spends in school: **900**

T.V.
TELEVISION

MERIT AWARD
CONSUMER TELEVISION
OVER :30 SINGLE

ART DIRECTOR
Paul Brazier

WRITER
Nick Worthington

AGENCY PRODUCER
Kate Taylor

PRODUCTION COMPANY
Outsider

DIRECTOR
Paul Gay

CREATIVE DIRECTOR
Peter Souter

CLIENT
Dulux

AGENCY
Abbott Mead Vickers.BBDO/London

02457A

MERIT AWARD
CONSUMER TELEVISION
OVER :30 SINGLE

ART DIRECTOR
Walter Campbell

WRITER
Walter Campbell

AGENCY PRODUCERS
Natalie Bright
Yvonne Chalkley

PRODUCTION COMPANY
Academy

DIRECTOR
Jonathan Glazer

CREATIVE DIRECTOR
Peter Souter

CLIENT
Guinness

AGENCY
Abbott Mead Vickers.BBDO/London

02458A

(Three clay figures—part of a child's diorama on display in a school corridor—are enjoying a cup of tea. They hear a door shut and freeze. Footsteps get closer. A teacher approaches and notices the figures. Checking that no one is watching, she pulls the head off one of the little clay men, then pops it in her bag.)

SUPER: You find the color. We'll match it.

(The headless clay man is crashing helplessly around the cardboard box set. His two friends attempt to fashion a new head for him.)

SUPER: Dulux.

ANNOUNCER: And then there's this guy, the dreamer, the champion of the Dream Club.

BARTENDER: What are you drinking?

QUINN: The usual.

ANNOUCER: He drifts off with questions anc wakes up with answers.

(Quinn faces a sleeping squirrel opposite him. The squir in a bar full of other squirrels drinking Guinness and rec newspapers.)

SQUIRREL: *(Wakes with a start.)* I've just had t weirdest dream.

ANNOUNCER: It's a gift. Tonight's dream—the big question...

(Quinn runs down a crowded street and climbs a huma pyramid at the top of which is a peep hole in a wall. Th scene closes with a close-up of Quinn's eye as he peers i the hole.)

ANNOUNCER: What's the meaning of life?

(Back in reality, Quinn, still asleep, starts to laugh. He discovered the meaning of life.)

ANNOUNCER: This is the Dream Club. Ladie and Gentleman, please charge your glasses.

SUPER: Good things come to those who wait.

.MAN: Great Neptune!

Do-do-do-do-do-do-do.

s trying to communicate with a fish, which just lies there. en tries with the canned tuna, which also just sits there.)

Do-do-do-do-do-do-do.

n falls off the shelf beside him. He looks down at the n the floor, dejected.)

UNCER: Cartoon Network. Clearly, the best place for cartoons.

(We cross through layers of the earth, from magma to rocks, to water and soil, then through a subway tunnel with a train speeding towards us. We see the hustle of a megalopolis from the hall of a large building, filled with stressed people. We move to the roof, above the city to reach the clouds, then stop on the beautiful calm blue sky.)

SUPER: Travel in peace. Airbus logo.

MERIT AWARD
CONSUMER TELEVISION
OVER :30 SINGLE

ART DIRECTOR
Damon Pittman

WRITERS
Hernán La Greca
Craig Adams
Steve Kuhn
Damon Pittman
Fernando Semenzato

AGENCY PRODUCER
Damon Pittman

PRODUCTION COMPANIES
Turner Studios
Wild Hare Studios

DIRECTOR
Larry Robertson

CREATIVE DIRECTOR
Fernando Semenzato

CLIENT
Cartoon Network Latin America

AGENCY
Cartoon Network Latin America/Atlanta

02460A

Also won:
MERIT AWARD
CONSUMER TELEVISION
UNDER $50,000 BUDGET: SINGLE

MERIT AWARD
CONSUMER TELEVISION
OVER :30 SINGLE

ART DIRECTOR
Bruno Banaszuk

WRITER
Chermine Assadian

AGENCY PRODUCER
Annie Moysan

PRODUCTION COMPANY
Entropie

DIRECTOR
Les Freres Poireaud

CREATIVE DIRECTORS
Jacques Seguela
Olivier Moulierac
Jerome Galinha

CLIENT
Airbus

AGENCY
Euro RSCG Corporate/Levallois

02461A

MERIT AWARD
CONSUMER TELEVISION
OVER :30 SINGLE

ART DIRECTOR
Eric Cosper

WRITER
Dean Buckhorn

AGENCY PRODUCER
Robert van de Weteringe Buys

PRODUCTION COMPANY
MJZ

DIRECTOR
Craig Gillespie

CREATIVE DIRECTORS
David Lubars
Peter McHugh

CLIENT
Citibank

AGENCY
Fallon/Minneapolis

02462A

MERIT AWARD
CONSUMER TELEVISION
OVER :30 SINGLE

ART DIRECTOR
Chris Lange

WRITER
Michael Hart

AGENCY PRODUCER
Brian DiLorenzo

PRODUCTION COMPANY
Director's Bureau

DIRECTOR
Mike Mills

CREATIVE DIRECTORS
David Lubars
Bruce Bildsten

CLIENT
PBS

AGENCY
Fallon/Minneapolis

02463A

(Through the night, a father keep his son from getting a good night's sleep by hammering nails, blow drying his hair, holding a booming stereo speaker up to the ceiling, and blowing an air horn.)

DAD: *(Hanging picture.)* Is that straight? *(Checking fire alarm.)* Battery's good! Hey, Jimbo! Good luck on those SATs.

SUPER: 80% of parents worry about paying for college. Maybe Citipro can help.

DAD: If he goes Ivy League, we're toast.

ANNOUNCER: Citipro free financial guidance to help you reach all your goals.

SUPER: Citibank logo. Live richly.

(Big Bird knocks on a front door. A young girl opens it takes Big Bird's hand. They walk through epic scenes, inclu the Berlin Wall coming down; a Wilson-era "Votes for Wo rally; on-stage with a professional ballet company; a cro street in southeast Asia; the surface of the moon. Finally, they return to the porch. The little girl waves good-bye.

ANNOUNCER: TV can be a child's window to t world. What will they see?

SUPER: PBS logo.

young guy is baking bread when the doorbell rings. He wers the intercom, then rushes into his neat living room. pulls stuff—empty beer cans, cigarette butts, dirty laundry ut of an IKEA cupboard and throws it around. Then he ets three of his fellow band members.)

ER: IKEA. Smart storage solutions.

MERIT AWARD CONSUMER TELEVISION OVER :30 SINGLE

ART DIRECTORS
Anders Eklind
Karin Jacobsson

WRITERS
Filip Nilsson
Hjalmar Delehag
Fredrik Jansson

AGENCY PRODUCER
Charlotte Most

PRODUCTION COMPANY
Anders Skog Films

DIRECTOR
Anders Skog

CLIENT
IKEA

AGENCY
Forsman & Bodenfors/
Göthenburg

02464A

(A tracking shot seamlessly revolves from one side of the earth and through to the other as a Land Rover Discovery is shown in various scenes—parked at a Chinese market, unloading schoolgirls, crossing a remote river on a makeshift raft, and, with a couple in formal attire, pulling up to an opera house.)

ANNOUNCER: The Discovery Series II. Uniquely equipped no matter what side of the planet you're on.

SUPER: Land Rover logo. The most well-traveled vehicles on earth.

MERIT AWARD CONSUMER TELEVISION OVER :30 SINGLE

ART DIRECTOR
Lou Flores

WRITER
Cameron Day

AGENCY PRODUCER
Peter Feldman

PRODUCTION COMPANY
Plum Production

CREATIVE DIRECTORS
Jeremy Postaer
David Crawford

CLIENT
Land Rover North America

AGENCY
GSD&M/Austin

02466A

MERIT AWARD
CONSUMER TELEVISION
OVER :30 SINGLE

ART DIRECTORS
Paul Westum
Erik Heisholt

WRITER
Erik Heisholt

AGENCY PRODUCER
Cyril Boye

PRODUCTION COMPANY
Leo Film

DIRECTORS
Paul Westum
Erik Heisholt

CREATIVE DIRECTOR
Erik Heisholt

CLIENT
Puls.no

AGENCY
Leo Burnett/Oslo

02468A

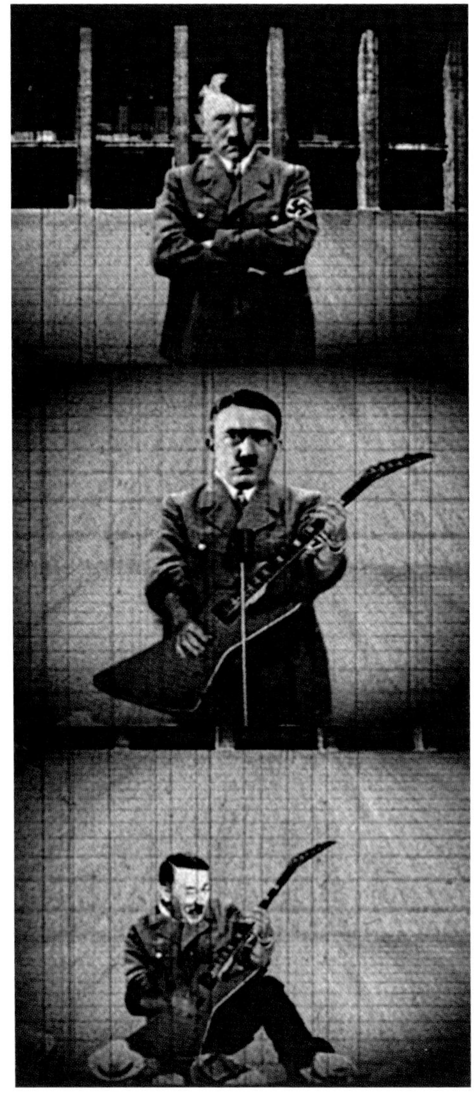

SUPER: Berlin 1935.

(Adolf Hitler plays an electric guitar. He's terrible.)

HITLER: Ja! Guitar-solo!

(The crowd throws bricks and stones, taking down the Nazi symbols.)

VOICE FROM AUDIENCE: Asshole!

SUPER: Music can change everything. A message from www.Puls.no. Logo. The online rock 'n roll magazine.

MERIT AWARD
CONSUMER TELEVISION
OVER :30 SINGLE

ART DIRECTOR
Vince Squibb

WRITER
Vince Squibb

AGENCY PRODUCER
Sarah Hallatt

PRODUCTION COMPANY
Stink

DIRECTOR
Ivan Zacharias

CREATIVE DIRECTOR
Charles Inge

CLIENT
Interbrew UK

AGENCY
Lowe/London

02469A

(A doctor does all he can to help the sick during a cholera outbreak. Despite his saintly behavior, the villagers shun h in fear that he has contracted the disease. But in the villag pub, their worries of contamination are soon forgotten on seeing a chance to sample his precious beer.)

SUPER: Stella Artois. Refreshingly expensiv

uy gets up off the sofa. Suddenly, the sofa springs to life, bing the guy and sending him to the floor. He tries to pe but the sofa hauls him back. The guy tumbles down tairs. He looks up in horror as the sofa launches itself n the stairs, only to get wedged in the doorframe.)

ER: Escape the sofa. Reebok logo.

(A young man is followed by thousands of men dressed as sperm. When he reaches a young woman, he is knocked to the ground by stampeding sperm. They throw themselves at the young woman, but bounce off an invisible barrier. The lovers kiss and walk away. The sperm men are trapped within a gigantic condom.)

SUPER: Durex. For a hundred million reasons.

MERIT AWARD
CONSUMER TELEVISION
OVER :30 SINGLE

ART DIRECTOR
Vince Squibb

WRITER
Vince Squibb

AGENCY PRODUCER
Sarah Hallatt

PRODUCTION COMPANY
Stink

DIRECTOR
Ivan Zacharias

CREATIVE DIRECTOR
Charles Inge

CLIENT
Reebok

AGENCY
Lowe/London

02465A

MERIT AWARD
CONSUMER TELEVISION
OVER :30 SINGLE

ART DIRECTOR
Dave Price

WRITER
Neil Lancaster

AGENCY PRODUCER
Sara Clementson

PRODUCTION COMPANY
Spectre

DIRECTOR
Daniel Kleinman

CREATIVE DIRECTOR
David George

CLIENT
Durex

AGENCY
McCann-Erickson/Manchester

02470A

MERIT AWARD
CONSUMER TELEVISION
OVER :30 SINGLE

ART DIRECTOR
Maximiliano Sanchez Correa

WRITER
Javier Campopiano

AGENCY PRODUCER
Marcelo Ramos

PRODUCTION COMPANY
Stuart Carbajal

CREATIVE DIRECTORS
Gustavo Reyes
Cesar Agost Carreño

CLIENT
Skin Less Skin

AGENCY
Ogilvy & Mather/Buenos Aires

02471A

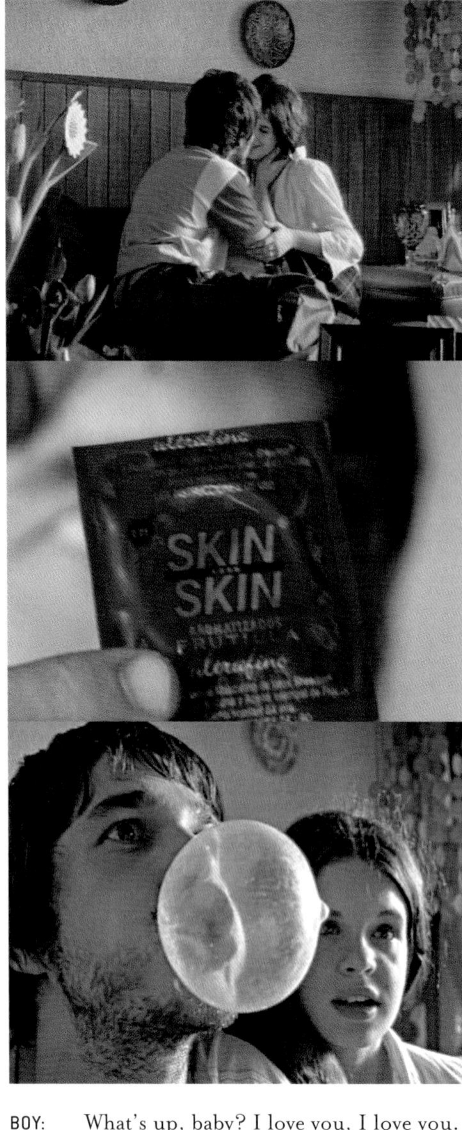

BOY: What's up, baby? I love you, I love you.

GIRL: No, no, wait, hold on, stop, stop.

BOY: What's wrong? It's our chance, sweetie. We are all alone now. You love me, I love you. I have everything we need. Look, come on. Don't give up on me now.

DAD: Hey, hey. What are you two doing?

BOY: Nothing. We were just talking.

DAD: What do you have over there?

BOY: A piece of gum.

SUPER: Logo. Ultra sensitivity. Strawberry flavor.

MERIT AWARD
CONSUMER TELEVISION
OVER :30 SINGLE

ART DIRECTOR
Michael Jansen

WRITERS
Bas Korsten
André Dammers

AGENCY PRODUCER
Marloes van den Berg

PRODUCTION COMPANY
De Schiettent

DIRECTOR
Sven Super

CREATIVE DIRECTOR
Michael Jansen

CLIENT
Pon's Automobielhandel B.V.

AGENCY
Result DDB/Amstelveen

02459A

MAN 1: If you take a corner too fast, it corre the wheels and engine, so that the ca remains stable. That's ESP.

MAN 2: On your Passat?

MAN 1: Yeah.

MAN 2: And status? My car has status. Standa

MAN 1: Status?

MAN 2: Yeah, imagine you're driving past a outdoor cafe. As you drive by everyb turns their head and they all think you're successful.

MAN 3: Oh, you mean status? My car has go that, too.

MAN 1: Eh, but how does that work on a we freeway? If you suddenly have to swe to avoid something?

MAN 2: Well, it's less effective there, of cour

MAN 3: Of course. There are no people wat ing alongside the freeway.

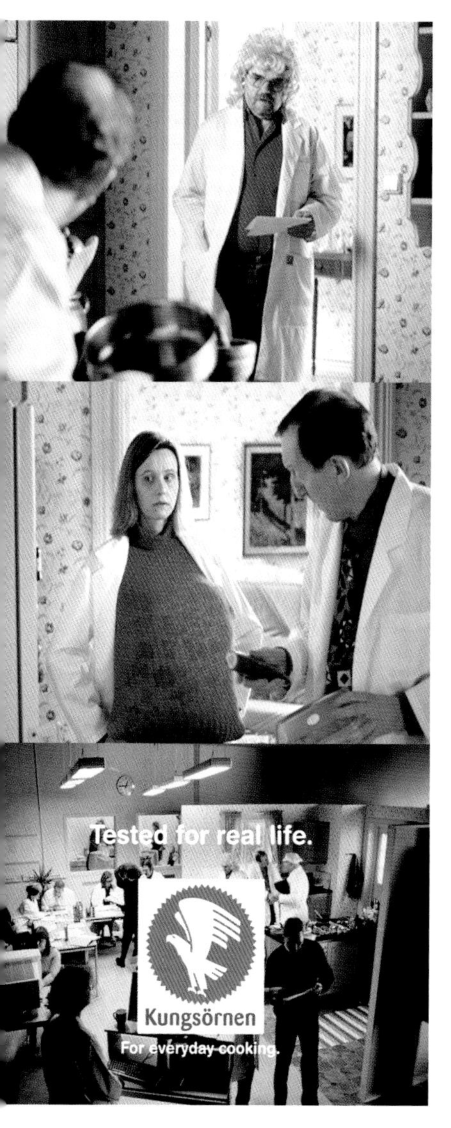

IN WIG: Do I look fat in this?

AS KID: I want ice cream.

AS SON: Dad, I think I'm gay.

ON TOILET: Ready, daddy, I'm ready!

IN WIG: You don't respect me at all.

TESTING FOOD: Mmm. Yummy!

ER: Tested for real life. Kungsornen. For everyday cooking.

MERIT AWARD CONSUMER TELEVISION OVER :30 SINGLE

ART DIRECTOR
Hans Ahlgren

WRITER
Olle Nordell

AGENCY PRODUCER
Johan Persson

PRODUCTION COMPANY
EPA International

DIRECTOR
Henrik Lagercrantz

CLIENT
Kungsornen

AGENCY
Stenstrom & Co./Stockholm

02472A

(A suburban neighborhood is bombarded by footballs, basketballs, and baseballs. An 18-wheeler plows through a hailstorm of classical instruments. A Nascar flattens a bus shelter. A jukebox splashes down in a lake. The XM Satellite mysteriously sweeps past.)

SUPER: XM logo.

ANNOUNCER: Coming soon. XM Satellite Radio.

MERIT AWARD CONSUMER TELEVISION OVER :30 SINGLE

ART DIRECTOR
Bill Kauker

WRITER
Brett Craig

AGENCY PRODUCERS
Richard O'Neill
Dan Connelly

PRODUCTION COMPANY
Propaganda Films

DIRECTOR
Dante Ariola

CREATIVE DIRECTOR
Lee Clow

CLIENT
XM Satellite Radio

AGENCY
TBWA/Chiat/Day/Los Angeles

02473A

MERIT AWARD
CONSUMER TELEVISION
OVER :30 SINGLE

ART DIRECTOR
Jon Soto

WRITER
Chuck McBride

AGENCY PRODUCER
Jennifer Golub

DIRECTOR
Spike Jonze

CREATIVE DIRECTOR
Chuck McBride

CLIENT
Levi's

AGENCY
TBWA/Chiat/Day/
San Francisco

02474A

(A man with headphones moves his legs in a dance-like but out-of-control way. The rest of his body remains motionless.)

SUPER: Flyweight Jeans. Levi's logo.

MERIT AWARD
CONSUMER TELEVISION
OVER :30 SINGLE

ART DIRECTORS
Hal Curtis
Tim Hanrahan

WRITER
Jimmy Smith

AGENCY PRODUCER
Vic Palumbo

PRODUCTION COMPANY
HSI

DIRECTOR
Paul Hunter

CREATIVE DIRECTORS
Dan Wieden
Hal Curtis
Jim Riswold

CLIENT
Nike

AGENCY
Wieden + Kennedy/Portland

02475A

(A series of shots shows basketball players—including Vin Carter, Darius Miles, Rasheed Wallace, Lamar Odom, and more—throwing a ball to each other, dribbling it low or between their legs, spinning it, dancing around it, going one-on-one, dunking it, kicking it, throwing it toward the camera, and break dancing.)

SUPER: Swoosh.

584 VHS
The beautifully crafted Passat W8.
You'll want to keep it that way.

STAFF NURSE: And the operation will involve a general anesthetic so you won't be able to go back to work this afternoon. And you can't drive. Did you drive here?

(The man begins to nod, then stops. He is motionless.)

MAN: Yes.

WOMAN: I'll drive.

(Man looks out window at his Passat.)

NURSE: And you've hadn't had anything to eat this morning?

MAN: No. Oh, yes. I had eggs and bacon this morning.

WOMAN: No you didn't.

MAN: Yes, I did. When you were in the bath.

NURSE: Look, you were told that you couldn't eat.

MAN: Yeah, sorry.

WOMAN: Are you sure that you had breakfast, darling?

MAN: Yeah, I had, um, full English breakfast. I had, um, toast and marmalade and, um, some baked beans and other bits and bobs. It was very nice, and I washed it back with...

SUPER: VW logo. The beautifully crafted Passat W8. You'll want to keep it that way.

MERIT AWARD
CONSUMER TELEVISION
OVER :30 CAMPAIGN

ART DIRECTORS
Ewan Patterson
Rob Jack

WRITERS
Ewan Patterson
Rob Jack

AGENCY PRODUCER
Rob Jack

PRODUCTION COMPANY
Partizan

CREATIVE DIRECTORS
Mike Hannett
Dave Buchanan

CLIENT
Volkswagen Passat

AGENCY
BMP DDB/London

02476A

MERIT AWARD
CONSUMER TELEVISION
:30/:25 SINGLE

ART DIRECTOR
Paul Brazier

WRITER
Nick Worthington

AGENCY PRODUCER
Carol Powell

PRODUCTION COMPANY
Outsider

DIRECTOR
Paul Gay

CREATIVE DIRECTOR
Peter Souter

CLIENT
Kaliber

AGENCY
Abbott Mead Vickers.BBDO/
London

02477A

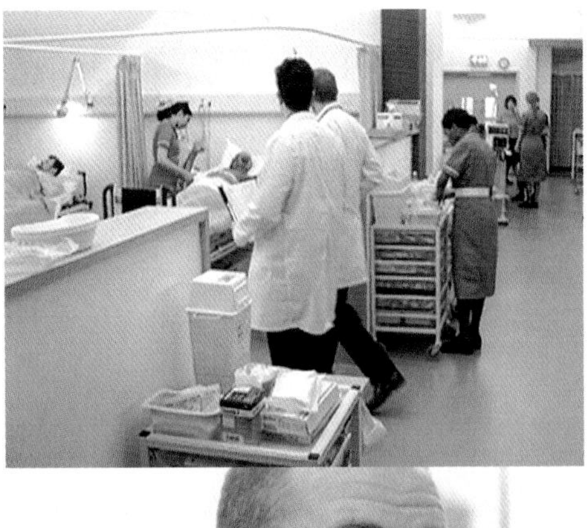

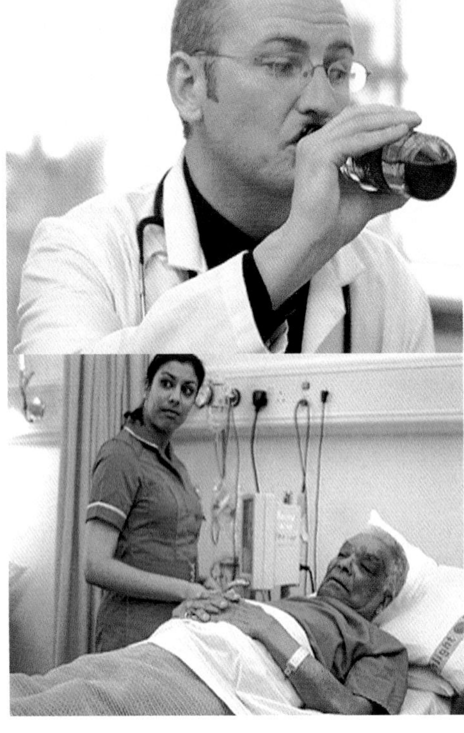

SURGEON: Hello, Charles, I'm Dr. Callaway. I'll be performing the operation today, as you know. This is Dr. Haig. I just wanted to reassure you that it's just a minor operation. Nothing to worry about, it's quite routine. Is there anything you'd like to ask us?

(The doctor swigs beer from a bottle.)

SURGEON: *(To Dr. Haig.)* Anything you want to say? Fine. See you in a few minutes then.

ANNOUNCER: New Kaliber. Only the beer gets drunk.

MERIT AWARD
CONSUMER TELEVISION
:30/:25 SINGLE

ART DIRECTOR
Don Shelford

WRITER
Susan Ebling Corbo

AGENCY PRODUCER
Paul Shannon

PRODUCTION COMPANY
Bob Industries

DIRECTOR
Dayton/Faris

CREATIVE DIRECTORS
Ron Lawner
Alan Pafenbach

CLIENT
Volkswagen of America

AGENCY
Arnold Worldwide/Boston

02478A

NARRATOR: The Roman Aqueducts have stoo here since 145 BC. Able to endu centuries because of an engineer marvel: The arch. A curved structu so strong that even when...

(New Beetle drives into frame behind him, lining up perfe with the arch.)

NARRATOR: ...great pressure is applied to it, holds its shape. A design with suc strength and integrity that to this day modern man has yet to impr on it.

SUPER: Round for a reason. Highest safe rating. VW logo. Drivers wanted

S: We have got to cut costs, people. Ideas?

: We could open an account on FedEx.com. Save 10% on express shipping.

S: Okay, how about this? We could open an account on FedEx.com. Save 10% on express shipping.

: You just said the same thing I did, except you did this. *(Hand gestures.)*

S: No, I did this.

LOYEES: Makes all the difference. Bingo. Right on the nose.

MAN: Red Stripe and reggae. Helping our white friends dance for over 70 years.

(A 20-something guy with a Red Stripe bounces back and forth to reggae music.)

MAN: Red Stripe. It's beer! Hooray Beer!

SUPER: Hooray beer.

MERIT AWARD
CONSUMER TELEVISION
:30/:25 SINGLE

ART DIRECTOR
Marianne Besch

WRITERS
Gerry Graf
Adam Goldstein
Earnest Lupinacci

AGENCY PRODUCERS
Sue Pettiti
Jeff Stock

PRODUCTION COMPANY
@radical.media

DIRECTOR
Frank Todaro

CREATIVE DIRECTORS
Ted Sann
Gerry Graf
Adam Goldstein
Marianne Besch

CLIENT
Federal Express

AGENCY
BBDO/New York

02499A

MERIT AWARD
CONSUMER TELEVISION
:30/:25 SINGLE

ART DIRECTORS
Gerry Graf
Harold Einstein

WRITERS
Gerry Graf
Harold Einstein

AGENCY PRODUCER
Elisa Greiche

PRODUCTION COMPANY
hungry man

DIRECTOR
Marcos Siega

CREATIVE DIRECTORS
Ted Sann
Gerry Graf
Harold Einstein

CLIENT
Guinness/Red Stripe

AGENCY
BBDO/New York

02479A

MERIT AWARD
CONSUMER TELEVISION
:30/:25 SINGLE

ART DIRECTORS
Libby Brockhoff
Randy Tatum

WRITERS
Tom Camp
Steve Casey

AGENCY PRODUCER
Sean Healey

PRODUCTION COMPANY
Head Gear Animation

DIRECTOR
Steve Angel

CREATIVE DIRECTOR
Jud Smith

CLIENT
IKEA

AGENCY
Carmichael Lynch/
Minneapolis

02480A

MAN: And so then I say to Warren, Warren, it's not a matter of requisitioning plastic fasteners, clearly it's a matter of following protocol. *(His wife pops off his head like a doll's.)* And what's more, all these forms need to be filled out in triplicate so don't look at me like it's my problem, mister. So I think I made my point. I mean, so there. *(She replaces it with a handsome Rhasta man with dreadlocks.)*

SUPER: Find your style. Ikea logo. Live better.

MERIT AWARD
CONSUMER TELEVISION
:30/:25 SINGLE

ART DIRECTOR
Jason Gaboriau

WRITER
Steve Doppelt

AGENCY PRODUCER
Kevin Diller

PRODUCTION COMPANY
Partizan

DIRECTOR
Traktor

CREATIVE DIRECTOR
Eric Silver

CLIENT
Budget

AGENCY
Cliff Freeman and Partners/
New York

02481A

EMPLOYEE 1: It takes less than a minute book at Budget.com.

EMPLOYEE 3: Great deals for just $19.99

EMPLOYEE 1: How can we let everyone k about Budget.com?

EMPLOYEE 2: We'll create a character to spread the word.

EMPLOYEE 3: Budget.com Man.

BUDGET.COM MAN: I'm Budget.com Man. I fig for justice and savings.

KID 1: Can you fly?

BUDGET.COM MAN: No

KID 2: Can you stop bullets?

BUDGET.COM MAN: No.

KID 2: You suck, Budget.com Man. *(Throws rock at Budget.co Man and knocks him unconscious.*

EMPLOYEES: Budget.com Man? Maybe It's a great deal, though. Excellent. $19.99. It's a gr price.

SUPER: Great deals for $19.99. O at Budget.com.

Time passes
and nothing
happens.

anti-wrinkle cream is shown for 30 seconds.)

ER: Neutrogena Healthy Skin. Time passes ...and nothing changes.

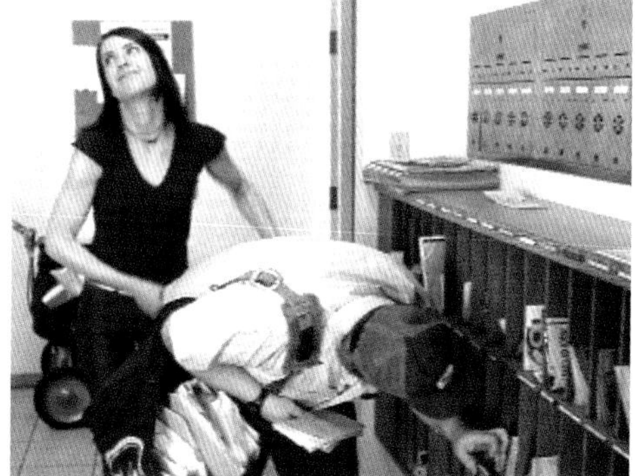

(An old lady struggles with her door because her light bulb has burned out. A young woman taps the light back on.)

SONG: I want to be like Buddy Lee.

(A small boy drops a sucker. The young woman pries it off the carpet and plops it back into his mouth.)

SONG: And help out everyone I see.

(A mail carrier bends over. He has "plumber's crack." The young woman casually tugs his pants up.)

SONG: There'd be no job too big for me. I want to be like Buddy Lee. But then it occurs to me.

(A piano falls, lands on Buddy Lee, and explodes. Buddy is unharmed.)

SONG: It might hurt to be like Buddy Lee.

SUPER: Be like Buddy Lee.

ANNOUNCER: Lee Dungarees. Can't bust 'em.

SUPER: Lee Dungarees. Can't bust 'em.

MERIT AWARD CONSUMER TELEVISION :30/:25 SINGLE

ART DIRECTOR
Felipe Massis

WRITER
Marcela Pagano

AGENCY PRODUCER
Nivio De Souza

PRODUCTION COMPANY
Tambor Filmes

DIRECTOR
Ciro Silva

CREATIVE DIRECTORS
Erh Ray
Jáder Rossetto
Pedro Cappeletti

CLIENT
Johnson & Johnson-Neutrogena

AGENCY
DM9 DDB Publicidade/São Paulo

02482A

MERIT AWARD CONSUMER TELEVISION :30/:25 SINGLE

ART DIRECTOR
Harvey Marco

WRITER
Dean Buckhorn

AGENCY PRODUCER
Marty Wetherall

PRODUCTION COMPANY
Partizan

DIRECTOR
Traktor

CREATIVE DIRECTORS
David Lubars
Bob Moore

CLIENT
The Lee Apparel Co./Buddy Lee

AGENCY
Fallon/Minneapolis

02483A

MERIT AWARD
CONSUMER TELEVISION
:30/:25 SINGLE

ART DIRECTORS
Chris Brignola
Matt Vescovo

WRITER
Bobby Pearce

AGENCY PRODUCER
Nancy Gentry

PRODUCTION COMPANY
Harry Nash

DIRECTOR
Fredrick Bond

CREATIVE DIRECTOR
Kevin Roddy

CLIENT
Conseco

AGENCY
Fallon/New York

02484A

MOM: There they are!

FATHER: Excuse me.

(A suitcase comes down the conveyer belt. Mother and daughter open the suitcase and let grandma out.)

GIRL: Gramma!

MOM: Hey, mom.

GRANNY: Hello.

MOM: How are you doing?

GRANNY: I'm okay. I'm just a little dizzy. Where's Stanley?

(Another suitcase with grandpa in it hits the bottom of the carousel.)

ANNOUNCER: How will you make your money last when you retire? Conseco offers a wide variety of retirement products that can help. Conseco. Step up.

MERIT AWARD
CONSUMER TELEVISION
:30/:25 SINGLE

ART DIRECTOR
Eric Rindal

WRITER
Clark Morgan

AGENCY PRODUCER
Steve Neely

PRODUCTION COMPANY
Moxie Pictures

DIRECTOR
Christopher Guest

CREATIVE DIRECTOR
Brian Bacino

CLIENT
Fox Sports

AGENCY
Foote Cone & Belding/
San Francisco

02485A

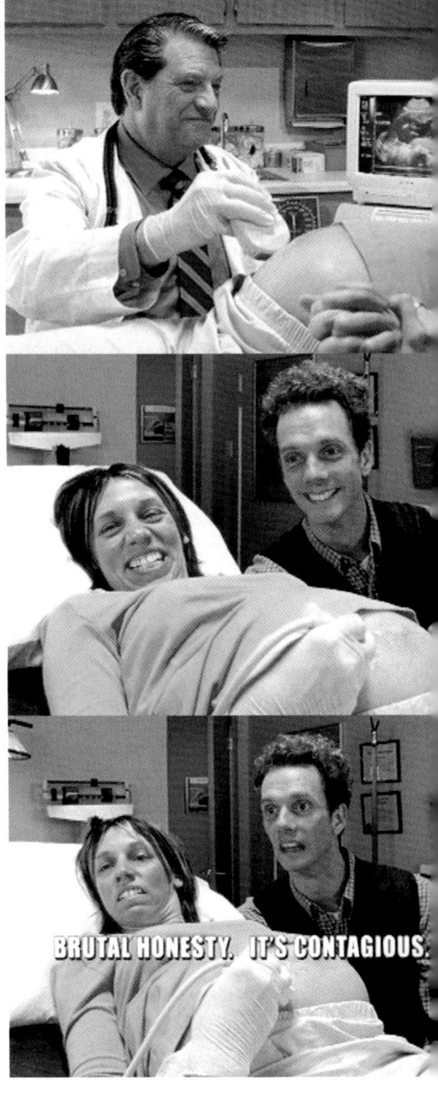

DOC: Hm mm. Everything looks in order.

DAD: So, Doc. What's it going to be?

(The doctor looks pointedly first at the father, then the mother.)

DOC: Ugly.

SUPER: Brutal honesty. It's contagious.

ANNOUNCER: The last word with Jim Rome. TV's only sports commentary that's truly brutally honest. Weeknights at 7 on Fox Sports.

ıonkey rides horseback through an abandoned dot-com
ɛ park. He passes the now out-of-business companies,
lasp.com" and "pimentoloaf.com." A wrecking ball
hes into the "LeSocks" factory. A LeSocks puppet mascot
ꞩ at the monkey's feet. He picks it up and begins to cry.)

ER: Invest wisely. E*Trade. It's your money.

SUPER: Rycharde Hawkes. HP labs.

(A group of Finnish children scroll through a display of tram arrival times their cell phones, then run outside to catch the tram.)

RYCHARDE HAWKES: *(On tram.)* It's very, very cold in Helsinki. It's no place to wait for a tram. But they embrace new technology in Finland, so at HP we're working on a way to use your mobile phone to find out exactly when your bus or tram will arrive...

KID: Let's go!

(They run outside as the tram arrives and pelt it with snowballs.)

RYCHARDE HAWKES: ...reducing the amount of time you have to wait outside. *(Snowballs hit his window.)* It's pretty cool.

SUPER: HP logo. Invent.

MERIT AWARD
CONSUMER TELEVISION
:30/:25 SINGLE

ART DIRECTORS
Stephen Pearson
David Gray

WRITER
Tom Miller

AGENCY PRODUCER
David Yost

PRODUCTION COMPANY
hungry man

DIRECTOR
Bryan Buckley

CREATIVE DIRECTORS
Rich Silverstein
David Gray

CLIENT
E*Trade

AGENCY
Goodby Silverstein & Partners/San Francisco

02486A

MERIT AWARD
CONSUMER TELEVISION
:30/:25 SINGLE

ART DIRECTOR
Rick Casteel

WRITER
John Matejczyk

AGENCY PRODUCER
Tanya LeSieur

PRODUCTION COMPANY
@radical.media

DIRECTOR
Erroll Morris

CREATIVE DIRECTORS
Rich Silverstein
Steve Simpson

CLIENT
Hewlett-Packard

AGENCY
Goodby Silverstein & Partners/San Francisco

02487A

MERIT AWARD
CONSUMER TELEVISION
:30/:25 SINGLE

ART DIRECTOR
Ralf Nolting

WRITER
Ralf Heuel

AGENCY PRODUCER
Natascha Teidler

PRODUCTION COMPANY
2am Films Ltd.

DIRECTOR
Paul Goldman

CREATIVE DIRECTORS
Ralf Heuel
Ralf Nolting

CLIENT
Volkswagen AG

AGENCY
Grabarz & Partners/Hamburg

02488A

(Important-looking ministers get out of limousines, accompanied by orderly motorcycle escorts. They are followed by a minister who has driven himself in a Passat W8 well ahead of a very disorganized, exhausted motorcycle escort.)

SUPER: The new Passat W8. The 8-Cylinder by Volkswagen. Volkswagen logo.

MERIT AWARD
CONSUMER TELEVISION
:30/:25 SINGLE

ART DIRECTOR
Jose Molla
Joaquin Molla

WRITER
Jose Molla
Joaquin Molla

AGENCY PRODUCERS
Eugenia Trujillo Viera
Graciella Creazzo

PRODUCTION COMPANY
Letca Films

DIRECTOR
Jorge Colon

CREATIVE DIRECTORS
Jose Molla
Joaquin Molla
Cristian Jofré

CLIENT
MTV

AGENCY
La Comunidad/Buenos Aires

02491A

(A man in a swimming pool stealthily looks around and apparently urinates in the pool.)

SUPER: We don't judge what people like. We j show it. The ten most requested vid MTV logo. Vote at MTVLA.com.

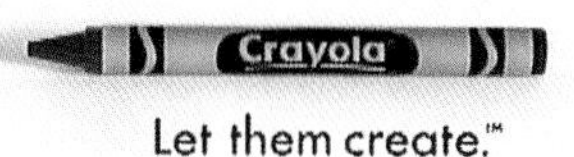

crayola.com

...r coloring an entire page brown, a young boy crumples ...is drawing and tosses it aside. He then bulldozes a huge ... of crumpled brown paper balls with his toy bulldozer. ...artist has made a mountain of fake boulders to haul.)

...ER: Crayola. Let them create. crayola.com.

(A young man in a bathroom is confronted by a sequence of i-zone photographs of two females. From the magnifying glasses that the females hold, it's obvious they're calling the guy's manhood into question.)

ANNOUNCER: The new i-zone convertible from Polaroid. The film is sticky. Not the camera.

SUPER: Polaroid. i-zone.com.

MERIT AWARD
CONSUMER TELEVISION
:30/:25 SINGLE

ART DIRECTOR
Jeannie Heilman Richardson

WRITER
John Nicolaides

AGENCY PRODUCER
Veronica Puc

PRODUCTION COMPANY
Biscuit Filmworks

DIRECTOR
Noam Murro

CREATIVE DIRECTORS
Jeannie Heilman Richardson
John Nicolaides
Jonathan Hoffman

CLIENT
Crayola

AGENCY
Leo Burnett/Chicago

02492A

MERIT AWARD
CONSUMER TELEVISION
:30/:25 SINGLE

ART DIRECTOR
Lisa Leone

WRITER
Matt Horton

AGENCY PRODUCER
Vince Geraghty

PRODUCTION COMPANY
Biscuit Filmworks

DIRECTOR
Noam Murro

CREATIVE DIRECTORS
Matt Horton
Kerry Keenan
Jonathan Hoffman

CLIENT
Polaroid iZone

AGENCY
Leo Burnett/Chicago

02494A

MERIT AWARD
CONSUMER TELEVISION
:30/:25 SINGLE

ART DIRECTOR
Anita Davis

WRITER
Jonathan Budds

AGENCY PRODUCER
Graeme Light

PRODUCTION COMPANY
Partizan

DIRECTOR
Joe Public

CREATIVE DIRECTOR
Nick Bell

CLIENT
Kellogg's

AGENCY
Leo Burnett/London

02493A

MUSIC: Born Free.

(A man interacts with a pack of tigers as though he is one of them, rolling around with them, grooming, tending to the young, stalking through the long grass, and lolling in the trees.)

ANNOUNCER: Can you do a really good impression of a tiger? Call the Kellogg's Frosties Growl for a Grand Competition. You could win a grand.

(The man growls into a mobile phone.)

MERIT AWARD
CONSUMER TELEVISION
:30/:25 SINGLE

ART DIRECTORS
Ryan Reed
Chris Gotz

WRITERS
Chris Gotz
Ryan Reed

AGENCY PRODUCERS
Iris Vinnicombe

PRODUCTION COMPANY
Egg Productions

CREATIVE DIRECTOR
Greg Burke

CLIENT
Volkswagen SA

AGENCY
Ogilvy & Mather Rightford Searle-Tripp & Makin/ Cape Town

02496A

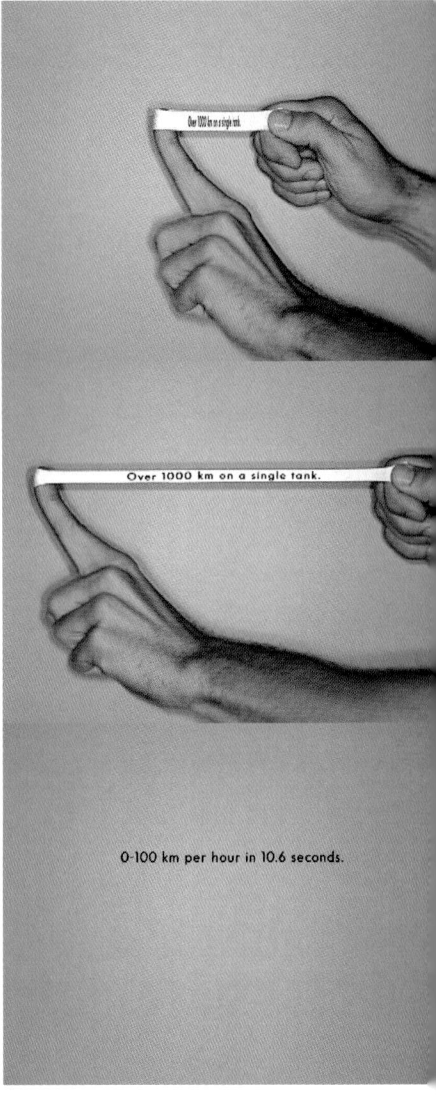

(A hand stretches out an rubber band.)

SUPER: Over 1000 km on a single tank.

(The hand lets the rubber band go and it shoots off.)

SUPER: 0-100 km per hour in 10.6 seconds. TDI Volkswagen. Isn't that what you expect from Volkswagen?

SYLVANIA
LONG LIFE

Kids can learn faster than 56k.

oung man replaces a blown light bulb with a Sylvania ; Life bulb and sits down to read. The light bulb blows ıgain. He takes out second bulb, now a very old man.)

ER: Sylvania long life bulbs.

TEACHER: Who is the President of the United States?

(Everyone except a boy with a loading strip on his forehead answers.)

CLASS: George Bush.

TEACHER: Very good! And the President of China, who is that?

(The boy is still loading.)

CLASS: Jiang Zemin.

TEACHER: Excellent! And the British Prime Minister?

(The boy is still loading.)

CLASS: Tony Blair.

TEACHER: Well done!

(Later, the boy is alone in the classroom. He raises his hand.)

BOY: George Bush!

SUPER: Kids can learn faster than 56k. Oxygen Broadband.

MERIT AWARD
CONSUMER TELEVISION
:30/:25 SINGLE

ART DIRECTOR
Joel Clement

WRITER
Jureeporn Thaidumrong

AGENCY PRODUCER
Yuthapong Varanukrohchoke

PRODUCTION COMPANY
Phenomena

DIRECTOR
Thanonchai Sornsriwichai

CREATIVE DIRECTOR
Jureeporn Thaidumrong

CLIENT
Sylvania

AGENCY
Saatchi & Saatchi/Bangkok

02503A

MERIT AWARD
CONSUMER TELEVISION
:30/:25 SINGLE

ART DIRECTORS
Francis Wee
Maurice Wee

WRITERS
Craig Davis
Renee Lim
Daniel Lim

AGENCY PRODUCER
Lara Bowden

PRODUCTION COMPANY
Film Factory

DIRECTOR
Chan Man Chung

CREATIVE DIRECTOR
Craig Davis

CLIENT
Oxygen Broadband

AGENCY
Saatchi & Saatchi/Hong Kong

02504A

MERIT AWARD
CONSUMER TELEVISION
:30/:25 SINGLE

ART DIRECTOR
Camilla Herberstein

WRITER
Gary du Toit

AGENCY PRODUCER
Helena Woodfine

PRODUCTION COMPANY
Velocity Afrika

DIRECTOR
Clive Will

CREATIVE DIRECTOR
Sue Anderson

CLIENT
Fresh

AGENCY
TBWA Hunt Lascaris/
Johannesburg

02506A

GRAN: Um...what about this one, darling? No? No, no....Ah! Isn't this pretty, darling?

GIRL: No, gran. It's fucking ugly.

GRAN: What? I'm going to wash your mouth out with soap, young lady.

SUPER: Butterscotch Soap. Logo.

GRAN: Honestly. What's got into you?

MERIT AWARD
CONSUMER TELEVISION
:30/:25 SINGLE

ART DIRECTOR
Greg Bell

WRITER
Paul Venables

AGENCY PRODUCER
Craig Allen

PRODUCTION COMPANY
hungry man

DIRECTOR
Hank Perlman

CREATIVE DIRECTORS
Greg Bell
Paul Venables

CLIENT
UltimateTV

AGENCY
Venables Bell & Partners/
San Francisco

02490A

ANNOUNCER: Ben has a serious, serious proble

WIFE: I am so upset.

(Ben's attention is split between watching a basketball ga and listening to his wife.)

SPOKESMAN: But then he got UltimateTV. A because it's always recording, he can use P-E-V-R. He Pauses th program. Empathizes. *(Ben pats h wife's knee.)* Validates.

BEN: Boy, you had a hard day.

(Satisfied, the wife leaves. Ben goes back to his game.)

SPOKESMAN: And Resumes. Ben has unleash digitally recorded television.

SUPER: UltimateTV logo.

WIFE: You are the sexiest man in the world right now.

›ofing scene from Bad News Bears.)

TERMAKER: Catfish. What a great arm. Who is that kid, anyway?

PBELL: Of course he's got a great arm, Buttermaker. He's the best athlete in the area. But you don't understand. That's Kelly Leek.

AD REYNOLDS: You guys talking about Kelly Leek?

TERMAKER: Yeah.

AD REYNOLDS: That dude is a bad mother. You talking about a loan shark. I borrowed a nickel from him last week. He said if I didn't give him a dime by Friday, he'd break my arm.

K SHOWALTER: Es un bandito.

ER: Baseball tonight. Lights. Camera. Baseball.

ANNOUNCER: Attention Newlywed Gal. Before you rush into a beer purchase, ask yourself this. What kind of man do you want?

(She pulls a six pack of Miller High Life out.)

ANNOUNCER: That's right, you want a High Life man. An investment in the high life is an investment in your future.

SUPER: Miller High Life logo.

MERIT AWARD
CONSUMER TELEVISION
:30/:25 SINGLE

ART DIRECTOR
Lance Ferguson

WRITER
Jon Goldberg

AGENCY PRODUCER
Tony Stearns

PRODUCTION COMPANY
Shelter Films

DIRECTOR
Tim Abshire

CREATIVE DIRECTORS
Ty Montague
Amy Nicholson

CLIENT
ESPN

AGENCY
Wieden + Kennedy/New York

02509A

MERIT AWARD
CONSUMER TELEVISION
:30/:25 SINGLE

ART DIRECTOR
Jeff Williams

WRITER
Jeff Kling

AGENCY PRODUCERS
Tieneke Pavesic
Jeff Selis

PRODUCTION COMPANY
@radical.media

DIRECTOR
Errol Morris

CREATIVE DIRECTORS
Dan Wieden
Rob Palmer

CLIENT
Miller High Life

AGENCY
Wieden + Kennedy/Portland

02500A

MERIT AWARD
CONSUMER TELEVISION
:30/:25 SINGLE

ART DIRECTOR
Jeff Williams

WRITER
Jeff Kling

AGENCY PRODUCERS
Jeff Selis
Tieneke Pavesic

PRODUCTION COMPANY
@radical.media

DIRECTOR
Errol Morris

CREATIVE DIRECTORS
Rob Palmer
Susan Hoffman

CLIENT
Miller High Life

AGENCY
Wieden + Kennedy/Portland

02508A

MERIT AWARD
CONSUMER TELEVISION
:30/:25 SINGLE

ART DIRECTOR
Jeff Williams

WRITER
Brant Mau

AGENCY PRODUCERS
Tieneke Pavesic
Jeff Selis

PRODUCTION COMPANY
@radical.media

DIRECTOR
Errol Morris

CREATIVE DIRECTORS
Dan Wieden
Susan Hoffman
Roger Camp
Rob Palmer

CLIENT
Miller High Life

AGENCY
Wieden + Kennedy/Portland

02501A

ANNOUNCER: This man may not bowl many strikes, but don't you think he's not still at the top of his game. His scores are not reflected in his average. His scores cannot be measured with hash marks and Xs. Even between frames he keeps his roll going. Here's to you, you old pole cat. You keep on living the High Life.

SUPER: Miller High Life logo.

ANNOUNCER: If anyone earned his Miller Tin tonight, it's the man in the red suit. But let's not jump the gun he's got to navigate a vehicle. Sorry, Pere Noel, it's cow juice for you. As for you, bring on th sugarplum fairies.

SUPER: Miller High Life logo.

GRIFFEY JR:	Take me out to the ballgame.
RODRIGUEZ:	*(In Spanish.)* Take me out with the crowd. *(Llé-va-me-a-go-zar.)*
HO PARK:	*(In Korean.)* Buy me some peanuts and crackerjacks. *(Sajuseyo Ttangkongua crackerjacks.)*
JHIRO SASAKI:	*(In Japanese.)* I don't care if I ever get back. *(Zutto kokoni iyoyo.)*
EME LLOYD:	*(With heavy Australian accent.)* 'Cause it's root root root for the home team.
GAGNE:	*(In French.)* If they don't win it's a shame. *(S'ils ne gagnent pas c'est dommage.)*
RUW JONES:	*(In Dutch.)* For it's one! *(Want't is een!)*
FRANCO:	*(In Italian.)* Two! *(Due!)*
RODRIGUEZ:	*(In Spanish.)* Three strikes you're out. *(Tres strikes, te vas!)*
MAGWIRE:	At the old ballgame.
R:	Bee-yooo-tiful. Swoosh.

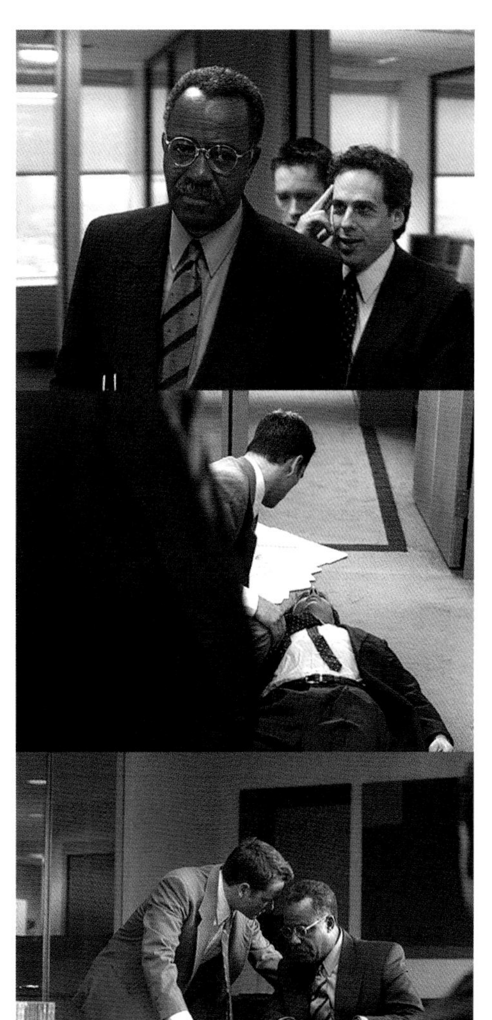

BOSS:	So, Dan, do we have everything we need for this meeting?
DAN:	It's all right here, sir. *(Points to his head, slams into a file cabinet and is knocked out cold.)*
ANNOUNCER:	Is your data back-up as reliable as it should be?
MAN 3:	Don't worry, sir, he told me everything.

(Man 3 slips, slams his head on the table, and passes out.)

ANNOUNCER:	Ours is. BrightStor storage software from Computer Associates.

MERIT AWARD
CONSUMER TELEVISION
:30/:25 SINGLE

ART DIRECTOR
Hal Curtis

WRITER
Mike Byrne

AGENCY PRODUCER
Jennifer Fiske

PRODUCTION COMPANY
@radical.media

DIRECTOR
Greg Kohs

CREATIVE DIRECTORS
Dan Wieden
Hal Curtis

CLIENT
Nike Baseball

AGENCY
Wieden + Kennedy/Portland

02502A

MERIT AWARD
CONSUMER TELEVISION
:30/:25 SINGLE

ART DIRECTOR
Ahmer Kalam

WRITER
Rachel Howald

AGENCY PRODUCER
Rich Rosenthal

PRODUCTION COMPANY
@radical.media

DIRECTOR
Lemoine Miller

CREATIVE DIRECTORS
Ann Hayden
Ahmer Kalam
Rachel Howald

CLIENT
Computer Associates

AGENCY
Young & Rubicam/New York

02498A

MERIT AWARD
CONSUMER TELEVISION
:30/:25 SINGLE

ART DIRECTORS
Ben Coulson
Ant Keogh

WRITERS
Ant Keogh
Ben Coulson

AGENCY PRODUCER
Nic Round

PRODUCTION COMPANY
Ghost

DIRECTOR
Clayton Jacobson

CREATIVE DIRECTOR
James McGrath

CLIENT
Melbourne International
Comedy Festival

AGENCY
Young & Rubicam Mattingly/
Melbourne

02510A

THERE'S A TIME AND A PLACE FOR COMEDY.
ten
MELBOURNE
INTERNATIONAL
COMEDY
FESTIVAL
MARCH 29-APRIL 22
www.comedyfestival.com.au

(A car pulls up next to a police car at an intersection. In the back seat a guy moons the cops. The cops notice him, then jump out of the car.)

SUPER: There's a time and a place for comedy. Melbourne International Comedy Festival, March 29 to April 22.

an walks down the street in a full-length fur coat.)

] & DARING MAN: Yes, my friend, you are bold but are you also daring?

man in the mink coat snaps his fingers, and 50 live s run off his body and into cages. The man is rewarded a bag of Doritos.)

]UNCER: New Doritos Extreme. Only for the bold and daring.

EMPLOYEE 1: Budget has all these cool cars.

EMPLOYEE 2: Jaguars, Rangers.

EMPLOYEE 4: Mustang Convertibles.

EMPLOYEE 1: Let's not forget the Explorer for only $39.99.

EMPLOYEE 3: Wow, how can we let everyone know about that?

EMPLOYEE 4: We'll send out a chain letter.

(A man throws out a chain letter. A light bulb on the wall goes out. Then a chandelier falls and levels him.)

EMPLOYEE 3: We don't need a chain letter.

SUPER: Rent the Ford Explorer for only $39.

MERIT AWARD
CONSUMER TELEVISION
:30/:25 CAMPAIGN

ART DIRECTORS
Gerry Graf
Harold Einstein

WRITERS
Gerry Graf
Harold Einstein

AGENCY PRODUCER
Elise Greiche

PRODUCTION COMPANY
hungry man

DIRECTOR
Marcos Siega

CREATIVE DIRECTORS
Ted Sann
Gerry Graf
Harold Einstein

CLIENT
Frito Lay/Doritos

AGENCY
BBDO/New York

02511A

MERIT AWARD
CONSUMER TELEVISION
:30/:25 CAMPAIGN

ART DIRECTORS
Jason Gaboriau
Scott Vitrone

WRITERS
Steve Doppelt
Ian Reichenthal

AGENCY PRODUCER
Kevin Diller

PRODUCTION COMPANY
Partizan

DIRECTOR
Traktor

CREATIVE DIRECTOR
Eric Silver

CLIENT
Budget

AGENCY
Cliff Freeman and Partners/
New York

02512A

MERIT AWARD
CONSUMER TELEVISION
:30/:25 CAMPAIGN

ART DIRECTORS
Guy Shelmerdine
Scott Vitrone

WRITERS
William Gelner
Ian Reichenthal
Garth Jennings

AGENCY PRODUCER
Ed Zazzera

PRODUCTION COMPANY
Partizan

DIRECTOR
Traktor

CREATIVE DIRECTOR
Eric Silver

CLIENT
Mike's Hard Lemonade

AGENCY
Cliff Freeman and Partners/
New York

02513A

MERIT AWARD
CONSUMER TELEVISION
:30/:25 CAMPAIGN

ART DIRECTOR
Lou Flores

WRITER
Cameron Day

AGENCY PRODUCER
Peter Feldman

PRODUCTION COMPANY
Plum Production

DIRECTOR
Eric Saarinen

CLIENT
Land Rover North America

AGENCY
GSD&M/Austin

02514A

FOREMAN: Hey, Ted!

(A lumberjack looks up and accidentally chops his foot off.)

FOREMAN: Tough break, buddy.

LUMBERJACK: Yeah, my wife just bought me them boots yesterday.

FOREMAN: Those are nice boots. Tell ya what. Let me buy you a tasty Mike's Hard Lemonade.

LUMBERJACK: Now you're talkin'.

ANNOUNCER: A hard day calls for a hard lemonade.

(A tracking shot seamlessly revolves from one side of the earth and through to the other as a Land Rover Discove shown in various scenes—parked at a Chinese market, unloading schoolgirls, crossing a remote river on a make raft. Multiple Discoveries are racing through a desert. A Discovery packed with emergency supplies arrives at a fl relief scene in an African village as international aid, ar an acheological dig site in Cairo. Finally, a couple in fo attire pulls up to an opera house in their Discovery Serie

ANNOUNCER: The Discovery Series II. Uniqu equipped no matter what side the planet you're on.

SUPER: Land Rover logo. The most we traveled vehicles on earth.

ung man and woman fall on the sofa, kissing tenderly. enly, the man discovers that a fork, which was lying on fa, is stuck in her back.)

R: Tidy up. IKEA. If not for yourself, at least for the others.

SEAL: Give a little bit. Give a little bit of your love to me...

ALANIS MORRISETTE: Now's the time that we need to share. So find yourself, we're...

MACY GRAY: ...on our way back home. Give a little bit...

ROBBIE ROBERTSON: ...give a little bit of my love to you. Um hmm.

SUPER: Gap logo. Give your gift.

MERIT AWARD
CONSUMER TELEVISION
:30/:25 CAMPAIGN

ART DIRECTOR
Sylvain Thirache

AGENCY PRODUCER
Marie Massis

PRODUCTION COMPANIES
Les Telecreateurs
Satellite Films

DIRECTOR
Brian Beletic

CREATIVE DIRECTOR
Pascal Gregoire

CLIENT
IKEA

AGENCY
Leagas Delaney/Paris

02515A

MERIT AWARD
CONSUMER TELEVISION
:30/:25 CAMPAIGN

ART DIRECTORS
Gary Koepke
Anthony Sperduti

WRITERS
Lance Jensen
Brian Lee Hughes

AGENCY PRODUCER
Leigh Donaldson

PRODUCTION COMPANY
HSI

DIRECTOR
Paul Hunter

CREATIVE DIRECTORS
Gary Koepke
Lance Jensen

CLIENT
The Gap

AGENCY
Modernista!/Boston

02516A

MERIT AWARD
CONSUMER TELEVISION
:30/:25 CAMPAIGN

ART DIRECTOR
Aaron Allen

WRITER
Mike McCommon

AGENCY PRODUCER
Frank Brooks

PRODUCTION COMPANY
Biscuit Filmworks

DIRECTOR
Noam Murro

CREATIVE DIRECTORS
Kevin Jones
Steve Luker

CLIENT
Sacramento Kings

AGENCY
Publicis & Hal Riney/
San Francisco

02517A

Also won:
MERIT AWARD
CONSUMER TELEVISION
:30/:25 SINGLE

(Although the man we see is clearly not Bobby Jackson, we hear Jackson's voice.)

ANNOUNCER: Bobby Jackson, your speed and quickness should really help you guys spread the court tonight. Besides hitting your outside shots, what else do you need to do tonight to be successful?

JACKSON'S VOICE: Just...doing things I normally do. Ah, scoring, rebounding, passing, playing D, getting move the ball. Ah, that's my game. I-I go out there and try to do the things and pick up the team an' give them energy. I feel like I'm gonna make every shot when I'm out there and that's how it should be. I mean, regardless what—how much time the clock, eh, eh, and what quarter it is, I feel like, I mean, and that's me, I want the ball in my hands, and I wanna make a play and I wanna make things happen.

SUPER: Sacramento Kings logo. Your team.

MERIT AWARD
CONSUMER TELEVISION
:30/:25 CAMPAIGN

ART DIRECTOR
Michael Robert

WRITER
Joachim Nielsen

AGENCY PRODUCER
Dorte Tellerup

PRODUCTION COMPANY
Bullet

DIRECTOR
Kasper Wedendahl

CREATIVE DIRECTOR
Michael Robert

CLIENT
Interflora

AGENCY
Robert/Boisen & Likeminded/
Copenhagen

02518A

(A man is holding a small and a huge drilling machine tool shop. His wife surprises him by letting him have the drilling machine.)

SUPER: The power of flowers. Interflora.

ouple is leaving a restaurant. The guy walks towards a
nd casually leans up against it.)*

: Would you like a lift home?

IAN: Yeah. Okay.

: Great, my car's just over here.

*guy turns away from the Corolla. The woman is very
pointed.)*

ER: The new Corolla. A car to be proud of.
Logo.

TV DOCTOR: For years, doctors have urged you to eat foods low in fat and high in fiber. Apparently, we got that all wrong. A new study shows that men and women should eat more stuffed jalapeños and bacon cheddar potato wedges. Tests prove that when added to your meal, whole jalapeños stuffed with three kinds of cheese and bacon cheddar potato wedges can remove wrinkles. Furthermore, I believe bacon prevents hair loss.

JACK: Where did you find this guy?

EXECUTIVE: A tobacco company.

SUPER: Make it a meal. Order a side.

MERIT AWARD
CONSUMER TELEVISION
:30/:25 CAMPAIGN

ART DIRECTORS
Jo Stafford
Brett Salmons

WRITERS
Brett Salmons
Jo Stafford
Justin Ruben

AGENCY PRODUCER
Chris Moore

PRODUCTION COMPANY
Outsider

DIRECTOR
John Madsen

CREATIVE DIRECTOR
David Droga

CLIENT
Toyota GB

AGENCY
Saatchi & Saatchi/London

02519A

MERIT AWARD
CONSUMER TELEVISION
:30/:25 CAMPAIGN

ART DIRECTOR
Dave Gassman

WRITERS
Dick Sittig
Rob Goldenberg

AGENCY PRODUCER
Fiona Forsyth

PRODUCTION COMPANY
@radical.media

DIRECTOR
Dick Sittig

CREATIVE DIRECTOR
Dick Sittig

CLIENT
Jack in the Box

AGENCY
Secret Weapon Marketing/
Santa Monica

02520A

Also won:
MERIT AWARD
CONSUMER TELEVISION
:30/:25 SINGLE

MERIT AWARD
CONSUMER TELEVISION
:30/:25 CAMPAIGN

ART DIRECTOR
Greg Bell

WRITER
Paul Venables

AGENCY PRODUCER
Craig Allen

PRODUCTION COMPANY
hungry man

DIRECTOR
Hank Perlman

CREATIVE DIRECTORS
Greg Bell
Paul Venables

CLIENT
UltimateTV

AGENCY
Venables Bell & Partners/
San Francisco

02521A

(A couple is watching TV. Phil switches channels from hockey to Monster Trucks to women's wrestling.)

SPOKESMAN: Phil hogs the remote in his house and so his wife is constantly subjected to his programming. Over time, this has had quite an effect on her.

(Wife crunches a can, buffed up like a female body builder.)

WIFE: Yes, yes, yes, yes. Go, go, go, go. Go.

SPOKESMAN: This could have been avoided with UltimateTV. Phil could've easily recorded both his shows, and shows for her, at the same time.

(Wife is now sprawled out on husband, who is too scared to move.)

SUPER: UltimateTV logo.

SPOKESMAN: Digitally recorded television could have preserved the woman he married.

MERIT AWARD
CONSUMER TELEVISION
:30/:25 CAMPAIGN

ART DIRECTOR
Ted Royer

WRITER
Jeff Bitsack

AGENCY PRODUCER
Gisellah Harvey

PRODUCTION COMPANY
hungry man

DIRECTOR
David Shane

CREATIVE DIRECTORS
Ty Montague
Amy Nicholson

CLIENT
ESPN Sportscenter

AGENCY
Wieden + Kennedy/New York

02522A

GEORGE: Like a lot of organizations, ESPN was having trouble with their carpet.

(Mascot takes a fall. Kenny tweaks a hamstring.)

DAN: Ow...ohh.

GEORGE: *(In a shirt that reads, "Marquis De Sod.")* So, they had me install more natural surface. This gr we installed is the best, it's a good Bermuda.

BRIAN BILLICK: *(Advising Trey about his grass stains.)* No hot water, okay? That'll s the stain.

GEORGE: Lays down very pretty.

(A groundskeeper cranks up a leaf blower. Dan and Stu attempt to do a show.)

GEORGE: Wherever you are, there's noth more beautiful than grass.

SUPER: This is SportsCenter.

.: There it is!

: Cracking of timber.

"H" of the "Hollywood" sign falls on her.)

ER: HBA logo. Health Insurance.

(A kid on a playground looks up into the sky, waiting for something to drop. After a while, a football falls from the sky. He kicks it, and the ball flies straight back into the sky at a very high speed.)

SUPER: Want to be stronger? Drink Bright School Milk.

MERIT AWARD
CONSUMER TELEVISION
:20 AND UNDER: SINGLE

ART DIRECTOR
Tony Rogers

WRITER
Emma Hill

AGENCY PRODUCER
Zaylee Saydam

DIRECTORS
Emma Hill
Tony Rogers

CREATIVE DIRECTOR
Antony Shannon

CLIENT
HBA Australia Health Insurance

AGENCY
Clemenger BBDO/Melbourne

02524A

MERIT AWARD
CONSUMER TELEVISION
:20 AND UNDER: SINGLE

ART DIRECTOR
Larry Ong

WRITER
Gladys Meng

AGENCY PRODUCER
Yuan Ye

PRODUCTION COMPANY
E&F Culture and Communication Co.

DIRECTOR
Yu Qing Lu

CREATIVE DIRECTOR
Larry Ong

CLIENT
Bright Dairy

AGENCY
D'Arcy/Shanghai

02525A

MERIT AWARD
CONSUMER TELEVISION
:20 AND UNDER: SINGLE

ART DIRECTORS
Sally Chu
Anna Lam

WRITERS
Milker Ho
Pauline Tsang

AGENCY PRODUCER
Anita Chan

PRODUCTION COMPANY
Cinetech

CREATIVE DIRECTORS
Eddie Booth
Milker Ho

CLIENT
IKEA

AGENCY
Leo Burnett/Hong Kong

02495A

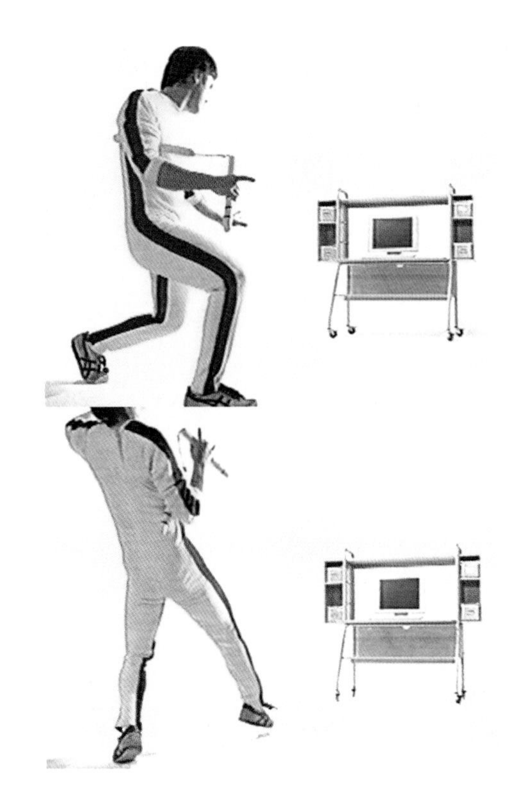

VOICEOVER: Watch out. They Move FAST! The IKEA Annual Sale.

SUPER: Annual sale.

MERIT AWARD
CONSUMER TELEVISION
:20 AND UNDER: SINGLE

ART DIRECTORS
Jeff Labbe
Eric King

WRITERS
Jeff Labbe
Eric King
Scott Wild

AGENCY PRODUCER
Betsy Beale

PRODUCTION COMPANY
Harvest Productions

DIRECTOR
Baker Smith

CREATIVE DIRECTOR
Chuck McBride

CLIENT
Fox Sports

AGENCY
TBWA/Chiat/Day/
San Francisco

02528A

SALESMAN: Why don't you shut her down a we'll talk price.

(Customer goes to hit the leaf blower's stop switch, but t mechanism falls off. It shoots heavy air followed by flam The panicked customer runs around the store spewing flam

SALESMAN: Put it down! What did you do, it down!

SUPER: Beware of things made in Octo

(A distracted worker, with his eyes glued to the 1988 Kirk Gibson 9th Inning Dodgers/A's World Series home loosely attaches a spark plug to a leaf blower.)

SUPER: MLB Playoffs are coming. Fox l

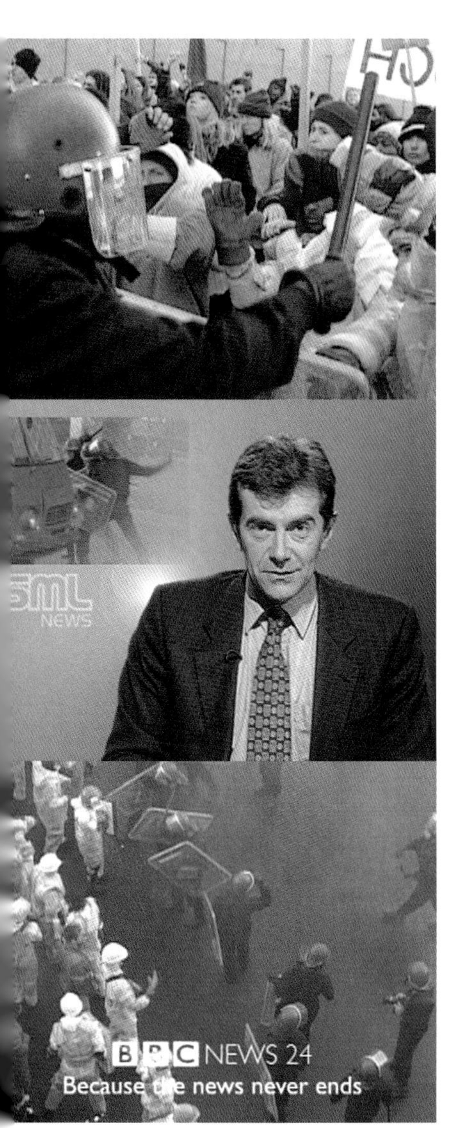

iolent demonstration is underway on the streets, the riot e trying to contain it.)

/SREADER: That's the end of the news.

:k at the demonstration, everybody stops fighting imme- ·ly.)

ER: BBC News 24. Because the news never ends.

GERMAN SOLDIER: And she has the prettiest blue eyes.

VOICEOVER: In the movies, German soldiers should never ever mention their sweethearts back home.

(German soldier gets shot.)

ANNOUNCER: Take fresh look at film with the Guardian's Friday review.

SUPER: Guardian logo.

MERIT AWARD
CONSUMER TELEVISION
:20 AND UNDER: CAMPAIGN

ART DIRECTOR
Dave Dye

WRITER
Sean Doyle

AGENCY PRODUCER
Edel Erickson

PRODUCTION COMPANY
Harry Nash

DIRECTOR
Ringan Ledwidge

CLIENT
BBC News 24

AGENCY
Abbott Mead Vickers.BBDO/London

02531A

Also won:
MERIT AWARD
CONSUMER TELEVISION
:20 AND UNDER: SINGLE

MERIT AWARD
CONSUMER TELEVISION
:20 AND UNDER: CAMPAIGN

ART DIRECTOR
Dean Webb

WRITER
Dean Webb

AGENCY PRODUCER
Richard Chambers

PRODUCTION COMPANY
The Mill

CREATIVE DIRECTOR
Andrew Fraser

CLIENT
Guardian Film 4

AGENCY
BMP DDB/London

02529A

MERIT AWARD
CONSUMER TELEVISION
:20 AND UNDER: CAMPAIGN

ART DIRECTOR
Damien Eley

WRITER
Scott Harris

AGENCY PRODUCER
Mandy Payne

PRODUCTION COMPANY
Pod Film

DIRECTOR
David Jagoda

CREATIVE DIRECTOR
Warren Brown

CLIENT
IKEA

AGENCY
Brown Melhuish Fishlock/
Sydney

02530A

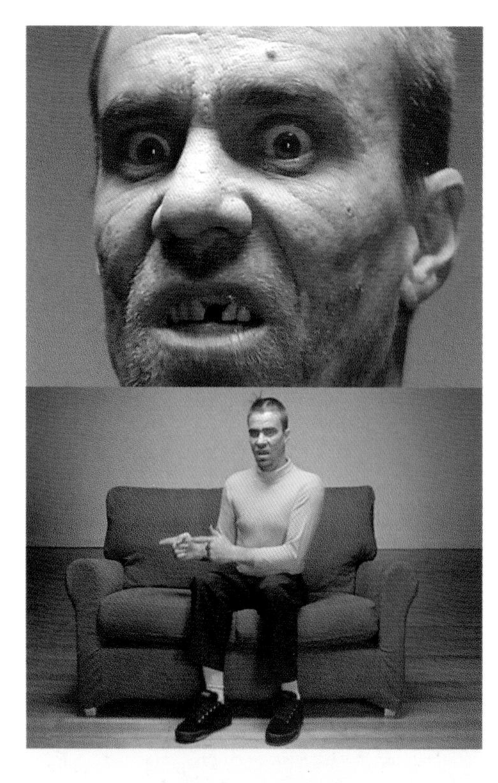

GUY: With the money I make doing kids' parties, I bought this nice couch.

SUPER: The IKEA catalogue clearance.

MERIT AWARD
CONSUMER TELEVISION
:20 AND UNDER: CAMPAIGN

ART DIRECTORS
Chris Garbutt
Paul Anderson
Paul Warner

WRITERS
Sue Anderson
Nicholas Hulley

AGENCY PRODUCER
Juanita Strydom

PRODUCTION COMPANY
Accelerator Films

DIRECTOR
David Gillard

CREATIVE DIRECTOR
Sue Anderson

CLIENT
Nashua

AGENCY
TBWA Hunt Lascaris/
Johannesburg

02532A

(A linesman's face is full of concentration. Slowly he tilt head and crouches even more. He is trying to peer up a te player's skirt.)

SUPER: Anna Kournikova's in South Africa Nashua Mobile. Associate sponsor.

RED STRIPE GUY: Red Stripe. The beer in the short and stubby bottle. And there's nothing wrong with being short and stubby.

SHORT & STUBBY GUY: I'll drink to that.

RED STRIPE GUY: Red Stripe! It's beer. Hooray Beer.

SHORT & STUBBY GUY: Yes, Hooray Beer.

SUPER: Hooray Beer.

MERIT AWARD
CONSUMER TELEVISION
VARYING LENGTHS CAMPAIGN

ART DIRECTORS
Gerry Graf
Harold Einstein

WRITERS
Gerry Graf
Harold Einstein

AGENCY PRODUCER
Elise Greiche

PRODUCTION COMPANY
hungry man

DIRECTOR
Marcos Siega

CREATIVE DIRECTORS
Ted Sann
Gerry Graf
Harold Einstein

CLIENT
Guinness/Red Stripe

AGENCY
BBDO/New York

02533A

MERIT AWARD
CONSUMER TELEVISION
VARYING LENGTHS CAMPAIGN

ART DIRECTORS
Stephen Pearson
Tom Miller

WRITERS
Stephen Pearson
Tom Miller

AGENCY PRODUCER
Angela Jones

PRODUCTION COMPANY
hungry man

DIRECTOR
Marcos Siega

CREATIVE DIRECTORS
Stephen Pearson
Tom Miller

CLIENT
Rainbow Media/Independent Film Channel

AGENCY
Pearson Miller/New York

02534A

Also won:
MERIT AWARD
CONSUMER TELEVISION
OVER :30 SINGLE

SUPER: Mike Jablonski, Independent Film Stuntman.

MIKE: Finding work as an independent stuntman can be difficult. You have to be proactive. Make your own opportunities. So when this buddy of mine told me Billy Bob was on the lot, I decided to pitch my own indie stunt movie to him.

(Mike looks through glass roof to see the meeting room and the tops of their heads.)

MAN: We're playing twins?

BILLY BOB: Yeah.

MAN: Identical twins?

BILLY BOB: Yeah.

MAN: *(Laughs)* Come on. Yeah right....Oh.

(Mike jumps through the glass roof and lands on the meeting room table.)

MIKE: Billy Bob freakin' Thorton. *(Sling Blade imitation.)* I love your work, uhm-hmm.

BILLY BOB: Exactly who are you?

MIKE: I am a stuntman slash screenwriter, uhm-hmm. I reckon you ought to read my script, uhm-hmm.

(He hands Billy Bob a script: "Punch Drunk, by Mike Jablonski.")

BILLY BOB: Why did you come through my ceili

MIKE: I, I don't reckon I know, uhm-hm

BILLY BOB: Don't, don't do that.

MIKE: Don't like that?

BILLY BOB: It's not fun for me.

MIKE: It's not fun, uhm-hmm.

BILLY BOB: I don't want you doing that voice. I don't want you doing the voice. Would you like me to call security

MIKE: Okay, see you later. *(He leaps throug glass window.)* We'll do lunch.

BILLY BOB: I read it. It sucks! *(Throws script out o window.)*

SUPER: The Independent Film Channel IF

MIKE: Once the restraining order lapses, gonna pitch him a revision. I thin tore my sac.

air of feet running in reflective shoes appears on lower side of screen).

ER: Just. Swoosh logo on screen.

(A runner follows a snowplow to be on a cleared path. Other runners join in. Marion Jones leads the pack. When the snowplow gets stuck, the runners stop and walk away.)

SUPER: Enjoy the weather. Swoosh. nike.com/enjoytheweather.

MERIT AWARD
CONSUMER TELEVISION
VARYING LENGTHS CAMPAIGN

ART DIRECTOR
Jayanta Jenkins

WRITER
Simon Mainwaring

AGENCY PRODUCER
Monika Prince

PRODUCTION COMPANY
Epoch Films

DIRECTOR
Jeff Preiss

CREATIVE DIRECTOR
Carlos Bayala

CLIENT
Nike

AGENCY
Wieden + Kennedy/Portland

02536A

MERIT AWARD
CONSUMER TELEVISION
VARYING LENGTHS CAMPAIGN

ART DIRECTORS
Bill Karow
Jayanta Jenkins

WRITERS
Mark Fitzloff
Simon Mainwaring

AGENCY PRODUCERS
Andrew Loevenguth
Jennifer Smieja

PRODUCTION COMPANIES
Harry Nash
Propaganda Films
Gorgeous Enterprises

DIRECTORS
Ringan Ledwidge
Dante Ariola
Chris Palmer

CREATIVE DIRECTORS
Dan Wieden
Hal Curtis
Jim Riswold

CLIENT
Nike

AGENCY
Wieden + Kennedy/Portland

02537A

MERIT AWARD
CONSUMER TELEVISION
UNDER $50,000 BUDGET:
SINGLE

ART DIRECTOR
Aaron Allen

WRITER
Mike McCommon

AGENCY PRODUCER
Frank Brooks

PRODUCTION COMPANY
Biscuit Filmworks

DIRECTOR
Noam Murro

CREATIVE DIRECTORS
Steve Luker
Kevin Jones

CLIENT
Sacramento Kings

AGENCY
Publicis & Hal Riney/
San Francisco

02539A

(Although we see a young girl being interviewed, we hear Vlade Divac's voice.)

ANNOUNCER: Vlade, you got a tough battle ahead of you tonight against one of the toughest teams in the league. You're a big man on this team. What are you guys going to do differently to control tonight's game? What's your strategy gonna be?

VLADE: Well, we have to just move the ball, ah, around. And, ah, get involved with everybody. We, ah, we have to be really focused on the game and don't think about what they're gonna do. If we play our game, like I said, you know, we-we-we, I think we be alright.

VOICEOVER: Vlade, I've asked you this before, but how hard is...

SUPER: Sacramento Kings logo. Your team.

MERIT AWARD
CONSUMER TELEVISION
UNDER $50,000 BUDGET:
SINGLE

ART DIRECTOR
Brett Wild

WRITER
Steve Straw

AGENCY PRODUCER
Barbara Clark

PRODUCTION COMPANY
The Box Office

DIRECTOR
Steve Straw

CREATIVE DIRECTOR
Brett Wild

CLIENT
Eukanuba

AGENCY
Saatchi & Saatchi/
Johannesburg

02540A

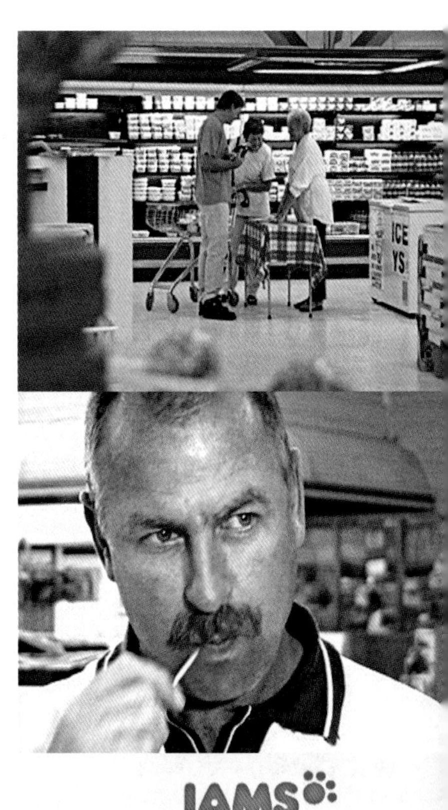

ANOUNCER: Try one.

MAN 1: Mm, this is good.

WOMAN 1: Tasty, there must be a lot of goo ness in there somewhere.

WOMAN 2: It's yum yum, I like it.

MAN 2: This is tasty, what is in it?

MAN 3: Mm, mm, very good, what is it

ANNOUNCER: IAMS not only provides the mo nutritious dog food, but the ta est, too.

SUPER: IAMS. Good for life. And not tested on animals.

-n to chef tasting the soup before serving.)*

-: Magnificent!

-IG ZI YI: The soup is too salty.

-ght scene ensues in martial arts style.)

-R: Dining out?

-ER: No charge for the soup, but this is for the "extras."

-ng fires something at the waiter, which to his relief turns -) be her Visa Gold card.)

MERIT AWARD NON BROADCAST CINEMA

ART DIRECTOR
David Guerrero

WRITER
David Guerrero

AGENCY PRODUCER
Bruce Davidson

PRODUCTION COMPANY
@radical.media

DIRECTOR
Bruce Hunt

CREATIVE DIRECTOR
David Guerrero

CLIENT
Visa International

AGENCY
BBDO/Guerrero Ortega/
Makati City

02541A

(An Arabic woman covered from head to toe in full-length garb crosses her legs like Sharon Stone in Basic Instinct.)

SUPER: Same planet. Different worlds. Vancouver International Film Festival logo. September 27–October 7, 2001.

COP 1: What was the nature of your relationship with Mr. Habiz?

COP 2: Did you kill him?

MERIT AWARD NON BROADCAST CINEMA

ART DIRECTOR
Lisa Francilia

WRITER
Dan Scherk

AGENCY PRODUCER
Valerie McTavish

PRODUCTION COMPANY
Rave Films

DIRECTOR
Trevor Cornish

CREATIVE DIRECTORS
Lisa Francilia
Dan Scherk

CLIENT
Vancouver International Film Festival

AGENCY
Bryant Fulton & Shee/
Vancouver

02542A

MERIT AWARD
NON BROADCAST
CINEMA

ART DIRECTOR
David Hillyard

WRITER
Ed Robinson

AGENCY PRODUCER
Manuela Franzini

PRODUCTION COMPANY
Stark Films

DIRECTOR
Jeff Stark

CREATIVE DIRECTOR
David Droga

CLIENT
Club 18-30

AGENCY
Saatchi & Saatchi/London

02543A

(A floating body, washed in by the tide, bangs into a couple kissing on the surf. She lets out a piercing scream.)

"DEAD" BODY: What a cracking night out! Morning!

SUPER: Club 18-30 logo.

MERIT AWARD
FOREIGN LANGUAGE

ART DIRECTOR
Sammy Law

WRITER
Valeria Au Yang

AGENCY PRODUCER
Ida Man

PRODUCTION COMPANY
Film Factory

DIRECTOR
Chan Man Chung

CREATIVE DIRECTORS
Gary Tranter
Matt Cullen

CLIENT
Sing Pao Daily News

AGENCY
Ogilvy & Mather/Hong Kong

02544A

(A man places his newspaper on the ground next to his c A woman, passing by, sees the paper on the ground, knc the dog out of the way, and picks it up for her own use.)

MERIT AWARD
INTEGRATED BRANDING

ART DIRECTORS
Matt Stein
Linda Knight

WRITERS
Kevin Proudfoot
Susan Newbauer-Hampton

DESIGNERS
Josh Whitlock
Alex Kerr

ILLUSTRATOR
James Jajac

PHOTOGRAPHER
Jake Chessum

CREATIVE DIRECTORS
Ty Montague
Amy Nicholson

AGENCY PRODUCER
Chris Noble

PRODUCTION COMPANY
Production League of America

DIRECTOR
Evan Bernard

CLIENT
ESPN-Summer X Games

AGENCY
Wieden + Kennedy/New York

02546A

NYQUIST: Let me show you guys something—but it's very important it doesn't leave the three of us, okay? Two counts of red—one one-thousand, two one-thousand, three—remember that, timing is everything. A quick dash of orange. The perfect icee. Woooo—slow down, you'll get a brain freeze—rookies.

(Nyquist takes the cup back, shaking his head, and drinks, giving himself an icee moustache.)

SUPER: No shirt no shoes no X Games. X Games. Watch August 18 – 23. ESPN. ESPN2. ABC.

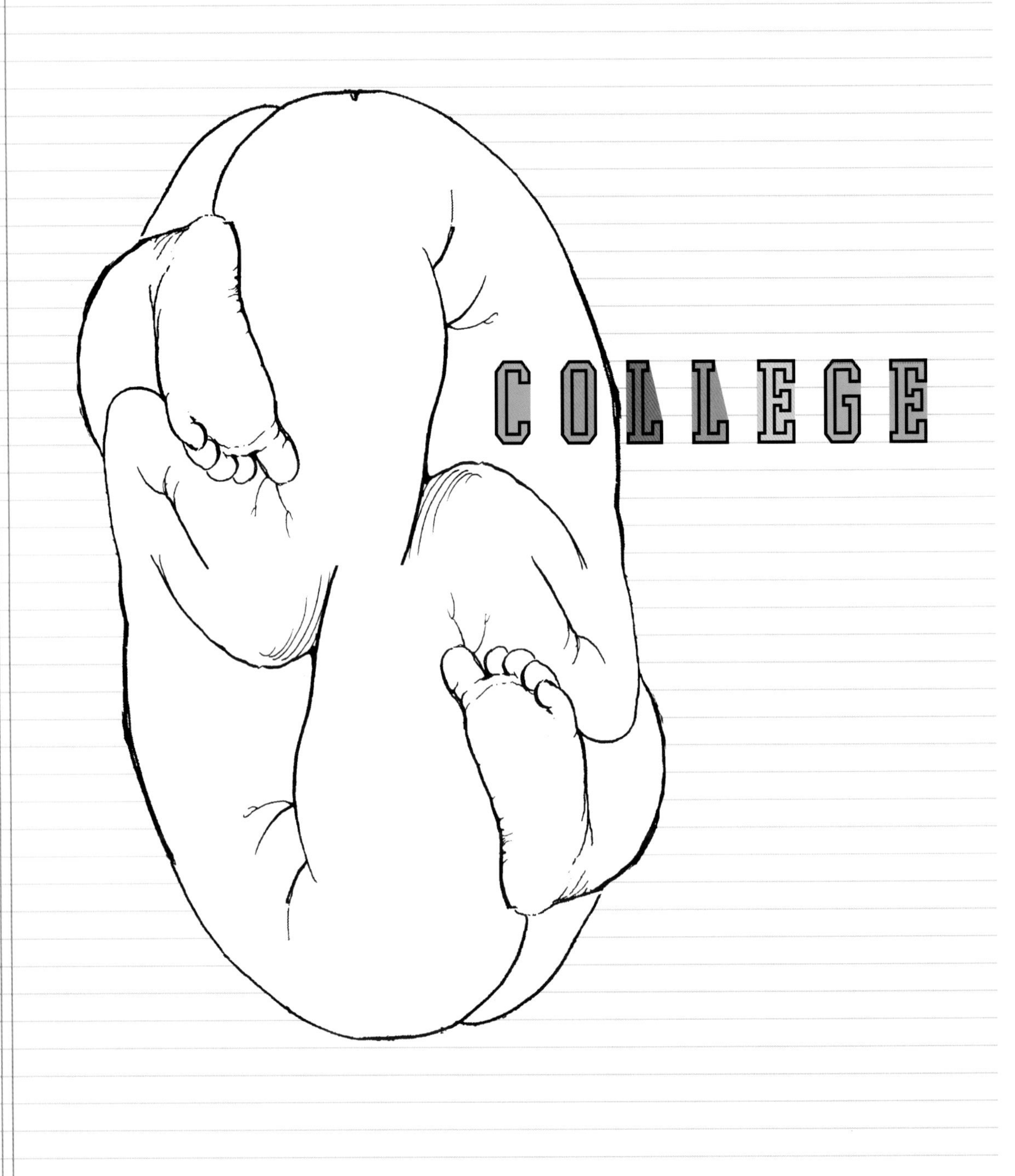
COLLEGE

innocence = unfallen = dupe = ignorance = immature = *bebé*

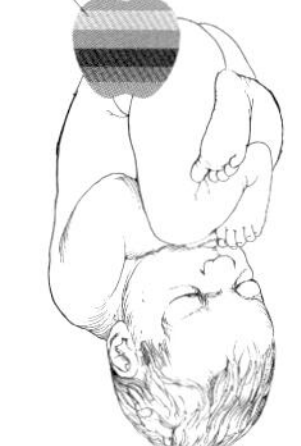

MERIT AWARD
COLLEGE: ADVERTISING

ART DIRECTOR
John Tso

WRITER
John Bollow

DESIGNER
John Tso

SCHOOL
Book Shop/Culver City

CC018

ASSIGNMENT:
Promote the United States as a nation with strong values and genuine concern for the welfare of the rest of the world.

MERIT AWARD
COLLEGE: ADVERTISING

ART DIRECTOR
Lisa Kaplowitz

WRITER
Patrick Miller

SCHOOL
Book Shop/Culver City

CC001

12:00 noon. Meditation room at IBM. Flint, Michigan.
America:
OPEN

Ethiopian Christians celebrating New Year's. Cambridge, Massachusetts.
America:
OPEN

MERIT AWARD
COLLEGE: ADVERTISING

ART DIRECTOR
Dave McClain

WRITER
Robin Jones

SCHOOL
Book Shop/Culver City

CC005

AMERICA · CUSTOMIZE ACCORDINGLY

AMERICA · CUSTOMIZE ACCORDINGLY

MERIT AWARD
COLLEGE: ADVERTISING

ART DIRECTORS
Joe Ringus
James Edin

WRITER
Matthew Bottkol

SCHOOL
Brainco/Minneapolis

CC047

MERIT AWARD
COLLEGE: ADVERTISING

ART DIRECTOR
Derek Till

WRITER
Brandon English

SCHOOL
Brainco/Minneapolis

CC063

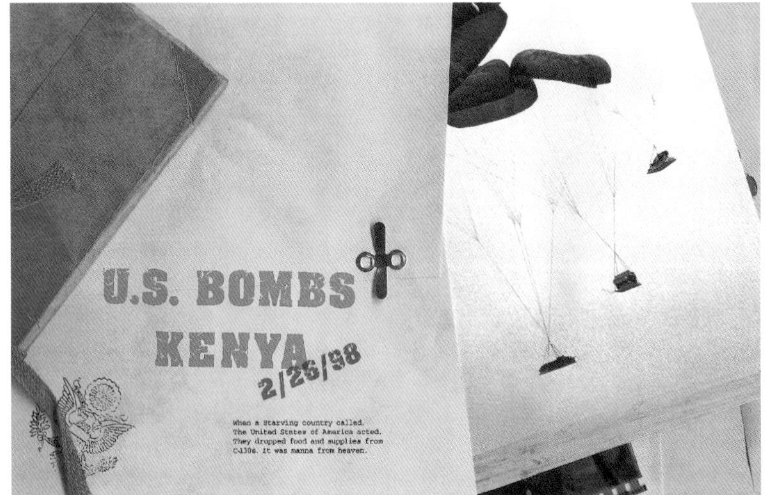

MERIT AWARD
COLLEGE: ADVERTISING

ART DIRECTOR
Stephanie Simpson

WRITER
Larry Johnson

PHOTOGRAPHER
Roy Beeson

SCHOOL
Creative Circus/Atlanta

CC045

COLLEGE MERIT

MERIT AWARD
COLLEGE: ADVERTISING

Actor/Comedian
WILL
FERRELL
Makes fun of the President of the United States of America every Saturday night on national television. Still alive.

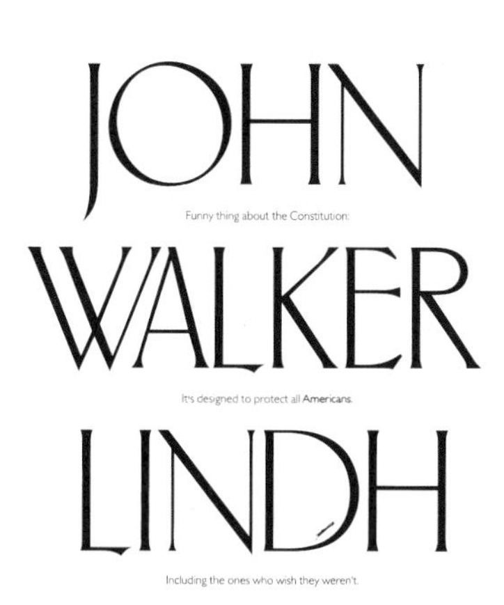

JOHN
Funny thing about the Constitution:
WALKER
It's designed to protect all Americans.
LINDH
Including the ones who wish they weren't.

Taliban Jihadi. American Citizen.
AMERICA
Justice for all.

ART DIRECTORS
Kristi Pagoulatos
Jessica Foster

WRITER
Jean Weisman

SCHOOL
Creative Circus/Atlanta

CC011

MERIT AWARD
COLLEGE: ADVERTISING

ART DIRECTORS
David Cuccinello
Jessica Boylston
Nina Orezzoli

WRITERS
Billy Leyhe
Nate Kneezel
Marc Pellmann

SCHOOL
Miami Ad School/
Miami Beach

CC010

COLLEGE MERIT

MERIT AWARD
COLLEGE: ADVERTISING

ART DIRECTOR
Troy Benson

WRITER
Lyle Shemer

SCHOOL
Miami Ad School/
Miami Beach

CC053

America's involvement in ________
is simply another example
of how a country that ________
is able to ________

____
____
____
________ Feel Free.

Without the basic right to freedom of expression, there can be no democracy. The United States of America is a country that protects and encourages free speech. Regardless of its content.

American culture is ________.
Its emphasis on ________
makes it a perfect example
of what happens when ________

____
____
____
________ Feel Free.

Without the basic right to freedom of expression, there can be no democracy. The United States of America is a country that protects and encourages free speech. Regardless of its content.

MERIT AWARD
COLLEGE: ADVERTISING

ART DIRECTOR
Gabe Seghi

WRITER
Leon Dekelbaum

SCHOOL
Miami Ad School/
Miami Beach

CC056

COLLEGE MERIT

you create **us**

you create **us**

MERIT AWARD
COLLEGE: ADVERTISING

ART DIRECTORS
David Cuccinello
Jessica Boylston
Nina Orezzoli

WRITERS
Billy Leyhe
Nate Kneezel
Marc Pellmann

SCHOOL
Miami Ad School/
Miami Beach

CC041

MERIT AWARD
COLLEGE: ADVERTISING

ART DIRECTOR
Matt Roberts

WRITER
Jim Korakis

SCHOOL
Miami Ad School/
San Francisco

CC020

MERIT AWARD
COLLEGE: ADVERTISING

ART DIRECTORS
Daniel Giachetti
John Clement

WRITERS
John Clement
Daniel Giachetti

SCHOOL
School of Visual Arts/
New York

CC052

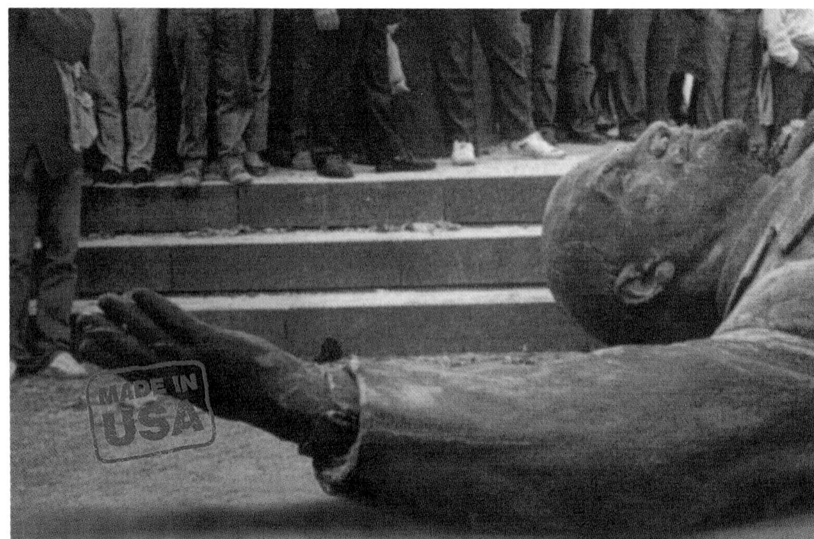

MERIT AWARD
COLLEGE: ADVERTISING

ART DIRECTOR
Amber Lashmett

WRITERS
Kate Ackerman
Jack Fahden
Amber Lashmett

SCHOOL
University of Colorado/
Boulder

CC006

MERIT AWARD
COLLEGE: ADVERTISING

ART DIRECTOR
Brandon Sides

WRITER
Reuben Hower

SCHOOL
University of Colorado/
Boulder

CC054

MERIT AWARD
COLLEGE: ADVERTISING

ART DIRECTOR
Adam Rand

WRITERS
Jeremy Seibold
Patrick Sullivan

SCHOOL
University of Colorado/
Boulder

CC003

MERIT AWARD
COLLEGE: ADVERTISING

ART DIRECTOR
Howard Grandison

WRITER
Howard Grandison

SCHOOL
University of Delaware/Newark

CC029

MERIT AWARD
COLLEGE: ADVERTISING

ART DIRECTOR
Josh Rosen

WRITER
Mark Svartz

SCHOOL
VCU Adcenter/Richmond

CC032

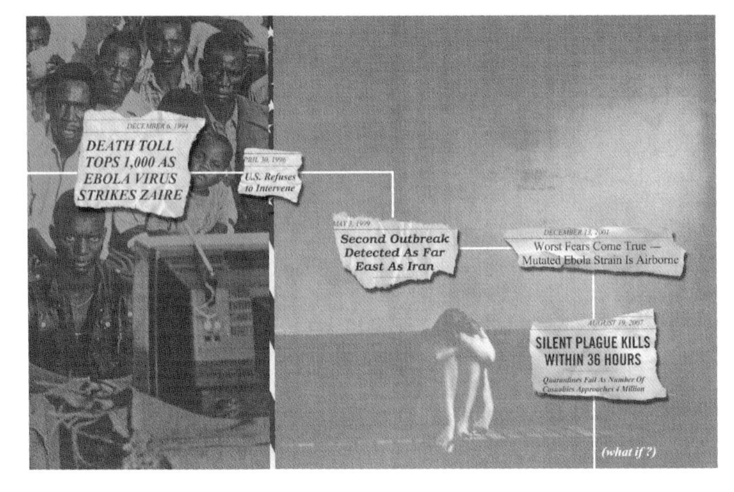

AMERICA INTERFERES WITH THE AFFAIRS OF OTHER COUNTRIES.

But in whose eyes? Somali children dying of starvation? Kuwaiti women being raped? Thousands of Bosnians facing genocide? At what point does interference become intervention?

AMERICA IS A SELF-SERVING BULLY.

Did the Roman Empire feed its starving neighbors? Did the Vikings bring medical aid along on their voyages? Did Napoleon bolster foreign economies? As the last superpower on earth, is America compelled to be benevolent? Or does it just choose to be?

COLLEGE MERIT

MERIT AWARD
COLLEGE: ADVERTISING

ART DIRECTOR
Nate Anderson

WRITER
Sean Vij

SCHOOL
VCU Adcenter/Richmond

CC023

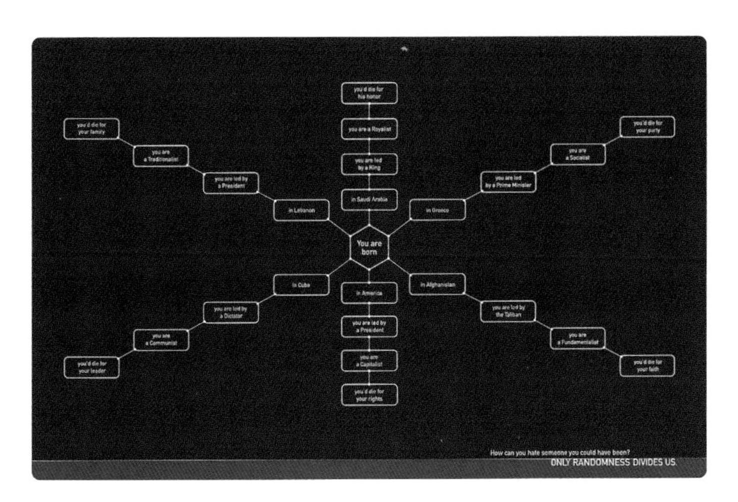

How can you hate someone you could have been?
ONLY RANDOMNESS DIVIDES US.

MERIT AWARD
COLLEGE: ADVERTISING

ART DIRECTOR
Mira Kaddoura

WRITERS
David Fredette
Beth Ryan
Mira Kaddoura

SCHOOL
VCU Adcenter/Richmond

CC025

MERIT AWARD
COLLEGE: ADVERTISING

ART DIRECTOR
Matt O'Malley

WRITER
Jon Graham

SCHOOL
VCU Adcenter/Richmond

CC002

MERIT AWARD
COLLEGE: ADVERTISING

ART DIRECTOR
Derrick J. Webb

WRITER
Julie Dulude

SCHOOL
VCU Adcenter/Richmond

CC049

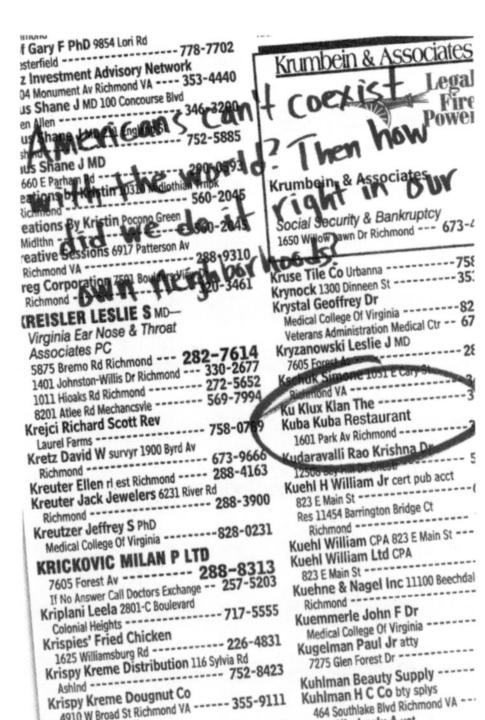

COLLEGE MERIT

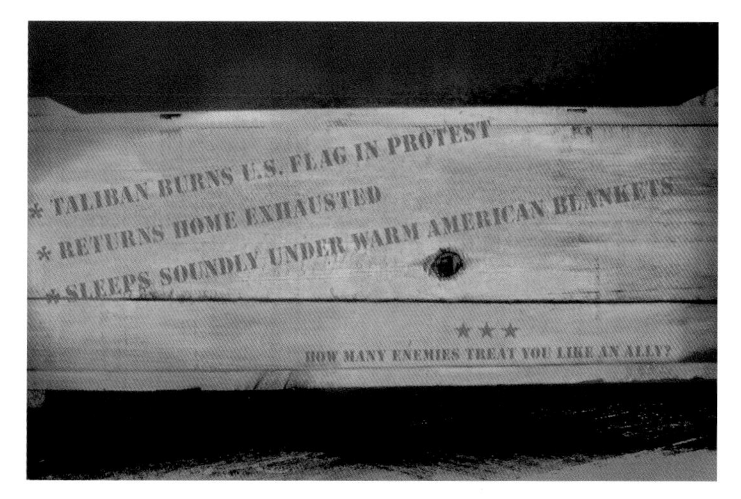

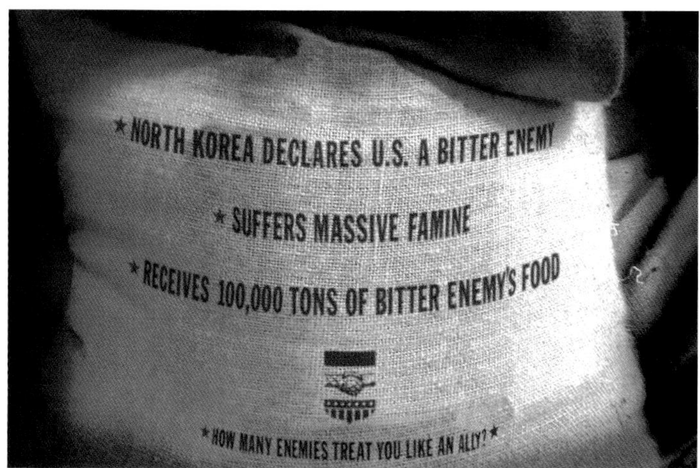

MERIT AWARD
COLLEGE: ADVERTISING

ART DIRECTOR
Barry Brothers

WRITER
Jeff Shill

SCHOOL
VCU Adcenter/Richmond

CC031

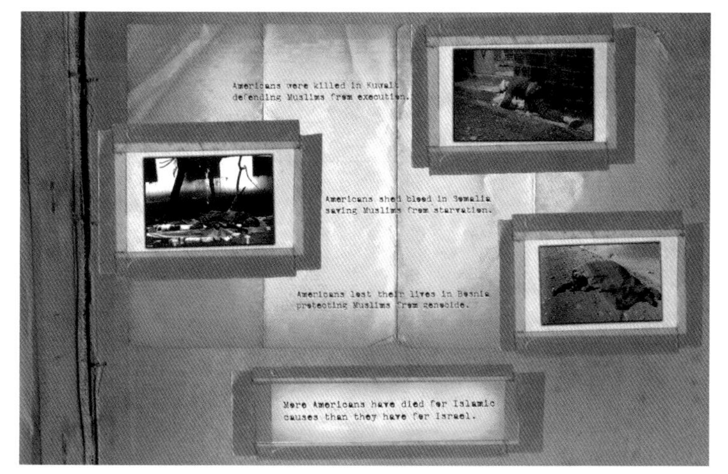

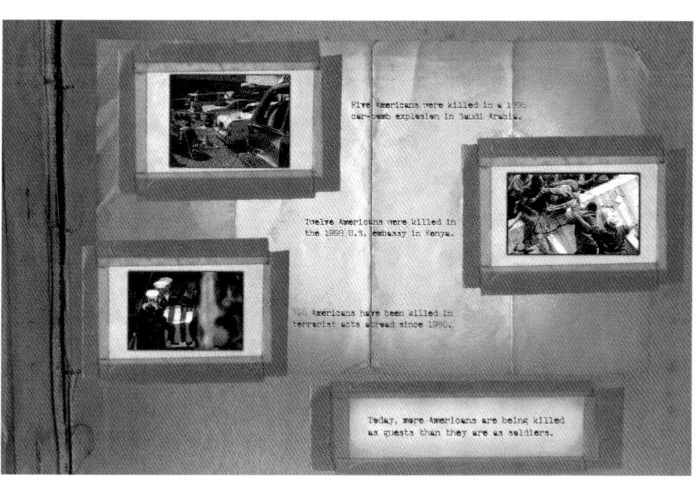

MERIT AWARD
COLLEGE: ADVERTISING

ART DIRECTOR
Matt Arnold

WRITER
Scott Johnson

SCHOOL
VCU Adcenter/Richmond

CC022

MERIT AWARD
COLLEGE: ADVERTISING

ART DIRECTOR
Whitney Jenkins

WRITER
Mark Maziarz

SCHOOL
VCU Adcenter/Richmond

CC036

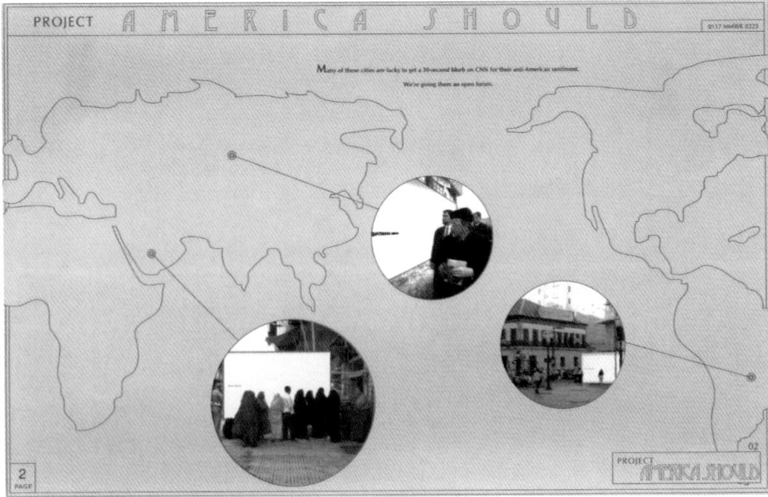

COLLEGE MERIT

IF YOU HAD ONE WISH FOR YOUR COUNTRY, WHAT WOULD IT BE?

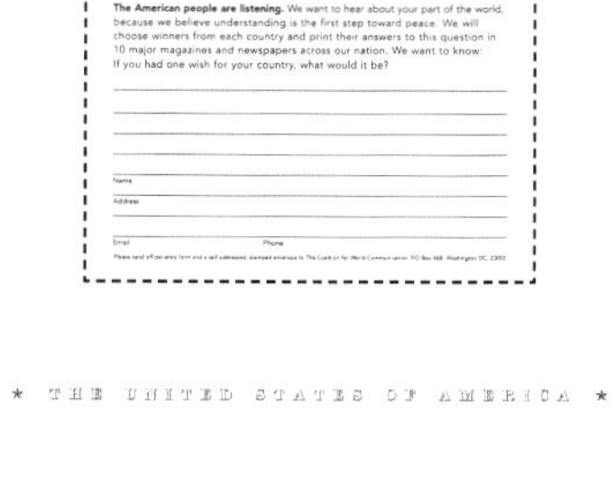

The American people are listening. We want to hear about your part of the world, because we believe understanding is the first step toward peace. We will choose winners from each country and print their answers to this question in 10 major magazines and newspapers across our nation. We want to know:
If you had one wish for your country, what would it be?
Name
Address
Email
Phone

★ THE UNITED STATES OF AMERICA ★

WHAT DO YOU LOVE MOST ABOUT YOUR COUNTRY?

The American people are listening. We want to hear about your part of the world, because we believe understanding is the first step toward peace. We will choose winners from each country and print their answers to this question in 10 major magazines and newspapers across our nation. We want to know:
What do you love most about your country?
Name
Address
Email
Phone

★ THE UNITED STATES OF AMERICA ★

MERIT AWARD
COLLEGE: ADVERTISING

ART DIRECTOR
Stuart Jennings

WRITER
Tannen Campbell

SCHOOL
VCU Adcenter/Richmond

CC030

MERIT AWARD
COLLEGE: ADVERTISING

ART DIRECTOR
Tik Kai Lau

WRITER
Michael Tuton

SCHOOL
VCU Adcenter/Richmond

CC044

MERIT AWARD
COLLEGE: ADVERTISING

ART DIRECTOR
Trevlin Utz - Boogie Woogie King of the Mountaintop

WRITER
Ravi Costa - International Pimp of the Year

SCHOOL
VCU Adcenter/Richmond

CC043

Hotmail's Creator Is Starting Up Again, and Again, and...

In 1988, Sabeer Bhatia left India for America. He's created Hotmail, sold it to Microsoft for $US400 million and is now on his next project.

By Ravi Costa

He's launched his second internet venture, writes Amanda Hall from California. Sabeer Bhatia's assistant says his company is in "stealth mode" - SiliconValley start-up speak for "it's all a big secret and we cannot tell you a thing about it".

Stealth mode. The very phrase is enough to lend even this dullest of offices in Fremont, south east of San Francisco, an excitement way beyond its low-rise, industrial greyness. Who knows what billion dollar business may be about to sprout right here?

Bhatia, meanwhile, has just flown in from Atlanta. He is tall, friendly, with an easy manner and a smiley face. He's been speaking at the Indian American Youth Conference.

"I tell them it's humans who go on to create great companies," he says.

"Everyone who is successful is human - just like you and me. You've got to pursue whatever it is you believe in, take it to completion and don't be afraid to dream big."

He disappears into his office to make some calls and his assistant begins the office tour.

She steers me past endless cubicles where Indian engineers sit quietly in front of screens tapping out long lines of gobbledegook. Past the de-bugging room where 20-year-olds in baseball caps try to bust the system, testing it to its limits. Past the kitchen stocked with drinks and snacks to fuel all this brain power 24 hours a day. And into what looks like the only meeting room in the building, a large, windowless space, empty save for a ping-pong table, some promotional boards and a large pile of mattresses. In start-up land, you never know if you'll make it home to sleep.

Hotmail's Creator Is Starting Up, continued, pg A6

This is America.

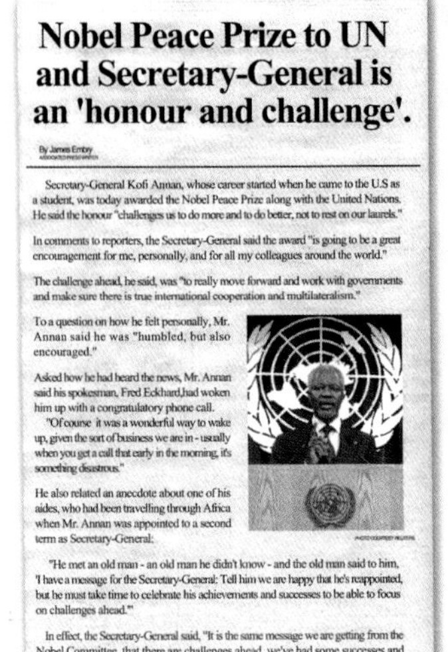

Nobel Peace Prize to UN and Secretary-General is an 'honour and challenge'.

By James Embry

Secretary-General Kofi Annan, whose career started when he came to the U.S as a student, was today awarded the Nobel Peace Prize along with the United Nations. He said the honour "challenges us to do more and to do better, not to rest on our laurels."

In comments to reporters, the Secretary-General said the award "is going to be a great encouragement for me, personally, and for all my colleagues around the world."

The challenge ahead, he said, was "to really move forward and work with governments and make sure there is true international cooperation and multilateralism."

To a question on how he felt personally, Mr. Annan said he was "humbled, but also encouraged."

Asked how he had heard the news, Mr. Annan said his spokesman, Fred Eckhard,had woken him up with a congratulatory phone call.

"Of course it was a wonderful way to wake up, given the sort of business we are in - usually when you get a call that early in the morning, it's something disastrous."

He also related an anecdote about one of his aides, who had been travelling through Africa when Mr. Annan was appointed to a second term as Secretary-General:

"He met an old man - an old man he didn't know - and the old man said to him, 'I have a message for the Secretary-General: Tell him we are happy that he's reappointed, but he must take time to celebrate his achievements and successes to be able to focus on challenges ahead.'"

In effect, the Secretary-General said, "It is the same message we are getting from the Nobel Committee, that there are challenges ahead, we've had some successes and failures, and they expect us to work hard and meet those challenges."

This is America.

MERIT AWARD
COLLEGE: ADVERTISING

ART DIRECTOR
Yosune George

WRITER
Jimbo Embry

SCHOOL
VCU Adcenter/Richmond

CC042

At first. America seemed like a big food chain. And it didn't impress me. Then, I began to notice little shops hidden in the city. Each with its own personality. That was the first part of America that felt real to me.

-Hsin-Yi Chen, China.

America Through Foreign Eyes. A Photo Essay of America by International Students.

I thought of America as a machine before I came. One Big Machine fueled by money. As I got around and outside the big cities, I saw a side of America they don't teach us about in History Books.

-Yosune Echeberrea, *Spain*.

America Through Foreign Eyes. A Photo Essay of America by International Students.

MERIT AWARD
COLLEGE: DESIGN

DESIGNERS
Derek Yoder
Milan Zori

WRITERS
Derek Yoder
Milan Zori

SCHOOL
Columbus College of Art & Design/Columbus

CCD001

MERIT AWARD
COLLEGE: DESIGN

DESIGNER
Jill Courtney Michel

SCHOOL
James Madison University/Harrisonburg

CCD009

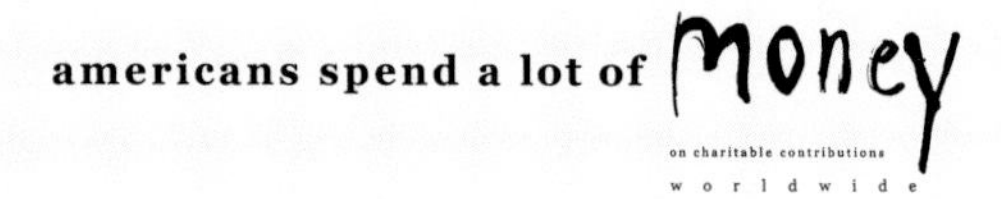

COLLEGE MERIT

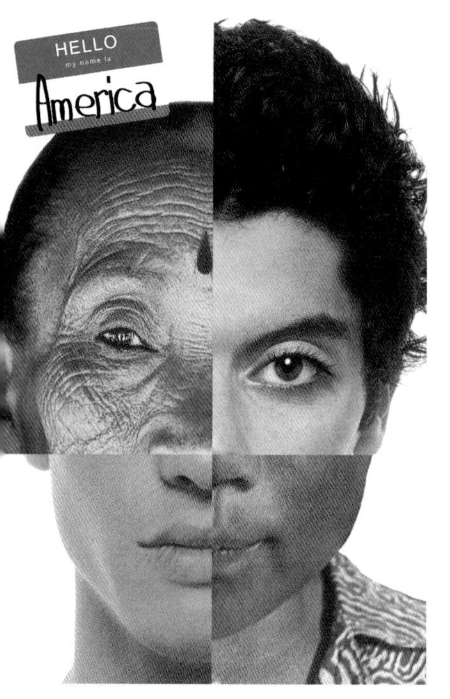

MERIT AWARD
COLLEGE: DESIGN

DESIGNER
H. Shane Grimes

WRITER
H. Shane Grimes

SCHOOL
James Madison University/
Harrisonburg

CCD021

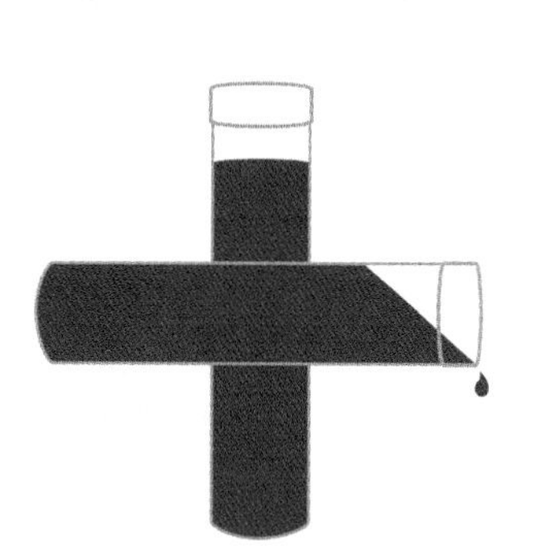

Having provided comfort and aid to those in need since 1881, the Red Cross quickly adopted Blood Services as a fundamental part of its humanitarian mission. Started as a war relief effort to provide life-saving blood for soldiers during World War II, Red Cross Blood Services has grown to become an industry leader - collecting and distributing half the nation's blood supply.
American Red Cross

For more than a century, the American Red Cross has been saving lives with health and safety education programs. Red Cross training ranges from first aid, CPR and AED to swimming and lifeguarding; from HIV/AIDS education to caregiving programs like Babysitter's Training. American Red Cross programs help people live safer and healthier lives.
American Red Cross

MERIT AWARD
COLLEGE: DESIGN

DESIGNER
Karen Kuebler

WRITERS
Karen Kuebler
American Red Cross Web Site

SCHOOL
James Madison University/
Harrisonburg

CCD004

MERIT AWARD
COLLEGE: DESIGN

DESIGNER
Mike Ryan

WRITER
Mike Ryan

SCHOOL
James Madison University/
Harrisonburg

CCD005

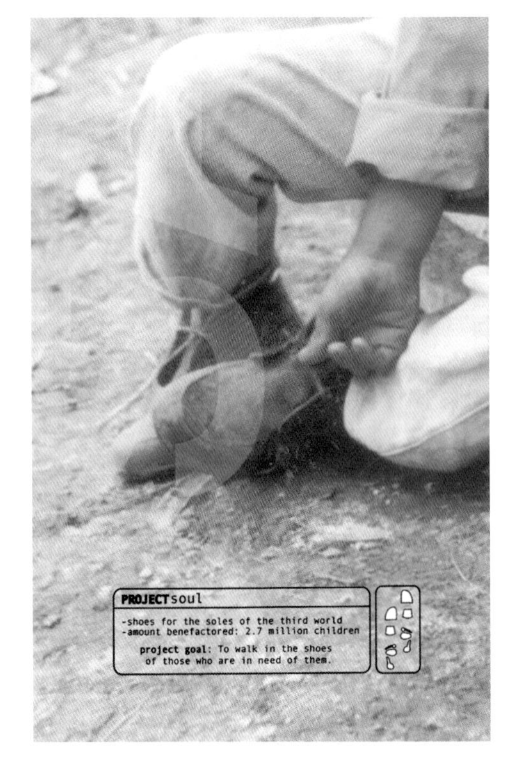

MERIT AWARD
COLLEGE: DESIGN

DESIGNER
Matt Thomas

SCHOOL
James Madison University/
Harrisonburg

CCD013

COLLEGE MERIT

MERIT AWARD
COLLEGE: DESIGN

DESIGNER
Miti Desai

SCHOOL
Portfolio Center/Atlanta

CCD020

MERIT AWARD
COLLEGE: DESIGN

DESIGNER
Kathryn Spitzberg

SCHOOL
Portfolio Center/Atlanta

CCD025

U.S. IMMIGRATION IS AT ITS HIGHEST LEVEL IN HISTORY.

8.47 billion
Made in USA
NOW SERVING 8.47 BILLION DOLLARS IN FOREIGN AID.

MERIT AWARD
COLLEGE: DESIGN

DESIGNER
Jim Lasser

SCHOOL
Portfolio Center/Atlanta

CCD017

YOUNG CREATIVE PROFESSIONALS COMPETITION

PRINT

TEAM
Tomizawa & Lee

MEMBERS
Jacqueline Lee
Al Tomizawa

TEAM SPONSOR
Creative Circus/Atlanta

ASSIGNMENT:
Create a campaign to promote a beverage targeted to the baby boom generation in one of three categories: print, television, or new media.

Dear Paul,
Last night Uncle Sam passed on due to complications from obesity. He'd be honored to have you serve as his pallbearer.
All my love
Aunt Anne
calcium fortified for life's surprises

YOUNG CREATIVE PROFESSIONALS COMPETITION

PRINT

TEAM
Oliviera/Durrett

MEMBERS
Christian Durrett
Demian Oliviera

TEAM SPONSOR
Creative Circus/Atlanta

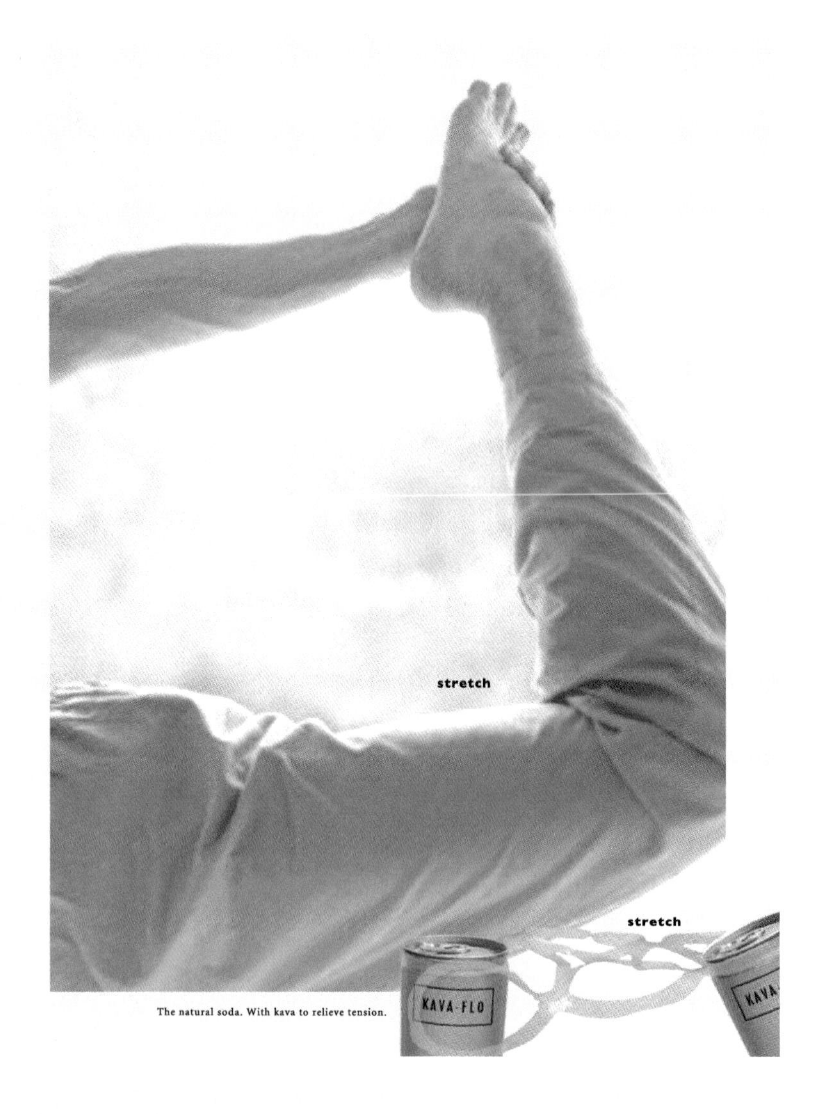

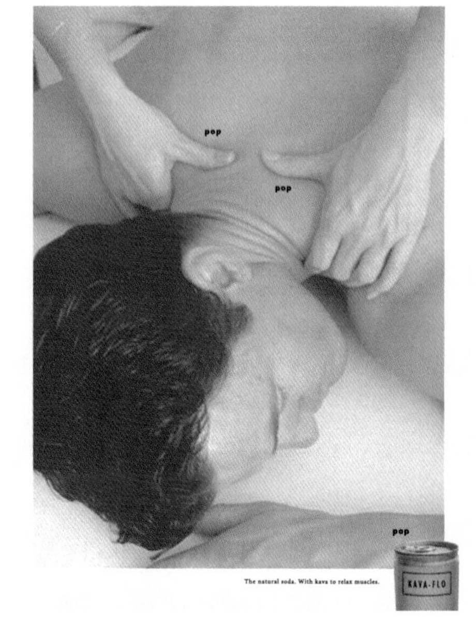

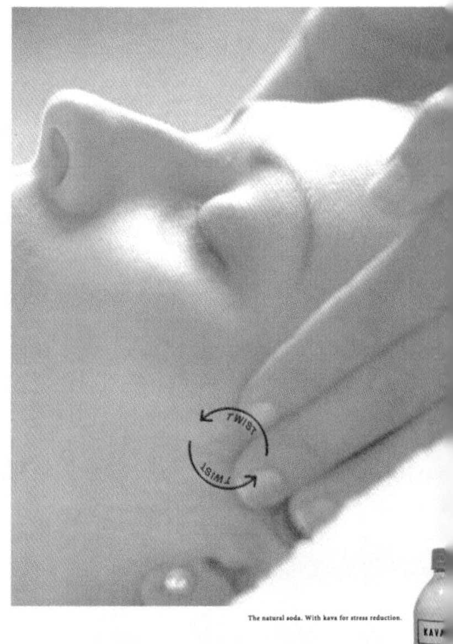

YOUNG CREATIVE PROFESSIONALS COMPETITION

TELEVISION

TEAM
Vertical Eye

MEMBERS
Miguel Fernandez
Roger Stephens
Ravi Subramanian
Roger H. Wong

TEAM SPONSOR
Vertical Eye/New York

SFX: Soft Bossa Nova throughout.

(Two businessmen are discussing a deal over lunch. Their waiter fills their glasses with Fjord Spring Water. The men taste their water and nod in approval as if it were wine. The waiter places the bottle of Fjord on the table. Suddenly, a cook bursts into the dinning room with his head on fire. He runs around the restaurant, begging for help. The businessmen and other patrons gulp down their glasses of water and hide their Fjord bottles, not wanting to waste it on the cook.)

SUPER: Precious.

YOUNG CREATIVE
PROFESSIONALS COMPETITION

NEW MEDIA

TEAM
Portfolio Center

MEMBERS
Brennan Boblett
Maria Brenny
Brad Gutting
Bryan Karr

TEAM SPONSOR
Portfolio Center/Atlanta

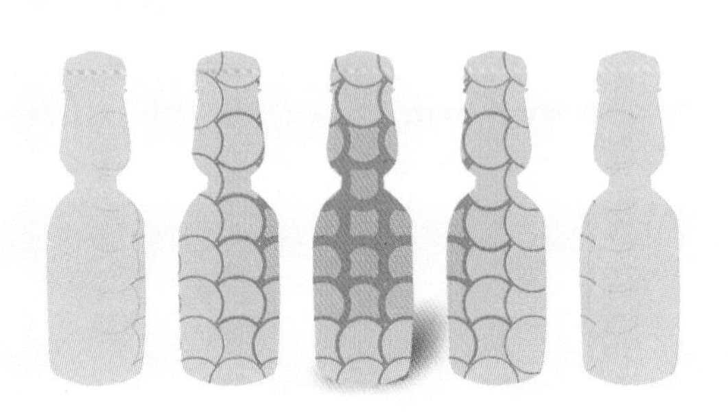

YOUNG CREATIVE PROFESSIONALS COMPETITION

NEW MEDIA: RUNNER UP

TEAM
Buttermilk

MEMBERS
Adam Dachis
Jarrod Riddle
Dan West

TEAM SPONSOR
Brainco/Minneapolis

SERENE

Lemonade (relaxant)

Sit back and relax with that old-time favorite lemonade. Let vitamins B2, B3, B12, C and E take you back to the summer of love, well almost. The Basis is you.

Close

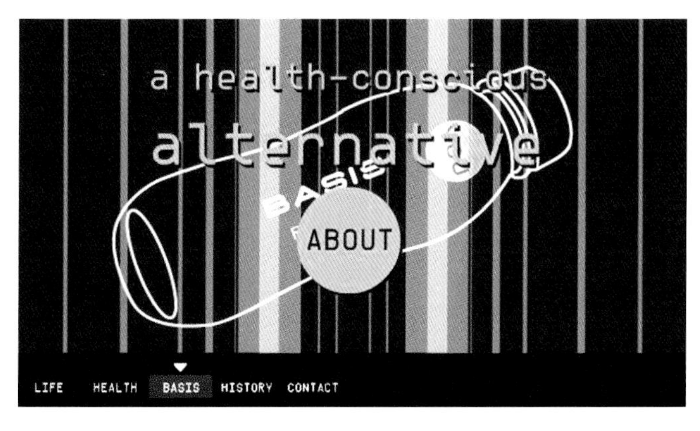

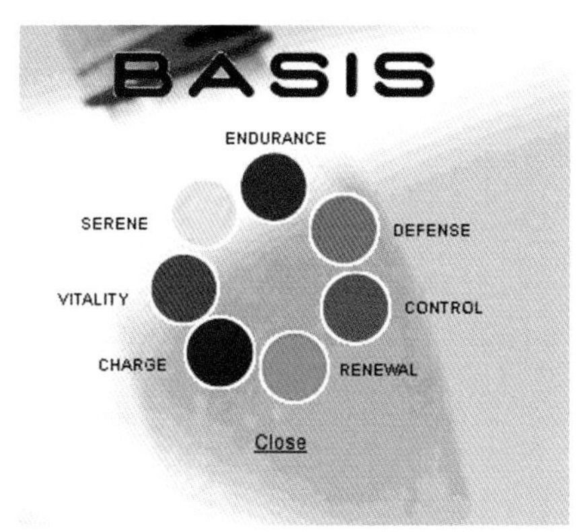

Index

AGENCY

AGENCY PRODUCER

ANIMATOR

ART DIRECTOR

CLIENT

COLLEGE

CREATIVE DIRECTOR

DESIGNER

DIRECTOR

ILLUSTRATOR

PHOTOGRAPHER

PRODUCTION COMPANY

TYPOGRAPHER

WRITER

YOUNG CREATIVE PROFESSIONAL COMPETITORS